The Franchise Ratings Guide

The Franchise Ratings Guide

3000 Franchisees Expose
the Best & Worst Franchise Opportunities

Gary M. Kowalski

iUniverse, Inc.
New York Lincoln Shanghai

The Franchise Ratings Guide
3000 Franchisees Expose the Best & Worst Franchise Opportunities

iUniverse books may be ordered through booksellers or by contacting:

iUniverse
2021 Pine Lake Road, Suite 100
Lincoln, NE 68512
www.iuniverse.com
1-800-Authors (1-800-288-4677)

ISBN-13: 978-0-595-38094-7 (pbk)
ISBN-13: 978-0-595-82462-5 (ebk)
ISBN-10: 0-595-38094-8 (pbk)
ISBN-10: 0-595-82462-5 (ebk)

Printed in the United States of America

Acknowledgments

This work was made possible through the love and support of many fine people I am fortunate to be acquainted with. Each individual or organization mentioned here was an ingredient in bringing the final product to life. Thank you all.

The Heart

George Kowalski
Erma Kowalski
Ellen and Ed Gouvier
Janet Kowalski
James and Tamra Kowalski
Bob and Terese Kowalski
Devon McCabe
Alex MacGregor
Fiona Rose
Reesa Guevara
Kelly Dorn

Mike Frank
Lisa Grippo
James Botti
Tom Harrington
Marie Harrington
Sean Jordan
Kirsten Smilge
Anna Florey
Lori Fritsche
Ashley Holloway
Chentelle Foret

The Lungs

3,000 hardworking franchisee respondents who shall remain nameless, and to whom I wish tremendous success
American Franchise Association
International Franchise Association (Terry Hill)
New York State Securities Division (Barbara Lasoff)
Penn State Law Review (Gabriel MacConaill & Fotini Skovakis)
SCORE

California Department of Corporations
Minnesota Department of Commerce
(Ann Hagestad and Dan Sexton)

The Compass

Susan Kezios
Sandy & Marilyn MacGregor
Laura Stapleton
Gordon Steele
Scott Shane

Paul Steinberg
Theme (Maureen Burdock)
Dan Weinfurter
Jessy Sullivan

CONTENTS

PREFACE

This project began as a labor of love. The idea came about in 1998, shortly after having sold my H2O Plus franchise back to the franchisor.[1] After having devoted body, mind and soul in an effort to see the business flourish, one of the many questions I asked myself was "What would have helped make the business more successful?" The answer that came to me was getting the perspectives of franchisees in a variety of franchises rather than just one. What also surfaced in my mind was that others could benefit from such insight. The result, many years later, is this book.

The objective of the book is to provide a "straight from the horse's mouth" perspective on what it's really like to own a franchise.[2] There are some excellent franchises to invest in as well as companies whose business tactics are at best questionable, with unwitting investors staking their lives' savings into them. This data is meant to shed light on, or "expose" both. My hope is that it will cause potential franchise investors to think twice before making any investment, and to underscore the importance of conducting thorough due diligence. **It is not meant to replace the due diligence process in any way.** Nor, despite the results, is it an attempt to imply that franchising is not a good investment. Franchising is, in fact, like any other investment: it is a risk. The more homework you do before investing, the better your chances of mitigating that risk and selecting the right one. This book is one element of the pre-investment process.

The information included provides a one-sided perspective, that of the franchisee.[3] The reasons for this are that there is no better source of insight on a franchise that its current owners, and because the information covered has not been easily available in any other forum, until now. While the perspectives of franchisors are readily available, those of franchisees are usually only heard after getting the sales pitch from the franchisor. These pitches can be quite persuasive, their statistics quite confidence building, enough so that many investors feel so optimistic that they fail to dedicate enough time to probing existing franchisees. Both perspectives are relevant.

Upon formulating questions that would uniformly apply to the broad range of franchises available, yet provide valuable insight to prospective investors, the next steps were to select the companies to survey and to secure contact information for current owners. Companies were selected based on their total number of outlets, their position within an industry segment, their potential for growth, and whether I could obtain contact information for franchise owners. This last point might be surprising, but suffice it to say the process is not always easy. With terrific support from state officials in California, Minnesota and New York, contact lists were provided and compiled for most of the companies that were initially identified. Actual surveying began in March 2004 and continued through February 2005. Along with a few dozen contacts by telephone, 20,165 surveys were mailed and 3,010 completed surveys were received, 99.2% from current owners. Data for 216 different franchises is included in this book, and every effort was made to secure 10 or more completed surveys for each franchise. The goal being to receive feedback from a greater number of owners than the average prospective franchise investor would contact on his or her own.

---

[1] The franchisor is the parent company that licenses the rights to use their trade name and marks.

[2] "For those of you thinking of purchasing a franchise, don't be mislead as to what it is: You're renting an income stream for a period of time. That's all it is." Susan Kezios, President of the American Franchisee Association, in an interview conducted by the author on January 28, 2005.

[3] The franchisee is the purchaser who leases the right to sell products and services under the parent company trade name.

Data from franchises that I received less than six completed surveys from were not included unless the number represented greater than 7% of the number of current franchisees (only one franchise fit this criteria). Only franchisees listed as "current" in the most recently available U.F.O.C.s[4] of each company were contacted, so that the data would not be tainted by any ill will potentially harbored by former franchisees. Company and cumulative data has been or will be shared free of charge with all survey respondents and their franchisors to thank them for their participation and support. As well, every effort has been made to provide completely unbiased information and to act merely as a conduit.

Thank you for your interest in this work.

---

[4]   U.F.O.C stands for "Uniform Franchise Offering Circular". This is the disclosure document that details the terms of your franchise agreement, including fees, royalties, and obligations of both the franchisor and franchisee. In theory, its terms should mirror those of the franchise agreement, which is the contract you ultimately sign when purchasing a franchise. Franchisors are required to provide prospective buyers copy of the UFOC at least 14 days (10 business days) before they can sign a franchise agreement. The UFOC is discussed in greater detail in Chapter 4.

CHAPTER 1

Why this Book is Important

To paraphrase a common statement of franchise owners, "My franchisor is more interested in selling franchises than in supporting the existing franchisees."[5] Pretty strong words, to be sure, but of the more than 1,100 direct quotes obtained from franchisees in my research, this was the most common statement made. Many others expressed thoughts such as their franchisor is "awesome"[6], that buying a franchise was "the best decision that we ever made"[7], and that they're making "10 times" more money than they thought they would[8]. So is franchising a good deal or not? The answer is that it can be. There are many good franchise opportunities as well as those that shouldn't be touched with a ten foot pole, and the moral of this book is to say do your homework thoroughly before you leap.

With sources touting the benefits of franchising everywhere you look, this may come as a bit of a surprise. Do a search on the internet for "95% of franchises succeed" and see how many different sites have that exact quotation. It's astounding, and usually accompanied by a reference such as "over 50% of non-franchise businesses fail". And take a look at these statistics, which are reprinted with permission from the International Franchise Association:

- There are an estimated 1,500 franchise companies operating in the U.S., doing business in 622,272 establishments
- A new franchise outlet opens somewhere in the U.S. every eight minutes
- Approximately one out of every 12 retail businesses in the U.S. is a franchise
- Franchising accounts for more than 40% of U.S. retail sales
- The total economic impact, that is, the effect of what occurs both in and as a result of franchised businesses, results in more than 18 million jobs or nearly 14% of the nation's private sector employment.[9]

---

[5] Here are two examples of the many who expressed this thought:

Sub-shop franchisee: "I am a franchisee for several concepts. All of them have their strengths and weaknesses. All of them have one consistent theme, they are in business to sell businesses, not products or services. They are more concerned about selling new stores than selling your products."

Financial Services franchisee: "They appear to be in the business of selling franchises and not making there (sic) existing franchises successful."

[6] Franchisee of a cosmetics store: "The…company is awesome; they are only a phone call away; always respond quickly; treat us wonderfully; put on a convention every year and at it gave each owner enough product (new) to pay for our room expense, also no charge for the convention. All but a couple products are U.S. made and packaged, all products are money-back guaranteed, they also co-op advertising by 60%! Can't say enough about their excellence in product, service and support."

[7] Home maintenance franchisee: "From our viewpoint this was the best decision that we ever made and it has enhanced our lives beyond all of our original expectations."

[8] Transmission repair franchisee: income is "10x more" than expected prior to opening for business.

[9] From the International Franchise Association publication: **The Economic Impact of Franchised Businesses**, available: http://www.franchise.org/edufound/profile/econo.asp

Given the explosive growth rate (the number of franchise outlets in the U.S. grew by 92% between 1992 and 2003[10]) and that "95% of franchises succeed", it would seem we should all jump on the bandwagon. But while these statistics may be impressive, franchising has one thing in common with every type of small business: It's a risk. And it's better to learn this now than after you've mortgaged your home to buy a franchise. Here are some of the cumulative survey results that are more relevant when deciding whether to invest in a franchise:

• 48% of franchisees are making less income than anticipated prior to opening their business

• 30% would not buy their franchise again, were they able to turn back the clock to the day they signed their franchise agreement

• 19% do not feel their franchisor equitably grants territories

Ouch! That's quite a different picture! So why the disparity between these figures and the survey findings? First of all, it helps to take a closer look at the "95% of franchises succeed" statistic. This figure references a study supposedly[11] conducted by the U.S. Department of Commerce of franchise companies doing business between 1971 and 1987. Although I have been unable to verify the authenticity of that claim, the Federal Trade Commission found a similar statement to be false and a misrepresentation[12]. The statement, made by the promoter of the International Franchise Expo and based on the results of a Gallup poll, was strikingly similar:

> "If you buy a Franchise Business, your chances of success are 94%! THAT'S A FACT, according to a recent Gallup poll. Conversely, it's estimated that only 35% of independent business start-ups survive 5 years."[13]

More credible is an in-depth study by Dr. Scott Shane of Case Western University, which showed vastly different results. Dr. Shane found that:

> "…despite the widespread reach of franchising, surprisingly few companies succeed at franchising. In fact, of the more than 200 new franchise systems established in the United States each year, 25% don't even make it to their first anniversary, approximately three quarters fail within a decade, and only 15% make it to 17 years."[14]

Casting further discredit on the "95% succeed" figure are the annual turnover rates of franchise outlets.[15] These range from 10% to 19% across industries, with the exception of the "Baked goods" industry with 50.5% annual turnover. The overall annual turnover rate is 16%.[16]

---

[10] Dr. Scott A. Shane, **From Ice Cream to the Internet**, Prentice Hall Publishing, Upper Saddle River, NJ, 2005, p. xiv.

[11] Inquiries I made to the Department of Commerce in an effort to find this study could not identify it.

[12] Press release, Federal Trade Commission, Franchise Show Promoter Agrees to settle FTC Charges of Misrepresenting Earnings and Success Rates of Franchises, September 27, 1995. Available at: http://www.ftc.gov/opa/1995/09/bexpo.htm (Identified first in the publication, **Beguiling Heresy: Regulating The Franchise Relationship**, by Paul Steinberg and Gerald Lescatre; published in the Penn State Law Review, Volume 109, pages 142 and 143, 2004

[13] Id.

[14] Shane, **From Ice Cream to the Internet**, Prentice Hall Publishing, Upper Saddle River, NJ, 2005, p. xvi.

[15] Although I did not verify the specific numbers of either statement, here are two noteworthy comments:
Stained glass franchisee: "In 2004 the number of…"zees" has dropped from over 160 to less than 115, even with new franchise sales."
Auto parts franchisee: "Over the past decade, store count has dropped over 300 sites."

[16] Shane, **From Ice Cream to the Internet**, p. 53, adapting data contained in the IFA Educational Foundation's "The Profile of Franchising (Washington, D.C., 1998).

Another reason for the disparity between the survey results and the statistics on franchising is that many franchise owners maintain their business because they simply can't get out.[17] [18] They're contractually bound by their franchise agreement, their lease, or both.[19] To walk away can lead to a legal squabble and substantial attorney's fees; or if they're personally liable for the lease, something fairly common, then to walk away can mean paying off the balance or declaring personal bankruptcy if funds are not available. So walking away is neither simple nor attractive.[20] Selling your business is also difficult as the franchisor must usually approve of any buyer, and will sometimes charge an administrative fee[21]; and even if a buyer is identified and approved, the price is likely to leave you with a substantial loss. So many decide to ride out the storm in the hope that things will improve.

Additionally, there are those who will attribute the survey results to disgruntled people being the most likely to respond to a survey. I respectfully disagree and here's why. First, although it's apparent many are angry, there are also plenty who are enthusiastic and complimentary toward their franchisors, even when their business is not profitable[22]. Many who rated their franchisor poorly did not fault them for their individual lack of success, but attributed external factors typical with any struggling business: the economy,[23] competition, their own ignorance in managing a business, etc.[24] This suggests that although respondents were critical, they were also fair. Another justification for discounting this theory is the several dozen phone calls I received from franchisees who often racked me over the coals with questions to understand the motives for the survey and who was funding it. These calls constituted the vast majority of all inquiries made, and occurred despite the clarifying explanation that accompanied the survey, which appeared exactly as follows in the cover letter: <u>I am not affiliated or contracted with "franchise name" or any other company.</u> Callers typically grilled me with several questions before even identifying themselves. Upon my explanation, they often would share their fear that I was a "corporate spy", or somehow working for the franchisor, and that they were fearful of repercussions for any criticisms. Many, even after long conversations, would still not identify themselves or their franchise. Supporting this claim further is the American Franchisee Association, which offers an "Anonymous" membership category for

---

[17] Sub-shop franchisee: "Easy to get in and hard to get out."

[18] Susan Kezios, President of the American Franchisee Association: "Franchisees are the only business people…that I know of who can't sell what they buy. Because when you want to sell your franchise, the new buyer will probably be signing the then current franchise contract which will probably have more restrictive terms in it than you had. So your equity has already been devalued, through no bad actions of your own…So if your royalty was 4%, the royalty now may be 6%. That man or woman is not going to make as much money as you were, because they've got to give two percentage points more to the franchisor for royalty and maybe another percentage for advertising…You cannot got into go franchising looking at this as a long-term deal, this is not like buying your own house and building equity in yourself. You may not be able to hand this on to your children, matter of fact you should not even think about handing this over to your children because it doesn't work that way. Franchise contracts are not written in that manner today. 25-30 years ago that's how they were written, but they're not written that way any more." Interview with Kezios conducted by the author on January 28, 2005.

[19] One print shop franchisee expressed: "I wish I could get out of my franchise agreement! I am in the fourth year of a 25 year agreement!"

[20] One franchisee of prominent women's fitness franchise recently paid $100,000 cash to their franchisor in order to release them from their contract.

[21] Candy store franchisee: "One other pricing problem is with the transfer fee if you try to sell your franchise. They want $4000 dollars just to transfer for paper work." A franchisee of tax preparation services noted similarly: "If a franchisee wants to re-sell an existing territory, the parent charges $5,000 off the top for 'paperwork' just to sell it."

[22] Sports photography franchisee who recently "folded" his business: "My decision had nothing to do with the company. They are wonderful. I needed to expand or fold up and decided to fold up. But it was a great experience and I learned a lot. The company made it as pleasant as possible."

[23] Financial franchisee: "I have failed in my business, but it may be due to the economy not (franchise name deleted)."

[24] Battery franchisee: "…the poor quality of my franchise experience is largely MY FAULT…mainly due to the fact that I have not been a strong presence in the management of the store…I believe that they have reasonably fulfilled the majority of their responsibilities to their franchisees."

franchisees fearful of franchisor retaliation.[25] So it's very clear that, whether warranted or not, these franchisees and no doubt hundreds of others felt such intimidation by their franchisors that they were too frightened to express their criticisms. Here are three true stories that illustrate how a franchisor can intimidate:

Franchisor of personal awards

Although I attempted to survey owners from this franchise, only three completed surveys were received back, with feedback mixed-to-poor. One day, while I was on the phone answering questions from one of its franchisees, who was concerned as to my ties to the company, another call came in. The call went into voicemail while we continued our discussion. About 10 minutes later, I checked the message, and found it to be from the head of franchising at their corporate office. He had called to inquire as to the motives of my survey, and I returned the call immediately, only to get his voicemail. I left him a message and said I'd be happy to speak with him. While this was occurring, he sent out an email to, I was told, all of the company's franchisees, under the subject heading "Suspicious survey". The franchisee I had been on the phone with only 10 minutes earlier was kind enough to share it with me, and it's transcribed below.

"Good afternoon,

Many storeowners have called regarding a survey fax they received from Gary Kowalski of Independent Franchise Research.

We know nothing about this individual or his motives for sending this questionnaire to our franchisees. I have placed a call to Mr. Kowalski and he has yet to call back.

I encourage everyone to simply disregard his correspondence and his future attempts to get information from you.

Regards,
(Name deleted)"

While I had "yet to call back", the gentleman had waited less than 10 minutes since leaving me a message before sending this email. And he obviously assumed the survey was being conducted by fax, as not one survey to its owners was actually sent by fax. I sure wouldn't want to do business with a company that operates like that! While certain factors give me reason to believe many other companies sent similar emails to their franchisees, I have no way of proving it.

Large sandwich franchisor

While surveying this company's franchisees, one of them must have shared my contact information with the company founder, as I received this email from him:

"Your survey has been sent to me in excess of 100 times by my franchisees.

Who is paying you and what is your goal?

(Name deleted)"

Aside from it having been written in a rather unprofessional tone, it's interesting to note that at the time this email was received I had only sent 83 surveys out to this company's franchisees. How many had actually contacted him I'll never know, but I would be surprised if it were more than four or five. Here was my reply to him:

---

[25] Paul Steinberg and Gerald Lescatre, **Beguiling Heresy: Regulating The Franchise Relationship**, published in the Penn State Law Review, Volume 109, pages 121, 2004.

"Dear (Name deleted):

To answer your two questions, my effort is entirely self-funded, i.e., no one is paying me, and my intention is to create a guidebook that will provide insight on franchising, from an owner's perspective, as a helpful tool for people thinking of investing in a franchise. If you have any additional questions, please contact me.

Sincerely,

Gary Kowalski
Independent Franchise Research"

It got more interesting over the next few days. For anyone completing the survey, there was a box on it that they could check if they would be open to having me follow-up with them regarding their answers. It also inquired whether email or telephone would be more convenient, and to please specify either/or. As part of my routine follow-up, I contacted one franchisee with the following email:

"Dear (name deleted):

Thank you very much for having completed my franchise owner survey. I really appreciate your kindness in having done so.

Thus far, I've received nine completed surveys from (franchise name deleted) owners with feedback on the franchise being mixed. Specifically, of the nine respondents, six would, if they could turn back time, make the same decision to buy their franchise, while two would not (one person said they are unsure); two of nine are making more money than expected, six are making less, and one is making about what they expected. I hope to have all the survey results completed and tabulated by next spring-summer, and will forward copy to you at that time.

Since you checked the box on the survey indicating you would be open to a follow-up conversation, I do have two additional questions for you. If you have time to complete them, I would genuinely appreciate it. Here they are:

You indicated on the survey that the initial and ongoing training provided by the franchisor has been good. What types of training have you received?

You indicated on the survey that the franchisor could improve the counsel/advice it provides on administrative/management issues. Can you elaborate on this?

Thank you again for your help and your time. I wish you the best, and will forward results to you once completed.

Sincerely,

Gary Kowalski
Independent Franchise Research"

Two days after sending it, I received a second and final email from the franchise founder, this one in reply to my questions above. It read as follows:

"Tell him to go pound sand".

It would seem, based on his writing "Tell him", that he wanted me to think the email was supposed to go to the franchisee. But this is difficult to believe since my address would need to have been typed into the address box. Either way he got the message across.

Commercial cleaning franchise

This is the story of "John", a former franchisee of one of the major commercial cleaning franchises.

In 1995, John purchased a franchise for his sister-in-law, also placing his name on the contract since he had made the actual investment. Three months later she decided to leave the system after being harassed by one of the franchisor's vice presidents. At this point, John decided to take over day-to-day running of the operations since his investment was at stake. Over the next four years, he worked hard and grew his business until he became the largest franchisee in the company. This is the story of how John went from being the most successful franchisee in the system to losing his entire operation overnight.

With this franchise you initially secure business by buying accounts from the franchisor. It works like this: Paying cash upfront buys you an account that will generate roughly 40% of your investment in monthly revenues. For example, if you pay $25,000 cash for an account, that account should generate about $10,000 gross revenue monthly. If you buy that same $10,000 a month account on credit, the franchisor will arrange a loan for you with a principal of $35,000 and an interest rate of 12% interest. Since John was able to purchase accounts for cash, he felt this was a great investment. And assuming you control your expenses reasonably, 40% gross return per month sure sounds like it. Unfortunately, this wasn't the whole story, and John learned the hard way how his franchisor really did business.

After you buy an account, you would think that you own it, but you don't. The franchisor retains the right to take back the account at any time if you fail to perform to the customer's satisfaction. That would seem reasonable since the franchisor needs to maintain a certain quality standard, and it can be easily tarnished if a franchisee is not meeting it. However, this franchisor wasn't as concerned about its image as it was its ability to churn and re-sell accounts, and used various excuses to tell franchisees their accounts had been cancelled. John said they typically told franchisees: "You have a personality conflict with them", and that "The customer does not want to see you anymore, he doesn't want you to disturb him…but he wants his (building access) key back because he has cancelled his account."

The unsuspecting franchisee wonders what went wrong, but follows orders not to contact the customer. In the meantime, the franchisor has already sold the account to a different franchisee, generating additional revenues for itself, but without regard for the interests of either the franchisee or the customer. There was no way for John to tell how many times accounts were churned in this way, but it was apparent to him that it was a regular part of how they conducted business.

Three months after this first happened to John, he bumped into one of one of his former customers whom he was told cancelled his account. The customer asked John, "I don't see you anymore, what happened?" The customer, who of course had not really cancelled the account, was told by the franchisor that John was "leaving the country". He was just as surprised as the franchisee to find out the truth.

So John quickly realized how the franchisor was doing business, and decided not to buy any additional accounts from the franchisor. Instead, he bought up accounts of financially distressed franchisees, the sale of which had to be approved by the franchisor. These were franchisees that could not afford to continue their operations, so were happy to sell to John. It's worth noting that the franchisees from which John bought these operations were all caucasian. This was not a coincidence—the franchisor, who must approve all franchisee transfers or sales, would not allow him to buy accounts from minorities or ethnic groups. The franchisor did not want these franchisees, who it deemed to be "unsophisticated", to be bought out as they were easy prey for the franchisor's account churning scheme, and helped pad revenues. Yet there were still enough "white" accounts for John to purchase, so many that within four years, he became their highest revenue franchisee. That led to another problem for him.

Once John became too large, the franchisor felt he was also becoming too powerful, and devised a plan to extricate him from their system. So one of their managers suggested to him that he was so successful in this industry, he should really start up his own business. Taking the advice, and with a verbal commitment from the franchisor that they would arrange for meeting with other franchisees who were willing to buy his accounts, John provided his 30 day notice to terminate his franchise agreement. The proceeds from these sales would allow him to start his own business and control his own destiny, without having to comply with the rules of the franchisor.

John met with the franchisor's staff and made handshake agreements to sell his accounts on the verbal agreement that he would receive sales proceeds from the buyers in 60 days. Shortly after John "sold" his accounts, the franchisor was presenting the buyers of these accounts with an ultimatum: "You either sign a new contract stating that you're buying these (formerly John's) accounts directly from us, and that proceeds go to us, or you forfeit your current franchise operation and your entire income stream." In essence, they stole John's accounts away from him, provided him with no compensation, re-sold them, and kept the proceeds for themselves. John had "sold" his franchise and all of its accounts, trusting in the franchisor that all proceeds would remit to him. In reality he received nothing.

Due to his contract stating that all disputes were to be settled by an arbitrator, John took this course. After spending over $500,000 fighting the franchisor, the arbitrator "changed the terms of the contract", allowing the franchisor to win. He is still fighting them, stating that "nobody cares". John admits his mistake was that he was too trusting.

Although what happened to John may not be the norm, it's a far more common occurrence than most prospective buyers realize. In addition to the cases above, there were other franchisors that implied, and one actually threatened, that they would sue me if I continued "harassing" their franchisees! In each case I explained that what I was doing was perfectly legal, and that these were independent business owners. It was up to them whether they chose to complete the survey.

On the positive side, several franchisors, upon learning of the survey and my motives, were quite supportive of the effort. Three of them, Colors on Parade, Keller Williams Realty, and United Check Cashing deserve special mention as they actually offered to assist my efforts. Each was encouraging and interested in benefiting from the results, and the offers of support impressive. Those that, while they did not offer to directly assist, still encouraged the effort were Children's Orchard, EmbroidMe, Express Personnel Services, MARS, Paul Davis Restoration, V2K The Virtual Window Fashion Store, and Visiting Angels.

In my mind there is no disparity. After communicating with hundreds of owners, reviewing all 3010 surveys, and sifting through a number of studies on the subject, I am completely convinced the data presents a fair and accurate portrait of the realities of franchising. And that is precisely the reason why this book is important: To challenge the common perception that franchising is an almost guaranteed formula for success.

CHAPTER 2

Understanding the Rating System, the Survey Questions, and the Results

This section provides insight on the questions asked in the survey, the overall scoring and ranking systems, and cumulative averages by question. In creating the survey, several objectives had to be met. The questions had to be substantive so that the answers would provide valuable insight to prospective franchise owners, yet short enough for franchisees to be willing to take the time to complete them. Questions also had to be phrased in such a way that they would be applicable to most any type of franchise, provide opportunity for respondents to be either complimentary or critical, and not be so intrusive that franchisees would feel uncomfortable answering them. This latter point was especially true of questions 10 and 12.

All franchisees were provided the same questions, and all franchises rated using the same formula. If a question went unanswered on a survey, it was simply disregarded since it had no impact on the rating. If a franchisee circled two different answers to the same question, each answer was considered 50% valid and points assigned at half the normal value for each.

Most franchises received both an "Overall Score" as well as an "Overall Rank". The Overall Score is on a 100-point scale, meaning zero was the minimum and 100 the maximum. Ranking is on a numerical scale, with the highest ranked company being number one and the lowest ranked company being number 193. While all franchises received a numerical rating (the Overall Score), those from which less than 10 completed surveys were received were not ranked unless the number of surveys received met or exceeded 7% of the total number of current franchise owners.

Here are the questions, the answer choices, and the cumulative averages for all 3010 survey respondents. Following these are some insight on the logic and weighting of each question and Best & Worst performers by question. (Highest percentage responses are boldfaced; percentages are rounded and so may not always total to exactly 100%; see alphabetized franchise listings for breakdown of specific franchise performance).

Q1: **About how many hours per week do you dedicate to your franchise business?**

	Cumulative Average	
A) Less than 40	18%	
B) **40–50**	**28%**	
C) 51–60	26%	**Summary:** 52% work 50 + hours per week
D) More than 60	26%	
E) Passive investment	1%	

This question was asked solely to provide insight and was not counted on the rating scale.

(Because hours worked per week is not necessarily reflective of a "Good" or "Bad" franchise, the following listing is of Highest and Lowest average number of hours worked per week):

<u>Highest/Most hours worked :</u>

Snap-on Tools
Deck The Walls
ServPro
Pizza Factory
Atlanta Bread Company
Meineke Car Care Centers
Property Damage Appraisers
Matco Tools
Tuffy Auto Service Centers
Jimmy John's Gourmet Sandwiches

<u>Lowest/Least hours worked:</u>

Gumball Gourmet
The Dentist's Choice
Vanguard Cleaning Systems
Interface Financial
Kinderdance International
Computertots
Christmas Decor
Pretzelmaker
Keller Williams Realty
Tutoring Club

Q2: **How would you describe your relations/communications with your franchisor?**

	<u>Cumulative Average</u>	
A) Excellent	27%	
B) **Good**	34%	
C) Adequate	18%	<u>Summary:</u> 61% Good to Excellent
D) Fair	12%	
E) Poor	9%	

Communications and relations are two of the most fundamental elements of the relationship between franchisor and franchisee, and the better they are between the parties, the easier it is to succeed. Weighted in the middle of the scale, and in theory should provide "easy" points for a franchisor that's diligently working to support their largest customers—their franchisees.

<u>Best:</u>

Computer Troubleshooters
HobbyTown USA
Assist-2-Sell
Keller Williams Realty
Culver's
DreamMaker Bath & Kitchen
Merle Norman
My Gym Children's Fitness Center
Express Personnel Services
Home Instead Senior Care

<u>Worst:</u>

The Maids International
Cottman Transmissions
Fiducial
Vanguard Cleaning Systems
Stained Glass Overlay
GNC
Deck The Walls
All Tune & Lube
TCBY
Huntington Learning Centers

Q3: **In terms of how your franchisor views your communications with other franchisees, it is:**

	<u>Cumulative Average</u>
A) **Very supportive**	63%
B) Not very supportive	14%
C) No influence	23%

One of the benefits gained by buying into a franchise network is the collective intelligence of its members. A good franchisor will work to foster an efficient communications network so that all involved will benefit. The franchisor may have the "expertise", having created and "proven" the concept, but franchisees working the field also have great ideas and insights that may be as good and are often better than those of the franchisor. This question is weighted lightly in the scale, and answering "no influence" had a minor negative impact on a franchise's overall score.

Best:	Worst:
American Poolplayers Association	Atlanta Bread Company
Computer Troubleshooters	Vanguard Cleaning Systems
Great Harvest	Diet Center
Sunbelt Business Advisors	Huntington Learning Centers
Paul Davis Restoration	All Tune & Lube
Budget Blinds	Mrs. Field's Cookies
The Sports Section	Subway
Allegra Network	Gloria Jean's Coffee
AlphaGraphics	The Medicine Shoppe
Carlson Wagonlit Travel (tie)	Pretzelmaker
Maid Brigade (tie)	

Q4: Is the franchisor fair with you in resolving any grievances?

	Cumulative Average	
A) Extremely fair	29%	
B) **Pretty fair**	32%	
C) Reasonably fair	25%	**Summary:** 86% Reasonably fair to Extremely fair
D) Not very fair	9%	
E) Not fair at all	4%	

Webster's defines a grievance as "a circumstance or condition thought to be unjust and ground for complaint or resentment". Hopefully, this won't come into play if and when you become a franchisee. But given that the term of most franchise agreements is 10 years, it may very well be of importance at some point. The weighting on this was light, and the difference in scoring between answering "Reasonably fair" and "Extremely fair" was not enough to materially affect the overall franchise rating.

Best:	Worst:
Culver's	GNC
Keller Williams Realty	Vanguard Cleaning Systems
My Gym Children's Fitness Center	Cottman Transmissions
Assist-2-Sell	Huntington Learning Centers
Learning Express	Baskin Robbins Ice Cream
Merle Norman	The Maids International
World Inspection Network	Jimmy John's Gourmet Sandwiches
Computer Troubleshooters	Quizno's
Heaven's Best Carpet	United Check Cashing
Kitchen Solvers	Subway

Q5: Are territories equitably granted?

	Cumulative Average
A) **Yes**	62%
B) No	19%
C) Not yet sure	18%

This is an extremely important question to have answered before buying any franchise, and Item 12 of your UFOC will define what territorial rights a franchisee has. If you feel your franchise agreement leaves the franchisor any room to infringe on your territory, then you should expect the worst and include the potential impact of it into your business plan and financial projections. You might want to steer clear of the company altogether. Remember, the most common quote obtained from franchise owners throughout the course of this survey can be paraphrased as "My franchisor is more interested in selling franchises than in supporting the existing franchisees." Given the chance, many franchisors will happily sell another franchise to add to their own revenues, while not being the least bit concerned as to how the sale might affect yours. And unless your contract has provided you with a clearly defined territory, which most do not, there will be very little you can do to stop the "cannibalization".

For the survey, "Yes" answers had a slight positive effect, while "No" answers had a more significant negative effect. "Not yet sure" answers were not weighted and thus had no impact on ratings.

Best: (Respondents from these 10 franchises unanimously answered "Yes, territories are equitably granted".)

Best	Worst
	Subway
ABC Seamless	Bruster's Real Ice Cream
Computer Troubleshooters	Snelling Personnel
Critter Control	Baskin Robbins Ice Cream
Culver's	GNC
Dr. Vinyl	Huntington Learning Centers
Fox's Den Pizza	ACE America's Cash Express
Ident-A-Kid	Dippin' Dots (tie)
PIP Printing	Domino's Pizza (tie)
Sunbelt Business Advisors	Interface Financial (tie)
Swisher Hygiene	Vanguard Cleaning Systems (tie)

Q6: How would you describe the initial and ongoing training provided by your franchisor?

	Cumulative Average	
A) Excellent	26%	
B) **Good**	32%	
C) Adequate	18%	**Summary:** 58% Good to Excellent
D) Fair	15%	
E) Poor	9%	

This question incorporates both "initial" and "ongoing" training to force respondents to grade them in a combined manner. When you invest hundreds of thousands of dollars into a franchise, you should expect all training to be good or excellent. This question was heavily weighted given that the training you and/or your staff receive is one of the foundation stones of your success.

Best:

Keller Williams Realty
Dunkin' Donuts
Fast Signs
Merle Norman
Cold Stone Creamery
Express Personnel Services
American Poolplayers Assocation
My Gym Children's Fitness Center
Management Recruiters International
Culver's

Worst:

Cottman Transmissions
Vanguard Cleaning Systems
Stained Glass Overlay
All Tune & Lube
GNC
Deck The Walls
Hungry Howie's Pizza & Subs
Gumball Gourmet
The Great Frame Up
Diet Center (tie)
Geeks On Call (tie)

Q7: **How well does the franchisor anticipate future trends in how it evolves and markets products and services?**

	Cumulative Average	
A) Extremely well	22%	
B) **Pretty well**	33%	**Summary:** 55% Pretty well to Extremely well
C) Adequately	21%	
D) Not very well	18%	
E) Terribly	5%	

Question seven aims to glean insight on the vision of the franchisor and how well it anticipates future trends in its industry. A franchise may be number one in one year, but can suffer significantly in the market if a competitor comes up with something the public perceives in a better way, or if it doesn't keep up with societal trends. They must be better than their competitors to maintain a leading edge.

This question was weighted in between light and medium on the scale. While it can be extremely important, its importance can vary among industries. For example, a dry cleaning franchise might not need to evolve as quickly as a fast food provider, which might have to start selling "low carb" alternative products to keep up with the latest fad diets.

Best:

Keller Williams Realty
Fast Signs
It's Just Lunch
Stanley Steemer
Merle Norman
Dunkin' Donuts
The Sports Section
HobbyTown USA
Curves
Budget Blinds

Worst:

Vanguard Cleaning Systems
GNC
Mr. Goodcents
Deck The Walls
Maui Wowi
Stained Glass Overlay
Cottman Transmissions
Baskin' Robbins
All Tune & Lube
KFC (tie)
Papa John's Pizza (tie)

Q8: How satisfied are you with your franchisor's spending of the royalty fees you pay?

	Cumulative Average
A) Extremely satisfied	10%
B) **Mostly satisfied**	35%
C) Somewhat satisfied	26%
D) Not very satisfied	17%
E) Not satisfied at all	11%

Summary: 45% Mostly satisfied to Extremely satisfied

Royalty fees also vary widely. Some franchisors have none, while others have a gross royalty fee and/or some form of advertising or marketing royalty. This question was worded in a general way to enable virtually all franchisees to respond to the question, and was weighted between light and medium on the scale. For those cases in which the franchisor requires no royalty fees whatsoever, the question was disregarded and it did not impact their rating.

Best:	Worst:
Sunbelt Business Advisors	Vanguard Cleaning Systems
Parcel Plus	Stained Glass Overlay
Keller Williams Realty	Diet Center
DreamMaker Bath & Kitchen	Cottman Transmissions
Curves	GNC
Computer Troubleshooters	All Tune & Lube
United Country Realty	Baskin Robbins Ice Cream
Visiting Angels	Fiducial
Taco Bell	Martinizing Dry Cleaning
Culver's	TCBY

Q9: In what ways could the parent company most improve? (Please check those that most <u>apply, no more than three</u>):

	Cumulative Average
☐ Communications	24%
☐ **Counsel/advice on administrative/management issues (THIRD)**	27%
☐ **Effectiveness of marketing/promotions (FIRST)**	47%
☐ Evolution of products/services	23%
☐ **Frequency of marketing/promotional campaigns (SECOND)**	29%
☐ Quality of products/services	9%
☐ Pricing of products/services to franchisees	26%
☐ Technology (Point of sale systems, usage of computers/email/software, etc.)	21%
☐ Training	23%

This question was asked solely to provide insight and was not counted on the rating scale.

Q10: Is your income A) more, B) less or C) about what you expected prior to opening your business?

A) More:	17%
B) **Less:**	48%
C) About what you expected:	35%

The importance of this question is apparent. Most people who buy a franchise do so for many different reasons, but if they don't think they can make money, they won't buy. What is virtually impossible to derive from this question is whether the initial financial projections made by franchisees were reasonable given the information available at the time.

However, since that cannot be determined without much more intensive research, if at all, this should act as a reasonable barometer.

This question was weighted heavily, surpassed on the scale only by question 12. Responses of "more" resulted in bonus points to the franchise.

Best:	**Worst:**
Heaven's Best Carpet	Gumball Gourmet
Health Mart	Maggie Moo's Ice Cream and Treatery
Critter Control	Deck The Walls
Sunbelt Business Advisors	Candy Bouquet
Cartex	EmbroidMe
Dunkin' Donuts	Stained Glass Overlay
ACE America's Cash Express	Tuffy Auto Service Centers
Curves	AAMCO
Snap-on Tools	Parcel Plus
ServiceMaster Clean	Cousin's Subs

Q11: **Prior to opening your franchise, which (if any) of the following did you underestimate? (Please check all that apply):**

	Cumulative Average
☐ **Amount of working capital required for your first year in business (THIRD)**	34%
☐ **Difficulty in hiring/retaining quality staff (FIRST)**	43%
☐ Expertise required to run the business	15%
☐ Impact of marketing/promotions	23%
☐ Start-up costs	19%
☐ **Degree of stress (SECOND)**	40%
☐ Workload	31%

This question was asked solely to provide insight and was not counted on the rating scale.

Q12: **If you could turn back time to the day you signed your franchise agreement, would you make the same decision to buy your franchise?**

	Cumulative Average
A) Yes	70%
B) No	30%

Once again, the importance of this question is apparent. We all wish we had the ability to benefit from hindsight to make better decisions. The answers to this question provide us with the hindsight of current franchise owners to truly assess whether it's a good decision to buy a given franchise. True, there were a few people who answered "No" even if their overall experience with the franchisor has been positive. But having sifted through all of the results, I would venture there were actually more who answered "Yes" even though their overall experience with the franchisor has been negative. People have many motivations for acting as they do. All in all, I am very confident that the results for this question do accurately and fairly reflect the sentiment of franchisees and assist in drawing a clear path toward the selection of a franchise.

Best:

(Respondents from these 15 franchises unanimously answered "Yes, they would make the same decision to buy their franchise if they could turn back time to the day they signed their franchise agreement".)

American Express Travel Service
American Poolplayers Association
Auntie Anne's Soft Rolled Pretzels
Computer Troubleshooters
Culligan Water Conditioning
Culver's
Curves
Dunkin's Donuts
Express Tax
Heaven's Best Carpet
HobbyTown USA
Little Caesar's Pizza
1-800-Got-Junk
Results! Travel
Rita's Italian Ice

Worst:

Cottman Transmissions
Stained Glass Overlay
Aussie Pet Mobile
CertaPro Painters
Maui Wowi
Vanguard Cleaning Systems
TCBY
All Tune & Lube
Business Cards Tomorrow
Gumball Gourmet (tie)
Maggie Moo's Ice Cream and Treatery (tie)
Quizno's (tie)

Overall Scores: (All franchises included, regardless of number of surveys received):

OVERALL AVERAGE SCORE OF 216 FRANCHISES: 66%

90 & Above:	Score:	Summary:
Culver's	98.44%	Of 216 franchises surveyed, seven, or 3%, scored 90 & above.
Heaven's Best Carpet	98.13%	
American Poolplayers Association	96.54%	
Curves	95.96%	
Home Instead Senior Care	93.98%	
Critter Control	91.76%	
California Closet Company	91.36%	

80–89:	Score:	Summary:
Auntie Anne's Soft Rolled Pretzels	89.29%	Of 216 franchises surveyed, 29, or 13%, scored 80–89.
HobbyTown USA	88.51%	
Results! Travel	87.64%	
Express Tax	86.93%	
Express Personnel Services	86.90%	
Dunkin' Donuts	86.72%	
Computer Troubleshooters	86.60%	
1-800-Got-Junk	86.07%	
World Inspection Network	85.66%	
Sunbelt Business Advisors	84.92%	
Rita's Italian Ice	84.83%	
Merle Norman	84.59%	
Fast Signs	84.25%	
Management Recruiters International	84.16%	
Cold Stone Creamery	83.68%	
DreamMaker Bath & Kitchen	83.48%	
Little Caesar's Pizza	83.45%	
Keller Williams Realty	83.20%	
Maid Brigade	83.14%	
United Country Realty	82.91%	
ServiceMaster Clean	82.62%	
American Express Travel Services	82.41%	
Snap-on Tools	81.91%	
Paul Davis Restoration	81.85%	
Health Mart	81.77%	
My Gym Children's Fitness Centers	80.92%	
Assist-2-Sell	80.64%	
Plato's Closet	80.55%	
Adventures In Advertising	80.34%	

Overall Franchise Scores, cont.:

70–79:	Score:
The Little Gym	79.88%
Visiting Angels	79.80%
Ident-A-Kid	79.76%
Taco John's	79.39%
Culligan Water Conditioning	79.26%
Budget Blinds	79.25%
L'il Angels	78.76%
Roto Rooter	78.42%
Re-Bath	78.40%
Carlson Wagonlit Travel	78.31%
The Dentist's Choice	78.29%
Taco Bell	78.01%
Merry Maids	77.90%
World Gym	77.28%
U.S. Lawns	76.33%
Allegra Network	76.25%
PIP Printing	76.13%
Kitchen Solvers	76.00%
Prudential Real Estate	75.76%
American Leak Detection	75.72%
The Sports Section	75.54%
Play It Again Sports	75.53%
Great Harvest	75.21%
Computer Tots	74.96%
Wild Bird Center	74.74%
Grease Monkey	74.50%
ACE America's Cash Express	74.24%
CFO Today	74.13%
AlphaGraphics	74.11%
HomeVestors	73.93%
Goddard Systems	73.93%
Remedy Intelligent Staffing	73.83%
Molly Maid	73.40%
Novus Auto Glass	73.26%
Pretzel Time	73.20%
Christmas Décor	72.99%
CruiseOne	72.90%
Once Upon A Child	72.83%
Help-U-Sell	72.82%
Sylvan Learning Center	72.47%
Wireless Zone	72.46%
Arby's	71.83%
Pillar To Post	71.63%
Kitchen Tune-Up	71.46%
Mr. Rooter	71.45%
Learning Express	71.32%

Summary:

Of 216 franchises surveyed, 53, or 25%, scored 70–79

Overall Franchise Scores, cont.:

Cartex	71.12%
Sandler Sales Institute	70.59%
Cost Cutters Family Hair Care	70.57%
Mr. Transmission	70.52%
Snelling Personnel	70.51%
Duraclean International	70.50%
HouseMaster Home Inspection	70.29%

<u>60–69</u>:	<u>Score:</u>
Pop-A-Lock	69.53%
Godfather's Pizza	69.40%
Lawn Doctor	69.02%
Kinderdance International	68.93%
Interiors by Decorating Den	68.84%
The Cleaning Authority	68.82%
Cruise Holidays	68.68%
Dr. Vinyl	68.64%
Dippin' Dots	68.60%
Stanley Steemer	68.57%
Fish Window Cleaning	68.34%
Two Men and a Truck, Int'l.	68.26%
Padgett Business Services	68.13%
Wild Birds Unlimited	68.11%
Batteries Plus	68.09%
Matco Tools	67.79%
MARS	67.69%
Uniglobe Travel	67.19%
Cash Plus	67.06%
AmeriSpec Home Inspection	67.02%
Dairy Queen	66.94%
Property Damage Apraisers	66.92%
Geeks On Call	66.74%
Domino's Pizza	66.53%
Kumon Math & Reading Ctrs.	66.31%
Pak Mail	66.19%
Minuteman Press	66.16%
Aero Colours	65.92%
It's Just Lunch	65.63%
Supercuts	65.52%
Purofirst	65.51%
Cookies By Design	65.35%
Sir Speedy	65.35%
Maaco	65.10%
Gymboree	64.96%
Ben & Jerry's	64.87%
The Mad Science Group	64.68%
Swisher Hygiene	64.62%

<u>Summary:</u>

Of 216 franchises surveyed, 63, or 29%, scored 60–69.

Overall Franchise Scores, cont.:

Parcel Plus	64.38%
Colors On Parade	63.99%
Papa Murphy's	63.69%
The Maids International	63.61%
Floor Coverings International	63.55%
Mrs. Field's	63.38%
Sign-A-Rama	63.29%
Mr. Electric	63.10%
Comfort Keepers	62.68%
Rocky Mountain Choc. Factory	62.41%
Interface Financial	62.33%
Signs By Tomorrow	61.89%
Great American Cookie Co.	61.86%
Carvel	61.85%
Pressed4Time	61.48%
KFC	61.38%
Leadership Management	61.36%
PostNet Postal & Business Services	61.32%
ServPro	61.25%
Jackson Hewitt	61.20%
Tutoring Club	61.13%
The UPS Store	60.84%
Maid To Perfection	60.54%
Gold's Gym	60.40%

Less than 60:	**Score:**
Meineke Car Care Centers	59.53%
Contours Express	59.39%
Line-X	59.39%
Ziebart	58.92%
Martinizing Dry Cleaning	58.79%
House Doctors	58.70%
The Medicine Shoppe	58.41%
Marble Slab Creamery	58.31%
Planet Beach	58.31%
United Check Cashing	57.91%
Bruster's Real Ice Cream	57.88%
Fast Frame USA	57.79%
Fox's Den Pizza	57.77%
Subway	57.67%
Papa John's Pizza	57.53%
Kwik Kopy Printing	57.44%
Pizza Factory	57.13%
Dollar Discount Stores	57.06%
Signs Now	57.05%
Steamatic	56.72%
Guardsman FurniturePro	56.57%

Summary:

Of 216 franchises surveyed, 64, or 30%, scored less than 60.

Overall Franchise Scores, cont.:

Nationwide Flr. & Window Cov.	56.30%
Home Helpers	56.15%
Midas International	55.56%
We The People	54.67%
MotoPhoto	54.51%
Childrens' Orchard	53.59%
Liberty Tax	53.56%
Jimmy John's Gourmet Sandw.	53.50%
V2K, Virtual Window Fashion Store	53.40%
Mr. Handyman	53.36%
Business Cards Tomorrow	53.21%
The Coffee Beanery	53.19%
Pretzelmaker	52.90%
Hungry Howie's Pizza & Subs	52.65%
Gloria Jean's Coffee	52.09%
Postal Annex+	49.58%
Furniture Medic	47.79%
Fiducial	47.04%
Cousin's Subs	45.99%
Baskin Robbins	45.53%
CertaPro Painters	44.97%
Aussie Pet Mobile	44.84%
EmbroidMe	44.33%
Quizno's	44.11%
Mr. Goodcents	43.73%
Huntington Learning Center	43.48%
AAMCO	43.38%
Atlanta Bread Company	42.25%
Smoothie King	41.51%
The Great Frame Up	41.24%
Diet Center	40.70%
Maui Wowi	40.31%
Candy Bouquet	40.21%
TCBY	40.13%
Tuffy Auto Service Centers	39.57%
Maggie Moo's Ice Cream and Try.	37.24%
Deck The Walls	35.19%
GNC	34.98%
All Tune & Lube	33.51%
Gumball Gourmet	30.89%
Cottman Transmissions	30.11%
Vanguard Cleaning Systems	29.66%
Stained Glass Overlay	25.89%

Top 15 Best & Worst Overall Scores
(includes only those franchises for which 10 or more surveys were received):

Best:	Score:	Worst:	Score:
Culver's	98.44%	Stained Glass Overlay	25.89%
Heaven's Best Carpet	98.13%	Vanguard Cleaning Systems	29.66%
American Poolplayers Associaton	96.54%	Cottman Transmissions	30.11%
Curves	95.96%	All Tune & Lube	33.51%
Home Instead Senior Care	93.98%	GNC	34.98%
Critter Control	91.76%	Deck The Walls	35.19%
California Closet Company	91.36%	Tuffy Auto Service Centers	39.57%
Auntie Anne's	89.29%	TCBY	40.13%
HobbyTown USA	88.51%	Candy Bouquet	40.21%
Results! Travel	87.64%	Maui Wowi	40.31%
Express Personnel Services	86.90%	Diet Center	40.70%
World Inspection Network	85.66%	The Great Frame Up	41.24%
Sunbelt Business Advisors	84.92%	Smoothie King	41.51%
Rita's Italian Ice	84.83%	Atlanta Bread Company	42.25%
Merle Norman	84.59%	AAMCO	43.38%

OVERALL AVERAGE SCORE OF 216 FRANCHISES: 66%

Percentage Results by Category (percentages rounded):

Automotive Detailing & Appearance

Franchise:	Score:
Cartex	71%
Dr. Vinyl	69%
MARS	68%
Aero Colours	66%
Colors On Parade	64%
Line-X	59%
Ziebart	59%
Category Average:	65%

Baked Goods

Franchise:	Score:
Auntie Anne's Soft Rolled Pretzels	89%
Dunkin's Donuts	87%
Great Harvest	75%
Pretzel Time	74%
Pretzelmaker	53%
Atlanta Bread Company	42%
Category Average:	70%

Automotive Maintenance & Repair

Franchise:	Score:
Grease Monkey	75%
Novus Auto Glass	73%
Mr. Transmission	71%
Maaco	65%
Meineke Car Care Centers	60%

Beauty

Franchise:	Score:
Merle Norman	85%
Cost Cutters Family Hair Care	71%
Supercuts	66%
Category Average:	74%

Performance by Category, cont.:

Automotive Maintenance & Repair, cont.

Franchise:	Score:
Midas International	56%
AAMCO Transmissions	43%
Tuffy Auto Service Centers	39%
All Tune & Lube	34%
Cottman Transmissions	30%
Category Average:	55%

Candy & Chocolates

Franchise:	Score:
Rocky Mountain Chocolate Factory	62%
Gumball Gourmet	31%
Category Average:	47%

Carpet & Upholstery Cleaning

Franchise:	Score:
Heaven's Best Carpet	98%
Stanley Steemer	69%
Category Average:	83%

Children's Products & Services

Franchise:	Score:
My Gym Children's Fitness Centers	81%
Plato's Closet	81%
The Little Gym	80%
Ident-A-Kid	80%
Goddard Systems	74%
Once Upon A Child	73%
Learning Express	71%
Kinderdance International	69%
Gymboree	65%
Children's Orchard	54%
Category Average:	73%

Coffee

Franchise:	Score:
The Coffee Beanery	53%
Gloria Jean's Coffee	52%
Category Average:	53%

Commercial Cleaning

Franchise:	Score:
ServiceMaster Clean	83%
Vanguard Cleaning Systems	30%
Category Average:	56%

Computer Services

Franchise:	Score:
Computer Troubleshooters	87%
Geeks On Call	67%
Category Average:	77%

Cookies

Franchise:	Score:
Mrs. Field's Cookies	63%
Great American Cookie Company	62%
Category Average:	63%

Dry Cleaning Services

Franchise:	Score:
Martinizing Dry Cleaning	59%
Pressed4Time	61%
Category Average:	60%

Performance by Category, cont.:

Education

Franchise:	Score:
Computertots	75%
Sylvan Learning Centers	72%
Kumon Math & Reading Centers	66%
The Mad Science Group	65%
Tutoring Club	61%
Huntington Learning Centers	43%
Category Average:	64%

Employment Services

Franchise:	Score:
Express Personnel Services	87%
Management Recruiters International	84%
Remedy Intelligent Staffing	74%
Snelling Personnel	71%
Category Average:	79%

Fast Food Frozen Desserts

Franchise:	Score:
Rita's Italian Ice	85%
Cold Stone Creamery	84%
Dippin' Dots	69%
Dairy Queen	67%
Ben & Jerry's	65%
Carvel	62%
Marble Slab Creamery	58%
Bruster's Old Fashioned Ice Cream	58%
Baskin Robbins	46%
Smoothie King	42%
Maui Wowi	40%
TCBY	40%
Maggie Moo's Ice Cream and Try.	37%
Category Average:	58%

Fast Food Miscellaneous

Franchise:	Score:
Culver's	98%
Taco John's	79%
Taco Bell	78%
KFC	61%
Category Average:	79%

Fast Food Sandwiches

Franchise:	Score:
Arby's	72%
Subway	58%
Jimmy John's Gourmet Sandwiches	54%
Cousin's Subs	46%
Quizno's	44%
Mr. Goodcents	44%
Category Average:	53%

Financial Services—Business

Franchise:	Score:
Sunbelt Business Advisors	85%
CFO Today	74%
Padgett Business Services	68%
Interface Financial	62%
Fiducial	47%
Category Average:	67%

Performance by Category, cont.:

Financial Services—Check Cashing

Franchise:	Score:
ACE America's Cash Express	74%
Cash Plus	67%
United Check Cashing Services	58%
Category Average:	66%

Financial Services—Tax Preparation

Franchise:	Score:
Express Tax	87%
Jackson Hewitt	61%
Liberty Tax Service	54%
Category Average:	67%

Framing Services

Franchise:	Score:
Fast Frame USA	58%
The Great Frame Up	41%
Deck The Walls	35%
Category Average:	45%

Furniture Repair

Franchise:	Score:
Guardsman FurniturePro	57%
Furniture Medic	48%
Category Average:	52%

Health Products & Services

Franchise:	Score:
Health Mart	82%
The Medicine Shoppe	58%
Diet Center	41%
GNC	35%
Category Average:	54%

Home Improvement

Franchise:	Score:
California Closet Company	91%
DreamMaker Bath & Kitchen	83%
Culligan Water Conditioning	79%
Budget Blinds	79%
Re-Bath	78%
Kitchen Solvers	76%
Christmas Décor	73%
Kitchen Tune-Up	71%
Interiors by Decorating Den	69%
Floor Coverings International	64%
ABC Seamless	62%
Nationwide Floor & Window Cov'g.	56%
V2K, Virtual Window Fashion Store	53%
Category Average:	72%

Home Inspection Services

Franchise:	Score:
World Inspection Network	86%
Pillar To Post	72%
HouseMaster Home Inspections	70%
AmeriSpec Home Inspection	67%
Category Average:	74%

Performance by Category, cont.:

Home or Business Maintenance/Repair

Franchise:	Score:
American Leak Detection	76%
Fish Window Cleaning	68%
Mr. Electric	63%
House Doctors	59%
Mr. Handyman	53%
CertaPro Painters	45%
Category Average:	61%

Home or Business Restoration

Franchise:	Score:
Paul Davis Restoration	82%
Duraclean International	71%
Purofirst	66%
ServPro	61%
Steamatic	57%
Category Average:	67%

Lawn Care:

Franchise:	Score:
U.S. Lawns	76%
Lawn Doctor	69%
Category Average:	73%

Personal Care Services

Franchise:	Score:
Home Instead Senior Care	94%
Visiting Angels	80%
Comfort Keepers	63%
Home Helpers	56%
Category Average:	73%

Personal Fitness

Franchise:	Score:
Curves	96%
World Gym	77%
Gold's Gym	60%
Contours Express	59%
Category Average:	73%

Pet Products or Services

Franchise:	Score:
Wild Bird Centers	75%
Wild Birds Unlimited	68%
Aussie Pet Mobile	45%
Category Average:	63%

Photography

Franchise:	Score:
L'il Angels	79%
The Sports Section	76%
MotoPhoto	55%
Category Average:	70%

Performance by Category, cont.:

Pizza

Franchise:	Score:
Little Caesar's Pizza	83%
Godfather's Pizza	69%
Domino's Pizza	67%
Papa Murphy's	64%
Fox's Den Pizza	58%
Papa John's	58%
Pizza Factory	57%
Hungry Howie's Pizza & Subs	53%
Category Average:	64%

Plumbing

Franchise:	Score:
Roto Rooter	78%
Mr. Rooter	71%
Category Average:	75%

Postal Services:

Franchise:	Score:
Pak Mail	66%
Parcel Plus	64%
PostNet Postal & Business Services	61%
The UPS Store	61%
Postal Annex+	50%
Category Average:	60%

Printing Services

Franchise:	Score:
Allegra Network	76%
PIP Printing	76%
AlphaGraphics	74%
MinuteMan Press	66%
Sir Speedy	65%
Kwik Kopy	57%
Category Average:	69%

Realty Services

Franchise:	Score:
Keller Williams Realty	83%
United Country Real Estate	83%
Assist-2-Sell	81%
Prudential Real Estate	76%
HomeVestors of America	74%
Help-U-Sell	73%
Category Average:	78%

Residential Cleaning Services

Franchise:	Score:
Maid Brigade	83%
Merry Maids	78%
Molly Maid	73%
The Cleaning Authority	69%
The Maids International	64%
Maid To Perfection	61%
Category Average:	71%

Performance by Category, cont.:

Sign Services

Franchise:	Score:
Fast Signs	84%
Sign-A-Rama	63%
Signs By Tomorrow	62%
Signs Now	57%
Category Average:	67%

Specialized Products & Services

Franchise:	Score:
American Poolplayers Association	97%
Critter Control	92%
HobbyTown USA	89%
1-800-Got-Junk	86%
Adventures in Advertising	80%
The Dentist's Choice	78%
Play It Again Sports	76%
Wireless Zone	72%
Sandler Sales Institute	71%
Pop-A-Lock	70%
Two Men and A Truck	68%
Batteries Plus	68%
Property Damage Appraisers	67%
It's Just Lunch	66%
Cookies By Design	65%
Swisher Hygiene	65%
Leadership Management	61%
Planet Beach	58%
Dollar Discount Stores	57%
We The People Forms & Services	55%
Business Cards Tomorrow	53%
EmbroidMe	44%
Candy Bouquet	40%
Stained Glass Overlay	26%
Category Average:	67%

Tools

Franchise:	Score:
Snap-on Tools	82%
Matco Tools	68%
Category Average:	75%

Travel

Franchise:	Score:
Results! Travel	88%
American Express Travel Svcs.	82%
Carlson Wagonlit Travel	78%
CruiseOne	73%
Cruise Holidays	69%
Uniglobe Travel	67%
Category Average:	76%

**OVERALL AVERAGE SCORE
OF 216 FRANCHISES: 66%**

CHAPTER 3

Top 10 Things to do Before
Buying a Franchise

1—Conduct due diligence on yourself

2—Find a great accountant

3—Find a great attorney specialized in franchise law

4—Conduct due diligence on the business

5—Refresh and enhance your business acumen

6—Write a business plan

7—Identify and hire a great team—then create a culture to retain it

8—Hone your leadership skills

9—Hone your sales skills

10—Create a schedule that allows some time for family and friends

1—Conduct due diligence on yourself

Do you have the right personality to manage a business? Owning and actively managing a business is like a marriage. It's time consuming[26], demanding, and stressful[27], and if you can't devote 100% of the time it needs, you are likely to fail. Among other things, you must be able and willing to:

- Promote and develop your brand[28]

- Sell your products and services[29]

---

[26] Survey results indicate that 52% of franchisees are working 50 or more hours per week.

[27] Survey results indicate that, prior to opening their franchises, 40% underestimated the degree of stress and 31% underestimated the workload.

[28] A franchisee of a candy store stated: "I believe there is only one reason for opening a franchise. Only one reason. Brand recognition. If the franchise does not have brand recognition, it's worthless. If it has brand recognition, it is probably doing things right."

[29] A franchisee of a staffing franchise has found that: "Most franchise models relegate the franchisee to: a role of sales & product/service fulfillment. The critical success factor is your ability to sell! Nothing happens 'til somebody sells something! The Pareto Principal applies here as well: 20% of the franchisees yield 80% of the business. The factor that separates those 20% from the others is their ability or willingness to sell!"

- Think creatively to get your business known in your community[30]
- Empathize with your customers to provide them value
- Make people like you so as to develop repeat business and retain employees
- Use your perceptiveness to hire the right people
- Manage a high level of stress and anxiety without them affecting your performance, and consider what effects this stress and anxiety will have on your personal life.[31]

Do you have the talent necessary to manage a business? You'll need to manage all of the following—or find and pay someone who can—and then manage them:

- Human Resources—Hiring, morale, legal requirements, benefits, etc.
- Financial—Accounting, budgeting, insurance, payroll, taxes, planning, etc.
- Operations—Earn respect and loyalty of employees, manage inventory, create controls to minimize pilferage, manage administrative tasks and franchisor communications, etc.
- Marketing—Advertising to develop your name and get people in the door, coordinating displays, signage, frequent buyer programs, promotions, etc.
- Maintenance—From the clogged sink to the broken cash register to washing the windows
- Sales—Get people to buy from you not just once, but again and again and again
- Software, computer and POS—Know how to operate, manipulate, manage and evolve them

What are your shortcomings, and how will you compensate for them? It's important to recognize these so that you can find someone who has the right skills to perform the task:

- Don't want to be the one selling? Better be able to find someone who is capable and be willing to compensate them commensurate with their performance.
- Don't know how to manage your payroll? Find a service you can trust and afford.
- Have a tendency to lose your temper? Be careful not to exhibit it around either customers or employees.

Do you have enough cash, and can you afford to lose it?

- While no one opens a business expecting to lose money, a lot of them do, franchises included.[32] It's wise to examine every possible scenario prior to committing to its opening. If losing your investment would be a devastating blow to your and/or your family, then take a long, thorough examination before making the leap.

---

[30] Here's a clever method used by one franchisee: (One of) "The two best advertising or marketing strategies I used…" was "Teaching a QuickBooks class at a local Accounting School where I got to meet with and train business owners and their staffs for an all day training seminar. The Accounting School paid me a small fee to do so, but in addition I offered a free 30 minute on-site consultation as part of the class. Any consulting work I was able to pick up from that was mine to keep. I paid the school a 10% referral fee and have received over $15,000 in added revenue. My only cost was my time. This was over a period of about 4 months."

[31] A home restoration franchisee noted: "Very stressful business. Always dealing with homeowners in crisis. Getting paid from the insurance companies is worse than pulling teeth. Cash flow is always difficult. It's nothing to be out $100,000+ on completed jobs."

[32] 48% of survey respondents are making less income than expected prior to opening their franchise.

- One of the most common reasons businesses fail is that they underestimate the working capital necessary to keep the business afloat in its first year.[33] [34] Make sure you work with your accountant or investment advisor to review all agreements with a fine-tooth comb, and to incorporate all possible capital outlays and expenditures into your financial projections.

If, after answering the questions above, you believe you still want to open a business, you then need to decide whether you'd be better off investing in a franchise or opening a business independently. What are the advantages to a franchise? Every franchise opportunity must be examined independently. As the overall results in this book demonstrate, there are many good franchise investments as well as bad ones, and some offer these advantages while others do not. As you evaluate, question current franchisees and consider only those companies whose owners say they purchased:

- A higher chance of succeeding than if they'd opened their own business independently

- A turn-key operation

- Training that assures you're ready to manage all facets of the business

- An effective plan to market and sell products and services

- A network of expertise for you to work with and benefit from

- A business from a franchisor who makes a genuine effort to help them be successful[35]

What are the disadvantages? As above, these will differ based on each company.

- Any franchise agreements you sign will be inherently one-sided, favoring the franchisor.[36] They are likely to place strict controls[37] and expensive standards on you and your business, from how it appears, to the products you sell, to the territory you operate within.

- Many franchisors will neglect your business shortly after you're up and running. Don't forget the most common statement of the franchisees in this survey: "My franchisor is more interested in selling franchises than in supporting

---

[33] "The underestimated startup capital was due to me expecting to make money (after buying a seeming profitable business) during the first 12 months. Three years later I am only giving 4 employees a living. My fault? maybe. I have probably put 100k into business that I didn't expect"…noted an auto repair franchisee. A residential cleaning service franchisee stated: "…the estimate of working capital was not estimated properly. The estimates (franchise name deleted) provided were NOT accurate. The amount estimated based on the information provided should have been doubled (possibly more). That has caused a huge problem for us."

[34] 34% of survey respondents underestimated the working capital necessary prior to opening their franchise.

[35] A realty services franchisee commented: "(Franchise name deleted) is a great franchise to have and the principals are very principled!"

From a carpet and upholstery services franchisee: "…owner (name deleted) is a "down to earth" company president that genuinely cares about all operators…The home office places high regard on helping everyone be successful. If you are not happy, it is not their fault. They are always there to help."

And a franchisee of a personal care company commented: "They give you the tools, the instruments, the means to succeed." The "only way you would fail is if you fail yourself."

[36] A franchisee of more than 25 fast food restaurants, who signed his first franchise agreement in the late 1970's, had this to say: "Franchising has evolved with tremendous power vested in the franchisor. The franchisee takes 99.9% of the risks and the franchisor has 110% of the power. Franchise law is tilted toward the franchisor. A balance of power must evolve."

Additional comment from an automotive detailing franchisee "As in most franchise agreements the franchisor has all the power and options and slanted legal ties. The franchisee(s) have few."

[37] The advantages and disadvantages through the eyes of a specialty retail franchisee: "When you own a franchise you get all the burdens/disadvantages of owning your own business (liability, total consumption of your life, etc. without any of the advantages—because you still "work for the franchisor" and have to do as they say. Obviously, there are numerous advantages to a franchise in terms of marketing, growth, name recognition, support, etc. All of which you pay for. Overall it has been an up and down experience for us."

the existing franchisees." Be careful, especially when dealing with a company that has lots of franchisees with multiple locations. These people will probably be well taken care of, while those with only one location may also be, but possibly to a lesser extent.[38]

- Most franchisors demand royalty payments as a percentage of gross income, whether you're making a profit or not. If the franchise demands a royalty for national marketing, make sure you'll stand to benefit from it.

- Once you sign your franchise agreement, you will be held accountable for honoring your commitments. On the other hand, the franchisor, which holds most of the cards, may change the terms periodically, and there will be little you can do about it short of forfeiting your franchise.[39]

- Even if you're franchise is successful, you may find when it's time to renew your franchise agreement that either you're not offered the option, or that you're precluded from renewing by new, more onerous stipulations.[40]

- You may be hard-pressed to transfer or sell your franchise if you've had enough of running it, are making only a meager return on your investment, or you become incapacitated.[41]

- Poor quality or service standards of other franchise locations may effect your own reputation for quality, and you may also be responsible for warranting the work of other locations. For example, let's say you're a franchisee of XYZ Transmission Repair. A customer whose vehicle was improperly repaired at another XYZ location 20 miles away may come to your location to have the problem corrected, and may expect it to be corrected at no cost.

2—Find a great accountant

If you're a great accountant, terrific, manage it all yourself. Unfortunately, most of us aren't, and the accounting is too important to not have it prepared well and with confidence. If you're part of the latter category, you'll need to find someone great <u>before</u> signing the agreement. They can work with you to help identify the type of opportunity that's best for you, whether it should be a franchise, the business entity that's best for you (C Corp., LLC, LLP, S Corp.?) and perform the necessary financial due diligence. And you'll need one after signing the agreement to create financial statements and tax returns, and provide sound advice on tax strategies, inventory levels and how best to manage your receivables. While the fees can add up, a competent accountant will often pay for his/her own fees through the sound advice and money-saving strategies they recommend.[42] Don't have a competent accountant and not sure how to find one? Here are:

---

[38] Feelings expressed by a hair-cutting franchisee: "…as an owner of just a few franchises it has become apparent that the small owners have become more of an "irritation" to (franchisor name deleted) than an asset. A fellow franchisee told me a couple of weeks ago that he had just opened his 10th salon and that corporate personnel were finally returning his phone calls. He thought maybe 10 salons were the magic number to be recognized."

[39] A candy store franchisee stated: "When we first started this, we signed our franchise agreement and UFOC. After seven or eight months, they made us re-sign an agreement with hundreds of changes from the original. They realized there were many mistakes in it…"You have to re-sign", they told us. They put tremendous pressure on us and called us every day." After that, they came back with changes another three or four times."

[40] The experience of one stained glass franchisee: "I did not anticipate my franchisor changing our agreement in very major ways upon renewal. I never dreamed that they would increase my minimum royalty amounts to a point where I would be unable to keep the franchise."

[41] The experience of one children's services franchisee: (Franchise name deleted was) "Very unsupportive in selling franchise. I recently sold and they did not follow through with their end of the transfer…Poor communication in the re-sell process; do not wish my experience on any other franchisee."
     And a franchisee of a printing services company noted: "If I could get out I would."

[42] With the benefit of hindsight, a realty services franchisee stated: "I believe (franchise name deleted) could have been more helpful in setting up corporate paperwork and hiring of accountants, lawyers, etc. I was told that this stuff was easy and not to hire them, save money and do it myself. It cost me triple than if I would of hired a professional."

A few sources:

- Ask friends or local business owners for referrals.
- If you have an attorney or financial planner, they may have recommendations.
- Contact your local chapter of the AICPA (American Institute of Certified Public Accountants).

Here are some questions to ask when trying to identify a great accountant. My recommendation is that you speak with a few if not several and compare them to one another.

- Are they a CPA (Certified Public Accountant)? CPA's generally have a greater depth of knowledge than most other accountants. However, depending upon the complexity of your business, it may not require the expertise of a CPA, which generally commands a higher hourly rate than most other accountants.
- What size is the firm? Most franchises are small businesses and don't require the breadth of knowledge offered by larger accounting firms. The smaller firms are likely to share greater empathy with your business as well as offer more attractive rates. Also be sure they're someone who will be able to competently manage your needs as your business grows and evolves.
- What rate will I be charged? (Don't forget to include this in your financial projections.)
- Is the person you're meeting with going to prepare your statements and returns, or are they going to have another staff member prepare them? If another staff member, who are they and what are their qualifications?
- How long will it generally take to prepare your statements and returns?
- What other services do they provide? Will they assist with tax or business planning? Can they assist with software or computer issues?
- Who are their clients? Have they worked with franchisees? Do they have clients in the same type of business?
- Has any legal action been taken against their firm for incorrect returns or statements?
- Will they provide you with other clients' names that you can contact as references?

Listen to what questions they ask you about your business goals. If they don't ask good questions of you and take an interest in how your business will grow, you may want to shop elsewhere.

3—Find a great attorney specialized in franchise law

If you're considering spending hundreds of thousands of dollars, taking on the obligations of business ownership, and signing a document that will commit you to a relationship that's generally 10 years in length, it's wise to spend some money on an attorney who **specializes in franchise law**. After reviewing your contracts, a good franchise attorney will assure you have a full understanding of all of your obligations and the controls and constraints placed upon you by these agreements.[43] As well, they will work to ensure you're getting the fairest contract possible. The smaller and "hungrier"

---

43   Susan Kezios, President of the American Franchisee Association: "If someone is going to buy a franchise, what they have to do is…when they receive the offering circular, and the franchise agreement, they have to read every word of it, whether they understand it or not. They need to take the offering circular, at a minimum, the franchise agreement—actually I suggest to folks that they try to avoid reading the marketing materials at all, and that they actually read the offering circular second, but what they read first is the franchise agreement because the franchise agreement is what they're going to sign. The offering circular makes representations about what is supposed to be in the franchise agreement. So I recommend people try to keep the blinders on to the marketing pitch and really don't pay too much attention at first to the UFOC but really read the franchise agreement…There's several handy checklists (you can find one on the AFA web page–www.franchisee.org), franchise agreement provisions you should avoid at all costs. They need to take that franchise agreement and the offering circular to someone who understands franchising, franchise law, preferably a franchisee attorney. And pay that $1,500, $2,500—whatever it might cost to have a proper review done, so they understand what a "covenant not to compete" means. (An example of the

the franchisor corporation, the greater your likelihood of negotiating change. Larger franchisors are more apt to make only make minor concessions. Regardless of what size franchisor you're dealing with, it is vital that your attorney possesses expertise specifically in franchise law as there are many nuances. Not sure how to identify a reputable attorney? Here are:

A few sources:

- Ask friends, local business, or current franchisees for referrals.
- If you have an accountant or financial planner, they may have recommendations.
- Contact the ABA (American Bar Association) at www.aba.org, or take a look at their national referral directory, at http://www.abanet.org/legalservices/findlegalhelp/lawrefdirectory.html#
- Also check the "Legal Resources" section of the American Franchisee Association's web page: www.franchisee.org

Some questions to ask:

- What rate will I be charged? (Don't forget to include this in your financial projections).
- How many UFOCs and/or franchise agreements have they reviewed?
- How successful have they been negotiating changes to the UFOC with franchisors?
- Will they provide you with other clients' names that you can contact as references?

4—Conduct due diligence on the business

The UFOC[44]

To do an in-depth investigation, the Uniform Franchise Offering Circular (UFOC) is a great source of information and a good place to start. Franchisors are required to provide you with a copy at least 14 calendar (10 business) days before you sign a franchise agreement. **(The terms found in the UFOC should theoretically mirror those in your franchise agreement, however, this is not always the case. The franchise agreement is the document you ultimately will have to sign and the terms of which you will be bound by when purchasing a franchise. Both you and your attorney should perform a thorough review of both documents).** While it can be difficult to get a copy of the UFOC without first disclosing extensive personal financial data, check the state agencies listed in Chapter 5 to see if they have a copy available for review. One, California, even offers online access for anyone to review them (http://134.186.208.228/caleasi/pub/Exsearch.htm). Unfortunately, all of the states, with the exception of Minnesota, allow filing exemptions (i.e., franchisors don't have to submit documents for review), the criteria of which can easily be met by many of these companies.

Here are some questions and the section within the UFOC for which you'll find the answers:

- How long has the franchisor been in business? (Item 1)
- How many years have they been selling franchises? (Item 1)

---

restrictions a "covenant not to compete" can have): They are running a tax preparation service now, but if they buy the H & R Block, it doesn't matter that they were running a tax preparation service for 15 years prior, but once they buy the H & R Block and after they leave the H & R Block they're going to be prohibited from operating tax preparation services for a certain number of years…and (within) a certain geographic radius. Doesn't matter what kind of franchise you pick."
Interview with Kezios conducted by the author on January 28, 2005.

44   U.F.O.C stands for "Uniform Franchise Offering Circular". This is the disclosure document that details the terms of your franchise agreement, including fees, royalties, and obligations of both the franchisor and franchisee. Its terms should, but don't necessarily, mirror those of the franchise agreement, which is the contract you ultimately sign when purchasing a franchise.

- What is the business experience of the company officers? (Item 2)

- What litigation, if any, has the franchisor been involved in? What was (were) the result(s)? (Item 3)

- What are the initial investment and ongoing fees? (Items 5, 6 and 7)

- Does the franchisor offer financing? (Item 10)

- What type of training is provided? (Item 11)

- Will you have a defined territory? How is it defined, and what about future expansion? (Item 12)

- What is your obligation to participate in the day-to-day operations of the business? (Item 15)

- What is the duration of the franchise agreement? (Item 17)

- What rules are you subject to should you decide to sell your franchise before your agreement terminates? (Item 17)

- Does the franchisor provide estimates as to how much money you can make? (Item 19)

- How many locations currently exist, where are these located, and how can you get in touch with them? (Item 20)

- Does the franchisor own and operate locations of its own, or are all locations owned by independent franchisees? (Item 20)

- Has the number of franchisees increased or decreased over the last three years? (Item 20. It is neither uncommon nor a very good sign to see that the number has diminished.)

- How many franchisees have "exited" the system, and how can I get in touch with them? (Item 20). Ask the franchisor why these owners have left, then contact some of the owners directly to hear their perspectives.

Contact Current and Past Franchisees

Identify owners who are both in and out of your geographic region, preferably in locations with similar demographic profiles to the area you're considering. Select them yourself from the UFOC as franchisors often "cherry-pick" their most enthusiastic supporters and then provide you this list to contact.[45] Speak with a minimum of 10 franchisees and ask them the same 12 questions asked in the survey for this book.[46] When those questions have been answered, ask more. Speak with your accountant and attorney beforehand to get their advice. And don't forget to contact several former franchisees to understand their perspectives. It may seem like a lot of work, but it's better to understand exactly what you're getting in to than to risk your hard earned money without a thorough examination of what it's being invested in. Here are some things to think about and possible questions to ask during your investigation:

Location

- What input do you have in selecting your location?[47]

- Who secures the necessary permits and approvals?

- Who negotiates the lease? Are the terms of the lease comparable to other tenants nearby?

- Will the duration of your lease and franchise agreement be the same?

- How much flexibility is there with regard to the lease terms?

---

[45]   As well, current franchisees will sometimes mislead you if their own business is losing money and they're trying to sell it. Being truthful only hurts their prospects of doing so. A mid-sized ice cream franchisee noted: "(Franchise name deleted) gave me a list (of names) to call. I called over 20 people and only one person told the truth" (that they were losing money).

[46]   Susan Kezios, President of the American Franchisee Association: "The other element (to steps that should be taken by a prospective franchise buyer) is to talk to as many of their existing franchisees and to visit as many as possible." Interview with Kezios conducted by the author on January 28, 2005.

[47]   Remarks from two national ice cream store franchisees: "Our lease payment was pre-negotiated, prior to us signing on. It's the highest in our state. This is a problem for us."

"My best advice…is to carefully pick your location. Lots of foot traffic, restaurant and evening entertainment districts are best."

- Will you be leasing, or sub-leasing the premises? If you are sub-leasing, make sure you're getting a fair deal and consider the ramifications if the lengths of the lease and your franchise agreement are different.
- Are you personally liable for the terms of the lease, or is your business?

Financial

First, find out your franchisor's:

- Costs of products to franchisees
- Revenues by product
- Monthly averages of gross revenues

And inquire whether:

- Volume discounts are offered, and if so, under what terms.
- The franchisor can designate the retail pricing of your products or services.
- The franchisor will assist in arranging credit card processing contracts, and if so, what the processing fees are.
- Franchisees are eligible for any special rates on insurance or health benefits. These are mentioned time-and-time again by franchise owners as unexpectedly heavy burdens.

These are essential for your financial projections, budgeting, managing inventory and supplies, hiring purposes, advertising and promotions and effective overall planning. For instance, in the franchise I owned, for four straight years 15% of my annual sales occurred during the seven-day period before Christmas and 40% of annual sales in the final six weeks of the year. You can imagine how helpful this knowledge would be in planning your first year in business!

Once you have these numbers, your accountant should then create three-to-five year projected net income under three scenarios: "Best Case", "Worst Case" and "Most Likely Case". To do so, you'll need to come up with good estimates for startup costs, including beginning inventory, grand opening promotions, working capital, etc. Include every possible expenditure, from workman's compensation, which is often under-estimated,[48] to unemployment insurance, payroll services, taxes, even a miscellaneous expense for things like bleach that you'll need to mop the floors. And be careful with income. It's fine to include an optimistic estimate for your "Best Case" scenario, but make sure you're realistic in your "Worst Case" too. You don't want surprises when it comes to your income; so if you can't live with all three scenarios, then consider it a red flag. You should also have your accountant review the financial statements of the franchisor to assess its stability (these can be found under Item 21 of the UFOC).

As an interesting side note, the average initial investment in a franchise, excluding real estate, is $318,975.[49] Average royalty fees range from 3% to 6% of monthly gross sales.

Marketing

- How important is the marketing of your business?
- How effective have the franchisor's advertising and promotions been?[50]

---

[48] In response to survey question 12, which asks "If you could turn back time to the day you signed your franchise agreement, would you make the same decision to buy your franchise?" a lawn care franchisee remarked: "My answer to # 12 (No) is based solely on the insurance (workers comp., general liability, auto, etc.) burden for operating this type of business in Florida."

[49] International Franchise Association website article "Answers to the 21 Most Commonly Asked Questions About Franchising", available at: http://www.franchise.org/resourcectr/faq/q15.asp

[50] 47% of franchisees in this survey indicated that the area in which their franchisor could most improve would be in the effectiveness of marketing and promotions. This was the most often cited area in which the franchisor could improve.

- Is the brand recognized by people?

- Inquire about current and future advertising and promotions, whether you will be required to conduct them and whether franchisees are given discounts to cover them.

- Is there a Marketing or Advertising royalty fee? If so, how much is it and how often do you pay it? How are these fees used? Is any of it dedicated to local marketing? If not, will you really benefit from it?

- Does the franchisor assist you with your own sales/marketing strategy?

- Will you be provided with demographic data to assess your location before signing any agreements?

- Assuming you've reviewed the demographics for your location, and that they are currently favorable, how are they expected to change over the next five to ten years? Are incomes projected to be on the rise? What about the average age? Percentage of teens?

- Are charges reasonable for advertising collateral purchased from the franchisor? Are you required to purchase these materials?

- How flexible/strict is the franchisor with regard to the products/services you offer? In other words, might you be able to sell products from outside vendors?

Risks

- What makes your product/service a better one to invest in?[51]

- How much of a threat to your success is competition? Research competitors, and then ask both the franchisor and franchisees about each.

- What impact might other franchisees in your region have on the brand image? While other franchisees are often your best source of insight, advice, ideas, and support, poor service quality by another franchisee may hurt your brand image.[52]

- What impact might a change in government policy or regulation have on your business?[53]

- How does the franchisor expect its business to expand and evolve over the next 10 years, the likely term of your agreement?

---

[51] Responses of two truck-bed liner franchisees to the question "What are the things you most admire about (franchise name deleted) as a company?" 1: "The chemical! I don't think there is a better polyurethane or system that can beat a (franchise name deleted) product."

2: "What I admire most about (franchise name deleted) is it is the best liner in the business and our cooperate (sic) office does a great job getting the word out about (product name deleted)."

[52] This insightful answer came from a franchisee of an automotive detailer, in response to a question about the importance of advertising: "I do not think that advertising by corporate would help me as an independent franchisee because (franchise name deleted) is only as good as the individual techs…in other words there is no real consistancy (sic) amongst technicians…for example just the other day I was at a dealership of mine and one of the manager(s) went to another city to pick up a vehicle for me to paint. While he was there he told the manager of that store that he was going to have his (franchise name deleted) tech paint the damage. The manager of that store said "really, our (franchise name deleted) guy is terrible" my manager replied "well our's (sic) is the best"…so you see (franchise name deleted) is only as good as the individual tech's ability. When I am in the market for a new account I go in personally with a referral from one of my other dealerships and speak to the management. This approach has worked well for me and my business."

[53] A franchisee offering children's educational services told to the author that, when new school board policies took effect, disallowing all but non-profit businesses from soliciting contracts within the school system, this completely took away the largest market for their services.

- Consider the risk of your franchisor being sold to another company. This may either improve or hinder your ability to succeed.[54]

- Will your local community support the type of business you intend to open?

- How quickly is the competition evolving and expanding?

- Are you in a "trendy" industry?

- How might the internet effect your business over time?[55]

- What type of legal liability would your business potentially be susceptible to—product, environmental, health, sexual harassment, slip-and-fall cases, etc.?[56]

- Is our national economy fairly stable? What about the local economy?

- Your franchise may be susceptible to bounced checks[57] and uncollectable accounts receivable[58]. Will the franchisor assist in bad debt collection?

- An additional risk noted in the Shane book:

  "Franchising is a useful tool for passing off risk to another party. When a company franchises, its franchisees bear some of the financial risk that comes from adding outlets in new locations that might or might not be successful. If the capital that a firm uses to establish the new outlet belongs to franchisees, the risk of expansion is borne by the franchisees. Therefore, one way for a firm to manage risk is to franchise outlets in new locations and have the franchisees bear the risk of figuring out whether the new locations will be successful. When the value of particular locations is known, the franchisor can buy back the successful locations and leave the unsuccessful ones franchised. **In fact, most franchisors tend to do just this, retaining the highest-performing outlets and franchising the lower-performing ones.**" (emphasis added by author)[59]

---

[54] Two examples: Franchisee of a financial/business services company: "When I bought in, we had a good franchisor, fair, worked with the franchisees. After two years, we were sold to a (foreign) company that has no idea how to be a franchisor and seems to just be using us to build their own company stores."

Franchisee of a health products company: "The latest owner appears only in maximizing his income while providing minimal to no support to the franchisees! The creator and original owner of (franchise name deleted) provided excellent support and advertising!!!"

[55] The perspective of a national travel services franchisee: "I look at the internet as our friend. I no longer have to spend a lot of productive (time) on non-productive transactions like airline tickets unless we receive compensation either from the customer or the airline. Because of the internet we have been able to reduce our headcount considerably and therefore increase our profitability."

[56] In response to survey question 11, a multiple-choice question which asks "Prior to opening your franchise, which (if any) of the following did you underestimate? a franchisee of a home inspection services firm, replied: "I underestimated the liability involved. The risk of lawsuits."

[57] In response to survey question 11, a multiple-choice questions which asks "Prior to opening your franchise, which (if any) of the following did you underestimate?" a check-cashing service franchisee replied: "How careful you have to be, especially at beginning to not take bad paper (checks)."

[58] Some thoughts from a tool products franchisee: "I enjoy the tool business. The money outlay is the hardest to manage. Would like to see company help more with bad debt collections."

[59] Shane, **From Ice Cream to the Internet**, Prentice Hall Publishing, Upper Saddle River, NJ, 2005, p. 36.

Miscellaneous

- Investigate whether to purchase a franchise, or whether you could be just as successful opening an independent business providing the same types of products and services.[60]

- Assuming your franchisor maintains a web site and toll-free ordering number, how will this effect your business? What restrictions will you be under in establishing a web site for your particular location and customers?

- If you are considering a franchise with only a few franchisees in place, are the existing owners independent of the parent. In other words, were the initial franchisees friends, relatives or acquaintances of the franchisor?

- Consider the effect other franchisees could have on your business.

- What reports will you be required to supply, how often, and what reports are provided to franchisees?

- If you sell or transfer your franchise, what types of non-compete and confidentiality agreements might you be required to sign?

- What restrictions will you be subject to with regard to outside business interests while running your franchise? Will these restrictions preclude you from operating other types of businesses or franchises?[61]

- What restrictions would you face if you wish to relocate your franchise to a new location?

- If you decide to enlist a new partner into the business, will the franchisor have to meet and approve them?

Training, Field Support & Technology

- Where is it conducted?

- What is the duration?

- Does it fully prepare you to successfully operate your business?[62]

---

[60]   The response of a home inspection services franchisee to the question, "What advice would you provide for someone considering investing in a (franchise name deleted) franchise?": "Explore the Independent route to reduce all franchise expenses as the independent inspectors get the equal training and are able to make more money than the franchised inspectors."

[61]   In a letter from John Rachide, Chairman of the International Franchisee Advisory Council (the Domino's Pizza franchisee association) to the F.T.C. (dated April 30, 1997), Mr. Rachide remarks: "All Domino's franchise contracts prohibit the franchisee from owning any other businesses. We cannot develop any other opportunities unless we sell our stores. When we sell our stores, few of us can command a price great enough to capitalize another business because of the small pool of potential buyers." Available at: http://www.ftc.gov/bcp/franchise/comments/rachid32.htm

[62]   Some positive experiences: From a furniture restoration franchisee: "We received 2 weeks of initial training at the corp. HQ upon purchasing the franchise. They not only have a very, very competent staff of trainers, but they also have "real-world" experience, just not someone who trains people for a living and doesn't know anything about what actually goes on outside their doors. They also have continuous free training at workshops and at their HQ, all you have to do is sign up if you're a franchisee. They also have normal working hours help available with only a phone call or page for free, this is way above what the other furniture repair franchise offers as far as I understand."

From a franchisee of an automotive detailer: "I was trained in all of the systems that I purchased in the franchise. The initial training was two weeks long at the corporate headquarters. It was well organized and was taught by qualified, experienced trainers. Step by step hands on training was done in each of the vehicle reconditioning systems as well as training on the business aspects such as bookkeeping and marketing. Instructions were also provided on how to set up the trailer that would be used for the business. Following the initial training…I spent a week with a mentor, who already had a business going…This was on-the-job training working with him in his established accounts. He also spent a week with me…to help me establish accounts and continue with hands on training. Each winter a conference is held where additional training on new techniques, products, and systems is provided. I have attended one conference so far and it was also beneficial in sharpening my skills and making me aware of new products. The trainers in the corporate office are available to the reps in the field at all times by phone to answer questions, provide technical support, and help in any way possible."

And one negative experience: "The training I received from (cookie franchisor name deleted) was at a cost of approx. $6000…My training…was given to me by a young lady from part of the (franchisor parent company name deleted) and she

- Ask current franchisees what training they wish they'd been provided.
- Can you review the operations manual before signing an agreement? If not, offer to sign a confidentiality agreement to see whether that would make a difference.
- If training is held at the franchisor's headquarters, who pays transportation and lodging costs?
- If training is held locally, who pays transportation costs for Corporate to fly in?
- Is there a fee for training? If yes, how much? If no, is there a maximum number of employees eligible before being charged a fee?
- What type(s) of ongoing training will me made available? At what intervals? Is there a fee?
- What type of field support is provided?
- How many field support staff are dedicated solely to franchisees?
- How often will field support staff visit your location?
- What's the turnover rate of field support staff?
- What typically occurs during their visits?
- How are training & new materials provided to existing franchise owners?
- What information technology support does the Franchisor provide?
- Is your P.O.S. (point of sale system, i.e., cash register) supported by a local technology firm? Is there a national support contract? If so, what is the annual fee to cover your equipment? If not, what is the hourly rate charged for service?
- Is the P.O.S. software proprietary or "off-the-shelf"? If proprietary, are updates provided free of charge?

5—Refresh and enhance your business acumen

Unless you employ the talent to manage the business for yourself, you'll need a solid and broad array of business skills. A great way to identify some of the skills you'll need for your particular business is to first work at an existing location.[63] I did this for a few weeks before opening my franchise and found the experience invaluable.[64] Of course, the degree of refresher necessary will vary from person-to-person, but most of us need to refresh in at least some of the following areas: Communications, Marketing, Sales, Human Resources, Technology, Finance.

Here are some good places to begin (Information provided by the Small Business Administration):

---

knew VERY little about the franchise…In my opinion, I could have learned the same amount of information in just 1 day at my own store, being taught by the current owner than (franchisor name deleted) own training. 1 week and $6000 wasted to be honest!"

[63] A home improvement franchisee had this thought: "Looking back I wish I would have worked at an existing franchise for six months or so to better learn the job."

And a smoothie franchisee responded to the question: "What advice would you provide to someone thinking of buying a (franchise name deleted) franchise?" as follows: "Work an event with a current franchise owner, set-up, work the event and tear down after. Had we done this I think we would have changed our mind."

[64] Susan Kezios, President of the American Franchisee Association: "If they're an engineer or a lawyer, and think they're going to go into a pizza franchise, or a pharmacy franchise, or a hobby franchise, go and work in a similar business part time for awhile…If you're going to buy a sub franchise, and you go and you work (in a sub franchise), and you learn the cost of the meat-slicer, and the countertops, and you learn those things from working part time there while you have your other full time job, and in the franchisor proposal you're buying a lot of the products and supplies from them…you see what the prices are, you're at least going to have some background that (shows) you're investing way too much money." Interview with Kezios conducted by the author on January 28, 2005.

<u>Small Business Administration (SBA)</u>: With offices nationally, they are an excellent resource for all types of counsel and advice for current and prospective small business owners, as well as a sponsor of the next two listings. For more information, call them at 1-800-U-ASK-SBA (1-800-827-5722) or visit their web site at: http://www.sbaonline.sba.gov

<u>Service Corps of Retired Executives (SCORE)</u>: A national organization sponsored by the Small Business Administration (SBA) of over 13,000 volunteer business executives who provide free counseling, workshops and seminars to prospective and existing small business people. There are 389 chapters nationwide. For more information, call them at 1-800-634-0245 or visit their web site at: http://www.score.org

<u>Small Business Development Centers</u>: Also sponsored by the SBA, in partnership with state and local governments, the educational community and the private sector. They provide assistance, counseling and training to prospective and existing business people, with 60 offices nationwide. For more information visit their web site at: http://www.sba.gov/sbdc or call the SBA at the number referenced above.

Another source of extremely helpful information is the "<u>All Experts</u>"™ web site, found at http://www.allexperts.com. There's no charge, and you can ask questions to thousands of volunteers in dozens of different categories, or search their extensive reservoir of previously asked questions and the answers that were given. I've received lots of timesaving help on questions about software, publishing, travel, and many other subjects.

6—Write a business plan

While writing a business plan may seem daunting or unnecessary to some, it is actually quite an important element of the process of starting a business.[65] [66] If you plan effectively upfront, your operation will run more smoothly and efficiently, more profitably, and with fewer surprises. And the good news is that, if you've already completed steps one through five above, you've already gathered much of the information needed to formulate a solid business plan. Your franchisor might also have already collected some of the data—ask them.

While business plans will vary by business type (e.g., Are you selling services, products, or both?), most will include the elements listed below. Some of these, such as a Management Summary, you may not feel are necessary for your particular business, so use your own judgment to create what you feel you will benefit from.

- Executive Summary—This includes a summary of the business itself, a Mission Statement, information on start-up costs and bank loans, and certain key operational or financial goals, such as a projected timeline for attaining profitability, gross margin objectives, or a goal for payroll expenses not to exceed a certain percentage of revenues.
- Market Analysis—This is an analysis of your sales territory, demographics, target customers, and competition. It should be analyzed not just in static terms, but also in terms of trends to understand how the market has changed over the past several years, and how it is expected to change over the next several. Don't forget to consider the impact of internet sales, whether yours or a competitor's, in this analysis.
- SWOT Analysis—A SWOT analysis identifies the Strengths, Weaknesses, Opportunities and Threats to your business, both on its own and relative to your future competition.

---

[65]   Some franchisors even require you to write a business plan. For instance, a franchisee from one of the highest performing franchises in this survey, stated that their franchisor "awards" franchises, and that "...you don't just write a check, you must have a business plan, a phone interview, financial backing..."

[66]   Susan Kezios, President of the American Franchisee Association, regarding steps that should be taken by a prospective franchise buyer: "I also tell people that they should really investigate if there's a small business development center, or a minority business development center or a women's business development center, and go and take some courses in "Starting a Business from Scratch" or "Writing a Business Plan", the kind of things you would do if you were not a person in a franchise...opening an independent, non-franchised firm, because your eyes will be opened...They might actually start to get the notion that they could do this on their own." Interview with Kezios conducted by the author on January 28, 2005.

- Marketing Strategy—A good marketing strategy will utilize the information from your Market Analysis to map out who you'll need to market to, effective methods of marketing to them, effective methods of selling to them, and how these might evolve over time.

- Operations Summary—This section summarizes the processes and procedures necessary for acquiring, producing, managing and fulfilling of the goods and/or services of your business. These will differ quite a bit from business to business. For instance, the processes, procedures, and customer interaction of a realtor will be markedly different from that of a sign maker.

- Management Summary—A summary of the management team and their backgrounds, as well as the expected personnel requirements of the business.

- Financial Plan—This should include a breakeven analysis and projections for cash flow, profit and loss, and balance sheet. This is one of, if not the most important section of your business plan, because if the financial projections are unappealing to you, there's no reason to move forward with buying the franchise. Make sure your projections are realistic, and include any assumptions you're making in the footnotes.

There are lots of helpful tools available for creating business plans, including books, software programs, and the internet. As with other sections, the local library and the Small Business Administration are good starting points. Here's the web link for the SBA's advice on business plans: http://www.sba.gov/starting_business/planning/basic.html

7—Identify and hire a great team—then create a culture to retain it

This is one of the most important and difficult challenges to making your business a success.[67] [68] Your team must be dedicated, productive, efficient, trustworthy, and provide excellent customer service. To create a team like this, they'll need to perceive that you provide them reasonable compensation, opportunity for personal growth and promotion, and that you manage them fairly, all in a trustworthy, team-oriented, friendly environment. How you lead them (point 9 below) will have a big impact on whether you'll be able to retain them. Your team is your business's face to the customer, and their morale can have tremendous implications for your business, either positive or negative. Make sure to hire well and manage employees fairly, and they'll be one of your best tools for helping your business grow.

8—Hone your leadership skills

Good leadership is essential to any business succeeding over the long run. You don't need to be a great leader, but you should at least be a good one. And don't fool yourself. Many of us feel we are excellent leaders when we're really not. There are vast differences between being decisive and being an <u>effective</u> leader. Describing all the characteristics of a great leader and how to attain them is beyond the scope of this book, however, and I would suggest looking at your local library, bookstore or the internet for some. You're sure to find plenty. For now, here are some things to consider:

- You should have a high degree of self-awareness and emotional control, and make decisions rationally rather than emotionally.

- Work to empathize with and involve your employees. This builds morale and productivity, and there's usually a lot you can learn from them.

---

[67] 43% of survey respondents indicated that they underestimated the difficulty of hiring and retaining quality staff prior to opening their franchise, the most often cited area of underestimation.

[68] A framing franchisee noted: "Finding good employees (is) the single most frustrating aspect of this business! Not to mention training them."

A second example, from a printing services franchisee: "Current problem? I cannot grow my business (i.e., add new services, increase sales, etc.) because of lack of capable (just capable!) employees. Whether this is a franchisor problem or not I don't know—it is not a hiring problem or even a training problem. (From my observation—this is not restricted to my franchise). It's just got to be a small businessman's problem, you eventually run out of family members to help out!"

- Work to empathize with the wants and needs of your customers. Meet their expectations of value in a welcoming, friendly environment, and they'll come back.

- Try to understand other people's perceptions of you. The better you do this, the more likely you'll be able to alter your behavior to mold those perceptions.

- Understand your short and long-term goals for the business. If you don't know where you want to go, you're unlikely to get there.

- Be self-motivated. As the leader, you've got to find the drive and tenacity to work your tail off. If you can't find this in yourself, who's going to light the spark under you?

- Accept mistakes as they're going to happen. Learn from them to improve and to set an example.

- Create an environment that's fair, respectful, trustworthy and team-oriented. People don't always have to agree with you, but they'll follow you if they respect you, believe you to be fair and honest, and if your decisions are generally wise.

9—Hone your sales skills

Few businesses have products or services that "sell themselves". Even if you believe that yours does, there's no product or service that won't benefit from the skills of a good sales person.

10—Create a schedule that allows some time for family and friends

It's likely that one of the main reasons you want to open a franchise is the expectation that it will improve the quality of life for your family and yourself.[69] Make sure you remember that, for your benefit and theirs.

---

[69] It's nice when things work out for all involved, like it did for this franchisee: "I have had a better life for myself and my family because of my decision to go into business for myself as a (franchise name deleted) franchisee."

CHAPTER 4

Understanding the UFOC

Bear in mind that the UFOC discloses many of your obligations and "rights" as a franchisee. It is generally regarded as very one-sided, with the franchisor retaining a tremendous degree of control over franchisees, and franchisees having few rights.[70][71] Regardless, if you're considering investing in a franchise then you need to review it in meticulous detail, preferably several times, before ever considering signing your franchise agreement. You should also have an attorney who is an expert in franchise law review it and provide counsel.[72] Note the cover page of the document, on which the Federal Trade Commission writes: "To protect you, we've required your franchisor to give you this information. **We haven't checked it and don't know if it's correct.**"[73] Examine this document, and all its accompanying schedules and exhibits, very carefully as its terms will govern your life for years to come once the franchise agreement has been signed (and assuming its terms mirror those of the franchise agreement).

---

[70] Also noteworthy, from Susan Kezios, President of the American Franchisee Association: "People have to understand what they're buying when they buy a franchise. The contracts are notoriously the same. The franchisor lawyers get together at the American Bar Association forum on franchising every year, they teach each other how to write these contracts, they teach each other how to disclose the minimum amount of information in the UFOC. The first time I was ever at an American Bar Association Forum on Franchising meeting, I remember a prominent franchisor lawyer standing in front of the room, holding up an offering circular saying (this was when the new regulatory guidelines came into effect) "The Federal Trade Commission wants us to disclose XYZ, now let me show you how we can avoid disclosing XYZ." Interview with Kezios conducted by the author on January 28, 2005.

[71] Further, in a letter from John Rachide, Chairman of the International Franchisee Advisory Council (the Domino's Pizza franchisee association) to the F.T.C. (April 30, 1997), Mr. Rachide remarks: "It is not likely that a new, young franchisee…is going to understand that they will be trapped by entering into the franchise agreement. Even though everything I describe above (in the letter) could be imagined after reading the UFOC, few honest business persons would have such an imagination. Franchisors have spent millions of dollars developing these elaborate traps.

Franchisees simply cannot see the situation until they are stuck in it." Available at:
http://www.ftc.gov/bcp/franchise/comments/rachid32.htm

[72] The terms found in the UFOC should theoretically mirror those in your franchise agreement, however, this is not always the case. The franchise agreement is the document you ultimately will have to sign and the terms of which you will be bound by when purchasing a franchise. Both you and your attorney should perform a thorough review of both documents.

[73] Thoughts from Susan Kezios on the effect of current franchise disclosure rules; i.e., the UFOC: "the patchwork quilt of Franchise Rule and existing state pre-sale disclosure laws have had little to no effect on the resulting franchise relationship and have been wholly inadequate in addressing the problems of overreaching and opportunism that current franchisees find themselves facing from certain franchisors. What is worse is that franchisors then justify their abuses by claiming that pre-sale disclosure makes abusive trade practices lawful and proper—because they were disclosed in advance. Little to no oversight compounds the problem by allowing certain franchisors and their lawyers to, quite simply, deceive franchise investors." Letter from Susan Kezios to the Secretary of the F.T.C (November 11, 2004), available at:
http://www.ftc.gov/os/comments/franrulestaffrpt/OL-100018.pdf

UFOC:

Item 1: The Franchisor, its predecessors, and affiliates

Provides information on the company, where it's headquartered, when and where it was incorporated, etc.

Item 2: Business experience

Provides the business backgrounds for each of the company's principal officers as well as any sub-franchisors or area developers who may have management responsibilities related to franchisees.

Item 3: Litigation

This section discloses the 10-year litigation history or the franchisor, its affiliates and those individuals whose experience is outlined in Item 2.[74]

Item 4: Bankruptcy

Discloses whether franchisor officers, affiliates or directors have been personally or professionally tied to bankruptcy proceedings over the prior 10-year period.

Item 5: Initial franchise fee

Discloses the upfront fee for usage of the franchise name and associated trademarks, whether, and if so under what circumstances, this fee might be refundable.

Item 6: Other fees

The franchisor must present, in tabular form, any and all of the various fees commonly assessed upon franchisees. You'll get to know this section well as you build your projected financial statements. Examples include royalty fees (generally as a percentage of gross revenues), marketing fees (also generally as a percentage of gross revenues), training fees, late payment fees, audit fees, fee for transferal of franchise, fees for duplicate copy of an operations manual, fee for a successor franchise agreement, an expense estimate for any mandatory store remodeling, etc. Examine each closely to assure an understanding.

If there's an advertising or promotions fee, look into how these funds are to be allocated. Will any of the fees come back to assist your region? Can any of your payments be used locally instead? If you're looking at a franchise that's not a household name, what type of national advertising is intended? Will it be effective for your needs?

If there are training fees, you'll need to know what upfront training you'll receive, how many of your staff are eligible for it, and whether and what you'll be charged for each person. What future training will be required? What future training might be offered? How much do you expect to need? Where will the training be held, and over what period of time? If you're a franchisee in Atlanta and your franchisor's headquartered in Minneapolis, a week's training at the headquarters for two employees could include training fees, airfare, lodging, meals, etc. If you find you're part of an industry that requires regular training updates, this can be a substantial amount of money. Are training sessions available via the internet or cd-rom? How helpful are these sessions? Some of these fees may be disclosed in greater detail in item 7. As always, I would recommend speaking with current franchisees to get their perspectives.

---

[74] However: "The disclosure document may not even be an accurate picture of litigation involving the parties that the franchisee will be dealing with: Actions brought by the franchisor against franchisees do not have to be disclosed, and actions brought by entities allegedly not parties to the agreement do not have to be disclosed." Paul Steinberg and Gerald Lescatre, **Beguiling Heresy: Regulating The Franchise Relationship**, published in the Penn State Law Review, Volume 109, pages 46, 2004.

Item 7: Initial investment

This section provides a range of estimates on the actual investment necessary to open your franchise for business, whether any of these payments are refundable, and under what conditions. In tabular form, it incorporates those fees disclosed in items five and six, as well as additional detail, which may include opening product inventory, lease estimates, leasehold improvements (this would include construction costs, labor and materials, fixtures, display cases, etc.), grand opening promotion expenses, security deposits, insurance requirements, computer hardware and software, etc. Be especially mindful of the allocation for working capital, which is often underestimated by franchisors and franchisees alike, as the survey in this book can attest to (34% of survey respondents indicated they underestimated working capital prior to opening their franchise).

Item 8: Restrictions on sources of products and services

Discloses what products, materials, supplies, fixtures, furniture, equipment, etc., you are required to purchase only from the franchisor or its designated sellers or suppliers. Generally, if you are interested in purchasing anything from non-designated sellers or suppliers, you must request and receive permission in writing from your franchisor.

It would be wise to discuss with current franchise owners what bearing this section will have on you. Often times franchisees can find necessary products or services that are the same price or less, and with lower or even no shipping costs if found locally (see Item 16 for more details). But their franchise agreement restricts them from taking advantage of the lower prices, and the franchisor will interpret the contract strictly so that this part of its profit center is not undermined. You should also inquire as to whether delivery of goods and/or services is efficient.

Item 9: Franchisee's obligations

This section details the obligations of the franchisee, from compliance standards to insurance, remodeling, audits, post-termination of agreements, etc.[75] The tabular format is useful as it cross-references the relevant sections of both the UFOC and the franchise agreement.

Item 10: Financing

Provides detail on whether the franchisor offers any forms of financing to franchisees, including all terms and conditions.

Item 11: Franchisor's obligations

The wording of this section is always interesting, and should be scrutinized carefully. It details the obligations of the franchisor both before you open your franchise as well as during its operation. It begins "**Except as set forth below, we need not provide any assistance to you**". And they mean it.

---

[75] "One of the dirtiest little secrets that just does not become apparent until you become a franchisee is when you sign a contract today, they need to understand that they are agreeing to at all times to be in compliance with the franchisor's policies and procedures **as they may change from time to time**. So the franchisor can change the operations manual overnight. It can change directive from the home office and if you don't want to be in default of the franchise agreement, you have to agree to change. The most visible change to anyone over the past couple of years was Mail Boxes, Etc., going to UPS. "First we're red, white and blue, we've paid off our $150,000 in leasehold improvements, and now we have to be brown"…So initially UPS paid for some of the changes from red, white and blue to brown. Franchisees who did not jump on board right away, they ended up having to pay for it themselves…. You are in effect signing a moving target. You don't know what you're signing, and you don't have the option to have much, if any input into that unless there's a strong, independent franchisee association within the chain.", Interview with Susan Kezios conducted by the author on January 28, 2005.

As you might expect, this section conveys a wealth of important information that you must understand before making the decision of whether to purchase the franchise. Distill it carefully to identify what the franchisor will provide, but also <u>what's not listed.</u> Among other things, this section includes whether the franchisor will assist with:

- Negotiation for purchase or lease of your site
- Products and/or services to be offered
- Pricing
- Procedures for internal controls
- Administration of and conditions for advertising
- Hardware and software requirements, etc.

Item 12: Territory

This disclosure describes whether any minimum area is granted to the franchisee, and what that is if there is one, policies regarding franchisee relocation of the business, and any restrictions placed upon the franchisee from accepting orders from outside its territory. This is important for mail order of merchandise, product sales through other stores, infomercials, etc. It is important you feel confident about the territorial rights within your contract. Don't just take someone's word as to how you will be protected—get it in writing. As is reflected in this survey, 19% of total respondents indicated that territories are inequitably granted.

Item 13: Trademarks

Item 14: Patents, Copyrights and Proprietary Information

Items 13 & 14 disclose the trademarks, patents, logos, symbols and intellectual information which franchisees have the right to use, and details how they can be used.

Item 15: Obligation to participate in the actual operation of the franchise business

This section covers the extent a franchisee is personally obligated to be involved in operation of the franchise, as well as any restrictions on the operation's manager. Some franchises require that the franchisee work a certain percentage of operating hours "on premises".

Item 16: Restrictions on what the franchisee may sell

Details any restrictions the franchisor requires on the goods and services that the franchisee may sell, whether the franchisee is required to sell only goods and services authorized by the franchisor, whether you'll be restricted from selling to certain customers, and whether the franchisor retains the right to change these. Franchisors will also sometimes impose specific operating hours for the franchised business. Don't underestimate the restrictions in this section. During the years I ran my franchise, my highest revenue-producing product line was one that was neither produced nor offered by my franchisor; i.e., I had to secure written authorization from the franchisor in order to sell it. You may wish to check with current franchisees on how flexible the franchisor is to their offering additional product lines or services.

Item 17: Renewal, termination, transfer and dispute resolution

This item, which is cross-referenced with the franchise agreement, details:

- The term of the franchise agreement
- Whether and under what conditions you or the franchisor may renew, extend, transfer or terminate the agreement
- How disputes will be resolved

(Franchise agreements generally require that disputes be resolved through arbitration. Some illuminating insight on arbitration comes from Steinberg and Lescatre: **Beguiling Heresy: Regulating The Franchise Relationship**, pages 251 & 252: "Franchisees are not alone in misunderstanding the seriousness of arbitration and its qualitative deficiencies. It would be difficult to conceive of a high court decision that a judge could be improvident or silly, yet the Supreme Court has said that the arbitrator may be "improvident, even silly".[76] "(F)actual errors" are not grounds for judicial review of the arbitrator's decision.[77] Even "the fact that 'a court is convinced (the arbitrator) committed serous error' does not suffice to overturn his decision."[78], nor does the arbitrator pleading guilty to criminal tax fraud invalidate the decision.")[79] [80]

Item 17 covers additional areas as well, but those listed above make up the bulk of it. Although most franchise investors don't anticipate selling their operation, many ultimately try to as a remedy for an underperforming business—and it's not easy. From this survey alone, I've received a few dozen requests from franchise owners, completely unsolicited on my part, inquiring whether I might like to buy their business, and if not, whether I know how they can go about selling it. If your business isn't generating a satisfactory income, or offer the potential to, few people will be interesting in buying it, and certainly not for the same price you paid. The lesson: You may not expect to want to sell your franchise, but if it does come to pass, expect to do so at a significant loss and likely with no assistance whatsoever from your franchisor.[81]

Item 18: Public figures

The section requires the franchisor to disclose whether it utilizes any "public figures", i.e., celebrities, to endorse or advertise its products, as well as any investment or managerial control that person has in the franchise.

---

[76] Steinberg and Lescatre cite Major League Baseball Players Association v. Garvey, 532 U.S. 1015, 509 (2001), (citing Paperworkers v. Misco, 484 U.S. 29, 39 (1987)).

[77] Steinberg and Lescatre citing Garvey, 532 U.S. at 509 (citing Misco, 484 U.S., at 36).

[78] Steinberg and Lescatre citing E. Associated Coal Corp. v. United Mine Workers of Am., 531 U.S. 57, 62 (2000) (quoting Misco, 484 U.S., at 38).

[79] Steinberg and Lescatre citing "See United Transp. Union v. Gateway W. Ry. Co., 284 F.3d 710, 712 (7th Cir. 2002).

[80] Also, from Kezios: "If a franchisee has the resources to challenge a franchisor's conduct in court, he or she is subject to highly subjective and inconsistent treatment within the legal system. Because there is no federal legislation establishing consistent standards, franchise agreements often contain choice of law and venue provisions which allow the franchisor to control the substantive law which will control any dispute including the place the matter has to be resolved. This means that a Nevada franchisee could be forced to litigate in Maine and be subject to Illinois law. This "forum shopping" allows franchisors to insulate themselves from a good number of lawsuits because of the great expense and inconvenience a small business person would have to incur to vindicate his or her rights even in the most egregious of cases." Letter from Susan Kezios, President of the American Franchise Association, to the Secretary of the F.T.C (January 31, 2000), available at www.ftc.gov/bcp/rulemaking/franchise/comments/comment037.htm

[81] This footnote appeared in Chapter 1, but is worth repeating: "Franchisees are the only business people…that I know of who can't sell what they buy. Because when you want to sell your franchise, the new buyer will probably be signing the then current franchise contract which will probably have more restrictive terms in it than you had. So your equity has already been devalued, through no bad actions of your own…So if your royalty was 4%, the royalty now may be 6%. That man or woman is not going to make as much money as you were, because they've got to give two percentage points more to the franchisor for royalty and maybe another percentage for advertising…You cannot got into go into franchising looking at this as a long-term deal, this is not like buying your own house and building equity in yourself. You may not be able to hand this on to your children, matter of fact you should not even think about handing this over to your children because it doesn't work that way. Franchise contracts are not written in that manner today. 25-30 years ago that's how they were written, but they're not written that way any more." Interview with Susan Kezios, conducted by the author on January 28, 2005.

Item 19: Earnings claim

If the franchisor intends to furnish estimates regarding potential income to be earned through franchise ownership, this is where it will do so. Most provide no written estimates[82], but if you're dealing with a franchisor that does provide them, examine them carefully to assure a correct interpretation. The reason for this is that estimates are sometimes generated from the gross sales of "certain franchisees". This may or may not be representive of their franchisees as a whole.

Item 20: List of outlets

This is one of the most important items of the UFOC as it requires the franchisor to disclose the names and contact information for its franchisees. They must also include contact information for any franchisee who, voluntarily or involuntarily, ceased to do business with them during the course of the past year. What makes this section valuable is that it gives you the key to conduct one of the most crucial steps of the due diligence process, contacting current and past owners to get "straight from the horse's mouth perspective" on what it's really like to own the franchise. If you're considering investing in a franchise, take the time to personally contact a minimum of 10 current franchisees and five former franchisees. You can use the survey questions in this book as a base, but come up with a list of your own, specific to the company you're investigating, and work with your financial advisor to expand the list. And don't be afraid to ask specific questions about income, margins, salaries, etc. You need to feel completely confident about each of them if you're going to invest. See the list in Chapter 3 for more ideas. Don't find out the hard way that you've made a bad investment. Use the information in this section to call them!

Item 21: Financial Statements

The audited financial statements of the franchisor. These are best interpreted by your CPA or financial advisor, who can review them to assure financial stability.

Item 22: Contracts

This section provides copies of any contracts you would be required to sign as a franchisee. It generally includes the Franchise Agreement, a Guaranty of Agreement, and often a Sublease Agreement. As is the case with the UFOC, it's best to have an your franchise attorney review these documents for you.

Item 23: Receipt

A detachable document which you sign to acknowledge receipt of the offering circular. Signing it does not oblige you to sign a franchise agreement or purchase a franchise.

---

[82] Be extremely wary of any verbal estimates that the franchisor is unwilling to put in writing.

CHAPTER 5

Franchise Organizations and Helpful Reference Sources

While some of these are listed elsewhere in this book, it's sometimes handy to have them in one concentrated section. I've tried to provide information on organizations that are unbiased in their thoughts about franchising, but there are some that may be biased one way or another, yet still provide extremely helpful information.

Franchise Organizations

North America

American Association of Franchise Dealers (AAFD): www.aafd.org

American Franchisee Association (AFA): http://www.franchisee.org

Canadian Alliance of Franchise Operators (CAFO): http://www.cafo.net

Canadian Franchise Association (CFA): http://www.cfa.ca

International Franchise Association (IFA): http://www.franchise.org

World Franchise Council (WFC): http://www.worldfranchisecouncil.org

Mexican Franchise Association:
Insurgentes Sur 1783 no 303
Colonia Guadeloupe Inn, Mexico City 01020
Phone: (52) 5 661 0655 Fax: (52) 5 663 2473
Contact: Mr Aldolfo Crespo
E-mail: amfl@prodigy.net.mx

Africa

Egypt: Egyptian Franchise Development Association: http://www.mife.com.eg

Nigeria: Nigerian International Franchise Association: http://www.nigerianfranchise.org (English language site)

South Africa: The Franchise Association of Southern Africa: http://www.fasa.co.za/

Zimbabwe:
Zimbabwe Franchise Association
C/O the ZNCC
P.O. Box 1934

Harare, Zimbabwe
Phone: (263) 4 753 444 Fax: (263) 4 753 450

Asia

China:

China International Franchisors Association:
Beijing International Club, Room 188
21 Jianguomenwai Dajie
Beijing, PRC 100020
Phone: (86-10) 6532-3861 Fax: (86-10) 6532-3877
E-mail: lalaw@chinalaw.cc
China Chain Store and Franchise Association: http://www.ccfa.org.cn (English available)

Hong Kong : Hong Kong Franchise Association : http://www.franchise.org.hk

India:
Franchising Association of India: http://www.franchisingassociationofindia.com
(domain expired Nov., 2004—Will it be renewed?).
Mr. C. Yoginder Pal, Chairman SIG
Veer Nariman Road
Churchgate, Mumbai 400-020, India
Phone: (91-22) 282-1413 Fax: (91-22) 204-6141
E-mail Address: faindia@usa.net

Indonesia:
Indonesian Franchise Association
Anang Sukandar, President
A 19 Darmawangsa X
Kebayoran Baru, Jakarta 12150, Indonesia
Phone: 62-21-739-5577 Fax: 62-21-723-4761

Israel:
Israel Franchise & Distribution Association: Israel Franchise & Distribution Association
P. O. Box 3093
Herzeliya 46590, Israel
Phone/Fax: 972-9-576-631
E-mail: emmers@netvision.net.il

Japan: Japan Franchise Association: http://jfa.jfa-fc.or.jp/(English available)

Korea:
South Korean Franchise Association
Lee Kyoung Woo, CEO
Hyosan B/D 3F
57-80, Gui-2Dong, Kwangjin-Gu
143-202 Seoul, South Korea
Phone: (82-2) 447-6094 Fax: (82-2) 3436-2162
E-mail Address: kfa01@netsgo.com

Malaysia: Malaysian Franchise Association: http://www.mfa.org.my (English language site)

Philippines:
Philippine Franchise Association:
Contact: Mrs. Ma. Alegria S. Limjoco
Unit 701, One Magnificent Mile (OMM-Citra)
San Miguel Ave., Ortigas Center
Pasig City, Philippines
Phone: (632) 687 0366 Fax: (632) 687 0365
E-mail: pfa@nwave.net

Singapore: Singapore International Franchise Association: www.sifa.org.sg (may not be available)
Contact: Mr Robert Leong
Informatics Building, 5 International Business Park, 609914
Phone: (65) 568 0802 Fax: (65) 568 0722
Email: sifa@pacific.net.sg

Taiwan: Taiwan Chain Store and Franchise Association: www.tcfa.org.tw

Thailand:
Thailand Franchise Association:
Managing Director: Somji Likhitsathaporn
20/25 Seri Village Onnui Sukhumvii 77
Pravate—BKK 10250, Thailand
Phone: (662) 321 2159 Fax: (662) 721 2795
Email: focus@bangkok.com

Turkey:
National Franchise Association of Turkey: www.ufrad.org.tr/(may not be available)
Chairman: Mr. Serdar Yanasan
Ergenekon cad. Pangalti Ishani 89/15
Istanbul 80240, Turkey
Phone: 90 212 296 6628 Fax: 90 212 224 5130
E-mail: ufrad@ufrad.com.tr

Central America

Dominican Republic:
Dominican Republic Franchise Association:
Mr. Oscar Luis Monzon, Executive Director
27 de Febrero # 340, Edif. Autoplaza
2do piso, suite A, Santo Domingo, Dominican Republic
Phone/Fax: (809) 563-1916
E-mail: c.nacional@codetel.net.do

Europe

Austria: Austrian Franchising Association: http://www.franchise.at (English available)

Belgium: Federation Belge de la Franchise: http://www.fbf-bff.be

Bulgaria:
Bulgarian Franchise Association:
Mrs. Lubka Kolarova, President

Phone/Fax (359) (52) 235 424; (359) (52) 600 724
E-mail: wan3vn@mbox.digsys.bg or kolarova@vega.bg

Czech Republic: The Czech Franchise Association: http://www.czech-franchise.cz (English available)

Denmark: Danish Franchise Association: http://www.dk-franchise.dk

Europe: European Franchise Federation: http://www.eff-franchise.com

Finland: Finland Franchise Association: http://www.franchising.fi

France: France Franchise Federation: http://www.franchise-fff.com

Germany: German Franchise Association: http://www.dfv-franchise.de (English available)

Great Britain: British Franchise Association: http://www.british-franchise.org

Greece: Franchise Association of Greece: http://www.franchising.gr (English available)

Hungary: Hungarian Franchise Association: http://www.franchise.hu (English available)

Iceland: Iceland Franchise Association: http://www.franchise.is (English available)

Ireland: Irish Franchise Association: http://www.irishfranchiseassociation.com

Italy: Italian Franchise Association: http://www.assofranchising.it

Latvia:
Latvian Franchise Association: http://www.franch.lv (may not be available)
Lachplesha 81, Daugavpils LV—5403—Latvia
Chairman: Mr. Victor Aldersberg (Arhis)
Director: Mrs. Olga Krumpane
Phone: 371 54 26349 Fax: 371 54 27374
E-mail: info@franch.lv or olga@franch.lv

Netherlands: Netherlands Franchise Association: http://www.nfv.nl (English available)

Norway: Norwegian Franchise Association: http://www.hsh-org.no (English available)

Poland: Polish Franchise Association: http://www.franchise.com.pl (English available)

Portugal: Portuguese Franchise Association: www.apfranchise.org

Romania:
Romanian Franchise Association:
Contact: Mr Florian Bolea
86 Bd. Aviatorilor, Bucharest
Phone: (40) 1 210 4881 Fax: (++40) 1 210 4832
E-mail: mbas@bah.logicnet.co

Russia: Russian Franchise Association: http://www.rarf.ru/(English available)

Spain: Spanish Franchise Association: www.franquiciadores.com

Sweden: Swedish Franchise Association: www.franchiseforeningen.se (English available)

Switzerland: Swiss Franchise Association: www.franchiseverband.ch (English available)

Ukraine:
Ukrainian Franchise Association
25 Bolshaya Morskaya Str, Sevaspol 99011 Ukraine
Phone: (380) 692 540 534 Fax: (380) 692 550 012
E-mail: tenaco@stel.sebaspol.ua

Oceania

Australia: Franchise Council of Australia: http://www.franchise.org.au

New Zealand: Franchise Association of New Zealand: http://www.franchise.org.nz

South America

Argentina: Argentina Franchise Association: http://www.aafranchising.com.ar

Brazil: Brazil Franchise Association: http://www.portaldofranchising.com.br

Chile:
Chilean Franchise Association
Asociacion de Franchising de Chile, Hernando de Aguirre 128
Office 904, Providencia, Santiago, Chile
Phone: 562 234 4189 Fax: 562 2341829
E-mail Address: negocio@netline.cl

Columbia: Columbian Franchise Association: http://www.centercourt.com/acolfran

Ecuador: Ecuador Franchise Assocation: http://www.aefran.homestead.com

Peru:
Peru Franchise Association
Gregorio Escobedo 396, Lima 11, Peru
Phone: (511) 464 851
Contact: Samuel Gleiser Katz
E-mail: cci-peru@camaralima.org.pe

Uruguay:
Uruguay Franchise Association
President: Mr. Rodolfo Montesdeoca
Daniel Munoz 2240
Av. 8 de Octubre 2688 7º # 702, CP. 11.600 CP 11.200, Montevideo, Uruguay
Phone: (598-2) 408-5189 Fax: (598-2) 408-5189
E-mail Address: milbea@adinet.com.uy

Venezuela:
Venezuela Chamber of Franchising
President: Rolando Seijas
Oficentro Neur, 3, Altamira, Oficina N 5

Caracas, Venezuela
Phone: (58) 2 261 8596 Fax: (58) 2 261 9620
E-mail: seibol@cantv.net

Venezuela Franchise Association
President: Arquimides Beliz
Calle Orinoco con Perija, Mini Centro Stela
Planta Alta, Oficina No. 5, Las Mercedes
Caracas, Venezuela
Phone: (58-2) 991-1401 Fax: (58-2) 991-4078

Reference Sources

Sources for viewing U.F.O.C.s

Easiest is the fantastic web site created by the California Department of Corporations. Here's a link to the search page. Remember, you won't always find the company by searching only its retail trade name. Search under the franchisor's actual name of incorporation, if you can identify it, and also try using the helpful "contains" function of the search engine.

http://134.186.208.228/caleasi/pub/Exsearch.htm

State agencies

Most state agencies, if not all, will require you to visit them in person to view the files. Due to limited state funds, most will also limit you to viewing a maximum of five per day. Call each for their individual policies. Photocopy machines are usually available for a fee.

California
Dept. of Corporations
State of California
320 W. 4th St., Suite 750
Los Angeles, CA 90013
213.576.7500
http://www.corp.ca.gov/

Hawaii
Dept. of Commerce and Consumer Affairs
State of Hawaii
1010 Richards St.
Honolulu, HI 96813
808-586-2722
http://www.state.hi.us/dcca/

Illinois
Franchise Bureau
Illinois Attorney General
500 South Second St.
Springfield, IL 62706
217-782-4465
http://www.ag.state.il.us/

Indiana
Indiana Securities Division
Room E-111
302 West Washington St.
Indianapolis, IN 46204
317-232-6681
http://www.in.gov/sos/securities/

Maryland
Office of the Attorney General
Securities Division
State of Maryland
200 St. Paul Place
Baltimore, MD 21202-2020
410.576.7042
http://www.oag.state.md.us/

Michigan
Consumer Protection Division
Antitrust and Franchise Unit
Michigan Dept. of Attorney General
670 Law Building
Lansing, MI 48933
517-373-7117
http://www.michigan.gov/ag/

Minnesota
Minnesota Dept. of Commerce
Franchise Section
85 7th Place East
St. Paul, MN 55101-2198
612-296-6328
http://www.state.mn.us

North Dakota
Office of Securities Commissioner
State of North Dakota
600 East Boulevard Avenue
Fifth Floor
Bismarck, ND 58505-0510
701-328-4712

Rhode Island
Division of Securities
State of Rhode Island
233 Richmond St., Suite 232
Providence, RI 02903
401.277.3048

Virginia
Division of Securities and
Retail Franchising
State Corporation Commission
Commonwealth of Virginia
1300 E. Main St., Ninth Floor
Richmond, VA 23219
804-371-9051

Wisconsin
Securities and Franchise Registration
Wisconsin Commissioner of Securities
P.O. Box 1768
345 West Washington
Madison, WI 53701-1768
608-266-8559

New York
Bureau of Investor Protection and Securities
New York State Dept. of Law
120 Broadway, 23rd Floor
New York, NY 10271
212-416-8211

Oregon
Dept. of Consumer and Business Services
Division of Finance and Corporate Securities
State of Oregon
350 Winter St., NE, Room 21
Salem, OR 97310
503-378-4140

South Dakota
Division of Securities
State of South Dakota
118 West Capitol Ave.
Pierre, SD 57501-2000
605-773-4823

Washington
Department of Financial Institutions
Securities Division
State of Washington
P.O. Box 9033
Olympia, WA 98507-9033
360-902-8738

General Franchise Information

Here are several of the dozens of sites dedicated to franchising. You'll find contacts, fees, corporate data, numbers of outlets, royalties, etc. I believe the first two to be particularly good.

http://www.worldfranchising.com

http://www.infonews.com

http://www.everyfranchise.com/pages/

http://www.franchise.com/
http://www.franchise1.com/
http://www.franchisedirectory.com/
http://www.franchisedirectory.ca/(Canada)

An interesting "chat room" dedicated to discussion on franchising. The site also offers a helpful free email newsletter, which provides updates on franchising internationally.

http://www.franchise-chat.com

These sites are dedicated to business re-sales and always have lots of franchises offered. Some are offered at a substantial discount to what you'd pay to open your own, and might offer good potential if they were not properly managed. On the other hand, it's interesting to see certain companies who have dozens of franchisees attempting to sell their outlets, generally not a good sign.

http://www.br-network.com/search.htm
http://www.businessbroker.net/franchise/franchise_resale.ihtml
http://www.franchisedatabase.com/

Business and Legal Advice

Small Business Support

SCORE: Excellent for expert advice on many facets of business: http://www.score.org

Small Business Administration: http://www.sbaonline.sba.gov

Small Business Development Centers: http://www.sba.gov/sbdc

All Experts: Good source on a broad range of topics, from small business to software and more: http://www.allexperts.com

Legal questions: http://www.lawguru.com

Professional Organizations

American Bar Association: http://www.aba.org
American Institute of Certified Public Accountants: www.aicpa.org

Periodicals

Always be mindful of those periodicals featuring franchises that advertise with them.

Canadian Business Franchise: http://www.cgb.ca/

Entrepreneur Magazine: http://www.entrepreneur.com/Franchise_Zone/FZ_FrontDoor/

Franchise Times: http://www.franchisetimes.com/

Franchising World: (Published by the IFA): http://www.franchise.org

Info Franchise Newsletter: http://www.infonews.com/newsletter.html

Books and Publications

Beguiling Heresy: Regulating The Franchise Relationship, by Paul Steinberg and Gerald Lescatre; published in the Penn State Law Review, Volume 109, 2004

This publication is the definitive insight guide on the inadequacies of current franchise regulations. It was written by an attorney and former franchisee of Subway, and is the most illuminating reference on franchising I have seen. Check with your local law library for availability.

Franchising Dreams, by Peter Birkeland

This book provides excellent insight on what it's like to own a franchise, as the author documents his conversations and experiences of three years of working side-by-side with franchisees of three different companies.

From Ice Cream to the Internet, by Dr. Scott Shane

Most helpful for those considering growing their business as a franchisor, but still provides valuable insight for prospective franchise owners.

CHAPTER 6

Alphabetized Survey Results For All 216 Franchises

AAMCO

www.aamco.com

The world's largest supplier of transmission repair services, with over 700 locations throughout the U.S. and Canada.

OVERALL SCORE: 43

One Presidential Blvd.
Bala Cynwyd, PA 19004
Fax: 610-664-5897
Total number of outlets: 700+
Total number of franchise outlets: 700+
International: Yes (Canada)

OVERALL RANK: 179

Phone: 800-GO-AAMCO
Investment, incl. franchise fee:
Franchise term:
Initial investment:
Royalty fee:
Advertising/Marketing fee:

SURVEY AND RESULTS *

Q1: **About how many hours per week do you dedicate to your franchise business?**

		% answering
A)	Less than 40	0%
B)	41–50	31%
C)	**51–60**	**38%**
D)	More than 60	31%
E)	Passive investment	0%

Q2: **How would you describe your relations/ communications with your franchisor?**

		% answering
A)	Excellent	8%
B)	Good	23%
C)	**Adequate**	**31%**
D)	Fair	23%
E)	Poor	15%

Q3: **In terms of how your franchisor views your communications with other franchisees, it is:**

		% answering
A)	**Very supportive**	**38%**
B)	Not very supportive	23%
C)	**No influence**	**38%**

Q4: **Is the franchisor fair with you in resolving any grievances?**

		% answering
A)	Extremely fair	0%
B)	**Pretty fair**	**38%**
C)	**Reasonably fair**	**38%**
D)	Not very fair	15%
E)	Not fair at all	8%

Q5: **Are territories equitably granted?**

		% answering
A)	Yes	31%
B)	No	31%
C)	**Not yet sure**	**38%**

Q6: **How would you describe the initial and ongoing training provided by your franchisor?**

		% answering
A)	Excellent	8%
B)	**Good**	**46%**
C)	Adequate	8%
D)	Fair	15%
E)	Poor	23%

Q7: **How well does the franchisor anticipate future trends in how it evolves and markets products and services?**

		% answering
A)	Extremely well	0%
B)	Pretty well	23%
C)	Adequately	31%
D)	**Not very well**	**38%**
E)	Terribly	8%

Q8: **How satisfied are you with your franchisor's spending of the royalty fees you pay?**

		% answering
A)	Extremely satisfied	0%
B)	Mostly satisfied	23%
C)	**Somewhat satisfied**	**38%**
D)	Not very satisfied	23%
E)	Not satisfied at all	15%

Q9: **In what ways could the parent company most improve? (Please check those that most apply, no more than three):**

❑ Communications

❑ Counsel/advice on administrative/management issues

❑ Effectiveness of marketing/promotions

❑ Evolution of products/services

❑ Frequency of marketing/promotional campaigns

❑ Quality of products/services

❑ Pricing of products/services to franchisees

❑ Technology (Point of sale systems, usage of computers/email/software, etc.)

❑ Training

Most frequent responses:	% answering
Effectiveness of marketing/promotions	38%
Frequency of marketing/promotional campaigns	31%
Pricing of products/services to franchisees	31%

Q10: **Is your income more, less or about what you expected prior to opening your business?**

	% answering	
More	8%	
Less	85%	**Summary: 16% making about what they**
About what was expected	8%	**expected, or more.**

Q11: **Prior to opening your franchise, which (if any) of the following did you underestimate?**

❑ Amount of working capital required for your 1st year in business

❑ Difficulty in hiring/retaining quality staff

❑ Expertise required to run the business

❑ Impact of marketing/promotions

❑ Start-up costs

❑ Degree of stress

❑ Workload

Most frequent responses:	% answering
Difficulty in hiring/retaining quality staff	69%
Degree of stress	62%
Amount of working capital required for 1st year in business	54%

Q12: **If you could turn back time to the day you signed your franchise agreement, would you make the same decision to buy your franchise?**

	% answering
Yes	46%
No	54%

* Number of survey respondents: 13 from 12 different states

Number of survey respondents as a % of total franchise units: 2%

ABC SEAMLESS

www.abcseamless.com

info@abcseamless.com

Franchisor of seamless steel siding, gutters and log home siding.

OVERALL SCORE: 62

3001 Fietchtner Drive

Fargo, ND 58103

Fax: 701-293-3107

Total number of outlets: 134

Total number of franchise outlets: 125

International: No

OVERALL RANK: 127

Phone: 800-732-6577

Franchise fee: $18,000 to $24,000

Franchise term: 10 years

Initial investment: $99,836 to $231,500

Advertising/Marketing fee: 1/2% of gross receipts, monthly

Royalty fee: 2% to 5% of gross receipts, monthly

SURVEY AND RESULTS *

Q1: About how many hours per week do you dedicate to your franchise business?

		% answering
A)	Less than 40	11%
B)	41–50	24%
C)	**51–60**	**48%**
D)	More than 60	17%
E)	Passive investment	0%

Q2: How would you describe your relations/ communications with your franchisor?

		% answering
A)	**Excellent**	**30%**
B)	Good	20%
C)	Adequate	28%
D)	Fair	9%
E)	Poor	13%

Q3: In terms of how your franchisor views your communications with other franchisees, it is:

		% answering
A)	**Very supportive**	**57%**
B)	Not very supportive	26%
C)	No influence	17%

Q4: Is the franchisor fair with you in resolving any grievances?

		% answering
A)	Extremely fair	27%
B)	**Pretty fair**	**36%**
C)	Reasonably fair	32%
D)	Not very fair	5%
E)	Not fair at all	0%

Q5: Are territories equitably granted?

		% answering
A)	**Yes**	**100%**
B)	No	0%
C)	Not yet sure	0%

Q6: How would you describe the initial and ongoing training provided by your franchisor?

		% answering
A)	**Excellent**	**35%**
B)	Good	26%
C)	Adequate	24%
D)	Fair	11%
E)	Poor	4%

Q7: How well does the franchisor anticipate future trends in how it evolves and markets products and services?

		% answering
A)	Extremely well	17%
B)	Pretty well	22%
C)	**Adequately**	**35%**
D)	Not very well	22%
E)	Terribly	4%

Q8: How satisfied are you with your franchisor's spending of the royalty fees you pay?

		% answering
A)	Extremely satisfied	5%
B)	Mostly satisfied	27%
C)	**Somewhat satisfied**	**32%**
D)	Not very satisfied	14%
E)	Not satisfied at all	23%

Q9: **In what ways could the parent company most improve? (Please check those that most apply, no more than three):**

❑ Communications

❑ Counsel/advice on administrative/management issues

❑ Effectiveness of marketing/promotions

❑ Evolution of products/services

❑ Frequency of marketing/promotional campaigns

❑ Quality of products/services

❑ Pricing of products/services to franchisees

❑ Technology (Point of sale systems, usage of computers/email/software, etc.)

❑ Training

Most frequent responses:	% answering
Effectiveness of marketing/promotions	52%
Counsel/advice on administrative/management issues	30%
Frequency of marketing/promotional campaigns (tie)	30%
Pricing of products/services to franchisees (tie)	30%

Q10: **Is your income more, less or about what you expected prior to opening your business?**

	% answering	
More	22%	
Less	48%	**Summary: 52% are making about what they**
About what was expected	30%	**expected, or more.**

Q11: **Prior to opening your franchise, which (if any) of the following did you underestimate?**

❑ Amount of working capital required for your 1st year in business

❑ Difficulty in hiring/retaining quality staff

❑ Expertise required to run the business

❑ Impact of marketing/promotions

❑ Start-up costs

❑ Degree of stress

❑ Workload

Most frequent responses:	% answering
Difficulty in hiring/retaining quality staff	70%
Degree of stress	65%
Amount of working capital required for 1st year in business	39%

Q12: **If you could turn back time to the day you signed your franchise agreement, would you make the same decision to buy your franchise?**

	% answering
Yes	65%
No	35%

*   Number of survey respondents: 23 from 18 different states

Number of survey respondents as a % of total franchise units: 17%

ACE America's Cash Express

www.acecashexpress.com
mmazer@acecashexpress.com

Ace Cash Express is the largest owner/operator of check-cashing stores in the United States.

OVERALL SCORE: 74

1231 Greenway Drive, Suite 600
Irving, TX 75038
Fax: 972-550-5150
Total number of outlets: 1,026
Total number of franchise outlets: 204
International: No

OVERALL RANK: 58

Phone: 800-713-3338
Franchise fee: $15,000–$30,000
Franchise term:
Initial investment: $143,200–$279,100
Advertising/Marketing fee:
Royalty fee: > of 6% or $850 to $1,000 monthly

SURVEY AND RESULTS *

Q1: About how many hours per week do you dedicate to your franchise business?

		% answering
A)	**Less than 40**	**31%**
B)	41–50	19%
C)	**51–60**	**31%**
D)	More than 60	19%
E)	Passive investment	0%

Q2: How would you describe your relations/ communications with your franchisor?

		% answering
A)	Excellent	13%
B)	**Good**	**50%**
C)	Adequate	31%
D)	Fair	6%
E)	Poor	0%

Q3: In terms of how your franchisor views your communications with other franchisees, it is:

		% answering
A)	**Very supportive**	**63%**
B)	Not very supportive	19%
C)	No influence	19%

Q4: Is the franchisor fair with you in resolving any grievances?

		% answering
A)	Extremely fair	25%
B)	Pretty fair	31%
C)	**Reasonably fair**	**44%**
D)	Not very fair	0%
E)	Not fair at all	0%

Q5: Are territories equitably granted?

		% answering
A)	Yes	25%
B)	**No**	**63%**
C)	Not yet sure	13%

Q6: How would you describe the initial and ongoing training provided by your franchisor?

		% answering
A)	Excellent	6%
B)	**Good**	**38%**
C)	Adequate	13%
D)	Fair	31%
E)	Poor	13%

Q7: How well does the franchisor anticipate future trends in how it evolves and markets products and services?

		% answering
A)	Extremely well	25%
B)	Pretty well	25%
C)	**Adequately**	**38%**
D)	Not very well	13%
E)	Terribly	0%

Q8: How satisfied are you with your franchisor's spending of the royalty fees you pay?

		% answering
A)	Extremely satisfied	6%
B)	**Mostly satisfied**	**38%**
C)	**Somewhat satisfied**	**38%**
D)	Not very satisfied	19%
E)	Not satisfied at all	0%

Q9: **In what ways could the parent company most improve? (Please check those that most apply, no more than three):**

- ❏ Communications
- ❏ Counsel/advice on administrative/management issues
- ❏ Effectiveness of marketing/promotions
- ❏ Evolution of products/services
- ❏ Frequency of marketing/promotional campaigns

- ❏ Quality of products/services
- ❏ Pricing of products/services to franchisees
- ❏ Technology (Point of sale systems, usage of computers/email/software, etc.)
- ❏ Training

Most frequent responses:	% answering
Effectiveness of marketing/promotions	69%
Communications	44%
Evolution of products/services (tie)	31%
Technology (tie)	31%
Training (tie)	31%

Q10: **Is your income more, less or about what you expected prior to opening your business?**

	% answering	
More	**57%**	
Less	14%	**Summary: 86% are making about what they**
About what was expected	29%	**expected, or more.**

Q11: **Prior to opening your franchise, which (if any) of the following did you underestimate?**

- ❏ Amount of working capital required for your 1st year in business
- ❏ Difficulty in hiring/retaining quality staff
- ❏ Expertise required to run the business
- ❏ Impact of marketing/promotions

- ❏ Start-up costs
- ❏ Degree of stress
- ❏ Workload

Most frequent responses:	% answering
Difficulty in hiring/retaining quality staff	31%
Amount of working capital required for your 1st year in business (tie)	25%
Start-up costs (tie)	25%
Degree of stress (tie)	25%
Workload (tie)	25%

Q12: **If you could turn back time to the day you signed your franchise agreement, would you make the same decision to buy your franchise?**

	% answering
Yes	**80%**
No	20%

* Number of survey respondents: 16 from 10 different states
Number of survey respondents as a % of total franchise units 7.84%

ADVENTURES IN ADVERTISING

www.discoveraia.com

Franchisor of promotional products, programs and gift items

OVERALL SCORE: 80

101 Commerce St.
Oshkosh, WI 54903
Fax: 920-303-4510
Total number of outlets: 464
Total number of franchise outlets: 464
International: Yes (Canada)

OVERALL RANK: 32

Phone: 920-236-7272
Franchise fee: $5,000 to $10,000
Franchise term: 5 years
Initial investment: $11,295 to $31,595
Advertising/Marketing fee: None currently
Royalty fee: 7% of first $75,000 in monthly gross revenue plus
6% of monthly gross revenue above $75,000

SURVEY AND RESULTS *

Q1: About how many hours per week do you dedicate to your franchise business?

		% answering
A)	Less than 40	0%
B)	41–50	25%
C)	51–60	33%
D)	**More than 60**	**42%**
E)	Passive investment	0%

Q2: How would you describe your relations/communications with your franchisor?

		% answering
A)	**Excellent**	**42%**
B)	**Good**	**42%**
C)	Adequate	17%
D)	Fair	17%
E)	Poor	0%

Q3: In terms of how your franchisor views your communications with other franchisees, it is:

		% answering
A)	**Very supportive**	**83%**
B)	Not very supportive	17%
C)	No influence	0%

Q4: Is the franchisor fair with you in resolving any grievances?

		% answering
A)	**Extremely fair**	**55%**
B)	Pretty fair	36%
C)	Reasonably fair	9%
D)	Not very fair	0%
E)	Not fair at all	0%

Q5: Are territories equitably granted?

		% answering
A)	Yes	36%
B)	**No**	**45%**
C)	Not yet sure	18%

Q6: How would you describe the initial and ongoing training provided by your franchisor?

		% answering
A)	**Excellent**	**50%**
B)	Good	42%
C)	Adequate	0%
D)	Fair	8%
E)	Poor	0%

Q7: How well does the franchisor anticipate future trends in how it evolves and markets products and services?

		% answering
A)	Extremely well	17%
B)	**Pretty well**	**58%**
C)	Adequately	17%
D)	Not very well	8%
E)	Terribly	0%

Q8: How satisfied are you with your franchisor's spending of the royalty fees you pay?

		% answering
A)	**Extremely satisfied**	**33%**
B)	**Mostly satisfied**	**33%**
C)	Somewhat satisfied	25%
D)	Not very satisfied	0%
E)	Not satisfied at all	8%

Q9: **In what ways could the parent company most improve? (Please check those that most apply, no more than three):**

- ❏ Communications
- ❏ Counsel/advice on administrative/management issues
- ❏ Effectiveness of marketing/promotions
- ❏ Evolution of products/services
- ❏ Frequency of marketing/promotional campaigns

- ❏ Quality of products/services
- ❏ Pricing of products/services to franchisees
- ❏ Technology (Point of sale systems, usage of computers/email/software, etc.)
- ❏ Training

Most frequent responses:

	% answering
Counsel/advice on administrative/management issues	58%
Frequency of marketing/promotional campaigns	33%
Effectiveness of marketing/promotional campaigns (tie)	25%
Pricing of products/services to franchisees (tie)	25%

Q10: **Is your income more, less or about what you expected prior to opening your business?**

	% answering	
More	25%	
Less	25%	**Summary: 75% are making about what they**
About what was expected	**50%**	**expected, or more.**

Q11: **Prior to opening your franchise, which (if any) of the following did you underestimate?**

- ❏ Amount of working capital required for your 1st year in business
- ❏ Difficulty in hiring/retaining quality staff
- ❏ Expertise required to run the business
- ❏ Impact of marketing/promotions

- ❏ Start-up costs
- ❏ Degree of stress
- ❏ Workload

Most frequent responses:

	% answering
Difficulty in hiring/retaining quality staff	42%
Degree of stress	42%
Workload	33%

Q12: **If you could turn back time to the day you signed your franchise agreement, would you make the same decision to buy your franchise?**

	% answering
Yes	**82%**
No	18%

*   Number of survey respondents: 12 from 11 different states
    Number of survey respondents as a % of total franchise units: 2.6%

AERO COLOURS

www.aerocolours.com

Specializing in vehicle paint chip and scratch repair, as well as bumper scratch and dent repair.

OVERALL SCORE: 66

6971 Washington Avenue South, Suite 102
Minneapolis, MN 55439
Fax: 952-942-0628
Total number of outlets: 82 (end of year 2003)
Total number of franchise outlets: 1
International: France, Costa Rica

OVERALL RANK: N/A

Phone: 800-696-AERO
Franchise fee: $25,000 to $125,000
Franchise term: 10 years
Initial investment: $57,400 to $165,400
Advertising/Marketing fee: None currently
Royalty fee: 7% of monthly gross revenue

SURVEY AND RESULTS *

Q1: **About how many hours per week do you dedicate to your franchise business?**

		% answering
A)	Less than 40	13%
B)	41–50	38%
C)	**51–60**	**50%**
D)	More than 60	0%
E)	Passive investment	0%

Q2: **How would you describe your relations/ communications with your franchisor?**

		% answering
A)	Excellent	13%
B)	Good	25%
C)	**Adequate**	**38%**
D)	Fair	13%
E)	Poor	13%

Q3: **In terms of how your franchisor views your communications with other franchisees, it is:**

		% answering
A)	**Very supportive**	**75%**
B)	Not very supportive	13%
C)	No influence	13%

Q4: **Is the franchisor fair with you in resolving any grievances?**

		% answering
A)	Extremely fair	25%
B)	**Pretty fair**	**38%**
C)	Reasonably fair	25%
D)	Not very fair	0%
E)	Not fair at all	13%

Q5: **Are territories equitably granted?**

		% answering
A)	**Yes**	**50%**
B)	No	25%
C)	Not yet sure	25%

Q6: **How would you describe the initial and ongoing training provided by your franchisor?**

		% answering
A)	Excellent	13%
B)	Good	13%
C)	**Adequate**	**38%**
D)	**Fair**	**38%**
E)	Poor	0%

Q7: **How well does the franchisor anticipate future trends in how it evolves and markets products and services?**

		% answering
A)	Extremely well	0%
B)	**Pretty well**	**50%**
C)	Adequately	13%
D)	Not very well	25%
E)	Terribly	13%

Q8: **How satisfied are you with your franchisor's spending of the royalty fees you pay?**

		% answering
A)	Extremely satisfied	0%
B)	Mostly satisfied	25%
C)	**Somewhat satisfied**	**38%**
D)	Not very satisfied	13%
E)	Not satisfied at all	25%

Q9: In what ways could the parent company most improve? (Please check those that most apply, no more than three):

❑   Communications
❑   Counsel/advice on administrative/management issues
❑   Effectiveness of marketing/promotions
❑   Evolution of products/services
❑   Frequency of marketing/promotional campaigns

❑   Quality of products/services
❑   Pricing of products/services to franchisees
❑   Technology (Point of sale systems, usage
     of computers/email/software, etc.)
❑   Training

Most frequent responses:

	% answering
Communications (tie)	50%
Evolution of products/services (tie)	50%
Pricing of products/services to franchisees (tie)	50%
Training (tie)	50%

Q10: Is your income more, less or about what you expected prior to opening your business?

	% answering	
More	25%	
Less	**38%**	**Summary: 63% are making about what they**
About what was expected	**38%**	**expected, or more.**

Q11: Prior to opening your franchise, which (if any) of the following did you underestimate?

❑   Amount of working capital required for your
     1st year in business
❑   Difficulty in hiring/retaining quality staff
❑   Expertise required to run the business
❑   Impact of marketing/promotions

❑   Start-up costs
❑   Degree of stress
❑   Workload

Most frequent responses:

	% answering
Difficulty in hiring/retaining quality staff	63%
Amount of working capital required for 1st year in business	50%
Degree of stress	25%

Q12: If you could turn back time to the day you signed your franchise agreement, would you make the same decision to buy your franchise?

	% answering
Yes	75%
No	25%

*   Number of survey respondents: 8 from 7 different states
    Number of survey respondents as a % of total franchise units: 6.48%

ALL TUNE & LUBE

www.alltuneandlube.com
info@alltuneand lube.com

All Tune and Lube is a provider full service vehicle maintenance and repair.

OVERALL SCORE: 34

OVERALL RANK: 190

8334 Veterans Highway
Millersville, MD 21108
Fax: 410-987-9080
Total number of outlets: 258*
Total number of franchise outlets: 257

Phone: 800-935-8863
Franchise fee: $31,000
Franchise term: 15 years
Initial investment: $95,000 to $144,500
International: Canada

Advertising/Marketing fee: Greater of 8% of wkly. gross sales <u>or</u> $685/week plus $60 monthly fee for "supplemental advertising"
Royalty fee: 7% of weekly gross sales ($250 minimum)
* Includes ATL Motor Mate & All Tune Transmission locations

SURVEY AND RESULTS **

Q1: About how many hours per week do you dedicate to your franchise business?

		% answering
A)	Less than 40	0%
B)	41–50	12%
C)	51–60	35%
D)	**More than 60**	**53%**
E)	Passive investment	0%

Q2: How would you describe your relations/communications with your franchisor?

		% answering
A)	Excellent	6%
B)	Good	6%
C)	Adequate	24%
D)	Fair	18%
E)	**Poor**	**47%**

Q3: In terms of how your franchisor views your communications with other franchisees, it is:

		% answering
A)	Very supportive	6%
B)	Not very supportive	38%
C)	**No influence**	**56%**

Q4: Is the franchisor fair with you in resolving any grievances?

		% answering
A)	Extremely fair	6%
B)	**Pretty fair**	**35%**
C)	Reasonably fair	18%
D)	Not very fair	29%
E)	Not fair at all	12%

Q5: Are territories equitably granted?

		% answering
A)	Yes	35%
B)	No	18%
C)	**Not yet sure**	**47%**

Q6: How would you describe the initial and ongoing training provided by your franchisor?

		% answering
A)	Excellent	6%
B)	Good	13%
C)	Adequate	25%
D)	Fair	19%
E)	**Poor**	**38%**

Q7: How well does the franchisor anticipate future trends in how it evolves and markets products and services?

		% answering
A)	Extremely well	0%
B)	Pretty well	12%
C)	Adequately	29%
D)	**Not very well**	**35%**
E)	Terribly	24%

Q8: How satisfied are you with your franchisor's spending of the royalty fees you pay?

		% answering
A)	Extremely satisfied	0%
B)	Mostly satisfied	12%
C)	Somewhat satisfied	6%
D)	Not very satisfied	35%
E)	**Not satisfied at all**	**47%**

Q9: **In what ways could the parent company most improve? (Please check those that most apply, no more than three):**

- ❏ Communications
- ❏ Counsel/advice on administrative/management issues
- ❏ Effectiveness of marketing/promotions
- ❏ Evolution of products/services
- ❏ Frequency of marketing/promotional campaigns

- ❏ Quality of products/services
- ❏ Pricing of products/services to franchisees
- ❏ Technology (Point of sale systems, usage of computers/email/software, etc.)
- ❏ Training

Most frequent responses:	% answering
Effectiveness of marketing/promotions	65%
Counsel/advice on administrative/management issues	35%
Evolution of products/services (tie)	24%
Pricing of products/services to franchisees (tie)	24%
Training (tie)	24%

Q10: **Is your income more, less or about what you expected prior to opening your business?**

	% answering	
More	6%	
Less	**75%**	**Summary: 25% are making about what they**
About what was expected	19%	**expected, or more.**

Q11: **Prior to opening your franchise, which (if any) of the following did you underestimate?**

- ❏ Amount of working capital required for your 1st year in business
- ❏ Difficulty in hiring/retaining quality staff
- ❏ Expertise required to run the business
- ❏ Impact of marketing/promotions

- ❏ Start-up costs
- ❏ Degree of stress
- ❏ Workload

Most frequent responses:	% answering
Amount of working capital required for 1st year in business	76%
Difficulty in hiring/retaining quality staff	59%
Degree of stress	53%

Q12: **If you could turn back time to the day you signed your franchise agreement, would you make the same decision to buy your franchise?**

	% answering
Yes	29%
No	**71%**

** Number of survey respondents: 17 from 14 different states

Number of survey respondents as a % of total franchise units: 6.59%

ALLEGRA NETWORK

www.allegranetwork.com

Full-service printer, copier, and document manager.

OVERALL SCORE: 76

OVERALL RANK: 48

21680 Haggerty Road, Suite 105S
Northville, MI 48167
Fax: 248-596-8601
Total number of outlets: 450+ (including all affiliates)
Total number of franchise outlets: 450+
International: Yes (Canada)

Phone: 248-596-8600
Franchise fee: $30,000
Franchise term: 20 years
Initial investment: $299,650 to 548,115
Advertising/Marketing fee: Varies
Royalty fee: Varies

SURVEY AND RESULTS *

Q1: About how many hours per week do you dedicate to your franchise business?

		% answering
A)	Less than 40	14%
B)	**41–50**	**29%**
C)	**51–60**	**29%**
D)	**More than 60**	**29%**
E)	Passive investment	0%

Q2: How would you describe your relations/communications with your franchisor?

		% answering
A)	Excellent	29%
B)	**Good**	**57%**
C)	Adequate	7%
D)	Fair	7%
E)	Poor	0%

Q3: In terms of how your franchisor views your communications with other franchisees, it is:

		% answering
A)	**Very supportive**	**93%**
B)	Not very supportive	0%
C)	No influence	7%

Q4: Is the franchisor fair with you in resolving any grievances?

		% answering
A)	Extremely fair	14%
B)	**Pretty fair**	**71%**
C)	Reasonably fair	7%
D)	Not very fair	7%
E)	Not fair at all	0%

Q5: Are territories equitably granted?

		% answering
A)	**Yes**	**50%**
B)	No	14%
C)	Not yet sure	36%

Q6: How would you describe the initial and ongoing training provided by your franchisor?

		% answering
A)	Excellent	21%
B)	**Good**	**50%**
C)	Adequate	7%
D)	Fair	21%
E)	Poor	0%

Q7: How well does the franchisor anticipate future trends in how it evolves and markets products and services?

		% answering
A)	Extremely well	14%
B)	**Pretty well**	**57%**
C)	Adequately	29%
D)	Not very well	0%
E)	Terribly	0%

Q8: How satisfied are you with your franchisor's spending of the royalty fees you pay?

		% answering
A)	Extremely satisfied	7%
B)	Mostly satisfied	36%
C)	**Somewhat satisfied**	**43%**
D)	Not very satisfied	0%
E)	Not satisfied at all	14%

Q9: **In what ways could the parent company most improve? (Please check those that most apply, no more than three):**

❑ Communications
❑ Counsel/advice on administrative/management issues
❑ Effectiveness of marketing/promotions
❑ Evolution of products/services
❑ Frequency of marketing/promotional campaigns

❑ Quality of products/services
❑ Pricing of products/services to franchisees
❑ Technology (Point of sale systems, usage of computers/email/software, etc.)
❑ Training

Most frequent responses:	% answering
Effectiveness of marketing/promotions	57%
Frequency of marketing/promotional campaigns	36%
Technology (tie)	29%
Training (tie)	29%

Q10: **Is your income more, less or about what you expected prior to opening your business?**

	% answering	
More	29%	
Less	**43%**	**Summary: 58% are making about what they**
About what was expected	29%	**expected, or more.**

Q11: **Prior to opening your franchise, which (if any) of the following did you underestimate?**

❑ Amount of working capital required for your 1st year in business
❑ Difficulty in hiring/retaining quality staff
❑ Expertise required to run the business
❑ Impact of marketing/promotions

❑ Start-up costs
❑ Degree of stress
❑ Workload

Most frequent responses:	% answering
Difficulty in hiring/retaining quality staff	64%
Degree of stress	64%
Workload	29%

Q12: **If you could turn back time to the day you signed your franchise agreement, would you make the same decision to buy your franchise?**

	% answering
Yes	**86%**
No	14%

*   Number of survey respondents: 14 from 14 different states
    Number of survey respondents as a % of total franchise units: 3.11%

ALPHAGRAPHICS

www.alphagraphics.com

Full-service printer, copier, and document manager.

OVERALL SCORE: 74

268 South State Street, Suite 300
Salt Lake City, UT 84111
Fax: 801-595-7271
Total number of outlets: 244
Total number of franchise outlets: 244
International: Yes (worldwide)

OVERALL RANK: 59

Phone: 800-955-6246
Franchise fee: $25,900
Franchise term: 20 years
Initial investment: $380,000 to $551,900
Advertising/Marketing fee: Multiple fees
Royalty fee:1.5% to 8% of monthly gross sales

SURVEY AND RESULTS *

Q1: **About how many hours per week do you dedicate to your franchise business?**

		% answering
A)	Less than 40	0%
B)	41–50	23%
C)	51–60	23%
D)	**More than 60**	**54%**
E)	Passive investment	0%

Q2: **How would you describe your relations/ communications with your franchisor?**

		% answering
A)	Excellent	42%
B)	**Good**	**50%**
C)	Adequate	8%
D)	Fair	0%
E)	Poor	0%

Q3: **In terms of how your franchisor views your communications with other franchisees, it is:**

		% answering
A)	**Very supportive**	**92%**
B)	Not very supportive	8%
C)	No influence	0%

Q4: **Is the franchisor fair with you in resolving any grievances?**

		% answering
A)	Extremely fair	33%
B)	**Pretty fair**	**42%**
C)	Reasonably fair	8%
D)	Not very fair	17%
E)	Not fair at all	0%

Q5: **Are territories equitably granted?**

		% answering
A)	**Yes**	**62%**
B)	No	31%
C)	Not yet sure	8%

Q6: **How would you describe the initial and ongoing training provided by your franchisor?**

		% answering
A)	**Excellent**	**46%**
B)	Good	38%
C)	Adequate	15%
D)	Fair	0%
E)	Poor	0%

Q7: **How well does the franchisor anticipate future trends in how it evolves and markets products and services?**

		% answering
A)	Extremely well	23%
B)	**Pretty well**	**54%**
C)	Adequately	15%
D)	Not very well	8%
E)	Terribly	0%

Q8: **How satisfied are you with your franchisor's spending of the royalty fees you pay?**

		% answering
A)	Extremely satisfied	8%
B)	**Mostly satisfied**	**62%**
C)	Somewhat satisfied	23%
D)	Not very satisfied	0%
E)	Not satisfied at all	8%

Q9: **In what ways could the parent company most improve? (Please check those that most apply, no more than three):**

❏ Communications

❏ Counsel/advice on administrative/management issues

❏ Effectiveness of marketing/promotions

❏ Evolution of products/services

❏ Frequency of marketing/promotional campaigns

❏ Quality of products/services

❏ Pricing of products/services to franchisees

❏ Technology (Point of sale systems, usage of computers/email/software, etc.)

❏ Training

Most frequent responses:	% answering
Effectiveness of marketing/promotions	69%
Evolution of products/services	38%
Training	31%

Q10: **Is your income more, less or about what you expected prior to opening your business?**

	% answering	
More	15%	
Less	38%	Summary: 61% are making about what they
About what was expected	**46%**	expected, or more.

Q11: **Prior to opening your franchise, which (if any) of the following did you underestimate?**

❏ Amount of working capital required for your 1st year in business

❏ Difficulty in hiring/retaining quality staff

❏ Expertise required to run the business

❏ Impact of marketing/promotions

❏ Start-up costs

❏ Degree of stress

❏ Workload

Most frequent responses:	% answering
Amount of working capital required for 1st year in business	62%
Difficulty in hiring/retaining quality staff	54%
Degree of stress	38%

Q12: **If you could turn back time to the day you signed your franchise agreement, would you make the same decision to buy your franchise?**

	% answering
Yes	**75%**
No	25%

*   Number of survey respondents: 13 from 12 different states

Number of survey respondents as a % of total franchise units: 5.33%

AMERICAN EXPRESS TRAVEL

OVERALL SCORE: 82

200 Vesey St., 44th Floor
New York, NY 10285
Total number of outlets: 1700+
(all worldwide affiliates included)
Total number of franchise/affiliate outlets: 1700+
International: Yes—(affiliates worldwide)

OVERALL RANK: 25

Phone:
Franchise fee:
Franchise term:
Initial investment:
Advertising/Marketing fee:
Royalty fee:

SURVEY AND RESULTS *

Q1: About how many hours per week do you dedicate to your franchise business?

		% answering
A)	Less than 40	7%
B)	**41–50**	**40%**
C)	51–60	27%
D)	More than 60	27%
E)	Passive investment	0%

Q2: How would you describe your relations/communications with your franchisor?

		% answering
A)	Excellent	27%
B)	**Good**	**47%**
C)	Adequate	20%
D)	Fair	7%
E)	Poor	0%

Q3: In terms of how your franchisor views your communications with other franchisees, it is:

		% answering
A)	**Very supportive**	**53%**
B)	Not very supportive	13%
C)	No influence	33%

Q4: Is the franchisor fair with you in resolving any grievances?

		% answering
A)	**Extremely fair**	**43%**
B)	Pretty fair	36%
C)	Reasonably fair	21%
D)	Not very fair	0%
E)	Not fair at all	0%

Q5: Are territories equitably granted?

		% answering
A)	**Yes**	**53%**
B)	No	27%
C)	Not yet sure	20%

Q6: How would you describe the initial and ongoing training provided by your franchisor?

		% answering
A)	Excellent	0%
B)	**Good**	**60%**
C)	Adequate	13%
D)	Fair	27%
E)	Poor	0%

Q7: How well does the franchisor anticipate future trends in how it evolves and markets products and services?

		% answering
A)	Extremely well	20%
B)	**Pretty well**	**47%**
C)	Adequately	20%
D)	Not very well	13%
E)	Terribly	0%

Q8: How satisfied are you with your franchisor's spending of the royalty fees you pay?

		% answering
A)	Extremely satisfied	13%
B)	**Mostly satisfied**	**33%**
C)	**Somewhat satisfied**	**33%**
D)	Not very satisfied	20%
E)	Not satisfied at all	0%

Q9: **In what ways could the parent company most improve? (Please check those that most apply, no more than three):**

❑ Communications
❑ Counsel/advice on administrative/management issues
❑ Effectiveness of marketing/promotions
❑ Evolution of products/services
❑ Frequency of marketing/promotional campaigns

❑ Quality of products/services
❑ Pricing of products/services to franchisees
❑ Technology (Point of sale systems, usage of computers/email/software, etc.)
❑ Training

Most frequent responses:	% answering
Pricing of products/services to franchisees	40%
Technology	33%
Effectiveness of marketing/promotions	27%
Frequency of marketing/promotional campaigns	13%

Q10: **Is your income more, less or about what you expected prior to opening your business?**

	% answering	
More	29%	
Less	21%	**Summary: 79% are making about what they**
About what was expected	**50%**	**expected, or more.**

Q11: **Prior to opening your franchise, which (if any) of the following did you underestimate?**

❑ Amount of working capital required for your 1st year in business
❑ Difficulty in hiring/retaining quality staff
❑ Expertise required to run the business
❑ Impact of marketing/promotions

❑ Start-up costs
❑ Degree of stress
❑ Workload

Most frequent responses:	% answering
Difficulty in hiring/retaining quality staff	40%
Degree of stress	27%
Amount of working capital required for 1st year in business	13%

Q12: **If you could turn back time to the day you signed your franchise agreement, would you make the same decision to buy your franchise?**

	% answering
Yes	**100%**
No	0%

* Number of survey respondents: 15 from 10 different states

Number of survey respondents as a % of total franchise units:

AMERICAN LEAK DETECTION

www.americanleakdetection.com
Email: info@americanleakdetection.com

Water, gas and related detection and repair services for both consumer and business customers.

OVERALL SCORE: 76

888 Research Drive, Suite 100
Palm Springs, CA 92262
Fax: 760-320-1288
Total number of outlets: 235
Total number of franchise outlets: 267
International: Yes (worldwide)

OVERALL RANK: 52

Phone: 800-755-6697
Franchise fee: $57,500 to $100,000
Franchise term: 10 years
Initial investment: $71,255 to $155,050
Advertising/Marketing fee: None currently
Royalty fee: 6 to 10% based on annual gross revenues

SURVEY AND RESULTS *

Q1: About how many hours per week do you dedicate to your franchise business?

		% answering
A)	Less than 40	0%
B)	41–50	27%
C)	**51–60**	**45%**
D)	More than 60	27%
E)	Passive investment	0%

Q2: How would you describe your relations/communications with your franchisor?

		% answering
A)	**Excellent**	**55%**
B)	Good	36%
C)	Adequate	0%
D)	Fair	9%
E)	Poor	0%

Q3: In terms of how your franchisor views your communications with other franchisees, it is:

		% answering
A)	**Very supportive**	**91%**
B)	Not very supportive	0%
C)	No influence	9%

Q4: Is the franchisor fair with you in resolving any grievances?

		% answering
A)	**Extremely fair**	**45%**
B)	Pretty fair	18%
C)	Reasonably fair	36%
D)	Not very fair	0%
E)	Not fair at all	0%

Q5: Are territories equitably granted?

		% answering
A)	**Yes**	**82%**
B)	No	9%
C)	Not yet sure	9%

Q6: How would you describe the initial and ongoing training provided by your franchisor?

		% answering
A)	Excellent	27%
B)	**Good**	**45%**
C)	Adequate	9%
D)	Fair	18%
E)	Poor	0%

Q7: How well does the franchisor anticipate future trends in how it evolves and markets products and services?

		% answering
A)	**Extremely well**	**36%**
B)	Pretty well	18%
C)	Adequately	18%
D)	Not very well	27%
E)	Terribly	0%

Q8: How satisfied are you with your franchisor's spending of the royalty fees you pay?

		% answering
A)	Extremely satisfied	9%
B)	**Mostly satisfied**	**36%**
C)	Somewhat satisfied	18%
D)	Not very satisfied	27%
E)	Not satisfied at all	9%

Q9:   In what ways could the parent company most improve? (Please check those that most apply, no more than three):

❑   Communications

❑   Counsel/advice on administrative/management issues

❑   Effectiveness of marketing/promotions

❑   Evolution of products/services

❑   Frequency of marketing/promotional campaigns

❑   Quality of products/services

❑   Pricing of products/services to franchisees

❑   Technology (Point of sale systems, usage of computers/email/software, etc.)

❑   Training

Most frequent responses:	% answering
Counsel/advice on administrative/management issues (tie)	36%
Evolution of products/services (tie)	36%
Pricing of products/services to franchisees	27%

Q10: Is your income more, less or about what you expected prior to opening your business?

	% answering	
More	36%	
Less	**45%**	**Summary: 54% are making about what they**
About what was expected	18%	**expected, or more.**

Q11: Prior to opening your franchise, which (if any) of the following did you underestimate?

❑   Amount of working capital required for your 1st year in business

❑   Difficulty in hiring/retaining quality staff

❑   Expertise required to run the business

❑   Impact of marketing/promotions

❑   Start-up costs

❑   Degree of stress

❑   Workload

Most frequent responses:	% answering
Degree of stress (tie)	36%
Workload (tie)	36%
Difficulty in hiring/retaining quality staff	27%

Q12: If you could turn back time to the day you signed your franchise agreement, would you make the same decision to buy your franchise?

	% answering
Yes	**80%**
No	20%

*   Number of survey respondents: 11 from 8 different states

Number of survey respondents as a % of total franchise units: 4.68%

AMERICAN POOLPLAYERS ASSOCIATION

www.poolplayers.com

Offers franchises for the operation of an amateur pool league.

OVERALL SCORE: 97

1000 Lake Saint Louis Blvd., Suite 325
Lake Saint Louis, MO 63367
Fax: 636-625-2975
Total number of outlets: 246
Total number of franchise outlets: 246
International: No
Advertising/Marketing fee: Up to 5% of gross
revenue, but only if plan approved by franchisees

OVERALL RANK: 3

Phone: 800-372-2536
Franchise fee: $5,000 (plus $100 for every
20,000 people in the territory)
Franchise term: 2 years
Initial investment: $11,969 to $14,779
Royalty fee: The greater of $2.50 per team or 20%
of the fee charged each team weekly

SURVEY AND RESULTS *

Q1: About how many hours per week do you dedicate to your franchise business?

		% answering
A)	Less than 40	25%
B)	41–50	20%
C)	51–60	25%
D)	**More than 60**	**30%**
E)	Passive investment	0%

Q2: How would you describe your relations/communications with your franchisor?

		% answering
A)	**Excellent**	**50%**
B)	**Good**	**50%**
C)	Adequate	0%
D)	Fair	0%
E)	Poor	0%

Q3: In terms of how your franchisor views your communications with other franchisees, it is:

		% answering
A)	**Very supportive**	**100%**
B)	Not very supportive	0%
C)	No influence	0%

Q4: Is the franchisor fair with you in resolving any grievances?

		% answering
A)	Extremely fair	40%
B)	**Pretty fair**	**50%**
C)	Reasonably fair	10%
D)	Not very fair	0%
E)	Not fair at all	0%

Q5: Are territories equitably granted?

		% answering
A)	**Yes**	**70%**
B)	No	0%
C)	Not yet sure	30%

Q6: How would you describe the initial and ongoing training provided by your franchisor?

		% answering
A)	**Excellent**	**70%**
B)	Good	20%
C)	Adequate	10%
D)	Fair	0%
E)	Poor	0%

Q7: How well does the franchisor anticipate future trends in how it evolves and markets products and services?

		% answering
A)	**Extremely well**	**50%**
B)	Pretty well	20%
C)	Adequately	30%
D)	Not very well	0%
E)	Terribly	0%

Q8: How satisfied are you with your franchisor's spending of the royalty fees you pay?

		% answering
A)	Extremely satisfied	10%
B)	**Mostly satisfied**	**50%**
C)	Somewhat satisfied	40%
D)	Not very satisfied	0%
E)	Not satisfied at all	0%

Q9: **In what ways could the parent company most improve? (Please check those that most apply, no more than three):**

❑ Communications
❑ Counsel/advice on administrative/management issues
❑ Effectiveness of marketing/promotions
❑ Evolution of products/services
❑ Frequency of marketing/promotional campaigns

❑ Quality of products/services
❑ Pricing of products/services to franchisees
❑ Technology (Point of sale systems, usage of computers/email/software, etc.)
❑ Training

Most frequent responses:	% answering
Effectiveness of marketing/promotions (tie)	40%
Technology (tie)	40%
Counsel/advice on administrative/management issues	30%

Q10: **Is your income more, less or about what you expected prior to opening your business?**

	% answering	
More	30%	
Less	20%	**Summary: 80% making about what they**
About what was expected	**50%**	**expected, or more**

Q11: **Prior to opening your franchise, which (if any) of the following did you underestimate?**

❑ Amount of working capital required for your 1st year in business
❑ Difficulty in hiring/retaining quality staff
❑ Expertise required to run the business
❑ Impact of marketing/promotions

❑ Start-up costs
❑ Degree of stress
❑ Workload

Most frequent responses:	% answering
Degree of stress	80%
Workload	50%
Amount of working capital required for 1st year in business (tie)	30%
Difficulty in hiring/retaining quality staff (tie)	30%
Expertise required to run the business (tie)	30%

Q12: **If you could turn back time to the day you signed your franchise agreement, would you make the same decision to buy your franchise?**

	% answering
Yes	**100%**
No	0%

* Number of survey respondents: 10 from 9 different states
Number of survey respondents as a % of total franchise units: 4.07%

AMERISPEC

www.amerispec.com

Residential and building inspection services.

OVERALL SCORE: 67

889 Ridge Lake Blvd.
Memphis, TN 38120
Total number of outlets:302
Total number of franchise outlets: 300
International: No
Advertising/Marketing fee: 3% of gross revenues
(minimum of $125 per month)

OVERALL RANK: 99

Phone: 800-426-2270
Franchise fee: $19,900 to $29,900
Franchise term: 5 years (10 in certain states)
Initial investment: $26,410 to 64,550
Royalty fee: 7% of gross revenues (minimum of
$250 per month)

SURVEY AND RESULTS *

Q1: **About how many hours per week do you dedicate to your franchise business?**

		% answering
A)	Less than 40	17%
B)	41–50	0%
C)	51–60	25%
D)	**More than 60**	**58%**
E)	Passive investment	0%

Q2: **How would you describe your relations/ communications with your franchisor?**

		% answering
A)	Excellent	25%
B)	**Good**	**33%**
C)	Adequate	8%
D)	Fair	25%
E)	Poor	8%

Q3: **In terms of how your franchisor views your communications with other franchisees, it is:**

		% answering
A)	**Very supportive**	**90%**
B)	Not very supportive	0%
C)	No influence	10%

Q4: **Is the franchisor fair with you in resolving any grievances?**

		% answering
A)	Extremely fair	9%
B)	Pretty fair	27%
C)	**Reasonably fair**	**55%**
D)	Not very fair	0%
E)	Not fair at all	9%

Q5: **Are territories equitably granted?**

		% answering
A)	**Yes**	**67%**
B)	No	17%
C)	Not yet sure	17%

Q6: **How would you describe the initial and ongoing training provided by your franchisor?**

		% answering
A)	**Excellent**	**50%**
B)	Good	8%
C)	Adequate	38%
D)	Fair	4%
E)	Poor	0%

Q7: **How well does the franchisor anticipate future trends in how it evolves and markets products and services?**

		% answering
A)	Extremely well	18%
B)	**Pretty well**	**36%**
C)	Adequately	9%
D)	Not very well	18%
E)	Terribly	18%

Q8: **How satisfied are you with your franchisor's spending of the royalty fees you pay?**

		% answering
A)	Extremely satisfied	25%
B)	**Mostly satisfied**	**33%**
C)	Somewhat satisfied	25%
D)	Not very satisfied	8%
E)	Not satisfied at all	8%

Q9: **In what ways could the parent company most improve? (Please check those that most apply, no more than three):**

❑ Communications

❑ Counsel/advice on administrative/management issues

❑ Effectiveness of marketing/promotions

❑ Evolution of products/services

❑ Frequency of marketing/promotional campaigns

❑ Quality of products/services

❑ Pricing of products/services to franchisees

❑ Technology (Point of sale systems, usage of computers/email/software, etc.)

❑ Training

Most frequent responses:	% answering
Effectiveness of marketing/promotions (tie)	33%
Evolution of products/services (tie)	33%
Pricing of products/services to franchisees (tie)	33%

Q10: **Is your income more, less or about what you expected prior to opening your business?**

	% answering
More	8%
Less	42%
About what was expected	**50%**

Q11: **Prior to opening your franchise, which (if any) of the following did you underestimate?**

❑ Amount of working capital required for your 1st year in business

❑ Difficulty in hiring/retaining quality staff

❑ Expertise required to run the business

❑ Impact of marketing/promotions

❑ Start-up costs

❑ Degree of stress

❑ Workload

Most frequent responses:	% answering
Difficulty in hiring/retaining quality staff (tie)	42%
Degree of stress (tie)	42%
Workload (tie)	42%

Q12: **If you could turn back time to the day you signed your franchise agreement, would you make the same decision to buy your franchise?**

	% answering
Yes	**64%**
No	36%

* Number of survey respondents: 12 from 11 different states

Number of survey respondents as a % of total franchise units: 4%

ARBY'S

www.arbys.com
Email:phultgren@arbys.com (Peter Hultgren)

Roast beef, chicken and deli-style sandwiches, drinks, and desserts.

OVERALL SCORE: 72

1000 Corporate Drive
Fort Lauderdale, FL 33334
Fax: 954-351-5222
Total number of outlets: 3400+
Total number of franchise outlets: 3400+
International: Yes (worldwide)

OVERALL RANK: 72

Phone: 954-351-5121
Franchise fee: $47,500
Franchise term: 20 years
Initial investment: $303,700 to 669,200
Advertising/Marketing fee: 1.2% of gross sales
Royalty fee: 4% of gross sales

SURVEY AND RESULTS *

Q1: About how many hours per week do you dedicate to your franchise business?

		% answering
A)	Less than 40	27%
B)	41–50	13%
C)	51–60	13%
D)	**More than 60**	**47%**
E)	Passive investment	0%

Q2: How would you describe your relations/communications with your franchisor?

		% answering
A)	Excellent	20%
B)	Good	20%
C)	**Adequate**	**47%**
D)	Fair	0%
E)	Poor	13%

Q3: In terms of how your franchisor views your communications with other franchisees, it is:

		% answering
A)	**Very supportive**	**40%**
B)	Not very supportive	20%
C)	**No influence**	**40%**

Q4: Is the franchisor fair with you in resolving any grievances?

		% answering
A)	Extremely fair	14%
B)	**Pretty fair**	**29%**
C)	Reasonably fair	21%
D)	Not very fair	21%
E)	Not fair at all	14%

Q5: Are territories equitably granted?

		% answering
A)	**Yes**	**50%**
B)	No	43%
C)	Not yet sure	7%

Q6: How would you describe the initial and ongoing training provided by your franchisor?

		% answering
A)	Excellent	20%
B)	Good	33%
C)	**Adequate**	**40%**
D)	Fair	0%
E)	Poor	7%

Q7: How well does the franchisor anticipate future trends in how it evolves and markets products and services?

		% answering
A)	Extremely well	13%
B)	**Pretty well**	**53%**
C)	Adequately	13%
D)	Not very well	7%
E)	Terribly	13%

Q8: How satisfied are you with your franchisor's spending of the royalty fees you pay?

		% answering
A)	Extremely satisfied	7%
B)	**Mostly satisfied**	**47%**
C)	Somewhat satisfied	27%
D)	Not very satisfied	0%
E)	Not satisfied at all	20%

Q9: **In what ways could the parent company most improve? (Please check those that most apply, no more than three):**

❑ Communications
❑ Counsel/advice on administrative/management issues
❑ Effectiveness of marketing/promotions
❑ Evolution of products/services
❑ Frequency of marketing/promotional campaigns

❑ Quality of products/services
❑ Pricing of products/services to franchisees
❑ Technology (Point of sale systems, usage of computers/email/software, etc.)
❑ Training

Most frequent responses:	% answering
Evolution of products/services	47%
Effectiveness of marketing/promotions	40%
Communications	33%

Q10: **Is your income more, less or about what you expected prior to opening your business?**

	% answering	
More	**36%**	
Less	29%	**Summary: 72% are making about what they**
About what was expected	**36%**	**expected, or more.**

Q11: **Prior to opening your franchise, which (if any) of the following did you underestimate?**

❑ Amount of working capital required for your 1st year in business
❑ Difficulty in hiring/retaining quality staff
❑ Expertise required to run the business
❑ Impact of marketing/promotions

❑ Start-up costs
❑ Degree of stress
❑ Workload

Most frequent responses:	% answering
Difficulty in hiring/retaining quality staff	60%
Degree of stress	33%
Impact of marketing/promotions (tie)	20%
Workload (tie)	20%

Q12: **If you could turn back time to the day you signed your franchise agreement, would you make the same decision to buy your franchise?**

	% answering
Yes	**87%**
No	13%

* Number of survey respondents: 15 from 12 different states
Number of survey respondents as a % of total franchise units: < 1%

ASSIST-2-SELL

www.assist2sell.com
Email: franchiseinfo@assist2sell.com

Real estate brokerage.

OVERALL SCORE: 81

1610 Meadow Wood Lane
Reno, NV 89502
Fax: 775-668-6069
Total number of outlets: 399
Total number of franchise outlets: 398
International: Yes (Canada)

OVERALL RANK: 30

Phone: 800-528-7816
Franchise fee: $19,500
Franchise term: 5 years
Initial investment: $30,000 to $62,000
Advertising/Marketing fee: > of $150 per month
or 1.5% of gross revenue (after nine months)
Royalty fee: 5% of monthly gross income

SURVEY AND RESULTS *

Q1: About how many hours per week do you dedicate to your franchise business?

		% answering
A)	Less than 40	8%
B)	41–50	25%
C)	51–60	17%
D)	**More than 60**	**50%**
E)	Passive investment	0%

Q2: How would you describe your relations/ communications with your franchisor?

		% answering
A)	Excellent	8%
B)	Good	25%
C)	Adequate	17%
D)	**Fair**	**50%**
E)	Poor	0%

Q3: In terms of how your franchisor views your communications with other franchisees, it is:

		% answering
A)	**Very supportive**	**83%**
B)	Not very supportive	0%
C)	No influence	17%

Q4: Is the franchisor fair with you in resolving any grievances?

		% answering
A)	**Extremely fair**	**82%**
B)	Pretty fair	9%
C)	Reasonably fair	9%
D)	Not very fair	0%
E)	Not fair at all	0%

Q5: Are territories equitably granted?

		% answering
A)	**Yes**	**83%**
B)	No	17%
C)	Not yet sure	0%

Q6: How would you describe the initial and ongoing training provided by your franchisor?

		% answering
A)	**Excellent**	**50%**
B)	Good	38%
C)	Adequate	8%
D)	Fair	0%
E)	Poor	4%

Q7: How well does the franchisor anticipate future trends in how it evolves and markets products and services?

		% answering
A)	**Extremely well**	**50%**
B)	Pretty well	42%
C)	Adequately	0%
D)	Not very well	8%
E)	Terribly	0%

Q8: How satisfied are you with your franchisor's spending of the royalty fees you pay?

		% answering
A)	**Extremely satisfied**	**42%**
B)	Mostly satisfied	25%
C)	Somewhat satisfied	25%
D)	Not very satisfied	0%
E)	Not satisfied at all	8%

Q9:   **In what ways could the parent company most improve? (Please check those that most apply, no more than three):**

❑   Communications

❑   Counsel/advice on administrative/management issues

❑   Effectiveness of marketing/promotions

❑   Evolution of products/services

❑   Frequency of marketing/promotional campaigns

❑   Quality of products/services

❑   Pricing of products/services to franchisees

❑   Technology (Point of sale systems, usage of computers/email/software, etc.)

❑   Training

Most frequent responses:	% answering
Effectiveness of marketing/promotions	42%
Technology	33%
Counsel/advice on administrative/management issues (tie)	17%
Evolution of products/services (tie)	17%
Frequency of marketing/promotional campaigns (tie)	17%

Q10: **Is your income more, less or about what you expected prior to opening your business?**

	% answering	
More	25%	
Less	33%	**Summary: 77% are making about what they**
About what was expected	**42%**	**expected, or more.**

Q11: **Prior to opening your franchise, which (if any) of the following did you underestimate?**

❑   Amount of working capital required for your 1st year in business

❑   Difficulty in hiring/retaining quality staff

❑   Expertise required to run the business

❑   Impact of marketing/promotions

❑   Start-up costs

❑   Degree of stress

❑   Workload

Most frequent responses:	% answering
Amount of working capital required for 1st year in business (tie)	42%
Difficulty in hiring/retaining quality staff (tie)	42%
Start-up costs	33%

Q12: **If you could turn back time to the day you signed your franchise agreement, would you make the same decision to buy your franchise?**

	% answering
Yes	**75%**
No	25%

*   Number of survey respondents: 12 from 10 different states

Number of survey respondents as a % of total franchise units: 3.02%

ATLANTA BREAD COMPANY

www.atlantabread.com

Cafe offering soups, salads, breads, sandwiches and pastries.

OVERALL SCORE: 42

1955 Lake Park Drive, Suite 400
Smyrna, GA 30080
Fax: 770-444-1991
Total number of outlets: 173
Total number of franchise outlets:
International: No

OVERALL RANK: 180

Phone: 800-398-3728
Franchise fee: $40,000
Franchise term: 10 years
Initial investment: $533,700 to $748,800
Advertising/Marketing fee: 3% of gross sales wkly.
Royalty fee: 5% of gross sales weekly

SURVEY AND RESULTS *

Q1: About how many hours per week do you dedicate to your franchise business?

		% answering
A)	Less than 40	0%
B)	41–50	0%
C)	**51–60**	**50%**
D)	**More than 60**	**50%**
E)	Passive investment	0%

Q2: How would you describe your relations/ communications with your franchisor?

		% answering
A)	Excellent	30%
B)	Good	0%
C)	**Adequate**	**40%**
D)	Fair	10%
E)	Poor	20%

Q3: In terms of how your franchisor views your communications with other franchisees, it is:

		% answering
A)	Very supportive	10%
B)	**Not very supportive**	**60%**
C)	No influence	30%

Q4: Is the franchisor fair with you in resolving any grievances?

		% answering
A)	Extremely fair	22%
B)	Pretty fair	11%
C)	**Reasonably fair**	**44%**
D)	Not very fair	11%
E)	Not fair at all	11%

Q5: Are territories equitably granted?

		% answering
A)	Yes	20%
B)	**No**	**40%**
C)	**Not yet sure**	**40%**

Q6: How would you describe the initial and ongoing training provided by your franchisor?

		% answering
A)	Excellent	10%
B)	**Good**	**40%**
C)	Adequate	0%
D)	Fair	35%
E)	Poor	15%

Q7: How well does the franchisor anticipate future trends in how it evolves and markets products and services?

		% answering
A)	Extremely well	0%
B)	Pretty well	30%
C)	Adequately	10%
D)	**Not very well**	**50%**
E)	Terribly	10%

Q8: How satisfied are you with your franchisor's spending of the royalty fees you pay?

		% answering
A)	Extremely satisfied	0%
B)	**Mostly satisfied**	**30%**
C)	**Somewhat satisfied**	**30%**
D)	**Not very satisfied**	**30%**
E)	Not satisfied at all	10%

Q9: **In what ways could the parent company most improve? (Please check those that most apply, no more than three):**

- ❑ Communications
- ❑ Counsel/advice on administrative/management issues
- ❑ Effectiveness of marketing/promotions
- ❑ Evolution of products/services
- ❑ Frequency of marketing/promotional campaigns

- ❑ Quality of products/services
- ❑ Pricing of products/services to franchisees
- ❑ Technology (Point of sale systems, usage of computers/email/software, etc.)
- ❑ Training

Most frequent responses:	% answering
Effectiveness of marketing/promotions	80%
Pricing of products/services to franchisees (tie)	50%
Communications (tie)	50%
Evolution of products/services	40%

Q10: **Is your income more, less or about what you expected prior to opening your business?**

	% answering	
More	0%	
Less	**70%**	**Summary: 30% are making about what they**
About what was expected	30%	**expected, or more.**

Q11: **Prior to opening your franchise, which (if any) of the following did you underestimate?**

- ❑ Amount of working capital required for your 1st year in business
- ❑ Difficulty in hiring/retaining quality staff
- ❑ Expertise required to run the business
- ❑ Impact of marketing/promotions

- ❑ Start-up costs
- ❑ Degree of stress
- ❑ Workload

Most frequent responses:	% answering
Difficulty in hiring/retaining quality staff (tie)	40%
Start-up costs (tie)	40%
Amount of working capital required for 1st year in business (tie)	40%

Q12: **If you could turn back time to the day you signed your franchise agreement, would you make the same decision to buy your franchise?**

	% answering
Yes	40%
No	**60%**

* Number of survey respondents: 10 from 8 different states
   Number of survey respondents as a % of total franchise units: 5.78%

AUNTIE ANNE'S HAND-ROLLED SOFT PRETZELS

www.auntieannes.com

Server of fresh pretzels, dips and drinks.

OVERALL SCORE: 89

160-A Route 41
Gap, PA 17527
Fax: 717-442-4139
Total number of outlets: 800+
Total number of franchise outlets: 800+
International: Yes (worldwide)

OVERALL RANK: 8

Phone: 717-442-4766
Franchise fee: $30,000
Franchise term: 10 years
Initial investment: $192,550 to $342,000
Advertising/Marketing fee: 6%
Royalty fee: 1%

SURVEY AND RESULTS *

Q1: About how many hours per week do you dedicate to your franchise business?

		% answering
A)	**Less than 40**	**45%**
B)	41–50	27%
C)	51–60	18%
D)	More than 60	9%
E)	Passive investment	0%

Q2: How would you describe your relations/ communications with your franchisor?

		% answering
A)	Excellent	27%
B)	**Good**	**72%**
C)	Adequate	0%
D)	Fair	0%
E)	Poor	0%

Q3: In terms of how your franchisor views your communications with other franchisees, it is:

		% answering
A)	**Very supportive**	**91%**
B)	Not very supportive	0%
C)	No influence	0%

Q4: Is the franchisor fair with you in resolving any grievances?

		% answering
A)	Extremely fair	27%
B)	**Pretty fair**	**55%**
C)	Reasonably fair	18%
D)	Not very fair	0%
E)	Not fair at all	0%

Q5: Are territories equitably granted?

		% answering
A)	**Yes**	**80%**
B)	No	20%
C)	Not yet sure	0%

Q6: How would you describe the initial and ongoing training provided by your franchisor?

		% answering
A)	**Excellent**	**55%**
B)	Good	27%
C)	Adequate	18%
D)	Fair	0%
E)	Poor	0%

Q7: How well does the franchisor anticipate future trends in how it evolves and markets products and services?

		% answering
A)	Extremely well	36%
B)	**Pretty well**	**45%**
C)	Adequately	18%
D)	Not very well	0%
E)	Terribly	0%

Q8: How satisfied are you with your franchisor's spending of the royalty fees you pay?

		% answering
A)	Extremely satisfied	0%
B)	**Mostly satisfied**	**64%**
C)	Somewhat satisfied	36%
D)	Not very satisfied	0%
E)	Not satisfied at all	0%

Q9: **In what ways could the parent company most improve? (Please check those that most apply, no more than three):**

❑ Communications
❑ Counsel/advice on administrative/management issues
❑ Effectiveness of marketing/promotions
❑ Evolution of products/services
❑ Frequency of marketing/promotional campaigns

❑ Quality of products/services
❑ Pricing of products/services to franchisees
❑ Technology (Point of sale systems, usage
    of computers/email/software, etc.)
❑ Training

Most frequent responses:	% answering
Effectiveness of marketing/promotions	55%
Technology	45%
Pricing of products/services to franchisees	45%

Q10: **Is your income more, less or about what you expected prior to opening your business?**

	% answering	
More	27%	
Less	27%	**Summary: 72% are making about what they**
About what was expected	**45%**	**expected, or more.**

Q11: **Prior to opening your franchise, which (if any) of the following did you underestimate?**

❑ Amount of working capital required for your
    1st year in business
❑ Difficulty in hiring/retaining quality staff
❑ Expertise required to run the business
❑ Impact of marketing/promotions

❑ Start-up costs
❑ Degree of stress
❑ Workload

Most frequent responses:	% answering
Degree of stress	55%
Difficulty in hiring/retaining quality staff	36%
Start-up costs	27%
Workload	27%

Q12: **If you could turn back time to the day you signed your franchise agreement, would you make the same decision to buy your franchise?**

	% answering
Yes	**100%**
No	0%

* Number of survey respondents: 11 from 7 different states
    Number of survey respondents as a % of total franchise units: 1.38%

AUSSIE PET MOBILE

www.aussiepetmobile.com
Email: corp@aussiepetmobile.com

Mobile pet grooming.

OVERALL SCORE: 45

34189 Pacific Coast Hwy.
Dana Point, CA 92629
Fax: 949-234-0688
Total number of outlets: 106
Total number of franchise outlets: 106
International: Yes (Mexico, Australia)

OVERALL RANK: 174

Phone: 949-234-0680
Franchise fee: $32,500
Franchise term: 10 years
Initial investment: $44,831 to $78,781
Advertising/Marketing fee: Greater of 4% of monthly gross revenues or $265
Royalty fee: Minimum 8% of mo. gross revenues

SURVEY AND RESULTS *

Q1: About how many hours per week do you dedicate to your franchise business?

		% answering
A)	Less than 40	23%
B)	41–50	15%
C)	51–60	23%
D)	**More than 60**	**38%**
E)	Passive investment	0%

Q2: How would you describe your relations/communications with your franchisor?

		% answering
A)	Excellent	15%
B)	**Good**	**38%**
C)	**Adequate**	**38%**
D)	Fair	8%
E)	Poor	0%

Q3: In terms of how your franchisor views your communications with other franchisees, it is:

		% answering
A)	**Very supportive**	**54%**
B)	Not very supportive	31%
C)	No influence	15%

Q4: Is the franchisor fair with you in resolving any grievances?

		% answering
A)	Extremely fair	9%
B)	Pretty fair	27%
C)	**Reasonably fair**	**45%**
D)	Not very fair	18%
E)	Not fair at all	0%

Q5: Are territories equitably granted?

		% answering
A)	**Yes**	**69%**
B)	No	8%
C)	Not yet sure	23%

Q6: How would you describe the initial and ongoing training provided by your franchisor?

		% answering
A)	Excellent	15%
B)	Good	0%
C)	Adequate	27%
D)	Fair	27%
E)	**Poor**	**31%**

Q7: How well does the franchisor anticipate future trends in how it evolves and markets products and services?

		% answering
A)	Extremely well	23%
B)	Pretty well	15%
C)	**Adequately**	**54%**
D)	Not very well	8%
E)	Terribly	0%

Q8: How satisfied are you with your franchisor's spending of the royalty fees you pay?

		% answering
A)	Extremely satisfied	8%
B)	Mostly satisfied	17%
C)	**Somewhat satisfied**	**25%**
D)	**Not very satisfied**	**25%**
E)	**Not satisfied at all**	**25%**

Q9:   **In what ways could the parent company most improve? (Please check those that most apply, no more than three):**

❑   Communications   ❑   Quality of products/services
❑   Counsel/advice on administrative/management issues   ❑   Pricing of products/services to franchisees
❑   Effectiveness of marketing/promotions   ❑   Technology (Point of sale systems, usage
❑   Evolution of products/services   of computers/email/software, etc.)
❑   Frequency of marketing/promotional campaigns   ❑   Training

Most frequent responses: % answering
Counsel/advice on administrative/management issues (tie)   46%
Effectiveness of marketing/promotions (tie)   46%
Training   38%

Q10:   **Is your income more, less or about what you expected prior to opening your business?**

                                        % answering
More   8%
Less   **69%**   **Summary: 31% are making about what they**
About what was expected   23%   **expected, or more.**

Q11:   **Prior to opening your franchise, which (if any) of the following did you underestimate?**

❑   Amount of working capital required for your   ❑   Start-up costs
     1st year in business   ❑   Degree of stress
❑   Difficulty in hiring/retaining quality staff   ❑   Workload
❑   Expertise required to run the business
❑   Impact of marketing/promotions

Most frequent responses: % answering
Workload   54%
Difficulty in hiring/retaining quality staff (tie)   46%
Degree of stress (tie)   46%

Q12:   **If you could turn back time to the day you signed your franchise agreement, would you make the same decision**
            to buy your franchise?

                                        % answering
                       Yes   31%
                       No   **69%**

*   Number of survey respondents: 13 from 6 different states
    Number of survey respondents as a % of total franchise units: 12.26%

BASKIN ROBBINS

www.baskinrobbins.com

Ice cream and frozen yogurt desserts.

OVERALL SCORE: 46

130 Royall St.
Canton, MA 02021
Fax: 818-996-5163
Total number of outlets: 5,000+
Total number of franchise outlets: 5,000+
International: Yes (worldwide)

OVERALL RANK: 172

Phone: 800-777-9983
Franchise fee:
Franchise term:
Initial investment:
Advertising/Marketing fee:
Royalty fee:

SURVEY AND RESULTS *

Q1: About how many hours per week do you dedicate to your franchise business?

		% answering
A)	Less than 40	28%
B)	41–50	17%
C)	51–60	6%
D)	**More than 60**	**39%**
E)	Passive investment	11%

Q2: How would you describe your relations/communications with your franchisor?

		% answering
A)	Excellent	6%
B)	Good	28%
C)	Adequate	6%
D)	**Fair**	**33%**
E)	Poor	28%

Q3: In terms of how your franchisor views your communications with other franchisees, it is:

		% answering
A)	**Very supportive**	**35%**
B)	**Not very supportive**	**35%**
C)	No influence	29%

Q4: Is the franchisor fair with you in resolving any grievances?

		% answering
A)	Extremely fair	6%
B)	Pretty fair	11%
C)	Reasonably fair	22%
D)	**Not very fair**	**50%**
E)	Not fair at all	11%

Q5: Are territories equitably granted?

		% answering
A)	Yes	18%
B)	**No**	**53%**
C)	Not yet sure	29%

Q6: How would you describe the initial and ongoing training provided by your franchisor?

		% answering
A)	Excellent	0%
B)	**Good**	**33%**
C)	Adequate	6%
D)	**Fair**	**33%**
E)	Poor	28%

Q7: How well does the franchisor anticipate future trends in how it evolves and markets products and services?

		% answering
A)	Extremely well	6%
B)	Pretty well	17%
C)	Adequately	17%
D)	**Not very well**	**33%**
E)	Terribly	28%

Q8: How satisfied are you with your franchisor's spending of the royalty fees you pay?

		% answering
A)	Extremely satisfied	0%
B)	Mostly satisfied	17%
C)	Somewhat satisfied	11%
D)	Not very satisfied	17%
E)	**Not satisfied at all**	**56%**

Q9: **In what ways could the parent company most improve? (Please check those that most apply, no more than three):**

- ❑ Communications
- ❑ Counsel/advice on administrative/management issues
- ❑ Effectiveness of marketing/promotions
- ❑ Evolution of products/services
- ❑ Frequency of marketing/promotional campaigns

- ❑ Quality of products/services
- ❑ Pricing of products/services to franchisees
- ❑ Technology (Point of sale systems, usage of computers/email/software, etc.)
- ❑ Training

Most frequent responses:	% answering
Effectiveness of marketing/promotions	83%
Evolution of products/services	50%
Communications (tie)	33%
Frequency of marketing/promotional campaigns (tie)	33%
Pricing of products/services to franchisees (tie)	33%

Q10: **Is your income more, less or about what you expected prior to opening your business?**

	% answering	
More	6%	
Less	**61%**	**Summary: 39% are making about what they**
About what was expected	33%	**expected, or more.**

Q11: **Prior to opening your franchise, which (if any) of the following did you underestimate?**

- ❑ Amount of working capital required for your 1st year in business
- ❑ Difficulty in hiring/retaining quality staff
- ❑ Expertise required to run the business
- ❑ Impact of marketing/promotions

- ❑ Start-up costs
- ❑ Degree of stress
- ❑ Workload

Most frequent responses:	% answering
Workload	39%
Degree of stress	33%
Difficulty in hiring/retaining quality staff	28%
Amount of working capital required for 1st year in business	28%

Q12: **If you could turn back time to the day you signed your franchise agreement, would you make the same decision to buy your franchise?**

	% answering
Yes	67%
No	33%

* Number of survey respondents: 18 from 11 different states

Number of survey respondents as a % of total franchise units: < 1%

BATTERIES PLUS

www.batteriesplus.com

The country's largest battery franchise.

OVERALL SCORE: 68

925 Walnut Ridge Drive, Suite 100
Hartland, WI 53029
Fax: 262-369-0215
Total number of outlets: 225+
Total number of franchise outlets: 211+
International: No

OVERALL RANK: 95

Phone: 262-912-3000
Franchise fee: $30,000
Franchise term: 10 years
Initial investment: $179,300–$315,300
Advertising/Marketing fee: 1% plus Advertising
Cooperative fee.
Royalty fee: 4%

SURVEY AND RESULTS *

Q1: About how many hours per week do you dedicate to your franchise business?

		% answering
A)	Less than 40	6%
B)	41–50	31%
C)	51–60	19%
D)	**More than 60**	**38%**
E)	Passive investment	6%

Q2: How would you describe your relations/ communications with your franchisor?

		% answering
A)	Excellent	31%
B)	**Good**	**50%**
C)	Adequate	13%
D)	Fair	6%
E)	Poor	0%

Q3: In terms of how your franchisor views your communications with other franchisees, it is:

		% answering
A)	**Very supportive**	**63%**
B)	Not very supportive	6%
C)	No influence	31%

Q4: Is the franchisor fair with you in resolving any grievances?

		% answering
A)	**Extremely fair**	**38%**
B)	Pretty fair	31%
C)	Reasonably fair	19%
D)	Not very fair	13%
E)	Not fair at all	0%

Q5: Are territories equitably granted?

		% answering
A)	**Yes**	**67%**
B)	No	7%
C)	Not yet sure	27%

Q6: How would you describe the initial and ongoing training provided by your franchisor?

		% answering
A)	Excellent	25%
B)	Good	19%
C)	**Adequate**	**50%**
D)	Fair	6%
E)	Poor	0%

Q7: How well does the franchisor anticipate future trends in how it evolves and markets products and services?

		% answering
A)	Extremely well	25%
B)	**Pretty well**	**31%**
C)	Adequately	28%
D)	Not very well	9%
E)	Terribly	6%

Q8: How satisfied are you with your franchisor's spending of the royalty fees you pay?

		% answering
A)	Extremely satisfied	13%
B)	**Mostly satisfied**	**50%**
C)	Somewhat satisfied	25%
D)	Not very satisfied	13%
E)	Not satisfied at all	0%

Q9: **In what ways could the parent company most improve? (Please check those that most apply, no more than three):**

❑ Communications

❑ Counsel/advice on administrative/management issues

❑ Effectiveness of marketing/promotions

❑ Evolution of products/services

❑ Frequency of marketing/promotional campaigns

❑ Quality of products/services

❑ Pricing of products/services to franchisees

❑ Technology (Point of sale systems, usage of computers/email/software, etc.)

❑ Training

Most frequent responses:	% answering
Quality of products/services	56%
Counsel/advice on administrative/management issues (tie)	38%
Evolution of products/services (tie)	38%
Pricing of products/services to franchisees (tie)	38%

Q10: **Is your income more, less or about what you expected prior to opening your business?**

	% answering	
More	13%	
Less	**50%**	**Summary: 51% are making about what they**
About what was expected	38%	**expected, or more.**

Q11: **Prior to opening your franchise, which (if any) of the following did you underestimate?**

❑ Amount of working capital required for your 1st year in business

❑ Difficulty in hiring/retaining quality staff

❑ Expertise required to run the business

❑ Impact of marketing/promotions

❑ Start-up costs

❑ Degree of stress

❑ Workload

Most frequent responses:	% answering
Amount of working capital required for your first year in business (tie)	63%
Difficulty in hiring/retaining quality staff (tie)	56%
Impact of marketing/promotions	25%
Start-up costs	25%

Q12: **If you could turn back time to the day you signed your franchise agreement, would you make the same decision to buy your franchise?**

	% answering
Yes	**67%**
No	33%

*   Number of survey respondents: 16 from 15 different states

    Number of survey respondents as a % of total franchise units: 7.11%

BEN & JERRY'S

www.benjerry.com

Ice cream and frozen yogurt desserts.

OVERALL SCORE: 65

30 Community Drive
South Burlington, VT 05403
Fax: 802-846-1610
Total number of outlets: 450+
Total number of franchise outlets: 450+
International: Yes (worldwide)

OVERALL RANK: 111

Phone: 802-846-1543, ext. 7485
Franchise fee: $5,000 to $30,000
Franchise term: 10 years
Initial investment: $129,500–$316,000
Advertising/Marketing fee: 4%
Royalty fee: 3%

SURVEY AND RESULTS *

Q1: About how many hours per week do you dedicate to your franchise business?

		% answering
A)	**Less than 40**	**27%**
B)	**41–50**	**27%**
C)	**51–60**	**27%**
D)	More than 60	18%
E)	Passive investment	18%

Q2: How would you describe your relations/communications with your franchisor?

		% answering
A)	**Excellent**	**45%**
B)	Good	27%
C)	Adequate	18%
D)	Fair	9%
E)	Poor	0%

Q3: In terms of how your franchisor views your communications with other franchisees, it is:

		% answering
A)	**Very supportive**	**82%**
B)	Not very supportive	18%
C)	No influence	0%

Q4: Is the franchisor fair with you in resolving any grievances?

		% answering
A)	**Extremely fair**	**40%**
B)	Pretty fair	30%
C)	Reasonably fair	10%
D)	Not very fair	20%
E)	Not fair at all	0%

Q5: Are territories equitably granted?

		% answering
A)	Yes	55%
B)	No	36%
C)	Not yet sure	9%

Q6: How would you describe the initial and ongoing training provided by your franchisor?

		% answering
A)	Excellent	18%
B)	**Good**	**36%**
C)	Adequate	23%
D)	Fair	14%
E)	Poor	9%

Q7: How well does the franchisor anticipate future trends in how it evolves and markets products and services?

		% answering
A)	Extremely well	18%
B)	Pretty well	27%
C)	Adequately	0%
D)	**Not very well**	**45%**
E)	Terribly	9%

Q8: How satisfied are you with your franchisor's spending of the royalty fees you pay?

		% answering
A)	Extremely satisfied	22%
B)	Mostly satisfied	22%
C)	**Somewhat satisfied**	**33%**
D)	Not very satisfied	22%
E)	Not satisfied at all	0%

Q9: In what ways could the parent company most improve? (Please check those that most apply, no more than three):

❑ Communications
❑ Counsel/advice on administrative/management issues
❑ Effectiveness of marketing/promotions
❑ Evolution of products/services
❑ Frequency of marketing/promotional campaigns

❑ Quality of products/services
❑ Pricing of products/services to franchisees
❑ Technology (Point of sale systems, usage of computers/email/software, etc.)
❑ Training

Most frequent responses: % answering

Effectiveness of marketing/promotions   82%
Evolution of products/services   55%
Pricing of products/services to franchisees   36%

Q10: Is your income more, less or about what you expected prior to opening your business?

	% answering	
More	9%	
Less	**64%**	**Summary: 36% are making about what they**
About what was expected	27%	**expected, or more.**

Q11: Prior to opening your franchise, which (if any) of the following did you underestimate?

❑ Amount of working capital required for your first year in business
❑ Difficulty in hiring/retaining quality staff
❑ Expertise required to run the business
❑ Impact of marketing/promotions

❑ Start-up costs
❑ Degree of stress
❑ Workload

Most frequent responses: % answering

Difficulty in hiring/retaining quality staff   45%
Impact of marketing/promotions   27%
Degree of stress (tie)   9%
Workload (tie)   9%

Q12: If you could turn back time to the day you signed your franchise agreement, would you make the same decision to buy your franchise?

	% answering
Yes	**82%**
No	18%

* Number of survey respondents: 11 from 8 different states
Number of survey respondents as a % of total franchise units: 2.44%

BRUSTER'S REAL ICE CREAM

www.brusters.com

Ice cream and frozen yogurt desserts.

OVERALL SCORE: 58

OVERALL RANK: N/A

730 Mulberry Street
Bridgewater, PA 15009
Fax: 724-774-0666
Total number of outlets: 200+
Total number of franchise outlets: 200+
International: No

Phone: 724-774-4250
Franchise fee:
Franchise term:
Initial investment:
Advertising/Marketing fee:
Royalty fee:

SURVEY AND RESULTS *

Q1: About how many hours per week do you dedicate to your franchise business?

		% answering
A)	**Less than 40**	**44%**
B)	41–50	11%
C)	51–60	11%
D)	More than 60	33%
E)	Passive investment	0%

Q2: How would you describe your relations/ communications with your franchisor?

		% answering
A)	**Excellent**	**33%**
B)	**Good**	**33%**
C)	Adequate	11%
D)	Fair	11%
E)	Poor	11%

Q3: In terms of how your franchisor views your communications with other franchisees, it is:

		% answering
A)	**Very supportive**	**44%**
B)	**Not very supportive**	**44%**
C)	No influence	11%

Q4: Is the franchisor fair with you in resolving any grievances?

		% answering
A)	Extremely fair	22%
B)	Pretty fair	22%
C)	**Reasonably fair**	**33%**
D)	Not very fair	11%
E)	Not fair at all	11%

Q5: Are territories equitably granted?

		% answering
A)	Yes	11%
B)	**No**	**56%**
C)	Not yet sure	33%

Q6: How would you describe the initial and ongoing training provided by your franchisor?

		% answering
A)	**Excellent**	**22%**
B)	Good	11%
C)	**Adequate**	**22%**
D)	**Fair**	**22%**
E)	**Poor**	**22%**

Q7: How well does the franchisor anticipate future trends in how it evolves and markets products and services?

		% answering
A)	Extremely well	11%
B)	**Pretty well**	**33%**
C)	Adequately	11%
D)	Not very well	22%
E)	Terribly	22%

Q8: How satisfied are you with your franchisor's spending of the royalty fees you pay?

		% answering
A)	Extremely satisfied	11%
B)	Mostly satisfied	33%
C)	Somewhat satisfied	0%
D)	**Not very satisfied**	**44%**
E)	Not satisfied at all	11%

Q9: **In what ways could the parent company most improve? (Please check those that most apply, no more than three):**

- ❑ Communications
- ❑ Counsel/advice on administrative/management issues
- ❑ Effectiveness of marketing/promotions
- ❑ Evolution of products/services
- ❑ Frequency of marketing/promotional campaigns

- ❑ Quality of products/services
- ❑ Pricing of products/services to franchisees
- ❑ Technology (Point of sale systems, usage of computers/email/software, etc.)
- ❑ Training

Most frequent responses: ……………………………………… % answering

	% answering
Pricing of products/services to franchisees	56%
Evolution of products/services (tie)	44%
Technology (tie)	44%

Q10: **Is your income more, less or about what you expected prior to opening your business?**

	% answering	
More	22%	
Less	44%	Summary: 55% are making about what they
About what was expected	33%	expected, or more.

Q11: Prior to opening your franchise, which (if any) of the following did you underestimate?

- ❑ Amount of working capital required for your first year in business
- ❑ Difficulty in hiring/retaining quality staff
- ❑ Expertise required to run the business
- ❑ Impact of marketing/promotions

- ❑ Start-up costs
- ❑ Degree of stress
- ❑ Workload

Most frequent responses: …………………………………………… % answering

	% answering
Degree of stress	67%
Workload	67%
Amount of working capital required for 1st year in business	33%

Q12: If you could turn back time to the day you signed your franchise agreement, would you make the same decision to buy your franchise?

	% answering
Yes	67%
No	33%

*   Number of survey respondents: 9 from 5 different states
      Number of survey respondents as a % of total franchise units: 4.5%

BUDGET BLINDS

www.budgetblinds.com
Email: franchise@budgetblinds.com

Mobile sales and installation of blinds, shades and drapes.

OVERALL SCORE: 79

1927 N. Glassell Street
Orange, CA 92865
Total number of outlets: 726
Total number of franchise outlets: 726
International: No

OVERALL RANK: 38

Phone: 800-420-5374
Franchise fee: $24,950
Franchise term: 10 years
Initial investment: $69,680 to $101,070
Advertising/Marketing fee: varies
Royalty fee: varies

SURVEY AND RESULTS *

Q1: About how many hours per week do you dedicate to your franchise business?

		% answering
A)	Less than 40	31%
B)	**41–50**	**44%**
C)	51–60	25%
D)	More than 60	0%
E)	Passive investment	0%

Q2: How would you describe your relations/communications with your franchisor?

		% answering
A)	**Excellent**	**44%**
B)	Good	31%
C)	Adequate	25%
D)	Fair	20%
E)	Poor	20%

Q3: In terms of how your franchisor views your communications with other franchisees, it is:

		% answering
A)	**Very supportive**	**94%**
B)	Not very supportive	6%
C)	No influence	0%

Q4: Is the franchisor fair with you in resolving any grievances?

		% answering
A)	Extremely fair	31%
B)	Pretty fair	31%
C)	**Reasonably fair**	**38%**
D)	Not very fair	0%
E)	Not fair at all	0%

Q5: Are territories equitably granted?

		% answering
A)	**Yes**	**75%**
B)	No	13%
C)	Not yet sure	13%

Q6: How would you describe the initial and ongoing training provided by your franchisor?

		% answering
A)	**Excellent**	**56%**
B)	Good	31%
C)	Adequate	13%
D)	Fair	0%
E)	Poor	0%

Q7: How well does the franchisor anticipate future trends in how it evolves and markets products and services?

		% answering
A)	Extremely well	44%
B)	**Pretty well**	**50%**
C)	Adequately	6%
D)	Not very well	0%
E)	Terribly	0%

Q8: How satisfied are you with your franchisor's spending of the royalty fees you pay?

		% answering
A)	Extremely satisfied	13%
B)	**Mostly satisfied**	**63%**
C)	Somewhat satisfied	25%
D)	Not very satisfied	0%
E)	Not satisfied at all	0%

Q9: **In what ways could the parent company most improve? (Please check those that most apply, no more than three):**

❑ Communications
❑ Counsel/advice on administrative/management issues
❑ Effectiveness of marketing/promotions
❑ Evolution of products/services
❑ Frequency of marketing/promotional campaigns

❑ Quality of products/services
❑ Pricing of products/services to franchisees
❑ Technology (Point of sale systems, usage of computers/email/software, etc.)
❑ Training

Most frequent responses:

	% answering
Counsel/advice on administrative/management issues	44%
Pricing of products/services to franchisees (tie)	38%
Technology (tie)	38%

Q10: **Is your income more, less or about what you expected prior to opening your business?**

	% answering	
More	25%	
Less	**44%**	**Summary: 56% are making about what they**
About what was expected	31%	**expected, or more.**

Q11: **Prior to opening your franchise, which (if any) of the following did you underestimate?**

❑ Amount of working capital required for your 1st year in business
❑ Difficulty in hiring/retaining quality staff
❑ Expertise required to run the business
❑ Impact of marketing/promotions

❑ Start-up costs
❑ Degree of stress
❑ Workload

Most frequent responses:

	% answering
Degree of stress	75%
Workload	50%
Difficulty in hiring/retaining quality staff	44%

Q12: **If you could turn back time to the day you signed your franchise agreement, would you make the same decision to buy your franchise?**

	% answering
Yes	**80%**
No	20%

* Number of survey respondents: 16 from 12 different states
Number of survey respondents as a % of total franchise units: 2.20%

BUSINESS CARDS TOMORROW

www.bct-net.com
Email: bob.dolan@bctonline.net

Business cards, stationery, and other office supply products.

OVERALL SCORE: 53

3000 NE 30th Place, Fifth Floor
Fort Lauderdale, FL 33306
Fax: 954-565-0742
Total number of outlets: 84
Total number of franchise outlets: 80
International: Yes (Canada)

OVERALL RANK: N/A

Phone: 800-627-9998
Franchise fee: $35,000
Franchise term: 25 years
Initial investment: $170,600 to $544,700
Advertising/Marketing fee: 1% of gross sales wkly.
Royalty fee: 6% of gross sales weekly

SURVEY AND RESULTS *

Q1: About how many hours per week do you dedicate to your franchise business?

		% answering
A)	Less than 40	0%
B)	41–50	13%
C)	**51–60**	**50%**
D)	More than 60	38%
E)	Passive investment	0%

Q2: How would you describe your relations/ communications with your franchisor?

		% answering
A)	Excellent	13%
B)	**Good**	**38%**
C)	Adequate	25%
D)	Fair	13%
E)	Poor	13%

Q3: In terms of how your franchisor views your communications with other franchisees, it is:

		% answering
A)	**Very supportive**	**75%**
B)	Not very supportive	13%
C)	No influence	13%

Q4: Is the franchisor fair with you in resolving any grievances?

		% answering
A)	Extremely fair	13%
B)	**Pretty fair**	**38%**
C)	Reasonably fair	25%
D)	Not very fair	13%
E)	Not fair at all	13%

Q5: Are territories equitably granted?

		% answering
A)	**Yes**	**88%**
B)	No	13%
C)	Not yet sure	0%

Q6: How would you describe the initial and ongoing training provided by your franchisor?

		% answering
A)	Excellent	13%
B)	**Good**	**63%**
C)	Adequate	13%
D)	Fair	13%
E)	Poor	0%

Q7: How well does the franchisor anticipate future trends in how it evolves and markets products and services?

		% answering
A)	Extremely well	0%
B)	**Pretty well**	**38%**
C)	Adequately	25%
D)	**Not very well**	**38%**
E)	Terribly	0%

Q8: How satisfied are you with your franchisor's spending of the royalty fees you pay?

		% answering
A)	Extremely satisfied	0%
B)	Mostly satisfied	25%
C)	Somewhat satisfied	25%
D)	**Not very satisfied**	**38%**
E)	Not satisfied at all	13%

Q9:   In what ways could the parent company most improve? (Please check those that most apply, no more than three):

❏ Communications

❏ Counsel/advice on administrative/management issues

❏ Effectiveness of marketing/promotions

❏ Evolution of products/services

❏ Frequency of marketing/promotional campaigns

❏ Quality of products/services

❏ Pricing of products/services to franchisees

❏ Technology (Point of sale systems, usage of computers/email/software, etc.)

❏ Training

Most frequent responses:	% answering
Evolution of products/services	63%
Effectiveness of marketing/promotions (tie)	38%
Frequency of marketing/promotional campaigns (tie)	38%
Technology (tie)	38%

Q10: Is your income more, less or about what you expected prior to opening your business?

	% answering	
More	0%	
Less	**63%**	**Summary: 38% are making about what they**
About what was expected	38%	**expected, or more.**

Q11: Prior to opening your franchise, which (if any) of the following did you underestimate?

❏ Amount of working capital required for your first year in business

❏ Difficulty in hiring/retaining quality staff

❏ Expertise required to run the business

❏ Impact of marketing/promotions

❏ Start-up costs

❏ Degree of stress

❏ Workload

Most frequent responses:	% answering
Difficulty in hiring/retaining quality staff	50%
Degree of stress (tie)	38%
Workload (tie)	38%

Q12: If you could turn back time to the day you signed your franchise agreement, would you make the same decision to buy your franchise?

	% answering
Yes	33%
No	**67%**

*   Number of survey respondents: 8 from 7 different states

Number of survey respondents as a % of total franchise units: 10%

CALIFORNIA CLOSET COMPANY

www.calclosets.com
Email: info@calclosets.com

Residential and commercial custom storage systems.

OVERALL SCORE: 91

1000 Fourth Street, #800
San Rafael, CA 94901
Fax: 415-256-8501
Total number of outlets: 156
Total number of franchise outlets: 148
International: Yes (worldwide)

OVERALL RANK: 7

Phone: 415-256-8500
Franchise fee: $45,900
Franchise term: 10 years
Initial investment: $121,500 to $341,900
Advertising/Marketing fee: 3%
Royalty fee: 11%

SURVEY AND RESULTS *

Q1: About how many hours per week do you dedicate to your franchise business?

		% answering
A)	Less than 40	7%
B)	41–50	29%
C)	51–60	29%
D)	**More than 60**	**36%**
E)	Passive investment	0%

Q2: How would you describe your relations/ communications with your franchisor?

		% answering
A)	Excellent	29%
B)	**Good**	**36%**
C)	Adequate	7%
D)	Fair	0%
E)	Poor	0%

Q3: In terms of how your franchisor views your communications with other franchisees, it is:

		% answering
A)	**Very supportive**	**79%**
B)	Not very supportive	7%
C)	No influence	14%

Q4: Is the franchisor fair with you in resolving any grievances?

		% answering
A)	**Extremely fair**	**50%**
B)	Pretty fair	14%
C)	Reasonably fair	36%
D)	Not very fair	20%
E)	Not fair at all	20%

Q5: Are territories equitably granted?

		% answering
A)	**Yes**	**93%**
B)	No	7%
C)	Not yet sure	0%

Q6: How would you describe the initial and ongoing training provided by your franchisor?

		% answering
A)	**Excellent**	**46%**
B)	Good	21%
C)	Adequate	25%
D)	Fair	0%
E)	Poor	7%

Q7: How well does the franchisor anticipate future trends in how it evolves and markets products and services?

		% answering
A)	**Extremely well**	**50%**
B)	Pretty well	29%
C)	Adequately	7%
D)	Not very well	14%
E)	Terribly	0%

Q8: How satisfied are you with your franchisor's spending of the royalty fees you pay?

		% answering
A)	Extremely satisfied	14%
B)	**Mostly satisfied**	**57%**
C)	Somewhat satisfied	21%
D)	Not very satisfied	7%
E)	Not satisfied at all	0%

Q9: **In what ways could the parent company most improve? (Please check those that most apply, no more than three):**

❏ Communications
❏ Counsel/advice on administrative/management issues
❏ Effectiveness of marketing/promotions
❏ Evolution of products/services
❏ Frequency of marketing/promotional campaigns

❏ Quality of products/services
❏ Pricing of products/services to franchisees
❏ Technology (Point of sale systems, usage of computers/email/software, etc.)
❏ Training

Most frequent responses:	% answering
Effectiveness of marketing/promotions	43%
Pricing of products/services to franchisees (tie)	36%
Training (tie)	36%

Q10: **Is your income more, less or about what you expected prior to opening your business?**

	% answering
More	36%
Less	21%
About what was expected	**43%**

Summary: 79% are making about what they expected, or more.

Q11: **Prior to opening your franchise, which (if any) of the following did you underestimate?**

❏ Amount of working capital required for your 1st year in business
❏ Difficulty in hiring/retaining quality staff
❏ Expertise required to run the business
❏ Impact of marketing/promotions

❏ Start-up costs
❏ Degree of stress
❏ Workload

Most frequent responses:	% answering
Difficulty in hiring/retaining quality staff	57%
Degree of stress (tie)	36%
Amount of working capital required for 1st year in business (tie)	36%

Q12: **If you could turn back time to the day you signed your franchise agreement, would you make the same decision to buy your franchise?**

	% answering
Yes	**93%**
No	7%

*   Number of survey respondents: 14 from 12 different states
    Number of survey respondents as a % of total franchise units: 8.97%

CANDY BOUQUET

www.candybouquet.com
Email: yumyum@candybouquet.com

Candy arrangements that appear as floral displays.

OVERALL SCORE: 40

OVERALL RANK: 186

423 East Third Street
Little Rock, AR 72201
Fax: 501-375-9998
Total number of outlets: 700+
Total number of franchise outlets: 700+
International: Yes (worldwide)

Phone: 877-CANDY01
Franchise fee: varies
Franchise term: 5 years
Initial investment: $7,270 to $46,130
Advertising/Marketing fee: none
Royalty fee: none (there is a monthly association fee, which varies by population of territory.

SURVEY AND RESULTS *

Q1: About how many hours per week do you dedicate to your franchise business?

		% answering
A)	Less than 40	21%
B)	**41–50**	**43%**
C)	51–60	29%
D)	More than 60	0%
E)	Passive investment	7%

Q2: How would you describe your relations/ communications with your franchisor?

		% answering
A)	Excellent	7%
B)	**Good**	**29%**
C)	Adequate	21%
D)	Fair	21%
E)	Poor	21%

Q3: In terms of how your franchisor views your communications with other franchisees, it is:

		% answering
A)	Very supportive	36%
B)	Not very supportive	21%
C)	**No influence**	**43%**

Q4: Is the franchisor fair with you in resolving any grievances?

		% answering
A)	Extremely fair	15%
B)	Pretty fair	15%
C)	**Reasonably fair**	**38%**
D)	Not very fair	8%
E)	Not fair at all	23%

Q5: Are territories equitably granted?

		% answering
A)	**Yes**	**86%**
B)	No	7%
C)	Not yet sure	7%

Q6: How would you describe the initial and ongoing training provided by your franchisor?

		% answering
A)	Excellent	14%
B)	**Good**	**29%**
C)	Adequate	21%
D)	Fair	14%
E)	Poor	21%

Q7: How well does the franchisor anticipate future trends in how it evolves and markets products and services?

		% answering
A)	Extremely well	7%
B)	Pretty well	21%
C)	**Adequately**	**36%**
D)	Not very well	14%
E)	Terribly	21%

Q8: How satisfied are you with your franchisor's spending of the royalty fees you pay?

		% answering
A)	Extremely satisfied	N/A
B)	Mostly satisfied	N/A
C)	Somewhat satisfied	N/A
D)	Not very satisfied	N/A
E)	Not satisfied at all	N/A

Q9: **In what ways could the parent company most improve? (Please check those that most apply, no more than three):**

❑ Communications
❑ Counsel/advice on administrative/management issues
❑ Effectiveness of marketing/promotions
❑ Evolution of products/services
❑ Frequency of marketing/promotional campaigns

❑ Quality of products/services
❑ Pricing of products/services to franchisees
❑ Technology (Point of sale systems, usage of computers/email/software, etc.)
❑ Training

Most frequent responses:	% answering
Effectiveness of marketing/promotions	79%
Frequency of marketing/promotional campaigns	64%
Pricing of products/services to franchisees (tie)	29%
Communications (tie)	29%
Quality of products/services (tie)	29%

Q10: **Is your income more, less or about what you expected prior to opening your business?**

	% answering	
More	0%	
Less	**86%**	**Summary: 14% are making about what they**
About what was expected	14%	**expected, or more.**

Q11: Prior to opening your franchise, which (if any) of the following did you underestimate?

❑ Amount of working capital required for your 1st year in business
❑ Difficulty in hiring/retaining quality staff
❑ Expertise required to run the business
❑ Impact of marketing/promotions

❑ Start-up costs
❑ Degree of stress
❑ Workload

Most frequent responses:	% answering
Impact of marketing/promotions	57%
Amount of working capital required for 1st year in business	50%
Degree of stress	43%

Q12: **If you could turn back time to the day you signed your franchise agreement, would you make the same decision to buy your franchise?**

	% answering
Yes	36%
No	**64%**

* Number of survey respondents: 14 from 12 different states
Number of survey respondents as a % of total franchise units: 2%

CARLSON WAGONLIT TRAVEL

www.carlsontravel.com
Email: clgfranchise@carlson.com

Travel agency.

OVERALL SCORE: 78

12755 State Highway 55
Plymouth, MN 55441
Fax: 763-212-2219
Total number of outlets: 900
Total number of franchise outlets: 900
International: Yes (worldwide)

OVERALL RANK: 42

Phone: 800-678-8241
Franchise fee: $10,000 to $29,900
Franchise term: 10 years
Initial investment: $55,580 to $161,880
Advertising/Marketing fee: varies
Royalty fee: varies

SURVEY AND RESULTS *

Q1: About how many hours per week do you dedicate to your franchise business?

		% answering
A)	Less than 40	0%
B)	**41–50**	**33%**
C)	51–60	25%
D)	**More than 60**	**33%**
E)	Passive investment	8%

Q2: How would you describe your relations/communications with your franchisor?

		% answering
A)	Excellent	42%
B)	**Good**	**50%**
C)	Adequate	8%
D)	Fair	0%
E)	Poor	0%

Q3: In terms of how your franchisor views your communications with other franchisees, it is:

		% answering
A)	**Very supportive**	**92%**
B)	Not very supportive	0%
C)	No influence	8%

Q4: Is the franchisor fair with you in resolving any grievances?

		% answering
A)	**Extremely fair**	**42%**
B)	**Pretty fair**	**42%**
C)	Reasonably fair	17%
D)	Not very fair	0%
E)	Not fair at all	0%

Q5: Are territories equitably granted?

		% answering
A)	**Yes**	**67%**
B)	No	17%
C)	Not yet sure	17%

Q6: How would you describe the initial and ongoing training provided by your franchisor?

		% answering
A)	Excellent	42%
B)	**Good**	**50%**
C)	Adequate	8%
D)	Fair	0%
E)	Poor	0%

Q7: How well does the franchisor anticipate future trends in how it evolves and markets products and services?

		% answering
A)	**Extremely well**	**42%**
B)	**Pretty well**	**42%**
C)	Adequately	0%
D)	Not very well	17%
E)	Terribly	17%

Q8: How satisfied are you with your franchisor's spending of the royalty fees you pay?

		% answering
A)	Extremely satisfied	25%
B)	**Mostly satisfied**	**33%**
C)	**Somewhat satisfied**	**33%**
D)	Not very satisfied	8%
E)	Not satisfied at all	0%

Q9: **In what ways could the parent company most improve? (Please check those that most apply, no more than three):**

- ❏ Communications
- ❏ Counsel/advice on administrative/management issues
- ❏ Effectiveness of marketing/promotions
- ❏ Evolution of products/services
- ❏ Frequency of marketing/promotional campaigns

- ❏ Quality of products/services
- ❏ Pricing of products/services to franchisees
- ❏ Technology (Point of sale systems, usage of computers/email/software, etc.)
- ❏ Training

Most frequent responses:

	% answering
Effectiveness of marketing/promotions	58%
Technology	50%
Evolution of products/services	42%

Q10: **Is your income more, less or about what you expected prior to opening your business?**

	% answering	
More	33%	
Less	**50%**	**Summary: 50% are making about what they**
About what was expected	17%	**expected, or more.**

Q11: **Prior to opening your franchise, which (if any) of the following did you underestimate?**

- ❏ Amount of working capital required for your 1st year in business
- ❏ Difficulty in hiring/retaining quality staff
- ❏ Expertise required to run the business
- ❏ Impact of marketing/promotions

- ❏ Start-up costs
- ❏ Degree of stress
- ❏ Workload

Most frequent responses:

	% answering
Degree of stress	50%
Amount of working capital required for 1st year in business (tie)	42%
Difficulty in hiring/retaining quality staff (tie)	42%

Q12: **If you could turn back time to the day you signed your franchise agreement, would you make the same decision to buy your franchise?**

	% answering
Yes	**83%**
No	17%

* Number of survey respondents: 12 from 11 different states

  Number of survey respondents as a % of total franchise units: 1.3%

CARTEX

www.fabrion.net
Email: franchiess@fabrion.net

Automotive interior restoration.

OVERALL SCORE: 71

42816 Mound Road
Sterling Heights, MI 48314
Fax: 586-739-4331
Total number of outlets: 118
Total number of franchise outlets: 118
International: No

OVERALL RANK: 77

Phone: 800-421-7328
Franchise fee: $25,000
Franchise term: years
Initial investment: $
Advertising/Marketing fee: %
Royalty fee: %

SURVEY AND RESULTS *

Q1: About how many hours per week do you dedicate to your franchise business?

		% answering
A)	**Less than 40**	**47%**
B)	41–50	40%
C)	51–60	7%
D)	More than 60	7%
E)	Passive investment	0%

Q2: How would you describe your relations/ communications with your franchisor?

		% answering
A)	**Excellent**	**40%**
B)	Good	20%
C)	Adequate	0%
D)	Fair	20%
E)	Poor	20%

Q3: In terms of how your franchisor views your communications with other franchisees, it is:

		% answering
A)	**Very supportive**	**53%**
B)	Not very supportive	13%
C)	No influence	33%

Q4: Is the franchisor fair with you in resolving any grievances?

		% answering
A)	**Extremely fair**	**43%**
B)	Pretty fair	21%
C)	Reasonably fair	21%
D)	Not very fair	7%
E)	Not fair at all	7%

Q5: Are territories equitably granted?

		% answering
A)	**Yes**	**73%**
B)	No	13%
C)	Not yet sure	13%

Q6: How would you describe the initial and ongoing training provided by your franchisor?

		% answering
A)	**Excellent**	**40%**
B)	Good	13%
C)	Adequate	20%
D)	Fair	20%
E)	Poor	7%

Q7: How well does the franchisor anticipate future trends in how it evolves and markets products and services?

		% answering
A)	**Extremely well**	**33%**
B)	Pretty well	20%
C)	Adequately	20%
D)	Not very well	20%
E)	Terribly	7%

Q8: How satisfied are you with your franchisor's spending of the royalty fees you pay?

		% answering
A)	**Extremely satisfied**	**43%**
B)	Mostly satisfied	7%
C)	Somewhat satisfied	7%
D)	Not very satisfied	7%
E)	Not satisfied at all	36%

Q9:   **In what ways could the parent company most improve? (Please check those that most apply, no more than three):**

❑   Communications

❑   Counsel/advice on administrative/management issues

❑   Effectiveness of marketing/promotions

❑   Evolution of products/services

❑   Frequency of marketing/promotional campaigns

❑   Quality of products/services

❑   Pricing of products/services to franchisees

❑   Technology (Point of sale systems, usage of computers/email/software, etc.)

❑   Training

Most frequent responses:	% answering
Effectiveness of marketing/promotions	47%
Evolution of products/services	40%
Pricing of products/services to franchisees	33%

Q10: **Is your income more, less or about what you expected prior to opening your business?**

	% answering	
More	**43%**	
Less	14%	**Summary: 86% are making about what they**
About what was expected	**43%**	**expected, or more.**

Q11: **Prior to opening your franchise, which (if any) of the following did you underestimate?**

❑   Amount of working capital required for your 1st year in business

❑   Difficulty in hiring/retaining quality staff

❑   Expertise required to run the business

❑   Impact of marketing/promotions

❑   Start-up costs

❑   Degree of stress

❑   Workload

Most frequent responses:	% answering
Difficulty in hiring/retaining quality staff	60%
Degree of stress (tie)	20%
Amount of working capital required for 1st year in business (tie)	20%
Start-up costs (tie)	20%

Q12: **If you could turn back time to the day you signed your franchise agreement, would you make the same decision to buy your franchise?**

	% answering
Yes	**60%**
No	40%

*   Number of survey respondents: 15 from 11 different states

Number of survey respondents as a % of total franchise units: 12.71%

CARVEL

www.carvel.com

Ice cream and frozen yogurt desserts.

OVERALL SCORE: 62

200 Glenridge Point Pkwy., Suite 200
Atlanta, GA 30342
Fax: 404-255-4978
Total number of outlets: 500
Total number of franchise outlets: 500
International: Yes (Canada & Puerto Rico)

OVERALL RANK: 126

Phone: 800-227-8353
Franchise fee: $15,000 to $30,000
Franchise term: 20 years
Initial investment: $30,330 to $355,497
Advertising/Marketing fee: varies
Royalty fee: varies

SURVEY AND RESULTS *

Q1: **About how many hours per week do you dedicate to your franchise business?**

		% answering
A)	Less than 40	10%
B)	41–50	30%
C)	51–60	10%
D)	**More than 60**	**50%**
E)	Passive investment	0%

Q2: **How would you describe your relations/ communications with your franchisor?**

		% answering
A)	**Excellent**	**30%**
B)	**Good**	**30%**
C)	Adequate	20%
D)	Fair	10%
E)	Poor	10%

Q3: **In terms of how your franchisor views your communications with other franchisees, it is:**

		% answering
A)	**Very supportive**	**50%**
B)	Not very supportive	10%
C)	No influence	40%

Q4: **Is the franchisor fair with you in resolving any grievances?**

		% answering
A)	Extremely fair	20%
B)	Pretty fair	30%
C)	**Reasonably fair**	**40%**
D)	Not very fair	10%
E)	Not fair at all	0%

Q5: **Are territories equitably granted?**

		% answering
A)	Yes	22%
B)	**No**	**44%**
C)	Not yet sure	33%

Q6: **How would you describe the initial and ongoing training provided by your franchisor?**

		% answering
A)	Excellent	20%
B)	**Good**	**30%**
C)	**Adequate**	**30%**
D)	Fair	10%
E)	Poor	10%

Q7: **How well does the franchisor anticipate future trends in how it evolves and markets products and services?**

		% answering
A)	Extremely well	10%
B)	**Pretty well**	**40%**
C)	Adequately	10%
D)	**Not very well**	**40%**
E)	Terribly	0%

Q8: **How satisfied are you with your franchisor's spending of the royalty fees you pay?**

		% answering
A)	Extremely satisfied	10%
B)	**Mostly satisfied**	**30%**
C)	**Somewhat satisfied**	**30%**
D)	Not very satisfied	20%
E)	Not satisfied at all	10%

Q9: **In what ways could the parent company most improve? (Please check those that most apply, no more than three):**

❑ Communications
❑ Counsel/advice on administrative/management issues
❑ Effectiveness of marketing/promotions
❑ Evolution of products/services
❑ Frequency of marketing/promotional campaigns

❑ Quality of products/services
❑ Pricing of products/services to franchisees
❑ Technology (Point of sale systems, usage of computers/email/software, etc.)
❑ Training

Most frequent responses: <u>% answering</u>

Frequency of marketing/promotional campaigns	50%
Effectiveness of marketing/promotions	40%
Pricing of products/services to franchisees	30%
Technology	30%

Q10: **Is your income more, less or about what you expected prior to opening your business?**

	<u>% answering</u>	
More	0%	
Less	**50%**	**Summary: 50% are making about what they**
About what was expected	**50%**	**expected, or more.**

Q11: **Prior to opening your franchise, which (if any) of the following did you underestimate?**

❑ Amount of working capital required for your 1st year in business
❑ Difficulty in hiring/retaining quality staff
❑ Expertise required to run the business
❑ Impact of marketing/promotions

❑ Start-up costs
❑ Degree of stress
❑ Workload

Most frequent responses: <u>% answering</u>

Difficulty in hiring/retaining quality staff	70%
Workload	50%
Degree of stress	30%

Q12: **If you could turn back time to the day you signed your franchise agreement, would you make the same decision to buy your franchise?**

	<u>% answering</u>
Yes	**70%**
No	30%

* Number of survey respondents: 10 from 6 different states
  Number of survey respondents as a % of total franchise units: 2%

CASH PLUS

www.cashplusinc.com
Email: gbade@cashplusinc.com (Greg Bade)

Check cashing services.

OVERALL SCORE: 67

3002 Dow Avenue, Suite 120
Tustin, CA 92780
Fax: 714-731-2099
Total number of outlets: 80+
Total number of franchise outlets: 80+
International: No

OVERALL RANK: N/A

Phone: 888-707-2274
Franchise fee: $15,000 to $30,000
Franchise term: 10 years
Initial investment: $53,000 to $231, 700
Advertising/Marketing fee: 3% of gross sales up to $16,667, then 1% of gross sales up to $66,667
Royalty fee: 6% of gross sales weekly (minimum $500 per month.

SURVEY AND RESULTS *

Q1: About how many hours per week do you dedicate to your franchise business?

		% answering
A)	Less than 40	13%
B)	41–50	13%
C)	51–60	25%
D)	**More than 60**	**50%**
E)	Passive investment	0%

Q2: How would you describe your relations/ communications with your franchisor?

		% answering
A)	Excellent	25%
B)	**Good**	**38%**
C)	Adequate	25%
D)	Fair	13%
E)	Poor	0%

Q3: In terms of how your franchisor views your communications with other franchisees, it is:

		% answering
A)	**Very supportive**	**63%**
B)	Not very supportive	25%
C)	No influence	13%

Q4: Is the franchisor fair with you in resolving any grievances?

		% answering
A)	Extremely fair	25%
B)	**Pretty fair**	**38%**
C)	Reasonably fair	13%
D)	Not very fair	25%
E)	Not fair at all	0%

Q5: Are territories equitably granted?

		% answering
A)	Yes	63%
B)	No	0%
C)	Not yet sure	38%

Q6: How would you describe the initial and ongoing training provided by your franchisor?

		% answering
A)	Excellent	13%
B)	**Good**	**63%**
C)	Adequate	13%
D)	Fair	0%
E)	Poor	13%

Q7: How well does the franchisor anticipate future trends in how it evolves and markets products and services?

		% answering
A)	Extremely well	0%
B)	Pretty well	63%
C)	Adequately	13%
D)	Not very well	13%
E)	Terribly	13%

Q8: How satisfied are you with your franchisor's spending of the royalty fees you pay?

		% answering
A)	Extremely satisfied	0%
B)	Mostly satisfied	25%
C)	Somewhat satisfied	25%
D)	Not very satisfied	25%
E)	Not satisfied at all	20%

Q9: **In what ways could the parent company most improve? (Please check those that most apply, no more than three):**

- ❏ Communications
- ❏ Counsel/advice on administrative/management issues
- ❏ Effectiveness of marketing/promotions
- ❏ Evolution of products/services
- ❏ Frequency of marketing/promotional campaigns

- ❏ Quality of products/services
- ❏ Pricing of products/services to franchisees
- ❏ Technology (Point of sale systems, usage of computers/email/software, etc.)
- ❏ Training

Most frequent responses:	% answering
Counsel/advice on administrative/management issues (tie)	38%
Effectiveness of marketing/promotions (tie)	38%
Evolution of products/services (tie)	38%

Q10: **Is your income more, less or about what you expected prior to opening your business?**

	% answering	
More	25%	
Less	**50%**	**Summary: 50% are making about what they**
About what was expected	25%	**expected, or more.**

Q11: **Prior to opening your franchise, which (if any) of the following did you underestimate?**

- ❏ Amount of working capital required for your 1st year in business
- ❏ Difficulty in hiring/retaining quality staff
- ❏ Expertise required to run the business
- ❏ Impact of marketing/promotions

- ❏ Start-up costs
- ❏ Degree of stress
- ❏ Workload

Most frequent responses:	% answering
Amount of working capital required for your first year in business	50%
Difficulty in hiring/retaining quality staff	38%
Impact of marketing/promotions (tie)	25%
Degree of stress (tie)	25%

Q12: **If you could turn back time to the day you signed your franchise agreement, would you make the same decision to buy your franchise?**

	% answering
Yes	**75%**
No	25%

* Number of survey respondents: 8 from 1 state.
Number of survey respondents as a % of total franchise units: 10%

CERTAPRO PAINTERS

www.certapro.com
Email: sholman@certapro.com

Residential and commercial painting services.

OVERALL SCORE: 45

150 Green Tree Road, Suite 1003
P.O. Box 836, Oaks, PA 19456
Total number of outlets: 141
Total number of franchise outlets: 141
International: Yes (several countries)
Royalty fee: up to 5% of monthly gross sales

OVERALL RANK: 173

Phone: 800-462-3782
Franchise fee: $40,000
Franchise term: 10 years
Initial investment: $76,200 to $94,250
Advertising/Marketing fee: up to 3% of monthly gross sales

SURVEY AND RESULTS *

Q1: About how many hours per week do you dedicate to your franchise business?

		% answering
A)	Less than 40	0%
B)	41–50	25%
C)	51–60	19%
D)	**More than 60**	**56%**
E)	Passive investment	0%

Q2: How would you describe your relations/communications with your franchisor?

		% answering
A)	Excellent	0%
B)	**Good**	**63%**
C)	Adequate	13%
D)	Fair	13%
E)	Poor	13%

Q3: In terms of how your franchisor views your communications with other franchisees, it is:

		% answering
A)	**Very supportive**	**75%**
B)	Not very supportive	19%
C)	No influence	6%

Q4: Is the franchisor fair with you in resolving any grievances?

		% answering
A)	Extremely fair	13%
B)	Pretty fair	31%
C)	**Reasonably fair**	**44%**
D)	Not very fair	6%
E)	Not fair at all	6%

Q5: Are territories equitably granted?

		% answering
A)	**Yes**	**60%**
B)	No	20%
C)	Not yet sure	20%

Q6: How would you describe the initial and ongoing training provided by your franchisor?

		% answering
A)	Excellent	19%
B)	Good	22%
C)	**Adequate**	**31%**
D)	Fair	19%
E)	Poor	9%

Q7: How well does the franchisor anticipate future trends in how it evolves and markets products and services?

		% answering
A)	Extremely well	20%
B)	**Pretty well**	**27%**
C)	Adequately	20%
D)	**Not very well**	**27%**
E)	Terribly	7%

Q8: How satisfied are you with your franchisor's spending of the royalty fees you pay?

		% answering
A)	Extremely satisfied	0%
B)	**Mostly satisfied**	**47%**
C)	Somewhat satisfied	0%
D)	Not very satisfied	40%
E)	Not satisfied at all	13%

Q9: **In what ways could the parent company most improve? (Please check those that most apply, no more than three):**

❏ Communications
❏ Counsel/advice on administrative/management issues
❏ Effectiveness of marketing/promotions
❏ Evolution of products/services
❏ Frequency of marketing/promotional campaigns

❏ Quality of products/services
❏ Pricing of products/services to franchisees
❏ Technology (Point of sale systems, usage of computers/email/software, etc.)
❏ Training

Most frequent responses:

	% answering
Counsel/advice on administrative/management issues	56%
Effectiveness of marketing/promotions	50%
Communications	44%

Q10: **Is your income more, less or about what you expected prior to opening your business?**

	% answering	
More	6%	
Less	**81%**	**Summary: 19% are making about what they**
About what was expected	13%	**expected, or more.**

Q11: **Prior to opening your franchise, which (if any) of the following did you underestimate?**

❏ Amount of working capital required for your 1st year in business
❏ Difficulty in hiring/retaining quality staff
❏ Expertise required to run the business
❏ Impact of marketing/promotions

❏ Start-up costs
❏ Degree of stress
❏ Workload

Most frequent responses:

	% answering
Difficulty in hiring/retaining quality staff	69%
Amount of working capital required for 1st year in business	63%
Degree of stress	56%

Q12: **If you could turn back time to the day you signed your franchise agreement, would you make the same decision to buy your franchise?**

	% answering
Yes	27%
No	**73%**

* Number of survey respondents: 16 from 15 different states
Number of survey respondents as a % of total franchise units: 11.35%

CFO TODAY

www.cfotoday.com
Email: info@cfotoday.com

Small business accounting and financial services.

OVERALL SCORE: 74

401 St. Francis Street
Tallahassee, FL 32301
Fax: 850-561-1374
Total number of outlets: 216
Total number of franchise outlets: 216
International: Yes (Canada & Puerto Rico)

OVERALL RANK: 60

Phone: 850-681-1941
Franchise fee: $24,000
Franchise term: 10 years
Initial investment: $24,400 to $37,000
Advertising/Marketing fee: 1-2%
Royalty fee: $100 to $300 per month

SURVEY AND RESULTS *

Q1: About how many hours per week do you dedicate to your franchise business?

		% answering
A)	**Less than 40**	31%
B)	**41–50**	31%
C)	**51–60**	31%
D)	More than 60	8%
E)	Passive investment	0%

Q2: How would you describe your relations/ communications with your franchisor?

		% answering
A)	Excellent	23%
B)	**Good**	54%
C)	Adequate	15%
D)	Fair	0%
E)	Poor	8%

Q3: In terms of how your franchisor views your communications with other franchisees, it is:

		% answering
A)	**Very supportive**	85%
B)	Not very supportive	15%
C)	No influence	0%

Q4: Is the franchisor fair with you in resolving any grievances?

		% answering
A)	**Extremely fair**	42%
B)	Pretty fair	33%
C)	Reasonably fair	25%
D)	Not very fair	0%
E)	Not fair at all	0%

Q5: Are territories equitably granted?

		% answering
A)	**Yes**	77%
B)	No	0%
C)	Not yet sure	23%

Q6: How would you describe the initial and ongoing training provided by your franchisor?

		% answering
A)	Excellent	0%
B)	**Good**	54%
C)	Adequate	31%
D)	Fair	8%
E)	Poor	8%

Q7: How well does the franchisor anticipate future trends in how it evolves and markets products and services?

		% answering
A)	Extremely well	8%
B)	Pretty well	8%
C)	Adequately	23%
D)	**Not very well**	54%
E)	Terribly	8%

Q8: How satisfied are you with your franchisor's spending of the royalty fees you pay?

		% answering
A)	Extremely satisfied	17%
B)	Mostly satisfied	17%
C)	**Somewhat satisfied**	42%
D)	Not very satisfied	25%
E)	Not satisfied at all	0%

Q9: In what ways could the parent company most improve? (Please check those that most apply, no more than three):

- ❏ Communications
- ❏ Counsel/advice on administrative/management issues
- ❏ Effectiveness of marketing/promotions
- ❏ Evolution of products/services
- ❏ Frequency of marketing/promotional campaigns

- ❏ Quality of products/services
- ❏ Pricing of products/services to franchisees
- ❏ Technology (Point of sale systems, usage of computers/email/software, etc.)
- ❏ Training

Most frequent responses:	% answering
Effectiveness of marketing/promotions	62%
Frequency of marketing/promotional campaigns	54%
Communications	46%

Q10: Is your income more, less or about what you expected prior to opening your business?

	% answering	
More	8%	
Less	**46%**	**Summary: 54% are making about what they**
About what was expected	**46%**	**expected, or more.**

Q11: Prior to opening your franchise, which (if any) of the following did you underestimate?

- ❏ Amount of working capital required for your 1st year in business
- ❏ Difficulty in hiring/retaining quality staff
- ❏ Expertise required to run the business
- ❏ Impact of marketing/promotions

- ❏ Start-up costs
- ❏ Degree of stress
- ❏ Workload

Most frequent responses:	% answering
Impact of marketing/promotions	38%
Amount of working capital required for your 1st year in business	31%
Workload	23%

Q12: If you could turn back time to the day you signed your franchise agreement, would you make the same decision to buy your franchise?

	% answering
Yes	**92%**
No	8%

* Number of survey respondents: 13 from 10 different states
  Number of survey respondents as a % of total franchise units: 6.02%

CHILDREN'S ORCHARD

www.childrensorchard.com

New and used children's clothing, books, toys, furniture, etc.

OVERALL SCORE: 54

2100 South Main Street, Suite B
Ann Arbor, MI 48103
Total number of outlets: 88
Total number of franchise outlets: 87
International: No
Royalty fee: > of 5% or $2,500 per quarter based
on gross sales, capped at $50,000/store/year

OVERALL RANK: 160

Phone: 800-999-KIDS
Franchise fee: $19,500
Franchise term: 10 years
Initial investment: $29,350 to $154,950
Advertising/Marketing fee: > of 1% or $500/quarter

SURVEY AND RESULTS *

Q1: About how many hours per week do you dedicate to your franchise business?

		% answering
A)	Less than 40	27%
B)	**41–50**	**40%**
C)	51–60	33%
D)	More than 60	0%
E)	Passive investment	0%

Q2: How would you describe your relations/communications with your franchisor?

		% answering
A)	Excellent	7%
B)	**Good**	**53%**
C)	Adequate	17%
D)	Fair	3%
E)	Poor	20%

Q3: In terms of how your franchisor views your communications with other franchisees, it is:

		% answering
A)	**Very supportive**	**47%**
B)	Not very supportive	7%
C)	**No influence**	**47%**

Q4: Is the franchisor fair with you in resolving any grievances?

		% answering
A)	**Extremely fair**	**42%**
B)	Pretty fair	33%
C)	Reasonably fair	0%
D)	Not very fair	8%
E)	Not fair at all	17%

Q5: Are territories equitably granted?

		% answering
A)	**Yes**	**47%**
B)	No	20%
C)	Not yet sure	33%

Q6: How would you describe the initial and ongoing training provided by your franchisor?

		% answering
A)	**Excellent**	**33%**
B)	Good	27%
C)	Adequate	20%
D)	Fair	13%
E)	Poor	13%

Q7: How well does the franchisor anticipate future trends in how it evolves and markets products and services?

		% answering
A)	Extremely well	20%
B)	**Pretty well**	**33%**
C)	Adequately	20%
D)	Not very well	13%
E)	Terribly	13%

Q8: How satisfied are you with your franchisor's spending of the royalty fees you pay?

		% answering
A)	Extremely satisfied	0%
B)	**Mostly satisfied**	**43%**
C)	Somewhat satisfied	29%
D)	Not very satisfied	0%
E)	Not satisfied at all	29%

Q9: **In what ways could the parent company most improve? (Please check those that most apply, no more than three):**

- ❏ Communications
- ❏ Counsel/advice on administrative/management issues
- ❏ Effectiveness of marketing/promotions
- ❏ Evolution of products/services
- ❏ Frequency of marketing/promotional campaigns

- ❏ Quality of products/services
- ❏ Pricing of products/services to franchisees
- ❏ Technology (Point of sale systems, usage of computers/email/software, etc.)
- ❏ Training

Most frequent responses:	% answering
Effectiveness of marketing/promotions	67%
Counsel/advice on administrative/management issues	40%
Communications	33%

Q10: **Is your income more, less or about what you expected prior to opening your business?**

	% answering	
More	0%	
Less	**67%**	**Summary: 33% are making about what they**
About what was expected	33%	**expected, or more.**

Q11: **Prior to opening your franchise, which (if any) of the following did you underestimate?**

- ❏ Amount of working capital required for your first year in business
- ❏ Difficulty in hiring/retaining quality staff
- ❏ Expertise required to run the business
- ❏ Impact of marketing/promotions

- ❏ Start-up costs
- ❏ Degree of stress
- ❏ Workload

Most frequent responses:	% answering
Amount of working capital required for 1st year in business	60%
Degree of stress	53%
Difficulty in hiring/retaining quality staff (tie)	33%
Workload (tie)	33%

Q12: **If you could turn back time to the day you signed your franchise agreement, would you make the same decision to buy your franchise?**

	% answering
Yes	**53%**
No	47%

* Number of survey respondents: 15 from 7 different states
Number of survey respondents as a % of total franchise units: 17.24%

CHRISTMAS DECOR

www.christmasdecor.net

Holiday and event decorating services.

OVERALL SCORE: 73

206 23rd Street
Lubbock, TX 79404
Fax:
Total number of outlets: 322
Total number of franchise outlets: 322
International: Yes (several countries)

OVERALL RANK: 66

Phone: 800-687-9551
Franchise fee: varies
Franchise term: 5 years
Initial investment: $9,350 to $42,350
Advertising/Marketing fee: > of $180 or 20% of annual royalty fee
Royalty fee: varies

SURVEY AND RESULTS *

Q1: About how many hours per week do you dedicate to your franchise business?

		% answering
A)	**Less than 40**	**72%**
B)	41–50	11%
C)	51–60	11%
D)	More than 60	0%
E)	Passive investment	6%

Q2: How would you describe your relations/ communications with your franchisor?

		% answering
A)	Excellent	11%
B)	**Good**	**44%**
C)	Adequate	22%
D)	Fair	22%
E)	Poor	0%

Q3: In terms of how your franchisor views your communications with other franchisees, it is:

		% answering
A)	**Very supportive**	**50%**
B)	Not very supportive	17%
C)	No influence	33%

Q4: Is the franchisor fair with you in resolving any grievances?

		% answering
A)	**Extremely fair**	**41%**
B)	Pretty fair	18%
C)	**Reasonably fair**	**41%**
D)	Not very fair	0%
E)	Not fair at all	0%

Q5: Are territories equitably granted?

		% answering
A)	**Yes**	**83%**
B)	No	6%
C)	Not yet sure	11%

Q6: How would you describe the initial and ongoing training provided by your franchisor?

		% answering
A)	Excellent	22%
B)	**Good**	**44%**
C)	Adequate	33%
D)	Fair	0%
E)	Poor	0%

Q7: How well does the franchisor anticipate future trends in how it evolves and markets products and services?

		% answering
A)	Extremely well	28%
B)	**Pretty well**	**33%**
C)	Adequately	28%
D)	Not very well	11%
E)	Terribly	0%

Q8: How satisfied are you with your franchisor's spending of the royalty fees you pay?

		% answering
A)	Extremely satisfied	6%
B)	**Mostly satisfied**	**35%**
C)	Somewhat satisfied	29%
D)	Not very satisfied	24%
E)	Not satisfied at all	6%

Q9: **In what ways could the parent company most improve? (Please check those that most apply, no more than three):**

- ❑ Communications
- ❑ Counsel/advice on administrative/management issues
- ❑ Effectiveness of marketing/promotions
- ❑ Evolution of products/services
- ❑ Frequency of marketing/promotional campaigns

- ❑ Quality of products/services
- ❑ Pricing of products/services to franchisees
- ❑ Technology (Point of sale systems, usage of computers/email/software, etc.)
- ❑ Training

Most frequent responses: % answering

Effectiveness of marketing/promotions   44%

Pricing of products/services to franchisees   39%

Communications   28%

Q10: **Is your income more, less or about what you expected prior to opening your business?**

	% answering	
More	28%	
Less	33%	**Summary: 67% are making about what they**
About what was expected	**39%**	**expected, or more.**

Q11: **Prior to opening your franchise, which (if any) of the following did you underestimate?**

- ❑ Amount of working capital required for your 1st year in business
- ❑ Difficulty in hiring/retaining quality staff
- ❑ Expertise required to run the business
- ❑ Impact of marketing/promotions

- ❑ Start-up costs
- ❑ Degree of stress
- ❑ Workload

Most frequent responses: % answering

Difficulty in hiring/retaining quality staff (tie)   39%

Impact of marketing/promotions (tie)   39%

Degree of stress   22%

Q12: **If you could turn back time to the day you signed your franchise agreement, would you make the same decision to buy your franchise?**

	% answering
Yes	**72%**
No	28%

* Number of survey respondents: 18 from 16 different states

Number of survey respondents as a % of total franchise units: 5.59%

THE CLEANING AUTHORITY

www.thecleaningauthority.com

Residential Cleaning services.

OVERALL SCORE: 69

6994 Columbia Gateway Drive
Columbia, MD 21046
Total number of outlets: 130
Total number of franchise outlets: 129
International: No

OVERALL RANK: 87

Phone: 800-783-6243
Franchise fee: $31,500 to $49,500
Franchise term: 10 years
Initial investment: $84,080 to $129,340
Advertising/Marketing fee: 1% of gross revenues
Royalty fee: varies

SURVEY AND RESULTS *

Q1: About how many hours per week do you dedicate to your franchise business?

		% answering
A)	Less than 40	7%
B)	41–50	14%
C)	51–60	36%
D)	**More than 60**	**43%**
E)	Passive investment	0%

Q2: How would you describe your relations/communications with your franchisor?

		% answering
A)	Excellent	29%
B)	**Good**	**57%**
C)	Adequate	14%
D)	Fair	0%
E)	Poor	0%

Q3: In terms of how your franchisor views your communications with other franchisees, it is:

		% answering
A)	**Very supportive**	**79%**
B)	Not very supportive	21%
C)	No influence	0%

Q4: Is the franchisor fair with you in resolving any grievances?

		% answering
A)	Extremely fair	36%
B)	**Pretty fair**	**43%**
C)	Reasonably fair	21%
D)	Not very fair	0%
E)	Not fair at all	0%

Q5: Are territories equitably granted?

		% answering
A)	**Yes**	**93%**
B)	No	0%
C)	Not yet sure	7%

Q6: How would you describe the initial and ongoing training provided by your franchisor?

		% answering
A)	Excellent	7%
B)	**Good**	**79%**
C)	Adequate	14%
D)	Fair	0%
E)	Poor	0%

Q7: How well does the franchisor anticipate future trends in how it evolves and markets products and services?

		% answering
A)	Extremely well	21%
B)	**Pretty well**	**43%**
C)	Adequately	36%
D)	Not very well	0%
E)	Terribly	0%

Q8: How satisfied are you with your franchisor's spending of the royalty fees you pay?

		% answering
A)	Extremely satisfied	29%
B)	**Mostly satisfied**	**43%**
C)	Somewhat satisfied	29%
D)	Not very satisfied	0%
E)	Not satisfied at all	0%

Q9: **In what ways could the parent company most improve? (Please check those that most apply, no more than three):**

❑ Communications
❑ Counsel/advice on administrative/management issues
❑ Effectiveness of marketing/promotions
❑ Evolution of products/services
❑ Frequency of marketing/promotional campaigns

❑ Quality of products/services
❑ Pricing of products/services to franchisees
❑ Technology (Point of sale systems, usage of computers/email/software, etc.)
❑ Training

Most frequent responses:

	% answering
Counsel/advice on administrative/management issues	50%
Frequency of marketing/promotional campaigns	36%
Effectiveness of marketing/promotions	29%

Q10: **Is your income more, less or about what you expected prior to opening your business?**

	% answering	
More	7%	
Less	**50%**	**Summary: 50% are making about what**
About what was expected	43%	**they expected, or more.**

Q11: **Prior to opening your franchise, which (if any) of the following did you underestimate?**

❑ Amount of working capital required for your 1st year in business
❑ Difficulty in hiring/retaining quality staff
❑ Expertise required to run the business
❑ Impact of marketing/promotions

❑ Start-up costs
❑ Degree of stress
❑ Workload

Most frequent responses:

	% answering
Degree of stress	71%
Amount of working capital required for your first year in business (tie)	57%
Difficulty in hiring/retaining quality staff (tie)	57%

Q12: **If you could turn back time to the day you signed your franchise agreement, would you make the same decision to buy your franchise?**

	% answering
Yes	**57%**
No	43%

* Number of survey respondents: 14 from 12 different states
Number of survey respondents as a % of total franchise units: 10.77%

THE COFFEE BEANERY

www.coffeebeanery.com
Email: franchiseinfo@beanerysupport.com

Specialty coffee.

OVERALL SCORE: 53

3429 Pierson Place
Flushing, MI 48433
Fax: 810-733-1536
Total number of outlets: 7 corporate
Total number of franchise outlets: 200+
International: Yes (several countries)

OVERALL RANK: 164

Phone: 800-728-2326
Franchise fee: $13,750 to $27,500
Franchise term: 15 years
Initial investment: $58,250 to $491,500
Advertising/Marketing fee: 2% of weekly gross sales for Brand Building Fund
Royalty fee: 6% of gross sales weekly

SURVEY AND RESULTS *

Q1: About how many hours per week do you dedicate to your franchise business?

		% answering
A)	Less than 40	0%
B)	**41–50**	**58%**
C)	51–60	25%
D)	More than 60	17%
E)	Passive investment	0%

Q2: How would you describe your relations/communications with your franchisor?

		% answering
A)	Excellent	25%
B)	Good	17%
C)	Adequate	8%
D)	**Fair**	**33%**
E)	Poor	17%

Q3: In terms of how your franchisor views your communications with other franchisees, it is:

		% answering
A)	**Very supportive**	**45%**
B)	Not very supportive	27%
C)	No influence	27%

Q4: Is the franchisor fair with you in resolving any grievances?

		% answering
A)	**Extremely fair**	**36%**
B)	Pretty fair	18%
C)	Reasonably fair	18%
D)	Not very fair	18%
E)	Not fair at all	9%

Q5: Are territories equitably granted?

		% answering
A)	**Yes**	**40%**
B)	No	20%
C)	**Not yet sure**	**40%**

Q6: How would you describe the initial and ongoing training provided by your franchisor?

		% answering
A)	Excellent	25%
B)	Good	17%
C)	**Adequate**	**38%**
D)	Fair	3%
E)	Poor	17%

Q7: How well does the franchisor anticipate future trends in how it evolves and markets products and services?

		% answering
A)	Extremely well	0%
B)	Pretty well	25%
C)	**Adequately**	**42%**
D)	Not very well	8%
E)	Terribly	25%

Q8: How satisfied are you with your franchisor's spending of the royalty fees you pay?

		% answering
A)	Extremely satisfied	0%
B)	Mostly satisfied	17%
C)	**Somewhat satisfied**	**42%**
D)	Not very satisfied	33%
E)	Not satisfied at all	8%

Q9: In what ways could the parent company most improve? (Please check those that most apply, no more than three):

❑ Communications
❑ Counsel/advice on administrative/management issues
❑ Effectiveness of marketing/promotions
❑ Evolution of products/services
❑ Frequency of marketing/promotional campaigns

❑ Quality of products/services
❑ Pricing of products/services to franchisees
❑ Technology (Point of sale systems, usage of computers/email/software, etc.)
❑ Training

Most frequent responses:

	% answering
Communications	58%
Evolution of products/services (tie)	50%
Pricing of products/services to franchisees (tie)	50%

Q10: Is your income more, less or about what you expected prior to opening your business?

	% answering	
More	0%	
Less	**67%**	**Summary: 33% are making about what they**
About what was expected	33%	**expected, or more.**

Q11: Prior to opening your franchise, which (if any) of the following did you underestimate?

❑ Amount of working capital required for your first year in business
❑ Difficulty in hiring/retaining quality staff
❑ Expertise required to run the business
❑ Impact of marketing/promotions

❑ Start-up costs
❑ Degree of stress
❑ Workload

Most frequent responses:

	% answering
Degree of stress	50%
Start-up costs (tie)	33%
Workload (tie)	33%

Q12: If you could turn back time to the day you signed your franchise agreement, would you make the same decision to buy your franchise?

	% answering
Yes	**64%**
No	36%

* Number of survey respondents: 12 from 10 different states
Number of survey respondents as a % of total franchise units: 6%

COLD STONE CREAMERY

www.coldstonecreamery.com

Premium ice cream and frozen yogurts.

OVERALL SCORE: 84

16101 N. 82nd Street, Suite A-4
Scottsdale, AZ 85260
Fax: 480-348-1718
Total number of outlets: 900+
Total number of franchise outlets: 900+
International: No (plans to be soon)

OVERALL RANK: 18

Phone: 866-464-9467
Franchise fee: $42,000
Franchise term: 10 years
Initial investment: $264,800 to $399,600
Advertising/Marketing fee: 3% of gross sales weekly
Royalty fee: 6% of gross sales weekly

SURVEY AND RESULTS *

Q1: **About how many hours per week do you dedicate to your franchise business?**

		% answering
A)	Less than 40	14%
B)	**41–50**	**57%**
C)	51–60	7%
D)	More than 60	21%
E)	Passive investment	0%

Q2: **How would you describe your relations/ communications with your franchisor?**

		% answering
A)	**Excellent**	**50%**
B)	Good	36%
C)	Adequate	7%
D)	Fair	7%
E)	Poor	0%

Q3: **In terms of how your franchisor views your communications with other franchisees, it is:**

		% answering
A)	**Very supportive**	**86%**
B)	Not very supportive	0%
C)	No influence	14%

Q4: **Is the franchisor fair with you in resolving any grievances?**

		% answering
A)	**Extremely fair**	**46%**
B)	Pretty fair	38%
C)	Reasonably fair	8%
D)	Not very fair	0%
E)	Not fair at all	8%

Q5: **Are territories equitably granted?**

		% answering
A)	Yes	36%
B)	**No**	**43%**
C)	Not yet sure	21%

Q6: **How would you describe the initial and ongoing training provided by your franchisor?**

		% answering
A)	**Excellent**	**71%**
B)	Good	29%
C)	Adequate	0%
D)	Fair	0%
E)	Poor	0%

Q7: **How well does the franchisor anticipate future trends in how it evolves and markets products and services?**

		% answering
A)	**Extremely well**	**64%**
B)	Pretty well	21%
C)	Adequately	7%
D)	Not very well	7%
E)	Terribly	0%

Q8: **How satisfied are you with your franchisor's spending of the royalty fees you pay?**

		% answering
A)	Extremely satisfied	21%
B)	**Mostly satisfied**	**57%**
C)	Somewhat satisfied	14%
D)	Not very satisfied	0%
E)	Not satisfied at all	0%

Q9: **In what ways could the parent company most improve? (Please check those that most apply, no more than three):**

☐ Communications
☐ Counsel/advice on administrative/management issues
☐ Effectiveness of marketing/promotions
☐ Evolution of products/services
☐ Frequency of marketing/promotional campaigns

☐ Quality of products/services
☐ Pricing of products/services to franchisees
☐ Technology (Point of sale systems, usage of computers/email/software, etc.)
☐ Training

Most frequent responses:

	% answering
Technology	64%
Communications	50%
Counsel/advice on administrative/management issues	36%

Q10: **Is your income more, less or about what you expected prior to opening your business?**

	% answering
More	8%
Less	38%
About what was expected	**54%**

Summary: 62% are making about what they expected, or more.

Q11: **Prior to opening your franchise, which (if any) of the following did you underestimate?**

☐ Amount of working capital required for your first year in business
☐ Difficulty in hiring/retaining quality staff
☐ Expertise required to run the business
☐ Impact of marketing/promotions

☐ Start-up costs
☐ Degree of stress
☐ Workload

Most frequent responses:

	% answering
Amount of working capital required for 1st year in business	50%
Degree of stress	50%
Workload	36%

Q12: **If you could turn back time to the day you signed your franchise agreement, would you make the same decision to buy your franchise?**

	% answering
Yes	**93%**
No	7%

* Number of survey respondents: 14 from 10 different states
Number of survey respondents as a % of total franchise units: 1.56%

COLORS ON PARADE

www.colorsfranchise.com

On-site mobile vehicle paint repair and refinishing.

OVERALL SCORE: 64

642 Century Circle,
Conway, SC 29526
Total number of outlets: 193
Total number of franchise outlets: 183
International: No

OVERALL RANK: 115

Phone: 800-929-3363
Franchise fee: $3,000
Franchise term: 10 years
Initial investment: $50,277 to $75,727
Advertising/Marketing fee: 7% of gross revenues
Royalty fee: 30% of gross revenues

SURVEY AND RESULTS *

Q1: About how many hours per week do you dedicate to your franchise business?

		% answering
A)	Less than 40	30%
B)	**41–50**	**40%**
C)	51–60	30%
D)	More than 60	0%
E)	Passive investment	0%

Q2: How would you describe your relations/ communications with your franchisor?

		% answering
A)	Excellent	10%
B)	Good	20%
C)	**Adequate**	**30%**
D)	**Fair**	**30%**
E)	Poor	10%

Q3: In terms of how your franchisor views your communications with other franchisees, it is:

		% answering
A)	**Very supportive**	**50%**
B)	Not very supportive	30%
C)	No influence	20%

Q4: Is the franchisor fair with you in resolving any grievances?

		% answering
A)	Extremely fair	20%
B)	**Pretty fair**	**40%**
C)	Reasonably fair	30%
D)	Not very fair	0%
E)	Not fair at all	10%

Q5: Are territories equitably granted?

		% answering
A)	**Yes**	**57%**
B)	No	43%
C)	Not yet sure	0%

Q6: How would you describe the initial and ongoing training provided by your franchisor?

		% answering
A)	Excellent	10%
B)	**Good**	**30%**
C)	**Adequate**	**30%**
D)	**Fair**	**30%**
E)	Poor	0%

Q7: How well does the franchisor anticipate future trends in how it evolves and markets products and services?

		% answering
A)	Extremely well	20%
B)	Pretty well	20%
C)	Adequately	10%
D)	**Not very well**	**40%**
E)	Terribly	10%

Q8: How satisfied are you with your franchisor's spending of the royalty fees you pay?

		% answering
A)	Extremely satisfied	20%
B)	Mostly satisfied	20%
C)	Somewhat satisfied	10%
D)	**Not very satisfied**	**30%**
E)	Not satisfied at all	20%

Q9: In what ways could the parent company most improve? (Please check those that most apply, no more than three):

❑ Communications
❑ Counsel/advice on administrative/management issues
❑ Effectiveness of marketing/promotions
❑ Evolution of products/services
❑ Frequency of marketing/promotional campaigns

❑ Quality of products/services
❑ Pricing of products/services to franchisees
❑ Technology (Point of sale systems, usage of computers/email/software, etc.)
❑ Training

Most frequent responses: % answering

Communications	70%
Pricing of products/services to franchisees	60%
Effectiveness of marketing/promotions (tie)	40%
Training (tie)	40%

Q10: Is your income more, less or about what you expected prior to opening your business?

           % answering

More	10%	
Less	30%	**Summary: 70% are making about what they**
About what was expected	**60%**	**expected, or more.**

Q11: Prior to opening your franchise, which (if any) of the following did you underestimate?

❑ Amount of working capital required for your first year in business
❑ Difficulty in hiring/retaining quality staff
❑ Expertise required to run the business
❑ Impact of marketing/promotions

❑ Start-up costs
❑ Degree of stress
❑ Workload

Most frequent responses: % answering

Degree of stress	60%
Amount of working capital required for 1st year in business (tie)	30%
Difficulty in hiring/retaining quality staff (tie)	30%

Q12: If you could turn back time to the day you signed your franchise agreement, would you make the same decision to buy your franchise?

           % answering

Yes	**70%**
No	30%

* Number of survey respondents: 10 from 8 different states
Number of survey respondents as a % of total franchise units: 5.18%

COMFORT KEEPERS

www.comfortkeepers.com
Email: contactus@comfortkeepers.com (U.S.) or admin@comfortkeepers.ca (Canada)

Assisted living in the home.

OVERALL SCORE: 63

6640 Poe Avenue, Suite 200
Dayton, OH 45414
Fax: 937-264-3103
Total number of outlets: 425
Total number of franchise outlets: 425
International: Yes (Canada)

OVERALL RANK: 121

Phone: 888-387-2415
Franchise fee: $18,750
Franchise term:
Initial investment:
Advertising/Marketing fee:
Royalty fee: 3 to 5%

SURVEY AND RESULTS *

Q1: About how many hours per week do you dedicate to your franchise business?

		% answering
A)	Less than 40	6%
B)	41–50	19%
C)	**51–60**	**38%**
D)	**More than 60**	**38%**
E)	Passive investment	0%

Q2: How would you describe your relations/communications with your franchisor?

		% answering
A)	Excellent	13%
B)	**Good**	**69%**
C)	Adequate	13%
D)	Fair	0%
E)	Poor	6%

Q3: In terms of how your franchisor views your communications with other franchisees, it is:

		% answering
A)	**Very supportive**	**69%**
B)	Not very supportive	13%
C)	No influence	19%

Q4: Is the franchisor fair with you in resolving any grievances?

		% answering
A)	Extremely fair	29%
B)	**Pretty fair**	**50%**
C)	Reasonably fair	14%
D)	Not very fair	0%
E)	Not fair at all	7%

Q5: Are territories equitably granted?

		% answering
A)	**Yes**	**75%**
B)	No	0%
C)	Not yet sure	25%

Q6: How would you describe the initial and ongoing training provided by your franchisor?

		% answering
A)	Excellent	13%
B)	**Good**	**50%**
C)	Adequate	13%
D)	Fair	19%
E)	Poor	6%

Q7: How well does the franchisor anticipate future trends in how it evolves and markets products and services?

		% answering
A)	Extremely well	31%
B)	**Pretty well**	**44%**
C)	Adequately	19%
D)	Not very well	6%
E)	Terribly	0%

Q8: How satisfied are you with your franchisor's spending of the royalty fees you pay?

		% answering
A)	Extremely satisfied	13%
B)	**Mostly satisfied**	**60%**
C)	Somewhat satisfied	13%
D)	Not very satisfied	7%
E)	Not satisfied at all	7%

Q9: **In what ways could the parent company most improve? (Please check those that most apply, no more than three):**

❑ Communications
❑ Counsel/advice on administrative/management issues
❑ Effectiveness of marketing/promotions
❑ Evolution of products/services
❑ Frequency of marketing/promotional campaigns

❑ Quality of products/services
❑ Pricing of products/services to franchisees
❑ Technology (Point of sale systems, usage of computers/email/software, etc.)
❑ Training

Most frequent responses:

	% answering
Effectiveness of marketing/promotions	56%
Counsel/advice on administrative/management issues (tie)	44%
Frequency of marketing/promotional campaigns (tie)	44%

Q10: **Is your income more, less or about what you expected prior to opening your business?**

	% answering	
More	7%	
Less	**67%**	**Summary: 34% are making about what**
About what was expected	27%	**they expected, or more.**

Q11: **Prior to opening your franchise, which (if any) of the following did you underestimate?**

❑ Amount of working capital required for your year in business
❑ Difficulty in hiring/retaining quality staff
❑ Expertise required to run the business
❑ Impact of marketing/promotions

❑ Start-up costs
❑ Degree of stress
❑ Workload

Most frequent responses:

	% answering
Degree of stress	75%
Difficulty in hiring/retaining quality staff	56%
Amount of working capital required for 1st year in business	50%

Q12: **If you could turn back time to the day you signed your franchise agreement, would you make the same decision to buy your franchise?**

	% answering
Yes	**60%**
No	40%

* Number of survey respondents: 16 from 11 different states
Number of survey respondents as a % of total franchise units: 3.76%

COMPUTER TROUBLESHOOTERS

www.comptroub.com

Email: info@comptroub.com or wilson@comptroub.com (International inquiries—Wilson McOrist)

On-site computer service and support for consumer and commercial customers.

OVERALL SCORE: 87

OVERALL RANK: N/A

755 Commerce Drive, Suite 412
Decatur, GA 30030
Total number of outlets: 400+ (150 in US & Canada)
Total number of franchise outlets: 400+
International: Yes (worldwide)
Advertising/Marketing fee: none. There is a $140 per month fee for the Regional Advertising Fund.

Phone: 877-704-1702
Franchise fee: $12,000
Franchise term: 10 years
Initial investment: $17,300 to 26,500
Royalty fee: none. There's a $240 per monthly administrative fee.

SURVEY AND RESULTS *

Q1: About how many hours per week do you dedicate to your franchise business?

		% answering
A)	Less than 40	17%
B)	41–50	33%
C)	51–60	0%
D)	**More than 60**	50%
E)	Passive investment	0%

Q2: How would you describe your relations/communications with your franchisor?

		% answering
A)	**Excellent**	83%
B)	Good	0%
C)	Adequate	17%
D)	Fair	0%
E)	Poor	0%

Q3: In terms of how your franchisor views your communications with other franchisees, it is:

		% answering
A)	**Very supportive**	100%
B)	Not very supportive	0%
C)	No influence	0%

Q4: Is the franchisor fair with you in resolving any grievances?

		% answering
A)	**Extremely fair**	80%
B)	Pretty fair	0%
C)	Reasonably fair	20%
D)	Not very fair	0%
E)	Not fair at all	0%

Q5: Are territories equitably granted?

		% answering
A)	**Yes**	100%
B)	No	0%
C)	Not yet sure	0%

Q6: How would you describe the initial and ongoing training provided by your franchisor?

		% answering
A)	**Excellent**	50%
B)	Good	17%
C)	Adequate	33%
D)	Fair	0%
E)	Poor	0%

Q7: How well does the franchisor anticipate future trends in how it evolves and markets products and services?

		% answering
A)	**Extremely well**	50%
B)	Pretty well	17%
C)	Adequately	17%
D)	Not very well	17%
E)	Terribly	0%

Q8: How satisfied are you with your franchisor's spending of the royalty fees you pay?

		% answering
A)	**Extremely satisfied**	67%
B)	Mostly satisfied	17%
C)	Somewhat satisfied	0%
D)	Not very satisfied	0%
E)	Not satisfied at all	17%

Q9: **In what ways could the parent company most improve? (Please check those that most apply, no more than three):**

☐ Communications
☐ Counsel/advice on administrative/management issues
☐ Effectiveness of marketing/promotions
☐ Evolution of products/services
☐ Frequency of marketing/promotional campaigns

☐ Quality of products/services
☐ Pricing of products/services to franchisees
☐ Technology (Point of sale systems, usage of computers/email/software, etc.)
☐ Training

Most frequent responses:

	% answering
Frequency of marketing/promotional campaigns	67%
Training	50%
Effectiveness of marketing/promotions	33%

Q10: Is your income more, less or about what you expected prior to opening your business?

	% answering
More	33%
Less	**50%**
About what was expected	17%

Summary: 50% are making about what they expected, or more.

Q11: Prior to opening your franchise, which (if any) of the following did you underestimate?

☐ Amount of working capital required for your first year in business
☐ Difficulty in hiring/retaining quality staff
☐ Expertise required to run the business
☐ Impact of marketing/promotions

☐ Start-up costs
☐ Degree of stress
☐ Workload

Most frequent responses:

	% answering
Difficulty in hiring/retaining quality staff (tie)	33%
Impact of marketing/promotions (tie)	33%
Degree of stress (tie)	33%
Workload (tie)	33%

Q12: If you could turn back time to the day you signed your franchise agreement, would you make the same decision to buy your franchise?

	% answering
Yes	**100%**
No	50%

* Number of survey respondents: 6 from 5 different states
Number of survey respondents as a % of total franchise units: 1.5%

COMPUTERTOTS/COMPUTER EXPLORERS

www.computertots.com
Email: cperkins@iced.net

Computer education for children ages 3-5 (Computertots) and ages 6-12 (Computer Explorers).

OVERALL SCORE: 75

12715 Telge Road
Cypress, TX 77429
Fax: 281-256-4178
Total number of outlets: 89
Total number of franchise outlets: 89
International: No

OVERALL RANK: N/A

Phone: 800-531-5053
Franchise fee: $30,000
Franchise term: 15 years
Initial investment: $47,725 to $66,250
Advertising/Marketing fee: > of 1% of gross sales
or $75 per month.
Royalty fee 8% of gross sales monthly, subject to
variable monthly minimum.

SURVEY AND RESULTS *

Q1: About how many hours per week do you dedicate to your franchise business?

		% answering
A)	**Less than 40**	**50%**
B)	41–50	38%
C)	51–60	0%
D)	More than 60	0%
E)	Passive investment	13%

Q2: How would you describe your relations/communications with your franchisor?

		% answering
A)	**Excellent**	**25%**
B)	**Good**	**25%**
C)	**Adequate**	**25%**
D)	**Fair**	**25%**
E)	Poor	0%

Q3: In terms of how your franchisor views your communications with other franchisees, it is:

		% answering
A)	**Very supportive**	**75%**
B)	Not very supportive	13%
C)	No influence	13%

Q4: Is the franchisor fair with you in resolving any grievances?

		% answering
A)	**Extremely fair**	**50%**
B)	Pretty fair	25%
C)	Reasonably fair	25%
D)	Not very fair	0%
E)	Not fair at all	0%

Q5: Are territories equitably granted?

		% answering
A)	**Yes**	**63%**
B)	No	13%
C)	Not yet sure	25%

Q6: How would you describe the initial and ongoing training provided by your franchisor?

		% answering
A)	**Excellent**	**63%**
B)	Good	0%
C)	Adequate	13%
D)	Fair	25%
E)	Poor	0%

Q7: How well does the franchisor anticipate future trends in how it evolves and markets products and services?

		% answering
A)	**Extremely well**	**38%**
B)	**Pretty well**	**38%**
C)	Adequately	0%
D)	Not very well	25%
E)	Terribly	0%

Q8: How satisfied are you with your franchisor's spending of the royalty fees you pay?

		% answering
A)	**Extremely satisfied**	**43%**
B)	Mostly satisfied	14%
C)	Somewhat satisfied	29%
D)	Not very satisfied	14%
E)	Not satisfied at all	0%

Q9: In what ways could the parent company most improve? (Please check those that most apply, no more than three):

- ❏ Communications
- ❏ Counsel/advice on administrative/management issues
- ❏ Effectiveness of marketing/promotions
- ❏ Evolution of products/services
- ❏ Frequency of marketing/promotional campaigns

- ❏ Quality of products/services
- ❏ Pricing of products/services to franchisees
- ❏ Technology (Point of sale systems, usage of computers/email/software, etc.)
- ❏ Training

Most frequent responses:

	% answering
Communications (tie)	38%
Effectiveness of marketing/promotions (tie)	38%
Quality of products/services (tie)	25%
Technology (tie)	25%
Training (tie)	25%

Q10: Is your income more, less or about what you expected prior to opening your business?

	% answering
More	25%
Less	**38%**
About what was expected	**38%**

Summary: 63% are making about what they expected, or more.

Q11: Prior to opening your franchise, which (if any) of the following did you underestimate?

- ❏ Amount of working capital required for your first year in business
- ❏ Difficulty in hiring/retaining quality staff
- ❏ Expertise required to run the business
- ❏ Impact of marketing/promotions

- ❏ Start-up costs
- ❏ Degree of stress
- ❏ Workload

Most frequent responses:

	% answering
Difficulty in hiring/retaining quality staff	63%
Amount of working capital required for 1st year in business	50%
Impact of marketing/promotions (tie)	25%
Start-up costs (tie)	25%
Degree of stress (tie)	25%

Q12: If you could turn back time to the day you signed your franchise agreement, would you make the same decision to buy your franchise?

	% answering
Yes	**75%**
No	25%

* Number of survey respondents: 8 from 6 different states
Number of survey respondents as a % of total franchise units: 8.99%

CONTOURS EXPRESS

www.contoursexpress.com

Women's only fitness and weight loss studio.

OVERALL SCORE: 59

156 Imperial Way
Nicholasville, KY 40356
Fax: 859-241-2234
Total number of outlets: 278
Total number of franchise outlets: 278
International: Yes (several countries)

OVERALL RANK: 138

Phone: 877-227-2282
Franchise fee: $12,495
Franchise term: 10 years
Initial investment: $37,895 to $63,020
Advertising/Marketing fee: 4% per month
Royalty fee: $395 per month

SURVEY AND RESULTS *

Q1: About how many hours per week do you dedicate to your franchise business?

		% answering
A)	Less than 40	24%
B)	**41–50**	**29%**
C)	**51–60**	**29%**
D)	More than 60	18%
E)	Passive investment	0%

Q2: How would you describe your relations/ communications with your franchisor?

		% answering
A)	**Excellent**	**35%**
B)	Good	18%
C)	Adequate	24%
D)	Fair	18%
E)	Poor	6%

Q3: In terms of how your franchisor views your communications with other franchisees, it is:

		% answering
A)	**Very supportive**	**65%**
B)	Not very supportive	6%
C)	No influence	29%

Q4: Is the franchisor fair with you in resolving any grievances?

		% answering
A)	**Extremely fair**	**42%**
B)	**Pretty fair**	**42%**
C)	Reasonably fair	17%
D)	Not very fair	0%
E)	Not fair at all	0%

Q5: Are territories equitably granted?

		% answering
A)	**Yes**	**76%**
B)	No	6%
C)	Not yet sure	18%

Q6: How would you describe the initial and ongoing training provided by your franchisor?

		% answering
A)	Excellent	12%
B)	**Good**	**41%**
C)	Adequate	24%
D)	Fair	0%
E)	Poor	24%

Q7: How well does the franchisor anticipate future trends in how it evolves and markets products and services?

		% answering
A)	Extremely well	24%
B)	Pretty well	18%
C)	**Adequately**	**35%**
D)	Not very well	24%
E)	Terribly	0%

Q8: How satisfied are you with your franchisor's spending of the royalty fees you pay?

		% answering
A)	Extremely satisfied	13%
B)	Mostly satisfied	27%
C)	Somewhat satisfied	13%
D)	**Not very satisfied**	**33%**
E)	Not satisfied at all	13%

Q9: **In what ways could the parent company most improve? (Please check those that most apply, no more than three):**

❑ Communications
❑ Counsel/advice on administrative/management issues
❑ Effectiveness of marketing/promotions
❑ Evolution of products/services
❑ Frequency of marketing/promotional campaigns

❑ Quality of products/services
❑ Pricing of products/services to franchisees
❑ Technology (Point of sale systems, usage of computers/email/software, etc.)
❑ Training

Most frequent responses:	% answering
Effectiveness of marketing/promotions	82%
Frequency of marketing/promotional campaigns	53%
Counsel/advice on administrative/management issues	41%

Q10: **Is your income more, less or about what you expected prior to opening your business?**

	% answering	
More	6%	
Less	**71%**	**Summary: 30% are making about what they**
About what was expected	24%	**expected, or more.**

Q11: **Prior to opening your franchise, which (if any) of the following did you underestimate?**

❑ Amount of working capital required for your first year in business
❑ Difficulty in hiring/retaining quality staff
❑ Expertise required to run the business
❑ Impact of marketing/promotions

❑ Start-up costs
❑ Degree of stress
❑ Workload

Most frequent responses:	% answering
Impact of marketing/promotions	71%
Amount of working capital required for 1st year in business	65%
Degree of stress	47%

Q12: **If you could turn back time to the day you signed your franchise agreement, would you make the same decision to buy your franchise?**

	% answering
Yes	**65%**
No	35%

* Number of survey respondents: 17 from 12 different states
  Number of survey respondents as a % of total franchise units: 6.12%

COOKIES BY DESIGN

www.cookiesbydesign.com
Email: franchisedevelopment@mgwmail.com

Plain and decorated cookie arrangements.

OVERALL SCORE: 65

1865 Summit Avenue, Suite 605
Plano, TX 75074
Fax: 972-398-9536
Total number of outlets: 252
Total number of franchise outlets: 252
International: No
Royalty fee: 6% of gross volume of business
monthly, subject to an annual minimum that
varies depending upon year of contract; fees
differ for kiosk and satellite locations

OVERALL RANK: 107

Phone: 800-945-2665
Franchise fee: $12,500 to $35,000
Franchise term: 1 year, with term extension if
all obligations of franchise agreement are
complied with in a timely manner
Advertising/Marketing fee: 1% of gross volume
of business, monthly

SURVEY AND RESULTS *

Q1: About how many hours per week do you dedicate to your franchise business?

		% answering
A)	Less than 40	23%
B)	41–50	23%
C)	51–60	23%
D)	**More than 60**	**31%**
E)	Passive investment	0%

Q2: How would you describe your relations/ communications with your franchisor?

		% answering
A)	Excellent	31%
B)	**Good**	**62%**
C)	Adequate	0%
D)	Fair	8%
E)	Poor	0%

Q3: In terms of how your franchisor views your communications with other franchisees, it is:

		% answering
A)	**Very supportive**	**83%**
B)	Not very supportive	0%
C)	No influence	17%

Q4: Is the franchisor fair with you in resolving any grievances?

		% answering
A)	Extremely fair	33%
B)	**Pretty fair**	**50%**
C)	Reasonably fair	17%
D)	Not very fair	0%
E)	Not fair at all	0%

Q5: Are territories equitably granted?

		% answering
A)	**Yes**	**64%**
B)	No	27%
C)	Not yet sure	9%

Q6: How would you describe the initial and ongoing training provided by your franchisor?

		% answering
A)	Excellent	31%
B)	**Good**	**46%**
C)	Adequate	15%
D)	Fair	8%
E)	Poor	0%

Q7: How well does the franchisor anticipate future trends in how it evolves and markets products and services?

		% answering
A)	Extremely well	31%
B)	Pretty well	8%
C)	**Adequately**	**54%**
D)	Not very well	8%
E)	Terribly	0%

Q8: How satisfied are you with your franchisor's spending of the royalty fees you pay?

		% answering
A)	Extremely satisfied	0%
B)	**Mostly satisfied**	**54%**
C)	Somewhat satisfied	38%
D)	Not very satisfied	0%
E)	Not satisfied at all	8%

Q9: **In what ways could the parent company most improve? (Please check those that most apply, no more than three):**

❑ Communications
❑ Counsel/advice on administrative/management issues
❑ Effectiveness of marketing/promotions
❑ Evolution of products/services
❑ Frequency of marketing/promotional campaigns

❑ Quality of products/services
❑ Pricing of products/services to franchisees
❑ Technology (Point of sale systems, usage of computers/email/software, etc.)
❑ Training

Most frequent responses:	% answering
Technology	62%
Effectiveness of marketing/promotions (tie)	54%
Evolution of products/services (tie)	54%

Q10: Is your income more, less or about what you expected prior to opening your business?

	% answering	
More	8%	
Less	**50%**	**Summary: 50% are making about what they**
About what was expected	42%	**expected, or more.**

Q11: Prior to opening your franchise, which (if any) of the following did you underestimate?

❑ Amount of working capital required for your 1st year in business
❑ Difficulty in hiring/retaining quality staff
❑ Expertise required to run the business
❑ Impact of marketing/promotions

❑ Start-up costs
❑ Degree of stress
❑ Workload

Most frequent responses:	% answering
Difficulty in hiring/retaining quality staff (tie)	46%
Impact of marketing/promotions (tie)	46%
Workload (tie)	46%

Q12: If you could turn back time to the day you signed your franchise agreement, would you make the same decision to buy your franchise?

	% answering
Yes	**54%**
No	46%

* Number of survey respondents: 13 from 10 different states
Number of survey respondents as a % of total franchise units: 5.16%

COST CUTTERS FAMILY HAIR CARE

www.costcutters.com or www.regisfranchise.com

Unisex hair salon.

OVERALL SCORE: 71

7201 Metro Boulevard
Edina, MN 55439
Fax: 952-947-7600
Total number of outlets: Approximately 1,000
Total number of franchise outlets:
Approximately 1,000
International: No

OVERALL RANK: 79

Phone: 952-947-7777
Franchise fee: $22,500
Franchise term:
Initial investment: $82,333 to $175,100
Advertising/Marketing fee:
Royalty fee:

SURVEY AND RESULTS *

Q1: **About how many hours per week do you dedicate to your franchise business?**

		% answering
A)	**Less than 40**	**36%**
B)	41–50	14%
C)	51–60	29%
D)	More than 60	21%
E)	Passive investment	0%

Q2: **How would you describe your relations/ communications with your franchisor?**

		% answering
A)	Excellent	21%
B)	**Good**	**36%**
C)	Adequate	21%
D)	Fair	7%
E)	Poor	14%

Q3: **In terms of how your franchisor views your communications with other franchisees, it is:**

		% answering
A)	**Very supportive**	**50%**
B)	Not very supportive	14%
C)	No influence	36%

Q4: **Is the franchisor fair with you in resolving any grievances?**

		% answering
A)	Extremely fair	23%
B)	**Pretty fair**	**46%**
C)	Reasonably fair	15%
D)	Not very fair	0%
E)	Not fair at all	15%

Q5: **Are territories equitably granted?**

		% answering
A)	**Yes**	**54%**
B)	No	31%
C)	Not yet sure	15%

Q6: **How would you describe the initial and ongoing training provided by your franchisor?**

		% answering
A)	Excellent	15%
B)	**Good**	**38%**
C)	Adequate	23%
D)	Fair	15%
E)	Poor	8%

Q7: **How well does the franchisor anticipate future trends in how it evolves and markets products and services?**

		% answering
A)	Extremely well	21%
B)	**Pretty well**	**64%**
C)	Adequately	0%
D)	Not very well	7%
E)	Terribly	7%

Q8: **How satisfied are you with your franchisor's spending of the royalty fees you pay?**

		% answering
A)	Extremely satisfied	0%
B)	**Mostly satisfied**	**42%**
C)	Somewhat satisfied	33%
D)	Not very satisfied	17%
E)	Not satisfied at all	8%

Q9: **In what ways could the parent company most improve? (Please check those that most apply, no more than three):**

- ❑ Communications
- ❑ Counsel/advice on administrative/management issues
- ❑ Effectiveness of marketing/promotions
- ❑ Evolution of products/services
- ❑ Frequency of marketing/promotional campaigns

- ❑ Quality of products/services
- ❑ Pricing of products/services to franchisees
- ❑ Technology (Point of sale systems, usage of computers/email/software, etc.)
- ❑ Training

Most frequent responses:

	% answering
Training	50%
Counsel/advice on administrative/management issues	36%
Communications (tie)	21%
Pricing of products/services to franchisees (tie)	21%
Technology (tie)	21%

Q10: **Is your income more, less or about what you expected prior to opening your business?**

	% answering	
More	**36%**	
Less	29%	**Summary: 72% are making about what they**
About what was expected	**36%**	**expected, or more.**

Q11: **Prior to opening your franchise, which (if any) of the following did you underestimate?**

- ❑ Amount of working capital required for your 1st year in business
- ❑ Difficulty in hiring/retaining quality staff
- ❑ Expertise required to run the business
- ❑ Impact of marketing/promotions

- ❑ Start-up costs
- ❑ Degree of stress
- ❑ Workload

Most frequent responses:

	% answering
Difficulty in hiring/retaining quality staff	64%
Start-up costs	50%
Amount of working capital required for 1st year in business	43%

Q12: **If you could turn back time to the day you signed your franchise agreement, would you make the same decision to buy your franchise?**

	% answering
Yes	**75%**
No	25%

* Number of survey respondents: 14 from 12 different states
Number of survey respondents as a % of total franchise units: 1.40%

COTTMAN TRANSMISSION

www.cottman.com

Nationwide automotive servicing centers.

OVERALL SCORE: 30

201 Gibraltar Road
Horsham, PA 19044
Fax: 801-640-7923
Total number of outlets: 400+
Total number of franchise outlets: 400+
International: Yes (Canada)

OVERALL RANK: 191

Phone: 800-394-6116
Franchise fee: $31,500
Franchise term: 15 years
Initial investment: $159,379 to $226,111
Advertising/Marketing fee: $709 per week
Royalty fee: 7 1/2% of gross sales weekly

SURVEY AND RESULTS *

Q1: About how many hours per week do you dedicate to your franchise business?

		% answering
A)	Less than 40	0%
B)	41–50	21%
C)	**51–60**	**43%**
D)	More than 60	36%
E)	Passive investment	0%

Q2: How would you describe your relations/ communications with your franchisor?

		% answering
A)	Excellent	7%
B)	Good	7%
C)	Adequate	7%
D)	Fair	21%
E)	**Poor**	**57%**

Q3: In terms of how your franchisor views your communications with other franchisees, it is:

		% answering
A)	Very supportive	36%
B)	Not very supportive	14%
C)	**No influence**	**50%**

Q4: Is the franchisor fair with you in resolving any grievances?

		% answering
A)	Extremely fair	8%
B)	Pretty fair	8%
C)	Reasonably fair	23%
D)	**Not very fair**	**38%**
E)	Not fair at all	23%

Q5: Are territories equitably granted?

		% answering
A)	**Yes**	**36%**
B)	**No**	**36%**
C)	Not yet sure	29%

Q6: How would you describe the initial and ongoing training provided by your franchisor?

		% answering
A)	Excellent	21%
B)	Good	7%
C)	Adequate	14%
D)	Fair	7%
E)	**Poor**	**50%**

Q7: How well does the franchisor anticipate future trends in how it evolves and markets products and services?

		% answering
A)	Extremely well	7%
B)	Pretty well	14%
C)	Adequately	21%
D)	**Not very well**	**36%**
E)	Terribly	21%

Q8: How satisfied are you with your franchisor's spending of the royalty fees you pay?

		% answering
A)	Extremely satisfied	7%
B)	Mostly satisfied	7%
C)	Somewhat satisfied	7%
D)	**Not very satisfied**	**43%**
E)	Not satisfied at all	36%

Q9: **In what ways could the parent company most improve? (Please check those that most apply, no more than three):**

❑ Communications
❑ Counsel/advice on administrative/management issues
❑ Effectiveness of marketing/promotions
❑ Evolution of products/services
❑ Frequency of marketing/promotional campaigns

❑ Quality of products/services
❑ Pricing of products/services to franchisees
❑ Technology (Point of sale systems, usage of computers/email/software, etc.)
❑ Training

Most frequent responses: % answering

	% answering
Communications	71%
Effectiveness of marketing/promotions	64%
Counsel/advice on administrative/management issues	50%

Q10: **Is your income more, less or about what you expected prior to opening your business?**

	% answering	
More	14%	
Less	**79%**	**Summary: 21% are making about what they**
About what was expected	7%	**expected, or more.**

Q11: **Prior to opening your franchise, which (if any) of the following did you underestimate?**

❑ Amount of working capital required for your 1st year in business
❑ Difficulty in hiring/retaining quality staff
❑ Expertise required to run the business
❑ Impact of marketing/promotions

❑ Start-up costs
❑ Degree of stress
❑ Workload

Most frequent responses: % answering

	% answering
Difficulty in hiring/retaining quality staff	79%
Amount of working capital required for 1st year in business (tie)	36%
Impact of marketing/promotions (tie)	36%

Q12: **If you could turn back time to the day you signed your franchise agreement, would you make the same decision to buy your franchise?**

	% answering
Yes	15%
No	**85%**

* Number of survey respondents: 14 from 12 different states
Number of survey respondents as a % of total franchise units: 3.5%

COUSIN'S SUBS

www.cousinssubs.com
Email: betterfranchise@cousinssubs.com

Fast food salad and sandwich retailer.

OVERALL SCORE: 46

N83 W 13400 Leon Road
Menomonee Falls, WI 53051
Fax: 262-253-7710
Total number of outlets: Approximately 175
Total number of franchise outlets: Approximately 175
International: No
Royalty fee: 6% of adjusted gross sales of less
than $150,000, 5% on the next $250,000,
and 4% on all sales over $1,000,000

OVERALL RANK: 171

Phone: 800-238-9736, ext. 2814
Franchise fee: $15,000 to $20,000
Franchise term:
Initial investment: $190,700–$276,300
Advertising/Marketing fee: 2% of adjusted gross sales

SURVEY AND RESULTS *

Q1: About how many hours per week do you dedicate to your franchise business?

		% answering
A)	**Less than 40**	**50%**
B)	41–50	30%
C)	51–60	0%
D)	More than 60	20%
E)	Passive investment	0%

Q2: How would you describe your relations/communications with your franchisor?

		% answering
A)	Excellent	15%
B)	Good	25%
C)	**Adequate**	**50%**
D)	Fair	0%
E)	Poor	10%

Q3: In terms of how your franchisor views your communications with other franchisees, it is:

		% answering
A)	Very supportive	30%
B)	Not very supportive	30%
C)	**No influence**	**40%**

Q4: Is the franchisor fair with you in resolving any grievances?

		% answering
A)	Extremely fair	10%
B)	**Pretty fair**	**40%**
C)	**Reasonably fair**	**40%**
D)	Not very fair	0%
E)	Not fair at all	10%

Q5: Are territories equitably granted?

		% answering
A)	**Yes**	**80%**
B)	No	0%
C)	Not yet sure	20%

Q6: How would you describe the initial and ongoing training provided by your franchisor?

		% answering
A)	Excellent	10%
B)	**Good**	**40%**
C)	Adequate	20%
D)	Fair	30%
E)	Poor	0%

Q7: How well does the franchisor anticipate future trends in how it evolves and markets products and services?

		% answering
A)	Extremely well	0%
B)	Pretty well	10%
C)	Adequately	20%
D)	**Not very well**	**70%**
E)	Terribly	0%

Q8: How satisfied are you with your franchisor's spending of the royalty fees you pay?

		% answering
A)	Extremely satisfied	0%
B)	Mostly satisfied	10%
C)	Somewhat satisfied	20%
D)	**Not very satisfied**	**60%**
E)	Not satisfied at all	10%

Q9: **In what ways could the parent company most improve? (Please check those that most apply, no more than three):**

❑ Communications

❑ Counsel/advice on administrative/management issues

❑ Effectiveness of marketing/promotions

❑ Evolution of products/services

❑ Frequency of marketing/promotional campaigns

❑ Quality of products/services

❑ Pricing of products/services to franchisees

❑ Technology (Point of sale systems, usage of computers/email/software, etc.)

❑ Training

Most frequent responses:	% answering
Effectiveness of marketing/promotions	70%
Evolution of products/services	50%
Frequency of marketing/promotional campaigns	40%

Q10: **Is your income more, less or about what you expected prior to opening your business?**

	% answering	
More	0%	
Less	**80%**	**Summary: 20% are making about what they**
About what was expected	20%	**expected, or more.**

Q11: **Prior to opening your franchise, which (if any) of the following did you underestimate?**

❑ Amount of working capital required for your 1st year in business

❑ Difficulty in hiring/retaining quality staff

❑ Expertise required to run the business

❑ Impact of marketing/promotions

❑ Start-up costs

❑ Degree of stress

❑ Workload

Most frequent responses:	% answering
Amount of working capital required for 1st year in business	50%
Degree of stress	40%
Workload	30%

Q12: **If you could turn back time to the day you signed your franchise agreement, would you make the same decision to buy your franchise?**

	% answering
Yes	40%
No	**60%**

* Number of survey respondents: 10 from 4 different states

Number of survey respondents as a % of total franchise units: 5.71%

CRITTER CONTROL

www.crittercontrol.com
Email: haps@crittercontrol.com

Wildlife management specialists.

OVERALL SCORE: 92

9435 E. Cherry Bend Road
Traverse City, MI 49684
Fax: 231-947-9440
Total number of outlets: 100+
Total number of franchise outlets: 100+
International: Yes (Canada)

OVERALL RANK: 6

Phone: 800-451-6544
Franchise fee: varies
Franchise term: 10 years
Initial investment: $10,250 to $69,000
Advertising/Marketing fee: 2% of monthly gross receipts
Royalty fee: varies

SURVEY AND RESULTS *

Q1: About how many hours per week do you dedicate to your franchise business?

		% answering
A)	Less than 40	0%
B)	41–50	25%
C)	51–60	25%
D)	**More than 60**	**50%**
E)	Passive investment	0%

Q2: How would you describe your relations/ communications with your franchisor?

		% answering
A)	Excellent	17%
B)	**Good**	**67%**
C)	Adequate	8%
D)	Fair	8%
E)	Poor	0%

Q3: In terms of how your franchisor views your communications with other franchisees, it is:

		% answering
A)	**Very supportive**	**83%**
B)	Not very supportive	0%
C)	No influence	17%

Q4: Is the franchisor fair with you in resolving any grievances?

		% answering
A)	Extremely fair	17%
B)	**Pretty fair**	**42%**
C)	Reasonably fair	25%
D)	Not very fair	17%
E)	Not fair at all	0%

Q5: Are territories equitably granted?

		% answering
A)	**Yes**	**100%**
B)	No	0%
C)	Not yet sure	0%

Q6: How would you describe the initial and ongoing training provided by your franchisor?

		% answering
A)	Excellent	17%
B)	**Good**	**58%**
C)	Adequate	17%
D)	Fair	8%
E)	Poor	0%

Q7: How well does the franchisor anticipate future trends in how it evolves and markets products and services?

		% answering
A)	**Extremely well**	**50%**
B)	Pretty well	25%
C)	Adequately	25%
D)	Not very well	0%
E)	Terribly	0%

Q8: How satisfied are you with your franchisor's spending of the royalty fees you pay?

		% answering
A)	Extremely satisfied	9%
B)	**Mostly satisfied**	**55%**
C)	Somewhat satisfied	18%
D)	Not very satisfied	9%
E)	Not satisfied at all	9%

Q9: **In what ways could the parent company most improve? (Please check those that most apply, no more than three):**

- ❏ Communications
- ❏ Counsel/advice on administrative/management issues
- ❏ Effectiveness of marketing/promotions
- ❏ Evolution of products/services
- ❏ Frequency of marketing/promotional campaigns

- ❏ Quality of products/services
- ❏ Pricing of products/services to franchisees
- ❏ Technology (Point of sale systems, usage of computers/email/software, etc.)
- ❏ Training

Most frequent responses:	% answering
Counsel/advice on administrative/management issues	67%
Technology	58%
Frequency of marketing/promotional campaigns	50%

Q10: **Is your income more, less or about what you expected prior to opening your business?**

	% answering	
More	**67%**	
Less	17%	**Summary: 84% are making about what they**
About what was expected	17%	**expected, or more.**

Q11: **Prior to opening your franchise, which (if any) of the following did you underestimate?**

- ❏ Amount of working capital required for your 1st year in business
- ❏ Difficulty in hiring/retaining quality staff
- ❏ Expertise required to run the business
- ❏ Impact of marketing/promotions

- ❏ Start-up costs
- ❏ Degree of stress
- ❏ Workload

Most frequent responses:	% answering
Workload	58%
Degree of stress	50%
Amount of working capital required for 1st year in business	33%

Q12: **If you could turn back time to the day you signed your franchise agreement, would you make the same decision to buy your franchise?**

	% answering
Yes	**92%**
No	8%

* Number of survey respondents: 12 from 11 different states
  Number of survey respondents as a % of total franchise units: 12%

CRUISE HOLIDAYS

www.cruiseholidays.com
Email: franchiseopportunities@cruiseholidays.com

Cruise vacation specialist.

OVERALL SCORE: 69

701 Carlson Parkway
Minneapolis, MN 55305
Fax:
Total number of outlets: 170
Total number of franchise outlets: 170
International: Yes (Canada)
Advertising/Marketing fee: $400 annual

OVERALL RANK: 88

Phone: 800-866-7245
Franchise fee: $30,000
Franchise term: 5 years
Initial investment: $78,169 to $136,719
($4,419 to $18,969 for an existing, independent,
cruise-only travel agency
Royalty fee: > of a minimum of $525 or a
maximum monthly license fee of $2,500, subject
to a maximum annual license fee of $15,000

SURVEY AND RESULTS *

Q1: About how many hours per week do you dedicate to your franchise business?

		% answering
A)	Less than 40	0%
B)	41–50	31%
C)	**51–60**	**44%**
D)	More than 60	25%
E)	Passive investment	0%

Q2: How would you describe your relations/ communications with your franchisor?

		% answering
A)	**Excellent**	**63%**
B)	Good	13%
C)	Adequate	19%
D)	Fair	0%
E)	Poor	6%

Q3: In terms of how your franchisor views your communications with other franchisees, it is:

		% answering
A)	**Very supportive**	**80%**
B)	Not very supportive	7%
C)	No influence	13%

Q4: Is the franchisor fair with you in resolving any grievances?

		% answering
A)	**Extremely fair**	**63%**
B)	Pretty fair	19%
C)	Reasonably fair	13%
D)	Not very fair	6%
E)	Not fair at all	0%

Q5: Are territories equitably granted?

		% answering
A)	**Yes**	**60%**
B)	No	33%
C)	Not yet sure	7%

Q6: How would you describe the initial and ongoing training provided by your franchisor?

		% answering
A)	**Excellent**	**50%**
B)	Good	38%
C)	Adequate	6%
D)	Fair	6%
E)	Poor	0%

Q7: How well does the franchisor anticipate future trends in how it evolves and markets products and services?

		% answering
A)	**Extremely well**	**38%**
B)	**Pretty well**	**38%**
C)	Adequately	19%
D)	Not very well	0%
E)	Terribly	6%

Q8: How satisfied are you with your franchisor's spending of the royalty fees you pay?

		% answering
A)	Extremely satisfied	25%
B)	**Mostly satisfied**	**50%**
C)	Somewhat satisfied	6%
D)	Not very satisfied	19%
E)	Not satisfied at all	0%

Q9:   **In what ways could the parent company most improve? (Please check those that most apply, no more than three):**

❏   Communications

❏   Counsel/advice on administrative/management issues

❏   Effectiveness of marketing/promotions

❏   Evolution of products/services

❏   Frequency of marketing/promotional campaigns

❏   Quality of products/services

❏   Pricing of products/services to franchisees

❏   Technology (Point of sale systems, usage of computers/email/software, etc.)

❏   Training

Most frequent responses:

	% answering
Technology	56%
Effectiveness of marketing/promotions	44%
Pricing of products/services to franchisees	38%

Q10: **Is your income more, less or about what you expected prior to opening your business?**

	% answering	
More	7%	
Less	**57%**	**Summary: 43% are making about what they**
About what was expected	36%	**expected, or more.**

Q11: **Prior to opening your franchise, which (if any) of the following did you underestimate?**

❏   Amount of working capital required for your first year in business

❏   Difficulty in hiring/retaining quality staff

❏   Expertise required to run the business

❏   Impact of marketing/promotions

❏   Start-up costs

❏   Degree of stress

❏   Workload

Most frequent responses:

	% answering
Amount of working capital required for your 1st year in business (tie)	44%
Difficulty in hiring/retaining quality staff (tie)	44%
Start-up costs (tie)	31%
Degree of stress (tie)	31%

Q12: **If you could turn back time to the day you signed your franchise agreement, would you make the same decision to buy your franchise?**

	% answering
Yes	**60%**
No	40%

*   Number of survey respondents: 16 from 11 different states

Number of survey respondents as a % of total franchise units: 9.41%

CRUISEONE

www.cruiseone.com

Cruise vacation specialist

OVERALL SCORE: 73

1415 NW 62nd Street, Suite 205
Fort Lauderdale, FL 33309
Fax: 954-958-3703
Total number of outlets: 437
Total number of franchise outlets: 437
International: Yes (Puerto Rico)

OVERALL RANK: 67

Phone: 954-958-3700
Franchise fee: $995 or $9,800
Franchise term: 5 years
Initial investment: $6,970 to $26,315
Advertising/Marketing fee: None
Royalty fee: 3% of annual gross sales up to $750,000

SURVEY AND RESULTS *

Q1: About how many hours per week do you dedicate to your franchise business?

		% answering
A)	**Less than 40**	**44%**
B)	41–50	31%
C)	51–60	19%
D)	More than 60	6%
E)	Passive investment	0%

Q2: How would you describe your relations/communications with your franchisor?

		% answering
A)	Excellent	19%
B)	**Good**	**63%**
C)	Adequate	6%
D)	Fair	13%
E)	Poor	0%

Q3: In terms of how your franchisor views your communications with other franchisees, it is:

		% answering
A)	**Very supportive**	**88%**
B)	Not very supportive	0%
C)	No influence	13%

Q4: Is the franchisor fair with you in resolving any grievances?

		% answering
A)	**Extremely fair**	**50%**
B)	Pretty fair	25%
C)	Reasonably fair	13%
D)	Not very fair	13%
E)	Not fair at all	0%

Q5: Are territories equitably granted?

		% answering
A)	**Yes**	**44%**
B)	No	31%
C)	Not yet sure	25%

Q6: How would you describe the initial and ongoing training provided by your franchisor?

		% answering
A)	Excellent	25%
B)	**Good**	**50%**
C)	Adequate	13%
D)	Fair	13%
E)	Poor	0%

Q7: How well does the franchisor anticipate future trends in how it evolves and markets products and services?

		% answering
A)	**Extremely well**	**44%**
B)	Pretty well	25%
C)	Adequately	25%
D)	Not very well	6%
E)	Terribly	0%

Q8: How satisfied are you with your franchisor's spending of the royalty fees you pay?

		% answering
A)	Extremely satisfied	31%
B)	**Mostly satisfied**	**44%**
C)	Somewhat satisfied	25%
D)	Not very satisfied	0%
E)	Not satisfied at all	0%

Q9: **In what ways could the parent company most improve? (Please check those that most apply, no more than three):**

❑ Communications

❑ Counsel/advice on administrative/management issues

❑ Effectiveness of marketing/promotions

❑ Evolution of products/services

❑ Frequency of marketing/promotional campaigns

❑ Quality of products/services

❑ Pricing of products/services to franchisees

❑ Technology (Point of sale systems, usage of computers/email/software, etc.)

❑ Training

Most frequent responses:

	% answering
Technology	63%
Training	38%
Communications (tie)	31%
Counsel/advice on administrative/management issues (tie)	31%
Effectiveness of marketing/promotions (tie)	31%

Q10: **Is your income more, less or about what you expected prior to opening your business?**

	% answering	
More	19%	
Less	**44%**	**Summary: 57% are making about what they**
About what was expected	38%	**expected, or more.**

Q11: **Prior to opening your franchise, which (if any) of the following did you underestimate?**

❑ Amount of working capital required for your 1st year in business

❑ Difficulty in hiring/retaining quality staff

❑ Expertise required to run the business

❑ Impact of marketing/promotions

❑ Start-up costs

❑ Degree of stress

❑ Workload

Most frequent responses:

	% answering
Amount of working capital required for 1st year in business (tie)	50%
Impact of marketing/promotions (tie)	50%
Degree of stress (tie)	31%
Workload (tie)	31%

Q12: **If you could turn back time to the day you signed your franchise agreement, would you make the same decision to buy your franchise?**

	% answering
Yes	75%
No	25%

* Number of survey respondents: 16 from 13 different states

Number of survey respondents as a % of total franchise units: 3.66%

CULLIGAN

www.culligan.com

Water treatment products and services.

OVERALL SCORE: 79

One Culligan Parkway
Northbrook, IL 60062
Fax: 847-205-6005
Total number of outlets: 721
Total number of franchise outlets: 647
International: Yes (worldwide)

OVERALL RANK: 37

Phone: 847-205-6000
Franchise fee: $5,000
Franchise term: 10 years
Initial investment: $104, 500 to $695,000
Advertising/Marketing fee: varies
Royalty fee: varies

SURVEY AND RESULTS *

Q1: About how many hours per week do you dedicate to your franchise business?

		% answering
A)	Less than 40	23%
B)	**41–50**	**38%**
C)	51–60	15%
D)	More than 60	23%
E)	Passive investment	0%

Q2: How would you describe your relations/communications with your franchisor?

		% answering
A)	Excellent	23%
B)	**Good**	**38%**
C)	Adequate	23%
D)	Fair	15%
E)	Poor	0%

Q3: In terms of how your franchisor views your communications with other franchisees, it is:

		% answering
A)	**Very supportive**	**38%**
B)	Not very supportive	23%
C)	**No influence**	**38%**

Q4: Is the franchisor fair with you in resolving any grievances?

		% answering
A)	Extremely fair	8%
B)	Pretty fair	38%
C)	**Reasonably fair**	**42%**
D)	Not very fair	12%
E)	Not fair at all	0%

Q5: Are territories equitably granted?

		% answering
A)	**Yes**	**69%**
B)	No	15%
C)	Not yet sure	15%

Q6: How would you describe the initial and ongoing training provided by your franchisor?

		% answering
A)	Excellent	15%
B)	**Good**	**38%**
C)	Adequate	31%
D)	Fair	8%
E)	Poor	8%

Q7: How well does the franchisor anticipate future trends in how it evolves and markets products and services?

		% answering
A)	Extremely well	8%
B)	**Pretty well**	**46%**
C)	Adequately	31%
D)	Not very well	15%
E)	Terribly	0%

Q8: How satisfied are you with your franchisor's spending of the royalty fees you pay?

		% answering
A)	Extremely satisfied	8%
B)	Mostly satisfied	23%
C)	**Somewhat satisfied**	**38%**
D)	Not very satisfied	31%
E)	Not satisfied at all	0%

Q9: **In what ways could the parent company most improve? (Please check those that most apply, no more than three):**

❏ Communications   ❏ Quality of products/services

❏ Counsel/advice on administrative/management issues   ❏ Pricing of products/services to franchisees

❏ Effectiveness of marketing/promotions   ❏ Technology (Point of sale systems, usage

❏ Evolution of products/services   of computers/email/software, etc.)

❏ Frequency of marketing/promotional campaigns   ❏ Training

Most frequent responses: <u>% answering</u>

Pricing of products/services to franchisees   62%

Effectiveness of marketing/promotions   38%

Training   31%

Q10: **Is your income more, less or about what you expected prior to opening your business?**

	<u>% answering</u>	
More	15%	
Less	**62%**	**Summary: 38% are making about what they**
About what was expected	23%	**expected, or more.**

Q11: **Prior to opening your franchise, which (if any) of the following did you underestimate?**

❏ Amount of working capital required for your   ❏ Start-up costs

    1st year in business   ❏ Degree of stress

❏ Difficulty in hiring/retaining quality staff   ❏ Workload

❏ Expertise required to run the business

❏ Impact of marketing/promotions

Most frequent responses: <u>% answering</u>

Difficulty in hiring/retaining quality staff   54%

Amount of working capital required for 1st year in business   31%

Expertise required to run the business (tie)   31%

Workload (tie)   31%

Q12: **If you could turn back time to the day you signed your franchise agreement, would you make the same decision to buy your franchise?**

		<u>% answering</u>
	Yes	**100%**
	No	0%

* Number of survey respondents: 13 from 12 different states

   Number of survey respondents as a % of total franchise units: 2%

CULVER'S

www.culvers.com

Fast food restaurants offering burgers, grilled sandwiches, salads, and frozen custard desserts.

OVERALL SCORE: 98

540 Water Street
Prairie du Sac, WI 53578
Fax: 608-643-7982
Total number of outlets: 285+
Total number of franchise outlets: 285+
International: No

OVERALL RANK: 1

Phone: 608-643-7980
Franchise fee: $30,000 to $55,000
Franchise term:
Initial investment: $185,000 to $2,923,000
Advertising/Marketing fee: 2% of gross sales monthly
Royalty fee: 4% of gross sales

SURVEY AND RESULTS *

Q1: About how many hours per week do you dedicate to your franchise business?

		% answering
A)	Less than 40	0%
B)	**41–50**	**40%**
C)	**51–60**	**40%**
D)	More than 60	20%
E)	Passive investment	0%

Q2: How would you describe your relations/communications with your franchisor?

		% answering
A)	**Excellent**	**60%**
B)	Good 4	0%
C)	Adequate	0%
D)	Fair	0%
E)	Poor	0%

Q3: In terms of how your franchisor views your communications with other franchisees, it is:

		% answering
A)	**Very supportive**	**70%**
B)	Not very supportive	0%
C)	No influence	30%

Q4: Is the franchisor fair with you in resolving any grievances?

		% answering
A)	Extremely fair	30%
B)	**Pretty fair**	**70%**
C)	Reasonably fair	0%
D)	Not very fair	0%
E)	Not fair at all	0%

Q5: Are territories equitably granted?

		% answering
A)	**Yes**	**90%**
B)	No	10%
C)	Not yet sure	0%

Q6: How would you describe the initial and ongoing training provided by your franchisor?

		% answering
A)	**Excellent**	**50%**
B)	**Good**	**50%**
C)	Adequate	0%
D)	Fair	0%
E)	Poor	0%

Q7: How well does the franchisor anticipate future trends in how it evolves and markets products and services?

		% answering
A)	Extremely well	30%
B)	**Pretty well**	**60%**
C)	Adequately	10%
D)	Not very well	20%
E)	Terribly	20%

Q8: How satisfied are you with your franchisor's spending of the royalty fees you pay?

		% answering
A)	Extremely satisfied	30%
B)	**Mostly satisfied**	**60%**
C)	Somewhat satisfied	0%
D)	Not very satisfied	10%
E)	Not satisfied at all	0%

Q9: **In what ways could the parent company most improve? (Please check those that most apply, no more than three):**

❑ Communications

❑ Counsel/advice on administrative/management issues

❑ Effectiveness of marketing/promotions

❑ Evolution of products/services

❑ Frequency of marketing/promotional campaigns

❑ Quality of products/services

❑ Pricing of products/services to franchisees

❑ Technology (Point of sale systems, usage of computers/email/software, etc.)

❑ Training

Most frequent responses:

	% answering
Evolution of products/services	40%
Effectiveness of marketing/promotions (tie)	30%
Frequency of marketing/promotional campaigns (tie)	30%

Q10: **Is your income more, less or about what you expected prior to opening your business?**

	% answering	
More	20%	
Less	10%	**Summary: 90% are making about what they**
About what was expected	**70%**	**expected, or more.**

Q11: **Prior to opening your franchise, which (if any) of the following did you underestimate?**

❑ Amount of working capital required for your 1st year in business

❑ Difficulty in hiring/retaining quality staff

❑ Expertise required to run the business

❑ Impact of marketing/promotions

❑ Start-up costs

❑ Degree of stress

❑ Workload

Most frequent responses:

	% answering
Difficulty in hiring/retaining quality staff (tie)	50%
Degree of stress (tie)	50%
Impact of marketing/promotions (tie)	20%
Start-up costs (tie)	20%

Q12: **If you could turn back time to the day you signed your franchise agreement, would you make the same decision to buy your franchise?**

	% answering
Yes	**100%**
No	0%

*   Number of survey respondents: 10 from 5 different states

Number of survey respondents as a % of total franchise units: 3.51%

CURVES

www.bodylines.com

Thirty minute workout centers for fitness and weight loss.

OVERALL SCORE: 96

100 Ritchie Road
Waco, TX 76712
Fax:254-399-9731
Total number of outlets: 8000+
Total number of franchise outlets: 8000+
International: Yes (worldwide)

OVERALL RANK: 4

Phone: 800-848-1096
Franchise fee: $29,900
Franchise term: 5 years
Initial investment: $36,425 to $42,850
Advertising/Marketing fee: 3% of gross income,
with a minimum payment of $195 and a maximum of $395.
Royalty fee: 5% of gross income, with a minimum
payment of $195 and a maximum of $795.

SURVEY AND RESULTS *

Q1: About how many hours per week do you dedicate to your franchise business?

		% answering
A)	**Less than 40**	**35%**
B)	41–50	22%
C)	51–60	30%
D)	More than 60	9%
E)	Passive investment	4%

Q2: How would you describe your relations/communications with your franchisor?

		% answering
A)	Excellent	39%
B)	**Good**	**48%**
C)	Adequate	9%
D)	Fair	4%
E)	Poor	0%

Q3: In terms of how your franchisor views your communications with other franchisees, it is:

		% answering
A)	**Very supportive**	**74%**
B)	Not very supportive	4%
C)	No influence	22%

Q4: Is the franchisor fair with you in resolving any grievances?

		% answering
A)	**Extremely fair**	**50%**
B)	Pretty fair	25%
C)	Reasonably fair	20%
D)	Not very fair	5%
E)	Not fair at all	0%

Q5: Are territories equitably granted?

		% answering
A)	Yes	85%
B)	No	5%
C)	Not yet sure	10%

Q6: How would you describe the initial and ongoing training provided by your franchisor?

		% answering
A)	**Excellent**	**61%**
B)	Good	30%
C)	Adequate	0%
D)	Fair	4%
E)	Poor	4%

Q7: How well does the franchisor anticipate future trends in how it evolves and markets products and services?

		% answering
A)	**Extremely well**	**57%**
B)	Pretty well	28%
C)	Adequately	15%
D)	Not very well	0%
E)	Terribly	0%

Q8: How satisfied are you with your franchisor's spending of the royalty fees you pay?

		% answering
A)	**Extremely satisfied**	**45%**
B)	Mostly satisfied	32%
C)	Somewhat satisfied	23%
D)	Not very satisfied	0%
E)	Not satisfied at all	0%

Q9: **In what ways could the parent company most improve? (Please check those that most apply, no more than three):**

❑ Communications
❑ Counsel/advice on administrative/management issues
❑ Effectiveness of marketing/promotions
❑ Evolution of products/services
❑ Frequency of marketing/promotional campaigns

❑ Quality of products/services
❑ Pricing of products/services to franchisees
❑ Technology (Point of sale systems, usage of computers/email/software, etc.)
❑ Training

Most frequent responses:

	% answering
Counsel/advice on administrative/management issues	30%
Pricing of products/services to franchisees	26%
Communications	22%

Q10: **Is your income more, less or about what you expected prior to opening your business?**

	% answering	
More	48%	
Less	19%	**Summary: 81% are making about what they**
About what was expected	33%	**expected, or more.**

Q11: **Prior to opening your franchise, which (if any) of the following did you underestimate?**

❑ Amount of working capital required for your 1st year in business
❑ Difficulty in hiring/retaining quality staff
❑ Expertise required to run the business
❑ Impact of marketing/promotions

❑ Start-up costs
❑ Degree of stress
❑ Workload

Most frequent responses:

	% answering
Difficulty in hiring/retaining quality staff	26%
Impact of marketing/promotions (tie)	22%
Degree of stress (tie)	22%

Q12: **If you could turn back time to the day you signed your franchise agreement, would you make the same decision to buy your franchise?**

	% answering
Yes	100%
No	0%

* Number of survey respondents: 23 from 11 different states
  Number of survey respondents as a % of total franchise units: < 1%

DAIRY QUEEN

www.dairyqueen.com

Fast food restaurant offering hamburgers, chicken sandwiches, ice cream, and more.

OVERALL SCORE: 67

7505 Metro Blvd.
Edina, MN 55439
Fax: 952-830-0301
Total number of outlets: 5,700+
Total number of franchise outlets: 5,700+
International: Yes (worldwide)

OVERALL RANK: 100

Phone: 952-830-0200
Franchise fee: $35,000
Franchise term: The shorter of 15 years or the term of the store's lease
Initial investment: $200,000 to $345,000
Advertising/Marketing fee: 4% of monthly sales
Royalty fee: 3 to 6% of monthly sales

SURVEY AND RESULTS *

Q1: About how many hours per week do you dedicate to your franchise business?

		% answering
A)	Less than 40	13%
B)	41–50	27%
C)	51–60	23%
D)	**More than 60**	**37%**
E)	Passive investment	0%

Q2: How would you describe your relations/communications with your franchisor?

		% answering
A)	Excellent	13%
B)	**Good**	**47%**
C)	Adequate	20%
D)	Fair	7%
E)	Poor	13%

Q3: In terms of how your franchisor views your communications with other franchisees, it is:

		% answering
A)	**Very supportive**	**53%**
B)	Not very supportive	27%
C)	No influence	20%

Q4: Is the franchisor fair with you in resolving any grievances?

		% answering
A)	Extremely fair	7%
B)	**Pretty fair**	**43%**
C)	Reasonably fair	36%
D)	Not very fair	7%
E)	Not fair at all	7%

Q5: Are territories equitably granted?

		% answering
A)	**Yes**	**53%**
B)	No	20%
C)	Not yet sure	27%

Q6: How would you describe the initial and ongoing training provided by your franchisor?

		% answering
A)	Excellent	20%
B)	**Good**	**33%**
C)	Adequate	27%
D)	Fair	7%
E)	Poor	13%

Q7: How well does the franchisor anticipate future trends in how it evolves and markets products and services?

		% answering
A)	**Extremely well**	**27%**
B)	**Pretty well**	**27%**
C)	**Adequately**	**27%**
D)	Not very well	13%
E)	Terribly	7%

Q8: How satisfied are you with your franchisor's spending of the royalty fees you pay?

		% answering
A)	Extremely satisfied	0%
B)	**Mostly satisfied**	**53%**
C)	Somewhat satisfied	20%
D)	Not very satisfied	20%
E)	Not satisfied at all	7%

Q9: **In what ways could the parent company most improve? (Please check those that most apply, no more than three):**

- ❏ Communications
- ❏ Counsel/advice on administrative/management issues
- ❏ Effectiveness of marketing/promotions
- ❏ Evolution of products/services
- ❏ Frequency of marketing/promotional campaigns
- ❏ Quality of products/services
- ❏ Pricing of products/services to franchisees
- ❏ Technology (Point of sale systems, usage of computers/email/software, etc.)
- ❏ Training

Most frequent responses:	% answering
Pricing of products/services to franchisees	53%
Evolution of products/services	47%
Communications	33%

Q10: **Is your income more, less or about what you expected prior to opening your business?**

	% answering	
More	27%	
Less	**40%**	**Summary: 60% are making about what they**
About what was expected	33%	**expected, or more.**

Q11: **Prior to opening your franchise, which (if any) of the following did you underestimate?**

- ❏ Amount of working capital required for your 1st year in business
- ❏ Difficulty in hiring/retaining quality staff
- ❏ Expertise required to run the business
- ❏ Impact of marketing/promotions
- ❏ Start-up costs
- ❏ Degree of stress
- ❏ Workload

Most frequent responses:	% answering
Degree of stress	67%
Difficulty in hiring/retaining quality staff (tie)	53%
Workload (tie)	53%

Q12: **If you could turn back time to the day you signed your franchise agreement, would you make the same decision to buy your franchise?**

	% answering
Yes	73%
No	27%

* Number of survey respondents: 15 from 13 different states
  Number of survey respondents as a % of total franchise units: < 1%

DECK THE WALLS

www.dtwfraninfo.com
Email: eellington@fcibiz.com

Custom framing and wall art.

OVERALL SCORE: 35

12707 North Freeway, Suite 330
Houston, TX 77060
Fax: 281-775-5250
Total number of outlets: 122
Total number of franchise outlets: 122
International: No

OVERALL RANK: 188

Phone: 800-543-3325
Franchise fee: $10,000 to $30,000
Franchise term: 10 years
Initial investment: $71,700 to $245,200
Advertising/Marketing fee: 2% of gross sales wkly.
Royalty fee: 6% of gross sales weekly

SURVEY AND RESULTS *

Q1: About how many hours per week do you dedicate to your franchise business?

		% answering
A)	Less than 40	0%
B)	41–50	0%
C)	51–60	36%
D)	**More than 60**	**64%**
E)	Passive investment	0%

Q2: How would you describe your relations/ communications with your franchisor?

		% answering
A)	Excellent	0%
B)	Good	9%
C)	Adequate	18%
D)	**Fair**	**36%**
E)	**Poor**	**36%**

Q3: In terms of how your franchisor views your communications with other franchisees, it is:

		% answering
A)	Very supportive	27%
B)	Not very supportive	9%
C)	No influence	64%

Q4: Is the franchisor fair with you in resolving any grievances?

		% answering
A)	Extremely fair	0%
B)	Pretty fair	20%
C)	**Reasonably fair**	**60%**
D)	Not very fair	20%
E)	Not fair at all	0%

Q5: Are territories equitably granted?

		% answering
A)	Yes	56%
B)	No	22%
C)	Not yet sure	22%

Q6: How would you describe the initial and ongoing training provided by your franchisor?

		% answering
A)	Excellent	0%
B)	Good	10%
C)	**Adequate**	**36%**
D)	Fair	18%
E)	**Poor**	**36%**

Q7: How well does the franchisor anticipate future trends in how it evolves and markets products and services?

		% answering
A)	Extremely well	0%
B)	Pretty well	0%
C)	Adequately	27%
D)	**Not very well**	**45%**
E)	Terribly	27%

Q8: How satisfied are you with your franchisor's spending of the royalty fees you pay?

		% answering
A)	Extremely satisfied	0%
B)	Mostly satisfied	0%
C)	Somewhat satisfied	18%
D)	Not very satisfied	36%
E)	**Not satisfied at all**	**45%**

Q9: **In what ways could the parent company most improve? (Please check those that most apply, no more than three):**

❏ Communications

❏ Counsel/advice on administrative/management issues

❏ Effectiveness of marketing/promotions

❏ Evolution of products/services

❏ Frequency of marketing/promotional campaigns

❏ Quality of products/services

❏ Pricing of products/services to franchisees

❏ Technology (Point of sale systems, usage of computers/email/software, etc.)

❏ Training

Most frequent responses:	% answering
Effectiveness of marketing/promotions (tie)	73%
Evolution of products/services (tie)	73%
Frequency of marketing/promotional campaigns	45%

Q10: **Is your income more, less or about what you expected prior to opening your business?**

| % answering | |
---|---|---
More | 0% |
Less | **91%** | **Summary: 9% are making about what they**
About what was expected | 9% | **expected, or more.**

Q11: **Prior to opening your franchise, which (if any) of the following did you underestimate?**

❏ Amount of working capital required for your 1st year in business

❏ Difficulty in hiring/retaining quality staff

❏ Expertise required to run the business

❏ Impact of marketing/promotions

❏ Start-up costs

❏ Degree of stress

❏ Workload

Most frequent responses:	% answering
Impact of marketing/promotions (tie)	73%
Workload (tie)	73%
Degree of stress	64%

Q12: **If you could turn back time to the day you signed your franchise agreement, would you make the same decision to buy your franchise?**

	% answering
Yes	45%
No	**55%**

*   Number of survey respondents: 11 from 10 different states

Number of survey respondents as a % of total franchise units: 9.02%

THE DENTIST'S CHOICE

www.thedentistschoice.com
Email: steve@thedentistschoice.com

Dental handpiece repair.

OVERALL SCORE: 78

34700 Coast Highway, Suite 307
Capistrano Beach, CA 92624
Fax: 949-443-2074
Total number of outlets: 69
Total number of franchise outlets: 69
International: No

OVERALL RANK: 43

Phone: 800-757-1333
Franchise fee: $17,500
Franchise term: 10 years
Initial investment: $25,950 to $30,090
Advertising/Marketing fee: None
Royalty fee: varies

SURVEY AND RESULTS *

Q1: About how many hours per week do you dedicate to your franchise business?

		% answering
A)	**Less than 40**	**80%**
B)	41–50	10%
C)	51–60	0%
D)	More than 60	0%
E)	Passive investment	10%

Q2: How would you describe your relations/communications with your franchisor?

		% answering
A)	**Excellent**	**50%**
B)	Good	10%
C)	Adequate	30%
D)	Fair	10%
E)	Poor	0%

Q3: In terms of how your franchisor views your communications with other franchisees, it is:

		% answering
A)	**Very supportive**	**60%**
B)	Not very supportive	0%
C)	No influence	40%

Q4: Is the franchisor fair with you in resolving any grievances?

		% answering
A)	**Extremely fair**	**44%**
B)	Pretty fair	33%
C)	Reasonably fair	22%
D)	Not very fair	0%
E)	Not fair at all	0%

Q5: Are territories equitably granted?

		% answering
A)	**Yes**	**67%**
B)	No	0%
C)	Not yet sure	33%

Q6: How would you describe the initial and ongoing training provided by your franchisor?

		% answering
A)	Excellent	20%
B)	**Good**	**50%**
C)	Adequate	20%
D)	Fair	0%
E)	Poor	10%

Q7: How well does the franchisor anticipate future trends in how it evolves and markets products and services?

		% answering
A)	Extremely well	10%
B)	Pretty well	30%
C)	**Adequately**	**60%**
D)	Not very well	0%
E)	Terribly	0%

Q8: How satisfied are you with your franchisor's spending of the royalty fees you pay?

		% answering
A)	Extremely satisfied	0%
B)	**Mostly satisfied**	**63%**
C)	Somewhat satisfied	38%
D)	Not very satisfied	0%
E)	Not satisfied at all	0%

Q9: **In what ways could the parent company most improve? (Please check those that most apply, no more than three):**

❏ Communications

❏ Counsel/advice on administrative/management issues

❏ Effectiveness of marketing/promotions

❏ Evolution of products/services

❏ Frequency of marketing/promotional campaigns

❏ Quality of products/services

❏ Pricing of products/services to franchisees

❏ Technology (Point of sale systems, usage of computers/email/software, etc.)

❏ Training

Most frequent responses: % answering

Effectiveness of marketing/promotions (tie)   40%

Frequency of marketing/promotional campaigns (tie)   40%

Training (tie)   40%

Q10: **Is your income more, less or about what you expected prior to opening your business?**

	% answering
More	0%
Less	22%
About what was expected	**78%**

Summary: 78% are making about what they expected, or more.

Q11: **Prior to opening your franchise, which (if any) of the following did you underestimate?**

❏ Amount of working capital required for your 1st year in business

❏ Difficulty in hiring/retaining quality staff

❏ Expertise required to run the business

❏ Impact of marketing/promotions

❏ Start-up costs

❏ Degree of stress

❏ Workload

Most frequent responses: % answering

Start-up costs   40%

Expertise required to run the business (tie)   30%

Workload (tie)   30%

Q12: **If you could turn back time to the day you signed your franchise agreement, would you make the same decision to buy your franchise?**

	% answering
Yes	**83%**
No	17%

* Number of survey respondents: 10 from 10 different states

Number of survey respondents as a % of total franchise units: 14.49%

DIET CENTER

www.dietcenterworldwide.com
Email: info@dietcenter.com

Weight loss and weight management program.

OVERALL SCORE: 41

395 Springside Drive
Akron, OH 44333
Fax: 330-666-2197
Total number of outlets: 114
Total number of franchise outlets: 114
International: Yes (Canada & Bermuda)

OVERALL RANK: 184

Phone: 800-656-3294
Franchise fee: $10,000
Franchise term: 10 years
Initial investment: $19,292 to $49,374
Advertising/Marketing fee: Currently $50/month
License fee: $350 per month

SURVEY AND RESULTS *

Q1: About how many hours per week do you dedicate to your franchise business?

		% answering
A)	Less than 40	25%
B)	**41–50**	**67%**
C)	51–60	8%
D)	More than 60	0%
E)	Passive investment	0%

Q2: How would you describe your relations/ communications with your franchisor?

		% answering
A)	Excellent	0%
B)	Good	17%
C)	Adequate	25%
D)	**Fair**	**33%**
E)	Poor	25%

Q3: In terms of how your franchisor views your communications with other franchisees, it is:

		% answering
A)	Very supportive	0%
B)	Not very supportive	36%
C)	**No influence**	**64%**

Q4: Is the franchisor fair with you in resolving any grievances?

		% answering
A)	Extremely fair	0%
B)	Pretty fair	20%
C)	**Reasonably fair**	**40%**
D)	Not very fair	30%
E)	Not fair at all	10%

Q5: Are territories equitably granted?

		% answering
A)	**Yes**	**60%**
B)	No	10%
C)	Not yet sure	30%

Q6: How would you describe the initial and ongoing training provided by your franchisor?

		% answering
A)	Excellent	0%
B)	Good	0%
C)	**Adequate**	**50%**
D)	**Fair**	**50%**
E)	Poor	0%

Q7: How well does the franchisor anticipate future trends in how it evolves and markets products and services?

		% answering
A)	Extremely well	0%
B)	Pretty well	9%
C)	**Adequately**	**55%**
D)	Not very well	36%
E)	Terribly	0%

Q8: How satisfied are you with your franchisor's spending of the royalty fees you pay?

		% answering
A)	Extremely satisfied	0%
B)	Mostly satisfied	0%
C)	Somewhat satisfied	8%
D)	**Not very satisfied**	**50%**
E)	Not satisfied at all	42%

Q9: **In what ways could the parent company most improve? (Please check those that most apply, no more than three):**

❑ Communications
❑ Counsel/advice on administrative/management issues
❑ Effectiveness of marketing/promotions
❑ Evolution of products/services
❑ Frequency of marketing/promotional campaigns

❑ Quality of products/services
❑ Pricing of products/services to franchisees
❑ Technology (Point of sale systems, usage of computers/email/software, etc.)
❑ Training

Most frequent responses:

	% answering
Effectiveness of marketing/promotions	50%
Quality of products/services (tie)	33%
Pricing of products/services to franchisees (tie)	33%
Training (tie)	33%

Q10: **Is your income more, less or about what you expected prior to opening your business?**

	% answering	
More	8%	
Less	**75%**	**Summary: 25% are making about what they**
About what was expected	17%	**expected, or more.**

Q11: **Prior to opening your franchise, which (if any) of the following did you underestimate?**

❑ Amount of working capital required for your 1st year in business
❑ Difficulty in hiring/retaining quality staff
❑ Expertise required to run the business
❑ Impact of marketing/promotions

❑ Start-up costs
❑ Degree of stress
❑ Workload

Most frequent responses:

	% answering
Difficulty in hiring/retaining quality staff (tie)	42%
Impact of marketing/promotions (tie)	42%
Degree of stress (tie)	25%
Workload (tie)	25%

Q12: **If you could turn back time to the day you signed your franchise agreement, would you make the same decision to buy your franchise?**

	% answering
Yes	**50%**
No	**50%**

* Number of survey respondents: 12 from 12 different states
Number of survey respondents as a % of total franchise units: 10.53%

DIPPIN' DOTS

www.dippindots.com

Flash frozen ice cream.

OVERALL SCORE: 69

5110 Charter Oak Drive
Paducah, KY 42001
Fax: 270-575-6997
Total number of outlets: 617
Total number of franchise outlets: 615
International: Yes (several)

OVERALL RANK: 90

Phone: 270-575-6990
Franchise fee: $12,500
Franchise term: 5 years
Initial investment: $69,539 to $214,750
Advertising/Marketing fee: 2% of gross sales wkly.
Royalty fee: 4% of gross sales weekly

SURVEY AND RESULTS *

Q1: About how many hours per week do you dedicate to your franchise business?

		% answering
A)	**Less than 40**	**38%**
B)	41–50	15%
C)	51–60	23%
D)	More than 60	23%
E)	Passive investment	0%

Q2: How would you describe your relations/ communications with your franchisor?

		% answering
A)	Excellent	31%
B)	**Good**	**35%**
C)	Adequate	8%
D)	Fair	19%
E)	Poor	8%

Q3: In terms of how your franchisor views your communications with other franchisees, it is:

		% answering
A)	**Very supportive**	**62%**
B)	Not very supportive	23%
C)	No influence	15%

Q4: Is the franchisor fair with you in resolving any grievances?

		% answering
A)	Extremely fair	23%
B)	**Pretty fair**	**31%**
C)	Reasonably fair	23%
D)	Not very fair	23%
E)	Not fair at all	0%

Q5: Are territories equitably granted?

		% answering
A)	Yes	25%
B)	**No**	**50%**
C)	Not yet sure	25%

Q6: How would you describe the initial and ongoing training provided by your franchisor?

		% answering
A)	**Excellent**	**23%**
B)	Good	15%
C)	**Adequate**	**23%**
D)	Fair	15%
E)	**Poor**	**23%**

Q7: How well does the franchisor anticipate future trends in how it evolves and markets products and services?

		% answering
A)	Extremely well	8%
B)	Pretty well	25%
C)	**Adequately**	**33%**
D)	Not very well	25%
E)	Terribly	8%

Q8: How satisfied are you with your franchisor's spending of the royalty fees you pay?

		% answering
A)	Extremely satisfied	0%
B)	**Mostly satisfied**	**54%**
C)	Somewhat satisfied	15%
D)	Not very satisfied	23%
E)	Not satisfied at all	8%

Q9: **In what ways could the parent company most improve? (Please check those that most apply, no more than three):**

❑ Communications
❑ Counsel/advice on administrative/management issues
❑ Effectiveness of marketing/promotions
❑ Evolution of products/services
❑ Frequency of marketing/promotional campaigns

❑ Quality of products/services
❑ Pricing of products/services to franchisees
❑ Technology (Point of sale systems, usage of computers/email/software, etc.)
❑ Training

Most frequent responses:

	% answering
Pricing of products/services to franchisees	46%
Communications	38%
Counsel/advice on administrative/management issues (tie)	23%
Effectiveness of marketing/promotions (tie)	23%
Evolution of products/services (tie)	23%
Frequency of marketing/promotional campaigns (tie)	23%

Q10: **Is your income more, less or about what you expected prior to opening your business?**

	% answering	
More	8%	
Less	23%	**Summary: 77% are making about what they**
About what was expected	**69%**	**expected, or more.**

Q11: **Prior to opening your franchise, which (if any) of the following did you underestimate?**

❑ Amount of working capital required for your 1st year in business
❑ Difficulty in hiring/retaining quality staff
❑ Expertise required to run the business
❑ Impact of marketing/promotions

❑ Start-up costs
❑ Degree of stress
❑ Workload

Most frequent responses:

	% answering
Difficulty in hiring/retaining quality staff (tie)	38%
Degree of stress (tie)	38%
Workload	23%

Q12: **If you could turn back time to the day you signed your franchise agreement, would you make the same decision to buy your franchise?**

	% answering
Yes	**83%**
No	17%

* Number of survey respondents: 13 from 11 different states
Number of survey respondents as a % of total franchise units: 2.11%

DOLLAR DISCOUNT STORES

www.dollardiscount.com
Email: info@dollardiscount.com

Retailer of a wide variety of items that sell for $1.00 or less.

OVERALL SCORE: 57

1362 Naamans Creek Road
Boothwyn, PA 19061
Fax: 610-485-6439
Total number of outlets: 140+
Total number of franchise outlets: 140+
International: No

OVERALL RANK: 152

Phone: 800-227-5314
Franchise fee: $18,000
Franchise term: 10 years
Initial investment: $99,000 to $195,000
Advertising/Marketing fee: 1% of gross receipts
Royalty fee: 3% of gross receipts weekly, up to
$1,000,000 per year; 1.5% of gross sales above
$1,000,000 during the same calendar year.

SURVEY AND RESULTS *

Q1: About how many hours per week do you dedicate to your franchise business?

		% answering
A)	Less than 40	6%
B)	41–50	25%
C)	51–60	31%
D)	**More than 60**	**38%**
E)	Passive investment	0%

Q2: How would you describe your relations/ communications with your franchisor?

		% answering
A)	Excellent	19%
B)	**Good**	**50%**
C)	Adequate	13%
D)	Fair	19%
E)	Poor	0%

Q3: In terms of how your franchisor views your communications with other franchisees, it is:

		% answering
A)	**Very supportive**	**50%**
B)	Not very supportive	0%
C)	**No influence**	**50%**

Q4: Is the franchisor fair with you in resolving any grievances?

		% answering
A)	Extremely fair	33%
B)	**Pretty fair**	**47%**
C)	Reasonably fair	20%
D)	Not very fair	0%
E)	Not fair at all	0%

Q5: Are territories equitably granted?

		% answering
A)	**Yes**	**44%**
B)	No	25%
C)	Not yet sure	31%

Q6: How would you describe the initial and ongoing training provided by your franchisor?

		% answering
A)	Excellent	25%
B)	**Good**	**31%**
C)	Adequate	0%
D)	Fair	19%
E)	Poor	25%

Q7: How well does the franchisor anticipate future trends in how it evolves and markets products and services?

		% answering
A)	Extremely well	13%
B)	**Pretty well**	**44%**
C)	Adequately	13%
D)	Not very well	25%
E)	Terribly	6%

Q8: How satisfied are you with your franchisor's spending of the royalty fees you pay?

		% answering
A)	Extremely satisfied	13%
B)	Mostly satisfied	25%
C)	**Somewhat satisfied**	**38%**
D)	Not very satisfied	19%
E)	Not satisfied at all	6%

Q9: **In what ways could the parent company most improve? (Please check those that most apply, no more than three):**

❏ Communications

❏ Counsel/advice on administrative/management issues

❏ Effectiveness of marketing/promotions

❏ Evolution of products/services

❏ Frequency of marketing/promotional campaigns

❏ Quality of products/services

❏ Pricing of products/services to franchisees

❏ Technology (Point of sale systems, usage of computers/email/software, etc.)

❏ Training

Most frequent responses: <u>% answering</u>

Frequency of marketing/promotional campaigns   63%

Effectiveness of marketing/promotions   44%

Communications   25%

Q10: **Is your income more, less or about what you expected prior to opening your business?**

	<u>% answering</u>	
More	0%	
Less	**69%**	**Summary: 31% are making about what they**
About what was expected	31%	**expected, or more.**

Q11: **Prior to opening your franchise, which (if any) of the following did you underestimate?**

❏ Amount of working capital required for your 1st year in business

❏ Difficulty in hiring/retaining quality staff

❏ Expertise required to run the business

❏ Impact of marketing/promotions

❏ Start-up costs

❏ Degree of stress

❏ Workload

Most frequent responses: <u>% answering</u>

Workload   50%

Difficulty in hiring/retaining quality staff   38%

Degree of stress   31%

Q12: **If you could turn back time to the day you signed your franchise agreement, would you make the same decision to buy your franchise?**

	<u>% answering</u>
Yes	**63%**
No	38%

*   Number of survey respondents: 16 from 12 different states

Number of survey respondents as a % of total franchise units: 11.43%

DOMINO'S PIZZA

www.dominos.com

Fast-food pizza, delivered.

OVERALL SCORE: 67

OVERALL RANK: 102

30 Frank Lloyd Wright Drive
Ann Arbor, MI 48106
Fax: 734-747-6210
Total number of outlets: 7,500+
Total number of franchise outlets: 6,375+
International: Yes (worldwide)

Phone: 888-366-4667
Franchise fee:
Franchise term:
Initial investment:
Advertising/Marketing fee:
Royalty fee:

SURVEY AND RESULTS *

Q1: About how many hours per week do you dedicate to your franchise business?

		% answering
A)	Less than 40	23%
B)	41–50	23%
C)	51–60	15%
D)	**More than 60**	**38%**
E)	Passive investment	0%

Q2: How would you describe your relations/communications with your franchisor?

		% answering
A)	Excellent	14%
B)	**Good**	**50%**
C)	Adequate	0%
D)	Fair	36%
E)	Poor	0%

Q3: In terms of how your fanchisor views your communications with other franchisees, it is:

		% answering
A)	**Very supportive**	**43%**
B)	Not very supportive	14%
C)	**No influence**	**43%**

Q4: Is the franchisor fair with you in resolving any grievances?

		% answering
A)	Extremely fair	21%
B)	Pretty fair	21%
C)	**Reasonably fair**	**43%**
D)	Not very fair	7%
E)	Not fair at all	7%

Q5: Are territories equitably granted?

		% answering
A)	Yes	36%
B)	**No**	**57%**
C)	Not yet sure	7%

Q6: How would you describe the initial and ongoing training provided by your franchisor?

		% answering
A)	Excellent	14%
B)	**Good**	**43%**
C)	Adequate	14%
D)	Fair	7%
E)	Poor	7%

Q7: How well does the franchisor anticipate future trends in how it evolves and markets products and services?

		% answering
A)	Extremely well	36%
B)	**Pretty well**	**50%**
C)	Adequately	7%
D)	Not very well	7%
E)	Terribly	0%

Q8: How satisfied are you with your franchisor's spending of the royalty fees you pay?

		% answering
A)	Extremely satisfied	7%
B)	Mostly satisfied	29%
C)	**Somewhat satisfied**	**43%**
D)	Not very satisfied	0%
E)	Not satisfied at all	21%

Q9: **In what ways could the parent company most improve? (Please check those that most apply, no more than three):**

❑ Communications
❑ Counsel/advice on administrative/management issues
❑ Effectiveness of marketing/promotions
❑ Evolution of products/services
❑ Frequency of marketing/promotional campaigns

❑ Quality of products/services
❑ Pricing of products/services to franchisees
❑ Technology (Point of sale systems, usage of computers/email/software, etc.)
❑ Training

Most frequent responses:	% answering
Effectiveness of marketing/promotions	50%
Frequency of marketing/promotional campaigns (tie)	36%
Pricing of products/services to franchisees (tie)	36%

Q10: **Is your income more, less or about what you expected prior to opening your business?**

	% answering	
More	14%	
Less	36%	**Summary: 64% are making about what they**
About what was expected	**50%**	**expected, or more.**

Q11: **Prior to opening your franchise, which (if any) of the following did you underestimate?**

❑ Amount of working capital required for your 1st year in business
❑ Difficulty in hiring/retaining quality staff
❑ Expertise required to run the business
❑ Impact of marketing/promotions

❑ Start-up costs
❑ Degree of stress
❑ Workload

Most frequent responses:	% answering
Degree of stress	50%
Amount of working capital required for 1st year in business (tie)	36%
Workload (tie)	36%

Q12: **If you could turn back time to the day you signed your franchise agreement, would you make the same decision to buy your franchise?**

	% answering
Yes	**79%**
No	21%

* Number of survey respondents: 14 from 12 different states
Number of survey respondents as a % of total franchise units: < 1%

DR. VINYL

www.drvinyl.com

Restoration and repair of vinyl, leather, and plastic covered surfaces.

OVERALL SCORE: 69

821 Northwest Commerce Drive
Lee's Summit, MO 64086
Fax:
Total number of outlets: 198
Total number of franchise outlets: 198
International: Yes (worldwide)
Advertising/Marketing fee: 1% of gross sales monthly

OVERALL RANK: 89

Phone: 816-525-6060
Franchise fee: $32,500 for territories up to
200,000; $32,500 plus $2,500 for each additional
10,000 in population over 200,000
Franchise term: 10 years
Initial investment: $44,000 to $69,500
Royalty fee: varies year-to-year

SURVEY AND RESULTS *

Q1: About how many hours per week do you dedicate to your franchise business?

		% answering
A)	Less than 40	14%
B)	**41–50**	**47%**
C)	51–60	25%
D)	More than 60	14%
E)	Passive investment	0%

Q2: How would you describe your relations/communications with your franchisor?

		% answering
A)	Excellent	29%
B)	**Good**	**43%**
C)	Adequate	21%
D)	Fair	7%
E)	Poor	0%

Q3: In terms of how your franchisor views your communications with other franchisees, it is:

		% answering
A)	**Very supportive**	**79%**
B)	Not very supportive	14%
C)	No influence	7%

Q4: Is the franchisor fair with you in resolving any grievances?

		% answering
A)	**Extremely fair**	**36%**
B)	**Pretty fair**	**36%**
C)	Reasonably fair	21%
D)	Not very fair	7%
E)	Not fair at all	0%

Q5: Are territories equitably granted?

		% answering
A)	**Yes**	**100%**
B)	No	0%
C)	Not yet sure	0%

Q6: How would you describe the initial and ongoing training provided by your franchisor?

		% answering
A)	**Excellent**	**36%**
B)	Good	29%
C)	Adequate	21%
D)	Fair	7%
E)	Poor	0%

Q7: How well does the franchisor anticipate future trends in how it evolves and markets products and services?

		% answering
A)	**Extremely well**	**36%**
B)	**Pretty well**	**36%**
C)	Adequately	21%
D)	Not very well	7%
E)	Terribly	0%

Q8: How satisfied are you with your franchisor's spending of the royalty fees you pay?

		% answering
A)	Extremely satisfied	15%
B)	Mostly satisfied	23%
C)	**Somewhat satisfied**	**38%**
D)	Not very satisfied	15%
E)	Not satisfied at all	8%

Q9: **In what ways could the parent company most improve? (Please check those that most apply, no more than three):**

- ❏ Communications
- ❏ Counsel/advice on administrative/management issues
- ❏ Effectiveness of marketing/promotions
- ❏ Evolution of products/services
- ❏ Frequency of marketing/promotional campaigns

- ❏ Quality of products/services
- ❏ Pricing of products/services to franchisees
- ❏ Technology (Point of sale systems, usage of computers/email/software, etc.)
- ❏ Training

Most frequent responses:	% answering
Effectiveness of marketing/promotions	50%
Frequency of marketing/promotional campaigns	36%
Pricing of products/services to franchisees (tie)	29%
Training (tie)	29%

Q10: **Is your income more, less or about what you expected prior to opening your business?**

	% answering	
More	29%	
Less	21%	**Summary: 79% are making about what they**
About what was expected	**50%**	**expected, or more.**

Q11: **Prior to opening your franchise, which (if any) of the following did you underestimate?**

- ❏ Amount of working capital required for your 1st year in business
- ❏ Difficulty in hiring/retaining quality staff
- ❏ Expertise required to run the business
- ❏ Impact of marketing/promotions

- ❏ Start-up costs
- ❏ Degree of stress
- ❏ Workload

Most frequent responses:	% answering
Difficulty in hiring/retaining quality staff	57%
Impact of marketing/promotions (tie)	21%
Degree of stress (tie)	21%

Q12: **If you could turn back time to the day you signed your franchise agreement, would you make the same decision to buy your franchise?**

	% answering
Yes	**57%**
No	43%

* Number of survey respondents: 14 from 13 different states
   Number of survey respondents as a % of total franchise units: 7.07%

DREAMMAKER BATH & KITCHEN

www.dreammaker-remodel.com
Email: dreammaker@dwyergroup.com

Refurbishing and remodeling of baths & kitchens to residential and commercial customers.

OVERALL SCORE: 83

1010-1020 North University Parks Drive
Waco, TX 76707
Fax: 254-745-2588
Total number of outlets: 235
Total number of franchise outlets: 235
International: Yes (worldwide)

OVERALL RANK: 19

Phone: 800-583-9099
Franchise fee: $27,000
Franchise term: 10 years
Initial investment: $64,092 to $113,000
Advertising/Marketing fee: varies
Royalty fee: varies

SURVEY AND RESULTS *

Q1: About how many hours per week do you dedicate to your franchise business?

		% answering
A)	Less than 40	20%
B)	**41–50**	**27%**
C)	**51–60**	**47%**
D)	More than 60	7%
E)	Passive investment	0%

Q2: How would you describe your relations/communications with your franchisor?

		% answering
A)	**Excellent**	**60%**
B)	Good	40%
C)	Adequate	0%
D)	Fair	0%
E)	Poor	0%

Q3: In terms of how your franchisor views your communications with other franchisees, it is:

		% answering
A)	**Very supportive**	**87%**
B)	Not very supportive	7%
C)	No influence	7%

Q4: Is the franchisor fair with you in resolving any grievances?

		% answering
A)	**Extremely fair**	**64%**
B)	Pretty fair	29%
C)	Reasonably fair	7%
D)	Not very fair	0%
E)	Not fair at all	0%

Q5: Are territories equitably granted?

		% answering
A)	**Yes**	**80%**
B)	No	0%
C)	Not yet sure	20%

Q6: How would you describe the initial and ongoing training provided by your franchisor?

		% answering
A)	Excellent	40%
B)	**Good**	**53%**
C)	Adequate	0%
D)	Fair	7%
E)	Poor	0%

Q7: How well does the franchisor anticipate future trends in how it evolves and markets products and services?

		% answering
A)	Extremely well	40%
B)	**Pretty well**	**53%**
C)	Adequately	7%
D)	Not very well	0%
E)	Terribly	0%

Q8: How satisfied are you with your franchisor's spending of the royalty fees you pay?

		% answering
A)	Extremely satisfied	33%
B)	**Mostly satisfied**	**60%**
C)	Somewhat satisfied	7%
D)	Not very satisfied	0%
E)	Not satisfied at all	0%

Q9: In what ways could the parent company most improve? (Please check those that most apply, no more than three):

- ❏ Communications
- ❏ Counsel/advice on administrative/management issues
- ❏ Effectiveness of marketing/promotions
- ❏ Evolution of products/services
- ❏ Frequency of marketing/promotional campaigns

- ❏ Quality of products/services
- ❏ Pricing of products/services to franchisees
- ❏ Technology (Point of sale systems, usage of computers/email/software, etc.)
- ❏ Training

Most frequent responses:	% answering
Pricing of products/services to franchisees (tie)	40%
Technology (tie)	40%
Frequency of marketing/promotional campaigns (tie)	27%
Quality of products/services (tie)	27%

Q10: Is your income more, less or about what you expected prior to opening your business?

	% answering	
More	15%	
Less	38%	**Summary: 61% are making about what they**
About what was expected	**46%**	**expected, or more.**

Q11: Prior to opening your franchise, which (if any) of the following did you underestimate?

- ❏ Amount of working capital required for your first year in business
- ❏ Difficulty in hiring/retaining quality staff
- ❏ Expertise required to run the business
- ❏ Impact of marketing/promotions

- ❏ Start-up costs
- ❏ Degree of stress
- ❏ Workload

Most frequent responses:	% answering
Amount of working capital required for your first year in business	53%
Degree of stress	47%
Expertise required to run the business (tie)	40%
Start-up costs (tie)	40%

Q12: If you could turn back time to the day you signed your franchise agreement, would you make the same decision to buy your franchise?

	% answering
Yes	**87%**
No	13%

* Number of survey respondents: 15 from 13 different states
   Number of survey respondents as a % of total franchise units: 6.38%

DUNKIN' DONUTS

www.dunkindonuts.com

Fast food coffee, donuts, and other breakfast items.

OVERALL SCORE: 82

130 Royall Street
Canton, MA 02021
Fax: 818-996-5163
Total number of outlets: 6,000+ (4,400 in U.S.)
Total number of franchise outlets: 6,000+
International:Yes (worldwide)

OVERALL RANK: N/A

Phone: 800-777-9983
Franchise fee:
Franchise term:
Initial investment:
Advertising/Marketing fee:
Royalty fee:

SURVEY AND RESULTS *

Q1: About how many hours per week do you dedicate to your franchise business?

		% answering
A)	Less than 40	11%
B)	**41–50**	**33%**
C)	**51–60**	**33%**
D)	More than 60	22%
E)	Passive investment	0%

Q2: How would you describe your relations/ communications with your franchisor?

		% answering
A)	Excellent	33%
B)	**Good**	**56%**
C)	Adequate	0%
D)	Fair	0%
E)	Poor	11%

Q3: In terms of how your franchisor views your communications with other franchisees, it is:

		% answering
A)	**Very supportive**	**78%**
B)	Not very supportive	22%
C)	No influence	0%

Q4: Is the franchisor fair with you in resolving any grievances?

		% answering
A)	**Extremely fair**	**33%**
B)	**Pretty fair**	**33%**
C)	Reasonably fair	22%
D)	Not very fair	0%
E)	Not fair at all	11%

Q5: Are territories equitably granted?

		% answering
A)	**Yes**	**63%**
B)	No	25%
C)	Not yet sure	13%

Q6: How would you describe the initial and ongoing training provided by your franchisor?

		% answering
A)	Excellent	22%
B)	**Good**	**78%**
C)	Adequate	0%
D)	Fair	0%
E)	Poor	0%

Q7: How well does the franchisor anticipate future trends in how it evolves and markets products and services?

		% answering
A)	Extremely well	22%
B)	**Pretty well**	**44%**
C)	Adequately	33%
D)	Not very well	0%
E)	Terribly	0%

Q8: How satisfied are you with your franchisor's spending of the royalty fees you pay?

		% answering
A)	Extremely satisfied	0%
B)	**Mostly satisfied**	**67%**
C)	Somewhat satisfied	22%
D)	Not very satisfied	11%
E)	Not satisfied at all	0%

Q9: **In what ways could the parent company most improve? (Please check those that most apply, no more than three):**

❏ Communications
❏ Counsel/advice on administrative/management issues
❏ Effectiveness of marketing/promotions
❏ Evolution of products/services
❏ Frequency of marketing/promotional campaigns

❏ Quality of products/services
❏ Pricing of products/services to franchisees
❏ Technology (Point of sale systems, usage of computers/email/software, etc.)
❏ Training

Most frequent responses:	% answering
Communications (tie)	44%
Evolution of products/services (tie)	44%
Effectiveness of marketing/promotions (tie)	33%
Technology (tie)	33%

Q10: **Is your income more, less or about what you expected prior to opening your business?**

	% answering	
More	33%	
Less	22%	**Summary: 77% are making about what they**
About what was expected	**44%**	**expected, or more.**

Q11: **Prior to opening your franchise, which (if any) of the following did you underestimate?**

❏ Amount of working capital required for your 1st year in business
❏ Difficulty in hiring/retaining quality staff
❏ Expertise required to run the business
❏ Impact of marketing/promotions

❏ Start-up costs
❏ Degree of stress
❏ Workload

Most frequent responses:	% answering
Difficulty in hiring/retaining quality staff	56%
Amount of working capital required for 1st year in business	44%
Start-up costs	33%

Q12: **If you could turn back time to the day you signed your franchise agreement, would you make the same decision to buy your franchise?**

	% answering
Yes	**89%**
No	11%

* Number of survey respondents: 9 from 8 different states
   Number of survey respondents as a % of total franchise units: <1%

DURACLEAN

www.duraclean.com
Email: franchise@duraclean.com

Various interior cleaning services to commercial and residential customers.

OVERALL SCORE: 71

220 West Campus Drive
Arlington Heights, IL 60006
Fax: 847-704-7101
Total number of outlets: 371 (213 in U.S.)
Total number of franchise outlets: 371
International:Yes (worldwide)

OVERALL RANK: 81

Phone: 800-251-7070
Franchise fee: $19,999 or $34,999
Franchise term: 5 years
Initial investment: $25,099 to $81,499
Advertising/Marketing fee: none
Royalty fee: varies

SURVEY AND RESULTS *

Q1: About how many hours per week do you dedicate to your franchise business?

		% answering
A)	Less than 40	23%
B)	**41–50**	**38%**
C)	51–60	31%
D)	More than 60	8%
E)	Passive investment	0%

Q2: How would you describe your relations/ communications with your franchisor?

		% answering
A)	**Excellent**	**46%**
B)	Good	38%
C)	Adequate	8%
D)	Fair	8%
E)	Poor	0%

Q3: In terms of how your franchisor views your communications with other franchisees, it is:

		% answering
A)	**Very supportive**	**46%**
B)	Not very supportive	8%
C)	**No influence**	**46%**

Q4: Is the franchisor fair with you in resolving any grievances?

		% answering
A)	**Extremely fair**	**46%**
B)	Pretty fair	23%
C)	Reasonably fair	23%
D)	Not very fair	8%
E)	Not fair at all	0%

Q5: Are territories equitably granted?

		% answering
A)	**Yes**	**92%**
B)	No	8%
C)	Not yet sure	0%

Q6: How would you describe the initial and ongoing training provided by your franchisor?

		% answering
A)	**Excellent**	**38%**
B)	Good	31%
C)	Adequate	23%
D)	Fair	8%
E)	Poor	0%

Q7: How well does the franchisor anticipate future trends in how it evolves and markets products and services?

		% answering
A)	Extremely well	23%
B)	**Pretty well**	**31%**
C)	Adequately	15%
D)	**Not very well**	**31%**
E)	Terribly	0%

Q8: How satisfied are you with your franchisor's spending of the royalty fees you pay?

		% answering
A)	Extremely satisfied	8%
B)	**Mostly satisfied**	**31%**
C)	**Somewhat satisfied**	**31%**
D)	Not very satisfied	23%
E)	Not satisfied at all	8%

Q9: **In what ways could the parent company most improve? (Please check those that most apply, no more than three):**

❑ Communications

❑ Counsel/advice on administrative/management issues

❑ Effectiveness of marketing/promotions

❑ Evolution of products/services

❑ Frequency of marketing/promotional campaigns

❑ Quality of products/services

❑ Pricing of products/services to franchisees

❑ Technology (Point of sale systems, usage of computers/email/software, etc.)

❑ Training

Most frequent responses:	% answering
Effectiveness of marketing/promotions (tie)	62%
Frequency of marketing/promotional campaigns (tie)	62%
Evolution of products/services (tie)	31%
Pricing of products/services to franchisees (tie)	31%

Q10: **Is your income more, less or about what you expected prior to opening your business?**

	% answering	
More	15%	
Less	**46%**	**Summary: 53% are making about what they**
About what was expected	38%	**expected, or more.**

Q11: **Prior to opening your franchise, which (if any) of the following did you underestimate?**

❑ Amount of working capital required for your 1st year in business

❑ Difficulty in hiring/retaining quality staff

❑ Expertise required to run the business

❑ Impact of marketing/promotions

❑ Start-up costs

❑ Degree of stress

❑ Workload

Most frequent responses:	% answering
Amount of working capital required for 1st year in business (tie)	54%
Difficulty in hiring/retaining quality staff (tie)	54%
Impact of marketing/promotions (tie)	23%
Start-up costs (tie)	23%
Workload (tie)	23%

Q12: **If you could turn back time to the day you signed your franchise agreement, would you make the same decision to buy your franchise?**

	% answering
Yes	**69%**
No	31%

* Number of survey respondents: 13 from 12 different states

Number of survey respondents as a % of total franchise units: 3.5%

EMBROIDME

www.embroidme.com

Logo customization or design embroidered on a wide range of apparel, gifts, and promotional items.

OVERALL SCORE: 44

1801 South Australian Avenue
West Palm Beach, FL 33409
Fax: 561-640-6062
Total number of outlets: 150+
Total number of franchise outlets: 150+
International: No

OVERALL RANK: 175

Phone: 800-727-6720
Franchise fee: $$19,500 or $35,500
Franchise term: 35 years
Initial investment: $44,560 to $216,413
Advertising/Marketing fee: 1% of gross revenues, monthly
Royalty fee: 5% of gross revenues, monthly

SURVEY AND RESULTS *

Q1: About how many hours per week do you dedicate to your franchise business?

		% answering
A)	Less than 40	10%
B)	41–50	2%
C)	51–60	36%
D)	**More than 60**	**52%**
E)	Passive investment	0%

Q2: How would you describe your relations/communications with your franchisor?

		% answering
A)	Excellent	16%
B)	**Good**	**30%**
C)	Adequate	18%
D)	Fair	23%
E)	Poor	14%

Q3: In terms of how your franchisor views your communications with other franchisees, it is:

		% answering
A)	**Very supportive**	**59%**
B)	Not very supportive	18%
C)	No influence	23%

Q4: Is the franchisor fair with you in resolving any grievances?

		% answering
A)	Extremely fair	11%
B)	**Pretty fair**	**39%**
C)	Reasonably fair	28%
D)	Not very fair	6%
E)	Not fair at all	17%

Q5: Are territories equitably granted?

		% answering
A)	**Yes**	**45%**
B)	No	23%
C)	Not yet sure	32%

Q6: How would you describe the initial and ongoing training provided by your franchisor?

		% answering
A)	Excellent	14%
B)	Good	23%
C)	**Adequate**	**27%**
D)	Fair	18%
E)	Poor	18%

Q7: How well does the franchisor anticipate future trends in how it evolves and markets products and services?

		% answering
A)	Extremely well	5%
B)	Pretty well	32%
C)	**Adequately**	**41%**
D)	Not very well	9%
E)	Terribly	14%

Q8: How satisfied are you with your franchisor's spending of the royalty fees you pay?

		% answering
A)	Extremely satisfied	9%
B)	Mostly satisfied	23%
C)	**Somewhat satisfied**	**27%**
D)	Not very satisfied	23%
E)	Not satisfied at all	18%

Q9: **In what ways could the parent company most improve? (Please check those that most apply, no more than three):**

❑ Communications
❑ Counsel/advice on administrative/management issues
❑ Effectiveness of marketing/promotions
❑ Evolution of products/services
❑ Frequency of marketing/promotional campaigns

❑ Quality of products/services
❑ Pricing of products/services to franchisees
❑ Technology (Point of sale systems, usage of computers/email/software, etc.)
❑ Training

Most frequent responses:	% answering
Effectiveness of marketing/promotions	59%
Frequency of marketing/promotional campaigns	45%
Technology	41%

Q10: **Is your income more, less or about what you expected prior to opening your business?**

	% answering	
More	0%	
Less	**86%**	**Summary: 14% are making about what they**
About what was expected	14%	**expected, or more.**

Q11: **Prior to opening your franchise, which (if any) of the following did you underestimate?**

❑ Amount of working capital required for your 1st year in business
❑ Difficulty in hiring/retaining quality staff
❑ Expertise required to run the business
❑ Impact of marketing/promotions

❑ Start-up costs
❑ Degree of stress
❑ Workload

Most frequent responses:	% answering
Amount of working capital required for 1st year in business	73%
Difficulty in hiring/retaining quality staff	55%
Degree of stress (tie)	50%
Workload (tie)	50%

Q12: **If you could turn back time to the day you signed your franchise agreement, would you make the same decision to buy your franchise?**

	% answering
Yes	40%
No	**60%**

* Number of survey respondents: 22 from 15 different states
Number of survey respondents as a % of total franchise units: 14.67%

EXPRESS PERSONNEL SERVICES

www.expressfranchising.com
Email: franchising@expresspersonnel.com

World's largest staffing and professional placement services firm.

OVERALL SCORE: 87

8516 Northwest Expressway
Oklahoma City, OK 73132
Total number of outlets: 400+
Total number of franchise outlets: 400+
International: Yes (several countries)

OVERALL RANK: 11

Phone: 877-652-6400
Franchise fee: $25,000
Franchise term: 5 years
Initial investment: $130,000–$160,000
Advertising/Marketing fee: varies
Royalty fee: varies

SURVEY AND RESULTS *

Q1: About how many hours per week do you dedicate to your franchise business?

		% answering
A)	Less than 40	0%
B)	41–50	33%
C)	51–60	25%
D)	**More than 60**	**42%**
E)	Passive investment	0%

Q2: How would you describe your relations/communications with your franchisor?

		% answering
A)	**Excellent**	**67%**
B)	Good	5%
C)	Adequate	0%
D)	Fair	8%
E)	Poor	0%

Q3: In terms of how your franchisor views your communications with other franchisees, it is:

		% answering
A)	**Very supportive**	**75%**
B)	Not very supportive	17%
C)	No influence	8%

Q4: Is the franchisor fair with you in resolving any grievances?

		% answering
A)	**Extremely fair**	**75%**
B)	Pretty fair	17%
C)	Reasonably fair	8%
D)	Not very fair	0%
E)	Not fair at all	0%

Q5: Are territories equitably granted?

		% answering
A)	**Yes**	**83%**
B)	No	8%
C)	Not yet sure	8%

Q6: How would you describe the initial and ongoing training provided by your franchisor?

		% answering
A)	**Excellent**	**71%**
B)	Good	21%
C)	Adequate	8%
D)	Fair	0%
E)	Poor	0%

Q7: How well does the franchisor anticipate future trends in how it evolves and markets products and services?

		% answering
A)	Extremely well	33%
B)	**Pretty well**	**42%**
C)	Adequately	17%
D)	Not very well	8%
E)	Terribly	0%

Q8: How satisfied are you with your franchisor's spending of the royalty fees you pay?

		% answering
A)	Extremely satisfied	8%
B)	**Mostly satisfied**	**50%**
C)	Somewhat satisfied	33%
D)	Not very satisfied	8%
E)	Not satisfied at all	0%

Q9: **In what ways could the parent company most improve? (Please check those that most apply, no more than three):**

❑ Communications
❑ Counsel/advice on administrative/management issues
❑ Effectiveness of marketing/promotions
❑ Evolution of products/services
❑ Frequency of marketing/promotional campaigns

❑ Quality of products/services
❑ Pricing of products/services to franchisees
❑ Technology (Point of sale systems, usage of computers/email/software, etc.)
❑ Training

Most frequent responses:

	% answering
Technology	50%
Effectiveness of marketing/promotions (tie)	33%
Evolution of products/services (tie)	33%
Pricing of products/services to franchisees (tie)	33%

Q10: **Is your income more, less or about what you expected prior to opening your business?**

	% answering
More	**42%**
Less	33%
About what was expected	25%

Summary: 77% are making about what they expected, or more.

Q11: **Prior to opening your franchise, which (if any) of the following did you underestimate?**

❑ Amount of working capital required for your 1st year in business
❑ Difficulty in hiring/retaining quality staff
❑ Expertise required to run the business
❑ Impact of marketing/promotions

❑ Start-up costs
❑ Degree of stress
❑ Workload

Most frequent responses:

	% answering
Difficulty in hiring/retaining quality staff	58%
Amount of working capital required for 1st year in business (tie)	42%
Degree of stress (tie)	42%

Q12: **If you could turn back time to the day you signed your franchise agreement, would you make the same decision to buy your franchise?**

	% answering
Yes	**92%**
No	8%

* Number of survey respondents: 12 from 11 different states
Number of survey respondents as a % of total franchise units: 3%

EXPRESS TAX

www.expresstaxservice.com
Email: franchise@expresstaxservice.com

Personal federal and state tax return preparation and filing.

OVERALL SCORE: 87

3030 Hartley Road, Suite 320
Jacksonville, FL 32257
Fax: 904-262-2864
Total number of outlets: 202
Total number of franchise outlets: 202
International: No

OVERALL RANK: N/A

Phone: 888-417-4461
Franchise fee: $5,000
Franchise term: 10 years
Initial investment: $9,900 to $16,550
Advertising/Marketing fee: none currently
Royalty fee: $2 to $12 per filed return

SURVEY AND RESULTS *

Q1: About how many hours per week do you dedicate to your franchise business?

		% answering
A)	**Less than 40**	**40%**
B)	41–50	20%
C)	**51–60**	**40%**
D)	More than 60	0%
E)	Passive investment	0%

Q2: How would you describe your relations/communications with your franchisor?

		% answering
A)	Excellent	33%
B)	**Good**	**50%**
C)	Adequate	17%
D)	Fair	0%
E)	Poor	0%

Q3: In terms of how your franchisor views your communications with other franchisees, it is:

		% answering
A)	**Very supportive**	**67%**
B)	Not very supportive	0%
C)	No influence	33%

Q4: Is the franchisor fair with you in resolving any grievances?

		% answering
A)	**Extremely fair**	**50%**
B)	**Pretty fair**	**50%**
C)	Reasonably fair	0%
D)	Not very fair	0%
E)	Not fair at all	0%

Q5: Are territories equitably granted?

		% answering
A)	**Yes**	**80%**
B)	No	0%
C)	Not yet sure	20%

Q6: How would you describe the initial and ongoing training provided by your franchisor?

		% answering
A)	Excellent	17%
B)	**Good**	**83%**
C)	Adequate	0%
D)	Fair	0%
E)	Poor	0%

Q7: How well does the franchisor anticipate future trends in how it evolves and markets products and services?

		% answering
A)	Extremely well	20%
B)	**Pretty well**	**80%**
C)	Adequately	0%
D)	Not very well	0%
E)	Terribly	0%

Q8: How satisfied are you with your franchisor's spending of the royalty fees you pay?

		% answering
A)	Extremely satisfied	20%
B)	**Mostly satisfied**	**60%**
C)	Somewhat satisfied	20%
D)	Not very satisfied	0%
E)	Not satisfied at all	0%

Q9: **In what ways could the parent company most improve? (Please check those that most apply, no more than three):**

❏ Communications
❏ Counsel/advice on administrative/management issues
❏ Effectiveness of marketing/promotions
❏ Evolution of products/services
❏ Frequency of marketing/promotional campaigns

❏ Quality of products/services
❏ Pricing of products/services to franchisees
❏ Technology (Point of sale systems, usage of computers/email/software, etc.)
❏ Training

Most frequent responses:	% answering
Frequency of marketing/promotional campaigns	50%
Communications (tie)	17%
Effectiveness of marketing/promotions (tie)	17%
Pricing of products/services to franchisees (tie)	17%
Training (tie)	17%

Q10: **Is your income more, less or about what you expected prior to opening your business?**

	% answering	
More	17%	
Less	33%	Summary: 67% are making about what they
About what was expected	**50%**	expected, or more.

Q11: **Prior to opening your franchise, which (if any) of the following did you underestimate?**

❏ Amount of working capital required for your 1st year in business
❏ Difficulty in hiring/retaining quality staff
❏ Expertise required to run the business
❏ Impact of marketing/promotions

❏ Start-up costs
❏ Degree of stress
❏ Workload

Most frequent responses:	% answering
Degree of stress	50%
Difficulty in hiring/retaining quality staff	33%
Impact of marketing/promotions (tie)	17%
Workload (tie)	17%

Q12: **If you could turn back time to the day you signed your franchise agreement, would you make the same decision to buy your franchise?**

	% answering
Yes	**100%**
No	0%

* Number of survey respondents: 6 from 3 different states
Number of survey respondents as a % of total franchise units: 2.97%

FAST FRAME

www.fastframe.com
Email: info@fastframe.com

Custom picture framing.

OVERALL SCORE: 58

1200 Lawrence Drive, Suite 300
Newbury Park, CA 91320
Total number of outlets: 250+
Total number of franchise outlets: 250+
International: Yes (several countries)

OVERALL RANK: 147

Phone: 888-TO-FRAME
Franchise fee: $25,000
Franchise term: 10 years
Initial investment: $105,700 to $150,200
Advertising/Marketing fee: 3%
Royalty fee: 7.5% of monthly gross receipts

SURVEY AND RESULTS *

Q1: About how many hours per week do you dedicate to your franchise business?

		% answering
A)	Less than 40	20%
B)	41–50	13%
C)	**51–60**	**53%**
D)	More than 60	7%
E)	Passive investment	7%

Q2: How would you describe your relations/ communications with your franchisor?

		% answering
A)	Excellent	27%
B)	**Good**	**47%**
C)	Adequate	13%
D)	Fair	0%
E)	Poor	13%

Q3: In terms of how your franchisor views your communications with other franchisees, it is:

		% answering
A)	**Very supportive**	**64%**
B)	Not very supportive	0%
C)	No influence	36%

Q4: Is the franchisor fair with you in resolving any grievances?

		% answering
A)	**Extremely fair**	**33%**
B)	**Pretty fair**	**33%**
C)	Reasonably fair	27%
D)	Not very fair	7%
E)	Not fair at all	0%

Q5: Are territories equitably granted?

		% answering
A)	**Yes**	**71%**
B)	No	21%
C)	Not yet sure	7%

Q6: How would you describe the initial and ongoing training provided by your franchisor?

		% answering
A)	Excellent	7%
B)	**Good**	**43%**
C)	Adequate	34%
D)	Fair	13%
E)	Poor	3%

Q7: How well does the franchisor anticipate future trends in how it evolves and markets products and services?

		% answering
A)	Extremely well	13%
B)	**Pretty well**	**60%**
C)	Adequately	20%
D)	Not very well	7%
E)	Terribly	0%

Q8: How satisfied are you with your franchisor's spending of the royalty fees you pay?

		% answering
A)	Extremely satisfied	13%
B)	**Mostly satisfied**	**33%**
C)	Somewhat satisfied	27%
D)	Not very satisfied	20%
E)	Not satisfied at all	7%

Q9: **In what ways could the parent company most improve? (Please check those that most apply, no more than three):**

- ❑ Communications
- ❑ Counsel/advice on administrative/management issues
- ❑ Effectiveness of marketing/promotions
- ❑ Evolution of products/services
- ❑ Frequency of marketing/promotional campaigns

- ❑ Quality of products/services
- ❑ Pricing of products/services to franchisees
- ❑ Technology (Point of sale systems, usage of computers/email/software, etc.)
- ❑ Training

Most frequent responses:

	% answering
Counsel/advice on administrative/management issues (tie)	33%
Effectiveness of marketing/promotions (tie)	33%
Technology (tie)	33%
Training (tie)	33%

Q10: **Is your income more, less or about what you expected prior to opening your business?**

	% answering	
More	0%	
Less	**53%**	**Summary: 47% are making about what they**
About what was expected	47%	**expected, or more.**

Q11: **Prior to opening your franchise, which (if any) of the following did you underestimate?**

- ❑ Amount of working capital required for your 1st year in business
- ❑ Difficulty in hiring/retaining quality staff
- ❑ Expertise required to run the business
- ❑ Impact of marketing/promotions

- ❑ Start-up costs
- ❑ Degree of stress
- ❑ Workload

Most frequent responses:

	% answering
Difficulty in hiring/retaining quality staff (tie)	33%
Degree of stress (tie)	33%
Amount of working capital required for 1st year in business	27%

Q12: **If you could turn back time to the day you signed your franchise agreement, would you make the same decision to buy your franchise?**

	% answering
Yes	**80%**
No	20%

* Number of survey respondents: 15 from 11 different states

Number of survey respondents as a % of total franchise units: 6%

FAST SIGNS

www.fastsigns.com
Email: bill.mcpherson@fastsigns.com

Computer-aided design of custom graphics, banners, and signs.

OVERALL SCORE: 84

2550 Midway Road, Suite 150
Carrollton, TX 75006
Fax: 972-248-8201
Total number of outlets: 492
Total number of franchise outlets: 492
International: Yes (several countries)

OVERALL RANK: 16

Phone: 800-827-7446
Franchise fee: $20,000
Franchise term: 20 years
Initial investment: $24,533 to $282,955
Advertising/Marketing fee: 2% of gross sales/mo.
Royalty fee: 6% of gross sales, monthly

SURVEY AND RESULTS *

Q1: About how many hours per week do you dedicate to your franchise business?

		% answering
A)	Less than 40	7%
B)	41–50	27%
C)	51–60	27%
D)	**More than 60**	**40%**
E)	Passive investment	0%

Q2: How would you describe your relations/ communications with your franchisor?

		% answering
A)	Excellent	47%
B)	**Good**	**53%**
C)	Adequate	0%
D)	Fair	0%
E)	Poor	0%

Q3: In terms of how your franchisor views your communications with other franchisees, it is:

		% answering
A)	**Very supportive**	**87%**
B)	Not very supportive	0%
C)	No influence	13%

Q4: Is the franchisor fair with you in resolving any grievances?

		% answering
A)	**Extremely fair**	**47%**
B)	**Pretty fair**	**47%**
C)	Reasonably fair	7%
D)	Not very fair	0%
E)	Not fair at all	0%

Q5: Are territories equitably granted?

		% answering
A)	**Yes**	**67%**
B)	No	20%
C)	Not yet sure	13%

Q6: How would you describe the initial and ongoing training provided by your franchisor?

		% answering
A)	**Excellent**	**73%**
B)	Good	27%
C)	Adequate	33%
D)	Fair	33%
E)	Poor	33%

Q7: How well does the franchisor anticipate future trends in how it evolves and markets products and services?

		% answering
A)	**Extremely well**	**80%**
B)	Pretty well	20%
C)	Adequately	0%
D)	Not very well	0%
E)	Terribly	0%

Q8: How satisfied are you with your franchisor's spending of the royalty fees you pay?

		% answering
A)	Extremely satisfied	13%
B)	**Mostly satisfied**	**73%**
C)	Somewhat satisfied	13%
D)	Not very satisfied	0%
E)	Not satisfied at all	0%

Q9: **In what ways could the parent company most improve? (Please check those that most apply, no more than three):**

❑ Communications
❑ Counsel/advice on administrative/management issues
❑ Effectiveness of marketing/promotions
❑ Evolution of products/services
❑ Frequency of marketing/promotional campaigns

❑ Quality of products/services
❑ Pricing of products/services to franchisees
❑ Technology (Point of sale systems, usage of computers/email/software, etc.)
❑ Training

Most frequent responses:

	% answering
Counsel/advice on administrative/management issues	33%
Effectiveness of marketing/promotions (tie)	20%
Pricing of products/services to franchisees (tie)	20%
Training (tie)	20%

Q10: **Is your income more, less or about what you expected prior to opening your business?**

	% answering	
More	23%	
Less	**38%**	**Summary: 61% are making about what they**
About what was expected	**38%**	**expected, or more.**

Q11: **Prior to opening your franchise, which (if any) of the following did you underestimate?**

❑ Amount of working capital required for your 1st year in business
❑ Difficulty in hiring/retaining quality staff
❑ Expertise required to run the business
❑ Impact of marketing/promotions

❑ Start-up costs
❑ Degree of stress
❑ Workload

Most frequent responses:

	% answering
Difficulty in hiring/retaining quality staff (tie)	47%
Workload (tie)	47%
Amount of working capital required for 1st year in business (tie)	40%
Degree of stress (tie)	40%

Q12: **If you could turn back time to the day you signed your franchise agreement, would you make the same decision to buy your franchise?**

	% answering
Yes	**87%**
No	13%

* Number of survey respondents: 15 from 13 different states
Number of survey respondents as a % of total franchise units: 3.05%

FIDUCIAL

www.fiducial.com

Email: franchise@fiducial.com

A full service provider of "back office" services to small businesses, including accounting, payroll, taxes and consulting services.

OVERALL SCORE: 47

10480 Little Patuxent Parkway, Third Floor
Columbia, MD 21044
Fax: 410-910-5903
Total number of outlets: 383
Total number of franchise outlets: 383
International: No

OVERALL RANK: 170

Phone: 800-323-9000
Franchise fee: $25,000
Franchise term: 10 years
Initial investment: $45,200 to $116,305
Advertising/Marketing fee: varies
Royalty fee: varies

SURVEY AND RESULTS *

Q1: About how many hours per week do you dedicate to your franchise business?

		% answering
A)	Less than 40	17%
B)	**41–50**	**44%**
C)	51–60	22%
D)	More than 60	17%
E)	Passive investment	0%

Q2: How would you describe your relations/communications with your franchisor?

		% answering
A)	Excellent	6%
B)	Good	6%
C)	Adequate	11%
D)	Fair	22%
E)	**Poor**	**56%**

Q3: In terms of how your franchisor views your communications with other franchisees, it is:

		% answering
A)	Very supportive	31%
B)	Not very supportive	31%
C)	**No influence**	**38%**

Q4: Is the franchisor fair with you in resolving any grievances?

		% answering
A)	Extremely fair	13%
B)	Pretty fair	6%
C)	**Reasonably fair**	**44%**
D)	Not very fair	13%
E)	Not fair at all	25%

Q5: Are territories equitably granted?

		% answering
A)	Yes	29%
B)	**No**	**35%**
C)	**Not yet sure**	**35%**

Q6: How would you describe the initial and ongoing training provided by your franchisor?

		% answering
A)	Excellent	11%
B)	Good	31%
C)	Adequate	0%
D)	Fair	22%
E)	**Poor**	**36%**

Q7: How well does the franchisor anticipate future trends in how it evolves and markets products and services?

		% answering
A)	Extremely well	6%
B)	Pretty well	17%
C)	**Adequately**	**28%**
D)	Not very well	22%
E)	**Terribly**	**28%**

Q8: How satisfied are you with your franchisor's spending of the royalty fees you pay?

		% answering
A)	Extremely satisfied	0%
B)	Mostly satisfied	6%
C)	Somewhat satisfied	22%
D)	Not very satisfied	28%
E)	**Not satisfied at all**	**44%**

Q9: **In what ways could the parent company most improve? (Please check those that most apply, no more than three):**

❑ Communications

❑ Counsel/advice on administrative/management issues

❑ Effectiveness of marketing/promotions

❑ Evolution of products/services

❑ Frequency of marketing/promotional campaigns

❑ Quality of products/services

❑ Pricing of products/services to franchisees

❑ Technology (Point of sale systems, usage of computers/email/software, etc.)

❑ Training

Most frequent responses:	**% answering**
Communications	61%
Effectiveness of marketing/promotions (tie)	50%
Training (tie)	50%

Q10: **Is your income more, less or about what you expected prior to opening your business?**

	% answering	
More	13%	
Less	38%	**Summary: 63% are making about what they**
About what was expected	**50%**	**expected, or more.**

Q11: **Prior to opening your franchise, which (if any) of the following did you underestimate?**

❑ Amount of working capital required for your 1st year in business

❑ Difficulty in hiring/retaining quality staff

❑ Expertise required to run the business

❑ Impact of marketing/promotions

❑ Start-up costs

❑ Degree of stress

❑ Workload

Most frequent responses:	**% answering**
Degree of stress	39%
Amount of working capital required for 1st year in business	33%
Workload	28%

Q12: **If you could turn back time to the day you signed your franchise agreement, would you make the same decision to buy your franchise?**

	% answering
Yes	**50%**
No	**50%**

* Number of survey respondents: 18 from 16 different states

Number of survey respondents as a % of total franchise units: 4.70%

FISH WINDOW CLEANING

www.fishwindowcleaning.com

Professional window cleaning.

OVERALL SCORE: 68

200 Enchanted Parkway
Manchester, MO 63021
Fax: 636-530-7856
Total number of outlets: 146
Total number of franchise outlets: 146
International: No
Royalty fee: 6% to 8% weekly, depending
upon amount of gross sales generated

OVERALL RANK: 92

Phone: 877-807-FISH
Franchise fee: $24,500 to $49,500
Franchise term: 10 years
Initial investment: $55,700 to $115,800
Advertising/Marketing fee: 1/2% of gross sales weekly

SURVEY AND RESULTS *

Q1: About how many hours per week do you dedicate to your franchise business?

		% answering
A)	Less than 40	13%
B)	**41–50**	**38%**
C)	51–60	25%
D)	More than 60	25%
E)	Passive investment	0%

Q2: How would you describe your relations/communications with your franchisor?

		% answering
A)	**Excellent**	**38%**
B)	Good	29%
C)	Adequate	10%
D)	Fair	14%
E)	Poor	10%

Q3: In terms of how your franchisor views your communications with other franchisees, it is:

		% answering
A)	**Very supportive**	**85%**
B)	Not very supportive	10%
C)	No influence	5%

Q4: Is the franchisor fair with you in resolving any grievances?

		% answering
A)	**Extremely fair**	**45%**
B)	Pretty fair	29%
C)	Reasonably fair	24%
D)	Not very fair	5%
E)	Not fair at all	0%

Q5: Are territories equitably granted?

		% answering
A)	**Yes**	**95%**
B)	No	5%
C)	Not yet sure	0%

Q6: How would you describe the initial and ongoing training provided by your franchisor?

		% answering
A)	**Excellent**	**43%**
B)	Good	40%
C)	Adequate	5%
D)	Fair	12%
E)	Poor	0%

Q7: How well does the franchisor anticipate future trends in how it evolves and markets products and services?

		% answering
A)	Extremely well	24%
B)	**Pretty well**	**52%**
C)	Adequately	14%
D)	Not very well	10%
E)	Terribly	0%

Q8: How satisfied are you with your franchisor's spending of the royalty fees you pay?

		% answering
A)	Extremely satisfied	10%
B)	**Mostly satisfied**	**43%**
C)	Somewhat satisfied	33%
D)	Not very satisfied	14%
E)	Not satisfied at all	0%

Q9: **In what ways could the parent company most improve? (Please check those that most apply, no more than three):**

❑ Communications

❑ Counsel/advice on administrative/management issues

❑ Effectiveness of marketing/promotions

❑ Evolution of products/services

❑ Frequency of marketing/promotional campaigns

❑ Quality of products/services

❑ Pricing of products/services to franchisees

❑ Technology (Point of sale systems, usage of computers/email/software, etc.)

❑ Training

Most frequent responses:	% answering
Effectiveness of marketing/promotions	57%
Communications (tie)	38%
Frequency of marketing/promotional campaigns (tie)	38%

Q10: **Is your income more, less or about what you expected prior to opening your business?**

	% answering	
More	5%	
Less	**70%**	**Summary: 30% are making about what they**
About what was expected	25%	**expected, or more.**

Q11: **Prior to opening your franchise, which (if any) of the following did you underestimate?**

❑ Amount of working capital required for your 1st year in business

❑ Difficulty in hiring/retaining quality staff

❑ Expertise required to run the business

❑ Impact of marketing/promotions

❑ Start-up costs

❑ Degree of stress

❑ Workload

Most frequent responses:	% answering
Difficulty in hiring/retaining quality staff	76%
Amount of working capital required for 1st year in business	38%
Start-up costs (tie)	33%
Degree of stress (tie)	33%

Q12: **If you could turn back time to the day you signed your franchise agreement, would you make the same decision to buy your franchise?**

	% answering
Yes	**75%**
No	25%

* Number of survey respondents: 21 from 16 different states

Number of survey respondents as a % of total franchise units: 14.38%

FLOOR COVERINGS INTERNATIONAL

www.floorcoveringsinternational.com
Email: info@carpetvan.com

Flooring specialist with mobile service to present over 3,000 styles and colors to you in your home.

OVERALL SCORE: 64

5182B Old Dixie Highway
Forest Park, GA 30297
Fax: 404-366-4406
Total number of outlets: 92 (# in United Kingdom not included)
Total number of franchise outlets: 92
International: Yes (Canada, United Kingdom)
Royalty fee: varies

OVERALL RANK: 118

Phone: 800-955-4324
Franchise fee: $30,000 plus an additional $0.35 for each additional household over 70,000 within your territory
Franchise term: 5 years
Initial investment: $65,600 to $99,900
Advertising/Marketing fee: > of $50 or 1% of gross sales monthly

SURVEY AND RESULTS *

Q1: About how many hours per week do you dedicate to your franchise business?

		% answering
A)	Less than 40	27%
B)	41–50	9%
C)	**51–60**	**55%**
D)	More than 60	9%
E)	Passive investment	0%

Q2: How would you describe your relations/communications with your franchisor?

		% answering
A)	**Excellent**	**27%**
B)	**Good**	**27%**
C)	Adequate	18%
D)	Fair	9%
E)	Poor	18%

Q3: In terms of how your franchisor views your communications with other franchisees, it is:

		% answering
A)	**Very supportive**	**55%**
B)	Not very supportive	18%
C)	No influence	27%

Q4: Is the franchisor fair with you in resolving any grievances?

		% answering
A)	**Extremely fair**	**36%**
B)	Pretty fair	27%
C)	Reasonably fair	27%
D)	Not very fair	9%
E)	Not fair at all	0%

Q5: Are territories equitably granted?

		% answering
A)	**Yes**	**82%**
B)	No	18%
C)	Not yet sure	0%

Q6: How would you describe the initial and ongoing training provided by your franchisor?

		% answering
A)	Excellent	18%
B)	**Good**	**45%**
C)	Adequate	9%
D)	Fair	18%
E)	Poor	9%

Q7: How well does the franchisor anticipate future trends in how it evolves and markets products and services?

		% answering
A)	Extremely well	0%
B)	**Pretty well**	**64%**
C)	Adequately	18%
D)	Not very well	18%
E)	Terribly	0%

Q8: How satisfied are you with your franchisor's spending of the royalty fees you pay?

		% answering
A)	Extremely satisfied	0%
B)	**Mostly satisfied**	**40%**
C)	Somewhat satisfied	30%
D)	Not very satisfied	0%
E)	Not satisfied at all	30%

Q9: **In what ways could the parent company most improve? (Please check those that most apply, no more than three):**

❏ Communications
❏ Counsel/advice on administrative/management issues
❏ Effectiveness of marketing/promotions
❏ Evolution of products/services
❏ Frequency of marketing/promotional campaigns

❏ Quality of products/services
❏ Pricing of products/services to franchisees
❏ Technology (Point of sale systems, usage of computers/email/software, etc.)
❏ Training

Most frequent responses:	% answering
Pricing of products/services to franchisees	55%
Effectiveness of marketing/promotions	45%
Frequency of marketing/promotional campaigns (tie)	27%
Technology (tie)	27%

Q10: **Is your income more, less or about what you expected prior to opening your business?**

	% answering	
More	20%	
Less	**50%**	**Summary: 50% are making about what they**
About what was expected	30%	**expected, or more.**

Q11: **Prior to opening your franchise, which (if any) of the following did you underestimate?**

❏ Amount of working capital required for your 1st year in business
❏ Difficulty in hiring/retaining quality staff
❏ Expertise required to run the business
❏ Impact of marketing/promotions

❏ Start-up costs
❏ Degree of stress
❏ Workload

Most frequent responses:	% answering
Amount of working capital required for 1st year in business (tie)	45%
Impact of marketing/promotions (tie)	45%
Expertise required to run the business	36%

Q12: **If you could turn back time to the day you signed your franchise agreement, would you make the same decision to buy your franchise?**

	% answering
Yes	**64%**
No	36%

*   Number of survey respondents: 11 from 9 different states
Number of survey respondents as a % of total franchise units: 11.96%

FOX'S PIZZA DEN

www.foxspizza.com
Email: info@foxspizza.com

Restaurant offering pizza, salads and sandwiches.

OVERALL SCORE: 58

3243 Old Frankstown Road
Pittsburgh, PA 15239
Total number of outlets: 220+
Total number of franchise outlets: 220+
International: No

OVERALL RANK: 148

Phone: 800-899-3697
Franchise fee: $8,000
Franchise term: 5 years
Initial investment: $68,250
Advertising/Marketing fee: none
Royalty fee: $200 per month

SURVEY AND RESULTS *

Q1: About how many hours per week do you dedicate to your franchise business?

		% answering
A)	Less than 40	0%
B)	41–50	25%
C)	51–60	25%
D)	**More than 60**	**50%**
E)	Passive investment	0%

Q2: How would you describe your relations/communications with your franchisor?

		% answering
A)	**Excellent**	**33%**
B)	Good	25%
C)	**Adequate**	**33%**
D)	Fair	0%
E)	Poor	8%

Q3: In terms of how your franchisor views your communications with other franchisees, it is:

		% answering
A)	Very supportive	27%
B)	Not very supportive	9%
C)	**No influence**	**64%**

Q4: Is the franchisor fair with you in resolving any grievances?

		% answering
A)	**Extremely fair**	**43%**
B)	Pretty fair	29%
C)	Reasonably fair	29%
D)	Not very fair	0%
E)	Not fair at all	0%

Q5: Are territories equitably granted?

		% answering
A)	**Yes**	**100%**
B)	No	0%
C)	Not yet sure	0%

Q6: How would you describe the initial and ongoing training provided by your franchisor?

		% answering
A)	Excellent	17%
B)	Good	25%
C)	**Adequate**	**33%**
D)	Fair	8%
E)	Poor	17%

Q7: How well does the franchisor anticipate future trends in how it evolves and markets products and services?

		% answering
A)	Extremely well	0%
B)	Pretty well	17%
C)	Adequately	17%
D)	**Not very well**	**58%**
E)	Terribly	8%

Q8: How satisfied are you with your franchisor's spending of the royalty fees you pay?

		% answering
A)	Extremely satisfied	13%
B)	Mostly satisfied	0%
C)	**Somewhat satisfied**	**50%**
D)	Not very satisfied	25%
E)	Not satisfied at all	13%

Q9: **In what ways could the parent company most improve? (Please check those that most apply, no more than three):**

❏ Communications
❏ Counsel/advice on administrative/management issues
❏ Effectiveness of marketing/promotions
❏ Evolution of products/services
❏ Frequency of marketing/promotional campaigns

❏ Quality of products/services
❏ Pricing of products/services to franchisees
❏ Technology (Point of sale systems, usage of computers/email/software, etc.)
❏ Training

Most frequent responses:

	% answering
Communications	50%
Effectiveness of marketing/promotions (tie)	42%
Frequency of marketing/promotional campaigns (tie)	42%
Pricing of products/services to franchisees (tie)	42%

Q10: **Is your income more, less or about what you expected prior to opening your business?**

	% answering	
More	8%	
Less	**67%**	**Summary: 33% are making about what they**
About what was expected	25%	**expected, or more.**

Q11: **Prior to opening your franchise, which (if any) of the following did you underestimate?**

❏ Amount of working capital required for your 1st year in business
❏ Difficulty in hiring/retaining quality staff
❏ Expertise required to run the business
❏ Impact of marketing/promotions

❏ Start-up costs
❏ Degree of stress
❏ Workload

Most frequent responses:

	% answering
Degree of stress	75%
Workload	50%
Amount of working capital required for 1st year in business (tie)	33%
Difficulty in hiring/retaining quality staff (tie)	33%

Q12: **If you could turn back time to the day you signed your franchise agreement, would you make the same decision to buy your franchise?**

	% answering
Yes	**67%**
No	33%

* Number of survey respondents: 12 from 8 different states
Number of survey respondents as a % of total franchise units: 5.45%

FURNITURE MEDIC

www.furnituremedicfranchise.com

The world's largest provider of furniture and wood restoration and repair.

OVERALL SCORE: 48

3839 Forest Hill-Irene Road
Memphis, TN 38125
Total number of outlets: 600
Total number of franchise outlets: 600
International: Yes (several countries)
Royalty fee: varies

OVERALL RANK: 169

Phone: 800-255-9687
Franchise fee: $4,500 to $22,500
Franchise term: 5 years
Initial investment: $17,105 to $81,894
Advertising/Marketing fee: > of $50 per month
or 1% of gross sales

SURVEY AND RESULTS *

Q1: About how many hours per week do you dedicate to your franchise business?

		% answering
A)	Less than 40	6%
B)	**41–50**	**33%**
C)	**51–60**	**33%**
D)	More than 60	28%
E)	Passive investment	0%

Q2: How would you describe your relations/communications with your franchisor?

		% answering
A)	Excellent	5%
B)	**Good**	**32%**
C)	Adequate	26%
D)	Fair	11%
E)	Poor	26%

Q3: In terms of how your franchisor views your communications with other franchisees, it is:

		% answering
A)	**Very supportive**	**42%**
B)	Not very supportive	18%
C)	No influence	4%

Q4: Is the franchisor fair with you in resolving any grievances?

		% answering
A)	Extremely fair	25%
B)	**Pretty fair**	**31%**
C)	Reasonably fair	25%
D)	Not very fair	19%
E)	Not fair at all	0%

Q5: Are territories equitably granted?

		% answering
A)	**Yes**	**58%**
B)	No	32%
C)	Not yet sure	11%

Q6: How would you describe the initial and ongoing training provided by your franchisor?

		% answering
A)	Excellent	11%
B)	Good	26%
C)	**Adequate**	**39%**
D)	Fair	13%
E)	Poor	11%

Q7: How well does the franchisor anticipate future trends in how it evolves and markets products and services?

		% answering
A)	Extremely well	11%
B)	Pretty well	22%
C)	**Adequately**	**28%**
D)	**Not very well**	**28%**
E)	Terribly	11%

Q8: How satisfied are you with your franchisor's spending of the royalty fees you pay?

		% answering
A)	Extremely satisfied	6%
B)	Mostly satisfied	22%
C)	Somewhat satisfied	28%
D)	Not very satisfied	11%
E)	**Not satisfied at all**	**33%**

Q9:   In what ways could the parent company most improve? (Please check those that most apply, no more than three):

❑   Communications   ❑   Quality of products/services
❑   Counsel/advice on administrative/management issues   ❑   Pricing of products/services to franchisees
❑   Effectiveness of marketing/promotions   ❑   Technology (Point of sale systems, usage
❑   Evolution of products/services   of computers/email/software, etc.)
❑   Frequency of marketing/promotional campaigns   ❑   Training

Most frequent responses: % answering
Frequency of marketing/promotional campaigns   58%
Pricing of products/services to franchisees   42%
Effectiveness of marketing/promotions   37%

Q10: Is your income more, less or about what you expected prior to opening your business?

	% answering	
More	0%	
Less	**72%**	**Summary: 28% are making about what they**
About what was expected	28%	**expected, or more.**

Q11: Prior to opening your franchise, which (if any) of the following did you underestimate?

❑   Amount of working capital required for your   ❑   Start-up costs
     1st year in business   ❑   Degree of stress
❑   Difficulty in hiring/retaining quality staff   ❑   Workload
❑   Expertise required to run the business
❑   Impact of marketing/promotions

Most frequent responses: % answering
Difficulty in hiring/retaining quality staff   42%
Amount of working capital required for 1st year in business   32%
Impact of marketing/promotions (tie)   26%
Degree of stress (tie)   26%

**Q12: If you could turn back time to the day you signed your franchise agreement, would you make the same decision
        to buy your franchise?**

	% answering
Yes	47%
No	**53%**

*   Number of survey respondents: 19 from 14 different states
     Number of survey respondents as a % of total franchise units: 3.17%

GEEKS ON CALL

www.geeksoncall.com
Email: info@geeksoncall.com

On-site computer service and support for consumer and commercial customers.

OVERALL SCORE: 67

814 Kempsville Road, Suite 106
Norfolk, VA 23502
Fax: 888-466-6946
Total number of outlets: 158
Total number of franchise outlets: 158
International: No

OVERALL RANK: N/A

Phone: 888-667-4577, ext. 307
Franchise fee: $25,000
Franchise term: 10 years
Initial investment: $53,350 to $82,150
Advertising/Marketing fee: $250 per week
Royalty fee: 11% of gross service revenues, wkly.

SURVEY AND RESULTS *

Q1: About how many hours per week do you dedicate to your franchise business?

		% answering
A)	Less than 40	17%
B)	41–50	0%
C)	51–60	17%
D)	**More than 60**	**33%**
E)	**Passive investment**	**33%**

Q2: How would you describe your relations/communications with your franchisor?

		% answering
A)	Excellent	17%
B)	**Good**	**50%**
C)	Adequate	0%
D)	Fair	3%
E)	Poor	0%

Q3: In terms of how your franchisor views your communications with other franchisees, it is:

		% answering
A)	**Very supportive**	**67%**
B)	Not very supportive	0%
C)	No influence	33%

Q4: Is the franchisor fair with you in resolving any grievances?

		% answering
A)	Extremely fair	0%
B)	**Pretty fair**	**50%**
C)	Reasonably fair	17%
D)	Not very fair	17%
E)	Not fair at all	17%

Q5: Are territories equitably granted?

		% answering
A)	**Yes**	**50%**
B)	No	33%
C)	Not yet sure	17%

Q6: How would you describe the initial and ongoing training provided by your franchisor?

		% answering
A)	Excellent	0%
B)	Good	17%
C)	**Adequate**	**33%**
D)	Fair	17%
E)	**Poor**	**33%**

Q7: How well does the franchisor anticipate future trends in how it evolves and markets products and services?

		% answering
A)	Extremely well	0%
B)	**Pretty well**	**50%**
C)	Adequately	17%
D)	Not very well	33%
E)	Terribly	0%

Q8: How satisfied are you with your franchisor's spending of the royalty fees you pay?

		% answering
A)	Extremely satisfied	0%
B)	**Mostly satisfied**	**33%**
C)	Somewhat satisfied	17%
D)	**Not very satisfied**	**33%**
E)	Not satisfied at all	17%

Q9: **In what ways could the parent company most improve? (Please check those that most apply, no more than three):**

❑ Communications
❑ Counsel/advice on administrative/management issues
❑ Effectiveness of marketing/promotions
❑ Evolution of products/services
❑ Frequency of marketing/promotional campaigns

❑ Quality of products/services
❑ Pricing of products/services to franchisees
❑ Technology (Point of sale systems, usage of computers/email/software, etc.)
❑ Training

Most frequent responses:	% answering
Communications (tie)	50%
Effectiveness of marketing/promotions (tie)	50%
Counsel/advice on administrative/management issues (tie)	33%
Frequency of marketing/promotional campaigns (tie)	33%
Pricing of products/services to franchisees (tie)	33%
Technology (tie)	33%

Q10: **Is your income more, less or about what you expected prior to opening your business?**

	% answering	
More	33%	
Less	33%	**Summary: 66% are making about what they**
About what was expected	33%	**expected, or more.**

Q11: **Prior to opening your franchise, which (if any) of the following did you underestimate?**

❑ Amount of working capital required for your 1st year in business
❑ Difficulty in hiring/retaining quality staff
❑ Expertise required to run the business
❑ Impact of marketing/promotions

❑ Start-up costs
❑ Degree of stress
❑ Workload

Most frequent responses:	% answering
Difficulty in hiring/retaining quality staff (tie)	83%
Degree of stress (tie)	83%
Workload	50%

Q12: **If you could turn back time to the day you signed your franchise agreement, would you make the same decision to buy your franchise?**

	% answering
Yes	83%
No	17%

* Number of survey respondents: 6 from 5 different states
Number of survey respondents as a % of total franchise units: 3.80%

GLORIA JEAN'S COFFEES

www.gloriajeans.com

Retailer of gourmet coffees, teas, and accessories.

OVERALL SCORE: 52

28 Executive Park, Suite 200
Irvine, CA 92614
Fax: 949-260-1610
Total number of outlets: 145
Total number of franchise outlets: 145
International:Yes/No

OVERALL RANK: 167

Phone: 949-260-1600
Franchise fee:
Franchise term:
Initial investment:
Advertising/Marketing fee:
Royalty fee:

SURVEY AND RESULTS *

Q1: **About how many hours per week do you dedicate to your franchise business?**

		% answering
A)	Less than 40	20%
B)	41–50	20%
C)	51–60	20%
D)	More than 60	20%
E)	Passive investment	20%

Q2: **How would you describe your relations/ communications with your franchisor?**

		% answering
A)	Excellent	20%
B)	Good	20%
C)	Adequate	20%
D)	Fair	20%
E)	Poor	20%

Q3: **In terms of how your franchisor views your communications with other franchisees, it is:**

		% answering
A)	Very supportive	33%
B)	Not very supportive	33%
C)	No influence	33%

Q4: **Is the franchisor fair with you in resolving any grievances?**

		% answering
A)	Extremely fair	20%
B)	Pretty fair	20%
C)	Reasonably fair	20%
D)	Not very fair	20%
E)	Not fair at all	20%

Q5: **Are territories equitably granted?**

		% answering
A)	Yes	33%
B)	No	33%
C)	Not yet sure	33%

Q6: **How would you describe the initial and ongoing training provided by your franchisor?**

		% answering
A)	Excellent	33%
B)	Good	33%
C)	Adequate	33%
D)	Fair	33%
E)	Poor	33%

Q7: **How well does the franchisor anticipate future trends in how it evolves and markets products and services?**

		% answering
A)	Extremely well	20%
B)	Pretty well	20%
C)	Adequately	20%
D)	Not very well	20%
E)	Terribly	20%

Q8: **How satisfied are you with your franchisor's spending of the royalty fees you pay?**

		% answering
A)	Extremely satisfied	20%
B)	Mostly satisfied	20%
C)	Somewhat satisfied	20%
D)	Not very satisfied	20%
E)	Not satisfied at all	20%

Q9: In what ways could the parent company most improve? (Please check those that most apply, no more than three):

❑ Communications
❑ Counsel/advice on administrative/management issues
❑ Effectiveness of marketing/promotions
❑ Evolution of products/services
❑ Frequency of marketing/promotional campaigns

❑ Quality of products/services
❑ Pricing of products/services to franchisees
❑ Technology (Point of sale systems, usage of computers/email/software, etc.)
❑ Training

Most frequent responses:

	% answering
Effectiveness of marketing/promotions	80%
Pricing of products/services to franchisees	60%
Evolution of products/services	40%

Q10: Is your income more, less or about what you expected prior to opening your business?

	% answering	
More	11%	
Less	44%	Summary: 55% are making about what they
About what was expected	44%	expected, or more.

Q11: Prior to opening your franchise, which (if any) of the following did you underestimate?

❑ Amount of working capital required for your 1st year in business
❑ Difficulty in hiring/retaining quality staff
❑ Expertise required to run the business
❑ Impact of marketing/promotions

❑ Start-up costs
❑ Degree of stress
❑ Workload

Most frequent responses:

	% answering
Difficulty in hiring/retaining quality staff	40%
Degree of stress	30%
Workload	20%

Q12: If you could turn back time to the day you signed your franchise agreement, would you make the same decision to buy your franchise?

	% answering
Yes	**70%**
No	30%

* Number of survey respondents: 10 from 7 different states
Number of survey respondents as a % of total franchise units: 6.90%

GNC (GENERAL NUTRITION CENTERS)

www.gncfranchising.com

World's largest retailer of vitamins and nutritional supplements.

OVERALL SCORE: 35

300 Sixth Avenue
Pittsburgh, PA 15222
Fax: 412-288-2033
Total number of outlets: 4,800 worldwide
Total number of franchise outlets: 4,800
worldwide (1,300 U.S.)
International: Yes/No

OVERALL RANK: 189

Phone: 800-766-7099
Franchise fee: $30,000 to $40,000
Franchise term: 10 years
Initial investment: $132,681 to $182,031
Advertising/Marketing fee: 3% of gross sales
Royalty fee: 6% of gross sales

SURVEY AND RESULTS *

Q1: About how many hours per week do you dedicate to your franchise business?

		% answering
A)	Less than 40	13%
B)	**41–50**	**48%**
C)	51–60	13%
D)	More than 60	26%
E)	Passive investment	0%

Q2: How would you describe your relations/communications with your franchisor?

		% answering
A)	Excellent	4%
B)	Good	9%
C)	Adequate	13%
D)	Fair	22%
E)	**Poor**	**52%**

Q3: In terms of how your franchisor views your communications with other franchisees, it is:

		% answering
A)	Very supportive	32%
B)	Not very supportive	27%
C)	**No influence**	**41%**

Q4: Is the franchisor fair with you in resolving any grievances?

		% answering
A)	Extremely fair	0%
B)	Pretty fair	5%
C)	**Reasonably fair**	**18%**
D)	Not very fair	55%
E)	Not fair at all	23%

Q5: Are territories equitably granted?

		% answering
A)	Yes	22%
B)	**No**	**52%**
C)	Not yet sure	26%

Q6: How would you describe the initial and ongoing training provided by your franchisor?

		% answering
A)	Excellent	0%
B)	Good	22%
C)	Adequate	22%
D)	Fair	13%
E)	**Poor**	**43%**

Q7: How well does the franchisor anticipate future trends in how it evolves and markets products and services?

		% answering
A)	Extremely well	0%
B)	Pretty well	4%
C)	Adequately	22%
D)	Not very well	35%
E)	**Terribly**	**39%**

Q8: How satisfied are you with your franchisor's spending of the royalty fees you pay?

		% answering
A)	Extremely satisfied	0%
B)	Mostly satisfied	9%
C)	Somewhat satisfied	9%
D)	Not very satisfied	32%
E)	**Not satisfied at all**	**50%**

Q9: **In what ways could the parent company most improve? (Please check those that most apply, no more than three):**

❑ Communications
❑ Counsel/advice on administrative/management issues
❑ Effectiveness of marketing/promotions
❑ Evolution of products/services
❑ Frequency of marketing/promotional campaigns

❑ Quality of products/services
❑ Pricing of products/services to franchisees
❑ Technology (Point of sale systems, usage of computers/email/software, etc.)
❑ Training

Most frequent responses:	% answering
Effectiveness of marketing/promotions (tie)	65%
Pricing of products/services to franchisees (tie)	65%
Communications (tie)	39%
Technology (tie)	39%

Q10: **Is your income more, less or about what you expected prior to opening your business?**

	% answering	
More	13%	
Less	**70%**	**Summary: 30% are making about what they**
About what was expected	17%	**expected, or more.**

Q11: **Prior to opening your franchise, which (if any) of the following did you underestimate?**

❑ Amount of working capital required for your 1st year in business
❑ Difficulty in hiring/retaining quality staff
❑ Expertise required to run the business
❑ Impact of marketing/promotions

❑ Start-up costs
❑ Degree of stress
❑ Workload

Most frequent responses:	% answering
Difficulty in hiring/retaining quality staff (tie)	43%
Degree of stress (tie)	43%
Workload	39%

Q12: **If you could turn back time to the day you signed your franchise agreement, would you make the same decision to buy your franchise?**

	% answering
Yes	48%
No	52%

* Number of survey respondents: 23 from 18 different states
  Number of survey respondents as a % of total franchise units: < 1%

THE GODDARD SCHOOL

www.goddardschool.com

Child care and early childhood development and education programs.

OVERALL SCORE: 74

1016 West Ninth Avenue
King of Prussia, PA 19406
Fax: 610-265-6931
Total number of outlets: 180
Total number of franchise outlets: 180
International: No

OVERALL RANK: 62

Phone: 800-272-4901
Franchise fee: $75,000
Franchise term: 15 years
Initial investment: $399,000
Advertising/Marketing fee: > of $2,000 or 4% of gross receipts monthly
Royalty fee: 7% of gross receipts monthly

SURVEY AND RESULTS *

Q1: About how many hours per week do you dedicate to your franchise business?

		% answering
A)	Less than 40	15%
B)	41–50	31%
C)	51–60	8%
D)	**More than 60**	**46%**
E)	Passive investment	0%

Q2: How would you describe your relations/ communications with your franchisor?

		% answering
A)	Excellent	31%
B)	**Good**	**38%**
C)	Adequate	23%
D)	Fair	8%
E)	Poor	0%

Q3: In terms of how your franchisor views your communications with other franchisees, it is:

		% answering
A)	**Very supportive**	**83%**
B)	Not very supportive	0%
C)	No influence	17%

Q4: Is the franchisor fair with you in resolving any grievances?

		% answering
A)	**Extremely fair**	**46%**
B)	Pretty fair	23%
C)	Reasonably fair	8%
D)	Not very fair	23%
E)	Not fair at all	0%

Q5: Are territories equitably granted?

		% answering
A)	Yes	33%
B)	**No**	**42%**
C)	Not yet sure	25%

Q6: How would you describe the initial and ongoing training provided by your franchisor?

		% answering
A)	Excellent	31%
B)	**Good**	**46%**
C)	Adequate	15%
D)	Fair	0%
E)	Poor	8%

Q7: How well does the franchisor anticipate future trends in how it evolves and markets products and services?

		% answering
A)	**Extremely well**	**62%**
B)	Pretty well	31%
C)	Adequately	0%
D)	Not very well	8%
E)	Terribly	0%

Q8: How satisfied are you with your franchisor's spending of the royalty fees you pay?

		% answering
A)	Extremely satisfied	0%
B)	**Mostly satisfied**	**54%**
C)	Somewhat satisfied	27%
D)	Not very satisfied	18%
E)	Not satisfied at all	0%

Q9: **In what ways could the parent company most improve? (Please check those that most apply, no more than three):**

❑ Communications
❑ Counsel/advice on administrative/management issues
❑ Effectiveness of marketing/promotions
❑ Evolution of products/services
❑ Frequency of marketing/promotional campaigns

❑ Quality of products/services
❑ Pricing of products/services to franchisees
❑ Technology (Point of sale systems, usage of computers/email/software, etc.)
❑ Training

Most frequent responses:

	% answering
Counsel/advice on administrative/management issues	46%
Effectiveness of marketing/promotions (tie)	38%
Technology (tie)	38%

Q10: **Is your income more, less or about what you expected prior to opening your business?**

	% answering	
More	8%	
Less	**46%**	**Summary: 54% are making about what they**
About what was expected	**46%**	**expected, or more.**

Q11: **Prior to opening your franchise, which (if any) of the following did you underestimate?**

❑ Amount of working capital required for your 1st year in business
❑ Difficulty in hiring/retaining quality staff
❑ Expertise required to run the business
❑ Impact of marketing/promotions

❑ Start-up costs
❑ Degree of stress
❑ Workload

Most frequent responses:

	% answering
Difficulty in hiring/retaining quality staff (tie)	69%
Degree of stress (tie)	69%
Amount of working capital required for 1st year in business	62%

Q12: **If you could turn back time to the day you signed your franchise agreement, would you make the same decision to buy your franchise?**

	% answering
Yes	**92%**
No	8%

* Number of survey respondents: 13 from 10 different states
Number of survey respondents as a % of total franchise units: 7.22%

GODFATHER'S PIZZA

www.godfathers.com

Pizzeria restaurants.

OVERALL SCORE: 69

9140 West Dodge Road
Omaha, NE 68814
Total number of outlets: 571
Total number of franchise outlets: 495
International: No
Service compensation: 3% of gross sales, weekly

OVERALL RANK: 83

Phone: 402-391-1452
Franchise fee: $150 to $20,150
Franchise term: 15 years
Initial investment: $158,500 to $575,500
Advertising/Marketing fee: none currently
Royalty fee: 2% of gross sales, weekly

SURVEY AND RESULTS *

Q1: About how many hours per week do you dedicate to your franchise business?

		% answering
A)	Less than 40	18%
B)	**41–50**	**36%**
C)	51–60	9%
D)	More than 60	27%
E)	Passive investment	9%

Q2: How would you describe your relations/communications with your franchisor?

		% answering
A)	Excellent	27%
B)	Good	27%
C)	**Adequate**	**45%**
D)	Fair	0%
E)	Poor	0%

Q3: In terms of how your franchisor views your communications with other franchisees, it is:

		% answering
A)	**Very supportive**	**70%**
B)	Not very supportive	0%
C)	No influence	30%

Q4: Is the franchisor fair with you in resolving any grievances?

		% answering
A)	Extremely fair	36%
B)	**Pretty fair**	**45%**
C)	Reasonably fair	18%
D)	Not very fair	0%
E)	Not fair at all	0%

Q5: Are territories equitably granted?

		% answering
A)	**Yes**	**73%**
B)	No	9%
C)	Not yet sure	18%

Q6: How would you describe the initial and ongoing training provided by your franchisor?

		% answering
A)	Excellent	18%
B)	**Good**	**36%**
C)	Adequate	27%
D)	Fair	18%
E)	Poor	0%

Q7: How well does the franchisor anticipate future trends in how it evolves and markets products and services?

		% answering
A)	Extremely well	0%
B)	**Pretty well**	**36%**
C)	Adequately	18%
D)	Not very well	27%
E)	Terribly	18%

Q8: How satisfied are you with your franchisor's spending of the royalty fees you pay?

		% answering
A)	Extremely satisfied	9%
B)	Mostly satisfied	27%
C)	Somewhat satisfied	14%
D)	**Not very satisfied**	**50%**
E)	Not satisfied at all	0%

Q9: **In what ways could the parent company most improve? (Please check those that most apply, no more than three):**

❑ Communications
❑ Counsel/advice on administrative/management issues
❑ Effectiveness of marketing/promotions
❑ Evolution of products/services
❑ Frequency of marketing/promotional campaigns

❑ Quality of products/services
❑ Pricing of products/services to franchisees
❑ Technology (Point of sale systems, usage of computers/email/software, etc.)
❑ Training

Most frequent responses:

	% answering
Effectiveness of marketing/promotions (tie)	45%
Evolution of products/services (tie)	45%
Pricing of products/services to franchisees (tie)	36%
Technology (tie)	36%

Q10: **Is your income more, less or about what you expected prior to opening your business?**

	% answering	
More	0%	
Less	45%	**Summary: 55% are making about what they**
About what was expected	**55%**	**expected, or more.**

Q11: **Prior to opening your franchise, which (if any) of the following did you underestimate?**

❑ Amount of working capital required for your 1st year in business
❑ Difficulty in hiring/retaining quality staff
❑ Expertise required to run the business
❑ Impact of marketing/promotions

❑ Start-up costs
❑ Degree of stress
❑ Workload

Most frequent responses:

	% answering
Degree of stress	55%
Impact of marketing/promotions	45%
Amount of working capital required for 1st year in business	36%

Q12: **If you could turn back time to the day you signed your franchise agreement, would you make the same decision to buy your franchise?**

	% answering
Yes	**82%**
No	18%

* Number of survey respondents: 11 from 9 different states
Number of survey respondents as a % of total franchise units: 2.22%

GOLD'S GYM

www.goldsgym.com

The world's largest fitness franchise.

OVERALL SCORE: 60

358 Hampton Drive
Venice, CA 90291
Total number of outlets: 600+
Total number of franchise outlets: 560+
International: Yes (worldwide)

OVERALL RANK: 136

Phone: 310-392-3005
Franchise fee: $20,000
Franchise term: 10 years
Initial investment: $916,000 to $2,736,500
Advertising/Marketing fee: $244 per month
Royalty fee: varies

SURVEY AND RESULTS *

Q1: About how many hours per week do you dedicate to your franchise business?

		% answering
A)	Less than 40	8%
B)	**41–50**	**46%**
C)	51–60	23%
D)	More than 60	23%
E)	Passive investment	0%

Q2: How would you describe your relations/communications with your franchisor?

		% answering
A)	Excellent	8%
B)	Good	23%
C)	**Adequate**	**31%**
D)	Fair	23%
E)	Poor	15%

Q3: In terms of how your franchisor views your communications with other franchisees, it is:

		% answering
A)	Very supportive	33%
B)	Not very supportive	17%
C)	**No influence**	**50%**

Q4: Is the franchisor fair with you in resolving any grievances?

		% answering
A)	Extremely fair	9%
B)	**Pretty fair**	**27%**
C)	**Reasonably fair**	**27%**
D)	Not very fair	18%
E)	Not fair at all	18%

Q5: Are territories equitably granted?

		% answering
A)	**Yes**	**54%**
B)	No	31%
C)	Not yet sure	15%

Q6: How would you describe the initial and ongoing training provided by your franchisor?

		% answering
A)	Excellent	15%
B)	Good	15%
C)	**Adequate**	**38%**
D)	Fair	0%
E)	Poor	31%

Q7: How well does the franchisor anticipate future trends in how it evolves and markets products and services?

		% answering
A)	Extremely well	8%
B)	Pretty well	33%
C)	Adequately	17%
D)	**Not very well**	**42%**
E)	Terribly	0%

Q8: How satisfied are you with your franchisor's spending of the royalty fees you pay?

		% answering
A)	Extremely satisfied	0%
B)	Mostly satisfied	8%
C)	Somewhat satisfied	25%
D)	**Not very satisfied**	**33%**
E)	**Not satisfied at all**	**33%**

Q9: **In what ways could the parent company most improve? (Please check those that most apply, no more than three):**

❑ Communications
❑ Counsel/advice on administrative/management issues
❑ Effectiveness of marketing/promotions
❑ Evolution of products/services
❑ Frequency of marketing/promotional campaigns

❑ Quality of products/services
❑ Pricing of products/services to franchisees
❑ Technology (Point of sale systems, usage of computers/email/software, etc.)
❑ Training

Most frequent responses:

	% answering
Communications	62%
Effectiveness of marketing/promotions	54%
Frequency of marketing/promotional campaigns	31%

Q10: **Is your income more, less or about what you expected prior to opening your business?**

	% answering	
More	15%	
Less	38%	**Summary: 61% are making about what they**
About what was expected	**46%**	**expected, or more.**

Q11: **Prior to opening your franchise, which (if any) of the following did you underestimate?**

❑ Amount of working capital required for your 1st year in business
❑ Difficulty in hiring/retaining quality staff
❑ Expertise required to run the business
❑ Impact of marketing/promotions

❑ Start-up costs
❑ Degree of stress
❑ Workload

Most frequent responses:

	% answering
Amount of working capital required for 1st year in business	46%
Difficulty in hiring/retaining quality staff (tie)	31%
Expertise required to run the business (tie)	31%
Start-up costs (tie)	31%

Q12: **If you could turn back time to the day you signed your franchise agreement, would you make the same decision to buy your franchise?**

	% answering
Yes	**75%**
No	25%

* Number of survey respondents: 13 from 12 different states
   Number of survey respondents as a % of total franchise units: 2.32%

GREASE MONKEY

www.greasemonkeyintl.com
Email: franchiseinfo@greasemonkeyintl.com

Quick-service lube and oil change centers.

OVERALL SCORE: 75

7100 E. Belleview Avenue, Suite 305
Greenwood Village, CO 80111
Fax: 303-308-5908
Total number of outlets: 240 (202 in U.S.)
Total number of franchise outlets: 237
International: Yes (Mexico)

OVERALL RANK: 57

Phone: 800-364-0352
Franchise fee: $30,000
Franchise term: 15 years
Initial investment: $136,068 to $313,343
Advertising/Marketing fee: 1% of gross receipts monthly
Royalty fee: 5% of gross receipts monthly

SURVEY AND RESULTS *

Q1: About how many hours per week do you dedicate to your franchise business?

		% answering
A)	Less than 40	20%
B)	41–50	27%
C)	51–60	20%
D)	**More than 60**	**33%**
E)	Passive investment	0%

Q2: How would you describe your relations/ communications with your franchisor?

		% answering
A)	Excellent	8%
B)	Good	25%
C)	**Adequate**	**33%**
D)	Fair	25%
E)	Poor	8%

Q3: In terms of how your franchisor views your communications with other franchisees, it is:

		% answering
A)	**Very supportive**	**67%**
B)	Not very supportive	13%
C)	No influence	20%

Q4: Is the franchisor fair with you in resolving any grievances?

		% answering
A)	**Extremely fair**	**46%**
B)	Pretty fair	23%
C)	Reasonably fair	23%
D)	Not very fair	8%
E)	Not fair at all	0%

Q5: Are territories equitably granted?

		% answering
A)	**Yes**	**67%**
B)	No	13%
C)	Not yet sure	20%

Q6: How would you describe the initial and ongoing training provided by your franchisor?

		% answering
A)	**Excellent**	**33%**
B)	**Good**	**33%**
C)	Adequate	30%
D)	Fair	7%
E)	Poor	20%

Q7: How well does the franchisor anticipate future trends in how it evolves and markets products and services?

		% answering
A)	Extremely well	27%
B)	**Pretty well**	**33%**
C)	Adequately	27%
D)	Not very well	13%
E)	Terribly	0%

Q8: How satisfied are you with your franchisor's spending of the royalty fees you pay?

		% answering
A)	Extremely satisfied	7%
B)	**Mostly satisfied**	**53%**
C)	Somewhat satisfied	27%
D)	Not very satisfied	7%
E)	Not satisfied at all	7%

Q9: **In what ways could the parent company most improve? (Please check those that most apply, no more than three):**

❑   Communications
❑   Counsel/advice on administrative/management issues
❑   Effectiveness of marketing/promotions
❑   Evolution of products/services
❑   Frequency of marketing/promotional campaigns

❑   Quality of products/services
❑   Pricing of products/services to franchisees
❑   Technology (Point of sale systems, usage
     of computers/email/software, etc.)
❑   Training

Most frequent responses:

	% answering
Effectiveness of marketing/promotions (tie)	47%
Technology (tie)	47%
Counsel/advice on administrative/management issues (tie)	40%
Training (tie)	40%

Q10: **Is your income more, less or about what you expected prior to opening your business?**

	% answering	
More	20%	
Less	27%	**Summary: 73% are making about what they**
About what was expected	**53%**	**expected, or more.**

Q11: **Prior to opening your franchise, which (if any) of the following did you underestimate?**

❑   Amount of working capital required for your
     1st year in business
❑   Difficulty in hiring/retaining quality staff
❑   Expertise required to run the business
❑   Impact of marketing/promotions

❑   Start-up costs
❑   Degree of stress
❑   Workload

Most frequent responses:

	% answering
Difficulty in hiring/retaining quality staff	67%
Degree of stress (tie)	47%
Workload (tie)	47%

Q12: **If you could turn back time to the day you signed your franchise agreement, would you make the same decision to buy your franchise?**

	% answering
Yes	**73%**
No	27%

*   Number of survey respondents: 15 from 9 different states
     Number of survey respondents as a % of total franchise units: 6.33%

GREAT AMERICAN COOKIES

www.greatamericancookies.com

Retail seller of cookies, brownies and drinks.

OVERALL SCORE: 62

2855 E. Cottonwood Parkway, Suite 400
Salt Lake City, UT 84121
Total number of outlets: 290
Total number of franchise outlets: 290
International: No
Advertising/Marketing fee: 1% of gross sales, monthly

OVERALL RANK: 125

Phone: 801-736-5600
Franchise fee: $30,000
Franchise term: Equal to term of lease
Initial investment: $116,500 to $274,000
Royalty fee: 6% of gross sales, monthly

SURVEY AND RESULTS *

Q1: About how many hours per week do you dedicate to your franchise business?

		% answering
A)	**Less than 40**	**33%**
B)	**41–50**	**33%**
C)	51–60	17%
D)	More than 60	17%
E)	Passive investment	0%

Q2: How would you describe your relations/communications with your franchisor?

		% answering
A)	Excellent	8%
B)	Good	25%
C)	**Adequate**	**33%**
D)	Fair	25%
E)	Poor	8%

Q3: In terms of how your franchisor views your communications with other franchisees, it is:

		% answering
A)	**Very supportive**	**58%**
B)	Not very supportive	0%
C)	No influence	42%

Q4: Is the franchisor fair with you in resolving any grievances?

		% answering
A)	Extremely fair	0%
B)	**Pretty fair**	**58%**
C)	Reasonably fair	25%
D)	Not very fair	17%
E)	Not fair at all	0%

Q5: Are territories equitably granted?

		% answering
A)	**Yes**	**50%**
B)	No	25%
C)	Not yet sure	25%

Q6: How would you describe the initial and ongoing training provided by your franchisor?

		% answering
A)	Excellent	0%
B)	**Good**	**45%**
C)	Adequate	0%
D)	**Fair**	**45%**
E)	Poor	9%

Q7: How well does the franchisor anticipate future trends in how it evolves and markets products and services?

		% answering
A)	Extremely well	0%
B)	Pretty well	33%
C)	**Adequately**	**50%**
D)	Not very well	8%
E)	Terribly	8%

Q8: How satisfied are you with your franchisor's spending of the royalty fees you pay?

		% answering
A)	Extremely satisfied	0%
B)	Mostly satisfied	8%
C)	**Somewhat satisfied**	**67%**
D)	Not very satisfied	17%
E)	Not satisfied at all	8%

Q9: **In what ways could the parent company most improve? (Please check those that most apply, no more than three):**

- ❑ Communications
- ❑ Counsel/advice on administrative/management issues
- ❑ Effectiveness of marketing/promotions
- ❑ Evolution of products/services
- ❑ Frequency of marketing/promotional campaigns

- ❑ Quality of products/services
- ❑ Pricing of products/services to franchisees
- ❑ Technology (Point of sale systems, usage of computers/email/software, etc.)
- ❑ Training

Most frequent responses:	% answering
Effectiveness of marketing/promotions	67%
Evolution of products/services	50%
Pricing of products/services to franchisees	42%

Q10: **Is your income more, less or about what you expected prior to opening your business?**

	% answering	
More	0%	
Less	45%	**Summary: 55% are making about what they**
About what was expected	**55%**	**expected, or more.**

Q11: **Prior to opening your franchise, which (if any) of the following did you underestimate?**

- ❑ Amount of working capital required for your 1st year in business
- ❑ Difficulty in hiring/retaining quality staff
- ❑ Expertise required to run the business
- ❑ Impact of marketing/promotions

- ❑ Start-up costs
- ❑ Degree of stress
- ❑ Workload

Most frequent responses:	% answering
Difficulty in hiring/retaining quality staff	58%
Degree of stress	33%
Amount of working capital required for 1st year in business	25%

Q12: **If you could turn back time to the day you signed your franchise agreement, would you make the same decision to buy your franchise?**

	% answering
Yes	**75%**
No	25%

* Number of survey respondents: 12 from 10 different states
  Number of survey respondents as a % of total franchise units: 4.14%

THE GREAT FRAME UP

www.tgfufraninfo.com

Retailer offering frames, framing, and do-it-yourself framing services.

OVERALL SCORE: 41

OVERALL RANK: 182

12707 North Freeway, Suite 330
Houston, TX 77251
Fax: 281-775-5250
Total number of outlets: 186
Total number of franchise outlets: 186
International: No

Phone: 800-543-3325
Franchise fee: $30,000
Franchise term: 10 years
Initial investment: $138,425 to $$188,150
Advertising/Marketing fee: 2% of gross sales wkly.
Royalty fee: 6% of gross sales weekly

SURVEY AND RESULTS *

Q1: About how many hours per week do you dedicate to your franchise business?

		% answering
A)	Less than 40	12%
B)	41–50	29%
C)	**51–60**	**47%**
D)	More than 60	12%
E)	Passive investment	0%

Q2: How would you describe your relations/ communications with your franchisor?

		% answering
A)	Excellent	0%
B)	**Good**	**32%**
C)	Adequate	27%
D)	Fair	12%
E)	Poor	29%

Q3: In terms of how your franchisor views your communications with other franchisees, it is:

		% answering
A)	Very supportive	41%
B)	Not very supportive	12%
C)	**No influence**	**47%**

Q4: Is the franchisor fair with you in resolving any grievances?

		% answering
A)	Extremely fair	13%
B)	Pretty fair	27%
C)	**Reasonably fair**	**33%**
D)	Not very fair	13%
E)	Not fair at all	13%

Q5: Are territories equitably granted?

		% answering
A)	Yes	31%
B)	No	31%
C)	**Not yet sure**	**38%**

Q6: How would you describe the initial and ongoing training provided by your franchisor?

		% answering
A)	Excellent	6%
B)	Good	18%
C)	Adequate	12%
D)	Fair	29%
E)	**Poor**	**35%**

Q7: How well does the franchisor anticipate future trends in how it evolves and markets products and services?

		% answering
A)	Extremely well	0%
B)	Pretty well	18%
C)	Adequately	29%
D)	**Not very well**	**35%**
E)	Terribly	18%

Q8: How satisfied are you with your franchisor's spending of the royalty fees you pay?

		% answering
A)	Extremely satisfied	0%
B)	Mostly satisfied	0%
C)	Somewhat satisfied	29%
D)	**Not very satisfied**	**35%**
E)	**Not satisfied at all**	**35%**

Q9: **In what ways could the parent company most improve? (Please check those that most apply, no more than three):**

- ❑ Communications
- ❑ Counsel/advice on administrative/management issues
- ❑ Effectiveness of marketing/promotions
- ❑ Evolution of products/services
- ❑ Frequency of marketing/promotional campaigns

- ❑ Quality of products/services
- ❑ Pricing of products/services to franchisees
- ❑ Technology (Point of sale systems, usage of computers/email/software, etc.)
- ❑ Training

Most frequent responses:

	% answering
Effectiveness of marketing/promotions	100%
Frequency of marketing/promotional campaigns	41%
Communications	29%

Q10: **Is your income more, less or about what you expected prior to opening your business?**

	% answering	
More	12%	
Less	76%	**Summary: 24% are making about what they**
About what was expected	12%	**expected, or more.**

Q11: **Prior to opening your franchise, which (if any) of the following did you underestimate?**

- ❑ Amount of working capital required for your 1st year in business
- ❑ Difficulty in hiring/retaining quality staff
- ❑ Expertise required to run the business
- ❑ Impact of marketing/promotions

- ❑ Start-up costs
- ❑ Degree of stress
- ❑ Workload

Most frequent responses:

	% answering
Amount of working capital required for your 1st year in business (tie)	41%
Difficulty in hiring/retaining quality staff (tie)	41%
Impact of marketing/promotions (tie)	41%
Degree of stress (tie)	41%

Q12: **If you could turn back time to the day you signed your franchise agreement, would you make the same decision to buy your franchise?**

	% answering
Yes	47%
No	**53%**

*   Number of survey respondents: 17 from 13 different states
    Number of survey respondents as a % of total franchise units: 9.14%

GREAT HARVEST BREAD COMPANY

www.greatharvest.com
Email: dawne@greatharvest.com

Baker of fresh breads, cookies, and sweets.

OVERALL SCORE: 75

28 South Montana Street
Dillon, MT 59725
Fax: 406-683-5537
Total number of outlets: 185
Total number of franchise outlets: 185
International: No

OVERALL RANK: 55

Phone: 800-442-0424
Franchise fee: $30,000
Franchise term: 10 years
Initial investment: $97,839 to $557,255
Advertising/Marketing fee: none
Royalty fee: 7% of gross sales for the first five
years, 6% for years six through 10, 5% thereafter

SURVEY AND RESULTS *

Q1: About how many hours per week do you dedicate to your franchise business?

		% answering
A)	Less than 40	14%
B)	41–50	18%
C)	51–60	32%
D)	**More than 60**	**36%**
E)	Passive investment	0%

Q2: How would you describe your relations/communications with your franchisor?

		% answering
A)	Excellent	29%
B)	**Good**	**50%**
C)	Adequate	14%
D)	Fair	7%
E)	Poor	0%

Q3: In terms of how your franchisor views your communications with other franchisees, it is:

		% answering
A)	**Very supportive**	**100%**
B)	Not very supportive	0%
C)	No influence	0%

Q4: Is the franchisor fair with you in resolving any grievances?

		% answering
A)	Extremely fair	42%
B)	**Pretty fair**	**50%**
C)	Reasonably fair	8%
D)	Not very fair	0%
E)	Not fair at all	0%

Q5: Are territories equitably granted?

		% answering
A)	**Yes**	**71%**
B)	No	0%
C)	Not yet sure	29%

Q6: How would you describe the initial and ongoing training provided by your franchisor?

		% answering
A)	Excellent	29%
B)	**Good**	**43%**
C)	Adequate	14%
D)	Fair	14%
E)	Poor	0%

Q7: How well does the franchisor anticipate future trends in how it evolves and markets products and services?

		% answering
A)	Extremely well	21%
B)	Pretty well	14%
C)	**Adequately**	**43%**
D)	Not very well	21%
E)	Terribly	0%

Q8: How satisfied are you with your franchisor's spending of the royalty fees you pay?

		% answering
A)	Extremely satisfied	7%
B)	**Mostly satisfied**	**57%**
C)	Somewhat satisfied	36%
D)	Not very satisfied	0%
E)	Not satisfied at all	0%

Q9: **In what ways could the parent company most improve? (Please check those that most apply, no more than three):**

❑ Communications

❑ Counsel/advice on administrative/management issues

❑ Effectiveness of marketing/promotions

❑ Evolution of products/services

❑ Frequency of marketing/promotional campaigns

❑ Quality of products/services

❑ Pricing of products/services to franchisees

❑ Technology (Point of sale systems, usage of computers/email/software, etc.)

❑ Training

Most frequent responses:	% answering
Evolution of products/services	57%
Effectiveness of marketing/promotions (tie)	50%
Pricing of products/services to franchisees (tie)	50%

Q10: **Is your income more, less or about what you expected prior to opening your business?**

	% answering	
More	23%	
Less	**46%**	**Summary: 54% are making about what they**
About what was expected	31%	**expected, or more.**

Q11: **Prior to opening your franchise, which (if any) of the following did you underestimate?**

❑ Amount of working capital required for your 1st year in business

❑ Difficulty in hiring/retaining quality staff

❑ Expertise required to run the business

❑ Impact of marketing/promotions

❑ Start-up costs

❑ Degree of stress

❑ Workload

Most frequent responses:	% answering
Degree of stress	64%
Workload	57%
Difficulty in hiring/retaining quality staff	36%

Q12: **If you could turn back time to the day you signed your franchise agreement, would you make the same decision to buy your franchise?**

	% answering
Yes	**77%**
No	23%

* Number of survey respondents: 14 from 13 different states

Number of survey respondents as a % of total franchise units: 7.57%

GUARDSMAN FURNITUREPRO

www.guardsmanfurniturepro.com
Email: furniturepro@valspar.com

Provider of furniture and wood repair and restoration.

OVERALL SCORE: 57

4999 36th Street SE
Grand Rapids, MI 49512
Fax: 616-285-7882
Total number of outlets: 100 (97 in U.S.)
Total number of franchise outlets: 100
International: Yes (Canada)

OVERALL RANK: 154

Phone: 800-496-6377
Franchise fee: $7,000
Franchise term: 5 years
Initial investment: $14,000 to $22,700
Advertising/Marketing fee: varies
Royalty fee: varies

SURVEY AND RESULTS *

Q1: About how many hours per week do you dedicate to your franchise business?

		% answering
A)	Less than 40	29%
B)	41–50	0%
C)	**51–60**	**36%**
D)	**More than 60**	**36%**
E)	Passive investment	0%

Q2: How would you describe your relations/communications with your franchisor?

		% answering
A)	Excellent	14%
B)	**Good**	**29%**
C)	**Adequate**	**29%**
D)	Fair	21%
E)	Poor	7%

Q3: In terms of how your franchisor views your communications with other franchisees, it is:

		% answering
A)	Very supportive	31%
B)	**Not very supportive**	**38%**
C)	No influence	31%

Q4: Is the franchisor fair with you in resolving any grievances?

		% answering
A)	Extremely fair	23%
B)	**Pretty fair**	**31%**
C)	**Reasonably fair**	**31%**
D)	Not very fair	8%
E)	Not fair at all	8%

Q5: Are territories equitably granted?

		% answering
A)	**Yes**	**85%**
B)	No	8%
C)	Not yet sure	8%

Q6: How would you describe the initial and ongoing training provided by your franchisor?

		% answering
A)	**Excellent**	**31%**
B)	Good	23%
C)	**Adequate**	**31%**
D)	Fair	8%
E)	Poor	8%

Q7: How well does the franchisor anticipate future trends in how it evolves and markets products and services?

		% answering
A)	Extremely well	15%
B)	Pretty well	8%
C)	**Adequately**	**38%**
D)	**Not very well**	**38%**
E)	Terribly	0%

Q8: How satisfied are you with your franchisor's spending of the royalty fees you pay?

		% answering
A)	Extremely satisfied	0%
B)	Mostly satisfied	15%
C)	**Somewhat satisfied**	**38%**
D)	**Not very satisfied**	**38%**
E)	Not satisfied at all	23%

Q9: **In what ways could the parent company most improve? (Please check those that most apply, no more than three):**

❑ Communications

❑ Counsel/advice on administrative/management issues

❑ Effectiveness of marketing/promotions

❑ Evolution of products/services

❑ Frequency of marketing/promotional campaigns

❑ Quality of products/services

❑ Pricing of products/services to franchisees

❑ Technology (Point of sale systems, usage of computers/email/software, etc.)

❑ Training

Most frequent responses:

	% answering
Communications	67%
Effectiveness of marketing/promotions	57%
Pricing of products/services to franchisees	43%

Q10: **Is your income more, less or about what you expected prior to opening your business?**

	% answering	
More	21%	
Less	**64%**	**Summary: 35% are making about what they**
About what was expected	14%	**expected, or more.**

Q11: **Prior to opening your franchise, which (if any) of the following did you underestimate?**

❑ Amount of working capital required for your 1st year in business

❑ Difficulty in hiring/retaining quality staff

❑ Expertise required to run the business

❑ Impact of marketing/promotions

❑ Start-up costs

❑ Degree of stress

❑ Workload

Most frequent responses:

	% answering
Difficulty in hiring/retaining quality staff	50%
Amount of working capital required for your 1st year in business	36%
Start-up costs (tie)	21%
Workload (tie)	21%

Q12: **If you could turn back time to the day you signed your franchise agreement, would you make the same decision to buy your franchise?**

	% answering
Yes	**57%**
No	43%

* Number of survey respondents: 14 from 14 different states

Number of survey respondents as a % of total franchise units: 14%

GUMBALL GOURMET

www.gumballgourmet.com

Gumball machines, kiosks, and retail stores.

OVERALL SCORE: 31

11622 McBean Drive
El Monte, CA 91732
Fax: 626-453-3892
Total number of outlets: 206
Total number of franchise outlets: 193
International: No

OVERALL RANK: N/A

Phone: 866-GUMBALL
Franchise fee: $17,200 to $313,960
Franchise term: 5 years
Initial investment: $24,620 to $462,081
Advertising/Marketing fee: none
Royalty fee: varies

SURVEY AND RESULTS *

Q1: About how many hours per week do you dedicate to your franchise business?

		% answering
A)	**Less than 40**	**78%**
B)	41–50	0%
C)	51–60	0%
D)	More than 60	0%
E)	Passive investment	22%

Q2: How would you describe your relations/ communications with your franchisor?

		% answering
A)	Excellent	0%
B)	Good	11%
C)	**Adequate**	**33%**
D)	Fair	22%
E)	**Poor**	**33%**

Q3: In terms of how your franchisor views your communications with other franchisees, it is:

		% answering
A)	Very supportive	22%
B)	Not very supportive	22%
C)	**No influence**	**56%**

Q4: Is the franchisor fair with you in resolving any grievances?

		% answering
A)	Extremely fair	0%
B)	**Pretty fair**	**56%**
C)	Reasonably fair	22%
D)	Not very fair	11%
E)	Not fair at all	11%

Q5: Are territories equitably granted?

		% answering
A)	Yes	44%
B)	**No**	**56%**
C)	Not yet sure	0%

Q6: How would you describe the initial and ongoing training provided by your franchisor?

		% answering
A)	Excellent	0%
B)	Good	11%
C)	**Adequate**	**33%**
D)	Fair	23%
E)	**Poor**	**33%**

Q7: How well does the franchisor anticipate future trends in how it evolves and markets products and services?

		% answering
A)	Extremely well	0%
B)	Pretty well	22%
C)	Adequately	22%
D)	**Not very well**	**33%**
E)	Terribly	22%

Q8: How satisfied are you with your franchisor's spending of the royalty fees you pay?

		% answering
A)	Extremely satisfied	0%
B)	Mostly satisfied	33%
C)	Somewhat satisfied	22%
D)	Not very satisfied	0%
E)	**Not satisfied at all**	**44%**

Q9: **In what ways could the parent company most improve? (Please check those that most apply, no more than three):**

❑ Communications
❑ Counsel/advice on administrative/management issues
❑ Effectiveness of marketing/promotions
❑ Evolution of products/services
❑ Frequency of marketing/promotional campaigns

❑ Quality of products/services
❑ Pricing of products/services to franchisees
❑ Technology (Point of sale systems, usage of computers/email/software, etc.)
❑ Training

Most frequent responses:	% answering
Quality of products/services	78%
Communications	56%
Frequency of marketing/promotional campaigns (tie)	44%
Pricing of products/services to franchisees (tie)	44%

Q10: **Is your income more, less or about what you expected prior to opening your business?**

	% answering	
More	0%	
Less	**100%**	**Summary: 0% are making about what they**
About what was expected	0%	**expected, or more.**

Q11: **Prior to opening your franchise, which (if any) of the following did you underestimate?**

❑ Amount of working capital required for your 1st year in business
❑ Difficulty in hiring/retaining quality staff
❑ Expertise required to run the business
❑ Impact of marketing/promotions

❑ Start-up costs
❑ Degree of stress
❑ Workload

Most frequent responses:	% answering
Start-up costs	44%
Impact of marketing/promotions	22%
Expertise required to run the business (tie)	11%
Degree of stress (tie)	11%

Q12: **If you could turn back time to the day you signed your franchise agreement, would you make the same decision to buy your franchise?**

	% answering
Yes	38%
No	**63%**

* Number of survey respondents: 9 from 6 different states
Number of survey respondents as a % of total franchise units: 4.66%

GYMBOREE PLAY & MUSIC

www.playandmusic.com

Interactive play & music programs for children.

OVERALL SCORE: 65

7000 Airport Blvd., Suite 200
Burlingame, CA 94010
Fax: 707-678-1315
Total number of outlets: 575+
Total number of franchise outlets: 575+
International: Yes (worldwide)

OVERALL RANK: 110

Phone: 877-4-GYMWEB
Franchise fee: $45,000
Franchise term: 10 years
Initial investment: $141,000 to $286,000
Advertising/Marketing fee: up to 5% of gross
receipts quarterly
Royalty fee: 6% of gross receipts, quarterly

SURVEY AND RESULTS *

Q1: About how many hours per week do you dedicate to your franchise business?

		% answering
A)	Less than 40	33%
B)	**41–50**	**42%**
C)	51–60	8%
D)	More than 60	17%
E)	Passive investment	0%

Q2: How would you describe your relations/ communications with your franchisor?

		% answering
A)	Excellent	25%
B)	**Good**	**42%**
C)	Adequate	25%
D)	Fair	8%
E)	Poor	0%

Q3: In terms of how your franchisor views your communications with other franchisees, it is:

		% answering
A)	**Very supportive**	**91%**
B)	Not very supportive	0%
C)	No influence	9%

Q4: Is the franchisor fair with you in resolving any grievances?

		% answering
A)	Extremely fair	10%
B)	Pretty fair	20%
C)	**Reasonably fair**	**60%**
D)	Not very fair	10%
E)	Not fair at all	0%

Q5: Are territories equitably granted?

		% answering
A)	**Yes**	**36%**
B)	No	27%
C)	**Not yet sure**	**36%**

Q6: How would you describe the initial and ongoing training provided by your franchisor?

		% answering
A)	Excellent	8%
B)	**Good**	**58%**
C)	Adequate	8%
D)	Fair	0%
E)	Poor	25%

Q7: How well does the franchisor anticipate future trends in how it evolves and markets products and services?

		% answering
A)	Extremely well	0%
B)	**Pretty well**	**42%**
C)	Adequately	33%
D)	Not very well	25%
E)	Terribly	0%

Q8: How satisfied are you with your franchisor's spending of the royalty fees you pay?

		% answering
A)	Extremely satisfied	0%
B)	**Mostly satisfied**	**55%**
C)	Somewhat satisfied	45%
D)	Not very satisfied	0%
E)	Not satisfied at all	0%

Q9: In what ways could the parent company most improve? (Please check those that most apply, no more than three):

- ❑ Communications
- ❑ Counsel/advice on administrative/management issues
- ❑ Effectiveness of marketing/promotions
- ❑ Evolution of products/services
- ❑ Frequency of marketing/promotional campaigns

- ❑ Quality of products/services
- ❑ Pricing of products/services to franchisees
- ❑ Technology (Point of sale systems, usage of computers/email/software, etc.)
- ❑ Training

Most frequent responses:

	% answering
Counsel/advice on administrative/management issues (tie)	50%
Technology (tie)	50%
Evolution of products/services	42%

Q10: Is your income more, less or about what you expected prior to opening your business?

	% answering	
More	0%	
Less	**55%**	Summary: 45% are making about what
About what was expected	45%	they expected, or more.

Q11: Prior to opening your franchise, which (if any) of the following did you underestimate?

- ❑ Amount of working capital required for your 1st year in business
- ❑ Difficulty in hiring/retaining quality staff
- ❑ Expertise required to run the business
- ❑ Impact of marketing/promotions

- ❑ Start-up costs
- ❑ Degree of stress
- ❑ Workload

Most frequent responses:

	% answering
Difficulty in hiring/retaining quality staff	75%
Workload	42%
Degree of stress	33%

Q12: If you could turn back time to the day you signed your franchise agreement, would you make the same decision to buy your franchise?

	% answering
Yes	**75%**
No	25%

* Number of survey respondents: 12 from 9 different states

Number of survey respondents as a % of total franchise units: 2.09%

HEALTH MART

www.healthmart.com
Email: investors@mckesson.com

Pharmacy retailer.

OVERALL SCORE: 82

1 Post Street
San Francisco, CA 94104
Fax: 415-983-8464
Total number of outlets:
Total number of franchise outlets:
International: No

OVERALL RANK: 28

Phone: 800-369-5467
Franchise fee: none
Franchise term: 5 years
Initial investment: $254,388 to $587,935
Advertising/Marketing fee: $50 to $150 per month
Royalty fee: $50 per month

SURVEY AND RESULTS *

Q1: About how many hours per week do you dedicate to your franchise business?

		% answering
A)	Less than 40	6%
B)	41–50	17%
C)	**51–60**	**44%**
D)	More than 60	33%
E)	Passive investment	0%

Q2: How would you describe your relations/ communications with your franchisor?

		% answering
A)	Excellent	0%
B)	**Good**	**39%**
C)	**Adequate**	**39%**
D)	Fair	17%
E)	Poor	6%

Q3: In terms of how your franchisor views your communications with other franchisees, it is:

		% answering
A)	Very supportive	18%
B)	Not very supportive	24%
C)	**No influence**	**59%**

Q4: Is the franchisor fair with you in resolving any grievances?

		% answering
A)	Extremely fair	7%
B)	Pretty fair	20%
C)	**Reasonably fair**	**67%**
D)	Not very fair	7%
E)	Not fair at all	0%

Q5: Are territories equitably granted?

		% answering
A)	**Yes**	**72%**
B)	No	11%
C)	Not yet sure	17%

Q6: How would you describe the initial and ongoing training provided by your franchisor?

		% answering
A)	Excellent	6%
B)	Good	24%
C)	Adequate	24%
D)	**Fair**	**35%**
E)	Poor	12%

Q7: How well does the franchisor anticipate future trends in how it evolves and markets products and services?

		% answering
A)	Extremely well	12%
B)	**Pretty well**	**35%**
C)	Adequately	24%
D)	Not very well	29%
E)	Terribly	0%

Q8: How satisfied are you with your franchisor's spending of the royalty fees you pay?

		% answering
A)	Extremely satisfied	6%
B)	Mostly satisfied	25%
C)	Somewhat satisfied	25%
D)	**Not very satisfied**	**38%**
E)	Not satisfied at all	6%

Q9: **In what ways could the parent company most improve? (Please check those that most apply, no more than three):**

❑ Communications

❑ Counsel/advice on administrative/management issues

❑ Effectiveness of marketing/promotions

❑ Evolution of products/services

❑ Frequency of marketing/promotional campaigns

❑ Quality of products/services

❑ Pricing of products/services to franchisees

❑ Technology (Point of sale systems, usage of computers/email/software, etc.)

❑ Training

Most frequent responses:	% answering
Effectiveness of marketing/promotions	61%
Frequency of marketing/promotional campaigns	50%
Evolution of products/services (tie)	33%
Pricing of products/services to franchisees (tie)	33%

Q10: **Is your income more, less or about what you expected prior to opening your business?**

	% answering	
More	35%	
Less	6%	**Summary: 94% are making about what they**
About what was expected	**59%**	**expected, or more.**

Q11: **Prior to opening your franchise, which (if any) of the following did you underestimate?**

❑ Amount of working capital required for your 1st year in business

❑ Difficulty in hiring/retaining quality staff

❑ Expertise required to run the business

❑ Impact of marketing/promotions

❑ Start-up costs

❑ Degree of stress

❑ Workload

Most frequent responses:	% answering
Degree of stress	39%
Workload	39%
Impact of marketing/promotions	22%

Q12: **If you could turn back time to the day you signed your franchise agreement, would you make the same decision to buy your franchise?**

	% answering
Yes	**94%**
No	6%

* Number of survey respondents: 18 from 14 different states

Number of survey respondents as a % of total franchise units:

HEAVEN'S BEST CARPET CLEANING

www.heavensbest.com
Email: mcoinc@heavensbest.com

Provides a unique "dry" method of carpet and upholstery cleaning.

OVERALL SCORE: 98

P.O. Box 607
Rexburg, ID 83440
Fax: 208-359-1236
Total number of outlets: 987
Total number of franchise outlets: 987
International: Yes (Bahamas, Canada, United Kingdom)

OVERALL RANK: 2

Phone: 800-359-2095
Franchise fee: $15,900
Franchise term: 5 years
Initial investment: $21,600 to $44,400
Advertising/Marketing fee: none
Royalty fee: $80 per month per van or set of equipment

SURVEY AND RESULTS *

Q1: About how many hours per week do you dedicate to your franchise business?

		% answering
A)	Less than 40	15%
B)	**41–50**	**54%**
C)	51–60	23%
D)	More than 60	8%
E)	Passive investment	0%

Q2: How would you describe your relations/ communications with your franchisor?

		% answering
A)	**Excellent**	**57%**
B)	Good	36%
C)	Adequate	7%
D)	Fair	0%
E)	Poor	0%

Q3: In terms of how your franchisor views your communications with other franchisees, it is:

		% answering
A)	**Very supportive**	**85%**
B)	Not very supportive	0%
C)	No influence	15%

Q4: Is the franchisor fair with you in resolving any grievances?

		% answering
A)	**Extremely fair**	**58%**
B)	Pretty fair	42%
C)	Reasonably fair	0%
D)	Not very fair	0%
E)	Not fair at all	0%

Q5: Are territories equitably granted?

		% answering
A)	**Yes**	**93%**
B)	No	0%
C)	Not yet sure	7%

Q6: How would you describe the initial and ongoing training provided by your franchisor?

		% answering
A)	Excellent	21%
B)	**Good**	**57%**
C)	Adequate	0%
D)	Fair	14%
E)	Poor	7%

Q7: How well does the franchisor anticipate future trends in how it evolves and markets products and services?

		% answering
A)	Extremely well	21%
B)	**Pretty well**	**50%**
C)	Adequately	29%
D)	Not very well	0%
E)	Terribly	0%

Q8: How satisfied are you with your franchisor's spending of the royalty fees you pay?

		% answering
A)	**Extremely satisfied**	**46%**
B)	Mostly satisfied	15%
C)	Somewhat satisfied	23%
D)	Not very satisfied	15%
E)	Not satisfied at all	0%

Q9:   **In what ways could the parent company most improve? (Please check those that most apply, no more than three):**

❑   Communications
❑   Counsel/advice on administrative/management issues
❑   Effectiveness of marketing/promotions
❑   Evolution of products/services
❑   Frequency of marketing/promotional campaigns

❑   Quality of products/services
❑   Pricing of products/services to franchisees
❑   Technology (Point of sale systems, usage of computers/email/software, etc.)
❑   Training

Most frequent responses:	% answering
Frequency of marketing/promotional campaigns	57%
Effectiveness of marketing/promotions	43%
Pricing of products/services to franchisees	29%

Q10:   **Is your income more, less or about what you expected prior to opening your business?**

	% answering	
More	**64%**	
Less	7%	**Summary: 93% are making about what they**
About what was expected	29%	**expected, or more.**

Q11:   Prior to opening your franchise, which (if any) of the following did you underestimate?

❑   Amount of working capital required for your 1st year in business
❑   Difficulty in hiring/retaining quality staff
❑   Expertise required to run the business
❑   Impact of marketing/promotions

❑   Start-up costs
❑   Degree of stress
❑   Workload

Most frequent responses:	% answering
Difficulty in hiring/retaining quality staff	43%
Impact of marketing/promotions	36%
Degree of stress (tie)	29%
Workload (tie)	29%

Q12:   If you could turn back time to the day you signed your franchise agreement, would you make the same decision to buy your franchise?

	% answering
Yes	**100%**
No	0%

*   Number of survey respondents: 14 from 10 different states
Number of survey respondents as a % of total franchise units: 1.42%

HELP-U-SELL

www.helpusell.com

A "fee-for-service" realty firm.

OVERALL SCORE: 73

900 West Castleton Road, #230
Castle Rock, CO 80109
Fax: 303-814-3400
Total number of outlets: 639
Total number of franchise outlets: 639
International: No
Royalty fee: > of $500 per month or 6% of
gross revenues monthly on the first $600,000
of office revenue, and 5% of subsequent gross
revenues for that calendar year

OVERALL RANK: 69

Phone: 800-366-1177
Franchise fee: $19,500
Franchise term: 5 years
Initial investment: $43,550 to $137,500
Advertising/Marketing fee: > of 1.5% of gross
revenues per month, or $150

SURVEY AND RESULTS *

Q1: About how many hours per week do you
dedicate to your franchise business?

		% answering
A)	Less than 40	7%
B)	**41–50**	**40%**
C)	51–60	20%
D)	More than 60	33%
E)	Passive investment	0%

Q2: How would you describe your relations/
communications with your franchisor?

		% answering
A)	Excellent	33%
B)	**Good**	**47%**
C)	Adequate	13%
D)	Fair	0%
E)	Poor	7%

Q3: In terms of how your franchisor views your
communications with other franchisees, it is:

		% answering
A)	**Very supportive**	**86%**
B)	Not very supportive	7%
C)	No influence	7%

Q4: Is the franchisor fair with you in
resolving any grievances?

		% answering
A)	**Extremely fair**	**40%**
B)	Pretty fair	40%
C)	Reasonably fair	13%
D)	Not very fair	7%
E)	Not fair at all	0%

Q5: Are territories equitably granted?

		% answering
A)	**Yes**	**73%**
B)	No	7%
C)	Not yet sure	20%

Q6: How would you describe the initial and
ongoing training provided by your franchisor?

		% answering
A)	**Excellent**	**40%**
B)	Good	27%
C)	Adequate	20%
D)	Fair	7%
E)	Poor	7%

Q7: How well does the franchisor anticipate
future trends in how it evolves and markets
products and services?

		% answering
A)	**Extremely well**	**40%**
B)	**Pretty well**	**40%**
C)	Adequately	13%
D)	Not very well	7%
E)	Terribly	0%

Q8: How satisfied are you with your franchisor's
spending of the royalty fees you pay?

		% answering
A)	Extremely satisfied	14%
B)	**Mostly satisfied**	**43%**
C)	Somewhat satisfied	14%
D)	Not very satisfied	21%
E)	Not satisfied at all	7%

Q9: **In what ways could the parent company most improve? (Please check those that most apply, no more than three):**

❏ Communications
❏ Counsel/advice on administrative/management issues
❏ Effectiveness of marketing/promotions
❏ Evolution of products/services
❏ Frequency of marketing/promotional campaigns

❏ Quality of products/services
❏ Pricing of products/services to franchisees
❏ Technology (Point of sale systems, usage of computers/email/software, etc.)
❏ Training

Most frequent responses:

	% answering
Frequency of marketing/promotional campaigns	47%
Counsel/advice on administrative/management issues (tie)	40%
Effectiveness of marketing/promotions (tie)	40%

Q10: **Is your income more, less or about what you expected prior to opening your business?**

	% answering	
More	13%	
Less	**60%**	**Summary: 40% are making about what they**
About what was expected	27%	**expected, or more.**

Q11: **Prior to opening your franchise, which (if any) of the following did you underestimate?**

❏ Amount of working capital required for your 1st year in business
❏ Difficulty in hiring/retaining quality staff
❏ Expertise required to run the business
❏ Impact of marketing/promotions

❏ Start-up costs
❏ Degree of stress
❏ Workload

Most frequent responses:

	% answering
Difficulty in hiring/retaining quality staff	53%
Amount of working capital required for 1st year in business	33%
Degree of stress	27%

Q12: **If you could turn back time to the day you signed your franchise agreement, would you make the same decision to buy your franchise?**

	% answering
Yes	**86%**
No	14%

* Number of survey respondents: 15 from 14 different states
Number of survey respondents as a % of total franchise units: 2.35%

HOBBYTOWN USA

www.hobbytown.com
Email: dfo@hobbytown.com (Nichole Ernst)

Retail hobby franchise.

OVERALL SCORE: 89

6301 South 58th Street
Lincoln, NE 68516
Total number of outlets: 150+
Total number of franchise outlets: 150+
International: No

OVERALL RANK: 9

Phone: 800-858-7370
Franchise fee: $10,000 or $19,500
Franchise term: 10 years
Initial investment: $134,825 to $693,000
Advertising/Marketing fee: 2% of gross sales
Royalty fee: varies from 2.5% to 3.5% of gross sales

SURVEY AND RESULTS *

Q1: About how many hours per week do you dedicate to your franchise business?

		% answering
A)	Less than 40	5%
B)	41–50	26%
C)	51–60	32%
D)	**More than 60**	**37%**
E)	Passive investment	0%

Q2: How would you describe your relations/communications with your franchisor?

		% answering
A)	**Excellent**	**68%**
B)	Good	26%
C)	Adequate	5%
D)	Fair	0%
E)	Poor	0%

Q3: In terms of how your franchisor views your communications with other franchisees, it is:

		% answering
A)	**Very supportive**	**84%**
B)	Not very supportive	16%
C)	No influence	0%

Q4: Is the franchisor fair with you in resolving any grievances?

		% answering
A)	**Extremely fair**	**56%**
B)	Pretty fair	39%
C)	Reasonably fair	6%
D)	Not very fair	0%
E)	Not fair at all	0%

Q5: Are territories equitably granted?

		% answering
A)	**Yes**	**95%**
B)	No	5%
C)	Not yet sure	0%

Q6: How would you describe the initial and ongoing training provided by your franchisor?

		% answering
A)	Excellent	37%
B)	**Good**	**47%**
C)	Adequate	16%
D)	Fair	0%
E)	Poor	0%

Q7: How well does the franchisor anticipate future trends in how it evolves and markets products and services?

		% answering
A)	**Extremely well**	**47%**
B)	**Pretty well**	**47%**
C)	Adequately	5%
D)	Not very well	0%
E)	Terribly	0%

Q8: How satisfied are you with your franchisor's spending of the royalty fees you pay?

		% answering
A)	Extremely satisfied	32%
B)	**Mostly satisfied**	**58%**
C)	Somewhat satisfied	5%
D)	Not very satisfied	0%
E)	Not satisfied at all	5%

Q9: In what ways could the parent company most improve? (Please check those that most apply, no more than three):

- ❑ Communications
- ❑ Counsel/advice on administrative/management issues
- ❑ Effectiveness of marketing/promotions
- ❑ Evolution of products/services
- ❑ Frequency of marketing/promotional campaigns

- ❑ Quality of products/services
- ❑ Pricing of products/services to franchisees
- ❑ Technology (Point of sale systems, usage of computers/email/software, etc.)
- ❑ Training

Most frequent responses:

	% answering
Effectiveness of marketing/promotions (tie)	42%
Technology (tie)	42%
Counsel/advice on administrative/management issues	32%

Q10: Is your income more, less or about what you expected prior to opening your business?

	% answering	
More	21%	
Less	37%	**Summary: 63% are making about what they**
About what was expected	**42%**	**expected, or more.**

Q11: Prior to opening your franchise, which (if any) of the following did you underestimate?

- ❑ Amount of working capital required for your 1st year in business
- ❑ Difficulty in hiring/retaining quality staff
- ❑ Expertise required to run the business
- ❑ Impact of marketing/promotions

- ❑ Start-up costs
- ❑ Degree of stress
- ❑ Workload

Most frequent responses:

	% answering
Workload	37%
Difficulty in hiring/retaining quality staff	32%
Degree of stress	26%

Q12: If you could turn back time to the day you signed your franchise agreement, would you make the same decision to buy your franchise?

	% answering
Yes	100%
No	0%

* Number of survey respondents: 19 from 16 different states
Number of survey respondents as a % of total franchise units: 12.67%

HOME HELPERS

www.homehelpers.cc
Email: inquiry@homehelpers.cc

Non-medical, personal, in-home care for seniors, expectant mothers, and those recuperating from injury or illness.

OVERALL SCORE: 56

10700 Montgomery Road
Cincinnati, OH 45242
Fax: 513-563-2691
Total number of outlets: 240 (238 in U.S.)
Total number of franchise outlets: 240 (238 in U.S.)
International: Yes (Canada)
Royalty fee: 6% of gross revenues up to $299,999, 5% of gross revenues
of $300,000 to $599,999, 4%of gross revenues of $600,000 and above,
subject to a minimum of $50 per week

OVERALL RANK: 156

Phone: 800-216-4196
Franchise fee: $18,900 for territory with population
up to 150,000, $200 per add'l. 1,000 in population
Franchise term: 10 years
Initial investment: $28,700 to $44,400
Advertising/Marketing fee: $75 per month

SURVEY AND RESULTS *

Q1: About how many hours per week do you dedicate to your franchise business?

		% answering
A)	**Less than 40**	**43%**
B)	**41–50**	**43%**
C)	51–60	7%
D)	More than 60	7%
E)	Passive investment	0%

Q2: How would you describe your relations/communications with your franchisor?

		% answering
A)	Excellent	7%
B)	**Good**	**57%**
C)	Adequate	21%
D)	Fair	0%
E)	Poor	14%

Q3: In terms of how your franchisor views your communications with other franchisees, it is:

		% answering
A)	**Very supportive**	**57%**
B)	Not very supportive	21%
C)	No influence	21%

Q4: Is the franchisor fair with you in resolving any grievances?

		% answering
A)	Extremely fair	29%
B)	**Pretty fair**	**36%**
C)	Reasonably fair	29%
D)	Not very fair	7%
E)	Not fair at all	0%

Q5: Are territories equitably granted?

		% answering
A)	**Yes**	**86%**
B)	No	0%
C)	Not yet sure	14%

Q6: How would you describe the initial and ongoing training provided by your franchisor?

		% answering
A)	Excellent	14%
B)	**Good**	**29%**
C)	Adequate	21%
D)	**Fair**	**29%**
E)	Poor	7%

Q7: How well does the franchisor anticipate future trends in how it evolves and markets products and services?

		% answering
A)	Extremely well	14%
B)	Pretty well	29%
C)	**Adequately**	**43%**
D)	Not very well	14%
E)	Terribly	0%

Q8: How satisfied are you with your franchisor's spending of the royalty fees you pay?

		% answering
A)	Extremely satisfied	7%
B)	Mostly satisfied	21%
C)	Somewhat satisfied	21%
D)	**Not very satisfied**	**36%**
E)	Not satisfied at all	14%

Q9: **In what ways could the parent company most improve? (Please check those that most apply, no more than three):**

❏ Communications

❏ Counsel/advice on administrative/management issues

❏ Effectiveness of marketing/promotions

❏ Evolution of products/services

❏ Frequency of marketing/promotional campaigns

❏ Quality of products/services

❏ Pricing of products/services to franchisees

❏ Technology (Point of sale systems, usage of computers/email/software, etc.)

❏ Training

Most frequent responses:

	% answering
Effectiveness of marketing/promotions	64%
Frequency of marketing/promotional campaigns	50%
Counsel/advice on administrative/management issues	36%

Q10: **Is your income more, less or about what you expected prior to opening your business?**

	% answering	
More	7%	
Less	**64%**	**Summary: 36% are making about what they**
About what was expected	29%	**expected, or more.**

Q11: **Prior to opening your franchise, which (if any) of the following did you underestimate?**

❏ Amount of working capital required for your 1st year in business

❏ Difficulty in hiring/retaining quality staff

❏ Expertise required to run the business

❏ Impact of marketing/promotions

❏ Start-up costs

❏ Degree of stress

❏ Workload

Most frequent responses:

	% answering
Difficulty in hiring/retaining quality staff	64%
Start-up costs (tie)	36%
Degree of stress (tie)	36%

Q12: **If you could turn back time to the day you signed your franchise agreement, would you make the same decision to buy your franchise?**

	% answering
Yes	**50%**
No	**50%**

*   Number of survey respondents: 14 from 13 different states

Number of survey respondents as a % of total franchise units: 5.83%

HOME INSTEAD SENIOR CARE

www.homeinstead.com
Email: franinfo@homeinstead.com

Non-medical companionship and home care services for the elderly.

OVERALL SCORE: 94

13330 California Street, Suite 200
Omaha, NE 68154
Fax: 402-498-5757
Total number of outlets: 575+
Total number of franchise outlets: 575+
International: Yes (several countries)

OVERALL RANK: 5

Phone: 888-484-5759
Franchise fee: $24,500
Franchise term: 10 years
Initial investment: $40,050 to $56,050
Advertising/Marketing fee: none
Royalty fee: 5% of gross sales, bi-weekly

SURVEY AND RESULTS *

Q1: About how many hours per week do you dedicate to your franchise business?

		% answering
A)	Less than 40	23%
B)	41–50	13%
C)	**51–60**	**42%**
D)	More than 60	23%
E)	Passive investment	0%

Q2: How would you describe your relations/communications with your franchisor?

		% answering
A)	**Excellent**	**66%**
B)	Good	25%
C)	Adequate	6%
D)	Fair	0%
E)	Poor	3%

Q3: In terms of how your franchisor views your communications with other franchisees, it is:

		% answering
A)	**Very supportive**	**90%**
B)	Not very supportive	3%
C)	No influence	6%

Q4: Is the franchisor fair with you in resolving any grievances?

		% answering
A)	**Extremely fair**	**70%**
B)	Pretty fair	7%
C)	Reasonably fair	19%
D)	Not very fair	0%
E)	Not fair at all	4%

Q5: Are territories equitably granted?

		% answering
A)	**Yes**	**68%**
B)	No	26%
C)	Not yet sure	6%

Q6: How would you describe the initial and ongoing training provided by your franchisor?

		% answering
A)	**Excellent**	**58%**
B)	Good	32%
C)	Adequate	6%
D)	Fair	3%
E)	Poor	0%

Q7: How well does the franchisor anticipate future trends in how it evolves and markets products and services?

		% answering
A)	**Extremely well**	**53%**
B)	Pretty well	31%
C)	Adequately	6%
D)	Not very well	9%
E)	Terribly	0%

Q8: How satisfied are you with your franchisor's spending of the royalty fees you pay?

		% answering
A)	Extremely satisfied	37%
B)	**Mostly satisfied**	**50%**
C)	Somewhat satisfied	7%
D)	Not very satisfied	7%
E)	Not satisfied at all	0%

Q9: **In what ways could the parent company most improve? (Please check those that most apply, no more than three):**

❑ Communications
❑ Counsel/advice on administrative/management issues
❑ Effectiveness of marketing/promotions
❑ Evolution of products/services
❑ Frequency of marketing/promotional campaigns

❑ Quality of products/services
❑ Pricing of products/services to franchisees
❑ Technology (Point of sale systems, usage of computers/email/software, etc.)
❑ Training

Most frequent responses:	% answering
Effectiveness of marketing/promotions (tie)	41%
Frequency of marketing/promotional campaigns (tie)	41%
Counsel/advice on administrative/management issues	38%

Q10: **Is your income more, less or about what you expected prior to opening your business?**

	% answering	
More	**47%**	
Less	23%	**Summary: 77% are making about what**
About what was expected	30%	**they expected, or more.**

Q11: **Prior to opening your franchise, which (if any) of the following did you underestimate?**

❑ Amount of working capital required for your 1st year in business
❑ Difficulty in hiring/retaining quality staff
❑ Expertise required to run the business
❑ Impact of marketing/promotions

❑ Start-up costs
❑ Degree of stress
❑ Workload

Most frequent responses:	% answering
Difficulty in hiring/retaining quality staff	44%
Degree of stress	41%
Amount of working capital required for 1st year in business	28%

Q12: **If you could turn back time to the day you signed your franchise agreement, would you make the same decision to buy your franchise?**

	% answering
Yes	**97%**
No	3%

* Number of survey respondents: 32 from 20 different states
  Number of survey respondents as a % of total franchise units: 5.57%

HOMEVESTORS OF AMERICA

www.homevestors.com

Buys and improves homes in need of repair and then re-sells them.

OVERALL SCORE: 74

10670 N. Central Expressway, Suite 700
Dallas, TX 75231
Fax: 972-761-9022
Total number of outlets: 200+
Total number of franchise outlets: 200+
International: No

OVERALL RANK: 61

Phone: 888-495-5220
Franchise fee: $46,000
Franchise term: 5 years
Initial investment: $139,150 to $219,450
Advertising/Marketing fee: varies
Royalty fee: $495 per month

SURVEY AND RESULTS *

Q1: About how many hours per week do you dedicate to your franchise business?

		% answering
A)	Less than 40	17%
B)	41–50	25%
C)	**51–60**	**33%**
D)	More than 60	25%
E)	Passive investment	0%

Q2: How would you describe your relations/ communications with your franchisor?

		% answering
A)	**Excellent**	**46%**
B)	Good	38%
C)	Adequate	8%
D)	Fair	8%
E)	Poor	0%

Q3: In terms of how your franchisor views your communications with other franchisees, it is:

		% answering
A)	**Very supportive**	**85%**
B)	Not very supportive	0%
C)	No influence	15%

Q4: Is the franchisor fair with you in resolving any grievances?

		% answering
A)	**Extremely fair**	**46%**
B)	Pretty fair	38%
C)	Reasonably fair	15%
D)	Not very fair	0%
E)	Not fair at all	0%

Q5: Are territories equitably granted?

		% answering
A)	**Yes**	**58%**
B)	No	25%
C)	Not yet sure	17%

Q6: How would you describe the initial and ongoing training provided by your franchisor?

		% answering
A)	**Excellent**	**46%**
B)	Good	38%
C)	Adequate	15%
D)	Fair	0%
E)	Poor	0%

Q7: How well does the franchisor anticipate future trends in how it evolves and markets products and services?

		% answering
A)	**Extremely well**	**46%**
B)	Pretty well	23%
C)	Adequately	8%
D)	Not very well	23%
E)	Terribly	0%

Q8: How satisfied are you with your franchisor's spending of the royalty fees you pay?

		% answering
A)	Extremely satisfied	15%
B)	**Mostly satisfied**	**54%**
C)	Somewhat satisfied	23%
D)	Not very satisfied	8%
E)	Not satisfied at all	0%

Q9: In what ways could the parent company most improve? (Please check those that most apply, no more than three):

❑ Communications
❑ Counsel/advice on administrative/management issues
❑ Effectiveness of marketing/promotions
❑ Evolution of products/services
❑ Frequency of marketing/promotional campaigns

❑ Quality of products/services
❑ Pricing of products/services to franchisees
❑ Technology (Point of sale systems, usage of computers/email/software, etc.)
❑ Training

Most frequent responses:	% answering
Counsel/advice on administrative/management issues (tie)	46%
Effectiveness of marketing/promotions (tie)	46%
Evolution of products/services	31%

Q10: Is your income more, less or about what you expected prior to opening your business?

	% answering	
More	0%	
Less	50%	Summary: 50% are making about what they
About what was expected	50%	expected, or more.

Q11: Prior to opening your franchise, which (if any) of the following did you underestimate?

❑ Amount of working capital required for your 1st year in business
❑ Difficulty in hiring/retaining quality staff
❑ Expertise required to run the business
❑ Impact of marketing/promotions

❑ Start-up costs
❑ Degree of stress
❑ Workload

Most frequent responses:	% answering
Degree of stress	54%
Amount of working capital required for 1st year in business (tie)	46%
Workload (tie)	46%

Q12: If you could turn back time to the day you signed your franchise agreement, would you make the same decision to buy your franchise?

	% answering
Yes	77%
No	23%

* Number of survey respondents: 13 from 5 different states
Number of survey respondents as a % of total franchise units: 6.50%

HOUSE DOCTORS

www.housedoctors.com
Email: info@housedoctor.com

Home handyman repair service.

OVERALL SCORE: 59

575 Chamber Drive
Milford, OH 45150
Fax: 513-831-6010
Total number of outlets: 200+
Total number of franchise outlets: 200+
International: No

OVERALL RANK: 143

Phone: 800-319-3359
Franchise fee: $13,900 to $32,900
Franchise term: 10 years
Initial investment: $25,450 to $55,550
Advertising/Marketing fee: 3% of gross revenues weekly, with a minimum of $12.50 per week
Royalty fee: 6% of gross revenues, weekly, with a minimum of $30 per week

SURVEY AND RESULTS *

Q1: About how many hours per week do you dedicate to your franchise business?

		% answering
A)	Less than 40	9%
B)	41–50	27%
C)	**51–60**	**41%**
D)	More than 60	23%
E)	Passive investment	0%

Q2: How would you describe your relations/ communications with your franchisor?

		% answering
A)	Excellent	18%
B)	**Good**	**36%**
C)	Adequate	18%
D)	Fair	20%
E)	Poor	7%

Q3: In terms of how your franchisor views your communications with other franchisees, it is:

		% answering
A)	**Very supportive**	**82%**
B)	Not very supportive	5%
C)	No influence	14%

Q4: Is the franchisor fair with you in resolving any grievances?

		% answering
A)	**Extremely fair**	**36%**
B)	Pretty fair	18%
C)	Reasonably fair	27%
D)	Not very fair	14%
E)	Not fair at all	5%

Q5: Are territories equitably granted?

		% answering
A)	**Yes**	**91%**
B)	No	5%
C)	Not yet sure	5%

Q6: How would you describe the initial and ongoing training provided by your franchisor?

		% answering
A)	Excellent	18%
B)	**Good**	**32%**
C)	Adequate	18%
D)	Fair	14%
E)	Poor	18%

Q7: How well does the franchisor anticipate future trends in how it evolves and markets products and services?

		% answering
A)	Extremely well	18%
B)	**Pretty well**	**32%**
C)	**Adequately**	**32%**
D)	Not very well	16%
E)	Terribly	2%

Q8: How satisfied are you with your franchisor's spending of the royalty fees you pay?

		% answering
A)	Extremely satisfied	14%
B)	**Mostly satisfied**	**23%**
C)	**Somewhat satisfied**	**23%**
D)	Not very satisfied	18%
E)	**Not satisfied at all**	**23%**

Q9: **In what ways could the parent company most improve? (Please check those that most apply, no more than three):**

❑ Communications
❑ Counsel/advice on administrative/management issues
❑ Effectiveness of marketing/promotions
❑ Evolution of products/services
❑ Frequency of marketing/promotional campaigns

❑ Quality of products/services
❑ Pricing of products/services to franchisees
❑ Technology (Point of sale systems, usage of computers/email/software, etc.)
❑ Training

Most frequent responses:	% answering
Effectiveness of marketing/promotions	50%
Counsel/advice on administrative/management issues	36%
Frequency of marketing/promotional campaigns	32%

Q10: **Is your income more, less or about what you expected prior to opening your business?**

	% answering	
More	0%	
Less	48%	**Summary: 52% are making about what they**
About what was expected	**52%**	**expected, or more.**

Q11: **Prior to opening your franchise, which (if any) of the following did you underestimate?**

❑ Amount of working capital required for your 1st year in business
❑ Difficulty in hiring/retaining quality staff
❑ Expertise required to run the business
❑ Impact of marketing/promotions

❑ Start-up costs
❑ Degree of stress
❑ Workload

Most frequent responses:	% answering
Difficulty in hiring/retaining quality staff	64%
Amount of working capital required for 1st year in business	32%
Start-up costs (tie)	27%
Degree of stress (tie)	27%

Q12: **If you could turn back time to the day you signed your franchise agreement, would you make the same decision to buy your franchise?**

	% answering
Yes	43%
No	**57%**

* Number of survey respondents: 22 from 17 different states
Number of survey respondents as a % of total franchise units: 11%

HOUSEMASTER HOME INSPECTIONS

www.housemaster.com
Email: sales@housemaster.com

Home inspection services.

OVERALL SCORE: 70

421 West Union Avenue
Bound Brook, NJ 08805
Total number of outlets: 380
Total number of franchise outlets: 380
International: Yes (Canada)

OVERALL RANK: 82

Phone: 800-526-3939
Franchise fee: $12,000 to $29,000
Franchise term: 5 years
Initial investment: $23,000 to $61,25
Advertising/Marketing fee: varies
Royalty fee: varies

SURVEY AND RESULTS *

Q1: About how many hours per week do you dedicate to your franchise business?

		% answering
A)	**Less than 40**	**39%**
B)	41–50	33%
C)	51–60	14%
D)	More than 60	7%
E)	Passive investment	7%

Q2: How would you describe your relations/communications with your franchisor?

		% answering
A)	Excellent	29%
B)	**Good**	**50%**
C)	Adequate	21%
D)	Fair	0%
E)	Poor	0%

Q3: In terms of how your franchisor views your communications with other franchisees, it is:

		% answering
A)	**Very supportive**	**79%**
B)	Not very supportive	0%
C)	No influence	21%

Q4: Is the franchisor fair with you in resolving any grievances?

		% answering
A)	**Extremely fair**	**42%**
B)	**Pretty fair**	**42%**
C)	Reasonably fair	17%
D)	Not very fair	0%
E)	Not fair at all	0%

Q5: Are territories equitably granted?

		% answering
A)	**Yes**	**43%**
B)	No	21%
C)	Not yet sure	36%

Q6: How would you describe the initial and ongoing training provided by your franchisor?

		% answering
A)	Excellent	43%
B)	**Good**	**50%**
C)	Adequate	7%
D)	Fair	0%
E)	Poor	0%

Q7: How well does the franchisor anticipate future trends in how it evolves and markets products and services?

		% answering
A)	**Extremely well**	**36%**
B)	**Pretty well**	**36%**
C)	Adequately	14%
D)	Not very well	14%
E)	Terribly	0%

Q8: How satisfied are you with your franchisor's spending of the royalty fees you pay?

		% answering
A)	Extremely satisfied	7%
B)	**Mostly satisfied**	**36%**
C)	**Somewhat satisfied**	**36%**
D)	Not very satisfied	14%
E)	Not satisfied at all	7%

Q9: **In what ways could the parent company most improve? (Please check those that most apply, no more than three):**

❑ Communications

❑ Counsel/advice on administrative/management issues

❑ Effectiveness of marketing/promotions

❑ Evolution of products/services

❑ Frequency of marketing/promotional campaigns

❑ Quality of products/services

❑ Pricing of products/services to franchisees

❑ Technology (Point of sale systems, usage of computers/email/software, etc.)

❑ Training

Most frequent responses:	% answering
Effectiveness of marketing/promotions (tie)	50%
Technology (tie)	50%
Pricing of products/services to franchisees	29%

Q10: **Is your income more, less or about what you expected prior to opening your business?**

	% answering	
More	21%	
Less	**57%**	**Summary: 42% are making about what they**
About what was expected	21%	**expected, or more.**

Q11: **Prior to opening your franchise, which (if any) of the following did you underestimate?**

❑ Amount of working capital required for your 1st year in business

❑ Difficulty in hiring/retaining quality staff

❑ Expertise required to run the business

❑ Impact of marketing/promotions

❑ Start-up costs

❑ Degree of stress

❑ Workload

Most frequent responses:	% answering
Difficulty in hiring/retaining quality staff	50%
Impact of marketing/promotions	36%
Degree of stress	29%

Q12: **If you could turn back time to the day you signed your franchise agreement, would you make the same decision to buy your franchise?**

	% answering
Yes	**69%**
No	31%

* Number of survey respondents: 14 from 12 different states

   Number of survey respondents as a % of total franchise units: 3.68%

HUNGRY HOWIE'S PIZZA & SUBS

www.hungryhowies.com
Email: franinfo@hungryhowies.com

Pizza, subs, and salads for carry-out or delivery.

OVERALL SCORE: 53

30300 Stephenson Highway
Madison Heights, MI 48071
Fax: 248-414-3301
Total number of outlets: 492
Total number of franchise outlets: 492
International: No

OVERALL RANK: 166

Phone: 248-414-3300
Franchise fee: $15,000
Franchise term: 20 years
Initial investment: $39,000 to $251,500
Advertising/Marketing fee: $0.20 for each pizza
box you purchase
Royalty fee: 5% of gross sales, minimum of $500 per month

SURVEY AND RESULTS *

Q1: About how many hours per week do you dedicate to your franchise business?

		% answering
A)	Less than 40	10%
B)	41–50	20%
C)	51–60	30%
D)	**More than 60**	**40%**
E)	Passive investment	0%

Q2: How would you describe your relations/communications with your franchisor?

		% answering
A)	Excellent	0%
B)	**Good**	**40%**
C)	Adequate	10%
D)	Fair	30%
E)	Poor	20%

Q3: In terms of how your franchisor views your communications with other franchisees, it is:

		% answering
A)	**Very supportive**	**40%**
B)	Not very supportive	30%
C)	No influence	30%

Q4: Is the franchisor fair with you in resolving any grievances?

		% answering
A)	Extremely fair	20%
B)	**Pretty fair**	**40%**
C)	Reasonably fair	20%
D)	Not very fair	20%
E)	Not fair at all	0%

Q5: Are territories equitably granted?

		% answering
A)	**Yes**	**60%**
B)	No	20%
C)	Not yet sure	20%

Q6: How would you describe the initial and ongoing training provided by your franchisor?

		% answering
A)	Excellent	0%
B)	Good	30%
C)	Adequate	20%
D)	Fair	0%
E)	**Poor**	**50%**

Q7: How well does the franchisor anticipate future trends in how it evolves and markets products and services?

		% answering
A)	Extremely well	10%
B)	Pretty well	20%
C)	**Adequately**	**50%**
D)	Not very well	20%
E)	Terribly	0%

Q8: How satisfied are you with your franchisor's spending of the royalty fees you pay?

		% answering
A)	Extremely satisfied	0%
B)	Mostly satisfied	20%
C)	**Somewhat satisfied**	**30%**
D)	**Not very satisfied**	**30%**
E)	Not satisfied at all	20%

Q9: **In what ways could the parent company most improve? (Please check those that most apply, no more than three):**

- ❏ Communications
- ❏ Counsel/advice on administrative/management issues
- ❏ Effectiveness of marketing/promotions
- ❏ Evolution of products/services
- ❏ Frequency of marketing/promotional campaigns
- ❏ Quality of products/services
- ❏ Pricing of products/services to franchisees
- ❏ Technology (Point of sale systems, usage of computers/email/software, etc.)
- ❏ Training

Most frequent responses:	% answering
Effectiveness of marketing/promotions	70%
Counsel/advice on administrative/management issues (tie)	40%
Frequency of marketing/promotional campaigns (tie)	40%
Training (tie)	40%

Q10: **Is your income more, less or about what you expected prior to opening your business?**

	% answering
More	11%
Less	**44%**
About what was expected	**44%**

Summary: 55% are making about what they expected, or more.

Q11: **Prior to opening your franchise, which (if any) of the following did you underestimate?**

- ❏ Amount of working capital required for your 1st year in business
- ❏ Difficulty in hiring/retaining quality staff
- ❏ Expertise required to run the business
- ❏ Impact of marketing/promotions
- ❏ Start-up costs
- ❏ Degree of stress
- ❏ Workload

Most frequent responses:	% answering
Impact of marketing/promotions (tie)	50%
Degree of stress (tie)	50%
Workload (tie)	50%

Q12: **If you could turn back time to the day you signed your franchise agreement, would you make the same decision to buy your franchise?**

	% answering
Yes	**50%**
No	**50%**

* Number of survey respondents: 10 from 6 different states
Number of survey respondents as a % of total franchise units: 2.03%

HUNTINGTON LEARNING CENTER

www.huntingtonlearning.com
Email: franchise@huntingtonlearningcenter.com

Tutoring and test preparation services.

OVERALL SCORE: 43

496 Kinderkamack Road
Oradell, NJ 07649
Total number of outlets: 230+
Total number of franchise outlets: 197
International: No

OVERALL RANK: 178

Phone: 800-653-8400
Franchise fee: $40,000
Franchise term: 10 years
Initial investment: $180,250 to $298,300
Advertising/Marketing fee: 2% of gross revenues, monthly
Royalty fee: 8% of gross revenues, monthly

SURVEY AND RESULTS *

Q1: About how many hours per week do you dedicate to your franchise business?

		% answering
A)	Less than 40	14%
B)	**41–50**	**36%**
C)	51–60	29%
D)	More than 60	21%
E)	Passive investment	0%

Q2: How would you describe your relations/communications with your franchisor?

		% answering
A)	Excellent	7%
B)	Good	13%
C)	Adequate	13%
D)	Fair	27%
E)	**Poor**	**40%**

Q3: In terms of how your franchisor views your communications with other franchisees, it is:

		% answering
A)	Very supportive	13%
B)	**Not very supportive**	**53%**
C)	No influence	33%

Q4: Is the franchisor fair with you in resolving any grievances?

		% answering
A)	Extremely fair	7%
B)	Pretty fair	20%
C)	Reasonably fair	13%
D)	**Not very fair**	**33%**
E)	Not fair at all	27%

Q5: Are territories equitably granted?

		% answering
A)	Yes	27%
B)	**No**	**53%**
C)	Not yet sure	20%

Q6: How would you describe the initial and ongoing training provided by your franchisor?

		% answering
A)	**Excellent**	**47%**
B)	Good	27%
C)	Adequate	13%
D)	Fair	13%
E)	Poor	0%

Q7: How well does the franchisor anticipate future trends in how it evolves and markets products and services?

		% answering
A)	Extremely well	0%
B)	Pretty well	20%
C)	**Adequately**	**40%**
D)	**Not very well**	**40%**
E)	Terribly	0%

Q8: How satisfied are you with your franchisor's spending of the royalty fees you pay?

		% answering
A)	Extremely satisfied	13%
B)	Mostly satisfied	7%
C)	Somewhat satisfied	27%
D)	**Not very satisfied**	**33%**
E)	Not satisfied at all	20%

Q9: **In what ways could the parent company most improve? (Please check those that most apply, no more than three):**

- ❏ Communications
- ❏ Counsel/advice on administrative/management issues
- ❏ Effectiveness of marketing/promotions
- ❏ Evolution of products/services
- ❏ Frequency of marketing/promotional campaigns

- ❏ Quality of products/services
- ❏ Pricing of products/services to franchisees
- ❏ Technology (Point of sale systems, usage of computers/email/software, etc.)
- ❏ Training

Most frequent responses:	% answering
Effectiveness of marketing/promotions (tie)	73%
Frequency of marketing/promotional campaigns (tie)	73%
Counsel/advice on administrative/management issues	47%

Q10: **Is your income more, less or about what you expected prior to opening your business?**

	% answering	
More	7%	
Less	**73%**	**Summary: 27% are making about what they**
About what was expected	20%	**expected, or more.**

Q11: **Prior to opening your franchise, which (if any) of the following did you underestimate?**

- ❏ Amount of working capital required for your 1st year in business
- ❏ Difficulty in hiring/retaining quality staff
- ❏ Expertise required to run the business
- ❏ Impact of marketing/promotions

- ❏ Start-up costs
- ❏ Degree of stress
- ❏ Workload

Most frequent responses:	% answering
Difficulty in hiring/retaining quality staff (tie)	47%
Impact of marketing/promotions (tie)	47%
Degree of stress	40%

Q12: **If you could turn back time to the day you signed your franchise agreement, would you make the same decision to buy your franchise?**

	% answering
Yes	43%
No	**57%**

* Number of survey respondents: 15 from 13 different states
Number of survey respondents as a % of total franchise units: 7.61%

IDENT-A-KID

www.ident-a-kid.com

Identification and tracking services.

OVERALL SCORE: 80

2810 Scherer Drive, Suite 100
Saint Petersburg, FL 33716
Fax: 727-576-8258
Total number of outlets: 200
Total number of franchise outlets: 200
International: Yes (Puerto Rico)

OVERALL RANK: 35

Phone: 727-577-4646
Franchise fee: $29,500
Franchise term: 10 years
Initial investment: $38,510 to $65,310
Advertising/Marketing fee: none
Royalty fee: none

SURVEY AND RESULTS *

Q1: About how many hours per week do you dedicate to your franchise business?

		% answering
A)	Less than 40	21%
B)	**41–50**	**57%**
C)	51–60	14%
D)	More than 60	7%
E)	Passive investment	0%

Q2: How would you describe your relations/communications with your franchisor?

		% answering
A)	Excellent	36%
B)	**Good**	**43%**
C)	Adequate	21%
D)	Fair	0%
E)	Poor	0%

Q3: In terms of how your franchisor views your communications with other franchisees, it is:

		% answering
A)	**Very supportive**	**68%**
B)	Not very supportive	21%
C)	No influence	11%

Q4: Is the franchisor fair with you in resolving any grievances?

		% answering
A)	Extremely fair	36%
B)	**Pretty fair**	**43%**
C)	Reasonably fair	21%
D)	Not very fair	0%
E)	Not fair at all	0%

Q5: Are territories equitably granted?

		% answering
A)	**Yes**	**100%**
B)	No	0%
C)	Not yet sure	0%

Q6: How would you describe the initial and ongoing training provided by your franchisor?

		% answering
A)	**Excellent**	**43%**
B)	Good	36%
C)	Adequate	14%
D)	Fair	7%
E)	Poor	0%

Q7: How well does the franchisor anticipate future trends in how it evolves and markets products and services?

		% answering
A)	Extremely well	36%
B)	**Pretty well**	**50%**
C)	Adequately	14%
D)	Not very well	0%
E)	Terribly	0%

Q8: How satisfied are you with your franchisor's spending of the royalty fees you pay?

		% answering
A)	Extremely satisfied	10%
B)	**Mostly satisfied**	**70%**
C)	Somewhat satisfied	20%
D)	Not very satisfied	0%
E)	Not satisfied at all	0%

Q9: **In what ways could the parent company most improve? (Please check those that most apply, no more than three):**

❑ Communications   ❑ Quality of products/services

❑ Counsel/advice on administrative/management issues   ❑ Pricing of products/services to franchisees

❑ Effectiveness of marketing/promotions   ❑ Technology (Point of sale systems, usage

❑ Evolution of products/services   of computers/email/software, etc.)

❑ Frequency of marketing/promotional campaigns   ❑ Training

Most frequent responses:	**% answering**
Pricing of products/services to franchisees	36%
Effectiveness of marketing/promotions (tie)	29%
Frequency of marketing/promotional campaigns (tie)	29%

Q10: **Is your income more, less or about what you expected prior to opening your business?**

	% answering	
More	14%	
Less	29%	**Summary: 71% are making about what they**
About what was expected	**57%**	**expected, or more.**

Q11: **Prior to opening your franchise, which (if any) of the following did you underestimate?**

❑ Amount of working capital required for your   ❑ Start-up costs

     1st year in business   ❑ Degree of stress

❑ Difficulty in hiring/retaining quality staff   ❑ Workload

❑ Expertise required to run the business

❑ Impact of marketing/promotions

Most frequent responses:	**% answering**
Impact of marketing/promotions (tie)	43%
Workload (tie)	43%
Amount of working capital required for 1st year in business (tie)	21%
Degree of stress (tie)	21%

Q12: **If you could turn back time to the day you signed your franchise agreement, would you make the same decision to buy your franchise?**

	% answering
Yes	**79%**
No	21%

* Number of survey respondents: 14 from 10 different states

   Number of survey respondents as a % of total franchise units: 7%

THE INTERFACE FINANCIAL GROUP

www.interfacefinancial.com
Email: ifg@interfacefinancial.com

Factoring services.

OVERALL SCORE: 62

2182 Dupont Drive, Suite 221
Irvine, CA 92612
Total number of outlets: 121 (72 in U.S.)
Total number of franchise outlets: 121
International: Yes (Canada)
Royalty fee: 8% of total gross profits, weekly

OVERALL RANK: 123

Phone: 800-387-0860
Franchise fee: $30,000
Franchise term: 10 years
Initial investment: $82,650 to $$133,800
Advertising/Marketing fee: 1% of gross profits
weekly (1/2% for regional, 1/2% for national)

SURVEY AND RESULTS *

Q1: About how many hours per week do you dedicate to your franchise business?

		% answering
A)	**Less than 40**	**89%**
B)	41–50	6%
C)	51–60	6%
D)	More than 60	0%
E)	Passive investment	0%

Q2: How would you describe your relations/ communications with your franchisor?

		% answering
A)	**Excellent**	**39%**
B)	**Good**	**39%**
C)	Adequate	11%
D)	Fair	11%
E)	Poor	0%

Q3: In terms of how your franchisor views your communications with other franchisees, it is:

		% answering
A)	**Very supportive**	**76%**
B)	Not very supportive	0%
C)	No influence	24%

Q4: Is the franchisor fair with you in resolving any grievances?

		% answering
A)	Extremely fair	31%
B)	**Pretty fair**	**46%**
C)	Reasonably fair	23%
D)	Not very fair	0%
E)	Not fair at all	0%

Q5: Are territories equitably granted?

		% answering
A)	Yes	15%
B)	**No**	**46%**
C)	Not yet sure	38%

Q6: How would you describe the initial and ongoing training provided by your franchisor?

		% answering
A)	Excellent	6%
B)	**Good**	**36%**
C)	Adequate	31%
D)	Fair	22%
E)	Poor	6%

Q7: How well does the franchisor anticipate future trends in how it evolves and markets products and services?

		% answering
A)	Extremely well	6%
B)	Pretty well	18%
C)	**Adequately**	**41%**
D)	Not very well	35%
E)	Terribly	0%

Q8: How satisfied are you with your franchisor's spending of the royalty fees you pay?

		% answering
A)	Extremely satisfied	0%
B)	Mostly satisfied	29%
C)	Somewhat satisfied	29%
D)	**Not very satisfied**	**35%**
E)	Not satisfied at all	6%

Q9: **In what ways could the parent company most improve? (Please check those that most apply, no more than three):**

❑ Communications

❑ Counsel/advice on administrative/management issues

❑ Effectiveness of marketing/promotions

❑ Evolution of products/services

❑ Frequency of marketing/promotional campaigns

❑ Quality of products/services

❑ Pricing of products/services to franchisees

❑ Technology (Point of sale systems, usage of computers/email/software, etc.)

❑ Training

Most frequent responses:	% answering
Effectiveness of marketing/promotions	61%
Frequency of marketing/promotional campaigns (tie)	39%
Training (tie)	39%

Q10: **Is your income more, less or about what you expected prior to opening your business?**

	% answering	
More	6%	
Less	**50%**	**Summary: 50% are making about what they**
About what was expected	44%	**expected, or more.**

Q11: **Prior to opening your franchise, which (if any) of the following did you underestimate?**

❑ Amount of working capital required for your 1st year in business

❑ Difficulty in hiring/retaining quality staff

❑ Expertise required to run the business

❑ Impact of marketing/promotions

❑ Start-up costs

❑ Degree of stress

❑ Workload

Most frequent responses:	% answering
Impact of marketing/promotions	28%
Expertise required to run the business	22%
Amount of working capital required for 1st year in business (tie)	17%
Degree of stress (tie)	17%

Q12: **If you could turn back time to the day you signed your franchise agreement, would you make the same decision to buy your franchise?**

	% answering
Yes	**59%**
No	41%

* Number of survey respondents: 18 from 13 different states

Number of survey respondents as a % of total franchise units: 6.48%

INTERIORS BY DECORATING DEN

www.decoratingden.com
Email: decden@decoratingden.com

Interior decorating services.

OVERALL SCORE: 69

8659 Commerce Drive
Easton, MD 21601
Fax: 410-820-5131
Total number of outlets: 500+
Total number of franchise outlets: 500+
International: Yes (Canada, United Kingdom)

OVERALL RANK: 86

Phone: 800-DEC-DENS
Franchise fee: $24,900
Franchise term: 10 years
Initial investment: $24,038 to $70,747
Advertising/Marketing fee: 4% of gross sales, with
a minimum payment of $100/month, twice monthly
Royalty fee: 7-9% of gross sales, twice monthly

SURVEY AND RESULTS *

Q1: About how many hours per week do you dedicate to your franchise business?

		% answering
A)	Less than 40	5%
B)	**41–50**	**58%**
C)	51–60	21%
D)	More than 60	16%
E)	Passive investment	0%

Q2: How would you describe your relations/ communications with your franchisor?

		% answering
A)	Excellent	32%
B)	**Good**	**42%**
C)	Adequate	11%
D)	Fair	11%
E)	Poor	5%

Q3: In terms of how your franchisor views your communications with other franchisees, it is:

		% answering
A)	Very supportive	79%
B)	Not very supportive	11%
C)	No influence	11%

Q4: Is the franchisor fair with you in resolving any grievances?

		% answering
A)	Extremely fair	29%
B)	**Pretty fair**	**35%**
C)	Reasonably fair	24%
D)	Not very fair	6%
E)	Not fair at all	6%

Q5: Are territories equitably granted?

		% answering
A)	**Yes**	**78%**
B)	No	6%
C)	Not yet sure	17%

Q6: How would you describe the initial and ongoing training provided by your franchisor?

		% answering
A)	Excellent	34%
B)	**Good**	**50%**
C)	Adequate	11%
D)	Fair	5%
E)	Poor	0%

Q7: How well does the franchisor anticipate future trends in how it evolves and markets products and services?

		% answering
A)	Extremely well	16%
B)	**Pretty well**	**47%**
C)	Adequately	32%
D)	Not very well	5%
E)	Terribly	0%

Q8: How satisfied are you with your franchisor's spending of the royalty fees you pay?

		% answering
A)	Extremely satisfied	16%
B)	Mostly satisfied	32%
C)	**Somewhat satisfied**	**37%**
D)	Not very satisfied	11%
E)	Not satisfied at all	5%

Q9: In what ways could the parent company most improve? (Please check those that most apply, no more than three):

- ❑ Communications
- ❑ Counsel/advice on administrative/management issues
- ❑ Effectiveness of marketing/promotions
- ❑ Evolution of products/services
- ❑ Frequency of marketing/promotional campaigns

- ❑ Quality of products/services
- ❑ Pricing of products/services to franchisees
- ❑ Technology (Point of sale systems, usage of computers/email/software, etc.)
- ❑ Training

Most frequent responses:	% answering
Counsel/advice on administrative/management issues	47%
Evolution of products/services (tie)	32%
Pricing of products/services to franchisees (tie)	32%

Q10: Is your income more, less or about what you expected prior to opening your business?

	% answering	
More	16%	
Less	**63%**	**Summary: 37% are making about what they**
About what was expected	21%	**expected, or more.**

Q11: Prior to opening your franchise, which (if any) of the following did you underestimate?

- ❑ Amount of working capital required for your 1st year in business
- ❑ Difficulty in hiring/retaining quality staff
- ❑ Expertise required to run the business
- ❑ Impact of marketing/promotions

- ❑ Start-up costs
- ❑ Degree of stress
- ❑ Workload

Most frequent responses:	% answering
Degree of stress (tie)	58%
Workload (tie)	58%
Amount of working capital required for 1st year in business	42%

Q12: If you could turn back time to the day you signed your franchise agreement, would you make the same decision to buy your franchise?

	% answering
Yes	74%
No	26%

*   Number of survey respondents: 19 from 15 different states
Number of survey respondents as a % of total franchise units: 3.80%

IT'S JUST LUNCH

www.itsjustlunch.com

Dating and matchmaking services.

OVERALL SCORE: 66

600 B Street, Suite 1850
San Diego, CA 92101
Total number of outlets: 70
Total number of franchise outlets: 70
International: Yes (Australia, Canada, Singapore)

OVERALL RANK: N/A

Phone: 619-234-7200
Franchise fee: $25,000 to $35,000
Franchise term: 10 years
Initial investment: $76,000 to $150,500
Advertising/Marketing fee: varies
Royalty fee: varies

SURVEY AND RESULTS *

Q1: About how many hours per week do you dedicate to your franchise business?

		% answering
A)	**Less than 40**	**60%**
B)	41–50	20%
C)	51–60	0%
D)	More than 60	20%
E)	Passive investment	0%

Q2: How would you describe your relations/communications with your franchisor?

		% answering
A)	Excellent	0%
B)	**Good**	**100%**
C)	Adequate	0%
D)	Fair	0%
E)	Poor	0%

Q3: In terms of how your franchisor views your communications with other franchisees, it is:

		% answering
A)	**Very supportive**	**60%**
B)	Not very supportive	40%
C)	No influence	0%

Q4: Is the franchisor fair with you in resolving any grievances?

		% answering
A)	Extremely fair	0%
B)	**Pretty fair**	**100%**
C)	Reasonably fair	0%
D)	Not very fair	0%
E)	Not fair at all	0%

Q5: Are territories equitably granted?

		% answering
A)	**Yes**	**80%**
B)	No	20%
C)	Not yet sure	0%

Q6: How would you describe the initial and ongoing training provided by your franchisor?

		% answering
A)	Excellent	0%
B)	**Good**	**40%**
C)	**Adequate**	**40%**
D)	Fair	0%
E)	Poor	20%

Q7: How well does the franchisor anticipate future trends in how it evolves and markets products and services?

		% answering
A)	**Extremely well**	**60%**
B)	Pretty well	40%
C)	Adequately	0%
D)	Not very well	0%
E)	Terribly	0%

Q8: How satisfied are you with your franchisor's spending of the royalty fees you pay?

		% answering
A)	Extremely satisfied	0%
B)	**Mostly satisfied**	**60%**
C)	Somewhat satisfied	20%
D)	Not very satisfied	20%
E)	Not satisfied at all	0%

Q9: **In what ways could the parent company most improve? (Please check those that most apply, no more than three):**

- ❑ Communications
- ❑ Counsel/advice on administrative/management issues
- ❑ Effectiveness of marketing/promotions
- ❑ Evolution of products/services
- ❑ Frequency of marketing/promotional campaigns

- ❑ Quality of products/services
- ❑ Pricing of products/services to franchisees
- ❑ Technology (Point of sale systems, usage of computers/email/software, etc.)
- ❑ Training

Most frequent responses:

	% answering
Counsel/advice on administrative/management issues (tie)	60%
Training (tie)	60%
Communications (tie)	40%
Effectiveness of marketing/promotions (tie)	40%

Q10: **Is your income more, less or about what you expected prior to opening your business?**

	% answering	
More	0%	
Less	**60%**	**Summary: 40% are making about what they**
About what was expected	40%	**expected, or more.**

Q11: **Prior to opening your franchise, which (if any) of the following did you underestimate?**

- ❑ Amount of working capital required for your 1st year in business
- ❑ Difficulty in hiring/retaining quality staff
- ❑ Expertise required to run the business
- ❑ Impact of marketing/promotions

- ❑ Start-up costs
- ❑ Degree of stress
- ❑ Workload

Most frequent responses:

	% answering
Difficulty in hiring/retaining quality staff	80%
Degree of stress	40%
Amount of working capital required for 1st year in business (tie)	20%
Impact of marketing/promotions (tie)	20%
Start-up costs (tie)	20%

Q12: **If you could turn back time to the day you signed your franchise agreement, would you make the same decision to buy your franchise?**

	% answering
Yes	**80%**
No	20%

* Number of survey respondents: 5 from 5 different states
Number of survey respondents as a % of total franchise units: 7.14%

JACKSON HEWITT TAX SERVICE

www.jacksonhewitt.com

The second largest tax preparation service in the United States.

OVERALL SCORE: 61

OVERALL RANK: 133

7 Sylvan Way
Parsippany, NJ 07054
Total number of outlets: 5,400+
Total number of franchise outlets: 5,400+
International: No

Phone: 800-475-2904
Franchise fee: $16,500 to $25,000
Franchise term: 10 years
Initial investment: $47,430 to $75,205
Advertising/Marketing fee: 6% of gross volume of business
Royalty fee: 15% of gross volume of business

SURVEY AND RESULTS *

Q1: **About how many hours per week do you dedicate to your franchise business?****

		% answering
A)	Less than 40	8%
B)	41–50	23%
C)	51–60	15%
D)	**More than 60**	**54%**
E)	Passive investment	0%

**Significantly heavier January through April

Q2: **How would you describe your relations/ communications with your franchisor?**

		% answering
A)	**Excellent**	**31%**
B)	Good	15%
C)	Adequate	14%
D)	**Fair**	**31%**
E)	Poor	8%

Q3: **In terms of how your franchisor views your communications with other franchisees, it is:**

		% answering
A)	**Very supportive**	**46%**
B)	Not very supportive	15%
C)	No influence	38%

Q4: **Is the franchisor fair with you in resolving any grievances?**

		% answering
A)	Extremely fair	0%
B)	Pretty fair	33%
C)	Reasonably fair	25%
D)	**Not very fair**	**42%**
E)	Not fair at all	0%

Q5: **Are territories equitably granted?**

		% answering
A)	**Yes**	**58%**
B)	No	25%
C)	Not yet sure	17%

Q6: **How would you describe the initial and ongoing training provided by your franchisor?**

		% answering
A)	**Excellent**	**38%**
B)	Good	23%
C)	Adequate	8%
D)	Fair	15%
E)	Poor	15%

Q7: **How well does the franchisor anticipate future trends in how it evolves and markets products and services?**

		% answering
A)	Extremely well	38%
B)	**Pretty well**	**46%**
C)	Adequately	8%
D)	Not very well	8%
E)	Terribly	0%

Q8: **How satisfied are you with your franchisor's spending of the royalty fees you pay?**

		% answering
A)	Extremely satisfied	0%
B)	**Mostly satisfied**	**46%**
C)	Somewhat satisfied	15%
D)	Not very satisfied	23%
E)	Not satisfied at all	15%

Q9: **In what ways could the parent company most improve? (Please check those that most apply, no more than three):**

❏ Communications
❏ Counsel/advice on administrative/management issues
❏ Effectiveness of marketing/promotions
❏ Evolution of products/services
❏ Frequency of marketing/promotional campaigns

❏ Quality of products/services
❏ Pricing of products/services to franchisees
❏ Technology (Point of sale systems, usage of computers/email/software, etc.)
❏ Training

Most frequent responses:	% answering
Effectiveness of marketing/promotions (tie)	62%
Frequency of marketing/promotional campaigns (tie)	62%
Communications (tie)	31%
Pricing of products/services to franchisees (tie)	31%

Q10: **Is your income more, less or about what you expected prior to opening your business?**

	% answering	
More	15%	
Less	**69%**	**Summary: 30% are making about what they**
About what was expected	15%	**expected, or more.**

Q11: **Prior to opening your franchise, which (if any) of the following did you underestimate?**

❏ Amount of working capital required for your 1st year in business
❏ Difficulty in hiring/retaining quality staff
❏ Expertise required to run the business
❏ Impact of marketing/promotions

❏ Start-up costs
❏ Degree of stress
❏ Workload

Most frequent responses:	% answering
Amount of working capital required for 1st year in business (tie)	54%
Difficulty in hiring/retaining quality staff (tie)	54%
Workload	46%

Q12: **If you could turn back time to the day you signed your franchise agreement, would you make the same decision to buy your franchise?**

	% answering
Yes	**77%**
No	23%

*   Number of survey respondents: 13 from 11 different states
Number of survey respondents as a % of total franchise units: < 1%

JIMMY JOHN'S GOURMET SANDWICHES

www.jimmyjohns.com

Gourmet sandwich shop.

OVERALL SCORE: 54

600 Tollgate Road
Elgin, IL 60123
Total number of outlets: 300+
Total number of franchise outlets: 300+
International: Yes (El Salvador, Guatemala)

OVERALL RANK: N/A

Phone: 847-888-7206
Franchise fee: $30,000
Franchise term: 10 years
Initial investment: $199,400 to $353,000
Advertising/Marketing fee: up to 4 1/2% of gross sales weekly
Royalty fee: 6% of gross sales weekly

SURVEY AND RESULTS *

Q1: About how many hours per week do you dedicate to your franchise business?

		% answering
A)	Less than 40	11%
B)	41–50	0%
C)	51–60	22%
D)	**More than 60**	**67%**
E)	Passive investment	0%

Q2: How would you describe your relations/communications with your franchisor?

		% answering
A)	Excellent	11%
B)	Good	22%
C)	**Adequate**	**33%**
D)	Fair	22%
E)	Poor	11%

Q3: In terms of how your franchisor views your communications with other franchisees, it is:

		% answering
A)	**Very supportive**	**50%**
B)	Not very supportive	13%
C)	No influence	38%

Q4: Is the franchisor fair with you in resolving any grievances?

		% answering
A)	Extremely fair	0%
B)	Pretty fair	22%
C)	**Reasonably fair**	**33%**
D)	Not very fair	22%
E)	Not fair at all	22%

Q5: Are territories equitably granted?

		% answering
A)	**Yes**	**33%**
B)	**No**	**33%**
C)	**Not yet sure**	**33%**

Q6: How would you describe the initial and ongoing training provided by your franchisor?

		% answering
A)	Excellent	11%
B)	Good	11%
C)	**Adequate**	**44%**
D)	Fair	11%
E)	Poor	22%

Q7: How well does the franchisor anticipate future trends in how it evolves and markets products and services?

		% answering
A)	Extremely well	0%
B)	Pretty well	22%
C)	Adequately	22%
D)	**Not very well**	**33%**
E)	Terribly	22%

Q8: How satisfied are you with your franchisor's spending of the royalty fees you pay?

		% answering
A)	Extremely satisfied	0%
B)	**Mostly satisfied**	**33%**
C)	**Somewhat satisfied**	**33%**
D)	Not very satisfied	11%
E)	Not satisfied at all	22%

Q9: **In what ways could the parent company most improve? (Please check those that most apply, no more than three):**

- ❏ Communications
- ❏ Counsel/advice on administrative/management issues
- ❏ Effectiveness of marketing/promotions
- ❏ Evolution of products/services
- ❏ Frequency of marketing/promotional campaigns

- ❏ Quality of products/services
- ❏ Pricing of products/services to franchisees
- ❏ Technology (Point of sale systems, usage of computers/email/software, etc.)
- ❏ Training

Most frequent responses:

	% answering
Communications	89%
Counsel/advice on administrative/management issues (tie)	56%
Effectiveness of marketing/promotions (tie)	56%

Q10: **Is your income more, less or about what you expected prior to opening your business?**

	% answering	
More	22%	
Less	**67%**	**Summary: 33% are making about what they**
About what was expected	11%	**expected, or more.**

Q11: **Prior to opening your franchise, which (if any) of the following did you underestimate?**

- ❏ Amount of working capital required for your 1st year in business
- ❏ Difficulty in hiring/retaining quality staff
- ❏ Expertise required to run the business
- ❏ Impact of marketing/promotions

- ❏ Start-up costs
- ❏ Degree of stress
- ❏ Workload

Most frequent responses:

	% answering
Impact of marketing/promotions	56%
Difficulty in hiring/retaining quality staff (tie)	44%
Degree of stress (tie)	44%

Q12: **If you could turn back time to the day you signed your franchise agreement, would you make the same decision to buy your franchise?**

	% answering
Yes	75%
No	25%

* Number of survey respondents: 9 from 6 different states
Number of survey respondents as a % of total franchise units: 3%

KELLER WILLIAMS REALTY

www.kw.com

Real estate services.

OVERALL SCORE: 83

807 Las Cimas Parkway, Suite 200
Austin, TX 78746
Fax: 512-328-1443
Total number of outlets: 437
Total number of franchise outlets: 437
International: Yes (Canada)

OVERALL RANK: 21

Phone: 512-327-3070
Franchise fee: $25,000
Franchise term: 5 years
Initial investment: $121,200 to $457,000
Advertising/Marketing fee: none currently
Royalty fee:6% of monthly gross revenues

SURVEY AND RESULTS *

Q1: About how many hours per week do you dedicate to your franchise business?

		% answering
A)	**Less than 40**	**65%**
B)	41–50	12%
C)	51–60	24%
D)	More than 60	0%
E)	Passive investment	0%

Q2: How would you describe your relations/communications with your franchisor?

		% answering
A)	**Excellent**	**65%**
B)	Good	29%
C)	Adequate	6%
D)	Fair	0%
E)	Poor	0%

Q3: In terms of how your franchisor views your communications with other franchisees, it is:

		% answering
A)	**Very supportive**	**79%**
B)	Not very supportive	21%
C)	No influence	0%

Q4: Is the franchisor fair with you in resolving any grievances?

		% answering
A)	**Extremely fair**	**53%**
B)	Pretty fair	29%
C)	Reasonably fair	18%
D)	Not very fair	0%
E)	Not fair at all	0%

Q5: Are territories equitably granted?

		% answering
A)	**Yes**	**47%**
B)	**No**	**47%**
C)	Not yet sure	6%

Q6: How would you describe the initial and ongoing training provided by your franchisor?

		% answering
A)	**Excellent**	**76%**
B)	Good	24%
C)	Adequate	0%
D)	Fair	0%
E)	Poor	0%

Q7: How well does the franchisor anticipate future trends in how it evolves and markets products and services?

		% answering
A)	**Extremely well**	**82%**
B)	Pretty well	18%
C)	Adequately	0%
D)	Not very well	0%
E)	Terribly	0%

Q8: How satisfied are you with your franchisor's spending of the royalty fees you pay?

		% answering
A)	**Extremely satisfied**	**53%**
B)	Mostly satisfied	29%
C)	Somewhat satisfied	12%
D)	Not very satisfied	6%
E)	Not satisfied at all	20%

Q9: **In what ways could the parent company most improve? (Please check those that most apply, no more than three):**

- ❏ Communications
- ❏ Counsel/advice on administrative/management issues
- ❏ Effectiveness of marketing/promotions
- ❏ Evolution of products/services
- ❏ Frequency of marketing/promotional campaigns

- ❏ Quality of products/services
- ❏ Pricing of products/services to franchisees
- ❏ Technology (Point of sale systems, usage of computers/email/software, etc.)
- ❏ Training

Most frequent responses:

	% answering
Communications (tie)	29%
Counsel/advice on administrative/management issues (tie)	29%
Frequency of marketing/promotional campaigns (tie)	29%

Q10: **Is your income more, less or about what you expected prior to opening your business?**

	% answering	
More	19%	
Less	**44%**	**Summary: 57% are making about what they**
About what was expected	38%	**expected, or more.**

Q11: **Prior to opening your franchise, which (if any) of the following did you underestimate?**

- ❏ Amount of working capital required for your 1st year in business
- ❏ Difficulty in hiring/retaining quality staff
- ❏ Expertise required to run the business
- ❏ Impact of marketing/promotions

- ❏ Start-up costs
- ❏ Degree of stress
- ❏ Workload

Most frequent responses:

	% answering
Difficulty in hiring/retaining quality staff (tie)	53%
Degree of stress (tie)	53%
Amount of working capital required for 1st year in business (tie)	35%
Workload (tie)	35%

Q12: **If you could turn back time to the day you signed your franchise agreement, would you make the same decision to buy your franchise?**

	% answering
Yes	**88%**
No	12%

* Number of survey respondents: 17 from 14 different states

Number of survey respondents as a % of total franchise units: 3.89%

KFC

www.yumfranchises.com
Email: 2yumyum@yum.com

World's largest fast-food chicken restaurants.

OVERALL SCORE: 61

1441 Gardiner Lane
Louisville, KY 40213
Fax: 502-874-8291
Total number of outlets: 13,000+
Total number of franchise outlets: 7,000+
International: Yes (worldwide)

OVERALL RANK: 129

Phone: 866-2YUMYUM
Franchise fee:
Franchise term:
Initial investment:
Advertising/Marketing fee:
Royalty fee:

SURVEY AND RESULTS *

Q1: About how many hours per week do you dedicate to your franchise business?

		% answering
A)	Less than 40	7%
B)	**41–50**	**43%**
C)	51–60	29%
D)	More than 60	21%
E)	Passive investment	0%

Q2: How would you describe your relations/communications with your franchisor?

		% answering
A)	Excellent	7%
B)	**Good**	**36%**
C)	Adequate	29%
D)	Fair	21%
E)	Poor	7%

Q3: In terms of how your franchisor views your communications with other franchisees, it is:

		% answering
A)	**Very supportive**	**50%**
B)	Not very supportive	29%
C)	No influence	21%

Q4: Is the franchisor fair with you in resolving any grievances?

		% answering
A)	Extremely fair	0%
B)	Pretty fair	29%
C)	**Reasonably fair**	**57%**
D)	Not very fair	7%
E)	Not fair at all	7%

Q5: Are territories equitably granted?

		% answering
A)	**Yes**	**86%**
B)	No	14%
C)	Not yet sure	0%

Q6: How would you describe the initial and ongoing training provided by your franchisor?

		% answering
A)	Excellent	7%
B)	Good	25%
C)	**Adequate**	**39%**
D)	Fair	21%
E)	Poor	7%

Q7: How well does the franchisor anticipate future trends in how it evolves and markets products and services?

		% answering
A)	Extremely well	0%
B)	Pretty well	14%
C)	Adequately	7%
D)	**Not very well**	**64%**
E)	Terribly	14%

Q8: How satisfied are you with your franchisor's spending of the royalty fees you pay?

		% answering
A)	Extremely satisfied	7%
B)	Mostly satisfied	14%
C)	**Somewhat satisfied**	**50%**
D)	Not very satisfied	29%
E)	Not satisfied at all	0%

Q9: **In what ways could the parent company most improve? (Please check those that most apply, no more than three):**

❑ Communications
❑ Counsel/advice on administrative/management issues
❑ Effectiveness of marketing/promotions
❑ Evolution of products/services
❑ Frequency of marketing/promotional campaigns

❑ Quality of products/services
❑ Pricing of products/services to franchisees
❑ Technology (Point of sale systems, usage of computers/email/software, etc.)
❑ Training

Most frequent responses:	% answering
Effectiveness of marketing/promotions (tie)	71%
Evolution of products/services (tie)	71%
Training	36%

Q10: **Is your income more, less or about what you expected prior to opening your business?**

	% answering	
More	21%	
Less	36%	**Summary: 64% are making about what they**
About what was expected	**43%**	**expected, or more.**

Q11: **Prior to opening your franchise, which (if any) of the following did you underestimate?**

❑ Amount of working capital required for your 1st year in businessq
❑ Difficulty in hiring/retaining quality staff
❑ Expertise required to run the business
❑ Impact of marketing/promotions

❑ Start-up costs
❑ Degree of stress
❑ Workload

Most frequent responses:	% answering
Degree of stress	50%
Difficulty in hiring/retaining quality staff	36%
Impact of marketing/promotions (tie)	29%
Workload (tie)	29%

Q12: **If you could turn back time to the day you signed your franchise agreement, would you make the same decision to buy your franchise?**

	% answering
Yes	**64%**
No	36%

* Number of survey respondents: 14 from 14 different states
   Number of survey respondents as a % of total franchise units: <1%

KINDERDANCE INTERNATIONAL

www.kinderdance.com

Educational dance, motor development programs, and gymnastics for boys and girls ages 2-8.

OVERALL SCORE: 69

OVERALL RANK: 85

1333 Gateway Drive, Suite 1003
Melbourne, FL 32901
Total number of outlets: 84 (83 in U.S.)
Total number of franchise outlets: 84
International: Yes (Canada)
Advertising/Marketing fee: 3% of gross sales, monthly

Phone: 800-554-2334
Franchise fee: $10,000 to $21,000
Franchise term: 10 years
Initial investment:
Royalty fee: 6-15% of gross sales monthly,
subject to minimums

SURVEY AND RESULTS *

Q1: About how many hours per week do you dedicate to your franchise business?

		% answering
A)	**Less than 40**	**77%**
B)	41–50	23%
C)	51–60	0%
D)	More than 60	0%
E)	Passive investment	0%

Q2: How would you describe your relations/ communications with your franchisor?

		% answering
A)	Excellent	23%
B)	**Good**	**54%**
C)	Adequate	8%
D)	Fair	8%
E)	Poor	8%

Q3: In terms of how your franchisor views your communications with other franchisees, it is:

		% answering
A)	**Very supportive**	**64%**
B)	Not very supportive	9%
C)	No influence	27%

Q4: Is the franchisor fair with you in resolving any grievances?

		% answering
A)	Extremely fair	25%
B)	**Pretty fair**	**33%**
C)	Reasonably fair	21%
D)	Not very fair	4%
E)	Not fair at all	17%

Q5: Are territories equitably granted?

		% answering
A)	**Yes**	**58%**
B)	No	33%
C)	Not yet sure	8%

Q6: How would you describe the initial and ongoing training provided by your franchisor?

		% answering
A)	Excellent	23%
B)	**Good**	**54%**
C)	Adequate	15%
D)	Fair	8%
E)	Poor	0%

Q7: How well does the franchisor anticipate future trends in how it evolves and markets products and services?

		% answering
A)	Extremely well	15%
B)	**Pretty well**	**31%**
C)	Adequately	8%
D)	**Not very well**	**31%**
E)	Terribly	15%

Q8: How satisfied are you with your franchisor's spending of the royalty fees you pay?

		% answering
A)	Extremely satisfied	0%
B)	**Mostly satisfied**	**46%**
C)	Somewhat satisfied	38%
D)	Not very satisfied	8%
E)	Not satisfied at all	8%

Q9: **In what ways could the parent company most improve? (Please check those that most apply, no more than three):**

- ❏ Communications
- ❏ Counsel/advice on administrative/management issues
- ❏ Effectiveness of marketing/promotions
- ❏ Evolution of products/services
- ❏ Frequency of marketing/promotional campaigns

- ❏ Quality of products/services
- ❏ Pricing of products/services to franchisees
- ❏ Technology (Point of sale systems, usage of computers/email/software, etc.)
- ❏ Training

Most frequent responses:

	% answering
Evolution of products/services	62%
Frequency of marketing/promotional campaigns	38%
Effectiveness of marketing/promotions (tie)	31%
Pricing of products/services to franchisees (tie)	31%

Q10: **Is your income more, less or about what you expected prior to opening your business?**

	% answering	
More	17%	
Less	33%	**Summary: 67% are making about what they**
About what was expected	**50%**	**expected, or more.**

Q11: **Prior to opening your franchise, which (if any) of the following did you underestimate?**

- ❏ Amount of working capital required for your 1st year in business
- ❏ Difficulty in hiring/retaining quality staff
- ❏ Expertise required to run the business
- ❏ Impact of marketing/promotions

- ❏ Start-up costs
- ❏ Degree of stress
- ❏ Workload

Most frequent responses:

	% answering
Difficulty in hiring/retaining quality staff	54%
Degree of stress	46%
Expertise required to run the business (tie)	23%
Workload (tie)	23%

Q12: **If you could turn back time to the day you signed your franchise agreement, would you make the same decision to buy your franchise?**

	% answering
Yes	**73%**
No	27%

* Number of survey respondents: 13 from 7 different states

Number of survey respondents as a % of total franchise units: 15.48%

KITCHEN SOLVERS

www.kitchensolvers.com

Kitchen & bath remodeling.

OVERALL SCORE: 76

401 Jay Street
La Crosse, WI 54601
Total number of outlets: 131
Total number of franchise outlets: 131
International: Yes (Canada)
Advertising/Marketing fee: 1% of monthly
gross sales

OVERALL RANK: 50

Phone: 800-845-6779
Franchise fee: $27,500 plus $150 for every 1,000
households over 100,000 households in territory
Franchise term: 10 years
Initial investment: $49,450 to $87,045
Royalty fee: varies from 4% to 8% of monthly
gross revenues

SURVEY AND RESULTS *

Q1: About how many hours per week do you dedicate to your franchise business?

		% answering
A)	Less than 40	8%
B)	41–50	25%
C)	51–60	25%
D)	**More than 60**	**42%**
E)	Passive investment	0%

Q2: How would you describe your relations/ communications with your franchisor?

		% answering
A)	**Excellent**	**42%**
B)	**Good**	**42%**
C)	Adequate	17%
D)	Fair	0%
E)	Poor	0%

Q3: In terms of how your franchisor views your communications with other franchisees, it is:

		% answering
A)	**Very supportive**	**75%**
B)	Not very supportive	0%
C)	No influence	25%

Q4: Is the franchisor fair with you in resolving any grievances?

		% answering
A)	**Extremely fair**	**58%**
B)	Pretty fair	42%
C)	Reasonably fair	0%
D)	Not very fair	0%
E)	Not fair at all	0%

Q5: Are territories equitably granted?

		% answering
A)	**Yes**	**92%**
B)	No	0%
C)	Not yet sure	8%

Q6: How would you describe the initial and ongoing training provided by your franchisor?

		% answering
A)	Excellent	25%
B)	**Good**	**58%**
C)	Adequate	17%
D)	Fair	0%
E)	Poor	0%

Q7: How well does the franchisor anticipate future trends in how it evolves and markets products and services?

		% answering
A)	Extremely well	25%
B)	**Pretty well**	**58%**
C)	Adequately	17%
D)	Not very well	0%
E)	Terribly	0%

Q8: How satisfied are you with your franchisor's spending of the royalty fees you pay?

		% answering
A)	Extremely satisfied	8%
B)	**Mostly satisfied**	**58%**
C)	Somewhat satisfied	25%
D)	Not very satisfied	8%
E)	Not satisfied at all	0%

Q9: **In what ways could the parent company most improve? (Please check those that most apply, no more than three):**

- ❏ Communications
- ❏ Counsel/advice on administrative/management issues
- ❏ Effectiveness of marketing/promotions
- ❏ Evolution of products/services
- ❏ Frequency of marketing/promotional campaigns

- ❏ Quality of products/services
- ❏ Pricing of products/services to franchisees
- ❏ Technology (Point of sale systems, usage of computers/email/software, etc.)
- ❏ Training

Most frequent responses:	% answering
Effectiveness of marketing/promotions (tie)	58%
Quality of products/services (tie)	58%
Pricing of products/services to franchisees	42%

Q10: **Is your income more, less or about what you expected prior to opening your business?**

	% answering	
More	8%	
Less	42%	**Summary: 58% are making about what they**
About what was expected	**50%**	**expected, or more.**

Q11: **Prior to opening your franchise, which (if any) of the following did you underestimate?**

- ❏ Amount of working capital required for your 1st year in business
- ❏ Difficulty in hiring/retaining quality staff
- ❏ Expertise required to run the business
- ❏ Impact of marketing/promotions

- ❏ Start-up costs
- ❏ Degree of stress
- ❏ Workload

Most frequent responses:	% answering
Workload	50%
Amount of working capital required for 1st year in business (tie)	33%
Impact of marketing/promotions (tie)	33%

Q12: **If you could turn back time to the day you signed your franchise agreement, would you make the same decision to buy your franchise?**

	% answering
Yes	**73%**
No	27%

* Number of survey respondents: 12 from 10 different states
Number of survey respondents as a % of total franchise units: 9.16%

KITCHEN TUNE-UP

www.kitchentuneup.com
Email: craig@kitchentuneup.com (Craig Green)

Kitchen and home remodeling.

OVERALL SCORE: 71

813 Circle Drive
Aberdeen, SD 57401
Fax: 605-225-1371
Total number of outlets: 300
Total number of franchise outlets: 300
International: No

OVERALL RANK: 74

Phone: 800-333-6385
Franchise fee: $9,995 to $25,000
Franchise term: 5 or 10 years
Initial investment: $410,050 to $50,065
Advertising/Marketing fee: none currently
Royalty fee: > of 7% or a monthly minimum that
varies as time passes

SURVEY AND RESULTS *

Q1: About how many hours per week do you dedicate to your franchise business?

		% answering
A)	Less than 40	13%
B)	**41–50**	**35%**
C)	51–60	17%
D)	**More than 60**	**35%**
E)	Passive investment	0%

Q2: How would you describe your relations/ communications with your franchisor?

		% answering
A)	**Excellent**	**43%**
B)	Good	35%
C)	Adequate	13%
D)	Fair	4%
E)	Poor	4%

Q3: In terms of how your franchisor views your communications with other franchisees, it is:

		% answering
A)	**Very supportive**	**74%**
B)	Not very supportive	4%
C)	No influence	22%

Q4: Is the franchisor fair with you in resolving any grievances?

		% answering
A)	**Extremely fair**	**41%**
B)	Pretty fair	27%
C)	Reasonably fair	23%
D)	Not very fair	9%
E)	Not fair at all	0%

Q5: Are territories equitably granted?

		% answering
A)	**Yes**	**73%**
B)	No	18%
C)	Not yet sure	9%

Q6: How would you describe the initial and ongoing training provided by your franchisor?

		% answering
A)	**Excellent**	**39%**
B)	Good	26%
C)	Adequate	22%
D)	Fair	9%
E)	Poor	4%

Q7: How well does the franchisor anticipate future trends in how it evolves and markets products and services?

		% answering
A)	**Extremely well**	**39%**
B)	Pretty well	35%
C)	Adequately	13%
D)	Not very well	13%
E)	Terribly	0%

Q8: How satisfied are you with your franchisor's spending of the royalty fees you pay?

		% answering
A)	Extremely satisfied	11%
B)	**Mostly satisfied**	**57%**
C)	Somewhat satisfied	23%
D)	Not very satisfied	5%
E)	Not satisfied at all	5%

Q9: **In what ways could the parent company most improve? (Please check those that most apply, no more than three):**

❏ Communications
❏ Counsel/advice on administrative/management issues
❏ Effectiveness of marketing/promotions
❏ Evolution of products/services
❏ Frequency of marketing/promotional campaigns

❏ Quality of products/services
❏ Pricing of products/services to franchisees
❏ Technology (Point of sale systems, usage of computers/email/software, etc.)
❏ Training

Most frequent responses: % answering

Frequency of marketing/promotional campaigns	43%
Effectiveness of marketing/promotions	39%
Counsel/advice on administrative/management issues	30%

Q10: **Is your income more, less or about what you expected prior to opening your business?**

% answering

More	18%	
Less	**55%**	**Summary: 45% are making about what they**
About what was expected	27%	**expected, or more.**

Q11: **Prior to opening your franchise, which (if any) of the following did you underestimate?**

❏ Amount of working capital required for your 1st year in business
❏ Difficulty in hiring/retaining quality staff
❏ Expertise required to run the business
❏ Impact of marketing/promotions

❏ Start-up costs
❏ Degree of stress
❏ Workload

Most frequent responses: % answering

Degree of stress	52%
Amount of working capital required for 1st year in business (tie)	39%
Difficulty in hiring/retaining quality staff (tie)	39%

Q12: **If you could turn back time to the day you signed your franchise agreement, would you make the same decision to buy your franchise?**

% answering

Yes	76%
No	24%

* Number of survey respondents: 23 from 19 different states
Number of survey respondents as a % of total franchise units: 7.67%

KUMON MATH & READING CENTERS

www.kumon.com

A unique learning system emphasizing math & reading.

OVERALL SCORE: 66

Glenpoint Centre East, 5th Floor
300 Frank W. Burr Blvd., Teaneck, NJ 07666
Fax: 201-928-0044
Total number of outlets: 1,500+ in U.S. and
Canada alone
Total number of franchise outlets: 1,500+ in
U.S. and Canada alone
International: Yes (worldwide)

OVERALL RANK: 103

Phone: 866-633-0740
Franchise fee:
Franchise term:
Initial investment:
Advertising/Marketing fee:
Royalty fee:

SURVEY AND RESULTS *

Q1: About how many hours per week do you dedicate to your franchise business?

		% answering
A)	**Less than 40**	**47%**
B)	41–50	33%
C)	51–60	7%
D)	More than 60	13%
E)	Passive investment	0%

Q2: How would you describe your relations/ communications with your franchisor?

		% answering
A)	Excellent	13%
B)	**Good**	**47%**
C)	Adequate	27%
D)	Fair	7%
E)	Poor	7%

Q3: In terms of how your franchisor views your communications with other franchisees, it is:

		% answering
A)	**Very supportive**	**50%**
B)	Not very supportive	14%
C)	No influence	36%

Q4: Is the franchisor fair with you in resolving any grievances?

		% answering
A)	Extremely fair	7%
B)	**Pretty fair**	**43%**
C)	Reasonably fair	21%
D)	Not very fair	21%
E)	Not fair at all	7%

Q5: Are territories equitably granted?

		% answering
A)	Yes	20%
B)	**No**	**40%**
C)	**Not yet sure**	**40%**

Q6: How would you describe the initial and ongoing training provided by your franchisor?

		% answering
A)	Excellent	20%
B)	**Good**	**40%**
C)	Adequate	33%
D)	Fair	7%
E)	Poor	0%

Q7: How well does the franchisor anticipate future trends in how it evolves and markets products and services?

		% answering
A)	Extremely well	21%
B)	Pretty well	21%
C)	Adequately	14%
D)	**Not very well**	**36%**
E)	Terribly	7%

Q8: How satisfied are you with your franchisor's spending of the royalty fees you pay?

		% answering
A)	Extremely satisfied	13%
B)	Mostly satisfied	20%
C)	Somewhat satisfied	13%
D)	**Not very satisfied**	**47%**
E)	Not satisfied at all	7%

Q9: **In what ways could the parent company most improve? (Please check those that most apply, no more than three):**

- ❏ Communications
- ❏ Counsel/advice on administrative/management issues
- ❏ Effectiveness of marketing/promotions
- ❏ Evolution of products/services
- ❏ Frequency of marketing/promotional campaigns

- ❏ Quality of products/services
- ❏ Pricing of products/services to franchisees
- ❏ Technology (Point of sale systems, usage of computers/email/software, etc.)
- ❏ Training

Most frequent responses:	% answering
Effectiveness of marketing/promotions	53%
Frequency of marketing/promotional campaigns	47%
Counsel/advice on administrative/management issues (tie)	40%
Pricing of products/services to franchisees (tie)	40%

Q10: **Is your income more, less or about what you expected prior to opening your business?**

	% answering	
More	7%	
Less	36%	**Summary: 64% are making about what they**
About what was expected	**57%**	**expected, or more.**

Q11: **Prior to opening your franchise, which (if any) of the following did you underestimate?**

- ❏ Amount of working capital required for your 1st year in business
- ❏ Difficulty in hiring/retaining quality staff
- ❏ Expertise required to run the business
- ❏ Impact of marketing/promotions

- ❏ Start-up costs
- ❏ Degree of stress
- ❏ Workload

Most frequent responses:	% answering
Workload	60%
Degree of stress	53%
Difficulty in hiring/retaining quality staff (tie)	27%
Impact of marketing/promotions (tie)	27%

Q12: **If you could turn back time to the day you signed your franchise agreement, would you make the same decision to buy your franchise?**

	% answering
Yes	**73%**
No	27%

* Number of survey respondents: 15 from 12 different states
Number of survey respondents as a % of total franchise units: <1%

KWIK KOPY PRINTING

www.kwikkopy.com
Email: kksales@kwikkopy.com

Full-service printer, copier, and document manager.

OVERALL SCORE: 57

12715 Telge Road
Cypress, TX 77429
Fax: 281-373-4450
Total number of outlets: 173
Total number of franchise outlets: 173
International: No

OVERALL RANK: 151

Phone: 888-280-2053
Franchise fee: $25,000
Franchise term:
Initial investment: $320,215 to $404,415
Advertising/Marketing fee:
Royalty fee:

SURVEY AND RESULTS *

Q1: About how many hours per week do you dedicate to your franchise business?

		% answering
A)	Less than 40	14%
B)	41–50	28%
C)	**51–60**	**38%**
D)	More than 60	21%
E)	Passive investment	0%

Q2: How would you describe your relations/ communications with your franchisor?

		% answering
A)	Excellent	10%
B)	**Good**	**36%**
C)	Adequate	31%
D)	Fair	14%
E)	Poor	9%

Q3: In terms of how your franchisor views your communications with other franchisees, it is:

		% answering
A)	**Very supportive**	**61%**
B)	Not very supportive	14%
C)	No influence	25%

Q4: Is the franchisor fair with you in resolving any grievances?

		% answering
A)	Extremely fair	4%
B)	Pretty fair	26%
C)	**Reasonably fair**	**52%**
D)	Not very fair	19%
E)	Not fair at all	0%

Q5: Are territories equitably granted?

		% answering
A)	**Yes**	**56%**
B)	No	22%
C)	Not yet sure	22%

Q6: How would you describe the initial and ongoing training provided by your franchisor?

		% answering
A)	Excellent	21%
B)	**Good**	**48%**
C)	Adequate	17%
D)	Fair	7%
E)	Poor	7%

Q7: How well does the franchisor anticipate future trends in how it evolves and markets products and services?

		% answering
A)	Extremely well	7%
B)	**Pretty well**	**39%**
C)	Adequately	29%
D)	Not very well	25%
E)	Terribly	0%

Q8: How satisfied are you with your franchisor's spending of the royalty fees you pay?

		% answering
A)	Extremely satisfied	0%
B)	Mostly satisfied	21%
C)	**Somewhat satisfied**	**31%**
D)	Not very satisfied	21%
E)	Not satisfied at all	28%

Q9: **In what ways could the parent company most improve? (Please check those that most apply, no more than three):**

- ❏ Communications
- ❏ Counsel/advice on administrative/management issues
- ❏ Effectiveness of marketing/promotions
- ❏ Evolution of products/services
- ❏ Frequency of marketing/promotional campaigns

- ❏ Quality of products/services
- ❏ Pricing of products/services to franchisees
- ❏ Technology (Point of sale systems, usage of computers/email/software, etc.)
- ❏ Training

Most frequent responses:	% answering
Effectiveness of marketing/promotions	38%
Frequency of marketing/promotional campaigns	34%
Pricing of products/services to franchisees	28%

Q10: **Is your income more, less or about what you expected prior to opening your business?**

	% answering	
More	14%	
Less	**50%**	**Summary: 50% are making about what they**
About what was expected	36%	**expected, or more.**

Q11: **Prior to opening your franchise, which (if any) of the following did you underestimate?**

- ❏ Amount of working capital required for your 1st year in business
- ❏ Difficulty in hiring/retaining quality staff
- ❏ Expertise required to run the business
- ❏ Impact of marketing/promotions

- ❏ Start-up costs
- ❏ Degree of stress
- ❏ Workload

Most frequent responses:	% answering
Difficulty in hiring/retaining quality staff	55%
Amount of working capital required for 1st year in business (tie)	38%
Degree of stress (tie)	38%

Q12: **If you could turn back time to the day you signed your franchise agreement, would you make the same decision to buy your franchise?**

	% answering
Yes	46%
No	**54%**

*   Number of survey respondents: 29 from 18 different states
Number of survey respondents as a % of total franchise units: 16.76%

LAWN DOCTOR

www.lawndoctor.com
Email: franchiseinformation@lawndoctor.com

Lawn, tree, and shrub care.

OVERALL SCORE: 69

142 State Route 34
Holmdel, NJ 07733
Total number of outlets: 450+
Total number of franchise outlets: 450+
International: No

OVERALL RANK: 84

Phone: 800-631-5660
Franchise fee: $74,900
Franchise term: 20 years
Initial investment: $82,900 to $83,300
Advertising/Marketing fee: none currently
Royalty fee:10% of net revenues weekly

SURVEY AND RESULTS *

Q1: About how many hours per week do you dedicate to your franchise business?

		% answering
A)	Less than 40	8%
B)	**41–50**	**42%**
C)	51–60	17%
D)	More than 60	33%
E)	Passive investment	0%

Q2: How would you describe your relations/communications with your franchisor?

		% answering
A)	Excellent	29%
B)	Good	21%
C)	**Adequate**	**33%**
D)	Fair	17%
E)	Poor	0%

Q3: In terms of how your franchisor views your communications with other franchisees, it is:

		% answering
A)	**Very supportive**	**58%**
B)	Not very supportive	17%
C)	No influence	25%

Q4: Is the franchisor fair with you in resolving any grievances?

		% answering
A)	**Extremely fair**	**36%**
B)	Pretty fair	27%
C)	**Reasonably fair**	**36%**
D)	Not very fair	0%
E)	Not fair at all	0%

Q5: Are territories equitably granted?

		% answering
A)	**Yes**	**83%**
B)	No	17%
C)	Not yet sure	0%

Q6: How would you describe the initial and ongoing training provided by your franchisor?

		% answering
A)	Excellent	25%
B)	**Good**	**38%**
C)	Adequate	33%
D)	Fair	0%
E)	Poor	4%

Q7: How well does the franchisor anticipate future trends in how it evolves and markets products and services?

		% answering
A)	Extremely well	29%
B)	**Pretty well**	**38%**
C)	Adequately	0%
D)	Not very well	33%
E)	Terribly	0%

Q8: How satisfied are you with your franchisor's spending of the royalty fees you pay?

		% answering
A)	Extremely satisfied	9%
B)	**Mostly satisfied**	**36%**
C)	**Somewhat satisfied**	**36%**
D)	Not very satisfied	9%
E)	Not satisfied at all	0%

Q9: **In what ways could the parent company most improve? (Please check those that most apply, no more than three):**

- ❏ Communications
- ❏ Counsel/advice on administrative/management issues
- ❏ Effectiveness of marketing/promotions
- ❏ Evolution of products/services
- ❏ Frequency of marketing/promotional campaigns

- ❏ Quality of products/services
- ❏ Pricing of products/services to franchisees
- ❏ Technology (Point of sale systems, usage of computers/email/software, etc.)
- ❏ Training

Most frequent responses:	% answering
Effectiveness of marketing/promotions (tie)	42%
Frequency of marketing/promotional campaigns (tie)	42%
Pricing of products/services to franchisees (tie)	42%

Q10: **Is your income more, less or about what you expected prior to opening your business?**

	% answering	
More	17%	
Less	**42%**	Summary: 59% are making about what they
About what was expected	**42%**	expected, or more.

Q11: **Prior to opening your franchise, which (if any) of the following did you underestimate?**

- ❏ Amount of working capital required for your 1st year in business
- ❏ Difficulty in hiring/retaining quality staff
- ❏ Expertise required to run the business
- ❏ Impact of marketing/promotions

- ❏ Start-up costs
- ❏ Degree of stress
- ❏ Workload

Most frequent responses:	% answering
Amount of working capital required for 1st year in business	42%
Impact of marketing/promotions (tie)	33%
Start-up costs (tie)	33%
Degree of stress (tie)	33%

Q12: **If you could turn back time to the day you signed your franchise agreement, would you make the same decision to buy your franchise?**

	% answering
Yes	**67%**
No	33%

*   Number of survey respondents: 12 from 10 different states

    Number of survey respondents as a % of total franchise units: 2.67%

LEADERSHIP MANAGEMENT

www.lmi-bus.com

Supervisory, leadership, and executive development training.

OVERALL SCORE: 61

4567 Lake Shore Drive
Waco, TX 76710
Total number of outlets: 249
Total number of franchise outlets: 249
International: Yes (worldwide)

OVERALL RANK: 130

Phone: 2554-776-2060
Franchise fee: $30,000
Franchise term: 10 years
Initial investment: $33,500 to $37,500
Advertising/Marketing fee: none currently
Royalty fee: 6% of monthly revenues, not to exceed $6,000 per year

SURVEY AND RESULTS *

Q1: About how many hours per week do you dedicate to your franchise business?

		% answering
A)	Less than 40	31%
B)	**41–50**	**44%**
C)	51–60	25%
D)	More than 60	0%
E)	Passive investment	0%

Q2: How would you describe your relations/communications with your franchisor?

		% answering
A)	Excellent	13%
B)	Good	27%
C)	**Adequate**	**47%**
D)	Fair	7%
E)	Poor	7%

Q3: In terms of how your franchisor views your communications with other franchisees, it is:

		% answering
A)	**Very supportive**	**47%**
B)	Not very supportive	27%
C)	No influence	27%

Q4: Is the franchisor fair with you in resolving any grievances?

		% answering
A)	Extremely fair	15%
B)	**Pretty fair**	**54%**
C)	Reasonably fair	23%
D)	Not very fair	8%
E)	Not fair at all	0%

Q5: Are territories equitably granted?

		% answering
A)	Yes	33%
B)	**No**	**50%**
C)	Not yet sure	17%

Q6: How would you describe the initial and ongoing training provided by your franchisor?

		% answering
A)	Excellent	25%
B)	**Good**	**31%**
C)	Adequate	25%
D)	Fair	6%
E)	Poor	13%

Q7: How well does the franchisor anticipate future trends in how it evolves and markets products and services?

		% answering
A)	Extremely well	6%
B)	**Pretty well**	**38%**
C)	**Adequately**	**38%**
D)	Not very well	13%
E)	Terribly	6%

Q8: How satisfied are you with your franchisor's spending of the royalty fees you pay?

		% answering
A)	Extremely satisfied	7%
B)	**Mostly satisfied**	**64%**
C)	Somewhat satisfied	7%
D)	Not very satisfied	14%
E)	Not satisfied at all	7%

Q9: **In what ways could the parent company most improve? (Please check those that most apply, no more than three):**

- ❏ Communications
- ❏ Counsel/advice on administrative/management issues
- ❏ Effectiveness of marketing/promotions
- ❏ Evolution of products/services
- ❏ Frequency of marketing/promotional campaigns

- ❏ Quality of products/services
- ❏ Pricing of products/services to franchisees
- ❏ Technology (Point of sale systems, usage of computers/email/software, etc.)
- ❏ Training

Most frequent responses: % answering

	% answering
Evolution of products/services (tie)	44%
Frequency of marketing/promotional campaigns (tie)	44%
Effectiveness of marketing/promotions	38%

Q10: **Is your income more, less or about what you expected prior to opening your business?**

	% answering	
More	13%	
Less	**63%**	**Summary: 38% are making about what they**
About what was expected	25%	**expected, or more.**

Q11: **Prior to opening your franchise, which (if any) of the following did you underestimate?**

- ❏ Amount of working capital required for your 1st year in business
- ❏ Difficulty in hiring/retaining quality staff
- ❏ Expertise required to run the business
- ❏ Impact of marketing/promotions

- ❏ Start-up costs
- ❏ Degree of stress
- ❏ Workload

Most frequent responses: % answering

	% answering
Difficulty in hiring/retaining quality staff	56%
Degree of stress	44%
Expertise required to run the business (tie)	38%
Impact of marketing/promotions (tie)	38%

Q12: **If you could turn back time to the day you signed your franchise agreement, would you make the same decision to buy your franchise?**

	% answering
Yes	**75%**
No	25%

*   Number of survey respondents: 16 from 13 different states

Number of survey respondents as a % of total franchise units: 6.43%

LEARNING EXPRESS

www.learningexpress.com
Email: info@learningexpress.com

The largest specialty toy retailer in the United States.

OVERALL SCORE: 71

29 Buena Vista Street
Devens, MA 01434
Fax: 978-889-1010
Total number of outlets: 107
Total number of franchise outlets: 107
International: No

OVERALL RANK: 76

Phone: 978-889-1000
Franchise fee: $30,000
Franchise term: 10 years
Initial investment: $167,000 to $277,000
Advertising/Marketing fee: none currently
Royalty fee: 5% of gross receipts, monthly

SURVEY AND RESULTS *

Q1: About how many hours per week do you dedicate to your franchise business?

		% answering
A)	Less than 40	9%
B)	41–50	18%
C)	**51–60**	**45%**
D)	More than 60	27%
E)	Passive investment	0%

Q2: How would you describe your relations/ communications with your franchisor?

		% answering
A)	Excellent	36%
B)	**Good**	**64%**
C)	Adequate	0%
D)	Fair	0%
E)	Poor	0%

Q3: In terms of how your franchisor views your communications with other franchisees, it is:

		% answering
A)	**Very supportive**	**82%**
B)	Not very supportive	18%
C)	No influence	0%

Q4: Is the franchisor fair with you in resolving any grievances?

		% answering
A)	Extremely fair	36%
B)	**Pretty fair**	**55%**
C)	Reasonably fair	9%
D)	Not very fair	0%
E)	Not fair at all	0%

Q5: Are territories equitably granted?

		% answering
A)	**Yes**	**91%**
B)	No	9%
C)	Not yet sure	0%

Q6: How would you describe the initial and ongoing training provided by your franchisor?

		% answering
A)	Excellent	18%
B)	**Good**	**50%**
C)	Adequate	27%
D)	Fair	0%
E)	Poor	5%

Q7: How well does the franchisor anticipate future trends in how it evolves and markets products and services?

		% answering
A)	Extremely well	27%
B)	Pretty well	27%
C)	**Adequately**	**36%**
D)	Not very well	9%
E)	Terribly	0%

Q8: How satisfied are you with your franchisor's spending of the royalty fees you pay?

		% answering
A)	Extremely satisfied	18%
B)	Mostly satisfied	18%
C)	**Somewhat satisfied**	**55%**
D)	Not very satisfied	9%
E)	Not satisfied at all	0%

Q9: **In what ways could the parent company most improve? (Please check those that most apply, no more than three):**

- ❏ Communications
- ❏ Counsel/advice on administrative/management issues
- ❏ Effectiveness of marketing/promotions
- ❏ Evolution of products/services
- ❏ Frequency of marketing/promotional campaigns

- ❏ Quality of products/services
- ❏ Pricing of products/services to franchisees
- ❏ Technology (Point of sale systems, usage of computers/email/software, etc.)
- ❏ Training

Most frequent responses:

	% answering
Counsel/advice on administrative/management issues (tie)	45%
Training (tie)	45%
Effectiveness of marketing/promotions	27%

Q10: **Is your income more, less or about what you expected prior to opening your business?**

	% answering	
More	9%	
Less	**55%**	**Summary: 45% are making about what they**
About what was expected	36%	**expected, or more.**

Q11: **Prior to opening your franchise, which (if any) of the following did you underestimate?**

- ❏ Amount of working capital required for your first year in business
- ❏ Difficulty in hiring/retaining quality staff
- ❏ Expertise required to run the business
- ❏ Impact of marketing/promotions

- ❏ Start-up costs
- ❏ Degree of stress
- ❏ Workload

Most frequent responses:

	% answering
Workload	73%
Expertise required to run the business	45%
Degree of stress	36%

Q12: **If you could turn back time to the day you signed your franchise agreement, would you make the same decision to buy your franchise?**

	% answering
Yes	**70%**
No	30%

* Number of survey respondents: 11 from 8 different states
   Number of survey respondents as a % of total franchise units: 10.28%

LIBERTY TAX SERVICE

www.libertytax.com
Email: sales@libtax.com

Income tax preparation service.

OVERALL SCORE: 54

1716 Corporate Landing Parkway
Virginia Beach, VA 23454
Fax: 757-301-8080
Total number of outlets: 1,735
Total number of franchise outlets: 1,735
International: Yes (Canada)

OVERALL RANK: 161

Phone: 800-790-3863, ext. 8130
Franchise fee: $28,000
Franchise term: 5 years
Initial investment: $38,800 to $50,400
Advertising/Marketing fee: 5% of gross receipts, monthly
Royalty fee: varies

SURVEY AND RESULTS *

Q1: About how many hours per week do you dedicate to your franchise business?

		% answering
A)	**Less than 40**	**29%**
B)	**41–50**	**29%**
C)	51–60	14%
D)	**More than 60**	**29%**
E)	Passive investment	0%

Q2: How would you describe your relations/communications with your franchisor?

		% answering
A)	Excellent	14%
B)	Good	18%
C)	**Adequate**	**39%**
D)	Fair	7%
E)	Poor	22%

Q3: In terms of how your franchisor views your communications with other franchisees, it is:

		% answering
A)	**Very supportive**	**71%**
B)	Not very supportive	21%
C)	No influence	7%

Q4: Is the franchisor fair with you in resolving any grievances?

		% answering
A)	Extremely fair	7%
B)	Pretty fair	32%
C)	**Reasonably fair**	**40%**
D)	Not very fair	14%
E)	Not fair at all	7%

Q5: Are territories equitably granted?

		% answering
A)	**Yes**	**36%**
B)	**No**	**36%**
C)	Not yet sure	29%

Q6: How would you describe the initial and ongoing training provided by your franchisor?

		% answering
A)	Excellent	21%
B)	**Good**	**29%**
C)	**Adequate**	**29%**
D)	Fair	21%
E)	Poor	0%

Q7: How well does the franchisor anticipate future trends in how it evolves and markets products and services?

		% answering
A)	Extremely well	25%
B)	**Pretty well**	**54%**
C)	Adequately	14%
D)	Not very well	7%
E)	Terribly	0%

Q8: How satisfied are you with your franchisor's spending of the royalty fees you pay?

		% answering
A)	Extremely satisfied	0%
B)	Mostly satisfied	21%
C)	**Somewhat satisfied**	**29%**
D)	Not very satisfied	21%
E)	**Not satisfied at all**	**29%**

Q9: In what ways could the parent company most improve? (Please check those that most apply, no more than three):

❑ Communications
❑ Counsel/advice on administrative/management issues
❑ Effectiveness of marketing/promotions
❑ Evolution of products/services
❑ Frequency of marketing/promotional campaigns

❑ Quality of products/services
❑ Pricing of products/services to franchisees
❑ Technology (Point of sale systems, usage of computers/email/software, etc.)
❑ Training

Most frequent responses:	% answering
Communications (tie)	50%
Technology (tie)	50%
Counsel/advice on administrative/management issues	43%

Q10: Is your income more, less or about what you expected prior to opening your business?

	% answering	
More	0%	
Less	**67%**	**Summary: 33% are making about what they**
About what was expected	33%	**expected, or more.**

Q11: Prior to opening your franchise, which (if any) of the following did you underestimate?

❑ Amount of working capital required for your 1st year in business
❑ Difficulty in hiring/retaining quality staff
❑ Expertise required to run the business
❑ Impact of marketing/promotions

❑ Start-up costs
❑ Degree of stress
❑ Workload

Most frequent responses:	% answering
Amount of working capital required for 1st year in business	93%
Start-up costs	64%
Difficulty in hiring/retaining quality staff	43%

Q12: If you could turn back time to the day you signed your franchise agreement, would you make the same decision to buy your franchise?

	% answering
Yes	**50%**
No	**50%**

* Number of survey respondents: 14 from 13 different states
Number of survey respondents as a % of total franchise units: <1%

LIL' ANGELS

www.lilangelsphoto.com
Email: sales@lilangelsphoto.com

Photography services to children's daycare, pre-school, and other child-focused organizations.

OVERALL SCORE: 79

4041 Hatcher Road
Memphis, TN 38118
Total number of outlets: 106
Total number of franchise outlets: 106
International: No

OVERALL RANK: 39

Phone: 800-358-9101
Franchise fee: $17,000
Franchise term: 10 years
Initial investment: $30,700 to $35,200
Advertising/Marketing fee: none currently
Royalty fee: none currently

SURVEY AND RESULTS *

Q1: About how many hours per week do you dedicate to your franchise business?

		% answering
A)	Less than 40	23%
B)	**41–50**	**38%**
C)	51–60	23%
D)	More than 60	8%
E)	Passive investment	8%

Q2: How would you describe your relations/communications with your franchisor?

		% answering
A)	**Excellent**	**38%**
B)	Good	23%
C)	Adequate	15%
D)	Fair	23%
E)	Poor	0%

Q3: In terms of how your franchisor views your communications with other franchisees, it is:

		% answering
A)	**Very supportive**	**69%**
B)	Not very supportive	23%
C)	No influence	8%

Q4: Is the franchisor fair with you in resolving any grievances?

		% answering
A)	Extremely fair	33%
B)	Pretty fair	8%
C)	**Reasonably fair**	**50%**
D)	Not very fair	8%
E)	Not fair at all	0%

Q5: Are territories equitably granted?

		% answering
A)	**Yes**	**62%**
B)	No	23%
C)	Not yet sure	15%

Q6: How would you describe the initial and ongoing training provided by your franchisor?

		% answering
A)	Excellent	23%
B)	**Good**	**38%**
C)	Adequate	31%
D)	Fair	0%
E)	Poor	8%

Q7: How well does the franchisor anticipate future trends in how it evolves and markets products and services?

		% answering
A)	Extremely well	15%
B)	**Pretty well**	**62%**
C)	Adequately	15%
D)	Not very well	8%
E)	Terribly	0%

Q8: How satisfied are you with your franchisor's spending of the royalty fees you pay?

		% answering
A)	Extremely satisfied	18%
B)	**Mostly satisfied**	**36%**
C)	**Somewhat satisfied**	**36%**
D)	Not very satisfied	9%
E)	Not satisfied at all	0%

Q9: **In what ways could the parent company most improve? (Please check those that most apply, no more than three):**

❑ Communications
❑ Counsel/advice on administrative/management issues
❑ Effectiveness of marketing/promotions
❑ Evolution of products/services
❑ Frequency of marketing/promotional campaigns

❑ Quality of products/services
❑ Pricing of products/services to franchisees
❑ Technology (Point of sale systems, usage of computers/email/software, etc.)
❑ Training

Most frequent responses:	% answering
Communications (tie)	46%
Training (tie)	46%
Effectiveness of marketing/promotions (tie)	31%
Quality of products/services (tie)	31%

Q10: **Is your income more, less or about what you expected prior to opening your business?**

	% answering	
More	31%	
Less	**38%**	**Summary: 62% are making about what they**
About what was expected	31%	**expected, or more.**

Q11: **Prior to opening your franchise, which (if any) of the following did you underestimate?**

❑ Amount of working capital required for your 1st year in business
❑ Difficulty in hiring/retaining quality staff
❑ Expertise required to run the business
❑ Impact of marketing/promotions

❑ Start-up costs
❑ Degree of stress
❑ Workload

Most frequent responses:	% answering
Degree of stress	62%
Workload	46%
Difficulty in hiring/retaining quality staff	38%

Q12: **If you could turn back time to the day you signed your franchise agreement, would you make the same decision to buy your franchise?**

	% answering
Yes	**92%**
No	8%

* Number of survey respondents: 13 from 9 different states
  Number of survey respondents as a % of total franchise units: 12.26%

LINE-X

www.linexcorp.com

Spray-on bed liners for trucks.

OVERALL SCORE: 59

2400 S. Garnsey Street
Santa Ana, CA 92707
Fax: 714-850-8759
Total number of outlets: 222
Total number of franchise outlets: 222
International: Yes (worldwide)

OVERALL RANK: 139

Phone: 800-831-3232
Franchise fee: $30,000
Franchise term: 5 years
Initial investment: $68,000 to $147,000
Advertising/Marketing fee: 1.5% of net sales quarterly
Royalty fee: none

SURVEY AND RESULTS *

Q1: About how many hours per week do you dedicate to your franchise business?

		% answering
A)	Less than 40	11%
B)	41–50	22%
C)	**51–60**	**33%**
D)	More than 60	28%
E)	Passive investment	6%

Q2: How would you describe your relations/communications with your franchisor?

		% answering
A)	**Excellent**	**39%**
B)	Good	17%
C)	Adequate	17%
D)	Fair	11%
E)	Poor	17%

Q3: In terms of how your franchisor views your communications with other franchisees, it is:

		% answering
A)	**Very supportive**	**44%**
B)	Not very supportive	28%
C)	No influence	28%

Q4: Is the franchisor fair with you in resolving any grievances?

		% answering
A)	Extremely fair	22%
B)	**Pretty fair**	**33%**
C)	Reasonably fair	11%
D)	Not very fair	28%
E)	Not fair at all	6%

Q5: Are territories equitably granted?

		% answering
A)	**Yes**	**39%**
B)	No	28%
C)	Not yet sure	33%

Q6: How would you describe the initial and ongoing training provided by your franchisor?

		% answering
A)	Excellent	6%
B)	**Good**	**44%**
C)	Adequate	11%
D)	Fair	22%
E)	Poor	17%

Q7: How well does the franchisor anticipate future trends in how it evolves and markets products and services?

		% answering
A)	Extremely well	17%
B)	**Pretty well**	**39%**
C)	Adequately	28%
D)	Not very well	6%
E)	Terribly	11%

Q8: How satisfied are you with your franchisor's spending of the royalty fees you pay?

		% answering
A)	Extremely satisfied	0%
B)	Mostly satisfied	29%
C)	**Somewhat satisfied**	**41%**
D)	Not very satisfied	6%
E)	Not satisfied at all	24%

Q9: **In what ways could the parent company most improve? (Please check those that most apply, no more than three):**

- ❑ Communications
- ❑ Counsel/advice on administrative/management issues
- ❑ Effectiveness of marketing/promotions
- ❑ Evolution of products/services
- ❑ Frequency of marketing/promotional campaigns
- ❑ Quality of products/services
- ❑ Pricing of products/services to franchisees
- ❑ Technology (Point of sale systems, usage of computers/email/software, etc.)
- ❑ Training

Most frequent responses:	% answering
Pricing of products/services to franchisees	67%
Effectiveness of marketing/promotions	56%
Frequency of marketing/promotional campaigns	39%

Q10: **Is your income more, less or about what you expected prior to opening your business?**

	% answering
More	6%
Less	**53%**
About what was expected	41%

Summary: 47% are making about what they expected, or more.

Q11: **Prior to opening your franchise, which (if any) of the following did you underestimate?**

- ❑ Amount of working capital required for your 1st year in business
- ❑ Difficulty in hiring/retaining quality staff
- ❑ Expertise required to run the business
- ❑ Impact of marketing/promotions
- ❑ Start-up costs
- ❑ Degree of stress
- ❑ Workload

Most frequent responses:	% answering
Difficulty in hiring/retaining quality staff	50%
Amount of working capital required for 1st year in business	39%
Impact of marketing/promotions	39%

Q12: **If you could turn back time to the day you signed your franchise agreement, would you make the same decision to buy your franchise?**

	% answering
Yes	**71%**
No	29%

* Number of survey respondents: 18 from 21 different states
  Number of survey respondents as a % of total franchise units: 18.14%

LITTLE CAESARS

www.littlecaesars.com

Fast-food pizza.

OVERALL SCORE: 83

OVERALL RANK: 20

2211 Woodward Avenue
Detroit, MI 48201
Fax: 313-983-6390
Total number of outlets: Approximately 3,000
Total number of franchise outlets:
Approximately 3,000
International: No

Phone: 313-983-6000
Franchise fee: $20,000
Franchise term:
Initial investment: $109,000 to $299,000
Advertising/Marketing fee: 1/4% of gross sales
Royalty fee: 6% of gross sales

SURVEY AND RESULTS *

Q1: About how many hours per week do you dedicate to your franchise business?

		% answering
A)	Less than 40	15%
B)	**41–50**	**69%**
C)	51–60	8%
D)	More than 60	8%
E)	Passive investment	0%

Q2: How would you describe your relations/ communications with your franchisor?

		% answering
A)	Excellent	0%
B)	**Good**	**46%**
C)	Adequate	23%
D)	Fair	23%
E)	Poor	8%

Q3: In terms of how your franchisor views your communications with other franchisees, it is:

		% answering
A)	**Very supportive**	**46%**
B)	Not very supportive	15%
C)	No influence	38%

Q4: Is the franchisor fair with you in resolving any grievances?

		% answering
A)	Extremely fair	0%
B)	**Pretty fair**	**38%**
C)	**Reasonably fair**	**38%**
D)	Not very fair	23%
E)	Not fair at all	0%

Q5: Are territories equitably granted?

		% answering
A)	**Yes**	**69%**
B)	No	15%
C)	Not yet sure	15%

Q6: How would you describe the initial and ongoing training provided by your franchisor?

		% answering
A)	Excellent	8%
B)	**Good**	**54%**
C)	Adequate	23%
D)	Fair	15%
E)	Poor	0%

Q7: How well does the franchisor anticipate future trends in how it evolves and markets products and services?

		% answering
A)	Extremely well	8%
B)	**Pretty well**	**31%**
C)	Adequately	46%
D)	Not very well	15%
E)	Terribly	0%

Q8: How satisfied are you with your franchisor's spending of the royalty fees you pay?

		% answering
A)	Extremely satisfied	8%
B)	Mostly satisfied	31%
C)	Somewhat satisfied	38%
D)	Not very satisfied	15%
E)	Not satisfied at all	8%

Q9: In what ways could the parent company most improve? (Please check those that most apply, no more than three):

- ❑ Communications
- ❑ Counsel/advice on administrative/management issues
- ❑ Effectiveness of marketing/promotions
- ❑ Evolution of products/services
- ❑ Frequency of marketing/promotional campaigns

- ❑ Quality of products/services
- ❑ Pricing of products/services to franchisees
- ❑ Technology (Point of sale systems, usage of computers/email/software, etc.)
- ❑ Training

Most frequent responses:	% answering
Evolution of products/services	62%
Pricing of products/services to franchisees	38%
Communications (tie)	31%
Technology (tie)	31%
Training (tie)	31%

Q10: Is your income more, less or about what you expected prior to opening your business?

	% answering
More	**54%**
Less	23%
About what was expected	23%

Summary: 77% are making about what they expected, or more.

Q11: Prior to opening your franchise, which (if any) of the following did you underestimate?

- ❑ Amount of working capital required for your 1st year in business
- ❑ Difficulty in hiring/retaining quality staff
- ❑ Expertise required to run the business
- ❑ Impact of marketing/promotions

- ❑ Start-up costs
- ❑ Degree of stress
- ❑ Workload

Most frequent responses:	% answering
Difficulty in hiring/retaining quality staff	46%
Impact of marketing/promotions	38%
Workload	23%

Q12: If you could turn back time to the day you signed your franchise agreement, would you make the same decision to buy your franchise?

	% answering
Yes	**100%**
No	0%

* Number of survey respondents: 13 from 10 different states
Number of survey respondents as a % of total franchise units: < 1%

THE LITTLE GYM

www.thelittlegym.com
Email: info@thelittlegym.com

Physical fitness, gymnastics, and motor skills development for children.

OVERALL SCORE: 80

8970 East Raintree Drive, Suite 200
Scottsdale, AZ 85260
Fax: 480-948-2765
Total number of outlets: 157 (130 in U.S.)
Total number of franchise outlets: 155
International: Yes (worldwide)

OVERALL RANK: 33

Phone: 888-228-2878
Franchise fee: $57,500
Franchise term: 10 years
Initial investment: $137,700 to $228,000
Advertising/Marketing fee: 1% of gross revenue, monthly
Royalty fee: 8% of gross revenue, monthly

SURVEY AND RESULTS *

Q1: About how many hours per week do you dedicate to your franchise business?

		% answering
A)	Less than 40	13%
B)	**41–50**	**47%**
C)	51–60	20%
D)	More than 60	20%
E)	Passive investment	0%

Q2: How would you describe your relations/ communications with your franchisor?

		% answering
A)	**Excellent**	**40%**
B)	**Good**	**40%**
C)	Adequate	13%
D)	Fair	7%
E)	Poor	0%

Q3: In terms of how your franchisor views your communications with other franchisees, it is:

		% answering
A)	**Very supportive**	**80%**
B)	Not very supportive	7%
C)	No influence	13%

Q4: Is the franchisor fair with you in resolving any grievances?

		% answering
A)	**Extremely fair**	**33%**
B)	**Pretty fair**	**33%**
C)	Reasonably fair	25%
D)	Not very fair	8%
E)	Not fair at all	0%

Q5: Are territories equitably granted?

		% answering
A)	**Yes**	**87%**
B)	No	7%
C)	Not yet sure	7%

Q6: How would you describe the initial and ongoing training provided by your franchisor?

		% answering
A)	**Excellent**	**53%**
B)	Good	40%
C)	Adequate	7%
D)	Fair	0%
E)	Poor	0%

Q7: How well does the franchisor anticipate future trends in how it evolves and markets products and services?

		% answering
A)	Extremely well	20%
B)	**Pretty well**	**47%**
C)	Adequately	13%
D)	Not very well	20%
E)	Terribly	0%

Q8: How satisfied are you with your franchisor's spending of the royalty fees you pay?

		% answering
A)	Extremely satisfied	23%
B)	**Mostly satisfied**	**31%**
C)	Somewhat satisfied	23%
D)	Not very satisfied	15%
E)	Not satisfied at all	8%

Q9: **In what ways could the parent company most improve? (Please check those that most apply, no more than three):**

❏ Communications

❏ Counsel/advice on administrative/management issues

❏ Effectiveness of marketing/promotions

❏ Evolution of products/services

❏ Frequency of marketing/promotional campaigns

❏ Quality of products/services

❏ Pricing of products/services to franchisees

❏ Technology (Point of sale systems, usage of computers/email/software, etc.)

❏ Training

Most frequent responses: % answering

Effectiveness of marketing/promotions   60%

Technology   47%

Frequency of marketing/promotional campaigns   40%

Q10: **Is your income more, less or about what you expected prior to opening your business?**

	% answering	
More	0%	
Less	36%	**Summary: 64% are making about what they**
About what was expected	**64%**	**expected, or more.**

Q11: **Prior to opening your franchise, which (if any) of the following did you underestimate?**

❏ Amount of working capital required for your 1st year in business

❏ Difficulty in hiring/retaining quality staff

❏ Expertise required to run the business

❏ Impact of marketing/promotions

❏ Start-up costs

❏ Degree of stress

❏ Workload

Most frequent responses: % answering

Difficulty in hiring/retaining quality staff   67%

Start-up costs (tie)   27%

Degree of stress (tie)   27%

Q12: **If you could turn back time to the day you signed your franchise agreement, would you make the same decision to buy your franchise?**

	% answering
Yes	**87%**
No	13%

* Number of survey respondents: 15 from 12 different states

Number of survey respondents as a % of total franchise units: 9.68%

MAACO

www.maaco.com

Vehicle painting and body repair services.

OVERALL SCORE: 65

381 Brooks Road
King of Prussia, PA 19406
Fax: 610-337-6113
Total number of outlets: Approximately 500
Total number of franchise outlets:
Approximately 500
International: Yes (Canada, Mexico)

OVERALL RANK: 109

Phone: 866-763-2579
Franchise fee:
Franchise term:
Initial investment:
Advertising/Marketing fee:
Royalty fee:

SURVEY AND RESULTS *

Q1: About how many hours per week do you dedicate to your franchise business?

		% answering
A)	Less than 40	0%
B)	41–50	27%
C)	51–60	23%
D)	**More than 60**	**43%**
E)	Passive investment	7%

Q2: How would you describe your relations/ communications with your franchisor?

		% answering
A)	Excellent	13%
B)	**Good**	**40%**
C)	Adequate	27%
D)	Fair	20%
E)	Poor	0%

Q3: In terms of how your franchisor views your communications with other franchisees, it is:

		% answering
A)	**Very supportive**	**80%**
B)	Not very supportive	13%
C)	No influence	7%

Q4: Is the franchisor fair with you in resolving any grievances?

		% answering
A)	Extremely fair	29%
B)	**Pretty fair**	**50%**
C)	Reasonably fair	21%
D)	Not very fair	0%
E)	Not fair at all	0%

Q5: Are territories equitably granted?

		% answering
A)	**Yes**	**60%**
B)	No	13%
C)	Not yet sure	27%

Q6: How would you describe the initial and ongoing training provided by your franchisor?

		% answering
A)	Excellent	7%
B)	**Good**	**47%**
C)	Adequate	7%
D)	Fair	33%
E)	Poor	7%

Q7: How well does the franchisor anticipate future trends in how it evolves and markets products and services?

		% answering
A)	Extremely well	20%
B)	**Pretty well**	**47%**
C)	Adequately	13%
D)	Not very well	20%
E)	Terribly	0%

Q8: How satisfied are you with your franchisor's spending of the royalty fees you pay?

		% answering
A)	Extremely satisfied	0%
B)	**Mostly satisfied**	**50%**
C)	Somewhat satisfied	36%
D)	Not very satisfied	14%
E)	Not satisfied at all	0%

Q9: **In what ways could the parent company most improve? (Please check those that most apply, no more than three):**

- ❑ Communications
- ❑ Counsel/advice on administrative/management issues
- ❑ Effectiveness of marketing/promotions
- ❑ Evolution of products/services
- ❑ Frequency of marketing/promotional campaigns

- ❑ Quality of products/services
- ❑ Pricing of products/services to franchisees
- ❑ Technology (Point of sale systems, usage of computers/email/software, etc.)
- ❑ Training

Most frequent responses:

	% answering
Training	53%
Communications (tie)	40%
Effectiveness of marketing/promotions (tie)	40%
Technology (tie)	40%

Q10: **Is your income more, less or about what you expected prior to opening your business?**

	% answering	
More	20%	
Less	**60%**	**Summary: 40% are making about what they**
About what was expected	20%	**expected, or more.**

Q11: **Prior to opening your franchise, which (if any) of the following did you underestimate?**

- ❑ Amount of working capital required for your 1st year in business
- ❑ Difficulty in hiring/retaining quality staff
- ❑ Expertise required to run the business
- ❑ Impact of marketing/promotions

- ❑ Start-up costs
- ❑ Degree of stress
- ❑ Workload

Most frequent responses:

	% answering
Difficulty in hiring/retaining quality staff	73%
Degree of stress	67%
Workload	40%

Q12: **If you could turn back time to the day you signed your franchise agreement, would you make the same decision to buy your franchise?**

	% answering
Yes	**73%**
No	27%

* Number of survey respondents: 15 from 12 different states

Number of survey respondents as a % of total franchise units: 3%

THE MAD SCIENCE GROUP

www.madscience.org
Email: joel@madscience.org (Joel Lazarovitz)

Science-focused educational programs.

OVERALL SCORE: 65

8360 Bougainville Street, Suite 201
Montreal, Quebec, Canada H4P 2G1
Fax: 514-344-6695
Total number of outlets: 100+ in North America
Total number of franchise outlets: 100+ in North America
International: Yes (worldwide)
Royalty fee: Generally 8% of gross revenues
monthly, but can vary

OVERALL RANK: 112

Phone: 514-344-4181
Franchise fee: $23,500
Franchise term: 10 years
Initial investment: $37,900 to $79,700
Advertising/Marketing fee: Greater of 3% of gross
revenues monthly, or $100

SURVEY AND RESULTS *

Q1: About how many hours per week do you dedicate to your franchise business?

		% answering
A)	Less than 40	7%
B)	**41–50**	**43%**
C)	51–60	17%
D)	More than 60	33%
E)	Passive investment	0%

Q2: How would you describe your relations/communications with your franchisor?

		% answering
A)	Excellent	13%
B)	**Good**	**40%**
C)	Adequate	27%
D)	Fair	13%
E)	Poor	7%

Q3: In terms of how your franchisor views your communications with other franchisees, it is:

		% answering
A)	**Very supportive**	**67%**
B)	Not very supportive	7%
C)	No influence	27%

Q4: Is the franchisor fair with you in resolving any grievances?

		% answering
A)	Extremely fair	8%
B)	Pretty fair	42%
C)	**Reasonably fair**	**50%**
D)	Not very fair	0%
E)	Not fair at all	0%

Q5: Are territories equitably granted?

		% answering
A)	**Yes**	**73%**
B)	No	0%
C)	Not yet sure	27%

Q6: How would you describe the initial and ongoing training provided by your franchisor?

		% answering
A)	Excellent	7%
B)	Good	27%
C)	**Adequate**	**40%**
D)	Fair	27%
E)	Poor	0%

Q7: How well does the franchisor anticipate future trends in how it evolves and markets products and services?

		% answering
A)	Extremely well	0%
B)	**Pretty well**	**57%**
C)	Adequately	21%
D)	Not very well	7%
E)	Terribly	14%

Q8: How satisfied are you with your franchisor's spending of the royalty fees you pay?

		% answering
A)	Extremely satisfied	7%
B)	**Mostly satisfied**	**36%**
C)	**Somewhat satisfied**	**36%**
D)	Not very satisfied	14%
E)	Not satisfied at all	7%

Q9: **In what ways could the parent company most improve? (Please check those that most apply, no more than three):**

- ❑ Communications
- ❑ Counsel/advice on administrative/management issues
- ❑ Effectiveness of marketing/promotions
- ❑ Evolution of products/services
- ❑ Frequency of marketing/promotional campaigns
- ❑ Quality of products/services
- ❑ Pricing of products/services to franchisees
- ❑ Technology (Point of sale systems, usage of computers/email/software, etc.)
- ❑ Training

Most frequent responses:	% answering
Counsel/advice on administrative/management issues	53%
Frequency of marketing/promotional campaigns	47%
Training	40%

Q10: **Is your income more, less or about what you expected prior to opening your business?**

	% answering	
More	0%	
Less	**53%**	**Summary: 53% are making about what they**
About what was expected	47%	**expected, or more.**

Q11: **Prior to opening your franchise, which (if any) of the following did you underestimate?**

- ❑ Amount of working capital required for your 1st year in business
- ❑ Difficulty in hiring/retaining quality staff
- ❑ Expertise required to run the business
- ❑ Impact of marketing/promotions
- ❑ Start-up costs
- ❑ Degree of stress
- ❑ Workload

Most frequent responses:	% answering
Difficulty in hiring/retaining quality staff	67%
Degree of stress	40%
Amount of working capital required for 1st year in business (tie)	33%
Workload (tie)	33%

Q12: **If you could turn back time to the day you signed your franchise agreement, would you make the same decision to buy your franchise?**

	% answering
Yes	**79%**
No	21%

* Number of survey respondents: 15 from 10 different states
   Number of survey respondents as a % of total franchise units: 15%

MAGGIE MOO'S ICE CREAM AND TREATERY

www.maggiemoos.com
Email: info@maggiemoos.com

Ice cream and other frozen desserts.

OVERALL SCORE: 37

10025 Governor Warfield Parkway, Suite 301
Columbia, MD 21044
Fax: 410-740-1500
Total number of outlets: 145
Total number of franchise outlets: 145
International: Yes (Thailand)
Advertising/Marketing fee: Currently 2% of
gross sales monthly

OVERALL RANK: N/A

Phone: 800-949-8114, ext. 140
Franchise fee: $30,000
Franchise term: The earlier of 10 years or the term
of your lease or sub-lease
Initial investment: $215,100 to $312,180
Royalty fee: 6% of gross sales monthly

SURVEY AND RESULTS *

Q1: About how many hours per week do you
dedicate to your franchise business?

		% answering
A)	Less than 40	33%
B)	41–50	17%
C)	51–60	0%
D)	**More than 60**	**50%**
E)	Passive investment	0%

Q2: How would you describe your relations/
communications with your franchisor?

		% answering
A)	Excellent	17%
B)	Good	17%
C)	**Adequate**	**33%**
D)	Fair	17%
E)	Poor	17%

Q3: In terms of how your franchisor views your
communications with other franchisees, it is:

		% answering
A)	**Very supportive**	**67%**
B)	Not very supportive	17%
C)	No influence	17%

Q4: Is the franchisor fair with you in
resolving any grievances?

		% answering
A)	**Extremely fair**	**33%**
B)	Pretty fair	0%
C)	**Reasonably fair**	**33%**
D)	**Not very fair**	**33%**
E)	Not fair at all	0%

Q5: Are territories equitably granted?

		% answering
A)	**Yes**	**40%**
B)	**No**	**40%**
C)	Not yet sure	20%

Q6: How would you describe the initial and
ongoing training provided by your franchisor?

		% answering
A)	Excellent	0%
B)	**Good**	**33%**
C)	**Adequate**	**33%**
D)	Fair	0%
E)	**Poor**	**33%**

Q7: How well does the franchisor anticipate
future trends in how it evolves and markets
products and services?

		% answering
A)	Extremely well	17%
B)	Pretty well	17%
C)	Adequately	0%
D)	**Not very well**	**67%**
E)	Terribly	0%

Q8: How satisfied are you with your franchisor's
spending of the royalty fees you pay?

		% answering
A)	Extremely satisfied	17%
B)	Mostly satisfied	17%
C)	Somewhat satisfied	0%
D)	**Not very satisfied**	**50%**
E)	Not satisfied at all	17%

Q9: **In what ways could the parent company most improve? (Please check those that most apply, no more than three):**

❑ Communications
❑ Counsel/advice on administrative/management issues
❑ Effectiveness of marketing/promotions
❑ Evolution of products/services
❑ Frequency of marketing/promotional campaigns

❑ Quality of products/services
❑ Pricing of products/services to franchisees
❑ Technology (Point of sale systems, usage of computers/email/software, etc.)
❑ Training

Most frequent responses:	% answering
Pricing of products/services to franchisees	67%
Counsel/advice on administrative/management issues (tie)	50%
Evolution of products/services (tie)	50%

Q10: **Is your income more, less or about what you expected prior to opening your business?**

	% answering	
More	0%	
Less	**100%**	Summary: 0% are making about what they
About what was expected	0%	expected, or more.

Q11: **Prior to opening your franchise, which (if any) of the following did you underestimate?**

❑ Amount of working capital required for your 1st year in business
❑ Difficulty in hiring/retaining quality staff
❑ Expertise required to run the business
❑ Impact of marketing/promotions

❑ Start-up costs
❑ Degree of stress
❑ Workload

Most frequent responses:	% answering
Workload	67%
Amount of working capital required for your 1st year in business	50%
Start-up costs (tie)	33%
Degree of stress (tie)	33%

Q12: **If you could turn back time to the day you signed your franchise agreement, would you make the same decision to buy your franchise?**

	% answering
Yes	33%
No	**67%**

* Number of survey respondents: 6 from 5 different states
  Number of survey respondents as a % of total franchise units: 4.14%

MAID BRIGADE

www.maidbrigade.com

Residential cleaning services.

OVERALL SCORE: 83

Four Concourse Parkway, Suite 200
Atlanta, GA 30328
Fax: 770-391-9092
Total number of outlets: 360+
Total number of franchise outlets: 360+
International: Yes (Canada, Ireland)

OVERALL RANK: 22

Phone: 800-722-6243
Franchise fee: $19,500 to $80,000
Franchise term: 10 years
Initial investment: $61,500 to $190,000
Advertising/Marketing fee: 2% of weekly gross revenues
Royalty fee: varies

SURVEY AND RESULTS *

Q1: About how many hours per week do you dedicate to your franchise business?

		% answering
A)	Less than 40	17%
B)	41–50	25%
C)	**51–60**	**58%**
D)	More than 60	0%
E)	Passive investment	0%

Q2: How would you describe your relations/communications with your franchisor?

		% answering
A)	**Excellent**	**50%**
B)	Good	33%
C)	Adequate	8%
D)	Fair	0%
E)	Poor	8%

Q3: In terms of how your franchisor views your communications with other franchisees, it is:

		% answering
A)	**Very supportive**	**92%**
B)	Not very supportive	8%
C)	No influence	0%

Q4: Is the franchisor fair with you in resolving any grievances?

		% answering
A)	Extremely fair	33%
B)	**Pretty fair**	**50%**
C)	Reasonably fair	8%
D)	Not very fair	8%
E)	Not fair at all	0%

Q5: Are territories equitably granted?

		% answering
A)	**Yes**	**67%**
B)	No	0%
C)	Not yet sure	33%

Q6: How would you describe the initial and ongoing training provided by your franchisor?

		% answering
A)	**Excellent**	**58%**
B)	Good	25%
C)	Adequate	8%
D)	Fair	8%
E)	Poor	0%

Q7: How well does the franchisor anticipate future trends in how it evolves and markets products and services?

		% answering
A)	Extremely well	25%
B)	**Pretty well**	**67%**
C)	Adequately	0%
D)	Not very well	8%
E)	Terribly	0%

Q8: How satisfied are you with your franchisor's spending of the royalty fees you pay?

		% answering
A)	Extremely satisfied	0%
B)	**Mostly satisfied**	**67%**
C)	Somewhat satisfied	8%
D)	Not very satisfied	8%
E)	Not satisfied at all	17%

Q9: **In what ways could the parent company most improve? (Please check those that most apply, no more than three):**

❑ Communications

❑ Counsel/advice on administrative/management issues

❑ Effectiveness of marketing/promotions

❑ Evolution of products/services

❑ Frequency of marketing/promotional campaigns

❑ Quality of products/services

❑ Pricing of products/services to franchisees

❑ Technology (Point of sale systems, usage of computers/email/software, etc.)

❑ Training

Most frequent responses:	% answering
Counsel/advice on administrative/management issues (tie)	50%
Effectiveness of marketing/promotions (tie)	50%
Evolution of products/services (tie)	33%
Frequency of marketing/promotional campaigns (tie)	33%

Q10: **Is your income more, less or about what you expected prior to opening your business?**

	% answering	
More	0%	
Less	17%	**Summary: 83% are making about what they**
About what was expected	**83%**	**expected, or more.**

Q11: **Prior to opening your franchise, which (if any) of the following did you underestimate?**

❑ Amount of working capital required for your 1st year in business

❑ Difficulty in hiring/retaining quality staff

❑ Expertise required to run the business

❑ Impact of marketing/promotions

❑ Start-up costs

❑ Degree of stress

❑ Workload

Most frequent responses:	% answering
Difficulty in hiring/retaining quality staff	75%
Amount of working capital required for 1st year in business (tie)	42%
Impact of marketing/promotions (tie)	42%

Q12: **If you could turn back time to the day you signed your franchise agreement, would you make the same decision to buy your franchise?**

	% answering
Yes	**83%**
No	17%

* Number of survey respondents: 12 from 9 different states

Number of survey respondents as a % of total franchise units: 3.33%

MAID TO PERFECTION

www.maidtoperfectioncorp.com
Email: maidsvc@aol.com

Residential and commercial cleaning services.

OVERALL SCORE: 61

1101 Opal Court
Hagerstown, MD 21740
Total number of outlets: 245
Total number of franchise outlets: 245
International: Yes (Canada)

OVERALL RANK: N/A

Phone: 800-648-6243
Franchise fee: $11,995
Franchise term: 10 years
Initial investment: $38,242.75 to $44,042.75
Advertising/Marketing fee: none
Royalty fee: varies

SURVEY AND RESULTS *

Q1: About how many hours per week do you dedicate to your franchise business?

		% answering
A)	Less than 40	0%
B)	**41–50**	**50%**
C)	**51–60**	**50%**
D)	More than 60	0%
E)	Passive investment	0%

Q2: How would you describe your relations/ communications with your franchisor?

		% answering
A)	**Excellent**	**50%**
B)	Good	33%
C)	Adequate	0%
D)	Fair	17%
E)	Poor	0%

Q3: In terms of how your franchisor views your communications with other franchisees, it is:

		% answering
A)	**Very supportive**	**50%**
B)	Not very supportive	33%
C)	No influence	17%

Q4: Is the franchisor fair with you in resolving any grievances?

		% answering
A)	**Extremely fair**	**33%**
B)	**Pretty fair**	**33%**
C)	Reasonably fair	17%
D)	Not very fair	0%
E)	Not fair at all	17%

Q5: Are territories equitably granted?

		% answering
A)	**Yes**	**50%**
B)	No	0%
C)	Not yet sure	50%

Q6: How would you describe the initial and ongoing training provided by your franchisor?

		% answering
A)	**Excellent**	**33%**
B)	**Good**	**33%**
C)	Adequate	17%
D)	Fair	0%
E)	Poor	17%

Q7: How well does the franchisor anticipate future trends in how it evolves and markets products and services?

		% answering
A)	Extremely well	17%
B)	**Pretty well**	**67%**
C)	Adequately	0%
D)	Not very well	0%
E)	Terribly	17%

Q8: How satisfied are you with your franchisor's spending of the royalty fees you pay?

		% answering
A)	**Extremely satisfied**	**20%**
B)	**Mostly satisfied**	**20%**
C)	**Somewhat satisfied**	**20%**
D)	**Not very satisfied**	**20%**
E)	**Not satisfied at all**	**20%**

Q9: **In what ways could the parent company most improve? (Please check those that most apply, no more than three):**

- ❏ Communications
- ❏ Counsel/advice on administrative/management issues
- ❏ Effectiveness of marketing/promotions
- ❏ Evolution of products/services
- ❏ Frequency of marketing/promotional campaigns

- ❏ Quality of products/services
- ❏ Pricing of products/services to franchisees
- ❏ Technology (Point of sale systems, usage of computers/email/software, etc.)
- ❏ Training

Most frequent responses:	% answering
Effectiveness of marketing/promotions (tie)	67%
Frequency of marketing/promotional campaigns (tie)	67%
Communications	33%

Q10: **Is your income more, less or about what you expected prior to opening your business?**

	% answering	
More	20%	
Less	**60%**	**Summary: 40% are making about what they**
About what was expected	20%	**expected, or more.**

Q11: **Prior to opening your franchise, which (if any) of the following did you underestimate?**

- ❏ Amount of working capital required for your 1st year in business
- ❏ Difficulty in hiring/retaining quality staff
- ❏ Expertise required to run the business
- ❏ Impact of marketing/promotions

- ❏ Start-up costs
- ❏ Degree of stress
- ❏ Workload

Most frequent responses:	% answering
Difficulty in hiring/retaining quality staff	50%
Amount of working capital required for your first year in business (tie)	33%
Degree of stress (tie)	33%
Workload (tie)	33%

Q12: **If you could turn back time to the day you signed your franchise agreement, would you make the same decision to buy your franchise?**

	% answering
Yes	**50%**
No	**50%**

* Number of survey respondents: 6 from 4 different states
Number of survey respondents as a % of total franchise units: 2.45%

THE MAIDS INTERNATIONAL

www.maids.com
Email: themaidsinfo@themaids.net

Residential cleaning services.

OVERALL SCORE: 64

4820 Dodge Street
Omaha, NE 68132
Fax: 402-558-4112
Total number of outlets: 699
Total number of franchise outlets: 684
International: Yes (Canada)
Royalty fee: varies

OVERALL RANK: 117

Phone: 800-843-6243
Franchise fee: $10,000 plus $0.95 for each
potential customer in your designated area
Franchise term: 20 years
Initial investment: $69,000 to $216,000
Advertising/Marketing fee: 2% of gross revenues weekly

SURVEY AND RESULTS *

Q1: About how many hours per week do you dedicate to your franchise business?

		% answering
A)	Less than 40	8%
B)	41–50	25%
C)	**51–60**	**50%**
D)	More than 60	17%
E)	Passive investment	0%

Q2: How would you describe your relations/ communications with your franchisor?

		% answering
A)	**Excellent**	**42%**
B)	Good	17%
C)	Adequate 1	7%
D)	Fair	25%
E)	Poor	0%

Q3: In terms of how your franchisor views your communications with other franchisees, it is:

		% answering
A)	**Very supportive**	**75%**
B)	Not very supportive	25%
C)	No influence	0%

Q4: Is the franchisor fair with you in resolving any grievances?

		% answering
A)	**Extremely fair**	**67%**
B)	Pretty fair	11%
C)	Reasonably fair	22%
D)	Not very fair	0%
E)	Not fair at all	0%

Q5: Are territories equitably granted?

		% answering
A)	**Yes**	**67%**
B)	No	8%
C)	Not yet sure	25%

Q6: How would you describe the initial and ongoing training provided by your franchisor?

		% answering
A)	**Excellent**	**42%**
B)	Good	17%
C)	Adequate	17%
D)	Fair	17%
E)	Poor	8%

Q7: How well does the franchisor anticipate future trends in how it evolves and markets products and services?

		% answering
A)	**Extremely well**	**33%**
B)	**Pretty well**	**33%**
C)	**Adequately**	**33%**
D)	Not very well	0%
E)	Terribly	0%

Q8: How satisfied are you with your franchisor's spending of the royalty fees you pay?

		% answering
A)	Extremely satisfied	25%
B)	**Mostly satisfied**	**33%**
C)	Somewhat satisfied	8%
D)	Not very satisfied	25%
E)	Not satisfied at all	8%

Q9: **In what ways could the parent company most improve? (Please check those that most apply, no more than three):**

❑ Communications

❑ Counsel/advice on administrative/management issues

❑ Effectiveness of marketing/promotions

❑ Evolution of products/services

❑ Frequency of marketing/promotional campaigns

❑ Quality of products/services

❑ Pricing of products/services to franchisees

❑ Technology (Point of sale systems, usage of computers/email/software, etc.)

❑ Training

Most frequent responses:	% answering
Effectiveness of marketing/promotions	58%
Technology	42%
Communications	33%

Q10: **Is your income more, less or about what you expected prior to opening your business?**

| % answering | |
--- | --- | ---
More | 0% |
Less | **75%** | **Summary: 25% are making about what they**
About what was expected | 25% | **expected, or more.**

Q11: **Prior to opening your franchise, which (if any) of the following did you underestimate?**

❑ Amount of working capital required for your first year in business

❑ Difficulty in hiring/retaining quality staff

❑ Expertise required to run the business

❑ Impact of marketing/promotions

❑ Start-up costs

❑ Degree of stress

❑ Workload

Most frequent responses:	% answering
Difficulty in hiring/retaining quality staff	67%
Amount of working capital required for your first year in business	33%
Expertise required to run the business (tie)	25%
Impact of marketing/promotions (tie)	25%
Degree of stress (tie)	25%
Workload (tie)	25%

Q12: **If you could turn back time to the day you signed your franchise agreement, would you make the same decision to buy your franchise?**

	% answering
Yes	**70%**
No	30%

* Number of survey respondents: 12 from 11 different states

Number of survey respondents as a % of total franchise units: 1.75%

MANAGEMENT RECRUITERS INTERNATIONAL (MRI)

www.brilliantpeople.com
Email: diane.schlosser@mrinetwork.com (Diane Schlosser)

Personnel search, recruiting, and placement firm.

OVERALL SCORE: 84

1801 Market Street, Suite 1350
Philadelphia, PA 19103
Fax: 216-696-6612
Total number of outlets: 1,100+
Total number of franchise outlets: 1,100+
International: Yes (worldwide)

OVERALL RANK: 17

Phone: 800-875-4000
Franchise fee:
Franchise term:
Initial investment:
Advertising/Marketing fee:
Royalty fee:

SURVEY AND RESULTS *

Q1: About how many hours per week do you dedicate to your franchise business?

		% answering
A)	Less than 40	12%
B)	41–50	29%
C)	**51–60**	**53%**
D)	More than 60	6%
E)	Passive investment	0%

Q2: How would you describe your relations/communications with your franchisor?

		% answering
A)	Excellent	35%
B)	**Good**	**41%**
C)	Adequate	6%
D)	Fair	18%
E)	Poor	0%

Q3: In terms of how your franchisor views your communications with other franchisees, it is:

		% answering
A)	**Very supportive**	**76%**
B)	Not very supportive	6%
C)	No influence	18%

Q4: Is the franchisor fair with you in resolving any grievances?

		% answering
A)	**Extremely fair**	**35%**
B)	**Pretty fair**	**35%**
C)	Reasonably fair	29%
D)	Not very fair	20%
E)	Not fair at all	20%

Q5: Are territories equitably granted?

		% answering
A)	**Yes**	**76%**
B)	No	12%
C)	Not yet sure	12%

Q6: How would you describe the initial and ongoing training provided by your franchisor?

		% answering
A)	**Excellent**	**65%**
B)	Good	24%
C)	Adequate	6%
D)	Fair	6%
E)	Poor	0%

Q7: How well does the franchisor anticipate future trends in how it evolves and markets products and services?

		% answering
A)	Extremely well	18%
B)	**Pretty well**	**35%**
C)	Adequately	12%
D)	**Not very well**	**35%**
E)	Terribly	0%

Q8: How satisfied are you with your franchisor's spending of the royalty fees you pay?

		% answering
A)	Extremely satisfied	12%
B)	**Mostly satisfied**	**59%**
C)	Somewhat satisfied	18%
D)	Not very satisfied	12%
E)	Not satisfied at all	0%

Q9: **In what ways could the parent company most improve? (Please check those that most apply, no more than three):**

- ❑ Communications
- ❑ Counsel/advice on administrative/management issues
- ❑ Effectiveness of marketing/promotions
- ❑ Evolution of products/services
- ❑ Frequency of marketing/promotional campaigns
- ❑ Quality of products/services
- ❑ Pricing of products/services to franchisees
- ❑ Technology (Point of sale systems, usage of computers/email/software, etc.)
- ❑ Training

Most frequent responses:	% answering
Counsel/advice on administrative/management issues	47%
Effectiveness of marketing/promotions (tie)	29%
Evolution of products/services (tie)	29%
Technology (tie)	29%

Q10: **Is your income more, less or about what you expected prior to opening your business?**

	% answering	
More	35%	
Less	35%	**Summary: 64% are making about what they**
About what was expected	29%	**expected, or more.**

Q11: **Prior to opening your franchise, which (if any) of the following did you underestimate?**

- ❑ Amount of working capital required for your 1st year in business
- ❑ Difficulty in hiring/retaining quality staff
- ❑ Expertise required to run the business
- ❑ Impact of marketing/promotions
- ❑ Start-up costs
- ❑ Degree of stress
- ❑ Workload

Most frequent responses:	% answering
Difficulty in hiring/retaining quality staff	71%
Degree of stress	53%
Workload	35%

Q12: **If you could turn back time to the day you signed your franchise agreement, would you make the same decision to buy your franchise?**

	% answering
Yes	**94%**
No	6%

* Number of survey respondents: 17 from 16 different states
Number of survey respondents as a % of total franchise units: 1.55%

MARBLE SLAB CREAMERY

www.marbleslab.com
Email: marbleslab@marbleslab.com

Ice cream, frozen yogurt, desserts, and specialty coffee.

OVERALL SCORE: 58

OVERALL RANK: N/A

3100 S. Gessner, Suite 305
Houston, TX 77063
Fax: 713-780-0264
Total number of outlets: 267
Total number of franchise outlets: 267
International: Yes (Canada)

Phone: 713-780-3601
Franchise fee: $28,000
Franchise term: 10 years
Initial investment: $205,175 to $313,275
Advertising/Marketing fee: 2% of gross sales weekly
Royalty fee: 6% of gross sales weekly

SURVEY AND RESULTS *

Q1: About how many hours per week do you dedicate to your franchise business?

		% answering
A)	Less than 40	33%
B)	41–50	0%
C)	51–60	22%
D)	**More than 60**	**44%**
E)	Passive investment	0%

Q2: How would you describe your relations/communications with your franchisor?

		% answering
A)	Excellent	0%
B)	**Good**	**44%**
C)	**Adequate**	**44%**
D)	Fair	11%
E)	Poor	0%

Q3: In terms of how your franchisor views your communications with other franchisees, it is:

		% answering
A)	Very supportive	33%
B)	Not very supportive	22%
C)	**No influence**	**44%**

Q4: Is the franchisor fair with you in resolving any grievances?

		% answering
A)	Extremely fair	0%
B)	**Pretty fair**	**56%**
C)	Reasonably fair	22%
D)	Not very fair	22%
E)	Not fair at all	0%

Q5: Are territories equitably granted?

		% answering
A)	**Yes**	**56%**
B)	No	33%
C)	Not yet sure	11%

Q6: How would you describe the initial and ongoing training provided by your franchisor?

		% answering
A)	**Excellent**	**50%**
B)	Good	22%
C)	Adequate	11%
D)	Fair	11%
E)	Poor	6%

Q7: How well does the franchisor anticipate future trends in how it evolves and markets products and services?

		% answering
A)	Extremely well	11%
B)	Pretty well	11%
C)	Adequately	33%
D)	**Not very well**	**44%**
E)	Terribly	0%

Q8: How satisfied are you with your franchisor's spending of the royalty fees you pay?

		% answering
A)	Extremely satisfied	11%
B)	**Mostly satisfied**	**33%**
C)	Somewhat satisfied	0%
D)	**Not very satisfied**	**33%**
E)	Not satisfied at all	22%

Q9: **In what ways could the parent company most improve? (Please check those that most apply, no more than three):**

- ❏ Communications
- ❏ Counsel/advice on administrative/management issues
- ❏ Effectiveness of marketing/promotions
- ❏ Evolution of products/services
- ❏ Frequency of marketing/promotional campaigns

- ❏ Quality of products/services
- ❏ Pricing of products/services to franchisees
- ❏ Technology (Point of sale systems, usage of computers/email/software, etc.)
- ❏ Training

Most frequent responses:	% answering
Effectiveness of marketing/promotions	67%
Evolution of products/services	56%
Frequency of marketing/promotional campaigns	44%

Q10: **Is your income more, less or about what you expected prior to opening your business?**

	% answering	
More	25%	
Less	**50%**	**Summary: 50% are making about what they**
About what was expected	25%	**expected, or more.**

Q11: **Prior to opening your franchise, which (if any) of the following did you underestimate?**

- ❏ Amount of working capital required for your 1st year in business
- ❏ Difficulty in hiring/retaining quality staff
- ❏ Expertise required to run the business
- ❏ Impact of marketing/promotions

- ❏ Start-up costs
- ❏ Degree of stress
- ❏ Workload

Most frequent responses:	% answering
Amount of working capital required for your first year in business (tie)	67%
Start-up costs (tie)	67%
Difficulty in hiring/retaining quality staff (tie)	56%
Workload (tie)	56%

Q12: **If you could turn back time to the day you signed your franchise agreement, would you make the same decision to buy your franchise?**

	% answering
Yes	**50%**
No	**50%**

* Number of survey respondents: 9 from 5 different states

Number of survey respondents as a % of total franchise units: 3.37%

(MARS) MIRACLE APPEARANCE RESTORATION SPECIALISTS

www.marsinternational.com
Email: mars@marsinternational.com

Vehicle appearance reconditioning services, equipment, supplies, and accessories.

OVERALL SCORE: 68

2001 East Division, Suite 101
Arlington, TX 76011
Fax: 800-230-2859
Total number of outlets:
Total number of franchise outlets:
International: No

OVERALL RANK: 97

Phone: 800-230-4106
Franchise fee: $5,000 to $20,000
Franchise term: 5 years
Initial investment: $10,750 to $100,850
Advertising/Marketing fee: 2% of gross sales weekly
Royalty fee: varies

SURVEY AND RESULTS *

Q1: About how many hours per week do you dedicate to your franchise business?

		% answering
A)	Less than 40	28%
B)	**41–50**	**39%**
C)	51–60	6%
D)	More than 60	28%
E)	Passive investment	0%

Q2: How would you describe your relations/ communications with your franchisor?

		% answering
A)	**Excellent**	**33%**
B)	Good	11%
C)	Adequate	11%
D)	Fair	22%
E)	Poor	22%

Q3: In terms of how your franchisor views your communications with other franchisees, it is:

		% answering
A)	**Very supportive**	**56%**
B)	Not very supportive	22%
C)	No influence	22%

Q4: Is the franchisor fair with you in resolving any grievances?

		% answering
A)	**Extremely fair**	**43%**
B)	Pretty fair	14%
C)	Reasonably fair	29%
D)	Not very fair	7%
E)	Not fair at all	7%

Q5: Are territories equitably granted?

		% answering
A)	**Yes**	**60%**
B)	No	33%
C)	Not yet sure	7%

Q6: How would you describe the initial and ongoing training provided by your franchisor?

		% answering
A)	**Excellent**	**28%**
B)	Good	22%
C)	Adequate	11%
D)	Fair	22%
E)	Poor	17%

Q7: How well does the franchisor anticipate future trends in how it evolves and markets products and services?

		% answering
A)	Extremely well	24%
B)	**Pretty well**	**35%**
C)	Adequately	24%
D)	Not very well	18%
E)	Terribly	0%

Q8: How satisfied are you with your franchisor's spending of the royalty fees you pay?

		% answering
A)	Extremely satisfied	6%
B)	**Mostly satisfied**	**29%**
C)	Somewhat satisfied	24%
D)	Not very satisfied	29%
E)	Not satisfied at all	12%

Q9: **In what ways could the parent company most improve? (Please check those that most apply, no more than three):**

❑ Communications

❑ Counsel/advice on administrative/management issues

❑ Effectiveness of marketing/promotions

❑ Evolution of products/services

❑ Frequency of marketing/promotional campaigns

❑ Quality of products/services

❑ Pricing of products/services to franchisees

❑ Technology (Point of sale systems, usage of computers/email/software, etc.)

❑ Training

Most frequent responses:	% answering
Training	67%
Effectiveness of marketing/promotions	44%
Counsel/advice on administrative/management issues (tie)	33%
Pricing of products/services to franchisees (tie)	33%

Q10: **Is your income more, less or about what you expected prior to opening your business?**

	% answering	
More	33%	
Less	33%	**Summary: 66% are making about what they**
About what was expected	33%	**expected, or more.**

Q11: **Prior to opening your franchise, which (if any) of the following did you underestimate?**

❑ Amount of working capital required for your 1st year in business

❑ Difficulty in hiring/retaining quality staff

❑ Expertise required to run the business

❑ Impact of marketing/promotions

❑ Start-up costs

❑ Degree of stress

❑ Workload

Most frequent responses:	% answering
Degree of stress	33%
Amount of working capital required for your 1st year in business (tie)	22%
Impact of marketing/promotions (tie)	22%
Workload (tie)	22%

Q12: **If you could turn back time to the day you signed your franchise agreement, would you make the same decision to buy your franchise?**

	% answering
Yes	**72%**
No	28%

* Number of survey respondents: 18 from 13 different states

   Number of survey respondents as a % of total franchise units:

MARTINIZING DRY CLEANING

www.martinizing.com

Dry cleaning services.

OVERALL SCORE: 59

422 Wards Corner Road
Loveland, OH45140
Fax: 513-731-0818
Total number of outlets: 600+
Total number of franchise outlets: 600+
International: Yes (Puerto Rico, Virgin Islands)
Royalty fee: > of 4% of total gross sales or
minimum royalty payment of $600 per month
after 24 months of operation

OVERALL RANK: 142

Phone: 800-827-0207
Franchise fee: $30,000
Franchise term: 20 years
Initial investment: $250,000–$396,000
Advertising/Marketing fee: 1/2% of total gross
sales monthly

SURVEY AND RESULTS *

Q1: About how many hours per week do you dedicate to your franchise business?

		% answering
A)	Less than 40	8%
B)	41–50	25%
C)	51–60	25%
D)	**More than 60**	**42%**
E)	Passive investment	0%

Q2: How would you describe your relations/communications with your franchisor?

		% answering
A)	Excellent	17%
B)	**Good**	**33%**
C)	Adequate	0%
D)	**Fair**	**33%**
E)	Poor	17%

Q3: In terms of how your franchisor views your communications with other franchisees, it is:

		% answering
A)	**Very supportive**	**50%**
B)	Not very supportive	33%
C)	No influence	17%

Q4: Is the franchisor fair with you in resolving any grievances?

		% answering
A)	Extremely fair	27%
B)	**Pretty fair**	**36%**
C)	Reasonably fair	9%
D)	Not very fair	18%
E)	Not fair at all	9%

Q5: Are territories equitably granted?

		% answering
A)	**Yes**	**50%**
B)	No	8%
C)	Not yet sure	42%

Q6: How would you describe the initial and ongoing training provided by your franchisor?

		% answering
A)	Excellent	17%
B)	Good	29%
C)	Adequate	8%
D)	Fair	8%
E)	**Poor**	**38%**

Q7: How well does the franchisor anticipate future trends in how it evolves and markets products and services?

		% answering
A)	Extremely well	33%
B)	Pretty well	17%
C)	Adequately	0%
D)	**Not very well**	**42%**
E)	Terribly	8%

Q8: How satisfied are you with your franchisor's spending of the royalty fees you pay?

		% answering
A)	Extremely satisfied	0%
B)	Mostly satisfied	20%
C)	Somewhat satisfied	20%
D)	**Not very satisfied**	**30%**
E)	**Not satisfied at all**	**30%**

Q9: **In what ways could the parent company most improve? (Please check those that most apply, no more than three):**

❑ Communications
❑ Counsel/advice on administrative/management issues
❑ Effectiveness of marketing/promotions
❑ Evolution of products/services
❑ Frequency of marketing/promotional campaigns

❑ Quality of products/services
❑ Pricing of products/services to franchisees
❑ Technology (Point of sale systems, usage of computers/email/software, etc.)
❑ Training

Most frequent responses:

	% answering
Communications	58%
Training	42%
Frequency of marketing/promotional campaigns (tie)	33%
Effectiveness of marketing/promotions (tie)	33%

Q10: **Is your income more, less or about what you expected prior to opening your business?**

	% answering	
More	17%	
Less	**58%**	**Summary: 42% are making about what they**
About what was expected	25%	**expected, or more.**

Q11: **Prior to opening your franchise, which (if any) of the following did you underestimate?**

❑ Amount of working capital required for your 1st year in business
❑ Difficulty in hiring/retaining quality staff
❑ Expertise required to run the business
❑ Impact of marketing/promotions

❑ Start-up costs
❑ Degree of stress
❑ Workload

Most frequent responses:

	% answering
Difficulty in hiring/retaining quality staff	42%
Start-up costs (tie)	33%
Degree of stress (tie)	33%

Q12: **If you could turn back time to the day you signed your franchise agreement, would you make the same decision to buy your franchise?**

	% answering
Yes	**75%**
No	25%

* Number of survey respondents: 12 from 6 different states
   Number of survey respondents as a % of total franchise units: 2.00%

MATCO TOOLS

www.matcotools.com

Manufacturer and distributor of automotive tools, equipment, and tool boxes.

OVERALL SCORE: 68

2000 Pennsylvania Avenue NW, 12th Floor
Washington, DC 20006
Fax: 330-926-5323
Total number of outlets: 448
Total number of franchise outlets: 380
International: Yes (Puerto Rico)

OVERALL RANK: 96

Phone: 866-BUY-TOOL
Franchise fee: none
Franchise term: 10 years
Initial investment: $150,000–$225,000
Advertising/Marketing fee: none
Royalty fee: none

SURVEY AND RESULTS *

Q1: About how many hours per week do you dedicate to your franchise business?

		% answering
A)	Less than 40	0%
B)	41–50	13%
C)	51–60	27%
D)	**More than 60**	**60%**
E)	Passive investment	0%

Q2: How would you describe your relations/ communications with your franchisor?

		% answering
A)	**Excellent**	**40%**
B)	Good	33%
C)	Adequate	27%
D)	Fair	0%
E)	Poor	0%

Q3: In terms of how your franchisor views your communications with other franchisees, it is:

		% answering
A)	**Very supportive**	**60%**
B)	Not very supportive	13%
C)	No influence	27%

Q4: Is the franchisor fair with you in resolving any grievances?

		% answering
A)	Extremely fair	27%
B)	**Pretty fair**	**40%**
C)	Reasonably fair	33%
D)	Not very fair	0%
E)	Not fair at all	0%

Q5: Are territories equitably granted?

		% answering
A)	**Yes**	**79%**
B)	No	14%
C)	Not yet sure	7%

Q6: How would you describe the initial and ongoing training provided by your franchisor?

		% answering
A)	Excellent	13%
B)	**Good**	**40%**
C)	Adequate	20%
D)	Fair	20%
E)	Poor	7%

Q7: How well does the franchisor anticipate future trends in how it evolves and markets products and services?

		% answering
A)	**Extremely well**	**33%**
B)	Pretty well	27%
C)	Adequately	20%
D)	Not very well	20%
E)	Terribly	0%

Q8: How satisfied are you with your franchisor's spending of the royalty fees you pay?

		% answering
A)	Extremely satisfied	N/A
B)	Mostly satisfied	N/A
C)	Somewhat satisfied	N/A
D)	Not very satisfied	N/A
E)	Not satisfied at all	N/A

Q9: **In what ways could the parent company most improve? (Please check those that most apply, no more than three):**

❑ Communications
❑ Counsel/advice on administrative/management issues
❑ Effectiveness of marketing/promotions
❑ Evolution of products/services
❑ Frequency of marketing/promotional campaigns

❑ Quality of products/services
❑ Pricing of products/services to franchisees
❑ Technology (Point of sale systems, usage of computers/email/software, etc.)
❑ Training

Most frequent responses:	% answering
Pricing of products/services to franchisees	80%
Training	40%
Counsel/advice on administrative/management issues	33%

Q10: **Is your income more, less or about what you expected prior to opening your business?**

	% answering	
More	0%	
Less	47%	**Summary: 53% are making about what they**
About what was expected	**53%**	**expected, or more.**

Q11: **Prior to opening your franchise, which (if any) of the following did you underestimate?**

❑ Amount of working capital required for your 1st year in business
❑ Difficulty in hiring/retaining quality staff
❑ Expertise required to run the business
❑ Impact of marketing/promotions

❑ Start-up costs
❑ Degree of stress
❑ Workload

Most frequent responses:	% answering
Degree of stress (tie)	67%
Workload (tie)	67%
Expertise required to run the business	13%

Q12: **If you could turn back time to the day you signed your franchise agreement, would you make the same decision to buy your franchise?**

	% answering
Yes	**71%**
No	29%

* Number of survey respondents: 15 from 4 different states
   Number of survey respondents as a % of total franchise units: 3.95%

MAUI WOWI FRESH HAWAIIAN BLENDS

www.mauiwowi.com

Fresh fruit smoothies and specialty coffees.

OVERALL SCORE: 40

5445 DTC Parkway, Suite 1050
Greenwood Village, CO 80111
Fax: 303-781-2438
Total number of outlets: 180
Total number of franchise outlets: 180
International: No

OVERALL RANK: 185

Phone: 877-862-8555
Franchise fee: $12,500 to $59,500
Franchise term: 10 years
Initial investment: $42,436 to $$318,865
Advertising/Marketing fee: 12% of the purchase
price of Maui Wowi products and equipment
Royalty fee: none

SURVEY AND RESULTS *

Q1: About how many hours per week do you dedicate to your franchise business?

		% answering
A)	Less than 40	41%
B)	**41–50**	**32%**
C)	51–60	5%
D)	More than 60	18%
E)	Passive investment	5%

Q2: How would you describe your relations/communications with your franchisor?

		% answering
A)	Excellent	13%
B)	Good	22%
C)	Adequate	17%
D)	Fair	22%
E)	**Poor**	**26%**

Q3: In terms of how your franchisor views your communications with other franchisees, it is:

		% answering
A)	**Very supportive**	**50%**
B)	Not very supportive	23%
C)	No influence	27%

Q4: Is the franchisor fair with you in resolving any grievances?

		% answering
A)	Extremely fair	5%
B)	**Pretty fair**	**43%**
C)	Reasonably fair	19%
D)	Not very fair	19%
E)	Not fair at all	14%

Q5: Are territories equitably granted?

		% answering
A)	Yes	50%
B)	No	30%
C)	Not yet sure	20%

Q6: How would you describe the initial and ongoing training provided by your franchisor?

		% answering
A)	Excellent	13%
B)	Good	17%
C)	Adequate	22%
D)	Fair	22%
E)	**Poor**	**26%**

Q7: How well does the franchisor anticipate future trends in how it evolves and markets products and services?

		% answering
A)	Extremely well	0%
B)	Pretty well	17%
C)	Adequately	17%
D)	**Not very well**	**39%**
E)	Terribly	26%

Q8: How satisfied are you with your franchisor's spending of the royalty fees you pay?

		% answering
A)	Extremely satisfied	0%
B)	Mostly satisfied	10%
C)	**Somewhat satisfied**	**40%**
D)	Not very satisfied	25%
E)	Not satisfied at all	25%

Q9: **In what ways could the parent company most improve? (Please check those that most apply, no more than three):**

❑   Communications

❑   Counsel/advice on administrative/management issues

❑   Effectiveness of marketing/promotions

❑   Evolution of products/services

❑   Frequency of marketing/promotional campaigns

❑   Quality of products/services

❑   Pricing of products/services to franchisees

❑   Technology (Point of sale systems, usage of computers/email/software, etc.)

❑   Training

Most frequent responses:

	% answering
Effectiveness of marketing/promotions (tie)	70%
Pricing of products/services to franchisees (tie)	70%
Evolution of products/services	35%

Q10: **Is your income more, less or about what you expected prior to opening your business?**

	% answering	
More	4%	
Less	**70%**	**Summary: 30% are making about what they**
About what was expected	26%	**expected, or more.**

Q11: **Prior to opening your franchise, which (if any) of the following did you underestimate?**

❑   Amount of working capital required for your 1st year in business

❑   Difficulty in hiring/retaining quality staff

❑   Expertise required to run the business

❑   Impact of marketing/promotions

❑   Start-up costs

❑   Degree of stress

❑   Workload

Most frequent responses:

	% answering
Degree of stress (tie)	43%
Workload (tie)	43%
Difficulty in hiring/retaining quality staff	39%

Q12: **If you could turn back time to the day you signed your franchise agreement, would you make the same decision to buy your franchise?**

	% answering
Yes	27%
No	**73%**

*   Number of survey respondents: 23 from 17 different states

Number of survey respondents as a % of total franchise units: 12.78%

THE MEDICINE SHOPPE

www.medicineshoppe.com
Email: franchisedevelopment@medshoppe.com

Retail pharmacies.

OVERALL SCORE: 58

OVERALL RANK: 144

7000 Cardinal Place
Dublin, OH 43017
Fax: 614-757-8871
Total number of outlets: 900+ (approximately
600 in U.S.)
Total number of franchise outlets: 900+
(approximately 600 in U.S.)
International: Yes (several countries)

Phone: 800-325-1397
Franchise fee:
Franchise term:
Initial investment: $198,000 to $254,000
Advertising/Marketing fee:
Royalty fee:

SURVEY AND RESULTS *

Q1: About how many hours per week do you dedicate to your franchise business?

		% answering
A)	Less than 40	6%
B)	**41–50**	**50%**
C)	51–60	25%
D)	More than 60	19%
E)	Passive investment	0%

Q2: How would you describe your relations/communications with your franchisor?

		% answering
A)	Excellent	13%
B)	**Good**	**40%**
C)	Adequate	7%
D)	Fair	13%
E)	Poor	27%

Q3: In terms of how your franchisor views your communications with other franchisees, it is:

		% answering
A)	Very supportive	25%
B)	**Not very supportive**	**44%**
C)	No influence	31%

Q4: Is the franchisor fair with you in resolving any grievances?

		% answering
A)	Extremely fair	6%
B)	Pretty fair	19%
C)	**Reasonably fair**	**38%**
D)	Not very fair	31%
E)	Not fair at all	6%

Q5: Are territories equitably granted?

		% answering
A)	**Yes**	**73%**
B)	No	7%
C)	Not yet sure	20%

Q6: How would you describe the initial and ongoing training provided by your franchisor?

		% answering
A)	Excellent	27%
B)	**Good**	**33%**
C)	Adequate	27%
D)	Fair	7%
E)	Poor	7%

Q7: How well does the franchisor anticipate future trends in how it evolves and markets products and services?

		% answering
A)	Extremely well	20%
B)	**Pretty well**	**27%**
C)	Adequately	20%
D)	Not very well	13%
E)	Terribly	20%

Q8: How satisfied are you with your franchisor's spending of the royalty fees you pay?

		% answering
A)	Extremely satisfied	0%
B)	Mostly satisfied	31%
C)	Somewhat satisfied	6%
D)	**Not very satisfied**	**38%**
E)	Not satisfied at all	25%

Q9: **In what ways could the parent company most improve? (Please check those that most apply, no more than three):**

❑ Communications
❑ Counsel/advice on administrative/management issues
❑ Effectiveness of marketing/promotions
❑ Evolution of products/services
❑ Frequency of marketing/promotional campaigns

❑ Quality of products/services
❑ Pricing of products/services to franchisees
❑ Technology (Point of sale systems, usage of computers/email/software, etc.)
❑ Training

Most frequent responses:	% answering
Pricing of products/services to franchisees	69%
Effectiveness of marketing/promotions	38%
Technology	31%

Q10: **Is your income more, less or about what you expected prior to opening your business?**

	% answering	
More	**44%**	
Less	38%	**Summary: 63% are making about what they**
About what was expected	19%	**expected, or more.**

Q11: **Prior to opening your franchise, which (if any) of the following did you underestimate?**

❑ Amount of working capital required for your 1st year in business
❑ Difficulty in hiring/retaining quality staff
❑ Expertise required to run the business
❑ Impact of marketing/promotions

❑ Start-up costs
❑ Degree of stress
❑ Workload

Most frequent responses:	% answering
Amount of working capital required for 1st year in business (tie)	44%
Start-up costs (tie)	44%
Degree of stress	38%

Q12: **If you could turn back time to the day you signed your franchise agreement, would you make the same decision to buy your franchise?**

	% answering
Yes	47%
No	**53%**

*   Number of survey respondents: 16 from 5 different states
    Number of survey respondents as a % of total franchise units: 1.78%

MEINEKE CAR CARE CENTERS

www.ownameineke.com

Vehicle repair services.

OVERALL SCORE: 60

OVERALL RANK: 137

128 South Tryon Street, Suite 900
Charlotte, NC 28202
Fax: 704-3771490
Total number of outlets: approximately 900
Total number of franchise outlets: approximately 900
International: Yes (several countries)

Phone: 800-Meineke
Franchise fee: $
Franchise term:
Initial investment:
Advertising/Marketing fee:
Royalty fee:

SURVEY AND RESULTS *

Q1: About how many hours per week do you dedicate to your franchise business?

		% answering
A)	Less than 40	0%
B)	41–50	8%
C)	51–60	33%
D)	**More than 60**	**58%**
E)	Passive investment	0%

Q2: How would you describe your relations/communications with your franchisor?

		% answering
A)	Excellent	8%
B)	**Good**	**50%**
C)	Adequate	13%
D)	Fair	0%
E)	**Poor**	**29%**

Q3: In terms of how your franchisor views your communications with other franchisees, it is:

		% answering
A)	**Very supportive**	**55%**
B)	Not very supportive	9%
C)	No influence	36%

Q4: Is the franchisor fair with you in resolving any grievances?

		% answering
A)	Extremely fair	10%
B)	**Pretty fair**	**30%**
C)	**Reasonably fair**	**30%**
D)	Not very fair	20%
E)	Not fair at all	10%

Q5: Are territories equitably granted?

		% answering
A)	**Yes**	**83%**
B)	No	8%
C)	Not yet sure	8%

Q6: How would you describe the initial and ongoing training provided by your franchisor?

		% answering
A)	Excellent	13%
B)	**Good**	**42%**
C)	Adequate	21%
D)	Fair	8%
E)	Poor	17%

Q7: How well does the franchisor anticipate future trends in how it evolves and markets products and services?

		% answering
A)	Extremely well	8%
B)	Pretty well	33%
C)	**Adequately**	**42%**
D)	Not very well	17%
E)	Terribly	0%

Q8: How satisfied are you with your franchisor's spending of the royalty fees you pay?

		% answering
A)	Extremely satisfied	8%
B)	**Mostly satisfied**	**50%**
C)	Somewhat satisfied	17%
D)	Not very satisfied	25%
E)	Not satisfied at all	0%

Q9: **In what ways could the parent company most improve? (Please check those that most apply, no more than three):**

- ❑ Communications
- ❑ Counsel/advice on administrative/management issues
- ❑ Effectiveness of marketing/promotions
- ❑ Evolution of products/services
- ❑ Frequency of marketing/promotional campaigns

- ❑ Quality of products/services
- ❑ Pricing of products/services to franchisees
- ❑ Technology (Point of sale systems, usage of computers/email/software, etc.)
- ❑ Training

Most frequent responses:	% answering
Counsel/advice on administrative/management issues	58%
Training	50%
Pricing of products/services to franchisees	42%

Q10: **Is your income more, less or about what you expected prior to opening your business?**

	% answering	
More	17%	
Less	**50%**	**Summary: 50% are making about what they**
About what was expected	33%	**expected, or more.**

Q11: **Prior to opening your franchise, which (if any) of the following did you underestimate?**

- ❑ Amount of working capital required for your 1st year in business
- ❑ Difficulty in hiring/retaining quality staff
- ❑ Expertise required to run the business
- ❑ Impact of marketing/promotions

- ❑ Start-up costs
- ❑ Degree of stress
- ❑ Workload

Most frequent responses:	% answering
Difficulty in hiring/retaining quality staff	75%
Degree of stress (tie)	58%
Workload (tie)	58%

Q12: **If you could turn back time to the day you signed your franchise agreement, would you make the same decision to buy your franchise?**

	% answering
Yes	**55%**
No	45%

* Number of survey respondents: 12 from 9 different states
  Number of survey respondents as a % of total franchise units: 1.33%

MERLE NORMAN COSMETICS

www.merlenorman.com

Developer, manufacturer, and distributor of cosmetics through retail stores.

OVERALL SCORE: 85

OVERALL RANK: 15

9130 Bellance Avenue
Los Angeles, CA 90045
Fax: 310-641-7744
Total number of outlets: Approximately 2,000
Total number of franchise outlets:
Approximately 2,000
International: Yes (several countries)

Phone: 800-421-6648
Franchise fee: none
Franchise term:
Initial investment:
Advertising/Marketing fee:
Royalty fee: none

SURVEY AND RESULTS *

Q1: About how many hours per week do you dedicate to your franchise business?

		% answering
A)	Less than 40	20%
B)	**41–50**	**67%**
C)	51–60	7%
D)	More than 60	7%
E)	Passive investment	0%

Q2: How would you describe your relations/communications with your franchisor?

		% answering
A)	**Excellent**	**67%**
B)	Good	27%
C)	Adequate	0%
D)	Fair	7%
E)	Poor	0%

Q3: In terms of how your franchisor views your communications with other franchisees, it is:

		% answering
A)	**Very supportive**	**71%**
B)	Not very supportive	0%
C)	No influence	29%

Q4: Is the franchisor fair with you in resolving any grievances?

		% answering
A)	**Extremely fair**	**80%**
B)	Pretty fair	7%
C)	Reasonably fair	13%
D)	Not very fair	0%
E)	Not fair at all	0%

Q5: Are territories equitably granted?

		% answering
A)	**Yes**	**50%**
B)	No	36%
C)	Not yet sure	14%

Q6: How would you describe the initial and ongoing training provided by your franchisor?

		% answering
A)	**Excellent**	**73%**
B)	Good	27%
C)	Adequate	0%
D)	Fair	0%
E)	Poor	0%

Q7: How well does the franchisor anticipate future trends in how it evolves and markets products and services?

		% answering
A)	**Extremely well**	**67%**
B)	Pretty well	27%
C)	Adequately	7%
D)	Not very well	0%
E)	Terribly	0%

Q8: How satisfied are you with your franchisor's spending of the royalty fees you pay?

		% answering
A)	Extremely satisfied	N/A
B)	Mostly satisfied	N/A
C)	Somewhat satisfied	N/A
D)	Not very satisfied	N/A
E)	Not satisfied at all	N/A

Q9: **In what ways could the parent company most improve? (Please check those that most apply, no more than three):**

❑ Communications
❑ Counsel/advice on administrative/management issues
❑ Effectiveness of marketing/promotions
❑ Evolution of products/services
❑ Frequency of marketing/promotional campaigns

❑ Quality of products/services
❑ Pricing of products/services to franchisees
❑ Technology (Point of sale systems, usage of computers/email/software, etc.)
❑ Training

Most frequent responses:

	% answering
Evolution of products/services	20%
Counsel/advice on administrative/management issues (tie)	13%
Frequency of marketing/promotional campaigns (tie)	13%

Q10: **Is your income more, less or about what you expected prior to opening your business?**

	% answering	
More	14%	
Less	29%	**Summary: 71% are making about what they**
About what was expected	**57%**	**expected, or more.**

Q11: **Prior to opening your franchise, which (if any) of the following did you underestimate?**

❑ Amount of working capital required for your 1st year in business
❑ Difficulty in hiring/retaining quality staff
❑ Expertise required to run the business
❑ Impact of marketing/promotions

❑ Start-up costs
❑ Degree of stress
❑ Workload

Most frequent responses:

	% answering
Difficulty in hiring/retaining quality staff	60%
Amount of working capital required for 1st year in business	47%
Impact of marketing/promotions (tie)	20%
Start-up costs (tie)	20%
Degree of stress (tie)	20%

Q12: **If you could turn back time to the day you signed your franchise agreement, would you make the same decision to buy your franchise?**

	% answering
Yes	**87%**
No	13%

* Number of survey respondents: 15 from 15 different states
Number of survey respondents as a % of total franchise units: < 1%

MERRY MAIDS

www.merrymaids.com

Residential cleaning services.

OVERALL SCORE: 78

3839 Forest Hill-Irene Road
Memphis, TN 38125
Fax: 901-597-8140
Total number of outlets: 900+
Total number of franchise outlets: 900+
International: Yes (several)

OVERALL RANK: 45

Phone: 800-798-8000
Franchise fee:
Franchise term:
Initial investment:
Advertising/Marketing fee:
Royalty fee:

SURVEY AND RESULTS *

Q1: About how many hours per week do you dedicate to your franchise business?

		% answering
A)	Less than 40	21%
B)	**41–50**	**29%**
C)	51–60	21%
D)	More than 60	21%
E)	Passive investment	7%

Q2: How would you describe your relations/ communications with your franchisor?

		% answering
A)	**Excellent**	**43%**
B)	Good	1%
C)	Adequate	29%
D)	Fair	7%
E)	Poor	0%

Q3: In terms of how your franchisor views your communications with other franchisees, it is:

		% answering
A)	**Very supportive**	**64%**
B)	Not very supportive	14%
C)	No influence	21%

Q4: Is the franchisor fair with you in resolving any grievances?

		% answering
A)	**Extremely fair**	**54%**
B)	Pretty fair	8%
C)	Reasonably fair	23%
D)	Not very fair	15%
E)	Not fair at all	0%

Q5: Are territories equitably granted?

		% answering
A)	**Yes**	**77%**
B)	No	23%
C)	Not yet sure	0%

Q6: How would you describe the initial and ongoing training provided by your franchisor?

		% answering
A)	**Excellent**	**50%**
B)	Good	21%
C)	Adequate	14%
D)	Fair	7%
E)	Poor	7%

Q7: How well does the franchisor anticipate future trends in how it evolves and markets products and services?

		% answering
A)	**Extremely well**	**50%**
B)	Pretty well	21%
C)	Adequately	29%
D)	Not very well	0%
E)	Terribly	0%

Q8: How satisfied are you with your franchisor's spending of the royalty fees you pay?

		% answering
A)	**Extremely satisfied**	**29%**
B)	**Mostly satisfied**	**29%**
C)	**Somewhat satisfied**	**29%**
D)	Not very satisfied	14%
E)	Not satisfied at all	14%

Q9: **In what ways could the parent company most improve? (Please check those that most apply, no more than three):**

❑ Communications
❑ Counsel/advice on administrative/management issues
❑ Effectiveness of marketing/promotions
❑ Evolution of products/services
❑ Frequency of marketing/promotional campaigns

❑ Quality of products/services
❑ Pricing of products/services to franchisees
❑ Technology (Point of sale systems, usage of computers/email/software, etc.)
❑ Training

Most frequent responses:	% answering
Communications	43%
Effectiveness of marketing/promotions (tie)	36%
Frequency of marketing/promotional campaigns (tie)	36%

Q10: **Is your income more, less or about what you expected prior to opening your business?**

	% answering	
More	29%	
Less	**36%**	**Summary: 65% are making about what they**
About what was expected	**36%**	**expected, or more.**

Q11: **Prior to opening your franchise, which (if any) of the following did you underestimate?**

❑ Amount of working capital required for your 1st year in business
❑ Difficulty in hiring/retaining quality staff
❑ Expertise required to run the business
❑ Impact of marketing/promotions

❑ Start-up costs
❑ Degree of stress
❑ Workload

Most frequent responses:	% answering
Difficulty in hiring/retaining quality staff	71%
Degree of stress	57%
Amount of working capital required for 1st year in business	36%

Q12: **If you could turn back time to the day you signed your franchise agreement, would you make the same decision to buy your franchise?**

	% answering
Yes	**86%**
No	14%

* Number of survey respondents: 14 from 11 different states
　Number of survey respondents as a % of total franchise units: 1.56%

MIDAS

www.midasfran.com

Vehicle repair services.

OVERALL SCORE: 56

OVERALL RANK: 157

1300 Arlington Heights Road
Itasca, IL 60143
Total number of outlets: 2,600+
Total number of franchise outlets: 2,600+
Royalty fee: 10%
International: Yes (worldwide)

Phone: 800-365-0007
Franchise fee: $20,000
Franchise term: 20 years
Initial investment:
Advertising/Marketing fee: none (1/2 of royalty
fee paid is currently dedicated by Midas to
national advertising

SURVEY AND RESULTS *

Q1: About how many hours per week do you dedicate to your franchise business?

		% answering
A)	Less than 40	8%
B)	41–50	15%
C)	51–60	23%
D)	**More than 60**	**54%**
E)	Passive investment	0%

Q2: How would you describe your relations/ communications with your franchisor?

		% answering
A)	Excellent	8%
B)	**Good**	**38%**
C)	Adequate	23%
D)	Fair	15%
E)	Poor	15%

Q3: In terms of how your franchisor views your communications with other franchisees, it is:

		% answering
A)	**Very supportive**	**83%**
B)	Not very supportive	0%
C)	No influence	17%

Q4: Is the franchisor fair with you in resolving any grievances?

		% answering
A)	Extremely fair	0%
B)	**Pretty fair**	**58%**
C)	Reasonably fair	33%
D)	Not very fair	8%
E)	Not fair at all	0%

Q5: Are territories equitably granted?

		% answering
A)	**Yes**	**62%**
B)	No	8%
C)	Not yet sure	31%

Q6: How would you describe the initial and ongoing training provided by your franchisor?

		% answering
A)	Excellent	8%
B)	Good	23%
C)	Adequate	23%
D)	Fair	15%
E)	**Poor**	**31%**

Q7: How well does the franchisor anticipate future trends in how it evolves and markets products and services?

		% answering
A)	Extremely well	8%
B)	**Pretty well**	**38%**
C)	Adequately	31%
D)	Not very well	15%
E)	Terribly	8%

Q8: How satisfied are you with your franchisor's spending of the royalty fees you pay?

		% answering
A)	Extremely satisfied	0%
B)	Mostly satisfied	23%
C)	**Somewhat satisfied**	**46%**
D)	Not very satisfied	15%
E)	Not satisfied at all	15%

Q9: **In what ways could the parent company most improve? (Please check those that most apply, no more than three):**

❑ Communications   ❑ Quality of products/services
❑ Counsel/advice on administrative/management issues   ❑ Pricing of products/services to franchisees
❑ Effectiveness of marketing/promotions   ❑ Technology (Point of sale systems, usage
❑ Evolution of products/services   of computers/email/software, etc.)
❑ Frequency of marketing/promotional campaigns   ❑ Training

Most frequent responses:	% answering
Effectiveness of marketing/promotions	69%
Training	62%
Frequency of marketing/promotional campaigns	46%

Q10: **Is your income more, less or about what you expected prior to opening your business?**

	% answering	
More	8%	
Less	**54%**	**Summary: 46% are making about what they**
About what was expected	38%	**expected, or more.**

Q11: **Prior to opening your franchise, which (if any) of the following did you underestimate?**

❑ Amount of working capital required for your   ❑ Start-up costs
    1st year in business   ❑ Degree of stress
❑ Difficulty in hiring/retaining quality staff   ❑ Workload
❑ Expertise required to run the business
❑ Impact of marketing/promotions

Most frequent responses:	% answering
Degree of stress	77%
Difficulty in hiring/retaining quality staff	69%
Workload	38%

Q12: **If you could turn back time to the day you signed your franchise agreement, would you make the same decision to buy your franchise?**

	% answering
Yes	**50%**
No	**50%**

* Number of survey respondents: 13 from 11 different states
    Number of survey respondents as a % of total franchise units: < 1%

MINUTEMAN PRESS

www.minutemanpress.com
Email: info@minutemanpress.com

Full service printing center.

OVERALL SCORE: 66

61 Executive Boulevard
Farmingdale, NY 11735
Fax: 631-249-5618
Total number of outlets: 873
Total number of franchise outlets: 873
International: Yes (several countries)

OVERALL RANK: 105

Phone: 800-645-3006
Franchise fee: $44,500
Franchise term: 35 years
Initial investment: $91,991 to $244,849
Advertising/Marketing fee: none
Royalty fee: 6% of total gross sales

SURVEY AND RESULTS *

Q1: About how many hours per week do you dedicate to your franchise business?

		% answering
A)	Less than 40	13%
B)	41–50	25%
C)	51–60	25%
D)	**More than 60**	**38%**
E)	Passive investment	0%

Q2: How would you describe your relations/ communications with your franchisor?

		% answering
A)	**Excellent**	**44%**
B)	Good	25%
C)	Adequate	19%
D)	Fair	6%
E)	Poor	6%

Q3: In terms of how your franchisor views your communications with other franchisees, it is:

		% answering
A)	**Very supportive**	**75%**
B)	Not very supportive	0%
C)	No influence	25%

Q4: Is the franchisor fair with you in resolving any grievances?

		% answering
A)	**Extremely fair**	**36%**
B)	Pretty fair	21%
C)	Reasonably fair	29%
D)	Not very fair	14%
E)	Not fair at all	0%

Q5: Are territories equitably granted?

		% answering
A)	**Yes**	**56%**
B)	No	31%
C)	Not yet sure	13%

Q6: How would you describe the initial and ongoing training provided by your franchisor?

		% answering
A)	Excellent	19%
B)	**Good**	**69%**
C)	Adequate	6%
D)	Fair	6%
E)	Poor	0%

Q7: How well does the franchisor anticipate future trends in how it evolves and markets products and services?

		% answering
A)	Extremely well	19%
B)	**Pretty well**	**38%**
C)	Adequately	19%
D)	Not very well	25%
E)	Terribly	0%

Q8: How satisfied are you with your franchisor's spending of the royalty fees you pay?

		% answering
A)	Extremely satisfied	14%
B)	**Mostly satisfied**	**36%**
C)	Somewhat satisfied	29%
D)	Not very satisfied	14%
E)	Not satisfied at all	7%

Q9: **In what ways could the parent company most improve? (Please check those that most apply, no more than three):**

❑ Communications
❑ Counsel/advice on administrative/management issues
❑ Effectiveness of marketing/promotions
❑ Evolution of products/services
❑ Frequency of marketing/promotional campaigns

❑ Quality of products/services
❑ Pricing of products/services to franchisees
❑ Technology (Point of sale systems, usage of computers/email/software, etc.)
❑ Training

Most frequent responses:	% answering
Frequency of marketing/promotional campaigns	38%
Communications (tie)	31%
Technology (tie)	31%

Q10: **Is your income more, less or about what you expected prior to opening your business?**

	% answering	
More	31%	
Less	**56%**	**Summary: 44% are making about what they**
About what was expected	13%	**expected, or more.**

Q11: **Prior to opening your franchise, which (if any) of the following did you underestimate?**

❑ Amount of working capital required for your 1st year in business
❑ Difficulty in hiring/retaining quality staff
❑ Expertise required to run the business
❑ Impact of marketing/promotions

❑ Start-up costs
❑ Degree of stress
❑ Workload

Most frequent responses:	% answering
Amount of working capital required for 1st year in business	50%
Workload	31%
Degree of stress	25%

Q12: **If you could turn back time to the day you signed your franchise agreement, would you make the same decision to buy your franchise?**

	% answering
Yes	**63%**
No	38%

* Number of survey respondents: 16 from 13 different states
   Number of survey respondents as a % of total franchise units: 1.83%

MOLLY MAID

www.mollymaid.com

Residential cleaning services.

OVERALL SCORE: 73

3948 Ranchero Drive
Ann Arbor, MI 48108
Fax: 734-822-6888
Total number of outlets: 291
Total number of franchise outlets: 291
International: Yes (several countries)
Royalty fee: varies

OVERALL RANK: 64

Phone: 800-665-5962
Franchise fee: $9,900 plus $1 for each targeted household in territory
Franchise term: 10 years
Initial investment: $70,000 to $100,000
Advertising/Marketing fee: $75 per month, not to exceed 2% of gross sales

SURVEY AND RESULTS *

Q1: About how many hours per week do you dedicate to your franchise business?

		% answering
A)	**Less than 40**	**50%**
B)	41–50	8%
C)	51–60	33%
D)	More than 60	8%
E)	Passive investment	0%

Q2: How would you describe your relations/ communications with your franchisor?

		% answering
A)	**Excellent**	**33%**
B)	**Good**	**33%**
C)	Adequate	8%
D)	Fair	25%
E)	Poor	0%

Q3: In terms of how your franchisor views your communications with other franchisees, it is:

		% answering
A)	**Very supportive**	**83%**
B)	Not very supportive	17%
C)	No influence	0%

Q4: Is the franchisor fair with you in resolving any grievances?

		% answering
A)	Extremely fair	22%
B)	**Pretty fair**	**44%**
C)	Reasonably fair	33%
D)	Not very fair	0%
E)	Not fair at all	0%

Q5: Are territories equitably granted?

		% answering
A)	Yes	40%
B)	No	0%
C)	**Not yet sure**	**60%**

Q6: How would you describe the initial and ongoing training provided by your franchisor?

		% answering
A)	Excellent	25%
B)	**Good**	**50%**
C)	Adequate	0%
D)	Fair	25%
E)	Poor	0%

Q7: How well does the franchisor anticipate future trends in how it evolves and markets products and services?

		% answering
A)	Extremely well	20%
B)	**Pretty well**	**30%**
C)	Adequately	20%
D)	Not very well	20%
E)	Terribly	10%

Q8: How satisfied are you with your franchisor's spending of the royalty fees you pay?

		% answering
A)	Extremely satisfied	0%
B)	**Mostly satisfied**	**67%**
C)	Somewhat satisfied	8%
D)	Not very satisfied	25%
E)	Not satisfied at all	0%

Q9: **In what ways could the parent company most improve? (Please check those that most apply, no more than three):**

❑ Communications
❑ Counsel/advice on administrative/management issues
❑ Effectiveness of marketing/promotions
❑ Evolution of products/services
❑ Frequency of marketing/promotional campaigns

❑ Quality of products/services
❑ Pricing of products/services to franchisees
❑ Technology (Point of sale systems, usage of computers/email/software, etc.)
❑ Training

Most frequent responses:

	% answering
Effectiveness of marketing/promotions	42%
Counsel/advice on administrative/management issues	33%
Frequency of marketing/promotional campaigns	25%

Q10: **Is your income more, less or about what you expected prior to opening your business?**

	% answering	
More	8%	
Less	**58%**	**Summary: 41% are making about what they**
About what was expected	33%	**expected, or more.**

Q11: **Prior to opening your franchise, which (if any) of the following did you underestimate?**

❑ Amount of working capital required for your 1st year in business
❑ Difficulty in hiring/retaining quality staff
❑ Expertise required to run the business
❑ Impact of marketing/promotions

❑ Start-up costs
❑ Degree of stress
❑ Workload

Most frequent responses:

	% answering
Amount of working capital required for 1st year in business	75%
Difficulty in hiring/retaining quality staff	50%
Impact of marketing/promotions	25%

Q12: **If you could turn back time to the day you signed your franchise agreement, would you make the same decision to buy your franchise?**

	% answering
Yes	**91%**
No	9%

* Number of survey respondents: 12 from 10 different states
  Number of survey respondents as a % of total franchise units: 4.12%

MOTOPHOTO

www.motophoto.com
Email: expert@motophoto.com

One hour photo processing.

OVERALL SCORE: 55

4444 Lake Center Drive
Dayton, OH 45426
Fax: 937-854-0140
Total number of outlets: 215+
Total number of franchise outlets: 208+
International: Yes (Canada)
Royalty fee 6% of net retail sales, 3% of net wholesale sales, payable weekly

OVERALL RANK: 159

Phone: 800-733-6686, ext. 313
Franchise fee: Re-sales only at this time
Franchise term: 10 years
Initial investment: Re-sales only at this time
Advertising/Marketing fee: 1/2% of net retail sales, payable weekly

SURVEY AND RESULTS *

Q1: About how many hours per week do you dedicate to your franchise business?

		% answering
A)	Less than 40	17%
B)	41–50	25%
C)	51–60	25%
D)	**More than 60**	**33%**
E)	Passive investment	0%

Q2: How would you describe your relations/ communications with your franchisor?

		% answering
A)	Excellent	%
B)	**Good**	**54%**
C)	Adequate	8%
D)	Fair	8%
E)	Poor	8%

Q3: In terms of how your franchisor views your communications with other franchisees, it is:

		% answering
A)	**Very supportive**	**77%**
B)	Not very supportive	15%
C)	No influence	8%

Q4: Is the franchisor fair with you in resolving any grievances?

		% answering
A)	**Extremely fair**	**31%**
B)	**Pretty fair**	**31%**
C)	Reasonably fair	23%
D)	Not very fair	15%
E)	Not fair at all	0%

Q5: Are territories equitably granted?

		% answering
A)	**Yes**	**62%**
B)	No	15%
C)	Not yet sure	23%

Q6: How would you describe the initial and ongoing training provided by your franchisor?

		% answering
A)	Excellent	0%
B)	**Good**	**54%**
C)	Adequate	31%
D)	Fair	8%
E)	Poor	8%

Q7: How well does the franchisor anticipate future trends in how it evolves and markets products and services?

		% answering
A)	Extremely well	8%
B)	Pretty well	23%
C)	Adequately	23%
D)	**Not very well**	**38%**
E)	Terribly	8%

Q8: How satisfied are you with your franchisor's spending of the royalty fees you pay?

		% answering
A)	Extremely satisfied	15%
B)	Mostly satisfied	15%
C)	**Somewhat satisfied**	**46%**
D)	Not very satisfied	15%
E)	Not satisfied at all	8%

Q9: **In what ways could the parent company most improve? (Please check those that most apply, no more than three):**

- ❑ Communications
- ❑ Counsel/advice on administrative/management issues
- ❑ Effectiveness of marketing/promotions
- ❑ Evolution of products/services
- ❑ Frequency of marketing/promotional campaigns

- ❑ Quality of products/services
- ❑ Pricing of products/services to franchisees
- ❑ Technology (Point of sale systems, usage of computers/email/software, etc.)
- ❑ Training

Most frequent responses:	% answering
Evolution of products/services	77%
Effectiveness of marketing/promotions	69%
Technology	31%

Q10: **Is your income more, less or about what you expected prior to opening your business?**

	% answering	
More	15%	
Less	**62%**	**Summary: 30% are making about what they**
About what was expected	15%	**expected, or more.**

Q11: **Prior to opening your franchise, which (if any) of the following did you underestimate?**

- ❑ Amount of working capital required for your 1st year in business
- ❑ Difficulty in hiring/retaining quality staff
- ❑ Expertise required to run the business
- ❑ Impact of marketing/promotions

- ❑ Start-up costs
- ❑ Degree of stress
- ❑ Workload

Most frequent responses:	% answering
Difficulty in hiring/retaining quality staff	54%
Amount of working capital required for your 1st year in business	46%
Degree of stress	38%

Q12: **If you could turn back time to the day you signed your franchise agreement, would you make the same decision to buy your franchise?**

	% answering
Yes	46%
No	**54%**

* Number of survey respondents: 13 from 8 different states
  Number of survey respondents as a % of total franchise units: 6.25%

MR. ELECTRIC

www.dwyergroup.com
Email: mrelectric@dwyergroup.com

Residential and commercial electrical service and repair.

OVERALL SCORE: 63

1010-1020 North University Parks Drive
Waco, TX 76707
Fax: 254-745-2501
Total number of outlets: 150
Total number of franchise outlets: 150
International: Yes (several countries)

OVERALL RANK: 120

Phone: 800-805-0575
Franchise fee: Minimum of $19,500
Franchise term: 10 years
Initial investment: $65,550 to $158,500
Advertising/Marketing fee: varies
Royalty fee varies

SURVEY AND RESULTS *

Q1: About how many hours per week do you dedicate to your franchise business?

		% answering
A)	Less than 40	31%
B)	**41–50**	**46%**
C)	51–60	23%
D)	More than 60	0%
E)	Passive investment	0%

Q2: How would you describe your relations/ communications with your franchisor?

		% answering
A)	**Excellent**	**38%**
B)	Good	23%
C)	Adequate	23%
D)	Fair	0%
E)	Poor	15%

Q3: In terms of how your franchisor views your communications with other franchisees, it is:

		% answering
A)	**Very supportive**	**67%**
B)	Not very supportive	8%
C)	No influence	25%

Q4: Is the franchisor fair with you in resolving any grievances?

		% answering
A)	**Extremely fair**	**38%**
B)	Pretty fair	31%
C)	Reasonably fair	15%
D)	Not very fair	8%
E)	Not fair at all	8%

Q5: Are territories equitably granted?

		% answering
A)	**Yes**	**62%**
B)	No	8%
C)	Not yet sure	31%

Q6: How would you describe the initial and ongoing training provided by your franchisor?

		% answering
A)	**Excellent**	**31%**
B)	**Good**	**31%**
C)	Adequate	15%
D)	Fair	15%
E)	Poor	8%

Q7: How well does the franchisor anticipate future trends in how it evolves and markets products and services?

		% answering
A)	Extremely well	23%
B)	**Pretty well**	**46%**
C)	Adequately	15%
D)	Not very well	0%
E)	Terribly	15%

Q8: How satisfied are you with your franchisor's spending of the royalty fees you pay?

		% answering
A)	Extremely satisfied	8%
B)	**Mostly satisfied**	**54%**
C)	Somewhat satisfied	23%
D)	Not very satisfied	0%
E)	Not satisfied at all	15%

Q9: **In what ways could the parent company most improve? (Please check those that most apply, no more than three):**

- ❑ Communications
- ❑ Counsel/advice on administrative/management issues
- ❑ Effectiveness of marketing/promotions
- ❑ Evolution of products/services
- ❑ Frequency of marketing/promotional campaigns

- ❑ Quality of products/services
- ❑ Pricing of products/services to franchisees
- ❑ Technology (Point of sale systems, usage of computers/email/software, etc.)
- ❑ Training

Most frequent responses:	% answering
Effectiveness of marketing/promotions	62%
Counsel/advice on administrative/management issues	54%
Communications (tie)	23%
Technology (tie)	23%
Pricing of products/services to franchisees (tie)	23%

Q10: **Is your income more, less or about what you expected prior to opening your business?**

	% answering	
More	0%	
Less	46%	**Summary: 54% are making about what they**
About what was expected	**54%**	**expected, or more.**

Q11: **Prior to opening your franchise, which (if any) of the following did you underestimate?**

- ❑ Amount of working capital required for your 1st year in business
- ❑ Difficulty in hiring/retaining quality staff
- ❑ Expertise required to run the business
- ❑ Impact of marketing/promotions

- ❑ Start-up costs
- ❑ Degree of stress
- ❑ Workload

Most frequent responses:	% answering
Difficulty in hiring/retaining quality staff	54%
Impact of marketing/promotions (tie)	38%
Degree of stress (tie)	38%

Q12: **If you could turn back time to the day you signed your franchise agreement, would you make the same decision to buy your franchise?**

	% answering
Yes	**54%**
No	46%

* Number of survey respondents: 13 from 10 different states

Number of survey respondents as a % of total franchise units: 8.67%

MR. GOODCENTS SUBS & PASTA

www.mrgoodcents.com

Fast food sandwich and pasta shops.

OVERALL SCORE: 44

OVERALL RANK: 177

8997 Commerce Drive
DeSoto, KS 66018
Fax: 913-583-3500
Total number of outlets: 134
Total number of franchise outlets: 130
International: No

Phone: 800-648-2368
Franchise fee: $5,000 to $12,500
Franchise term: 10 years
Initial investment: $100,250 to $228,750
Advertising/Marketing fee: 3.5% of gross
revenue, payable weekly
Royalty fee: 5% of gross revenue, payable weekly

SURVEY AND RESULTS *

Q1: About how many hours per week do you dedicate to your franchise business?

		% answering
A)	Less than 40	0%
B)	41–50	30%
C)	**51–60**	**50%**
D)	More than 60	20%
E)	Passive investment	0%

Q2: How would you describe your relations/communications with your franchisor?

		% answering
A)	Excellent	10%
B)	Good	20%
C)	Adequate	20%
D)	Fair	20%
E)	**Poor**	**30%**

Q3: In terms of how your franchisor views your communications with other franchisees, it is:

		% answering
A)	**Very supportive**	**40%**
B)	Not very supportive	30%
C)	No influence	30%

Q4: Is the franchisor fair with you in resolving any grievances?

		% answering
A)	Extremely fair	10%
B)	Pretty fair	30%
C)	Reasonably fair	20%
D)	**Not very fair**	**40%**
E)	Not fair at all	0%

Q5: Are territories equitably granted?

		% answering
A)	**Yes**	**40%**
B)	**No**	**40%**
C)	Not yet sure	20%

Q6: How would you describe the initial and ongoing training provided by your franchisor?

		% answering
A)	Excellent	10%
B)	Good	10%
C)	Adequate	10%
D)	**Fair**	**50%**
E)	Poor	20%

Q7: How well does the franchisor anticipate future trends in how it evolves and markets products and services?

		% answering
A)	Extremely well	0%
B)	Pretty well	20%
C)	Adequately	20%
D)	Not very well	20%
E)	**Terribly**	**40%**

Q8: How satisfied are you with your franchisor's spending of the royalty fees you pay?

		% answering
A)	Extremely satisfied	0%
B)	Mostly satisfied	20%
C)	Somewhat satisfied	20%
D)	**Not very satisfied**	**30%**
E)	**Not satisfied at all**	**30%**

Q9: **In what ways could the parent company most improve? (Please check those that most apply, no more than three):**

- ❏ Communications
- ❏ Counsel/advice on administrative/management issues
- ❏ Effectiveness of marketing/promotions
- ❏ Evolution of products/services
- ❏ Frequency of marketing/promotional campaigns

- ❏ Quality of products/services
- ❏ Pricing of products/services to franchisees
- ❏ Technology (Point of sale systems, usage of computers/email/software, etc.)
- ❏ Training

Most frequent responses:	% answering
Effectiveness of marketing/promotions	80%
Evolution of products/services	50%
Communications (tie)	40%
Frequency of marketing/promotional campaigns (tie)	40%

Q10: **Is your income more, less or about what you expected prior to opening your business?**

	% answering	
More	10%	
Less	**50%**	**Summary: 50% are making about what they**
About what was expected	40%	**expected, or more.**

Q11: **Prior to opening your franchise, which (if any) of the following did you underestimate?**

- ❏ Amount of working capital required for your 1st year in business
- ❏ Difficulty in hiring/retaining quality staff
- ❏ Expertise required to run the business
- ❏ Impact of marketing/promotions

- ❏ Start-up costs
- ❏ Degree of stress
- ❏ Workload

Most frequent responses:	% answering
Impact of marketing/promotions	80%
Amount of working capital required for your 1st year in business	60%
Start-up costs	50%

Q12: **If you could turn back time to the day you signed your franchise agreement, would you make the same decision to buy your franchise?**

	% answering
Yes	40%
No	**60%**

*   Number of survey respondents: 10 from 5 different states

Number of survey respondents as a % of total franchise units: 7.69%

MR. HANDYMAN

www.mrhandyman.com

Home maintenance and repair services.

OVERALL SCORE: 53

3948 Ranchero Drive
Ann Arbor, MI 48108
Fax: 734-822-6888
Total number of outlets: 111
Total number of franchise outlets: 111
Advertising/Marketing fee: 1.25% of gross
sales, payable weekly

OVERALL RANK: 163

Phone: 800-289-4600
Franchise fee: $9,900 plus $30,000 territory fee
Franchise term: 10 years
Initial investment: $86,200 to $$127,300
International: No
Royalty fee: 7% of gross sales less material
revenue generated, payable weekly; (3.5% of
gross sales on material revenue generated)

SURVEY AND RESULTS *

Q1: About how many hours per week do you dedicate to your franchise business?

		% answering
A)	Less than 40	11%
B)	**41–50**	**39%**
C)	51–60	22%
D)	More than 60	28%
E)	Passive investment	0%

Q2: How would you describe your relations/ communications with your franchisor?

		% answering
A)	**Excellent**	**33%**
B)	**Good**	**33%**
C)	Adequate	17%
D)	Fair	11%
E)	Poor	6%

Q3: In terms of how your franchisor views your communications with other franchisees, it is:

		% answering
A)	**Very supportive**	**78%**
B)	Not very supportive	6%
C)	No influence	17%

Q4: Is the franchisor fair with you in resolving any grievances?

		% answering
A)	Extremely fair	18%
B)	**Pretty fair**	**53%**
C)	Reasonably fair	29%
D)	Not very fair	0%
E)	Not fair at all	0%

Q5: Are territories equitably granted?

		% answering
A)	**Yes**	**61%**
B)	No	17%
C)	Not yet sure	22%

Q6: How would you describe the initial and ongoing training provided by your franchisor?

		% answering
A)	Excellent	6%
B)	**Good**	**39%**
C)	Adequate	28%
D)	Fair	6%
E)	Poor	22%

Q7: How well does the franchisor anticipate future trends in how it evolves and markets products and services?

		% answering
A)	Extremely well	11%
B)	Pretty well	28%
C)	**Adequately**	**39%**
D)	Not very well	22%
E)	Terribly	0%

Q8: How satisfied are you with your franchisor's spending of the royalty fees you pay?

		% answering
A)	Extremely satisfied	6%
B)	Mostly satisfied	18%
C)	**Somewhat satisfied**	**53%**
D)	Not very satisfied	24%
E)	Not satisfied at all	0%

Q9: **In what ways could the parent company most improve? (Please check those that most apply, no more than three):**

❑ Communications
❑ Counsel/advice on administrative/management issues
❑ Effectiveness of marketing/promotions
❑ Evolution of products/services
❑ Frequency of marketing/promotional campaigns

❑ Quality of products/services
❑ Pricing of products/services to franchisees
❑ Technology (Point of sale systems, usage of computers/email/software, etc.)
❑ Training

Most frequent responses:	% answering
Effectiveness of marketing/promotions	61%
Frequency of marketing/promotional campaigns	50%
Training	33%

Q10: **Is your income more, less or about what you expected prior to opening your business?**

	% answering	
More	6%	
Less	**72%**	**Summary: 28% are making about what they**
About what was expected	22%	**expected, or more.**

Q11: **Prior to opening your franchise, which (if any) of the following did you underestimate?**

❑ Amount of working capital required for your 1st year in business
❑ Difficulty in hiring/retaining quality staff
❑ Expertise required to run the business
❑ Impact of marketing/promotions

❑ Start-up costs
❑ Degree of stress
❑ Workload

Most frequent responses:	% answering
Difficulty in hiring/retaining quality staff	61%
Amount of working capital required for your 1st year in business (tie)	44%
Impact of marketing/promotions (tie)	44%

Q12: **If you could turn back time to the day you signed your franchise agreement, would you make the same decision to buy your franchise?**

	% answering
Yes	44%
No	**56%**

* Number of survey respondents: 18 from 11 different states
Number of survey respondents as a % of total franchise units: 16.22%

MR. ROOTER

www.mrrooter.com
Email: mrrooter@dwyergroup.com

Plumbing and drain cleaning services.

OVERALL SCORE: 71

OVERALL RANK: 75

1010 North University Parks Drive
Waco, TX 76707
Fax: 254-745-2501
Total number of outlets: 300+
Total number of franchise outlets: 300+
International:

Phone: 800-583-8003
Franchise fee:
Franchise term:
Initial investment: $
Advertising/Marketing fee:
Royalty fee:

SURVEY AND RESULTS *

Q1: About how many hours per week do you dedicate to your franchise business?

		% answering
A)	Less than 40	21%
B)	41–50	29%
C)	**51–60**	**36%**
D)	More than 60	14%
E)	Passive investment	0%

Q2: How would you describe your relations/ communications with your franchisor?

		% answering
A)	Excellent	36%
B)	**Good**	**43%**
C)	Adequate	14%
D)	Fair	0%
E)	Poor	7%

Q3: In terms of how your franchisor views your communications with other franchisees, it is:

		% answering
A)	**Very supportive**	**64%**
B)	Not very supportive	14%
C)	No influence	21%

Q4: Is the franchisor fair with you in resolving any grievances?

		% answering
A)	**Extremely fair**	**36%**
B)	**Pretty fair**	**36%**
C)	Reasonably fair	18%
D)	Not very fair	9%
E)	Not fair at all	0%

Q5: Are territories equitably granted?

		% answering
A)	**Yes**	**75%**
B)	No	8%
C)	Not yet sure	17%

Q6: How would you describe the initial and ongoing training provided by your franchisor?

		% answering
A)	**Excellent**	**46%**
B)	Good	31%
C)	Adequate	15%
D)	Fair	8%
E)	Poor	0%

Q7: How well does the franchisor anticipate future trends in how it evolves and markets products and services?

		% answering
A)	Extremely well	21%
B)	Pretty well	50%
C)	Adequately	21%
D)	Not very well	7%
E)	Terribly	0%

Q8: How satisfied are you with your franchisor's spending of the royalty fees you pay?

		% answering
A)	Extremely satisfied	14%
B)	**Mostly satisfied**	**50%**
C)	Somewhat satisfied	21%
D)	Not very satisfied	14%
E)	Not satisfied at all	0%

Q9: **In what ways could the parent company most improve? (Please check those that most apply, no more than three):**

❑ Communications
❑ Counsel/advice on administrative/management issues
❑ Effectiveness of marketing/promotions
❑ Evolution of products/services
❑ Frequency of marketing/promotional campaigns

❑ Quality of products/services
❑ Pricing of products/services to franchisees
❑ Technology (Point of sale systems, usage of computers/email/software, etc.)
❑ Training

Most frequent responses:	% answering
Effectiveness of marketing/promotions	50%
Counsel/advice on administrative/management issues	43%
Frequency of marketing/promotional campaigns	36%

Q10: **Is your income more, less or about what you expected prior to opening your business?**

	% answering	
More	36%	
Less	**50%**	**Summary: 50% are making about what they**
About what was expected	14%	**expected, or more.**

Q11: **Prior to opening your franchise, which (if any) of the following did you underestimate?**

❑ Amount of working capital required for your 1st year in business
❑ Difficulty in hiring/retaining quality staff
❑ Expertise required to run the business
❑ Impact of marketing/promotions

❑ Start-up costs
❑ Degree of stress
❑ Workload

Most frequent responses:	% answering
Difficulty in hiring/retaining quality staff	43%
Amount of working capital required for 1st year in business (tie)	29%
Degree of stress (tie)	29%

Q12: **If you could turn back time to the day you signed your franchise agreement, would you make the same decision to buy your franchise?**

	% answering
Yes	**67%**
No	33%

* Number of survey respondents: 14 from 11 different states
   Number of survey respondents as a % of total franchise units: 4.67%

MR. TRANSMISSION

www.mrtransmission.com

Auto service center specializing in transmission and other repairs.

OVERALL SCORE: 71

4444 West 147th Street
Midlothian, IL 60445
Total number of outlets: 153
Total number of franchise outlets: 153
International: No
Royalty fee: 7% of gross sales weekly

OVERALL RANK: N/A

Phone: 800-377-9247
Franchise fee: $27,500
Franchise term: 20 years
Initial investment: $149,000
Advertising/Marketing fee: Currently $100 per month

SURVEY AND RESULTS *

Q1: About how many hours per week do you dedicate to your franchise business?

		% answering
A)	Less than 40	13%
B)	41–50	13%
C)	**51–60**	**38%**
D)	**More than 60**	**38%**
E)	Passive investment	0%

Q2: How would you describe your relations/communications with your franchisor?

		% answering
A)	**Excellent**	**25%**
B)	**Good**	**25%**
C)	Adequate	13%
D)	**Fair**	**25%**
E)	Poor	13%

Q3: In terms of how your franchisor views your communications with other franchisees, it is:

		% answering
A)	**Very supportive**	**63%**
B)	Not very supportive	13%
C)	No influence	25%

Q4: Is the franchisor fair with you in resolving any grievances?

		% answering
A)	**Extremely fair**	**38%**
B)	Pretty fair	13%
C)	**Reasonably fair**	**38%**
D)	Not very fair	0%
E)	Not fair at all	13%

Q5: Are territories equitably granted?

		% answering
A)	**Yes**	**75%**
B)	No	25%
C)	Not yet sure	0%

Q6: How would you describe the initial and ongoing training provided by your franchisor?

		% answering
A)	Excellent	25%
B)	Good	13%
C)	Adequate	13%
D)	Fair	13%
E)	**Poor**	**38%**

Q7: How well does the franchisor anticipate future trends in how it evolves and markets products and services?

		% answering
A)	Extremely well	13%
B)	Pretty well	25%
C)	**Adequately**	**50%**
D)	Not very well	13%
E)	Terribly	0%

Q8: How satisfied are you with your franchisor's spending of the royalty fees you pay?

		% answering
A)	Extremely satisfied	13%
B)	Mostly satisfied	25%
C)	Somewhat satisfied	13%
D)	**Not very satisfied**	**25%**
E)	**Not satisfied at all**	**25%**

Q9: **In what ways could the parent company most improve? (Please check those that most apply, no more than three):**

❑ Communications
❑ Counsel/advice on administrative/management issues
❑ Effectiveness of marketing/promotions
❑ Evolution of products/services
❑ Frequency of marketing/promotional campaigns

❑ Quality of products/services
❑ Pricing of products/services to franchisees
❑ Technology (Point of sale systems, usage of computers/email/software, etc.)
❑ Training

Most frequent responses:	% answering
Effectiveness of marketing/promotions	50%
Evolution of products/services (tie)	38%
Training (tie)	38%

Q10: **Is your income more, less or about what you expected prior to opening your business?**

	% answering	
More	50%	
Less	25%	Summary: 75% are making about what they
About what was expected	25%	expected, or more.

Q11: **Prior to opening your franchise, which (if any) of the following did you underestimate?**

❑ Amount of working capital required for your 1st year in business
❑ Difficulty in hiring/retaining quality staff
❑ Expertise required to run the business
❑ Impact of marketing/promotions

❑ Start-up costs
❑ Degree of stress
❑ Workload

Most frequent responses:	% answering
Amount of working capital required for your 1st year in business (tie)	50%
Difficulty in hiring/retaining quality staff (tie)	50%
Degree of stress (tie)	50%

Q12: **If you could turn back time to the day you signed your franchise agreement, would you make the same decision to buy your franchise?**

	% answering
Yes	**88%**
No	13%

* Number of survey respondents: 8 from 5 different states
Number of survey respondents as a % of total franchise units: 5.23%

MRS. FIELD'S COOKIES

www.mrsfieldfranchise.com
Email: eliseh@mrsfields.com

Fresh-baked cookies, brownies, muffins, coffee and other beverages.

OVERALL SCORE: 63

2855 East Cottonwood Parkway
Salt Lake City, UT 84121
Fax: 425-377-0963 (Lake Stevens, WA office)
Total number of outlets: 392
Total number of franchise outlets: 317
International: Yes (several countries)

OVERALL RANK: N/A

Phone: 800-336-6551, ext. 5611
Franchise fee: $30,000
Franchise term: 7 years
Initial investment: $162,400 to $247,100
Advertising/Marketing fee: 1 to 3% of gross
revenues monthly
Royalty fee: 6% of monthly gross revenues

SURVEY AND RESULTS *

Q1: About how many hours per week do you dedicate to your franchise business?

		% answering
A)	Less than 40	17%
B)	**41–50**	**33%**
C)	**51–60**	**33%**
D)	More than 60	17%
E)	Passive investment	0%

Q2: How would you describe your relations/ communications with your franchisor?

		% answering
A)	Excellent	0%
B)	Good	17%
C)	**Adequate**	**67%**
D)	Fair	17%
E)	Poor	0%

Q3: In terms of how your franchisor views your communications with other franchisees, it is:

		% answering
A)	Very supportive	20%
B)	**Not very supportive**	**40%**
C)	**No influence**	**40%**

Q4: Is the franchisor fair with you in resolving any grievances?

		% answering
A)	Extremely fair	0%
B)	Pretty fair	25%
C)	**Reasonably fair**	**75%**
D)	Not very fair	0%
E)	Not fair at all	0%

Q5: Are territories equitably granted?

		% answering
A)	**Yes**	**50%**
B)	**No**	**0%**
C)	**Not yet sure**	**50%**

Q6: How would you describe the initial and ongoing training provided by your franchisor?

		% answering
A)	Excellent	0%
B)	Good	33%
C)	**Adequate**	**50%**
D)	Fair	17%
E)	Poor	0%

Q7: How well does the franchisor anticipate future trends in how it evolves and markets products and services?

		% answering
A)	Extremely well	17%
B)	Pretty well	17%
C)	**Adequately**	**33%**
D)	**Not very well**	**33%**
E)	Terribly	0%

Q8: How satisfied are you with your franchisor's spending of the royalty fees you pay?

		% answering
A)	Extremely satisfied	0%
B)	Mostly satisfied	17%
C)	**Somewhat satisfied**	**50%**
D)	Not very satisfied	33%
E)	Not satisfied at all	0%

Q9: **In what ways could the parent company most improve? (Please check those that most apply, no more than three):**

- ❏ Communications
- ❏ Counsel/advice on administrative/management issues
- ❏ Effectiveness of marketing/promotions
- ❏ Evolution of products/services
- ❏ Frequency of marketing/promotional campaigns
- ❏ Quality of products/services
- ❏ Pricing of products/services to franchisees
- ❏ Technology (Point of sale systems, usage of computers/email/software, etc.)
- ❏ Training

Most frequent responses:	% answering
Pricing of products/services to franchisees	67%
Communications (tie)	50%
Effectiveness of marketing/promotions (tie)	50%

Q10: **Is your income more, less or about what you expected prior to opening your business?**

	% answering	
More	0%	
Less	33%	**Summary: 67% are making about what they**
About what was expected	**67%**	**expected, or more.**

Q11: **Prior to opening your franchise, which (if any) of the following did you underestimate?**

- ❏ Amount of working capital required for your 1st year in business
- ❏ Difficulty in hiring/retaining quality staff
- ❏ Expertise required to run the business
- ❏ Impact of marketing/promotions
- ❏ Start-up costs
- ❏ Degree of stress
- ❏ Workload

Most frequent responses:	% answering
Amount of working capital required for your 1st year in business	50%
Difficulty in hiring/retaining quality staff (tie)	33%
Start-up costs (tie)	33%

Q12: **If you could turn back time to the day you signed your franchise agreement, would you make the same decision to buy your franchise?**

	% answering
Yes	**67%**
No	33%

* Number of survey respondents: 6 from 6 different states
  Number of survey respondents as a % of total franchise units: 1.89%

MY GYM CHILDREN'S FITNESS CENTER

www.my-gym.com
Email: franchises@my-gym.com

Fitness center for children aged three months to nine years old.

OVERALL SCORE: 81

15300 Ventura Boulevard, Suite 423
Sherman Oaks, CA 91403
Fax: 818-907-0735
Total number of outlets: Approximately 150
Total number of franchise outlets:
Approximately 150
International: Yes (several countries)

OVERALL RANK: 29

Phone: 800-469-4967
Franchise fee: $49,500
Franchise term: 12 years
Initial investment: $132,010 to $232,560
Advertising/Marketing fee: 1% of gross revenues
Royalty fee: 6% of gross revenues monthly

SURVEY AND RESULTS *

Q1: About how many hours per week do you dedicate to your franchise business?

		% answering
A)	**Less than 40**	**36%**
B)	41–50	29%
C)	**51–60**	**36%**
D)	More than 60	0%
E)	Passive investment	0%

Q2: How would you describe your relations/communications with your franchisor?

		% answering
A)	**Excellent**	**60%**
B)	Good	33%
C)	Adequate	7%
D)	Fair	0%
E)	Poor	0%

Q3: In terms of how your franchisor views your communications with other franchisees, it is:

		% answering
A)	**Very supportive**	**93%**
B)	Not very supportive	7%
C)	No influence	0%

Q4: Is the franchisor fair with you in resolving any grievances?

		% answering
A)	**Extremely fair**	**73%**
B)	Pretty fair	27%
C)	Reasonably fair	0%
D)	Not very fair	0%
E)	Not fair at all	0%

Q5: Are territories equitably granted?

		% answering
A)	**Yes**	**80%**
B)	No	7%
C)	Not yet sure	13%

Q6: How would you describe the initial and ongoing training provided by your franchisor?

		% answering
A)	**Excellent**	**67%**
B)	Good	20%
C)	Adequate	13%
D)	Fair	0%
E)	Poor	0%

Q7: How well does the franchisor anticipate future trends in how it evolves and markets products and services?

		% answering
A)	**Extremely well**	**47%**
B)	Pretty well	27%
C)	Adequately	27%
D)	Not very well	0%
E)	Terribly	0%

Q8: How satisfied are you with your franchisor's spending of the royalty fees you pay?

		% answering
A)	Extremely satisfied	20%
B)	Mostly satisfied	20%
C)	**Somewhat satisfied**	**40%**
D)	Not very satisfied	20%
E)	Not satisfied at all	0%

Q9: **In what ways could the parent company most improve? (Please check those that most apply, no more than three):**

❑ Communications
❑ Counsel/advice on administrative/management issues
❑ Effectiveness of marketing/promotions
❑ Evolution of products/services
❑ Frequency of marketing/promotional campaigns

❑ Quality of products/services
❑ Pricing of products/services to franchisees
❑ Technology (Point of sale systems, usage of computers/email/software, etc.)
❑ Training

Most frequent responses: % answering

Effectiveness of marketing/promotions   67%
Frequency of marketing/promotional campaigns   40%
Training   33%

Q10: **Is your income more, less or about what you expected prior to opening your business?**

	% answering	
More	13%	
Less	**47%**	**Summary: 53% are making about what they**
About what was expected	40%	**expected, or more.**

Q11: **Prior to opening your franchise, which (if any) of the following did you underestimate?**

❑ Amount of working capital required for your 1st year in business
❑ Difficulty in hiring/retaining quality staff
❑ Expertise required to run the business
❑ Impact of marketing/promotions

❑ Start-up costs
❑ Degree of stress
❑ Workload

Most frequent responses: % answering

Difficulty in hiring/retaining quality staff   73%
Degree of stress (tie)   40%
Workload (tie)   40%

Q12: **If you could turn back time to the day you signed your franchise agreement, would you make the same decision to buy your franchise?**

	% answering
Yes	**87%**
No	13%

* Number of survey respondents: 15 from 9 different states
   Number of survey respondents as a % of total franchise units: 10%

NATIONWIDE FLOOR & WINDOW COVERING

www.floorsandwindows.com

Floor and window installer with mobile showrooms that go to you.

OVERALL SCORE: 56

OVERALL RANK: 155

111 East Kilbourn Avenue, 24th Floor
Milwaukee, WI 53202
Fax: 414-765-1300
Total number of outlets: 93 (87 in U.S.)
Total number of franchise outlets: 93 (87 in U.S.)
International: Yes (Canada)
Royalty fee: varies

Phone: 800-366-8088
Franchise fee: $36,900 to $51,900 plus variable
fee for additional households in territory
Franchise term: 10 years
Initial investment: $59,340 to $142,400
Advertising/Marketing fee: Currently $400 per
month

SURVEY AND RESULTS *

Q1: About how many hours per week do you dedicate to your franchise business?

		% answering
A)	Less than 40	5%
B)	41–50	10%
C)	51–60	25%
D)	**More than 60**	**60%**
E)	Passive investment	0%

Q2: How would you describe your relations/communications with your franchisor?

		% answering
A)	Excellent	25%
B)	**Good**	**45%**
C)	Adequate	10%
D)	Fair	20%
E)	Poor	0%

Q3: In terms of how your franchisor views your communications with other franchisees, it is:

		% answering
A)	**Very supportive**	**75%**
B)	Not very supportive	15%
C)	No influence	10%

Q4: Is the franchisor fair with you in resolving any grievances?

		% answering
A)	Extremely fair	17%
B)	**Pretty fair**	**39%**
C)	Reasonably fair	28%
D)	Not very fair	17%
E)	Not fair at all	0%

Q5: Are territories equitably granted?

		% answering
A)	**Yes**	**80%**
B)	No	10%
C)	Not yet sure	10%

Q6: How would you describe the initial and ongoing training provided by your franchisor?

		% answering
A)	**Excellent**	**50%**
B)	Good	16%
C)	Adequate	29%
D)	Fair	0%
E)	Poor	5%

Q7: How well does the franchisor anticipate future trends in how it evolves and markets products and services?

		% answering
A)	Extremely well	15%
B)	**Pretty well**	**35%**
C)	Adequately	30%
D)	Not very well	20%
E)	Terribly	0%

Q8: How satisfied are you with your franchisor's spending of the royalty fees you pay?

		% answering
A)	Extremely satisfied	0%
B)	**Mostly satisfied**	**45%**
C)	Somewhat satisfied	25%
D)	Not very satisfied	25%
E)	Not satisfied at all	5%

Q9: **In what ways could the parent company most improve? (Please check those that most apply, no more than three):**

- ❏ Communications
- ❏ Counsel/advice on administrative/management issues
- ❏ Effectiveness of marketing/promotions
- ❏ Evolution of products/services
- ❏ Frequency of marketing/promotional campaigns

- ❏ Quality of products/services
- ❏ Pricing of products/services to franchisees
- ❏ Technology (Point of sale systems, usage of computers/email/software, etc.)
- ❏ Training

Most frequent responses:	% answering
Pricing of products/services to franchisees	80%
Effectiveness of marketing/promotions	55%
Counsel/advice on administrative/management issues	40%

Q10: **Is your income more, less or about what you expected prior to opening your business?**

	% answering	
More	0%	
Less	**79%**	**Summary: 21% are making about what they**
About what was expected	21%	**expected, or more.**

Q11: **Prior to opening your franchise, which (if any) of the following did you underestimate?**

- ❏ Amount of working capital required for your 1st year in business
- ❏ Difficulty in hiring/retaining quality staff
- ❏ Expertise required to run the business
- ❏ Impact of marketing/promotions

- ❏ Start-up costs
- ❏ Degree of stress
- ❏ Workload

Most frequent responses:	% answering
Amount of working capital required for your 1st year in business	80%
Difficulty in hiring/retaining quality staff (tie)	40%
Workload (tie)	40%

Q12: **If you could turn back time to the day you signed your franchise agreement, would you make the same decision to buy your franchise?**

	% answering
Yes	47%
No	**53%**

* Number of survey respondents: 20 from 14 different states

Number of survey respondents as a % of total franchise units: 21.51%

NOVUS AUTO GLASS REPAIR & REPLACEMENT

www.novusglass.com

Email: joyceo@novusglass.com

Vehicle glass repair and replacement services.

OVERALL SCORE: 73

Eagle Creek Commerce Center East
12800 Highway 13 South, Suite 500
Savage, MN 55378
Fax: 952-946-0481
Total number of outlets: 500+
Total number of franchise outlets: 500+
International: Yes (worldwide)

OVERALL RANK: 65

Phone: 800-944-6811
Franchise fee: $7,500
Franchise term: 10 years
Initial investment: $37,979 to $98,099
Advertising/Marketing fee: none
Royalty fee: varies

SURVEY AND RESULTS *

Q1: About how many hours per week do you dedicate to your franchise business?

		% answering
A)	Less than 40	13%
B)	**41–50**	**40%**
C)	**51–60**	**40%**
D)	More than 60	7%
E)	Passive investment	7%

Q2: How would you describe your relations/ communications with your franchisor?

		% answering
A)	**Excellent**	**27%**
B)	**Good**	**27%**
C)	Adequate	13%
D)	Fair	13%
E)	Poor	0%

Q3: In terms of how your franchisor views your communications with other franchisees, it is:

		% answering
A)	**Very supportive**	**64%**
B)	Not very supportive	14%
C)	No influence	21%

Q4: Is the franchisor fair with you in resolving any grievances?

		% answering
A)	Extremely fair	23%
B)	Pretty fair	23%
C)	**Reasonably fair**	**38%**
D)	Not very fair	8%
E)	Not fair at all	8%

Q5: Are territories equitably granted?

		% answering
A)	**Yes**	**64%**
B)	No	7%
C)	Not yet sure	29%

Q6: How would you describe the initial and ongoing training provided by your franchisor?

		% answering
A)	Excellent	33%
B)	**Good**	**47%**
C)	Adequate	13%
D)	Fair	0%
E)	Poor	7%

Q7: How well does the franchisor anticipate future trends in how it evolves and markets products and services?

		% answering
A)	Extremely well	7%
B)	Pretty well	13%
C)	Adequately	33%
D)	**Not very well**	**40%**
E)	Terribly	7%

Q8: How satisfied are you with your franchisor's spending of the royalty fees you pay?

		% answering
A)	Extremely satisfied	7%
B)	Mostly satisfied	20%
C)	**Somewhat satisfied**	**27%**
D)	Not very satisfied	20%
E)	**Not satisfied at all**	**27%**

Q9: **In what ways could the parent company most improve? (Please check those that most apply, no more than three):**

- ❏ Communications
- ❏ Counsel/advice on administrative/management issues
- ❏ Effectiveness of marketing/promotions
- ❏ Evolution of products/services
- ❏ Frequency of marketing/promotional campaigns
- ❏ Quality of products/services
- ❏ Pricing of products/services to franchisees
- ❏ Technology (Point of sale systems, usage of computers/email/software, etc.)
- ❏ Training

Most frequent responses:	% answering
Effectiveness of marketing/promotions	80%
Frequency of marketing/promotional campaigns	47%
Evolution of products/services	27%

Q10: **Is your income more, less or about what you expected prior to opening your business?**

	% answering	
More	14%	
Less	29%	**Summary: 71% are making about what they**
About what was expected	**57%**	**expected, or more.**

Q11: **Prior to opening your franchise, which (if any) of the following did you underestimate?**

- ❏ Amount of working capital required for your 1st year in business
- ❏ Difficulty in hiring/retaining quality staff
- ❏ Expertise required to run the business
- ❏ Impact of marketing/promotions
- ❏ Start-up costs
- ❏ Degree of stress
- ❏ Workload

Most frequent responses:	% answering
Difficulty in hiring/retaining quality staff (tie)	27%
Impact of marketing/promotions (tie)	27%
Workload (tie)	27%

Q12: **If you could turn back time to the day you signed your franchise agreement, would you make the same decision to buy your franchise?**

	% answering
Yes	**85%**
No	15%

* Number of survey respondents: 15 from 15 different states
    Number of survey respondents as a % of total franchise units: 3%

1-800-GOT-JUNK?

www.1800gotjunk.com

Rubbish removal services.

OVERALL SCORE: 86

1523 West 3rd Avenue, 2nd Avenue
Vancouver, BC Canada V6J 1J8
Fax: 801-751-0634
Total number of outlets: 99 (88 in U.S.)
Total number of franchise outlets: 99 (88 in U.S.)
International: Yes (Canada)

OVERALL RANK: N/A

Phone: 800-468-5865
Franchise fee: $16,000
Franchise term: 5 years
Initial investment: $66,675 to $92,575
Advertising/Marketing fee: 1% of gross revenue, semi-monthly
Royalty fee: 8% of gross revenue, semi-monthly

SURVEY AND RESULTS *

Q1: About how many hours per week do you dedicate to your franchise business?

		% answering
A)	Less than 40	22%
B)	41–50	22%
C)	**51–60**	**33%**
D)	More than 60	22%
E)	Passive investment	0%

Q2: How would you describe your relations/communications with your franchisor?

		% answering
A)	Excellent	33%
B)	**Good**	**56%**
C)	Adequate	11%
D)	Fair	0%
E)	Poor	0%

Q3: In terms of how your franchisor views your communications with other franchisees, it is:

		% answering
A)	**Very supportive**	**78%**
B)	Not very supportive	11%
C)	No influence	11%

Q4: Is the franchisor fair with you in resolving any grievances?

		% answering
A)	Extremely fair	22%
B)	**Pretty fair**	**44%**
C)	Reasonably fair	22%
D)	Not very fair	11%
E)	Not fair at all	0%

Q5: Are territories equitably granted?

		% answering
A)	**Yes**	**67%**
B)	No	11%
C)	Not yet sure	22%

Q6: How would you describe the initial and ongoing training provided by your franchisor?

		% answering
A)	Excellent	0%
B)	**Good**	**100%**
C)	Adequate	0%
D)	Fair	0%
E)	Poor	0%

Q7: How well does the franchisor anticipate future trends in how it evolves and markets products and services?

		% answering
A)	Extremely well	22%
B)	**Pretty well**	**44%**
C)	Adequately	33%
D)	Not very well	0%
E)	Terribly	0%

Q8: How satisfied are you with your franchisor's spending of the royalty fees you pay?

		% answering
A)	Extremely satisfied	0%
B)	**Mostly satisfied**	**50%**
C)	Somewhat satisfied	17%
D)	Not very satisfied	33%
E)	Not satisfied at all	0%

Q9: **In what ways could the parent company most improve? (Please check those that most apply, no more than three):**

☐ Communications
☐ Counsel/advice on administrative/management issues
☐ Effectiveness of marketing/promotions
☐ Evolution of products/services
☐ Frequency of marketing/promotional campaigns

☐ Quality of products/services
☐ Pricing of products/services to franchisees
☐ Technology (Point of sale systems, usage of computers/email/software, etc.)
☐ Training

Most frequent responses:	% answering
Frequency of marketing/promotional campaigns	78%
Effectiveness of marketing/promotions	67%
Counsel/advice on administrative/management issues	33%

Q10: **Is your income more, less or about what you expected prior to opening your business?**

	% answering	
More	22%	
Less	22%	**Summary: 88% are making about what they**
About what was expected	**56%**	**expected, or more.**

Q11: **Prior to opening your franchise, which (if any) of the following did you underestimate?**

☐ Amount of working capital required for your 1st year in business
☐ Difficulty in hiring/retaining quality staff
☐ Expertise required to run the business
☐ Impact of marketing/promotions

☐ Start-up costs
☐ Degree of stress
☐ Workload

Most frequent responses:	% answering
Difficulty in hiring/retaining quality staff	67%
Amount of working capital required for your 1st year in business	33%
Impact of marketing/promotions	22%

Q12: **If you could turn back time to the day you signed your franchise agreement, would you make the same decision to buy your franchise?**

	% answering
Yes	**100%**
No	0%

* Number of survey respondents: 9 from 8 different states
   Number of survey respondents as a % of total franchise units: 9.09%

ONCE UPON A CHILD

www.ouac.com
Email: ouac-corporate-operations@ouac.com

Retailer of children's new and used clothing, toys, furniture, etc.

OVERALL SCORE: 73

4200 Dahlberg Drive, Suite 100
Minneapolis, MN 55422
Fax: 763-520-8410
Total number of outlets: 211
Total number of franchise outlets: 210
International: Yes (Canada)

OVERALL RANK: 68

Phone: 800-567-6600
Franchise fee: $20,000
Franchise term: 10 years
Initial investment: $129,675 to $224,197
Advertising/Marketing fee: $500 annually
Royalty fee: 5% of gross sales

SURVEY AND RESULTS *

Q1: About how many hours per week do you dedicate to your franchise business?

		% answering
A)	**Less than 40**	**38%**
B)	41–50	15%
C)	51–60	15%
D)	More than 60	31%
E)	Passive investment	0%

Q2: How would you describe your relations/ communications with your franchisor?

		% answering
A)	Excellent	31%
B)	**Good**	**54%**
C)	Adequate	8%
D)	Fair	8%
E)	Poor	0%

Q3: In terms of how your franchisor views your communications with other franchisees, it is:

		% answering
A)	**Very supportive**	**85%**
B)	Not very supportive	0%
C)	No influence	15%

Q4: Is the franchisor fair with you in resolving any grievances?

		% answering
A)	Extremely fair	17%
B)	**Pretty fair**	**50%**
C)	Reasonably fair	25%
D)	Not very fair	8%
E)	Not fair at all	0%

Q5: Are territories equitably granted?

		% answering
A)	**Yes**	**69%**
B)	No	0%
C)	Not yet sure	31%

Q6: How would you describe the initial and ongoing training provided by your franchisor?

		% answering
A)	**Excellent**	**31%**
B)	**Good**	**31%**
C)	Adequate	23%
D)	Fair	15%
E)	Poor	0%

Q7: How well does the franchisor anticipate future trends in how it evolves and markets products and services?

		% answering
A)	Extremely well	23%
B)	**Pretty well**	**46%**
C)	Adequately	19%
D)	Not very well	12%
E)	Terribly	0%

Q8: How satisfied are you with your franchisor's spending of the royalty fees you pay?

		% answering
A)	Extremely satisfied	8%
B)	**Mostly satisfied**	**38%**
C)	**Somewhat satisfied**	**38%**
D)	Not very satisfied	15%
E)	Not satisfied at all	0%

Q9: In what ways could the parent company most improve? (Please check those that most apply, no more than three):

- ❑ Communications
- ❑ Counsel/advice on administrative/management issues
- ❑ Effectiveness of marketing/promotions
- ❑ Evolution of products/services
- ❑ Frequency of marketing/promotional campaigns
- ❑ Quality of products/services
- ❑ Pricing of products/services to franchisees
- ❑ Technology (Point of sale systems, usage of computers/email/software, etc.)
- ❑ Training

Most frequent responses:	% answering
Counsel/advice on administrative/management issues (tie)	46%
Effectiveness of marketing/promotions (tie)	46%
Training	31%

Q10: Is your income more, less or about what you expected prior to opening your business?

	% answering	
More	17%	
Less	**50%**	**Summary: 50% are making about what they**
About what was expected	33%	**expected, or more.**

Q11: Prior to opening your franchise, which (if any) of the following did you underestimate?

- ❑ Amount of working capital required for your 1st year in business
- ❑ Difficulty in hiring/retaining quality staff
- ❑ Expertise required to run the business
- ❑ Impact of marketing/promotions
- ❑ Start-up costs
- ❑ Degree of stress
- ❑ Workload

Most frequent responses:	% answering
Difficulty in hiring/retaining quality staff	54%
Start-up costs	38%
Amount of working capital required for 1st year in business	31%

Q12: If you could turn back time to the day you signed your franchise agreement, would you make the same decision to buy your franchise?

	% answering
Yes	**77%**
No	23%

* Number of survey respondents: 13 from 11 different states
Number of survey respondents as a % of total franchise units: 6.19%

PADGETT BUSINESS SERVICES

www.smallbizpros.com

Accounting, tax, and payroll services for small businesses.

OVERALL SCORE: 68

160 Hawthorne Park
Athens, GA 30606
Fax: 800-548-1040
Total number of outlets: 276
Total number of franchise outlets: 275
International: Yes (Canada)

OVERALL RANK: 94

Phone: 800-723-4388, ext. 290
Franchise fee: $37,500
Franchise term: 10 years
Initial investment: $49,500
Advertising/Marketing fee: none currently
Royalty fee: > of 9% of gross receipts or a
variable monthly minimum

SURVEY AND RESULTS *

Q1: About how many hours per week do you dedicate to your franchise business?

		% answering
A)	Less than 40	35%
B)	**41–50**	**41%**
C)	51–60	12%
D)	More than 60	12%
E)	Passive investment	0%

Q2: How would you describe your relations/communications with your franchisor?

		% answering
A)	Excellent	12%
B)	**Good**	**47%**
C)	Adequate	24%
D)	Fair	12%
E)	Poor	6%

Q3: In terms of how your franchisor views your communications with other franchisees, it is:

		% answering
A)	**Very supportive**	**76%**
B)	Not very supportive	6%
C)	No influence	18%

Q4: Is the franchisor fair with you in resolving any grievances?

		% answering
A)	**Extremely fair**	**35%**
B)	Pretty fair	24%
C)	Reasonably fair	29%
D)	Not very fair	12%
E)	Not fair at all	0%

Q5: Are territories equitably granted?

		% answering
A)	**Yes**	**82%**
B)	No	6%
C)	Not yet sure	12%

Q6: How would you describe the initial and ongoing training provided by your franchisor?

		% answering
A)	Excellent	31%
B)	**Good**	**44%**
C)	Adequate	13%
D)	Fair	6%
E)	Poor	6%

Q7: How well does the franchisor anticipate future trends in how it evolves and markets products and services?

		% answering
A)	Extremely well	18%
B)	**Pretty well**	**53%**
C)	Adequately	29%
D)	Not very well	0%
E)	Terribly	0%

Q8: How satisfied are you with your franchisor's spending of the royalty fees you pay?

		% answering
A)	Extremely satisfied	0%
B)	**Mostly satisfied**	**76%**
C)	Somewhat satisfied	18%
D)	Not very satisfied	6%
E)	Not satisfied at all	0%

Q9: **In what ways could the parent company most improve? (Please check those that most apply, no more than three):**

- ❑ Communications
- ❑ Counsel/advice on administrative/management issues
- ❑ Effectiveness of marketing/promotions
- ❑ Evolution of products/services
- ❑ Frequency of marketing/promotional campaigns

- ❑ Quality of products/services
- ❑ Pricing of products/services to franchisees
- ❑ Technology (Point of sale systems, usage of computers/email/software, etc.)
- ❑ Training

Most frequent responses:	% answering
Effectiveness of marketing/promotions	65%
Communications (tie)	24%
Evolution of products/services (tie)	24%
Technology (tie)	24%

Q10: **Is your income more, less or about what you expected prior to opening your business?**

	% answering	
More	0%	
Less	**63%**	**Summary: 38% are making about what they**
About what was expected	38%	**expected, or more.**

Q11: **Prior to opening your franchise, which (if any) of the following did you underestimate?**

- ❑ Amount of working capital required for your 1st year in business
- ❑ Difficulty in hiring/retaining quality staff
- ❑ Expertise required to run the business
- ❑ Impact of marketing/promotions

- ❑ Start-up costs
- ❑ Degree of stress
- ❑ Workload

Most frequent responses:	% answering
Impact of marketing/promotions	47%
Amount of working capital required for your 1st year in business (tie)	41%
Workload (tie)	41%

Q12: **If you could turn back time to the day you signed your franchise agreement, would you make the same decision to buy your franchise?**

	% answering
Yes	**76%**
No	24%

* Number of survey respondents: 17 from 15 different states

Number of survey respondents as a % of total franchise units: 6.18%

PAK MAIL

www.pakmail.com

Packing, shipping, and mailing services.

OVERALL SCORE: 66

7173 South Havana Street, Suite 600
Englewood, CO 80112
Total number of outlets: 372
Total number of franchise outlets: 372
International: No
Royalty fee: varies

OVERALL RANK: 104

Phone: 800-833-2821
Franchise fee: $29,950
Franchise term: 10 years
Initial investment: $114,998 to $147,773
Advertising/Marketing fee: 2% of all revenues, monthly

SURVEY AND RESULTS *

Q1: About how many hours per week do you dedicate to your franchise business?

		% answering
A)	Less than 40	6%
B)	**41–50**	**44%**
C)	**51–60**	**44%**
D)	More than 60	6%
E)	Passive investment	0%

Q2: How would you describe your relations/ communications with your franchisor?

		% answering
A)	**Excellent**	**50%**
B)	Good	38%
C)	Adequate	0%
D)	Fair	0%
E)	Poor	13%

Q3: In terms of how your franchisor views your communications with other franchisees, it is:

		% answering
A)	**Very supportive**	**88%**
B)	Not very supportive	0%
C)	No influence	13%

Q4: Is the franchisor fair with you in resolving any grievances?

		% answering
A)	**Extremely fair**	**56%**
B)	Pretty fair	25%
C)	Reasonably fair	19%
D)	Not very fair	0%
E)	Not fair at all	0%

Q5: Are territories equitably granted?

		% answering
A)	**Yes**	**69%**
B)	No	13%
C)	Not yet sure	19%

Q6: How would you describe the initial and ongoing training provided by your franchisor?

		% answering
A)	**Excellent**	**40%**
B)	Good	33%
C)	Adequate	13%
D)	Fair	0%
E)	Poor	13%

Q7: How well does the franchisor anticipate future trends in how it evolves and markets products and services?

		% answering
A)	Extremely well	31%
B)	**Pretty well**	**38%**
C)	Adequately	19%
D)	Not very well	6%
E)	Terribly	6%

Q8: How satisfied are you with your franchisor's spending of the royalty fees you pay?

		% answering
A)	Extremely satisfied	19%
B)	**Mostly satisfied**	**44%**
C)	Somewhat satisfied	13%
D)	Not very satisfied	13%
E)	Not satisfied at all	13%

Q9: **In what ways could the parent company most improve? (Please check those that most apply, no more than three):**

- ❑ Communications
- ❑ Counsel/advice on administrative/management issues
- ❑ Effectiveness of marketing/promotions
- ❑ Evolution of products/services
- ❑ Frequency of marketing/promotional campaigns
- ❑ Quality of products/services
- ❑ Pricing of products/services to franchisees
- ❑ Technology (Point of sale systems, usage of computers/email/software, etc.)
- ❑ Training

Most frequent responses:	% answering
Effectiveness of marketing/promotions	69%
Technology	56%
Frequency of marketing/promotional campaigns	31%

Q10: **Is your income more, less or about what you expected prior to opening your business?**

	% answering	
More	0%	
Less	**53%**	**Summary: 53% are making about what they**
About what was expected	47%	**expected, or more.**

Q11: **Prior to opening your franchise, which (if any) of the following did you underestimate?**

- ❑ Amount of working capital required for your 1st year in business
- ❑ Difficulty in hiring/retaining quality staff
- ❑ Expertise required to run the business
- ❑ Impact of marketing/promotions
- ❑ Start-up costs
- ❑ Degree of stress
- ❑ Workload

Most frequent responses:	% answering
Amount of working capital required for your 1st year in business	69%
Degree of stress	38%
Expertise required to run the business (tie)	31%
Impact of marketing/promotions (tie)	31%

Q12: **If you could turn back time to the day you signed your franchise agreement, would you make the same decision to buy your franchise?**

	% answering
Yes	**56%**
No	44%

* Number of survey respondents: 16 from 14 different states
Number of survey respondents as a % of total franchise units: 4.30%

PAPA JOHN'S PIZZA

www.papajohns.com

The world's third largest pizza delivery company.

OVERALL SCORE: 58

2002 Papa John's Boulevard
Louisville, KY 40299
Fax: 502-266-2925
Total number of outlets: Approximately 3,000 worldwide
Total number of franchise outlets:
Approximately 3,000 worldwide
International: Yes (worldwide)

OVERALL RANK: 150

Phone: 888-777-7272
Franchise fee: $25,000
Franchise term:
Initial investment: $160,000 to $395,000
Advertising/Marketing fee: 2.25% of net sales, monthly
Royalty fee: 4% of net sales, monthly

SURVEY AND RESULTS *

Q1: About how many hours per week do you dedicate to your franchise business?

		% answering
A)	Less than 40	8%
B)	**41–50**	**42%**
C)	51–60	8%
D)	**More than 60**	**42%**
E)	Passive investment	0%

Q2: How would you describe your relations/communications with your franchisor?

		% answering
A)	Excellent	17%
B)	Good	17%
C)	Adequate	17%
D)	**Fair**	**42%**
E)	Poor	8%

Q3: In terms of how your franchisor views your communications with other franchisees, it is:

		% answering
A)	**Very supportive**	**42%**
B)	Not very supportive	25%
C)	No influence	33%

Q4: Is the franchisor fair with you in resolving any grievances?

		% answering
A)	Extremely fair	25%
B)	Pretty fair	8%
C)	**Reasonably fair**	**33%**
D)	Not very fair	25%
E)	Not fair at all	8%

Q5: Are territories equitably granted?

		% answering
A)	**Yes**	**58%**
B)	No	33%
C)	Not yet sure	8%

Q6: How would you describe the initial and ongoing training provided by your franchisor?

		% answering
A)	Excellent	17%
B)	**Good**	**42%**
C)	Adequate	0%
D)	Fair	17%
E)	Poor	25%

Q7: How well does the franchisor anticipate future trends in how it evolves and markets products and services?

		% answering
A)	Extremely well	0%
B)	Pretty well	17%
C)	Adequately	8%
D)	**Not very well**	**58%**
E)	Terribly	17%

Q8: How satisfied are you with your franchisor's spending of the royalty fees you pay?

		% answering
A)	Extremely satisfied	0%
B)	Mostly satisfied	18%
C)	**Somewhat satisfied**	**36%**
D)	Not very satisfied	18%
E)	Not satisfied at all	27%

Q9: **In what ways could the parent company most improve? (Please check those that most apply, no more than three):**

❏ Communications

❏ Counsel/advice on administrative/management issues

❏ Effectiveness of marketing/promotions

❏ Evolution of products/services

❏ Frequency of marketing/promotional campaigns

❏ Quality of products/services

❏ Pricing of products/services to franchisees

❏ Technology (Point of sale systems, usage of computers/email/software, etc.)

❏ Training

Most frequent responses:	% answering
Effectiveness of marketing/promotions	67%
Evolution of products/services	50%
Counsel/advice on administrative/management issues	42%

Q10: **Is your income more, less or about what you expected prior to opening your business?**

	% answering	
More	18%	
Less	36%	**Summary: 63% are making about what they**
About what was expected	**45%**	**expected, or more.**

Q11: **Prior to opening your franchise, which (if any) of the following did you underestimate?**

❏ Amount of working capital required for your 1st year in business

❏ Difficulty in hiring/retaining quality staff

❏ Expertise required to run the business

❏ Impact of marketing/promotions

❏ Start-up costs

❏ Degree of stress

❏ Workload

Most frequent responses:	% answering
Difficulty in hiring/retaining quality staff (tie)	42%
Degree of stress (tie)	42%
Amount of working capital required for 1st year in business	33%

Q12: **If you could turn back time to the day you signed your franchise agreement, would you make the same decision to buy your franchise?**

	% answering
Yes	**64%**
No	36%

* Number of survey respondents: 12 from 10 different states

    Number of survey respondents as a % of total franchise units: < 1%

PAPA MURPHY'S PIZZA

www.papamurphys.com

Take-and-bake pizza, calzone, lasagna, and other foods.

OVERALL SCORE: 64

8000 NE Parkway Drive, Suite 350
Vancouver, WA 98662
Fax: 360-26-0500
Total number of outlets: 786
Total number of franchise outlets: 786
International: Yes/No

OVERALL RANK: 116

Phone: 360-260-7272
Franchise fee: $25,000
Franchise term: 10 years
Initial investment: $140,600–$225,000
Advertising/Marketing fee: 1% of weekly gross revenue
Royalty fee: 5% of weekly gross revenue

SURVEY AND RESULTS *

Q1: About how many hours per week do you dedicate to your franchise business?

		% answering
A)	**Less than 40**	23%
B)	**41–50**	23%
C)	**51–60**	23%
D)	**More than 60**	23%
E)	Passive investment	8%

Q2: How would you describe your relations/communications with your franchisor?

		% answering
A)	Excellent	8%
B)	**Good**	38%
C)	Adequate	31%
D)	Fair	8%
E)	Poor	15%

Q3: In terms of how your franchisor views your communications with other franchisees, it is:

		% answering
A)	**Very supportive**	58%
B)	Not very supportive	8%
C)	No influence	33%

Q4: Is the franchisor fair with you in resolving any grievances?

		% answering
A)	Extremely fair	8%
B)	Pretty fair	17%
C)	**Reasonably fair**	50%
D)	Not very fair	25%
E)	Not fair at all	0%

Q5: Are territories equitably granted?

		% answering
A)	Yes	42%
B)	**No**	50%
C)	Not yet sure	8%

Q6: How would you describe the initial and ongoing training provided by your franchisor?

		% answering
A)	Excellent	15%
B)	**Good**	54%
C)	Adequate	8%
D)	Fair	15%
E)	Poor	8%

Q7: How well does the franchisor anticipate future trends in how it evolves and markets products and services?

		% answering
A)	Extremely well	14%
B)	**Pretty well**	31%
C)	**Adequately**	31%
D)	Not very well	15%
E)	Terribly	8%

Q8: How satisfied are you with your franchisor's spending of the royalty fees you pay?

		% answering
A)	Extremely satisfied	0%
B)	**Mostly satisfied**	54%
C)	Somewhat satisfied	23%
D)	Not very satisfied	8%
E)	Not satisfied at all	15%

Q9: **In what ways could the parent company most improve? (Please check those that most apply, no more than three):**

❏ Communications

❏ Counsel/advice on administrative/management issues

❏ Effectiveness of marketing/promotions

❏ Evolution of products/services

❏ Frequency of marketing/promotional campaigns

❏ Quality of products/services

❏ Pricing of products/services to franchisees

❏ Technology (Point of sale systems, usage of computers/email/software, etc.)

❏ Training

Most frequent responses:	% answering
Communications	62%
Effectiveness of marketing/promotions	31%
Counsel/advice on administrative/management issues (tie)	23%
Evolution of products/services (tie)	23%
Frequency of marketing/promotional campaigns (tie)	23%
Technology (tie)	23%

Q10: **Is your income more, less or about what you expected prior to opening your business?**

	% answering	
More	17%	
Less	**50%**	**Summary: 50% are making about what they**
About what was expected	33%	**expected, or more.**

Q11: Prior to opening your franchise, which (if any) of the following did you underestimate?

❏ Amount of working capital required for your 1st year in business

❏ Difficulty in hiring/retaining quality staff

❏ Expertise required to run the business

❏ Impact of marketing/promotions

❏ Start-up costs

❏ Degree of stress

❏ Workload

Most frequent responses:	% answering
Difficulty in hiring/retaining quality staff (tie)	38%
Degree of stress (tie)	38%
Amount of working capital required for 1st year in business (tie)	38%
Workload (tie)	38%

Q12: If you could turn back time to the day you signed your franchise agreement, would you make the same decision to buy your franchise?

	% answering
Yes	**77%**
No	23%

* Number of survey respondents: 13 from 10 different states

Number of survey respondents as a % of total franchise units: 1.65%

PARCEL PLUS

www.parcelplus.com
Email: info@iced.net

Packing, shipping, and mailing services.

OVERALL SCORE: 64

12715 Telge Road
Cypress, TX 77429
Fax: 281-373-4450
Total number of outlets: 85
Total number of franchise outlets: 85
International: No

OVERALL RANK: 114

Phone: 888-280-2053
Franchise fee: $30,000
Franchise term:
Initial investment: $150,425 to $$209,600
Advertising/Marketing fee:
Royalty fee:

SURVEY AND RESULTS *

Q1: About how many hours per week do you dedicate to your franchise business?

		% answering
A)	Less than 40	8%
B)	41–50	17%
C)	**51–60**	**42%**
D)	More than 60	33%
E)	Passive investment	0%

Q2: How would you describe your relations/communications with your franchisor?

		% answering
A)	Excellent	17%
B)	**Good**	**50%**
C)	Adequate	17%
D)	Fair	8%
E)	Poor	8%

Q3: In terms of how your franchisor views your communications with other franchisees, it is:

		% answering
A)	**Very supportive**	**75%**
B)	Not very supportive	0%
C)	No influence	25%

Q4: Is the franchisor fair with you in resolving any grievances?

		% answering
A)	Extremely fair	20%
B)	Pretty fair	30%
C)	**Reasonably fair**	**40%**
D)	Not very fair	10%
E)	Not fair at all	0%

Q5: Are territories equitably granted?

		% answering
A)	**Yes**	**75%**
B)	No	0%
C)	Not yet sure	25%

Q6: How would you describe the initial and ongoing training provided by your franchisor?

		% answering
A)	**Excellent**	**42%**
B)	**Good**	**42%**
C)	Adequate	17%
D)	Fair	0%
E)	Poor	0%

Q7: How well does the franchisor anticipate future trends in how it evolves and markets products and services?

		% answering
A)	Extremely well	17%
B)	**Pretty well**	**50%**
C)	Adequately	25%
D)	Not very well	0%
E)	Terribly	0%

Q8: How satisfied are you with your franchisor's spending of the royalty fees you pay?

		% answering
A)	Extremely satisfied	0%
B)	**Mostly satisfied**	**58%**
C)	Somewhat satisfied	17%
D)	Not very satisfied	25%
E)	Not satisfied at all	0%

Q9: **In what ways could the parent company most improve? (Please check those that most apply, no more than three):**

- ❑ Communications
- ❑ Counsel/advice on administrative/management issues
- ❑ Effectiveness of marketing/promotions
- ❑ Evolution of products/services
- ❑ Frequency of marketing/promotional campaigns

- ❑ Quality of products/services
- ❑ Pricing of products/services to franchisees
- ❑ Technology (Point of sale systems, usage of computers/email/software, etc.)
- ❑ Training

Most frequent responses:	% answering
Evolution of products/services	42%
Communications (tie)	33%
Effectiveness of marketing/promotions (tie)	33%

Q10: **Is your income more, less or about what you expected prior to opening your business?**

	% answering	
More	8%	
Less	**83%**	**Summary: 16% are making about what they**
About what was expected	8%	**expected, or more.**

Q11: **Prior to opening your franchise, which (if any) of the following did you underestimate?**

- ❑ Amount of working capital required for your 1st year in business
- ❑ Difficulty in hiring/retaining quality staff
- ❑ Expertise required to run the business
- ❑ Impact of marketing/promotions

- ❑ Start-up costs
- ❑ Degree of stress
- ❑ Workload

Most frequent responses:	% answering
Difficulty in hiring/retaining quality staff (tie)	33%
Impact of marketing/promotions (tie)	33%
Degree of stress (tie)	33%

Q12: **If you could turn back time to the day you signed your franchise agreement, would you make the same decision to buy your franchise?**

	% answering
Yes	**75%**
No	25%

* Number of survey respondents: 12 from 7 different states
 Number of survey respondents as a % of total franchise units: 14.12%

PAUL DAVIS RESTORATION

www.pdrestoration.com
Email: sales@pdrestoration.com

Restoration and reconstruction services in the event of fire, flood, break-in, or other disasters.

OVERALL SCORE: 82

One Independent Drive, Suite 2300
Jacksonville, FL 32202
Fax: 904-737-4204
Total number of outlets: 210
Total number of franchise outlets: 210
International: No
Advertising/Marketing fee: $125 per month
plus 0.2% of closed gross sales but no more
than $6,000 per year

OVERALL RANK: 27

Phone: 904-737-2779
Franchise fee: $52,500 plus $0.10 for every
person in territory should population exceed 300,000
Franchise term: 5 years
Initial investment: $104,464 to $164,774
Royalty fee: 3.5% of gross sales monthly, subject
to an annual minimum

SURVEY AND RESULTS *

Q1: About how many hours per week do you dedicate to your franchise business?

		% answering
A)	Less than 40	5%
B)	**41–50**	**37%**
C)	51–60	26%
D)	More than 60	32%
E)	Passive investment	0%

Q2: How would you describe your relations/ communications with your franchisor?

		% answering
A)	**Excellent**	**42%**
B)	Good	37%
C)	Adequate	11%
D)	Fair	11%
E)	Poor	0%

Q3: In terms of how your franchisor views your communications with other franchisees, it is:

		% answering
A)	**Very supportive**	**95%**
B)	Not very supportive	5%
C)	No influence	0%

Q4: Is the franchisor fair with you in resolving any grievances?

		% answering
A)	**Extremely fair**	**53%**
B)	Pretty fair	32%
C)	Reasonably fair	11%
D)	Not very fair	5%
E)	Not fair at all	0%

Q5: Are territories equitably granted?

		% answering
A)	**Yes**	**84%**
B)	No	5%
C)	Not yet sure	11%

Q6: How would you describe the initial and ongoing training provided by your franchisor?

		% answering
A)	**Excellent**	**58%**
B)	Good	26%
C)	Adequate	11%
D)	Fair	0%
E)	Poor	5%

Q7: How well does the franchisor anticipate future trends in how it evolves and markets products and services?

		% answering
A)	Extremely well	26%
B)	**Pretty well**	**68%**
C)	Adequately	0%
D)	Not very well	5%
E)	Terribly	0%

Q8: How satisfied are you with your franchisor's spending of the royalty fees you pay?

		% answering
A)	Extremely satisfied	21%
B)	**Mostly satisfied**	**47%**
C)	Somewhat satisfied	32%
D)	Not very satisfied	0%
E)	Not satisfied at all	0%

Q9: **In what ways could the parent company most improve? (Please check those that most apply, no more than three):**

❏ Communications
❏ Counsel/advice on administrative/management issues
❏ Effectiveness of marketing/promotions
❏ Evolution of products/services
❏ Frequency of marketing/promotional campaigns

❏ Quality of products/services
❏ Pricing of products/services to franchisees
❏ Technology (Point of sale systems, usage of computers/email/software, etc.)
❏ Training

Most frequent responses:	% answering
Effectiveness of marketing/promotions	68%
Frequency of marketing/promotional campaigns	47%
Counsel/advice on administrative/management issues	32%

Q10: **Is your income more, less or about what you expected prior to opening your business?**

	% answering
More	**44%**
Less	28%
About what was expected	28%

Summary: 72% are making about what they expected, or more.

Q11: **Prior to opening your franchise, which (if any) of the following did you underestimate?**

❏ Amount of working capital required for your 1st year in business
❏ Difficulty in hiring/retaining quality staff
❏ Expertise required to run the business
❏ Impact of marketing/promotions

❏ Start-up costs
❏ Degree of stress
❏ Workload

Most frequent responses:	% answering
Amount of working capital required for your 1st year in business (tie)	58%
Difficulty in hiring/retaining quality staff (tie)	58%
Degree of stress	53%

Q12: **If you could turn back time to the day you signed your franchise agreement, would you make the same decision to buy your franchise?**

	% answering
Yes	**72%**
No	28%

* Number of survey respondents: 19 from 17 different states
Number of survey respondents as a % of total franchise units: 9.05%

PILLAR TO POST

www.pillartopost.com
Email: tampa@pillartopost.com

Home inspection services.

OVERALL SCORE: 72

13902 North Dale Mabry Highway, Suite 300
Tampa, FL 33618
Fax: 813-963-5301
Total number of outlets: 400+
Total number of franchise outlets: 400+
International: No
Royalty fee: 7% of gross revenues subject to
monthly and annual minimums

OVERALL RANK: 73

Phone: 800-294-5591
Franchise fee: $18,900 to $28,900
Franchise term: 5 years
Initial investment: $28,700 to $44,500
Advertising/Marketing fee: 2% of gross revenues
monthly, subject to $100 minimum

SURVEY AND RESULTS *

Q1: About how many hours per week do you dedicate to your franchise business?

		% answering
A)	Less than 40	10%
B)	41–50	25%
C)	51–60	30%
D)	**More than 60**	**35%**
E)	Passive investment	0%

Q2: How would you describe your relations/ communications with your franchisor?

		% answering
A)	Excellent	20%
B)	**Good**	**35%**
C)	Adequate	25%
D)	Fair	15%
E)	Poor	5%

Q3: In terms of how your franchisor views your communications with other franchisees, it is:

		% answering
A)	**Very supportive**	**79%**
B)	Not very supportive	5%
C)	No influence	16%

Q4: Is the franchisor fair with you in resolving any grievances?

		% answering
A)	Extremely fair	19%
B)	**Pretty fair**	**38%**
C)	Reasonably fair	31%
D)	Not very fair	6%
E)	Not fair at all	6%

Q5: Are territories equitably granted?

		% answering
A)	**Yes**	**79%**
B)	No	5%
C)	Not yet sure	16%

Q6: How would you describe the initial and ongoing training provided by your franchisor?

		% answering
A)	**Excellent**	**40%**
B)	Good	28%
C)	Adequate	13%
D)	Fair	8%
E)	Poor	13%

Q7: How well does the franchisor anticipate future trends in how it evolves and markets products and services?

		% answering
A)	**Extremely well**	**35%**
B)	Pretty well	30%
C)	Adequately	20%
D)	Not very well	10%
E)	Terribly	5%

Q8: How satisfied are you with your franchisor's spending of the royalty fees you pay?

		% answering
A)	Extremely satisfied	0%
B)	**Mostly satisfied**	**60%**
C)	Somewhat satisfied	20%
D)	Not very satisfied	0%
E)	Not satisfied at all	20%

Q9: **In what ways could the parent company most improve? (Please check those that most apply, no more than three):**

- ❑ Communications
- ❑ Counsel/advice on administrative/management issues
- ❑ Effectiveness of marketing/promotions
- ❑ Evolution of products/services
- ❑ Frequency of marketing/promotional campaigns
- ❑ Quality of products/services
- ❑ Pricing of products/services to franchisees
- ❑ Technology (Point of sale systems, usage of computers/email/software, etc.)
- ❑ Training

Most frequent responses:	% answering
Effectiveness of marketing/promotions	50%
Counsel/advice on administrative/management issues (tie)	40%
Frequency of marketing/promotional campaigns (tie)	40%
Training (tie)	40%

Q10: **Is your income more, less or about what you expected prior to opening your business?**

	% answering	
More	20%	
Less	**40%**	**Summary: 60% are making about what they**
About what was expected	**40%**	**expected, or more.**

Q11: **Prior to opening your franchise, which (if any) of the following did you underestimate?**

- ❑ Amount of working capital required for your 1st year in business
- ❑ Difficulty in hiring/retaining quality staff
- ❑ Expertise required to run the business
- ❑ Impact of marketing/promotions
- ❑ Start-up costs
- ❑ Degree of stress
- ❑ Workload

Most frequent responses:	% answering
Degree of stress	40%
Impact of marketing/promotions	35%
Workload	30%

Q12: **If you could turn back time to the day you signed your franchise agreement, would you make the same decision to buy your franchise?**

	% answering
Yes	**75%**
No	25%

* Number of survey respondents: 20 from 12 different states
  Number of survey respondents as a % of total franchise units: 5%

PIP PRINTING

www.pip.com
Email: franchisesales@pip.com

Printing, copying, and document management.

OVERALL SCORE: 76

26722 Plaza Drive, Suite 200
Mission Viejo, CA 92691
Fax: 949-282-3899
Total number of outlets: 400+
Total number of franchise outlets: 400+
International: Yes (United Kingdom)

OVERALL RANK: 49

Phone: 949-282-3800
Franchise fee: $40,000
Franchise term: 10 years
Initial investment: $53,000 to $442,316
Advertising/Marketing fee: 2% of gross sales, up
to a maximum of $975 per month
Royalty fee: varies

SURVEY AND RESULTS *

Q1: About how many hours per week do you dedicate to your franchise business?

		% answering
A)	Less than 40	23%
B)	**41–50**	**46%**
C)	51–60	31%
D)	More than 60	0%
E)	Passive investment	0%

Q2: How would you describe your relations/communications with your franchisor?

		% answering
A)	**Excellent**	**54%**
B)	Good	38%
C)	Adequate	0%
D)	Fair	0%
E)	Poor	8%

Q3: In terms of how your franchisor views your communications with other franchisees, it is:

		% answering
A)	**Very supportive**	**85%**
B)	Not very supportive	8%
C)	No influence	8%

Q4: Is the franchisor fair with you in resolving any grievances?

		% answering
A)	**Extremely fair**	**64%**
B)	Pretty fair	27%
C)	Reasonably fair	0%
D)	Not very fair	9%
E)	Not fair at all	0%

Q5: Are territories equitably granted?

		% answering
A)	**Yes**	**100%**
B)	No	0%
C)	Not yet sure	0%

Q6: How would you describe the initial and ongoing training provided by your franchisor?

		% answering
A)	Excellent	38%
B)	**Good**	**46%**
C)	Adequate	8%
D)	Fair	0%
E)	Poor	8%

Q7: How well does the franchisor anticipate future trends in how it evolves and markets products and services?

		% answering
A)	**Extremely well**	**69%**
B)	Pretty well	15%
C)	Adequately	8%
D)	Not very well	8%
E)	Terribly	0%

Q8: How satisfied are you with your franchisor's spending of the royalty fees you pay?

		% answering
A)	Extremely satisfied	0%
B)	**Mostly satisfied**	**85%**
C)	Somewhat satisfied	0%
D)	Not very satisfied	8%
E)	Not satisfied at all	8%

Q9: **In what ways could the parent company most improve? (Please check those that most apply, no more than three):**

❑ Communications
❑ Counsel/advice on administrative/management issues
❑ Effectiveness of marketing/promotions
❑ Evolution of products/services
❑ Frequency of marketing/promotional campaigns

❑ Quality of products/services
❑ Pricing of products/services to franchisees
❑ Technology (Point of sale systems, usage of computers/email/software, etc.)
❑ Training

Most frequent responses:

	% answering
Effectiveness of marketing/promotions	85%
Counsel/advice on administrative/management issues (tie)	38%
Training (tie)	38%

Q10: **Is your income more, less or about what you expected prior to opening your business?**

	% answering	
More	8%	
Less	**54%**	**Summary: 46% are making about what they**
About what was expected	38%	**expected, or more.**

Q11: **Prior to opening your franchise, which (if any) of the following did you underestimate?**

❑ Amount of working capital required for your 1st year in business
❑ Difficulty in hiring/retaining quality staff
❑ Expertise required to run the business
❑ Impact of marketing/promotions

❑ Start-up costs
❑ Degree of stress
❑ Workload

Most frequent responses:

	% answering
Difficulty in hiring/retaining quality staff	77%
Amount of working capital required for 1st year in business	31%
Degree of stress	23%

Q12: **If you could turn back time to the day you signed your franchise agreement, would you make the same decision to buy your franchise?**

	% answering
Yes	**85%**
No	15%

* Number of survey respondents: 13 from 9 different states
Number of survey respondents as a % of total franchise units: 3.25%

PIZZA FACTORY

www.pizzafactory.com
Email: pfinc@sti.net

Pizza and pasta restaurant.

OVERALL SCORE: 59

49430 Road 426, Suite D, P.O. Box 989
Oakhurst, CA 93644
Total number of outlets: 125
Total number of franchise outlets: 125
International: No
Royalty fee: 5% of gross sales monthly

OVERALL RANK: 140

Phone: 800-654-4840
Franchise fee: $5,000 to $20,000
Franchise term: 20 years
Initial investment: $69,200 to $300,000
Advertising/Marketing fee: 2% of gross sales monthly

SURVEY AND RESULTS *

Q1: About how many hours per week do you dedicate to your franchise business?

		% answering
A)	Less than 40	7%
B)	41–50	7%
C)	51–60	13%
D)	**More than 60**	**73%**
E)	Passive investment	0%

Q2: How would you describe your relations/communications with your franchisor?

		% answering
A)	**Excellent**	**40%**
B)	**Good**	**40%**
C)	Adequate	20%
D)	Fair	7%
E)	Poor	13%

Q3: In terms of how your franchisor views your communications with other franchisees, it is:

		% answering
A)	**Very supportive**	**86%**
B)	Not very supportive	0%
C)	No influence	14%

Q4: Is the franchisor fair with you in resolving any grievances?

		% answering
A)	**Extremely fair**	**43%**
B)	Pretty fair	29%
C)	Reasonably fair	14%
D)	Not very fair	7%
E)	Not fair at all	7%

Q5: Are territories equitably granted?

		% answering
A)	Yes	79%
B)	No	7%
C)	Not yet sure	14%

Q6: How would you describe the initial and ongoing training provided by your franchisor?

		% answering
A)	Excellent	27%
B)	Good	13%
C)	**Adequate**	**33%**
D)	Fair	13%
E)	Poor	13%

Q7: How well does the franchisor anticipate future trends in how it evolves and markets products and services?

		% answering
A)	Extremely well	7%
B)	**Pretty well**	**43%**
C)	Adequately	14%
D)	Not very well	29%
E)	Terribly	7%

Q8: How satisfied are you with your franchisor's spending of the royalty fees you pay?

		% answering
A)	Extremely satisfied	7%
B)	**Mostly satisfied**	**33%**
C)	Somewhat satisfied	23%
D)	Not very satisfied	30%
E)	Not satisfied at all	7%

Q9: **In what ways could the parent company most improve? (Please check those that most apply, no more than three):**

❑ Communications

❑ Counsel/advice on administrative/management issues

❑ Effectiveness of marketing/promotions

❑ Evolution of products/services

❑ Frequency of marketing/promotional campaigns

❑ Quality of products/services

❑ Pricing of products/services to franchisees

❑ Technology (Point of sale systems, usage of computers/email/software, etc.)

❑ Training

Most frequent responses:

	% answering
Effectiveness of marketing/promotions	80%
Frequency of marketing/promotional campaigns	67%
Evolution of products/services	40%

Q10: **Is your income more, less or about what you expected prior to opening your business?**

	% answering	
More	13%	
Less	**53%**	**Summary: 46% are making about what they**
About what was expected	33%	**expected, or more.**

Q11: **Prior to opening your franchise, which (if any) of the following did you underestimate?**

❑ Amount of working capital required for your 1st year in business

❑ Difficulty in hiring/retaining quality staff

❑ Expertise required to run the business

❑ Impact of marketing/promotions

❑ Start-up costs

❑ Degree of stress

❑ Workload

Most frequent responses:

	% answering
Degree of stress	80%
Difficulty in hiring/retaining quality staff (tie)	67%
Workload (tie)	67%

Q12: **If you could turn back time to the day you signed your franchise agreement, would you make the same decision to buy your franchise?**

	% answering
Yes	43%
No	**57%**

* Number of survey respondents: 15 from 4 different states

Number of survey respondents as a % of total franchise units: 12%

PLANET BEACH

www.planetbeach.com

Tanning salon.

OVERALL SCORE: 58

5161 Taravella Road
Marrero, LA 70072
Fax: 504-361-5540
Total number of outlets: 173 (154 in U.S.)
Total number of franchise outlets: 173 (154 in U.S.)
International: Yes (Australia, Canada)

OVERALL RANK: 145

Phone: 888-290-8266
Franchise fee: $25,000 to $35,000
Franchise term: 10 years
Initial investment: $213,547 to $368,489
Advertising/Marketing fee: 1% of gross sales monthly
Royalty fee: 6% of gross sales monthly

SURVEY AND RESULTS *

Q1: About how many hours per week do you dedicate to your franchise business?

		% answering
A)	Less than 40	33%
B)	**41–50**	**40%**
C)	51–60	13%
D)	More than 60	13%
E)	Passive investment	0%

Q2: How would you describe your relations/communications with your franchisor?

		% answering
A)	Excellent	20%
B)	**Good**	**47%**
C)	Adequate	13%
D)	Fair	0%
E)	Poor	20%

Q3: In terms of how your franchisor views your communications with other franchisees, it is:

		% answering
A)	**Very supportive**	**53%**
B)	Not very supportive	27%
C)	No influence	20%

Q4: Is the franchisor fair with you in resolving any grievances?

		% answering
A)	Extremely fair	14%
B)	**Pretty fair**	**29%**
C)	**Reasonably fair**	**29%**
D)	Not very fair	21%
E)	Not fair at all	7%

Q5: Are territories equitably granted?

		% answering
A)	**Yes**	**40%**
B)	No	27%
C)	Not yet sure	33%

Q6: How would you describe the initial and ongoing training provided by your franchisor?

		% answering
A)	Excellent	20%
B)	**Good**	**53%**
C)	Adequate	7%
D)	Fair	13%
E)	Poor	7%

Q7: How well does the franchisor anticipate future trends in how it evolves and markets products and services?

		% answering
A)	Extremely well	20%
B)	**Pretty well**	**53%**
C)	Adequately	7%
D)	Not very well	13%
E)	Terribly	7%

Q8: How satisfied are you with your franchisor's spending of the royalty fees you pay?

		% answering
A)	Extremely satisfied	7%
B)	Mostly satisfied	13%
C)	**Somewhat satisfied**	**47%**
D)	Not very satisfied	20%
E)	Not satisfied at all	13%

Q9: **In what ways could the parent company most improve? (Please check those that most apply, no more than three):**

☐ Communications
☐ Counsel/advice on administrative/management issues
☐ Effectiveness of marketing/promotions
☐ Evolution of products/services
☐ Frequency of marketing/promotional campaigns

☐ Quality of products/services
☐ Pricing of products/services to franchisees
☐ Technology (Point of sale systems, usage of computers/email/software, etc.)
☐ Training

Most frequent responses: % answering

Frequency of marketing/promotional campaigns   53%
Effectiveness of marketing/promotions   47%
Communications   40%

Q10: **Is your income more, less or about what you expected prior to opening your business?**

	% answering	
More	0%	
Less	**53%**	**Summary: 47% are making about what they**
About what was expected	47%	**expected, or more.**

Q11: **Prior to opening your franchise, which (if any) of the following did you underestimate?**

☐ Amount of working capital required for your 1st year in business
☐ Difficulty in hiring/retaining quality staff
☐ Expertise required to run the business
☐ Impact of marketing/promotions

☐ Start-up costs
☐ Degree of stress
☐ Workload

Most frequent responses: % answering

Amount of working capital required for your 1st year in business   67%
Difficulty in hiring/retaining quality staff   47%
Start-up costs   40%

Q12: **If you could turn back time to the day you signed your franchise agreement, would you make the same decision to buy your franchise?**

	% answering
Yes	**57%**
No	43%

* Number of survey respondents: 15 from 13 different states
Number of survey respondents as a % of total franchise units: 8.67%

PLATO'S CLOSET

www.platoscloset.com
Email: pc-corporate-operations@platoscloset.com

"Recycled" clothing for teens and young adults.

OVERALL SCORE: 81

4200 Dahlberg Drive, Suite 100
Minneapolis, MN 55422
Fax: 763-520-8410
Total number of outlets: 125
Total number of franchise outlets: 124
International: Yes (Canada)

OVERALL RANK: 31

Phone: 800-567-6600
Franchise fee: $20,000
Franchise term: 10 years
Initial investment: $134,808 to $286,497
Advertising/Marketing fee: none currently
Royalty fee: 4% of gross sales weekly

SURVEY AND RESULTS *

Q1: About how many hours per week do you dedicate to your franchise business?

		% answering
A)	Less than 40	18%
B)	**41–50**	**27%**
C)	51–60	18%
D)	**More than 60**	**27%**
E)	Passive investment	9%

Q2: How would you describe your relations/ communications with your franchisor?

		% answering
A)	**Excellent**	**36%**
B)	**Good**	**36%**
C)	Adequate	9%
D)	Fair	5%
E)	Poor	14%

Q3: In terms of how your franchisor views your communications with other franchisees, it is:

		% answering
A)	**Very supportive**	**82%**
B)	Not very supportive	9%
C)	No influence	9%

Q4: Is the franchisor fair with you in resolving any grievances?

		% answering
A)	**Extremely fair**	**50%**
B)	Pretty fair	30%
C)	Reasonably fair	10%
D)	Not very fair	10%
E)	Not fair at all	0%

Q5: Are territories equitably granted?

		% answering
A)	**Yes**	**55%**
B)	No	18%
C)	Not yet sure	27%

Q6: How would you describe the initial and ongoing training provided by your franchisor?

		% answering
A)	**Excellent**	**55%**
B)	Good	18%
C)	Adequate	9%
D)	Fair	18%
E)	Poor	0%

Q7: How well does the franchisor anticipate future trends in how it evolves and markets products and services?

		% answering
A)	Extremely well	36%
B)	**Pretty well**	**55%**
C)	Adequately	0%
D)	Not very well	5%
E)	Terribly	5%

Q8: How satisfied are you with your franchisor's spending of the royalty fees you pay?

		% answering
A)	Extremely satisfied	27%
B)	**Mostly satisfied**	**36%**
C)	Somewhat satisfied	27%
D)	Not very satisfied	9%
E)	Not satisfied at all	0%

Q9: **In what ways could the parent company most improve? (Please check those that most apply, no more than three):**

- ❏ Communications
- ❏ Counsel/advice on administrative/management issues
- ❏ Effectiveness of marketing/promotions
- ❏ Evolution of products/services
- ❏ Frequency of marketing/promotional campaigns

- ❏ Quality of products/services
- ❏ Pricing of products/services to franchisees
- ❏ Technology (Point of sale systems, usage of computers/email/software, etc.)
- ❏ Training

Most frequent responses:	% answering
Effectiveness of marketing/promotions	73%
Counsel/advice on administrative/management issues (tie)	55%
Frequency of marketing/promotional campaigns (tie)	55%

Q10: **Is your income more, less or about what you expected prior to opening your business?**

	% answering	
More	36%	
Less	**45%**	**Summary: 54% are making about what they**
About what was expected	18%	**expected, or more.**

Q11: **Prior to opening your franchise, which (if any) of the following did you underestimate?**

- ❏ Amount of working capital required for your 1st year in business
- ❏ Difficulty in hiring/retaining quality staff
- ❏ Expertise required to run the business
- ❏ Impact of marketing/promotions

- ❏ Start-up costs
- ❏ Degree of stress
- ❏ Workload

Most frequent responses:	% answering
Impact of marketing/promotions	45%
Amount of working capital required for your 1st year in business (tie)	36%
Difficulty in hiring/retaining quality staff (tie)	36%

Q12: **If you could turn back time to the day you signed your franchise agreement, would you make the same decision to buy your franchise?**

	% answering
Yes	**91%**
No	9%

* Number of survey respondents: 11 from 10 different states
  Number of survey respondents as a % of total franchise units: 8.87%

PLAY IT AGAIN SPORTS

www.playitagainsports.com

Used and new sporting goods and equipment.

OVERALL SCORE: 76

4200 Dahlberg Drive, Suite 100
Minneapolis, MN 55422
Fax: 763-520-8410
Total number of outlets: 430+
Total number of franchise outlets: 430+
International: Yes (Canada)

OVERALL RANK: 54

Phone: 800-567-6600
Franchise fee: $20,000
Franchise term: 10 years
Initial investment: $209,422 to $339,371
Advertising/Marketing fee: $500 per year
Royalty fee: 5% of gross sales weekly

SURVEY AND RESULTS *

Q1: About how many hours per week do you dedicate to your franchise business?

		% answering
A)	Less than 40	10%
B)	**41–50**	**60%**
C)	51–60	10%
D)	More than 60	20%
E)	Passive investment	0%

Q2: How would you describe your relations/communications with your franchisor?

		% answering
A)	Excellent	10%
B)	**Good**	**50%**
C)	Adequate	30%
D)	Fair	10%
E)	Poor	0%

Q3: In terms of how your franchisor views your communications with other franchisees, it is:

		% answering
A)	**Very supportive**	**60%**
B)	Not very supportive	20%
C)	No influence	20%

Q4: Is the franchisor fair with you in resolving any grievances?

		% answering
A)	Extremely fair	22%
B)	Pretty fair	33%
C)	**Reasonably fair**	**44%**
D)	Not very fair	0%
E)	Not fair at all	0%

Q5: Are territories equitably granted?

		% answering
A)	**Yes**	**80%**
B)	No	0%
C)	Not yet sure	20%

Q6: How would you describe the initial and ongoing training provided by your franchisor?

		% answering
A)	Excellent	40%
B)	**Good**	**50%**
C)	Adequate	10%
D)	Fair	0%
E)	Poor	0%

Q7: How well does the franchisor anticipate future trends in how it evolves and markets products and services?

		% answering
A)	Extremely well	10%
B)	**Pretty well**	**70%**
C)	Adequately	20%
D)	Not very well	0%
E)	Terribly	0%

Q8: How satisfied are you with your franchisor's spending of the royalty fees you pay?

		% answering
A)	Extremely satisfied	0%
B)	**Mostly satisfied**	**50%**
C)	Somewhat satisfied	40%
D)	Not very satisfied	10%
E)	Not satisfied at all	0%

Q9: **In what ways could the parent company most improve? (Please check those that most apply, no more than three):**

❑ Communications

❑ Counsel/advice on administrative/management issues

❑ Effectiveness of marketing/promotions

❑ Evolution of products/services

❑ Frequency of marketing/promotional campaigns

❑ Quality of products/services

❑ Pricing of products/services to franchisees

❑ Technology (Point of sale systems, usage of computers/email/software, etc.)

❑ Training

Most frequent responses:	% answering
Counsel/advice on administrative/management issues (tie)	60%
Effectiveness of marketing/promotions (tie)	60%
Frequency of marketing/promotional campaigns	40%

Q10: **Is your income more, less or about what you expected prior to opening your business?**

	% answering	
More	20%	
Less	**40%**	**Summary: 60% are making about what they**
About what was expected	**40%**	**expected, or more.**

Q11: **Prior to opening your franchise, which (if any) of the following did you underestimate?**

❑ Amount of working capital required for your 1st year in business

❑ Difficulty in hiring/retaining quality staff

❑ Expertise required to run the business

❑ Impact of marketing/promotions

❑ Start-up costs

❑ Degree of stress

❑ Workload

Most frequent responses:	% answering
Difficulty in hiring/retaining quality staff (tie)	50%
Workload (tie)	50%
Amount of working capital required for 1st year in business	30%

Q12: **If you could turn back time to the day you signed your franchise agreement, would you make the same decision to buy your franchise?**

	% answering
Yes	**80%**
No	20%

* Number of survey respondents: 10 from 10 different states

Number of survey respondents as a % of total franchise units: 2.33%

POP-A-LOCK

www.pop-a-lock.com
Email: info@pop-a-lock.com

Locksmithing services.

OVERALL SCORE: 70

1018 Harding Street, Suite 101
Lafayette, LA 70503
Fax: 337-233-6555
Total number of outlets: 115
Total number of franchise outlets: 115
International: No
Advertising/Marketing fee:

OVERALL RANK: N/A

Phone: 337-233-6211
Franchise fee: $20,000 plus $40 per one thousand
of population in your territory (maximum of Total $100,000)
Franchise term:
Initial investment:
Royalty fee:

SURVEY AND RESULTS *

Q1: About how many hours per week do you dedicate to your franchise business?

		% answering
A)	Less than 40	14%
B)	**41–50**	**43%**
C)	51–60	0%
D)	**More than 60**	**43%**
E)	Passive investment	0%

Q2: How would you describe your relations/ communications with your franchisor?

		% answering
A)	**Excellent**	**43%**
B)	Good	14%
C)	Adequate	0%
D)	Fair	14%
E)	Poor	29%

Q3: In terms of how your franchisor views your communications with other franchisees, it is:

		% answering
A)	**Very supportive**	**71%**
B)	Not very supportive	0%
C)	No influence	29%

Q4: Is the franchisor fair with you in resolving any grievances?

		% answering
A)	**Extremely fair**	**43%**
B)	Pretty fair	29%
C)	Reasonably fair	14%
D)	Not very fair	0%
E)	Not fair at all	14%

Q5: Are territories equitably granted?

		% answering
A)	**Yes**	**71%**
B)	No	0%
C)	Not yet sure	29%

Q6: How would you describe the initial and ongoing training provided by your franchisor?

		% answering
A)	**Excellent**	**43%**
B)	Good	0%
C)	Adequate	14%
D)	Fair	14%
E)	Poor	29%

Q7: How well does the franchisor anticipate future trends in how it evolves and markets products and services?

		% answering
A)	Extremely well	14%
B)	Pretty well	14%
C)	**Adequately**	**29%**
D)	**Not very well**	**29%**
E)	Terribly	14%

Q8: How satisfied are you with your franchisor's spending of the royalty fees you pay?

		% answering
A)	Extremely satisfied	14%
B)	Mostly satisfied	14%
C)	**Somewhat satisfied**	**43%**
D)	Not very satisfied	14%
E)	Not satisfied at all	14%

Q9: **In what ways could the parent company most improve? (Please check those that most apply, no more than three):**

- ❑ Communications
- ❑ Counsel/advice on administrative/management issues
- ❑ Effectiveness of marketing/promotions
- ❑ Evolution of products/services
- ❑ Frequency of marketing/promotional campaigns

- ❑ Quality of products/services
- ❑ Pricing of products/services to franchisees
- ❑ Technology (Point of sale systems, usage of computers/email/software, etc.)
- ❑ Training

Most frequent responses:	% answering
Communications (tie)	43%
Frequency of marketing/promotional campaigns (tie)	43%
Counsel/advice on administrative/management issues (tie)	29%
Evolution of products/services (tie)	29%
Quality of products/services (tie)	29%

Q10: **Is your income more, less or about what you expected prior to opening your business?**

	% answering	
More	**50%**	
Less	33%	**Summary: 67% are making about what they**
About what was expected	17%	**expected, or more.**

Q11: **Prior to opening your franchise, which (if any) of the following did you underestimate?**

- ❑ Amount of working capital required for your 1st year in business
- ❑ Difficulty in hiring/retaining quality staff
- ❑ Expertise required to run the business
- ❑ Impact of marketing/promotions

- ❑ Start-up costs
- ❑ Degree of stress
- ❑ Workload

Most frequent responses:	% answering
Difficulty in hiring/retaining quality staff	71%
Degree of stress	57%
Amount of working capital required for 1st year in business (tie)	43%
Workload (tie)	43%

Q12: **If you could turn back time to the day you signed your franchise agreement, would you make the same decision to buy your franchise?**

	% answering
Yes	**71%**
No	29%

* Number of survey respondents: 7 from 5 different states
Number of survey respondents as a % of total franchise units: 6.09%

POSTAL ANNEX+

www.postalannex.com

Packing, shipping, and mailing services.

OVERALL SCORE: 50

7850 Metropolitan Drive, Suite 200
San Diego, CA 92108
Fax: 619-563-9850
Total number of outlets: 305
Total number of franchise outlets: 305
International: Yes (Austria)
Royalty fee: 5% of gross receipts monthly

OVERALL RANK: 168

Phone: 800-456-1525
Franchise fee: $29,950 (20% discount for eligible veterans)
Franchise term: 20 years
Initial investment: $121,100 to $180,650
Advertising/Marketing fee: 2% of gross receipts monthly

SURVEY AND RESULTS *

Q1: About how many hours per week do you dedicate to your franchise business?

		% answering
A)	Less than 40	11%
B)	41–50	17%
C)	**51–60**	**39%**
D)	More than 60	33%
E)	Passive investment	0%

Q2: How would you describe your relations/ communications with your franchisor?

		% answering
A)	Excellent	22%
B)	**Good**	**39%**
C)	Adequate	11%
D)	Fair	17%
E)	Poor	11%

Q3: In terms of how your franchisor views your communications with other franchisees, it is:

		% answering
A)	**Very supportive**	**63%**
B)	Not very supportive	13%
C)	No influence	25%

Q4: Is the franchisor fair with you in resolving any grievances?

		% answering
A)	Extremely fair	24%
B)	**Pretty fair**	**41%**
C)	Reasonably fair	18%
D)	Not very fair	6%
E)	Not fair at all	12%

Q5: Are territories equitably granted?

		% answering
A)	**Yes**	**72%**
B)	No	22%
C)	Not yet sure	6%

Q6: How would you describe the initial and ongoing training provided by your franchisor?

		% answering
A)	Excellent	22%
B)	Good	22%
C)	Adequate	11%
D)	**Fair**	**28%**
E)	Poor	17%

Q7: How well does the franchisor anticipate future trends in how it evolves and markets products and services?

		% answering
A)	Extremely well	11%
B)	Pretty well	22%
C)	**Adequately**	**39%**
D)	Not very well	28%
E)	Terribly	0%

Q8: How satisfied are you with your franchisor's spending of the royalty fees you pay?

		% answering
A)	Extremely satisfied	0%
B)	**Mostly satisfied**	**39%**
C)	Somewhat satisfied	22%
D)	Not very satisfied	22%
E)	Not satisfied at all	17%

Q9: **In what ways could the parent company most improve? (Please check those that most apply, no more than three):**

❑ Communications

❑ Counsel/advice on administrative/management issues

❑ Effectiveness of marketing/promotions

❑ Evolution of products/services

❑ Frequency of marketing/promotional campaigns

❑ Quality of products/services

❑ Pricing of products/services to franchisees

❑ Technology (Point of sale systems, usage of computers/email/software, etc.)

❑ Training

Most frequent responses:	% answering
Effectiveness of marketing/promotions	50%
Evolution of products/services (tie)	33%
Training (tie)	33%

Q10: **Is your income more, less or about what you expected prior to opening your business?**

	% answering	
More	6%	
Less	**72%**	**Summary: 28% are making about what they**
About what was expected	22%	**expected, or more.**

Q11: **Prior to opening your franchise, which (if any) of the following did you underestimate?**

❑ Amount of working capital required for your 1st year in business

❑ Difficulty in hiring/retaining quality staff

❑ Expertise required to run the business

❑ Impact of marketing/promotions

❑ Start-up costs

❑ Degree of stress

❑ Workload

Most frequent responses:	% answering
Amount of working capital required for your 1st year in business (tie)	44%
Degree of stress (tie)	44%
Workload	33%

Q12: **If you could turn back time to the day you signed your franchise agreement, would you make the same decision to buy your franchise?**

	% answering
Yes	39%
No	**61%**

* Number of survey respondents: 18 from 9 different states

Number of survey respondents as a % of total franchise units: 5.90%

POSTNET POSTAL & BUSINESS CENTERS

www.postnet.com
Email: info@postnet.com

Packing, shipping, copying, and printing.

OVERALL SCORE: 61

181 North Arroyo Grande Boulevard, Bldg. A, Suite 100
Henderson, NV 89074
Fax: 702-792-7115
Total number of outlets: 819 (485 in U.S.)
Total number of franchise outlets: 819 (485 in U.S.)
International: Yes (worldwide)

OVERALL RANK: 131

Phone: 702-792-7100
Franchise fee: $29,900
Franchise term: 15 years
Initial investment: $174,325 to $195,800
Advertising/Marketing fee: 2% of gross sales weekly
Royalty fee: 4% of gross sales weekly

SURVEY AND RESULTS *

Q1: About how many hours per week do you dedicate to your franchise business?

		% answering
A)	Less than 40	17%
B)	41–50	17%
C)	**51–60**	**42%**
D)	More than 60	25%
E)	Passive investment	0%

Q2: How would you describe your relations/communications with your franchisor?

		% answering
A)	Excellent	33%
B)	**Good**	**50%**
C)	Adequate	0%
D)	Fair	8%
E)	Poor	8%

Q3: In terms of how your franchisor views your communications with other franchisees, it is:

		% answering
A)	**Very supportive**	**83%**
B)	Not very supportive	17%
C)	No influence	0%

Q4: Is the franchisor fair with you in resolving any grievances?

		% answering
A)	**Extremely fair**	**45%**
B)	Pretty fair	27%
C)	Reasonably fair	9%
D)	Not very fair	9%
E)	Not fair at all	9%

Q5: Are territories equitably granted?

		% answering
A)	**Yes**	**75%**
B)	No	0%
C)	Not yet sure	25%

Q6: How would you describe the initial and ongoing training provided by your franchisor?

		% answering
A)	**Excellent**	**42%**
B)	Good	25%
C)	Adequate	25%
D)	Fair	0%
E)	Poor	8%

Q7: How well does the franchisor anticipate future trends in how it evolves and markets products and services?

		% answering
A)	**Extremely well**	**45%**
B)	**Pretty well**	**45%**
C)	Adequately	9%
D)	Not very well	0%
E)	Terribly	0%

Q8: How satisfied are you with your franchisor's spending of the royalty fees you pay?

		% answering
A)	Extremely satisfied	17%
B)	**Mostly satisfied**	**50%**
C)	Somewhat satisfied	17%
D)	Not very satisfied	0%
E)	Not satisfied at all	17%

Q9: **In what ways could the parent company most improve? (Please check those that most apply, no more than three):**

- ❏ Communications
- ❏ Counsel/advice on administrative/management issues
- ❏ Effectiveness of marketing/promotions
- ❏ Evolution of products/services
- ❏ Frequency of marketing/promotional campaigns

- ❏ Quality of products/services
- ❏ Pricing of products/services to franchisees
- ❏ Technology (Point of sale systems, usage of computers/email/software, etc.)
- ❏ Training

Most frequent responses:	% answering
Effectiveness of marketing/promotions	58%
Pricing of products/services to franchisees	42%
Counsel/advice on administrative/management issues (tie)	33%
Frequency of marketing/promotional campaigns (tie)	33%

Q10: **Is your income more, less or about what you expected prior to opening your business?**

	% answering	
More	8%	
Less	**58%**	**Summary: 41% are making about what they**
About what was expected	33%	**expected, or more.**

Q11: **Prior to opening your franchise, which (if any) of the following did you underestimate?**

- ❏ Amount of working capital required for your 1st year in business
- ❏ Difficulty in hiring/retaining quality staff
- ❏ Expertise required to run the business
- ❏ Impact of marketing/promotions

- ❏ Start-up costs
- ❏ Degree of stress
- ❏ Workload

Most frequent responses:	% answering
Amount of working capital required for your 1st year in business	50%
Degree of stress	33%
Difficulty in hiring/retaining quality staff	25%

Q12: **If you could turn back time to the day you signed your franchise agreement, would you make the same decision to buy your franchise?**

	% answering
Yes	42%
No	**58%**

* Number of survey respondents: 12 from 11 different states

Number of survey respondents as a % of total franchise units: 1.47%

PRESSED 4 TIME

www.pressed4time.com
Email: franchiseinfo@pressed4time.com

Mobile dry cleaning services.

OVERALL SCORE: 61

8 Clock Tower Place, Suite 110
Maynard, MA 01754
Fax: 978823-8301
Total number of outlets: 163
Total number of franchise outlets: 163
International: No

OVERALL RANK: 128

Phone: 800-423-8711
Franchise fee: $18,500
Franchise term: 10 years
Initial investment: $23,890 to $32,330
Advertising/Marketing fee: none currently
Royalty fee: varies

SURVEY AND RESULTS *

Q1: About how many hours per week do you dedicate to your franchise business?

		% answering
A)	Less than 40	8%
B)	**41–50**	**33%**
C)	**51–60**	**33%**
D)	More than 60	25%
E)	Passive investment	0%

Q2: How would you describe your relations/ communications with your franchisor?

		% answering
A)	Excellent	25%
B)	**Good**	**33%**
C)	Adequate	8%
D)	**Fair**	**33%**
E)	Poor	0%

Q3: In terms of how your franchisor views your communications with other franchisees, it is:

		% answering
A)	Very supportive	40%
B)	Not very supportive	0%
C)	**No influence**	**60%**

Q4: Is the franchisor fair with you in resolving any grievances?

		% answering
A)	**Extremely fair**	**36%**
B)	Pretty fair	27%
C)	Reasonably fair	27%
D)	Not very fair	0%
E)	Not fair at all	9%

Q5: Are territories equitably granted?

		% answering
A)	**Yes**	**83%**
B)	No	8%
C)	Not yet sure	8%

Q6: How would you describe the initial and ongoing training provided by your franchisor?

		% answering
A)	Excellent	25%
B)	Good	17%
C)	**Adequate**	**42%**
D)	Fair	8%
E)	Poor	8%

Q7: How well does the franchisor anticipate future trends in how it evolves and markets products and services?

		% answering
A)	Extremely well	9%
B)	**Pretty well**	**45%**
C)	Adequately	18%
D)	Not very well	27%
E)	Terribly	0%

Q8: How satisfied are you with your franchisor's spending of the royalty fees you pay?

		% answering
A)	Extremely satisfied	0%
B)	**Mostly satisfied**	**40%**
C)	Somewhat satisfied	20%
D)	Not very satisfied	20%
E)	Not satisfied at all	20%

Q9: In what ways could the parent company most improve? (Please check those that most apply, no more than three):

❑ Communications

❑ Counsel/advice on administrative/management issues

❑ Effectiveness of marketing/promotions

❑ Evolution of products/services

❑ Frequency of marketing/promotional campaigns

❑ Quality of products/services

❑ Pricing of products/services to franchisees

❑ Technology (Point of sale systems, usage of computers/email/software, etc.)

❑ Training

Most frequent responses:

	% answering
Technology	67%
Effectiveness of marketing/promotions	50%
Training	33%

Q10: Is your income more, less or about what you expected prior to opening your business?

	% answering
More	8%
Less	**58%**
About what was expected	33%

Summary: 41% are making about what they expected, or more.

Q11: Prior to opening your franchise, which (if any) of the following did you underestimate?

❑ Amount of working capital required for your 1st year in business

❑ Difficulty in hiring/retaining quality staff

❑ Expertise required to run the business

❑ Impact of marketing/promotions

❑ Start-up costs

❑ Degree of stress

❑ Workload

Most frequent responses:

	% answering
Workload	50%
Amount of working capital required for your 1st year in business	33%
Impact of marketing/promotions	25%

Q12: If you could turn back time to the day you signed your franchise agreement, would you make the same decision to buy your franchise?

	% answering
Yes	**64%**
No	36%

*   Number of survey respondents: 12 from 11 different states

Number of survey respondents as a % of total franchise units: 7.36%

PRETZELMAKER

www.pretzelmaker.com
Email: eliseh@mrsfields.com

Fresh-backed soft pretzels and beverages.

OVERALL SCORE: 53

OVERALL RANK: 165

2855 East Cottonwood Parkway, Suite 200
Salt Lake City, UT 84121
Fax: 425-377-0963 (Lake Stevens, WA office)
Total number of outlets: 200+
Total number of franchise outlets: 200+
International: Yes (Canada)

Phone: 800-348-6311
Franchise fee: $25,000
Franchise term: 7 years
Initial investment: $107,000 to $238,500
Advertising/Marketing fee: 1-3% of gross sales
Royalty fee: 7% of gross sales

SURVEY AND RESULTS *

Q1: About how many hours per week do you dedicate to your franchise business?

		% answering
A)	**Less than 40**	**55%**
B)	41–50	27%
C)	51–60	9%
D)	More than 60	0%
E)	Passive investment	9%

Q2: How would you describe your relations/ communications with your franchisor?

		% answering
A)	Excellent	0%
B)	Good	27%
C)	**Adequate**	**45%**
D)	Fair	18%
E)	Poor	9%

Q3: In terms of how your franchisor views your communications with other franchisees, it is:

		% answering
A)	Very supportive	30%
B)	**Not very supportive**	**50%**
C)	No influence	20%

Q4: Is the franchisor fair with you in resolving any grievances?

		% answering
A)	Extremely fair	0%
B)	Pretty fair	36%
C)	**Reasonably fair**	**64%**
D)	Not very fair	0%
E)	Not fair at all	0%

Q5: Are territories equitably granted?

		% answering
A)	Yes	18%
B)	No	36%
C)	**Not yet sure**	**45%**

Q6: How would you describe the initial and ongoing training provided by your franchisor?

		% answering
A)	Excellent	9%
B)	**Good**	**27%**
C)	**Adequate**	**27%**
D)	**Fair**	**27%**
E)	Poor	9%

Q7: How well does the franchisor anticipate future trends in how it evolves and markets products and services?

		% answering
A)	Extremely well	0%
B)	Pretty well	18%
C)	**Adequately**	**36%**
D)	**Not very well**	**36%**
E)	Terribly	9%

Q8: How satisfied are you with your franchisor's spending of the royalty fees you pay?

		% answering
A)	Extremely satisfied	0%
B)	Mostly satisfied	0%
C)	**Somewhat satisfied**	**55%**
D)	Not very satisfied	18%
E)	Not satisfied at all	27%

Q9: **In what ways could the parent company most improve? (Please check those that most apply, no more than three):**

- ❏ Communications
- ❏ Counsel/advice on administrative/management issues
- ❏ Effectiveness of marketing/promotions
- ❏ Evolution of products/services
- ❏ Frequency of marketing/promotional campaigns

- ❏ Quality of products/services
- ❏ Pricing of products/services to franchisees
- ❏ Technology (Point of sale systems, usage of computers/email/software, etc.)
- ❏ Training

Most frequent responses:	% answering
Training	50%
Effectiveness of marketing/promotions (tie)	33%
Evolution of products/services (tie)	33%

Q10: **Is your income more, less or about what you expected prior to opening your business?**

	% answering	
More	0%	
Less	**58%**	**Summary: 42% are making about what they**
About what was expected	42%	**expected, or more.**

Q11: **Prior to opening your franchise, which (if any) of the following did you underestimate?**

- ❏ Amount of working capital required for your 1st year in business
- ❏ Difficulty in hiring/retaining quality staff
- ❏ Expertise required to run the business
- ❏ Impact of marketing/promotions

- ❏ Start-up costs
- ❏ Degree of stress
- ❏ Workload

Most frequent responses:	% answering
Difficulty in hiring/retaining quality staff (tie)	33%
Impact of marketing/promotions (tie)	33%
Workload	25%

Q12: **If you could turn back time to the day you signed your franchise agreement, would you make the same decision to buy your franchise?**

	% answering
Yes	**67%**
No	33%

* Number of survey respondents: 12 from 9 different states
Number of survey respondents as a % of total franchise units: 6%

PRETZEL TIME

www.pretzeltime.com
Email: eliseh@mrsfields.com

Fresh-baked pretzels, and other snacks and beverages.

OVERALL SCORE: 73

2855 East Cottonwood Parkway, Suite 200
Salt Lake City, UT 84121
Fax: 425-377-0963 (Lake Stevens, WA office)
Total number of outlets: 300+
Total number of franchise outlets: 250+
International: Yes (Canada)

OVERALL RANK: N/A

Phone: 800-348-6311
Franchise fee: $25,000
Franchise term: 7 years
Initial investment: $107,000 to $238,500
Advertising/Marketing fee: 1-3% of gross sales
Royalty fee: 7% of gross sales

SURVEY AND RESULTS *

Q1: About how many hours per week do you dedicate to your franchise business?

		% answering
A)	Less than 40	0%
B)	**41–50**	**67%**
C)	51–60	17%
D)	More than 60	17%
E)	Passive investment	0%

Q2: How would you describe your relations/communications with your franchisor?

		% answering
A)	Excellent	33%
B)	**Good**	**50%**
C)	Adequate	0%
D)	Fair	0%
E)	Poor	17%

Q3: In terms of how your franchisor views your communications with other franchisees, it is:

		% answering
A)	**Very supportive**	**80%**
B)	Not very supportive	20%
C)	No influence	0%

Q4: Is the franchisor fair with you in resolving any grievances?

		% answering
A)	Extremely fair	20%
B)	**Pretty fair**	**60%**
C)	Reasonably fair	20%
D)	Not very fair	0%
E)	Not fair at all	0%

Q5: Are territories equitably granted?

		% answering
A)	Yes	33%
B)	No	17%
C)	**Not yet sure**	**50%**

Q6: How would you describe the initial and ongoing training provided by your franchisor?

		% answering
A)	Excellent	17%
B)	**Good**	**50%**
C)	Adequate	0%
D)	Fair	0%
E)	Poor	33%

Q7: How well does the franchisor anticipate future trends in how it evolves and markets products and services?

		% answering
A)	Extremely well	17%
B)	Pretty well	17%
C)	**Adequately**	**50%**
D)	Not very well	17%
E)	Terribly	0%

Q8: How satisfied are you with your franchisor's spending of the royalty fees you pay?

		% answering
A)	Extremely satisfied	0%
B)	Mostly satisfied	33%
C)	**Somewhat satisfied**	**50%**
D)	Not very satisfied	17%
E)	Not satisfied at all	0%

Q9: In what ways could the parent company most improve? (Please check those that most apply, no more than three):

- ❑ Communications
- ❑ Counsel/advice on administrative/management issues
- ❑ Effectiveness of marketing/promotions
- ❑ Evolution of products/services
- ❑ Frequency of marketing/promotional campaigns
- ❑ Quality of products/services
- ❑ Pricing of products/services to franchisees
- ❑ Technology (Point of sale systems, usage of computers/email/software, etc.)
- ❑ Training

Most frequent responses:	% answering
Effectiveness of marketing/promotions (tie)	50%
Frequency of marketing/promotional campaigns (tie)	50%
Communications	33%

Q10: Is your income more, less or about what you expected prior to opening your business?

	% answering	
More	33%	
Less	33%	**Summary: 66% are making about what they**
About what was expected	33%	**expected, or more.**

Q11: Prior to opening your franchise, which (if any) of the following did you underestimate?

- ❑ Amount of working capital required for your 1st year in business
- ❑ Difficulty in hiring/retaining quality staff
- ❑ Expertise required to run the business
- ❑ Impact of marketing/promotions
- ❑ Start-up costs
- ❑ Degree of stress
- ❑ Workload

Most frequent responses:	% answering
Difficulty in hiring/retaining quality staff	33%
Degree of stress	33%
Amount of working capital required for 1st year in business (tie)	17%
Start-up costs (tie)	17%
Workload (tie)	17%

Q12: If you could turn back time to the day you signed your franchise agreement, would you make the same decision to buy your franchise?

	% answering
Yes	83%
No	17%

* Number of survey respondents: 6 from 6 different states
Number of survey respondents as a % of total franchise units: 2.40%

PROPERTY DAMAGE APPRAISERS

www.pdahomeoffice.com

Vehicle and property damage appraisal services.

OVERALL SCORE: 67

6100 Southwest Boulevard, Suite 200
Fort Worth, TX 76109
Fax: 817-731-5550
Total number of outlets: 260
Total number of franchise outlets: 260
International: No

OVERALL RANK: 101

Phone: 800-749-7324, ext. 23
Franchise fee: none
Franchise term: 3 years
Initial investment: $18,330 to $35,950
Advertising/Marketing fee: none
Royalty fee: 15% of weekly gross invoice fees

SURVEY AND RESULTS *

Q1: About how many hours per week do you dedicate to your franchise business?

		% answering
A)	Less than 40	0%
B)	41–50	10%
C)	51–60	30%
D)	**More than 60**	**60%**
E)	Passive investment	0%

Q2: How would you describe your relations/ communications with your franchisor?

		% answering
A)	Excellent	20%
B)	Good	30%
C)	**Adequate**	**40%**
D)	Fair	10%
E)	Poor	0%

Q3: In terms of how your franchisor views your communications with other franchisees, it is:

		% answering
A)	**Very supportive**	**50%**
B)	Not very supportive	30%
C)	No influence	20%

Q4: Is the franchisor fair with you in resolving any grievances?

		% answering
A)	Extremely fair	10%
B)	Pretty fair	30%
C)	**Reasonably fair**	**40%**
D)	Not very fair	10%
E)	Not fair at all	10%

Q5: Are territories equitably granted?

		% answering
A)	**Yes**	**60%**
B)	No	20%
C)	Not yet sure	20%

Q6: How would you describe the initial and ongoing training provided by your franchisor?

		% answering
A)	Excellent	20%
B)	Good	20%
C)	**Adequate**	**30%**
D)	Fair	10%
E)	Poor	20%

Q7: How well does the franchisor anticipate future trends in how it evolves and markets products and services?

		% answering
A)	**Extremely well**	**40%**
B)	Pretty well	30%
C)	Adequately	20%
D)	Not very well	10%
E)	Terribly	0%

Q8: How satisfied are you with your franchisor's spending of the royalty fees you pay?

		% answering
A)	Extremely satisfied	11%
B)	Mostly satisfied	22%
C)	**Somewhat satisfied**	**33%**
D)	**Not very satisfied**	**33%**
E)	Not satisfied at all	0%

Q9: **In what ways could the parent company most improve? (Please check those that most apply, no more than three):**

❑ Communications

❑ Counsel/advice on administrative/management issues

❑ Effectiveness of marketing/promotions

❑ Evolution of products/services

❑ Frequency of marketing/promotional campaigns

❑ Quality of products/services

❑ Pricing of products/services to franchisees

❑ Technology (Point of sale systems, usage of computers/email/software, etc.)

❑ Training

Most frequent responses:

	% answering
Effectiveness of marketing/promotions	60%
Pricing of products/services to franchisees	50%
Counsel/advice on administrative/management issues (tie)	30%
Frequency of marketing/promotional campaigns (tie)	30%

Q10: **Is your income more, less or about what you expected prior to opening your business?**

	% answering	
More	30%	
Less	**50%**	**Summary: 50% are making about what they**
About what was expected	20%	**expected, or more.**

Q11: **Prior to opening your franchise, which (if any) of the following did you underestimate?**

❑ Amount of working capital required for your 1st year in business

❑ Difficulty in hiring/retaining quality staff

❑ Expertise required to run the business

❑ Impact of marketing/promotions

❑ Start-up costs

❑ Degree of stress

❑ Workload

Most frequent responses:

	% answering
Difficulty in hiring/retaining quality staff	70%
Degree of stress	40%
Workload	30%

Q12: **If you could turn back time to the day you signed your franchise agreement, would you make the same decision to buy your franchise?**

	% answering
Yes	**80%**
No	20%

*   Number of survey respondents: 10 from 9 different states

Number of survey respondents as a % of total franchise units: 3.85%

PRUDENTIAL REAL ESTATE

www.prudential.com/realestate

Real estate services.

OVERALL SCORE: 76

OVERALL RANK: 51

751 Broad Street
Newark, NJ 07102
Fax: 973-367-6476
Total number of outlets:
Total number of franchise outlets:
International: Yes (Australia, Canada, New Zealand)

Phone: 866-224-8895
Franchise fee:
Franchise term:
Initial investment:
Advertising/Marketing fee:
Royalty fee:

SURVEY AND RESULTS *

Q1: **About how many hours per week do you dedicate to your franchise business?**

		% answering
A)	Less than 40	0%
B)	**41–50**	**38%**
C)	51–60	23%
D)	**More than 60**	**38%**
E)	Passive investment	0%

Q2: **How would you describe your relations/ communications with your franchisor?**

		% answering
A)	Excellent	15%
B)	**Good**	**54%**
C)	Adequate	23%
D)	Fair	8%
E)	Poor	0%

Q3: **In terms of how your franchisor views your communications with other franchisees, it is:**

		% answering
A)	**Very supportive**	**54%**
B)	Not very supportive	23%
C)	No influence	23%

Q4: **Is the franchisor fair with you in resolving any grievances?**

		% answering
A)	**Extremely fair**	**42%**
B)	Pretty fair	33%
C)	Reasonably fair	17%
D)	Not very fair	8%
E)	Not fair at all	0%

Q5: **Are territories equitably granted?**

		% answering
A)	**Yes**	**77%**
B)	No	23%
C)	Not yet sure	0%

Q6: **How would you describe the initial and ongoing training provided by your franchisor?**

		% answering
A)	Excellent	31%
B)	**Good**	**46%**
C)	Adequate	23%
D)	Fair	0%
E)	Poor	0%

Q7: **How well does the franchisor anticipate future trends in how it evolves and markets products and services?**

		% answering
A)	Extremely well	38%
B)	**Pretty well**	**46%**
C)	Adequately	0%
D)	Not very well	15%
E)	Terribly	0%

Q8: **How satisfied are you with your franchisor's spending of the royalty fees you pay?**

		% answering
A)	Extremely satisfied	15%
B)	**Mostly satisfied**	**54%**
C)	Somewhat satisfied	15%
D)	Not very satisfied	8%
E)	Not satisfied at all	8%

Q9: **In what ways could the parent company most improve? (Please check those that most apply, no more than three):**

❏ Communications
❏ Counsel/advice on administrative/management issues
❏ Effectiveness of marketing/promotions
❏ Evolution of products/services
❏ Frequency of marketing/promotional campaigns

❏ Quality of products/services
❏ Pricing of products/services to franchisees
❏ Technology (Point of sale systems, usage of computers/email/software, etc.)
❏ Training

Most frequent responses: % answering

Effectiveness of marketing/promotions (tie)   46%
Frequency of marketing/promotional campaigns (tie)   46%
Counsel/advice on administrative/management issues (tie)   31%
Technology (tie)   31%

Q10: **Is your income more, less or about what you expected prior to opening your business?**

	% answering	
More	23%	
Less	**38%**	**Summary: 61% are making about what they**
About what was expected	**38%**	**expected, or more.**

Q11: **Prior to opening your franchise, which (if any) of the following did you underestimate?**

❏ Amount of working capital required for your 1st year in business
❏ Difficulty in hiring/retaining quality staff
❏ Expertise required to run the business
❏ Impact of marketing/promotions

❏ Start-up costs
❏ Degree of stress
❏ Workload

Most frequent responses: % answering

Degree of stress   62%
Workload   46%
Difficulty in hiring/retaining quality staff (tie)   23%
Impact of marketing/promotions (tie)   23%

Q12: **If you could turn back time to the day you signed your franchise agreement, would you make the same decision to buy your franchise?**

	% answering
Yes	**85%**
No	15%

*   Number of survey respondents: 13 from 11 different states
    Number of survey respondents as a % of total franchise units: 6.48%

PUROSYSTEMS

www.purosystems.com
Email: info@puroclean.com

Fire and water damage restoration and reconstruction

OVERALL SCORE: 66

6001 Hiatus Road, Suite 13
Tamarac, FL 33321
Fax: 800-955-8527
Total number of outlets: 84
Total number of franchise outlets: 84
International: No

OVERALL RANK: 106

Phone: 800-351-2282
Franchise fee: $25,000 or $30,000 plus $0.10 per
person in excess of 100,000 within your territory
Franchise term: 20 years
Initial investment: $54,250 to $78,900
Advertising/Marketing fee: none currently
Royalty fee: varies

SURVEY AND RESULTS *

Q1: About how many hours per week do you dedicate to your franchise business?

		% answering
A)	Less than 40	15%
B)	**41–50**	**43%**
C)	51–60	33%
D)	More than 60	10%
E)	Passive investment	0%

Q2: How would you describe your relations/ communications with your franchisor?

		% answering
A)	Excellent	26%
B)	Good	21%
C)	**Adequate**	**29%**
D)	Fair	3%
E)	Poor	21%

Q3: In terms of how your franchisor views your communications with other franchisees, it is:

		% answering
A)	**Very supportive**	**65%**
B)	Not very supportive	20%
C)	No influence	15%

Q4: Is the franchisor fair with you in resolving any grievances?

		% answering
A)	**Extremely fair**	**30%**
B)	**Pretty fair**	**30%**
C)	Reasonably fair	23%
D)	Not very fair	18%
E)	Not fair at all	0%

Q5: Are territories equitably granted?

		% answering
A)	**Yes**	**65%**
B)	No	15%
C)	Not yet sure	20%

Q6: How would you describe the initial and ongoing training provided by your franchisor?

		% answering
A)	Excellent	30%
B)	**Good**	**40%**
C)	Adequate	8%
D)	Fair	13%
E)	Poor	10%

Q7: How well does the franchisor anticipate future trends in how it evolves and markets products and services?

		% answering
A)	Extremely well	5%
B)	Pretty well	25%
C)	Adequately	25%
D)	**Not very well**	**30%**
E)	Terribly	15%

Q8: How satisfied are you with your franchisor's spending of the royalty fees you pay?

		% answering
A)	Extremely satisfied	0%
B)	Mostly satisfied	25%
C)	**Somewhat satisfied**	**40%**
D)	Not very satisfied	10%
E)	Not satisfied at all	25%

Q9: **In what ways could the parent company most improve? (Please check those that most apply, no more than three):**

❑ Communications
❑ Counsel/advice on administrative/management issues
❑ Effectiveness of marketing/promotions
❑ Evolution of products/services
❑ Frequency of marketing/promotional campaigns

❑ Quality of products/services
❑ Pricing of products/services to franchisees
❑ Technology (Point of sale systems, usage of computers/email/software, etc.)
❑ Training

Most frequent responses:	% answering
Effectiveness of marketing/promotions	90%
Frequency of marketing/promotional campaigns	70%
Communications	35%

Q10: **Is your income more, less or about what you expected prior to opening your business?**

	% answering	
More	35%	
Less	**45%**	**Summary: 55% are making about what they**
About what was expected	20%	**expected, or more.**

Q11: **Prior to opening your franchise, which (if any) of the following did you underestimate?**

❑ Amount of working capital required for your 1st year in business
❑ Difficulty in hiring/retaining quality staff
❑ Expertise required to run the business
❑ Impact of marketing/promotions

❑ Start-up costs
❑ Degree of stress
❑ Workload

Most frequent responses:	% answering
Degree of stress	65%
Amount of working capital required for your 1st year in business	60%
Difficulty in hiring/retaining quality staff (tie)	40%
Start-up costs (tie)	40%

Q12: **If you could turn back time to the day you signed your franchise agreement, would you make the same decision to buy your franchise?**

	% answering
Yes	**70%**
No	30%

* Number of survey respondents: 20 from 14 different states
Number of survey respondents as a % of total franchise units: 23.81%

QUIZNO'S

www.quiznos.com

Toasted sub-sandwiches.

OVERALL SCORE: 44

1475 Lawrence Street, Suite 400
Denver, CO 80202
Fax: 720-359-3399
Total number of outlets: approximately 3,500
Total number of franchise outlets:
approximately 3,500
International: Yes (worldwide)

OVERALL RANK: 176

Phone: 800-335-4782
Franchise fee: $25,000
Franchise term:
Initial investment: $176,050 to $236,900
Advertising/Marketing fee: 3% regional fee, 1% national fee
Royalty fee: 7%

SURVEY AND RESULTS *

Q1: About how many hours per week do you dedicate to your franchise business?

		% answering
A)	Less than 40	13%
B)	41–50	20%
C)	51–60	13%
D)	**More than 60**	**47%**
E)	Passive investment	7%

Q2: How would you describe your relations/communications with your franchisor?

		% answering
A)	Excellent	0%
B)	Good	23%
C)	Adequate	30%
D)	Fair	14%
E)	**Poor**	**33%**

Q3: In terms of how your franchisor views your communications with other franchisees, it is:

		% answering
A)	Very supportive	33%
B)	Not very supportive	13%
C)	**No influence**	**53%**

Q4: Is the franchisor fair with you in resolving any grievances?

		% answering
A)	Extremely fair	7%
B)	Pretty fair	14%
C)	Reasonably fair	29%
D)	**Not very fair**	**36%**
E)	Not fair at all	14%

Q5: Are territories equitably granted?

		% answering
A)	Yes	33%
B)	**No**	**53%**
C)	Not yet sure	13%

Q6: How would you describe the initial and ongoing training provided by your franchisor?

		% answering
A)	Excellent	20%
B)	**Good**	**33%**
C)	Adequate	27%
D)	Fair	20%
E)	Poor	0%

Q7: How well does the franchisor anticipate future trends in how it evolves and markets products and services?

		% answering
A)	Extremely well	20%
B)	Pretty well	13%
C)	**Adequately**	**33%**
D)	Not very well	27%
E)	Terribly	7%

Q8: How satisfied are you with your franchisor's spending of the royalty fees you pay?

		% answering
A)	Extremely satisfied	0%
B)	Mostly satisfied	20%
C)	**Somewhat satisfied**	**33%**
D)	Not very satisfied	27%
E)	Not satisfied at all	20%

Q9: **In what ways could the parent company most improve? (Please check those that most apply, no more than three):**

- ❏ Communications
- ❏ Counsel/advice on administrative/management issues
- ❏ Effectiveness of marketing/promotions
- ❏ Evolution of products/services
- ❏ Frequency of marketing/promotional campaigns

- ❏ Quality of products/services
- ❏ Pricing of products/services to franchisees
- ❏ Technology (Point of sale systems, usage of computers/email/software, etc.)
- ❏ Training

Most frequent responses:

	% answering
Effectiveness of marketing/promotions	60%
Communications (tie)	40%
Pricing of products/services to franchisees (tie)	40%

Q10: **Is your income more, less or about what you expected prior to opening your business?**

	% answering	
More	13%	
Less	**67%**	**Summary: 67% are making about what they**
About what was expected	20%	**expected, or more.**

Q11: **Prior to opening your franchise, which (if any) of the following did you underestimate?**

- ❏ Amount of working capital required for your 1st year in business
- ❏ Difficulty in hiring/retaining quality staff
- ❏ Expertise required to run the business
- ❏ Impact of marketing/promotions

- ❏ Start-up costs
- ❏ Degree of stress
- ❏ Workload

Most frequent responses:

	% answering
Start-up costs	67%
Workload	53%
Difficulty in hiring/retaining quality staff	40%

Q12: **If you could turn back time to the day you signed your franchise agreement, would you make the same decision to buy your franchise?**

	% answering
Yes	33%
No	**67%**

* Number of survey respondents: 15 from 12 different states

Number of survey respondents as a % of total franchise units: < 1%

RE-BATH

www.rebath.com

Seller and installer of customized bathtub liners, shower base liners/replacement shower base liners, wall surround systems, and other bath-related products.

OVERALL SCORE: 78

1055 South Country Club Drive, Building 2
Mesa, AZ 85210
Total number of outlets: 156
Total number of franchise outlets: 156
International: Yes (Bahamas, Bermuda, Canada, Puerto Rico)
Royalty fee: $25 per unit sold; A unit is s bath tub liner or shower base liner/replacement shower base liner

OVERALL RANK: 41

Phone: 800-426-4573
Franchise fee: $6,000 to $40,000 ($3,500 for a Small Market Dealership of less than 150,000 in population
Franchise term: 5 years
Initial investment: $33,900 to $216,000
Advertising/Marketing fee: none currently

SURVEY AND RESULTS *

Q1: About how many hours per week do you dedicate to your franchise business?

		% answering
A)	Less than 40	33%
B)	41–50	17%
C)	**51–60**	**44%**
D)	More than 60	6%
E)	Passive investment	0%

Q2: How would you describe your relations/ communications with your franchisor?

		% answering
A)	**Excellent**	**50%**
B)	Good	39%
C)	Adequate	11%
D)	Fair	0%
E)	Poor	0%

Q3: In terms of how your franchisor views your communications with other franchisees, it is:

		% answering
A)	**Very supportive**	**89%**
B)	Not very supportive	0%
C)	No influence	11%

Q4: Is the franchisor fair with you in resolving any grievances?

		% answering
A)	**Extremely fair**	**44%**
B)	Pretty fair	33%
C)	Reasonably fair	22%
D)	Not very fair	0%
E)	Not fair at all	0%

Q5: Are territories equitably granted?

		% answering
A)	**Yes**	**89%**
B)	No	6%
C)	Not yet sure	6%

Q6: How would you describe the initial and ongoing training provided by your franchisor?

		% answering
A)	**Excellent**	**50%**
B)	Good	44%
C)	Adequate	3%
D)	Fair	0%
E)	Poor	3%

Q7: How well does the franchisor anticipate future trends in how it evolves and markets products and services?

		% answering
A)	**Extremely well**	**50%**
B)	Pretty well	39%
C)	Adequately	6%
D)	Not very well	6%
E)	Terribly	0%

Q8: How satisfied are you with your franchisor's spending of the royalty fees you pay?

		% answering
A)	Extremely satisfied	6%
B)	**Mostly satisfied**	**56%**
C)	Somewhat satisfied	25%
D)	Not very satisfied	13%
E)	Not satisfied at all	0%

Q9: **In what ways could the parent company most improve? (Please check those that most apply, no more than three):**

❑ Communications

❑ Counsel/advice on administrative/management issues

❑ Effectiveness of marketing/promotions

❑ Evolution of products/services

❑ Frequency of marketing/promotional campaigns

❑ Quality of products/services

❑ Pricing of products/services to franchisees

❑ Technology (Point of sale systems, usage of computers/email/software, etc.)

❑ Training

Most frequent responses:	% answering
Effectiveness of marketing/promotions	56%
Pricing of products/services to franchisees	39%
Counsel/advice on administrative/management issues	33%

Q10: Is your income more, less or about what you expected prior to opening your business?

	% answering	
More	6%	
Less	**50%**	**Summary: 50% are making about what they**
About what was expected	44%	**expected, or more.**

Q11: Prior to opening your franchise, which (if any) of the following did you underestimate?

❑ Amount of working capital required for your 1st year in business

❑ Difficulty in hiring/retaining quality staff

❑ Expertise required to run the business

❑ Impact of marketing/promotions

❑ Start-up costs

❑ Degree of stress

❑ Workload

Most frequent responses:	% answering
Difficulty in hiring/retaining quality staff	56%
Amount of working capital required for your 1st year in business	33%
Impact of marketing/promotions (tie)	28%
Degree of stress (tie)	28%
Workload (tie)	28%

Q12: If you could turn back time to the day you signed your franchise agreement, would you make the same decision to buy your franchise?

	% answering
Yes	**83%**
No	17%

* Number of survey respondents: 18 from 16 different states

Number of survey respondents as a % of total franchise units: 11.54%

REMEDY INTELLIGENT STAFFING

www.remedystaff.com

Temporary and permanent staffing and placement firm.

OVERALL SCORE: 74

101 Enterprise
Aliso Viejo, CA 92656
Fax: 949-425-7800
Total number of outlets: 140+
Total number of franchisees: 100+
International: No

OVERALL RANK: 63

Phone: 800-736-3392
Franchise fee: $18,000
Franchise term: 10 years
Initial investment: $92,120 to $202,260
Advertising/Marketing fee: none currently
Royalty fee: varies

SURVEY AND RESULTS *

Q1: About how many hours per week do you dedicate to your franchise business?

		% answering
A)	Less than 40	0%
B)	41–50	40%
C)	51–60	10%
D)	**More than 60**	**50%**
E)	Passive investment	0%

Q2: How would you describe your relations/communications with your franchisor?

		% answering
A)	**Excellent**	**30%**
B)	**Good**	**30%**
C)	Adequate	20%
D)	Fair	10%
E)	Poor	10%

Q3: In terms of how your franchisor views your communications with other franchisees, it is:

		% answering
A)	**Very supportive**	**70%**
B)	Not very supportive	0%
C)	No influence	30%

Q4: Is the franchisor fair with you in resolving any grievances?

		% answering
A)	Extremely fair	10%
B)	**Pretty fair**	**50%**
C)	Reasonably fair	30%
D)	Not very fair	10%
E)	Not fair at all	0%

Q5: Are territories equitably granted?

		% answering
A)	**Yes**	**80%**
B)	No	0%
C)	Not yet sure	20%

Q6: How would you describe the initial and ongoing training provided by your franchisor?

		% answering
A)	**Excellent**	**50%**
B)	Good	30%
C)	Adequate	10%
D)	Fair	10%
E)	Poor	0%

Q7: How well does the franchisor anticipate future trends in how it evolves and markets products and services?

		% answering
A)	Extremely well	30%
B)	Pretty well	20%
C)	Adequately	10%
D)	**Not very well**	**40%**
E)	Terribly	0%

Q8: How satisfied are you with your franchisor's spending of the royalty fees you pay?

		% answering
A)	Extremely satisfied	0%
B)	**Mostly satisfied**	**40%**
C)	Somewhat satisfied	30%
D)	Not very satisfied	30%
E)	Not satisfied at all	0%

Q9: **In what ways could the parent company most improve? (Please check those that most apply, no more than three):**

❑ Communications
❑ Counsel/advice on administrative/management issues
❑ Effectiveness of marketing/promotions
❑ Evolution of products/services
❑ Frequency of marketing/promotional campaigns

❑ Quality of products/services
❑ Pricing of products/services to franchisees
❑ Technology (Point of sale systems, usage of computers/email/software, etc.)
❑ Training

Most frequent responses:	% answering
Communications (tie)	30%
Counsel/advice on administrative/management issues (tie)	30%
Frequency of marketing/promotional campaigns (tie)	30%
Pricing of products/services to franchisees (tie)	30%
Technology (tie)	30%
Training (tie)	30%

Q10: **Is your income more, less or about what you expected prior to opening your business?**

	% answering	
More	40%	
Less	40%	**Summary: 60% are making about what they**
About what was expected	20%	**expected, or more.**

Q11: **Prior to opening your franchise, which (if any) of the following did you underestimate?**

❑ Amount of working capital required for your 1st year in business
❑ Difficulty in hiring/retaining quality staff
❑ Expertise required to run the business
❑ Impact of marketing/promotions

❑ Start-up costs
❑ Degree of stress
❑ Workload

Most frequent responses:	% answering
Difficulty in hiring/retaining quality staff	70%
Degree of stress	60%
Amount of working capital required for 1st year in business (tie)	40%
Workload (tie)	40%

Q12: **If you could turn back time to the day you signed your franchise agreement, would you make the same decision to buy your franchise?**

	% answering
Yes	75%
No	25%

* Number of survey respondents: 10 from 10 different states
Number of survey respondents as a % of total franchise units: 10%

RESULTS! TRAVEL

www.resultstravel.com

Travel agency.

OVERALL SCORE: 88

701 Carlson Parkway
Minneapolis, MN 55305
Total number of outlets: 715
Total number of franchise outlets: 715
Franchise term: 1 year
International: No
Advertising/Marketing fee: none

OVERALL RANK: 10

Phone: 763-212-8587
Franchise fee: $1,500 for "conversion"agencies;
"conversion agencies", which are the only eligible
licensees of Results!, are those converting an
existing travel agency to Results! Fee is currently waived
Initial investment: $25 to $8,925
Royalty fee: none ($600 annual license fee; currently reduced)

SURVEY AND RESULTS *

Q1: About how many hours per week do you dedicate to your franchise business?

		% answering
A)	Less than 40	8%
B)	41–50	31%
C)	**51–60**	**46%**
D)	More than 60	8%
E)	Passive investment	8%

Q2: How would you describe your relations/ communications with your franchisor?

		% answering
A)	Excellent	31%
B)	**Good**	**38%**
C)	Adequate	23%
D)	Fair	0%
E)	Poor	8%

Q3: In terms of how your franchisor views your communications with other franchisees, it is:

		% answering
A)	**Very supportive**	**64%**
B)	Not very supportive	0%
C)	No influence	36%

Q4: Is the franchisor fair with you in resolving any grievances?

		% answering
A)	Extremely fair	33%
B)	**Pretty fair**	**56%**
C)	Reasonably fair	11%
D)	Not very fair	0%
E)	Not fair at all	0%

Q5: Are territories equitably granted?

		% answering
A)	Yes	33%
B)	No	0%
C)	**Not yet sure**	**67%**

Q6: How would you describe the initial and ongoing training provided by your franchisor?

		% answering
A)	**Excellent**	**50%**
B)	Good	33%
C)	Adequate	8%
D)	Fair	0%
E)	Poor	8%

Q7: How well does the franchisor anticipate future trends in how it evolves and markets products and services?

		% answering
A)	Extremely well	38%
B)	**Pretty well**	**46%**
C)	Adequately	8%
D)	Not very well	8%
E)	Terribly	0%

Q8: How satisfied are you with your franchisor's spending of the royalty fees you pay?

		% answering
A)	Extremely satisfied	8%
B)	**Mostly satisfied**	**75%**
C)	Somewhat satisfied	17%
D)	Not very satisfied	0%
E)	Not satisfied at all	0%

Q9: **In what ways could the parent company most improve? (Please check those that most apply, no more than three):**

❑ Communications

❑ Counsel/advice on administrative/management issues

❑ Effectiveness of marketing/promotions

❑ Evolution of products/services

❑ Frequency of marketing/promotional campaigns

❑ Quality of products/services

❑ Pricing of products/services to franchisees

❑ Technology (Point of sale systems, usage of computers/email/software, etc.)

❑ Training

Most frequent responses:	% answering
Training	38%
Evolution of products/services (tie)	23%
Frequency of marketing/promotional campaigns (tie)	23%
Pricing of products/services to franchisees (tie)	23%

Q10: **Is your income more, less or about what you expected prior to opening your business?**

	% answering	
More	**33%**	
Less	**33%**	**Summary: 66% are making about what they**
About what was expected	**33%**	**expected, or more.**

Q11: **Prior to opening your franchise, which (if any) of the following did you underestimate?**

❑ Amount of working capital required for your 1st year in business

❑ Difficulty in hiring/retaining quality staff

❑ Expertise required to run the business

❑ Impact of marketing/promotions

❑ Start-up costs

❑ Degree of stress

❑ Workload

Most frequent responses:	% answering
Difficulty in hiring/retaining quality staff	46%
Degree of stress (tie)	31%
Workload (tie)	31%

Q12: **If you could turn back time to the day you signed your franchise agreement, would you make the same decision to buy your franchise?**

	% answering
Yes	**100%**
No	0%

* Number of survey respondents: 13 from 13 different states

Number of survey respondents as a % of total franchise units: 1.82%

RITA'S

www.ritasice.com

Email: franchise_sales@ritascorp.com
Italian ices and other frozen desserts.

OVERALL SCORE: 85

1525 Ford Road, P.O. Box 1147
Bensalem, PA 19020
Fax: 215-633-9922
Total number of outlets: 330
Total number of franchise outlets:
International: No

OVERALL RANK: 14

Phone: 800-677-RITA
Franchise fee: $22,500 to $25,000
Franchise term:
Initial investment: $137,150 to $$259,400
Advertising/Marketing fee: 2.5%
Royalty fee:6.5% of gross sales

SURVEY AND RESULTS *

Q1: About how many hours per week do you dedicate to your franchise business?

		% answering
A)	Less than 40	6%
B)	41–50	25%
C)	51–60	19%
D)	**More than 60**	**44%**
E)	Passive investment	6%

Q2: How would you describe your relations/ communications with your franchisor?

		% answering
A)	**Excellent**	**41%**
B)	**Good**	**41%**
C)	Adequate	12%
D)	Fair	6%
E)	Poor	0%

Q3: In terms of how your franchisor views your communications with other franchisees, it is:

		% answering
A)	**Very supportive**	**53%**
B)	Not very supportive	12%
C)	No influence	35%

Q4: Is the franchisor fair with you in resolving any grievances?

		% answering
A)	Extremely fair	35%
B)	Pretty fair	24%
C)	**Reasonably fair**	**41%**
D)	Not very fair	0%
E)	Not fair at all	0%

Q5: Are territories equitably granted?

		% answering
A)	**Yes**	**63%**
B)	No	19%
C)	Not yet sure	19%

Q6: How would you describe the initial and ongoing training provided by your franchisor?

		% answering
A)	**Excellent**	**47%**
B)	Good	29%
C)	Adequate	24%
D)	Fair	0%
E)	Poor	0%

Q7: How well does the franchisor anticipate future trends in how it evolves and markets products and services?

		% answering
A)	**Extremely well**	**53%**
B)	Pretty well	29%
C)	Adequately	12%
D)	Not very well	6%
E)	Terribly	0%

Q8: How satisfied are you with your franchisor's spending of the royalty fees you pay?

		% answering
A)	Extremely satisfied	13%
B)	Mostly satisfied	38%
C)	**Somewhat satisfied**	**44%**
D)	Not very satisfied	6%
E)	Not satisfied at all	0%

Q9: **In what ways could the parent company most improve? (Please check those that most apply, no more than three):**

❑ Communications
❑ Counsel/advice on administrative/management issues
❑ Effectiveness of marketing/promotions
❑ Evolution of products/services
❑ Frequency of marketing/promotional campaigns

❑ Quality of products/services
❑ Pricing of products/services to franchisees
❑ Technology (Point of sale systems, usage of computers/email/software, etc.)
❑ Training

Most frequent responses:

	% answering
Counsel/advice on administrative/management issues	41%
Evolution of products/services	29%
Frequency of marketing/promotional campaigns (tie)	24%
Pricing of products/services to franchisees (tie)	24%

Q10: **Is your income more, less or about what you expected prior to opening your business?**

	% answering	
More	20%	
Less	33%	**Summary: 67% are making about what they**
About what was expected	**47%**	**expected, or more.**

Q11: **Prior to opening your franchise, which (if any) of the following did you underestimate?**

❑ Amount of working capital required for your 1st year in business
❑ Difficulty in hiring/retaining quality staff
❑ Expertise required to run the business
❑ Impact of marketing/promotions

❑ Start-up costs
❑ Degree of stress
❑ Workload

Most frequent responses:

	% answering
Start-up costs	35%
Amount of working capital required for your 1st year in business (tie)	29%
Workload (tie)	29%

Q12: **If you could turn back time to the day you signed your franchise agreement, would you make the same decision to buy your franchise?**

	% answering
Yes	**100%**
No	0%

* Number of survey respondents: 17 from 3 different states
Number of survey respondents as a % of total franchise units:

ROCKY MOUNTAIN CHOCOLATE FACTORY

www.rmcf.com

Gourmet chocolate and other premium confectionery products.

OVERALL SCORE: 62

265 Turner Drive
Durango, CO 81303
Fax: 970-259-5895
Total number of outlets: 284
Total number of franchise outlets: 276
International: Yes (Abu Dhabi, Canada, Guam)

OVERALL RANK: 122

Phone: 800-438-7623
Franchise fee: $24,500
Franchise term: 10 years
Initial investment: $88,500 to $447,686
Advertising/Marketing fee: 1% of gross retail sales
Royalty fee: 5% of gross retail sales

SURVEY AND RESULTS *

Q1: About how many hours per week do you dedicate to your franchise business?

		% answering
A)	Less than 40	23%
B)	**41–50**	**31%**
C)	51–60	15%
D)	**More than 60**	**31%**
E)	Passive investment	0%

Q2: How would you describe your relations/ communications with your franchisor?

		% answering
A)	Excellent	23%
B)	**Good**	**54%**
C)	Adequate	8%
D)	Fair	8%
E)	Poor	8%

Q3: In terms of how your franchisor views your communications with other franchisees, it is:

		% answering
A)	**Very supportive**	**38%**
B)	Not very supportive	23%
C)	**No influence**	**38%**

Q4: Is the franchisor fair with you in resolving any grievances?

		% answering
A)	Extremely fair	33%
B)	Pretty fair	17%
C)	**Reasonably fair**	**33%**
D)	Not very fair	8%
E)	Not fair at all	8%

Q5: Are territories equitably granted?

		% answering
A)	**Yes**	**46%**
B)	No	15%
C)	Not yet sure	38%

Q6: How would you describe the initial and ongoing training provided by your franchisor?

		% answering
A)	**Excellent**	**46%**
B)	Good	23%
C)	Adequate	23%
D)	Fair	0%
E)	Poor	8%

Q7: How well does the franchisor anticipate future trends in how it evolves and markets products and services?

		% answering
A)	Extremely well	17%
B)	**Pretty well**	**42%**
C)	Adequately	33%
D)	Not very well	0%
E)	Terribly	8%

Q8: How satisfied are you with your franchisor's spending of the royalty fees you pay?

		% answering
A)	Extremely satisfied	17%
B)	**Mostly satisfied**	**25%**
C)	**Somewhat satisfied**	**25%**
D)	**Not very satisfied**	**25%**
E)	Not satisfied at all	8%

Q9: In what ways could the parent company most improve? (Please check those that most apply, no more than three):

- ❏ Communications
- ❏ Counsel/advice on administrative/management issues
- ❏ Effectiveness of marketing/promotions
- ❏ Evolution of products/services
- ❏ Frequency of marketing/promotional campaigns

- ❏ Quality of products/services
- ❏ Pricing of products/services to franchisees
- ❏ Technology (Point of sale systems, usage of computers/email/software, etc.)
- ❏ Training

Most frequent responses:	% answering
Effectiveness of marketing/promotions	69%
Frequency of marketing/promotional campaigns	62%
Counsel/advice on administrative/management issues (tie)	31%
Pricing of products/services to franchisees (tie)	31%

Q10: Is your income more, less or about what you expected prior to opening your business?

	% answering	
More	0%
Less	54%	Summary: 46% are making about what they
About what was expected	46%	expected, or more.

Q11: Prior to opening your franchise, which (if any) of the following did you underestimate?

- ❏ Amount of working capital required for your 1st year in business
- ❏ Difficulty in hiring/retaining quality staff
- ❏ Expertise required to run the business
- ❏ Impact of marketing/promotions

- ❏ Start-up costs
- ❏ Degree of stress
- ❏ Workload

Most frequent responses:	% answering
Degree of stress	62%
Workload	54%
Difficulty in hiring/retaining quality staff	38%

Q12: If you could turn back time to the day you signed your franchise agreement, would you make the same decision to buy your franchise?

	% answering
Yes	62%
No	38%

* Number of survey respondents: 13 from 13 different states
  Number of survey respondents as a % of total franchise units: 4.70%

ROTO ROOTER

www.rotorooter.com
Email: franchising@rotorootercorp.com

Plumbing and drain cleaning services.

OVERALL SCORE: 78

300 Ashworth Road
West Des Moines, IA 50265
Fax: 515-223-6109
Total number of outlets: 600+
Total number of franchise outlets: 500+
International: Yes (worldwide)

OVERALL RANK: 40

Phone: 515-213-1343, ext. 1920
Franchise fee:
Franchise term: 10 years
Initial investment
Advertising/Marketing fee:
Royalty fee:

SURVEY AND RESULTS *

Q1: About how many hours per week do you dedicate to your franchise business?

		% answering
A)	Less than 40	12%
B)	41–50	24%
C)	51–60	29%
D)	**More than 60**	**35%**
E)	Passive investment	0%

Q2: How would you describe your relations/communications with your franchisor?

		% answering
A)	Excellent	24%
B)	**Good**	**35%**
C)	Adequate	29%
D)	Fair	12%
E)	Poor	0%

Q3: In terms of how your franchisor views your communications with other franchisees, it is:

		% answering
A)	Very supportive	35%
B)	Not very supportive	24%
C)	**No influence**	**41%**

Q4: Is the franchisor fair with you in resolving any grievances?

		% answering
A)	Extremely fair	21%
B)	**Pretty fair**	**43%**
C)	Reasonably fair	36%
D)	Not very fair	0%
E)	Not fair at all	0%

Q5: Are territories equitably granted?

		% answering
A)	**Yes**	**82%**
B)	No	6%
C)	Not yet sure	12%

Q6: How would you describe the initial and ongoing training provided by your franchisor?

		% answering
A)	Excellent	7%
B)	Good	20%
C)	**Adequate**	**33%**
D)	Fair	7%
E)	**Poor**	**33%**

Q7: How well does the franchisor anticipate future trends in how it evolves and markets products and services?

		% answering
A)	Extremely well	13%
B)	**Pretty well**	**44%**
C)	Adequately	31%
D)	Not very well	9%
E)	Terribly	3%

Q8: How satisfied are you with your franchisor's spending of the royalty fees you pay?

		% answering
A)	Extremely satisfied	13%
B)	**Mostly satisfied**	**33%**
C)	**Somewhat satisfied**	**33%**
D)	Not very satisfied	13%
E)	Not satisfied at all	7%

Q9:   In what ways could the parent company most improve? (Please check those that most apply, no more than three):

❏ Communications
❏ Counsel/advice on administrative/management issues
❏ Effectiveness of marketing/promotions
❏ Evolution of products/services
❏ Frequency of marketing/promotional campaigns

❏ Quality of products/services
❏ Pricing of products/services to franchisees
❏ Technology (Point of sale systems, usage of computers/email/software, etc.)
❏ Training

Most frequent responses:	% answering
Pricing of products/services to franchisees	41%
Effectiveness of marketing/promotions (tie)	35%
Frequency of marketing/promotional campaigns (tie)	35%

Q10: Is your income more, less or about what you expected prior to opening your business?

	% answering	
More	31%	
Less	25%	**Summary: 75% are making about what they**
About what was expected	**44%**	**expected, or more.**

Q11: Prior to opening your franchise, which (if any) of the following did you underestimate?

❏ Amount of working capital required for your 1st year in business
❏ Difficulty in hiring/retaining quality staff
❏ Expertise required to run the business
❏ Impact of marketing/promotions

❏ Start-up costs
❏ Degree of stress
❏ Workload

Most frequent responses:	% answering
Difficulty in hiring/retaining quality staff	65%
Degree of stress (tie)	35%
Workload (tie)	35%

Q12: If you could turn back time to the day you signed your franchise agreement, would you make the same decision to buy your franchise?

	% answering
Yes	**94%**
No	6%

*   Number of survey respondents: 17 from 14 different states
    Number of survey respondents as a % of total franchise units: 3.4%

SANDLER SALES INSTITUTE

www.sandler.com
Email: info@sandler.com

Sales and sales management training to individuals and businesses.

OVERALL SCORE: 71

10411 Stevenson Road
Stevenson, MD 21153
Fax: 410-358-7858
Total number of outlets: 157
Total number of franchise outlets: 157
International: Yes (Canada)

OVERALL RANK: 78

Phone: 800-669-3537, ext. 2033 (Ron Taylor)
Franchise fee: $50,000
Franchise term: 5 years
Initial investment: $56,450 to $73,250
Advertising/Marketing fee: none
Royalty fee: $1,160 monthly service charge

SURVEY AND RESULTS *

Q1: About how many hours per week do you dedicate to your franchise business?

		% answering
A)	Less than 40	14%
B)	**41–50**	**38%**
C)	51–60	33%
D)	More than 60	14%
E)	Passive investment	0%

Q2: How would you describe your relations/ communications with your franchisor?

		% answering
A)	Excellent	24%
B)	**Good**	**38%**
C)	Adequate	19%
D)	Fair	19%
E)	Poor	0%

Q3: In terms of how your franchisor views your communications with other franchisees, it is:

		% answering
A)	**Very supportive**	**62%**
B)	Not very supportive	5%
C)	No influence	33%

Q4: Is the franchisor fair with you in resolving any grievances?

		% answering
A)	Extremely fair	30%
B)	**Pretty fair**	**35%**
C)	Reasonably fair	28%
D)	Not very fair	3%
E)	Not fair at all	5%

Q5: Are territories equitably granted?

		% answering
A)	**Yes**	**60%**
B)	No	25%
C)	Not yet sure	15%

Q6: How would you describe the initial and ongoing training provided by your franchisor?

		% answering
A)	**Excellent**	**36%**
B)	Good	14%
C)	Adequate	19%
D)	Fair	17%
E)	Poor	14%

Q7: How well does the franchisor anticipate future trends in how it evolves and markets products and services?

		% answering
A)	Extremely well	10%
B)	Pretty well	14%
C)	**Adequately**	**38%**
D)	**Not very well**	**38%**
E)	Terribly	0%

Q8: How satisfied are you with your franchisor's spending of the royalty fees you pay?

		% answering
A)	Extremely satisfied	11%
B)	Mostly satisfied	21%
C)	**Somewhat satisfied**	**42%**
D)	Not very satisfied	16%
E)	Not satisfied at all	11%

Q9: **In what ways could the parent company most improve? (Please check those that most apply, no more than three):**

❑ Communications
❑ Counsel/advice on administrative/management issues
❑ Effectiveness of marketing/promotions
❑ Evolution of products/services
❑ Frequency of marketing/promotional campaigns

❑ Quality of products/services
❑ Pricing of products/services to franchisees
❑ Technology (Point of sale systems, usage of computers/email/software, etc.)
❑ Training

Most frequent responses: % answering
Effectiveness of marketing/promotions   67%
Evolution of products/services   52%
Counsel/advice on administrative/management issues   38%

Q10: Is your income more, less or about what you expected prior to opening your business?

	% answering
More	24%
Less	**38%**
About what was expected	**38%**

Summary: 62% are making about what they expected, or more.

Q11: Prior to opening your franchise, which (if any) of the following did you underestimate?

❑ Amount of working capital required for your 1st year in business
❑ Difficulty in hiring/retaining quality staff
❑ Expertise required to run the business
❑ Impact of marketing/promotions

❑ Start-up costs
❑ Degree of stress
❑ Workload

Most frequent responses: % answering
Impact of marketing/promotions   48%
Amount of working capital required for your 1st year in business   43%
Degree of stress (tie)   33%
Workload (tie)   33%

Q12: If you could turn back time to the day you signed your franchise agreement, would you make the same decision to buy your franchise?

	% answering
Yes	**81%**
No	19%

* Number of survey respondents: 21 from 16 different states
Number of survey respondents as a % of total franchise units: 13.38%

SERVICEMASTER CLEAN

www.servicemaster.com

Residential and commercial cleaning and disaster restoration services.

OVERALL SCORE: 83

3250 Lacey Road, Suite 600
Downers Grove, IL 60515
Fax: 630-663-2001
Total number of outlets: 4,500+
Total number of franchise outlets: 4,500+
International: Yes (worldwide)

OVERALL RANK: 24

Phone: 800-255-9687
Franchise fee:
Franchise term:
Initial investment: $20,283 to $84,525
Advertising/Marketing fee:
Royalty fee:

SURVEY AND RESULTS *

Q1: About how many hours per week do you dedicate to your franchise business?

		% answering
A)	Less than 40	0%
B)	41–50	23%
C)	**51–60**	**46%**
D)	More than 60	15%
E)	Passive investment	15%

Q2: How would you describe your relations/communications with your franchisor?

		% answering
A)	Excellent	31%
B)	**Good**	**46%**
C)	Adequate	8%
D)	Fair	15%
E)	Poor	0%

Q3: In terms of how your franchisor views your communications with other franchisees, it is:

		% answering
A)	**Very supportive**	**85%**
B)	Not very supportive	15%
C)	No influence	0%

Q4: Is the franchisor fair with you in resolving any grievances?

		% answering
A)	**Extremely fair**	**38%**
B)	**Pretty fair**	**38%**
C)	Reasonably fair	15%
D)	Not very fair	8%
E)	Not fair at all	0%

Q5: Are territories equitably granted?

		% answering
A)	**Yes**	**67%**
B)	No	17%
C)	Not yet sure	17%

Q6: How would you describe the initial and ongoing training provided by your franchisor?

		% answering
A)	Excellent	15%
B)	**Good**	**46%**
C)	Adequate	38%
D)	Fair	0%
E)	Poor	0%

Q7: How well does the franchisor anticipate future trends in how it evolves and markets products and services?

		% answering
A)	**Extremely well**	**46%**
B)	Pretty well	31%
C)	Adequately	15%
D)	Not very well	8%
E)	Terribly	0%

Q8: How satisfied are you with your franchisor's spending of the royalty fees you pay?

		% answering
A)	Extremely satisfied	0%
B)	**Mostly satisfied**	**54%**
C)	Somewhat satisfied	46%
D)	Not very satisfied	0%
E)	Not satisfied at all	0%

Q9: **In what ways could the parent company most improve? (Please check those that most apply, no more than three):**

❏ Communications
❏ Counsel/advice on administrative/management issues
❏ Effectiveness of marketing/promotions
❏ Evolution of products/services
❏ Frequency of marketing/promotional campaigns

❏ Quality of products/services
❏ Pricing of products/services to franchisees
❏ Technology (Point of sale systems, usage of computers/email/software, etc.)
❏ Training

Most frequent responses:	% answering
Effectiveness of marketing/promotions	54%
Training Training	38%
Frequency of marketing/promotional campaigns (tie)	31%
Pricing of products/services to franchisees (tie)	31%

Q10: **Is your income more, less or about what you expected prior to opening your business?**

	% answering	
More	31%	
Less	15%	**Summary: 85% are making about what they**
About what was expected	**54%**	**expected, or more.**

Q11: **Prior to opening your franchise, which (if any) of the following did you underestimate?**

❏ Amount of working capital required for your 1st year in business
❏ Difficulty in hiring/retaining quality staff
❏ Expertise required to run the business
❏ Impact of marketing/promotions

❏ Start-up costs
❏ Degree of stress
❏ Workload

Most frequent responses:	% answering
Difficulty in hiring/retaining quality staff	62%
Degree of stress	46%
Impact of marketing/promotions	38%

Q12: **If you could turn back time to the day you signed your franchise agreement, would you make the same decision to buy your franchise?**

	% answering
Yes	**86%**
No	14%

*   Number of survey respondents: 13 from 11 different states
Number of survey respondents as a % of total franchise units: < 1%

SERVPRO

www.servpro.com
Email: jvaughn@servpronet.com

Fire and water clean up and restoration services.

OVERALL SCORE: 61

575 Airport Road
Gallatin, TN 37066
Fax: 615-451-1602
Total number of outlets: 1,250+
Total number of franchise outlets: 1,250+
International: No

OVERALL RANK: 132

Phone: 800-826-9586
Franchise fee:
Franchise term:
Initial investment:
Advertising/Marketing fee:
Royalty fee:

SURVEY AND RESULTS *

Q1: About how many hours per week do you dedicate to your franchise business?

		% answering
A)	Less than 40	0%
B)	41–50	0%
C)	51–60	46%
D)	**More than 60**	**54%**
E)	Passive investment	0%

Q2: How would you describe your relations/communications with your franchisor?

		% answering
A)	Excellent	15%
B)	**Good**	**46%**
C)	Adequate	31%
D)	Fair	0%
E)	Poor	8%

Q3: In terms of how your franchisor views your communications with other franchisees, it is:

		% answering
A)	**Very supportive**	**62%**
B)	Not very supportive	8%
C)	No influence	31%

Q4: Is the franchisor fair with you in resolving any grievances?

		% answering
A)	Extremely fair	8%
B)	**Pretty fair**	**46%**
C)	Reasonably fair	38%
D)	Not very fair	0%
E)	Not fair at all	8%

Q5: Are territories equitably granted?

		% answering
A)	**Yes**	**46%**
B)	No	31%
C)	Not yet sure	23%

Q6: How would you describe the initial and ongoing training provided by your franchisor?

		% answering
A)	Excellent	23%
B)	**Good**	**54%**
C)	Adequate	15%
D)	Fair	8%
E)	Poor	0%

Q7: How well does the franchisor anticipate future trends in how it evolves and markets products and services?

		% answering
A)	**Extremely well**	**46%**
B)	Pretty well	31%
C)	Adequately	15%
D)	Not very well	0%
E)	Terribly	8%

Q8: How satisfied are you with your franchisor's spending of the royalty fees you pay?

		% answering
A)	Extremely satisfied	8%
B)	Mostly satisfied	23%
C)	**Somewhat satisfied**	**46%**
D)	Not very satisfied	15%
E)	Not satisfied at all	8%

Q9: **In what ways could the parent company most improve? (Please check those that most apply, no more than three):**

❑ Communications

❑ Counsel/advice on administrative/management issues

❑ Effectiveness of marketing/promotions

❑ Evolution of products/services

❑ Frequency of marketing/promotional campaigns

❑ Quality of products/services

❑ Pricing of products/services to franchisees

❑ Technology (Point of sale systems, usage of computers/email/software, etc.)

❑ Training

Most frequent responses:

	% answering
Effectiveness of marketing/promotions	54%
Counsel/advice on administrative/management issues	36%
Pricing of products/services to franchisees	38%

Q10: **Is your income more, less or about what you expected prior to opening your business?**

	% answering	
More	38%	
Less	**46%**	**Summary: 53% are making about what they**
About what was expected	15%	**expected, or more.**

Q11: **Prior to opening your franchise, which (if any) of the following did you underestimate?**

❑ Amount of working capital required for your 1st year in business

❑ Difficulty in hiring/retaining quality staff

❑ Expertise required to run the business

❑ Impact of marketing/promotions

❑ Start-up costs

❑ Degree of stress

❑ Workload

Most frequent responses:

	% answering
Degree of stress	62%
Difficulty in hiring/retaining quality staff	54%
Amount of working capital required for 1st year in business	46%

Q12: **If you could turn back time to the day you signed your franchise agreement, would you make the same decision to buy your franchise?**

	% answering
Yes	**77%**
No	23%

* Number of survey respondents: 13 from 11 different states

Number of survey respondents as a % of total franchise units: 1.04%

SIGN-A-RAMA

www.sign-a-rama.com
Email: signinfo@signarama.com

Full-service sign business.

OVERALL SCORE: 63

1801 South Australian Avenue
West Palm Beach, FL 33409
Fax: 561-640-5580
Total number of outlets: 700+
Total number of franchise outlets: 700+
International: Yes (Worldwide)

OVERALL RANK: 119

Phone: 561-640-5570
Franchise fee: $39,500
Franchise term: 35 years
Initial investment: $50,260 to $198,158
Advertising/Marketing fee: none
Royalty fee: 6% of gross sales monthly

SURVEY AND RESULTS *

Q1: About how many hours per week do you dedicate to your franchise business?

		% answering
A)	Less than 40	0%
B)	41–50	14%
C)	**51–60**	**57%**
D)	More than 60	29%
E)	Passive investment	0%

Q2: How would you describe your relations/ communications with your franchisor?

		% answering
A)	**Excellent**	**36%**
B)	Good	29%
C)	Adequate	21%
D)	Fair	0%
E)	Poor	14%

Q3: In terms of how your franchisor views your communications with other franchisees, it is:

		% answering
A)	**Very supportive**	**64%**
B)	Not very supportive	14%
C)	No influence	21%

Q4: Is the franchisor fair with you in resolving any grievances?

		% answering
A)	**Extremely fair**	**42%**
B)	Pretty fair	17%
C)	**Reasonably fair**	**42%**
D)	Not very fair	0%
E)	Not fair at all	0%

Q5: Are territories equitably granted?

		% answering
A)	**Yes**	**42%**
B)	No	33%
C)	Not yet sure	25%

Q6: How would you describe the initial and ongoing training provided by your franchisor?

		% answering
A)	Excellent	18%
B)	**Good**	**50%**
C)	Adequate	21%
D)	Fair	7%
E)	Poor	4%

Q7: How well does the franchisor anticipate future trends in how it evolves and markets products and services?

		% answering
A)	Extremely well	14%
B)	**Pretty well**	**43%**
C)	Adequately	29%
D)	Not very well	14%
E)	Terribly	0%

Q8: How satisfied are you with your franchisor's spending of the royalty fees you pay?

		% answering
A)	Extremely satisfied	8%
B)	**Mostly satisfied**	**38%**
C)	Somewhat satisfied	31%
D)	Not very satisfied	23%
E)	Not satisfied at all	0%

Q9: **In what ways could the parent company most improve? (Please check those that most apply, no more than three):**

❑ Communications

❑ Counsel/advice on administrative/management issues

❑ Effectiveness of marketing/promotions

❑ Evolution of products/services

❑ Frequency of marketing/promotional campaigns

❑ Quality of products/services

❑ Pricing of products/services to franchisees

❑ Technology (Point of sale systems, usage of computers/email/software, etc.)

❑ Training

Most frequent responses:

	% answering
Counsel/advice on administrative/management issues	50%
Pricing of products/services to franchisees	43%
Effectiveness of marketing/promotions (tie)	36%
Training (tie)	36%

Q10: **Is your income more, less or about what you expected prior to opening your business?**

	% answering	
More	14%	
Less	**64%**	**Summary: 35% are making about what they**
About what was expected	21%	**expected, or more.**

Q11: **Prior to opening your franchise, which (if any) of the following did you underestimate?**

❑ Amount of working capital required for your 1st year in business

❑ Difficulty in hiring/retaining quality staff

❑ Expertise required to run the business

❑ Impact of marketing/promotions

❑ Start-up costs

❑ Degree of stress

❑ Workload

Most frequent responses:

	% answering
Difficulty in hiring/retaining quality staff	71%
Amount of working capital required for your 1st year in business	64%
Start-up costs	50%

Q12: **If you could turn back time to the day you signed your franchise agreement, would you make the same decision to buy your franchise?**

	% answering
Yes	**69%**
No	31%

* Number of survey respondents: 14 from 13 different states

Number of survey respondents as a % of total franchise units: 2%

SIGNS BY TOMORROW

www.signsbytomorrow.com
Email: sales@signsbytomorrow.com (Marty Rockenstire)

Computer-generated signs and graphics.

OVERALL SCORE: 62

OVERALL RANK: 125

6460 Dobbin Road
Columbia, MD 21045
Fax: 410-992-7675
Total number of outlets: 152
Total number of franchise outlets: 150
International: No
Royalty fee: 6% of monthly store-produced
product sales, 3% of sub-contracted sales
(payment not to exceed $3,000 per month)

Phone: 800-765-7446
Franchise fee: $28,500
Franchise term: 20 years
Initial investment: $117,000 to $193,500
Advertising/Marketing fee: 1% of monthly net
royalty sales

SURVEY AND RESULTS *

Q1: About how many hours per week do you dedicate to your franchise business?

		% answering
A)	Less than 40	0%
B)	41–50	13%
C)	**51–60**	**60%**
D)	More than 60	27%
E)	Passive investment	0%

Q2: How would you describe your relations/communications with your franchisor?

		% answering
A)	Excellent	27%
B)	**Good**	**33%**
C)	Adequate	7%
D)	Fair	20%
E)	Poor	13%

Q3: In terms of how your franchisor views your communications with other franchisees, it is:

		% answering
A)	**Very supportive**	**77%**
B)	Not very supportive	8%
C)	No influence	15%

Q4: Is the franchisor fair with you in resolving any grievances?

		% answering
A)	Extremely fair	21%
B)	Pretty fair	14%
C)	**Reasonably fair**	**36%**
D)	Not very fair	21%
E)	Not fair at all	7%

Q5: Are territories equitably granted?

		% answering
A)	**Yes**	**46%**
B)	No	15%
C)	Not yet sure	38%

Q6: How would you describe the initial and ongoing training provided by your franchisor?

		% answering
A)	**Excellent**	**27%**
B)	**Good**	**27%**
C)	**Adequate**	**27%**
D)	Fair	13%
E)	Poor	7%

Q7: How well does the franchisor anticipate future trends in how it evolves and markets products and services?

		% answering
A)	**Extremely well**	**29%**
B)	Pretty well	21%
C)	Adequately	21%
D)	Not very well	21%
E)	Terribly	7%

Q8: How satisfied are you with your franchisor's spending of the royalty fees you pay?

		% answering
A)	Extremely satisfied	7%
B)	**Mostly satisfied**	**40%**
C)	Somewhat satisfied	27%
D)	Not very satisfied	13%
E)	Not satisfied at all	13%

Q9: In what ways could the parent company most improve? (Please check those that most apply, no more than three):

- ❑ Communications
- ❑ Counsel/advice on administrative/management issues
- ❑ Effectiveness of marketing/promotions
- ❑ Evolution of products/services
- ❑ Frequency of marketing/promotional campaigns

- ❑ Quality of products/services
- ❑ Pricing of products/services to franchisees
- ❑ Technology (Point of sale systems, usage of computers/email/software, etc.)
- ❑ Training

Most frequent responses:

	% answering
Communications	47%
Effectiveness of marketing/promotions (tie)	40%
Frequency of marketing/promotional campaigns (tie)	40%

Q10: Is your income more, less or about what you expected prior to opening your business?

	% answering	
More	0%	
Less	**57%**	**Summary: 57% are making about what they**
About what was expected	43%	**expected, or more.**

Q11: Prior to opening your franchise, which (if any) of the following did you underestimate?

- ❑ Amount of working capital required for your 1st year in business
- ❑ Difficulty in hiring/retaining quality staff
- ❑ Expertise required to run the business
- ❑ Impact of marketing/promotions

- ❑ Start-up costs
- ❑ Degree of stress
- ❑ Workload

Most frequent responses:

	% answering
Amount of working capital required for your 1st year in business	53%
Degree of stress (tie)	47%
Workload (tie)	47%

Q12: If you could turn back time to the day you signed your franchise agreement, would you make the same decision to buy your franchise?

	% answering
Yes	**67%**
No	33%

* Number of survey respondents: 15 from 12 different states
Number of survey respondents as a % of total franchise units: 10%

SIGNS NOW

www.signsnow.com

Full-service sign business.

OVERALL SCORE: 57

4900 Manatee Avenue West, Suite 201
Bradenton, FL 34209
Total number of outlets: 247 (217 in U.S.)
Total number of franchise outlets: 245
International: Yes (several countries
Advertising/Marketing fee: 2% of gross sales) monthly

OVERALL RANK: 153

Phone: 800-356-3373
Franchise fee: $25,000
Franchise term: 20 years
Initial investment: $139,525 to $362,775
Royalty fee: 5% of gross sales monthly

SURVEY AND RESULTS *

Q1: About how many hours per week do you dedicate to your franchise business?

		% answering
A)	Less than 40	8%
B)	**41–50**	**38%**
C)	**51–60**	**38%**
D)	More than 60	15%
E)	Passive investment	0%

Q2: How would you describe your relations/ communications with your franchisor?

		% answering
A)	Excellent	0%
B)	**Good**	**36%**
C)	Adequate	29%
D)	Fair	21%
E)	Poor	14%

Q3: In terms of how your franchisor views your communications with other franchisees, it is:

		% answering
A)	**Very supportive**	**50%**
B)	Not very supportive	7%
C)	No influence	43%

Q4: Is the franchisor fair with you in resolving any grievances?

		% answering
A)	Extremely fair	8%
B)	**Pretty fair**	**46%**
C)	Reasonably fair	31%
D)	Not very fair	0%
E)	Not fair at all	15%

Q5: Are territories equitably granted?

		% answering
A)	**Yes**	**50%**
B)	No	7%
C)	Not yet sure	43%

Q6: How would you describe the initial and ongoing training provided by your franchisor?

		% answering
A)	Excellent	14%
B)	**Good**	**36%**
C)	Adequate	14%
D)	Fair	14%
E)	Poor	21%

Q7: How well does the franchisor anticipate future trends in how it evolves and markets products and services?

		% answering
A)	Extremely well	0%
B)	**Pretty well**	**43%**
C)	Adequately	29%
D)	Not very well	21%
E)	Terribly	7%

Q8: How satisfied are you with your franchisor's spending of the royalty fees you pay?

		% answering
A)	Extremely satisfied	0%
B)	Mostly satisfied	29%
C)	Somewhat satisfied	14%
D)	**Not very satisfied**	**36%**
E)	Not satisfied at all	21%

Q9: **In what ways could the parent company most improve? (Please check those that most apply, no more than three):**

❑ Communications

❑ Counsel/advice on administrative/management issues

❑ Effectiveness of marketing/promotions

❑ Evolution of products/services

❑ Frequency of marketing/promotional campaigns

❑ Quality of products/services

❑ Pricing of products/services to franchisees

❑ Technology (Point of sale systems, usage of computers/email/software, etc.)

❑ Training

Most frequent responses:

	% answering
Effectiveness of marketing/promotions	71%
Counsel/advice on administrative/management issues (tie)	29%
Pricing of products/services to franchisees (tie)	29%
Training (tie)	29%

Q10: **Is your income more, less or about what you expected prior to opening your business?**

	% answering	
More	14%	
Less	**64%**	**Summary: 35% are making about what they**
About what was expected	21%	**expected, or more.**

Q11: **Prior to opening your franchise, which (if any) of the following did you underestimate?**

❑ Amount of working capital required for your 1st year in business

❑ Difficulty in hiring/retaining quality staff

❑ Expertise required to run the business

❑ Impact of marketing/promotions

❑ Start-up costs

❑ Degree of stress

❑ Workload

Most frequent responses:

	% answering
Degree of stress	50%
Difficulty in hiring/retaining quality staff (tie)	43%
Expertise required to run the business (tie)	43%

Q12: **If you could turn back time to the day you signed your franchise agreement, would you make the same decision to buy your franchise?**

	% answering
Yes	**71%**
No	29%

* Number of survey respondents: 14 from 12 different states

Number of survey respondents as a % of total franchise units: 5.71%

SIR SPEEDY

www.sirspeedy.com
Email: marketing@sirspeedy.com

Full-service printer, copier, and document manager.

OVERALL SCORE: 65

26722 Plaza Drive, P.O. Box 9077
Mission Viejo, CA 92690
Fax: 949-348-5066
Total number of outlets: over 1,000
Total number of franchise outlets: over 1,000
International: Yes (worldwide)

OVERALL RANK: 108

Phone: 800-747-7733
Franchise fee: $25,000
Franchise term: 20 years
Initial investment: $188,000 to $478,000
Advertising: 1% of gross sales for 1st 12 months,
2% of gross sales thereafter, payable weekly
Royalty fee: 4% of gross sales for 1st 12 months,
6% of gross sales thereafter, payable weekly

SURVEY AND RESULTS *

Q1: About how many hours per week do you dedicate to your franchise business?

		% answering
A)	Less than 40	0%
B)	41–50	31%
C)	**51–60**	**38%**
D)	More than 60	23%
E)	Passive investment	8%

Q2: How would you describe your relations/communications with your franchisor?

		% answering
A)	**Excellent**	**46%**
B)	Good	0%
C)	Adequate	23%
D)	Fair	15%
E)	Poor	15%

Q3: In terms of how your franchisor views your communications with other franchisees, it is:

		% answering
A)	**Very supportive**	**62%**
B)	Not very supportive	8%
C)	No influence	31%

Q4: Is the franchisor fair with you in resolving any grievances?

		% answering
A)	**Extremely fair**	**42%**
B)	Pretty fair	8%
C)	Reasonably fair	33%
D)	Not very fair	8%
E)	Not fair at all	8%

Q5: Are territories equitably granted?

		% answering
A)	**Yes**	**77%**
B)	No	15%
C)	Not yet sure	8%

Q6: How would you describe the initial and ongoing training provided by your franchisor?

		% answering
A)	**Excellent**	**54%**
B)	Good	8%
C)	Adequate	8%
D)	Fair	23%
E)	Poor	8%

Q7: How well does the franchisor anticipate future trends in how it evolves and markets products and services?

		% answering
A)	**Extremely well**	**62%**
B)	Pretty well	15%
C)	Adequately	8%
D)	Not very well	8%
E)	Terribly	8%

Q8: How satisfied are you with your franchisor's spending of the royalty fees you pay?

		% answering
A)	**Extremely satisfied**	**38%**
B)	Mostly satisfied	23%
C)	Somewhat satisfied	8%
D)	Not very satisfied	23%
E)	Not satisfied at all	8%

Q9: **In what ways could the parent company most improve? (Please check those that most apply, no more than three):**

❑ Communications

❑ Counsel/advice on administrative/management issues

❑ Effectiveness of marketing/promotions

❑ Evolution of products/services

❑ Frequency of marketing/promotional campaigns

❑ Quality of products/services

❑ Pricing of products/services to franchisees

❑ Technology (Point of sale systems, usage of computers/email/software, etc.)

❑ Training

Most frequent responses:

	% answering
Counsel/advice on administrative/management issues (tie)	38%
Effectiveness of marketing/promotions (tie)	38%
Communications (tie)	23%
Pricing of products/services to franchisees (tie)	23%

Q10: **Is your income more, less or about what you expected prior to opening your business?**

	% answering	
More	23%	
Less	**62%**	**Summary: 38% are making about what they**
About what was expected	15%	**expected, or more.**

Q11: **Prior to opening your franchise, which (if any) of the following did you underestimate?**

❑ Amount of working capital required for your 1st year in business

❑ Difficulty in hiring/retaining quality staff

❑ Expertise required to run the business

❑ Impact of marketing/promotions

❑ Start-up costs

❑ Degree of stress

❑ Workload

Most frequent responses:

	% answering
Workload	46%
Difficulty in hiring/retaining quality staff	38%
Amount of working capital required for 1st year in business (tie)	31%
Expertise required to run the business (tie)	31%
Start-up costs (tie)	31%
Degree of stress (tie)	31%

Q12: **If you could turn back time to the day you signed your franchise agreement, would you make the same decision to buy your franchise?**

	% answering
Yes	**67%**
No	33%

* Number of survey respondents: 13 from 9 different states

Number of survey respondents as a % of total franchise units: 1.3%

SMOOTHIE KING

www.smoothieking.com
Email: franchise@smoothieking.com

Smoothies and other nutritional drinks and products.

OVERALL SCORE: 42

2400 Veterans Memorial Boulevard, Suite 110
Kenner, LA 70062
Fax: 504-469-1274
Total number of outlets: 370
Total number of franchise outlets: 369
International: No

OVERALL RANK: 181

Phone: 800-577-4200
Franchise fee: $25,000
Franchise term: 10 years
Initial investment: $91,000 to $239,000
Advertising/Marketing fee: 1% of gross sales, monthly
Royalty fee: 6% of gross sales monthly

SURVEY AND RESULTS *

Q1: About how many hours per week do you dedicate to your franchise business?

		% answering
A)	Less than 40	25%
B)	41–50	25%
C)	51–60	17%
D)	**More than 60**	**33%**
E)	Passive investment	0%

Q2: How would you describe your relations/ communications with your franchisor?

		% answering
A)	Excellent	0%
B)	Good	17%
C)	**Adequate**	**33%**
D)	**Fair**	**33%**
E)	Poor	17%

Q3: In terms of how your franchisor views your communications with other franchisees, it is:

		% answering
A)	Very supportive	20%
B)	Not very supportive	30%
C)	**No influence**	**50%**

Q4: Is the franchisor fair with you in resolving any grievances?

		% answering
A)	Extremely fair	0%
B)	Pretty fair	25%
C)	**Reasonably fair**	**50%**
D)	Not very fair	17%
E)	Not fair at all	8%

Q5: Are territories equitably granted?

		% answering
A)	Yes	33%
B)	**No**	**42%**
C)	Not yet sure	25%

Q6: How would you describe the initial and ongoing training provided by your franchisor?

		% answering
A)	Excellent	0%
B)	Good	25%
C)	**Adequate**	**33%**
D)	**Fair**	**33%**
E)	Poor	8%

Q7: How well does the franchisor anticipate future trends in how it evolves and markets products and services?

		% answering
A)	Extremely well	0%
B)	Pretty well	25%
C)	**Adequately**	**42%**
D)	Not very well	33%
E)	Terribly	0%

Q8: How satisfied are you with your franchisor's spending of the royalty fees you pay?

		% answering
A)	Extremely satisfied	0%
B)	Mostly satisfied	0%
C)	**Somewhat satisfied**	**50%**
D)	Not very satisfied	25%
E)	Not satisfied at all	25%

Q9: **In what ways could the parent company most improve? (Please check those that most apply, no more than three):**

- ❏ Communications
- ❏ Counsel/advice on administrative/management issues
- ❏ Effectiveness of marketing/promotions
- ❏ Evolution of products/services
- ❏ Frequency of marketing/promotional campaigns

- ❏ Quality of products/services
- ❏ Pricing of products/services to franchisees
- ❏ Technology (Point of sale systems, usage of computers/email/software, etc.)
- ❏ Training

Most frequent responses:	% answering
Effectiveness of marketing/promotions	67%
Communications (tie)	42%
Frequency of marketing/promotional campaigns (tie)	42%

Q10: **Is your income more, less or about what you expected prior to opening your business?**

	% answering	
More	0%	
Less	**75%**	**Summary: 25% are making about what they**
About what was expected	25%	**expected, or more.**

Q11: **Prior to opening your franchise, which (if any) of the following did you underestimate?**

- ❏ Amount of working capital required for your 1st year in business
- ❏ Difficulty in hiring/retaining quality staff
- ❏ Expertise required to run the business
- ❏ Impact of marketing/promotions

- ❏ Start-up costs
- ❏ Degree of stress
- ❏ Workload

Most frequent responses:	% answering
Amount of working capital required for your 1st year in business	58%
Impact of marketing/promotions (tie)	50%
Start-up costs (tie)	50%
Amount of working capital required for 1st year in business (tie)	50%

Q12: **If you could turn back time to the day you signed your franchise agreement, would you make the same decision to buy your franchise?**

	% answering
Yes	42%
No	**58%**

* Number of survey respondents: 12 from 11 different states
Number of survey respondents as a % of total franchise units: 3.25%

SNAP-ON-TOOLS

www.snapon.com

Manufacturer and distributor of automotive tools, equipment, and tool boxes.

OVERALL SCORE: 82

10801 Corporate Drive
Pleasant Prairie, WI 53158
Fax: 262-656-5577
Total number of outlets:
Total number of franchise outlets:
International: Yes (worldwide)

OVERALL RANK: 26

Phone: 262-656-5200
Franchise fee:
Franchise term:
Initial investment:
Advertising/Marketing fee:
Royalty fee:

SURVEY AND RESULTS *

Q1: About how many hours per week do you dedicate to your franchise business?

		% answering
A)	Less than 40	0%
B)	41–50	0%
C)	51–60	13%
D)	**More than 60**	**88%**
E)	Passive investment	0%

Q2: How would you describe your relations/communications with your franchisor?

		% answering
A)	Excellent	19%
B)	**Good**	**38%**
C)	Adequate	19%
D)	Fair	19%
E)	Poor	6%

Q3: In terms of how your franchisor views your communications with other franchisees, it is:

		% answering
A)	**Very supportive**	**44%**
B)	Not very supportive	19%
C)	No influence	38%

Q4: Is the franchisor fair with you in resolving any grievances?

		% answering
A)	Extremely fair	19%
B)	Pretty fair	25%
C)	**Reasonably fair**	**38%**
D)	Not very fair	19%
E)	Not fair at all	0%

Q5: Are territories equitably granted?

		% answering
A)	**Yes**	**44%**
B)	**No**	**44%**
C)	Not yet sure	13%

Q6: How would you describe the initial and ongoing training provided by your franchisor?

		% answering
A)	Excellent	19%
B)	**Good**	**50%**
C)	Adequate	19%
D)	Fair	0%
E)	Poor	13%

Q7: How well does the franchisor anticipate future trends in how it evolves and markets products and services?

		% answering
A)	Extremely well	6%
B)	**Pretty well**	**50%**
C)	Adequately	25%
D)	Not very well	19%
E)	Terribly	0%

Q8: How satisfied are you with your franchisor's spending of the royalty fees you pay?

		% answering
A)	Extremely satisfied	0%
B)	**Mostly satisfied**	**47%**
C)	Somewhat satisfied	27%
D)	Not very satisfied	27%
E)	Not satisfied at all	0%

Q9: In what ways could the parent company most improve? (Please check those that most apply, no more than three):

- ❑ Communications
- ❑ Counsel/advice on administrative/management issues
- ❑ Effectiveness of marketing/promotions
- ❑ Evolution of products/services
- ❑ Frequency of marketing/promotional campaigns

- ❑ Quality of products/services
- ❑ Pricing of products/services to franchisees
- ❑ Technology (Point of sale systems, usage of computers/email/software, etc.)
- ❑ Training

Most frequent responses:

	% answering
Pricing of products/services to franchisees	56%
Effectiveness of marketing/promotions	44%
Communications (tie)	31%
Evolution of products/services (tie)	31%
Quality of products/services (tie)	31%

Q10: Is your income more, less or about what you expected prior to opening your business?

	% answering	
More	**44%**	
Less	19%	**Summary: 82% are making about what they**
About what was expected	38%	**expected, or more.**

Q11: Prior to opening your franchise, which (if any) of the following did you underestimate?

- ❑ Amount of working capital required for your 1st year in business
- ❑ Difficulty in hiring/retaining quality staff
- ❑ Expertise required to run the business
- ❑ Impact of marketing/promotions

- ❑ Start-up costs
- ❑ Degree of stress
- ❑ Workload

Most frequent responses:

	% answering
Workload	69%
Degree of stress	56%
Expertise required to run the business	19%

Q12: If you could turn back time to the day you signed your franchise agreement, would you make the same decision to buy your franchise?

	% answering
Yes	**93%**
No	7%

* Number of survey respondents: 16 from 10 different states

Number of survey respondents as a % of total franchise units:

SNELLING PERSONNEL

www.snelling.com
Email: franchise.sales@snelling.com

Temporary and permanent staffing and placement firm.

OVERALL SCORE: 71

12801 North Central Expressway, Suite 700
Dallas, TX 75243
Fax: 972-239-6881
Total number of outlets: 194
Total number of franchise outlets: 194
International: No

OVERALL RANK: 80

Phone: 800-776-5556
Franchise fee: $0 to 20,000
Franchise term: 5 years
Initial investment: $75,290 to $181,000
Advertising/Marketing fee: varies
Royalty fee: varies

SURVEY AND RESULTS *

Q1: About how many hours per week do you dedicate to your franchise business?

		% answering
A)	Less than 40	21%
B)	**41–50**	**37%**
C)	51–60	26%
D)	More than 60	16%
E)	Passive investment	0%

Q2: How would you describe your relations/communications with your franchisor?

		% answering
A)	Excellent	37%
B)	**Good**	**42%**
C)	Adequate	8%
D)	Fair	3%
E)	Poor	11%

Q3: In terms of how your franchisor views your communications with other franchisees, it is:

		% answering
A)	**Very supportive**	**68%**
B)	Not very supportive	11%
C)	No influence	21%

Q4: Is the franchisor fair with you in resolving any grievances?

		% answering
A)	**Extremely fair**	**32%**
B)	Pretty fair	26%
C)	**Reasonably fair**	**32%**
D)	Not very fair	5%
E)	Not fair at all	5%

Q5: Are territories equitably granted?

		% answering
A)	Yes	27%
B)	**No**	**60%**
C)	Not yet sure	13%

Q6: How would you describe the initial and ongoing training provided by your franchisor?

		% answering
A)	Excellent	28%
B)	**Good**	**39%**
C)	Adequate	17%
D)	Fair	11%
E)	Poor	6%

Q7: How well does the franchisor anticipate future trends in how it evolves and markets products and services?

		% answering
A)	**Extremely well**	**32%**
B)	**Pretty well**	**32%**
C)	Adequately	11%
D)	Not very well	21%
E)	Terribly	5%

Q8: How satisfied are you with your franchisor's spending of the royalty fees you pay?

		% answering
A)	Extremely satisfied	16%
B)	Mostly satisfied	26%
C)	**Somewhat satisfied**	**32%**
D)	Not very satisfied	11%
E)	Not satisfied at all	16%

Q9: **In what ways could the parent company most improve? (Please check those that most apply, no more than three):**

❑ Communications
❑ Counsel/advice on administrative/management issues
❑ Effectiveness of marketing/promotions
❑ Evolution of products/services
❑ Frequency of marketing/promotional campaigns

❑ Quality of products/services
❑ Pricing of products/services to franchisees
❑ Technology (Point of sale systems, usage of computers/email/software, etc.)
❑ Training

Most frequent responses:

	% answering
Effectiveness of marketing/promotions	58%
Frequency of marketing/promotional campaigns	37%
Counsel/advice on administrative/management issues (tie)	26%
Training (tie)	26%

Q10: **Is your income more, less or about what you expected prior to opening your business?**

	% answering	
More	39%	
Less	**50%**	**Summary: 50% are making about what they**
About what was expected	11%	**expected, or more.**

Q11: **Prior to opening your franchise, which (if any) of the following did you underestimate?**

❑ Amount of working capital required for your 1st year in business
❑ Difficulty in hiring/retaining quality staff
❑ Expertise required to run the business
❑ Impact of marketing/promotions

❑ Start-up costs
❑ Degree of stress
❑ Workload

Most frequent responses:

	% answering
Difficulty in hiring/retaining quality staff	79%
Degree of stress	63%
Workload	26%

Q12: **If you could turn back time to the day you signed your franchise agreement, would you make the same decision to buy your franchise?**

	% answering
Yes	**84%**
No	16%

* Number of survey respondents: 19 from 16 different states
Number of survey respondents as a % of total franchise units: 9.79%

THE SPORTS SECTION

www.sports-section.com

Specialized sports-themed photography for youth sports and other school groups.

OVERALL SCORE: 76

2150 Boggs Road, Suite 200
Duluth, GA 30096
Total number of outlets: 184
Total number of franchise outlets: 184
International: Yes (Canada, New Zealand,
Puerto Rico)
Advertising/Marketing fee: none

OVERALL RANK: 53

Phone: 800-321-9127
Franchise fee: $12,900 to $33,900, plus variable
additional amount if increased population is
purchased for your territory
Franchise term: 10 years
Initial investment: $21,150 to $56,715
Royalty fee: none

SURVEY AND RESULTS *

Q1: About how many hours per week do you dedicate to your franchise business?

		% answering
A)	Less than 40	9%
B)	41–50	28%
C)	**51–60**	**38%**
D)	More than 60	25%
E)	Passive investment	0%

Q2: How would you describe your relations/ communications with your franchisor?

		% answering
A)	**Excellent**	**69%**
B)	Good	13%
C)	Adequate	6%
D)	Fair	6%
E)	Poor	6%

Q3: In terms of how your franchisor views your communications with other franchisees, it is:

		% answering
A)	**Very supportive**	**93%**
B)	Not very supportive	0%
C)	No influence	7%

Q4: Is the franchisor fair with you in resolving any grievances?

		% answering
A)	**Extremely fair**	**56%**
B)	Pretty fair	13%
C)	Reasonably fair	19%
D)	Not very fair	6%
E)	Not fair at all	6%

Q5: Are territories equitably granted?

		% answering
A)	Yes	81%
B)	No	19%
C)	Not yet sure	0%

Q6: How would you describe the initial and ongoing training provided by your franchisor?

		% answering
A)	Excellent	44%
B)	Good	44%
C)	Adequate	0%
D)	Fair	13%
E)	Poor	0%

Q7: How well does the franchisor anticipate future trends in how it evolves and markets products and services?

		% answering
A)	Extremely well	44%
B)	Pretty well	56%
C)	Adequately	0%
D)	Not very well	0%
E)	Terribly	0%

Q8: How satisfied are you with your franchisor's spending of the royalty fees you pay?

		% answering
A)	Extremely satisfied	N/A
B)	Mostly satisfied	N/A
C)	Somewhat satisfied	N/A
D)	Not very satisfied	N/A
E)	Not satisfied at all	N/A

Q9: **In what ways could the parent company most improve? (Please check those that most apply, no more than three):**

❑ Communications
❑ Counsel/advice on administrative/management issues
❑ Effectiveness of marketing/promotions
❑ Evolution of products/services
❑ Frequency of marketing/promotional campaigns

❑ Quality of products/services
❑ Pricing of products/services to franchisees
❑ Technology (Point of sale systems, usage of computers/email/software, etc.)
❑ Training

Most frequent responses:

	% answering
Pricing of products/services to franchisees	75%
Effectiveness of marketing/promotions	31%
Counsel/advice on administrative/management issues (tie)	25%
Frequency of marketing/promotional campaigns (tie)	25%

Q10: **Is your income more, less or about what you expected prior to opening your business?**

	% answering	
More	13%	
Less	**50%**	**Summary: 51% are making about what they**
About what was expected	38%	**expected, or more.**

Q11: **Prior to opening your franchise, which (if any) of the following did you underestimate?**

❑ Amount of working capital required for your 1st year in business
❑ Difficulty in hiring/retaining quality staff
❑ Expertise required to run the business
❑ Impact of marketing/promotions

❑ Start-up costs
❑ Degree of stress
❑ Workload

Most frequent responses:

	% answering
Difficulty in hiring/retaining quality staff	63%
Degree of stress	50%
Workload	44%

Q12: **If you could turn back time to the day you signed your franchise agreement, would you make the same decision to buy your franchise?**

	% answering
Yes	**88%**
No	13%

* Number of survey respondents: 16 from 13 different states
Number of survey respondents as a % of total franchise units: 8.70%

STAINED GLASS OVERLAY

www.stainedglassoverlay.com

Seller, fabricator, and installer of simulated stained and leaded glass, beveled glass and other related products.

OVERALL SCORE: 26

1827 North Case Street
Orange, CA 92865
Total number of outlets: 300+
Total number of franchise outlets: 300+
International: Yes (worldwide)
Royalty fee: 5% of gross sales monthly, subject
to annual minimums

OVERALL RANK: 193

Phone: 800-944-4746
Franchise fee: $45,000
Franchise term: 5 years
Initial investment: $88,200 to $117,500
Advertising/Marketing fee: 2% of gross sales monthly

SURVEY AND RESULTS *

Q1: **About how many hours per week do you dedicate to your franchise business?**

		% answering
A)	**Less than 40**	**29%**
B)	**41–50**	**29%**
C)	**51–60**	**29%**
D)	More than 60	14%
E)	Passive investment	0%

Q2: **How would you describe your relations/ communications with your franchisor?**

		% answering
A)	Excellent	0%
B)	Good	7%
C)	Adequate	18%
D)	Fair	29%
E)	**Poor**	**46%**

Q3: **In terms of how your franchisor views your communications with other franchisees, it is:**

		% answering
A)	Very supportive	27%
B)	Not very supportive	18%
C)	**No influence**	**55%**

Q4: **Is the franchisor fair with you in resolving any grievances?**

		% answering
A)	Extremely fair	8%
B)	Pretty fair	8%
C)	**Reasonably fair**	**42%**
D)	Not very fair	33%
E)	Not fair at all	8%

Q5: **Are territories equitably granted?**

		% answering
A)	**Yes**	**43%**
B)	No	29%
C)	Not yet sure	29%

Q6: **How would you describe the initial and ongoing training provided by your franchisor?**

		% answering
A)	Excellent	0%
B)	Good	7%
C)	Adequate	21%
D)	**Fair**	**36%**
E)	**Poor**	**36%**

Q7: **How well does the franchisor anticipate future trends in how it evolves and markets products and services?**

		% answering
A)	Extremely well	0%
B)	Pretty well	21%
C)	Adequately	14%
D)	**Not very well**	**36%**
E)	Terribly	29%

Q8: **How satisfied are you with your franchisor's spending of the royalty fees you pay?**

		% answering
A)	Extremely satisfied	0%
B)	Mostly satisfied	0%
C)	Somewhat satisfied	0%
D)	**Not very satisfied**	**57%**
E)	Not satisfied at all	43%

Q9: **In what ways could the parent company most improve? (Please check those that most apply, no more than three):**

- ❑ Communications
- ❑ Counsel/advice on administrative/management issues
- ❑ Effectiveness of marketing/promotions
- ❑ Evolution of products/services
- ❑ Frequency of marketing/promotional campaigns

- ❑ Quality of products/services
- ❑ Pricing of products/services to franchisees
- ❑ Technology (Point of sale systems, usage of computers/email/software, etc.)
- ❑ Training

Most frequent responses:	% answering
Effectiveness of marketing/promotions	79%
Frequency of marketing/promotional campaigns (tie)	50%
Training (tie)	50%

Q10: **Is your income more, less or about what you expected prior to opening your business?**

	% answering	
More	0%	
Less	**86%**	**Summary: 14% are making about what they**
About what was expected	14%	**expected, or more.**

Q11: **Prior to opening your franchise, which (if any) of the following did you underestimate?**

- ❑ Amount of working capital required for your 1st year in business
- ❑ Difficulty in hiring/retaining quality staff
- ❑ Expertise required to run the business
- ❑ Impact of marketing/promotions

- ❑ Start-up costs
- ❑ Degree of stress
- ❑ Workload

Most frequent responses:	% answering
Amount of working capital required for your 1st year in business	71%
Degree of stress	64%
Start-up costs	43%

Q12: **If you could turn back time to the day you signed your franchise agreement, would you make the same decision to buy your franchise?**

	% answering
Yes	15%
No	**85%**

* Number of survey respondents: 14 from 13 different states
Number of survey respondents as a % of total franchise units: 4.67%

STANLEY STEEMER

www.stanleysteemer.com

Residential and commercial carpet and upholstery cleaning.

OVERALL SCORE: 69

550 Stanley Steemer Parkway
Dublin, OH 43016
Fax: 614-764-1506
Total number of outlets: 270+
Total number of franchise outlets:
International:

OVERALL RANK: 91

Phone: 614-764-2007
Franchise fee:
Franchise term:
Initial investment:
Advertising/Marketing fee
Royalty fee:

SURVEY AND RESULTS *

Q1: About how many hours per week do you dedicate to your franchise business?

		% answering
A)	Less than 40	20%
B)	41–50	20%
C)	**51–60**	**30%**
D)	**More than 60**	**30%**
E)	Passive investment	0%

Q2: How would you describe your relations/ communications with your franchisor?

		% answering
A)	**Excellent**	**50%**
B)	Good	20%
C)	Adequate	20%
D)	Fair	0%
E)	Poor	10%

Q3: In terms of how your franchisor views your communications with other franchisees, it is:

		% answering
A)	**Very supportive**	**56%**
B)	Not very supportive	33%
C)	No influence	11%

Q4: Is the franchisor fair with you in resolving any grievances?

		% answering
A)	**Extremely fair**	**56%**
B)	Pretty fair	22%
C)	Reasonably fair	11%
D)	Not very fair	0%
E)	Not fair at all	11%

Q5: Are territories equitably granted?

		% answering
A)	**Yes**	**80%**
B)	No	10%
C)	Not yet sure	10%

Q6: How would you describe the initial and ongoing training provided by your franchisor?

		% answering
A)	**Excellent**	**60%**
B)	Good	20%
C)	Adequate	20%
D)	Fair	0%
E)	Poor	0%

Q7: How well does the franchisor anticipate future trends in how it evolves and markets products and services?

		% answering
A)	**Extremely well**	**70%**
B)	Pretty well	20%
C)	Adequately	10%
D)	Not very well	0%
E)	Terribly	0%

Q8: How satisfied are you with your franchisor's spending of the royalty fees you pay?

		% answering
A)	**Extremely satisfied**	**33%**
B)	**Mostly satisfied**	**33%**
C)	Somewhat satisfied	11%
D)	Not very satisfied	11%
E)	Not satisfied at all	11%

Q9: **In what ways could the parent company most improve? (Please check those that most apply, no more than three):**

❑ Communications
❑ Counsel/advice on administrative/management issues
❑ Effectiveness of marketing/promotions
❑ Evolution of products/services
❑ Frequency of marketing/promotional campaigns

❑ Quality of products/services
❑ Pricing of products/services to franchisees
❑ Technology (Point of sale systems, usage of computers/email/software, etc.)
❑ Training

Most frequent responses:

	% answering
Communications	40%
Pricing of products/services to franchisees	30%
Counsel/advice on administrative/management issues (tie)	20%
Effectiveness of marketing/promotions (tie)	20%
Training (tie)	20%

Q10: **Is your income more, less or about what you expected prior to opening your business?**

	% answering	
More	30%	
Less	**60%**	**Summary: 40% are making about what they**
About what was expected	10%	**expected, or more.**

Q11: **Prior to opening your franchise, which (if any) of the following did you underestimate?**

❑ Amount of working capital required for your 1st year in business
❑ Difficulty in hiring/retaining quality staff
❑ Expertise required to run the business
❑ Impact of marketing/promotions

❑ Start-up costs
❑ Degree of stress
❑ Workload

Most frequent responses:

	% answering
Degree of stress	60%
Amount of working capital required for your 1st year in business	40%
Difficulty in hiring/retaining quality staff (tie)	30%
Expertise required to run the business (tie)	30%
Workload (tie)	30%

Q12: **If you could turn back time to the day you signed your franchise agreement, would you make the same decision to buy your franchise?**

	% answering
Yes	**60%**
No	40%

* Number of survey respondents: 10 from 8 different states
Number of survey respondents as a % of total franchise units: 3.70%

STEAMATIC

www.steamatic.com

Commercial and residential cleaning and restoration services.

OVERALL SCORE: 57

303 Arthur Street
Fort Worth, TX 76107
Fax: 817-810-9226
Total number of outlets: 361
Total number of franchise outlets: 327
International: Yes (worldwide)

OVERALL RANK: N/A

Phone: 800-527-1295
Franchise fee: $7,000 to $24,000 (plus $80 per for
every 1,000 people exceeding 350,000 in territory
Franchise term: 10 years
Initial investment: $100,552 to $171,312
Advertising/Marketing fee: 5% of gross revenues
Royalty fee: varies

SURVEY AND RESULTS *

Q1: About how many hours per week do you dedicate to your franchise business?

		% answering
A)	Less than 40	0%
B)	**41–50**	**56%**
C)	51–60	44%
D)	More than 60	0%
E)	Passive investment	0%

Q2: How would you describe your relations/ communications with your franchisor?

		% answering
A)	Excellent	11%
B)	Good	22%
C)	Adequate	11%
D)	**Fair**	**33%**
E)	Poor	22%

Q3: In terms of how your franchisor views your communications with other franchisees, it is:

		% answering
A)	**Very supportive**	**67%**
B)	Not very supportive	0%
C)	No influence	33%

Q4: Is the franchisor fair with you in resolving any grievances?

		% answering
A)	Extremely fair	11%
B)	**Pretty fair**	**33%**
C)	**Reasonably fair**	**33%**
D)	Not very fair	22%
E)	Not fair at all	0%

Q5: Are territories equitably granted?

		% answering
A)	**Yes**	**89%**
B)	No	11%
C)	Not yet sure	0%

Q6: How would you describe the initial and ongoing training provided by your franchisor?

		% answering
A)	Excellent	22%
B)	Good	11%
C)	**Adequate**	**44%**
D)	Fair	22%
E)	Poor	0%

Q7: How well does the franchisor anticipate future trends in how it evolves and markets products and services?

		% answering
A)	Extremely well	11%
B)	Pretty well	11%
C)	**Adequately**	**44%**
D)	Not very well	33%
E)	Terribly	0%

Q8: How satisfied are you with your franchisor's spending of the royalty fees you pay?

		% answering
A)	Extremely satisfied	0%
B)	Mostly satisfied	11%
C)	**Somewhat satisfied**	**56%**
D)	Not very satisfied	22%
E)	Not satisfied at all	11%

Q9: **In what ways could the parent company most improve? (Please check those that most apply, no more than three):**

❑ Communications

❑ Counsel/advice on administrative/management issues

❑ Effectiveness of marketing/promotions

❑ Evolution of products/services

❑ Frequency of marketing/promotional campaigns

❑ Quality of products/services

❑ Pricing of products/services to franchisees

❑ Technology (Point of sale systems, usage of computers/email/software, etc.)

❑ Training

Most frequent responses:

	% answering
Communications (tie)	44%
Counsel/advice on administrative/management issues (tie)	44%
Effectiveness of marketing/promotions (tie)	44%

Q10: **Is your income more, less or about what you expected prior to opening your business?**

	% answering	
More	13%	
Less	**63%**	**Summary: 38% are making about what they**
About what was expected	25%	**expected, or more.**

Q11: **Prior to opening your franchise, which (if any) of the following did you underestimate?**

❑ Amount of working capital required for your 1st year in business

❑ Difficulty in hiring/retaining quality staff

❑ Expertise required to run the business

❑ Impact of marketing/promotions

❑ Start-up costs

❑ Degree of stress

❑ Workload

Most frequent responses:

	% answering
Difficulty in hiring/retaining quality staff	56%
Degree of stress (tie)	56%
Workload (tie)	44%

Q12: **If you could turn back time to the day you signed your franchise agreement, would you make the same decision to buy your franchise?**

	% answering
Yes	**56%**
No	44%

* Number of survey respondents: 9 from 9 different states

Number of survey respondents as a % of total franchise units: 2.75%

SUBWAY

www.subway.com
Email: franchise@subway.com

Fast food soup and sandwich retailer.

OVERALL SCORE: 58

325 Bic Drive
Milford, CT 06460
Fax: 203-876-6674
Total number of outlets: 23,066
Total number of franchise outlets: 23,065
International: Yes (worldwide)

OVERALL RANK: 149

Phone: 800-888-4848
Franchise fee: $12,500
Franchise term:
Initial investment: $69,300 to $191,000
Advertising/Marketing fee: 4.5%
Royalty fee: 8%

SURVEY AND RESULTS *

Q1: About how many hours per week do you dedicate to your franchise business?

		% answering
A)	Less than 40	25%
B)	**41–50**	**31%**
C)	51–60	19%
D)	More than 60	25%
E)	Passive investment	0%

Q2: How would you describe your relations/communications with your franchisor?

		% answering
A)	Excellent	6%
B)	**Good**	**25%**
C)	**Adequate**	**25%**
D)	**Fair**	**25%**
E)	Poor	19%

Q3: In terms of how your franchisor views your communications with other franchisees, it is:

		% answering
A)	Very supportive	31%
B)	**Not very supportive**	**56%**
C)	No influence	13%

Q4: Is the franchisor fair with you in resolving any grievances?

		% answering
A)	Extremely fair	0%
B)	Pretty fair	31%
C)	Reasonably fair	19%
D)	**Not very fair**	**38%**
E)	Not fair at all	13%

Q5: Are territories equitably granted?

		% answering
A)	Yes	7%
B)	**No**	**93%**
C)	Not yet sure	0%

Q6: How would you describe the initial and ongoing training provided by your franchisor?

		% answering
A)	Excellent	19%
B)	**Good**	**41%**
C)	Adequate	19%
D)	Fair	9%
E)	Poor	13%

Q7: How well does the franchisor anticipate future trends in how it evolves and markets products and services?

		% answering
A)	Extremely well	19%
B)	**Pretty well**	**25%**
C)	**Adequately**	**25%**
D)	Not very well	19%
E)	Terribly	13%

Q8: How satisfied are you with your franchisor's spending of the royalty fees you pay?

		% answering
A)	Extremely satisfied	13%
B)	Mostly satisfied	13%
C)	Somewhat satisfied	19%
D)	Not very satisfied	25%
E)	**Not satisfied at all**	**31%**

Q9: **In what ways could the parent company most improve? (Please check those that most apply, no more than three):**

❑ Communications   ❑ Quality of products/services
❑ Counsel/advice on administrative/management issues   ❑ Pricing of products/services to franchisees
❑ Effectiveness of marketing/promotions   ❑ Technology (Point of sale systems, usage
❑ Evolution of products/services   of computers/email/software, etc.)
❑ Frequency of marketing/promotional campaigns   ❑ Training

Most frequent responses: % answering
Effectiveness of marketing/promotions   63%
Pricing of products/services to franchisees   50%
Evolution of products/services   44%

Q10: **Is your income more, less or about what you expected prior to opening your business?**

	% answering
More	25%
Less	25%
About what was expected	**50%**

Summary: 75% are making about what they expected, or more.

Q11: **Prior to opening your franchise, which (if any) of the following did you underestimate?**

❑ Amount of working capital required for your   ❑ Start-up costs
   1st year in business   ❑ Degree of stress
❑ Difficulty in hiring/retaining quality staff   ❑ Workload
❑ Expertise required to run the business
❑ Impact of marketing/promotions

Most frequent responses: % answering
Difficulty in hiring/retaining quality staff   63%
Degree of stress   44%
Workload   31%

Q12: **If you could turn back time to the day you signed your franchise agreement, would you make the same decision to buy your franchise?**

	% answering
Yes	**63%**
No	38%

* Number of survey respondents: 16 from 15 different states
  Number of survey respondents as a % of total franchise units: < 1%

SUNBELT BUSINESS ADVISORS

www.sunbeltnetwork.com

The world's largest business broker network.

OVERALL SCORE: 85

7301 Rivers Avenue, Suite 230
Charleston, SC 29406
Total number of outlets: 350 (in U.S.; additional
offices in 11 other countries)
Total number of franchise outlets: 350 in U.S.
International: Yes (worldwide)
Royalty fee: $500 to $700 per month,
depending upon size of territory

OVERALL RANK: 13

Phone: 800-771-7866
Franchise fee: $15,000 to $25,000
Franchise term: 10 years
Initial investment: $51,300 to $102,500
Advertising/Marketing fee: 20% of monthly royalty

SURVEY AND RESULTS *

Q1: About how many hours per week do you dedicate to your franchise business?

		% answering
A)	Less than 40	28%
B)	41–50	33%
C)	51–60	23%
D)	More than 60	17%
E)	Passive investment	0%

Q2: How would you describe your relations/communications with your franchisor?

		% answering
A)	**Excellent**	**28%**
B)	**Good**	**28%**
C)	Adequate	17%
D)	**Fair**	**28%**
E)	Poor	0%

Q3: In terms of how your franchisor views your communications with other franchisees, it is:

		% answering
A)	Very supportive	82%
B)	Not very supportive	6%
C)	No influence	12%

Q4: Is the franchisor fair with you in resolving any grievances?

		% answering
A)	Extremely fair	24%
B)	**Pretty fair**	**53%**
C)	Reasonably fair	24%
D)	Not very fair	0%
E)	Not fair at all	0%

Q5: Are territories equitably granted?

		% answering
A)	**Yes**	**76%**
B)	No	6%
C)	Not yet sure	18%

Q6: How would you describe the initial and ongoing training provided by your franchisor?

		% answering
A)	Excellent	6%
B)	**Good**	**50%**
C)	Adequate	17%
D)	Fair	11%
E)	Poor	17%

Q7: How well does the franchisor anticipate future trends in how it evolves and markets products and services?

		% answering
A)	Extremely well	0%
B)	**Pretty well**	**56%**
C)	Adequately	11%
D)	Not very well	33%
E)	Terribly	0%

Q8: How satisfied are you with your franchisor's spending of the royalty fees you pay?

		% answering
A)	Extremely satisfied	11%
B)	**Mostly satisfied**	**50%**
C)	Somewhat satisfied	22%
D)	Not very satisfied	17%
E)	Not satisfied at all	0%

Q9: In what ways could the parent company most improve? (Please check those that most apply, no more than three):

❑ Communications
❑ Counsel/advice on administrative/management issues
❑ Effectiveness of marketing/promotions
❑ Evolution of products/services
❑ Frequency of marketing/promotional campaigns

❑ Quality of products/services
❑ Pricing of products/services to franchisees
❑ Technology (Point of sale systems, usage of computers/email/software, etc.)
❑ Training

Most frequent responses:	% answering
Effectiveness of marketing/promotions (tie)	72%
Training (tie)	72%
Communications	44%

Q10: Is your income more, less or about what you expected prior to opening your business?

	% answering	
More	17%	
Less	17%	**Summary: 84% are making about what they**
About what was expected	**67%**	**expected, or more.**

Q11: Prior to opening your franchise, which (if any) of the following did you underestimate?

❑ Amount of working capital required for your 1st year in business
❑ Difficulty in hiring/retaining quality staff
❑ Expertise required to run the business
❑ Impact of marketing/promotions

❑ Start-up costs
❑ Degree of stress
❑ Workload

Most frequent responses:	% answering
Difficulty in hiring/retaining quality staff	67%
Amount of working capital required for your 1st year in business (tie)	22%
Expertise required to run the business (tie)	22%
Impact of marketing/promotions (tie)	22%
Degree of stress (tie)	22%

Q12: If you could turn back time to the day you signed your franchise agreement, would you make the same decision to buy your franchise?

	% answering
Yes	**94%**
No	6%

* Number of survey respondents: 18 from 13 different states
  Number of survey respondents as a % of total franchise units: 5.14%

SUPERCUTS

www.supercuts.com or www.regisfranchise.com

Unisex hair salon.

OVERALL SCORE: 66

7201 Metro Boulevard
Edina, MN 55439
Fax: 952-947-7600
Total number of outlets: 2,000+
Total number of franchise outlets: 2,000+
International: (Canada, Puerto Rico,
United Kingdom)

OVERALL RANK: N/A

Phone: 952-947-7777
Franchise fee: $22,500
Franchise term:
Initial investment: $106,860 to $169,080
Advertising/Marketing fee:
Royalty fee:

SURVEY AND RESULTS *

Q1: About how many hours per week do you dedicate to your franchise business?

		% answering
A)	Less than 40	33%
B)	**41–50**	**44%**
C)	51–60	22%
D)	More than 60	0%
E)	Passive investment	0%

Q2: How would you describe your relations/communications with your franchisor?

		% answering
A)	Excellent	0%
B)	**Good**	**44%**
C)	Adequate	33%
D)	Fair	11%
E)	Poor	11%

Q3: In terms of how your franchisor views your communications with other franchisees, it is:

		% answering
A)	**Very supportive**	**67%**
B)	Not very supportive	33%
C)	No influence	0%

Q4: Is the franchisor fair with you in resolving any grievances?

		% answering
A)	Extremely fair	22%
B)	**Pretty fair**	**33%**
C)	Reasonably fair	22%
D)	Not very fair	11%
E)	Not fair at all	11%

Q5: Are territories equitably granted?

		% answering
A)	**Yes**	**44%**
B)	No	11%
C)	**Not yet sure**	**44%**

Q6: How would you describe the initial and ongoing training provided by your franchisor?

		% answering
A)	Excellent	22%
B)	Good	11%
C)	**Adequate**	**33%**
D)	Fair	22%
E)	Poor	11%

Q7: How well does the franchisor anticipate future trends in how it evolves and markets products and services?

		% answering
A)	Extremely well	11%
B)	**Pretty well**	**44%**
C)	Adequately	11%
D)	Not very well	22%
E)	Terribly	11%

Q8: How satisfied are you with your franchisor's spending of the royalty fees you pay?

		% answering
A)	Extremely satisfied	0%
B)	**Mostly satisfied**	**39%**
C)	**Somewhat satisfied**	**39%**
D)	Not very satisfied	11%
E)	Not satisfied at all	11%

Q9: **In what ways could the parent company most improve? (Please check those that most apply, no more than three):**

❑ Communications
❑ Counsel/advice on administrative/management issues
❑ Effectiveness of marketing/promotions
❑ Evolution of products/services
❑ Frequency of marketing/promotional campaigns

❑ Quality of products/services
❑ Pricing of products/services to franchisees
❑ Technology (Point of sale systems, usage of computers/email/software, etc.)
❑ Training

Most frequent responses:	% answering
Effectiveness of marketing/promotions (tie)	44%
Training (tie)	44%
Counsel/advice on administrative/management issues	33%

Q10: **Is your income more, less or about what you expected prior to opening your business?**

	% answering	
More	13%	
Less	38%	**Summary: 63% are making about what they**
About what was expected	**50%**	**expected, or more.**

Q11: Prior to opening your franchise, which (if any) of the following did you underestimate?

❑ Amount of working capital required for your 1st year in business
❑ Difficulty in hiring/retaining quality staff
❑ Expertise required to run the business
❑ Impact of marketing/promotions

❑ Start-up costs
❑ Degree of stress
❑ Workload

Most frequent responses:	% answering
Difficulty in hiring/retaining quality staff	56%
Amount of working capital required for your 1st year in business	44%
Impact of marketing/promotions (tie)	22%
Degree of stress (tie)	22%

Q12: **If you could turn back time to the day you signed your franchise agreement, would you make the same decision to buy your franchise?**

	% answering
Yes	**75%**
No	25%

*   Number of survey respondents: 9 from 7 different states
    Number of survey respondents as a % of total franchise units: < 1%

SWISHER HYGIENE

www.swisheronline.com

Commercial hygiene services.

OVERALL SCORE: 65

6849 Fairview Road
Charlotte, NC 28210
Fax: 704-365-8941
Total number of outlets: 127
Total number of franchise outlets: 126 (88 in U.S.)
International: Yes (worldwide)
Royalty fee: Generally 6% of monthly gross
revenues, but can vary

OVERALL RANK: 113

Phone: 800-444-4138
Franchise fee: $35,000 to $85,000, depending
upon population of territory
Franchise term: 5 years
Initial investment: $89,200 to $170,050
Advertising/Marketing fee: 2% of monthly gross revenues

SURVEY AND RESULTS *

Q1: About how many hours per week do you dedicate to your franchise business?

		% answering
A)	**Less than 40**	**30%**
B)	**41–50**	**30%**
C)	51–60	10%
D)	**More than 60**	**30%**
E)	Passive investment	0%

Q2: How would you describe your relations/ communications with your franchisor?

		% answering
A)	Excellent	0%
B)	Good	25%
C)	**Adequate**	**45%**
D)	Fair	10%
E)	Poor	20%

Q3: In terms of how your franchisor views your communications with other franchisees, it is:

		% answering
A)	**Very supportive**	**50%**
B)	Not very supportive	40%
C)	No influence	10%

Q4: Is the franchisor fair with you in resolving any grievances?

		% answering
A)	Extremely fair	10%
B)	Pretty fair	10%
C)	**Reasonably fair**	**50%**
D)	Not very fair	20%
E)	Not fair at all	10%

Q5: Are territories equitably granted?

		% answering
A)	**Yes**	**100%**
B)	No	0%
C)	Not yet sure	0%

Q6: How would you describe the initial and ongoing training provided by your franchisor?

		% answering
A)	Excellent	0%
B)	Good	20%
C)	**Adequate**	**50%**
D)	Fair	10%
E)	Poor	20%

Q7: How well does the franchisor anticipate future trends in how it evolves and markets products and services?

		% answering
A)	Extremely well	10%
B)	Pretty well	0%
C)	**Adequately**	**70%**
D)	Not very well	20%
E)	Terribly	0%

Q8: How satisfied are you with your franchisor's spending of the royalty fees you pay?

		% answering
A)	Extremely satisfied	0%
B)	Mostly satisfied	20%
C)	Somewhat satisfied	30%
D)	**Not very satisfied**	**40%**
E)	Not satisfied at all	10%

Q9: In what ways could the parent company most improve? (Please check those that most apply, no more than three):

- ❏ Communications
- ❏ Counsel/advice on administrative/management issues
- ❏ Effectiveness of marketing/promotions
- ❏ Evolution of products/services
- ❏ Frequency of marketing/promotional campaigns

- ❏ Quality of products/services
- ❏ Pricing of products/services to franchisees
- ❏ Technology (Point of sale systems, usage of computers/email/software, etc.)
- ❏ Training

Most frequent responses:

	% answering
Effectiveness of marketing/promotions (tie)	40%
Pricing of products/services to franchisees (tie)	40%
Communications (tie)	30%
Counsel/advice on administrative/management issues (tie)	30%
Frequency of marketing/promotional campaigns (tie)	30%
Technology (tie)	30%

Q10: Is your income more, less or about what you expected prior to opening your business?

	% answering	
More	10%	
Less	30%	**Summary: 70% are making about what they**
About what was expected	**60%**	**expected, or more.**

Q11: Prior to opening your franchise, which (if any) of the following did you underestimate?

- ❏ Amount of working capital required for your 1st year in business
- ❏ Difficulty in hiring/retaining quality staff
- ❏ Expertise required to run the business
- ❏ Impact of marketing/promotions

- ❏ Start-up costs
- ❏ Degree of stress
- ❏ Workload

Most frequent responses:

	% answering
Difficulty in hiring/retaining quality staff	60%
Amount of working capital required for your 1st year in business (tie)	40%
Degree of stress (tie)	40%

Q12: If you could turn back time to the day you signed your franchise agreement, would you make the same decision to buy your franchise?

	% answering
Yes	**78%**
No	22%

* Number of survey respondents: 10 from 9 different states
  Number of survey respondents as a % of total franchise units: 7.94%

SYLVAN LEARNING CENTERS

www.educate.com

Educational and tutoring services for students in kindergarten through grade 12.

OVERALL SCORE: 72

1001 Fleet Street
Baltimore, MD 21202
Fax: 410-843-8441
Total number of outlets: 1,000+ in North America
Total number of franchise outlets: 1,000+ in
North America
International: Yes (worldwide)

OVERALL RANK: 70

Phone: 888-EDUCATE
Franchise fee: $38,000 to $46,000
Franchise term:
Initial investment:
Advertising/Marketing fee:
Royalty fee:

SURVEY AND RESULTS *

Q1: About how many hours per week do you dedicate to your franchise business?

		% answering
A)	Less than 40	27%
B)	41–50	20%
C)	**51–60**	**33%**
D)	More than 60	20%
E)	Passive investment	0%

Q2: How would you describe your relations/communications with your franchisor?

		% answering
A)	Excellent	20%
B)	**Good**	**40%**
C)	Adequate	13%
D)	Fair	20%
E)	Poor	7%

Q3: In terms of how your franchisor views your communications with other franchisees, it is:

		% answering
A)	**Very supportive**	**73%**
B)	Not very supportive	0%
C)	No influence	27%

Q4: Is the franchisor fair with you in resolving any grievances?

		% answering
A)	**Extremely fair**	**36%**
B)	Pretty fair	21%
C)	Reasonably fair	14%
D)	Not very fair	29%
E)	Not fair at all	0%

Q5: Are territories equitably granted?

		% answering
A)	Yes	40%
B)	**No**	**47%**
C)	Not yet sure	13%

Q6: How would you describe the initial and ongoing training provided by your franchisor?

		% answering
A)	Excellent	20%
B)	**Good**	**40%**
C)	Adequate	27%
D)	Fair	7%
E)	Poor	7%

Q7: How well does the franchisor anticipate future trends in how it evolves and markets products and services?

		% answering
A)	**Extremely well**	**33%**
B)	**Pretty well**	**33%**
C)	Adequately	13%
D)	Not very well	20%
E)	Terribly	0%

Q8: How satisfied are you with your franchisor's spending of the royalty fees you pay?

		% answering
A)	Extremely satisfied	7%
B)	**Mostly satisfied**	**47%**
C)	Somewhat satisfied	20%
D)	Not very satisfied	20%
E)	Not satisfied at all	7%

Q9: **In what ways could the parent company most improve? (Please check those that most apply, no more than three):**

❑ Communications

❑ Counsel/advice on administrative/management issues

❑ Effectiveness of marketing/promotions

❑ Evolution of products/services

❑ Frequency of marketing/promotional campaigns

❑ Quality of products/services

❑ Pricing of products/services to franchisees

❑ Technology (Point of sale systems, usage of computers/email/software, etc.)

❑ Training

Most frequent responses:

	% answering
Technology	60%
Counsel/advice on administrative/management issues (tie)	33%
Training (tie)	33%

Q10: **Is your income more, less or about what you expected prior to opening your business?**

	% answering	
More	33%	
Less	**40%**	**Summary: 60% are making about what they**
About what was expected	27%	**expected, or more.**

Q11: **Prior to opening your franchise, which (if any) of the following did you underestimate?**

❑ Amount of working capital required for your 1st year in business

❑ Difficulty in hiring/retaining quality staff

❑ Expertise required to run the business

❑ Impact of marketing/promotions

❑ Start-up costs

❑ Degree of stress

❑ Workload

Most frequent responses:

	% answering
Difficulty in hiring/retaining quality staff	47%
Degree of stress	40%
Amount of working capital required for 1st year in business	33%

Q12: **If you could turn back time to the day you signed your franchise agreement, would you make the same decision to buy your franchise?**

	% answering
Yes	**87%**
No	13%

*   Number of survey respondents: 15 from 12 different states

Number of survey respondents as a % of total franchise units: 1.50%

TACO BELL

www.yumfranchises.com

Fast-food Mexican restaurant.

OVERALL SCORE: 78

17901 Von Karman
Irvine, CA 92614
Fax: 949-863-2252
Total number of outlets: 6,500+
Total number of franchise outlets: 5,000+
International: Yes (worldwide)

OVERALL RANK: 44

Phone: 949-863-4500
Franchise fee:
Franchise term:
Initial investment:
Advertising/Marketing fee:
Royalty fee:

SURVEY AND RESULTS *

Q1: About how many hours per week do you dedicate to your franchise business?

		% answering
A)	Less than 40	15%
B)	**41–50**	**38%**
C)	51–60	0%
D)	**More than 60**	**38%**
E)	Passive investment	8%

Q2: How would you describe your relations/ communications with your franchisor?

		% answering
A)	Excellent	31%
B)	**Good**	**46%**
C)	Adequate	8%
D)	Fair	0%
E)	Poor	15%

Q3: In terms of how your franchisor views your communications with other franchisees, it is:

		% answering
A)	**Very supportive**	**75%**
B)	Not very supportive	0%
C)	No influence	25%

Q4: Is the franchisor fair with you in resolving any grievances?

		% answering
A)	Extremely fair	15%
B)	**Pretty fair**	**38%**
C)	Reasonably fair	31%
D)	Not very fair	8%
E)	Not fair at all	8%

Q5: Are territories equitably granted?

		% answering
A)	**Yes**	**50%**
B)	**No**	**50%**
C)	Not yet sure	0%

Q6: How would you describe the initial and ongoing training provided by your franchisor?

		% answering
A)	Excellent	23%
B)	Good	31%
C)	**Adequate**	**38%**
D)	Fair	0%
E)	Poor	8%

Q7: How well does the franchisor anticipate future trends in how it evolves and markets products and services?

		% answering
A)	Extremely well	31%
B)	**Pretty well**	**46%**
C)	Adequately	15%
D)	Not very well	8%
E)	Terribly	0%

Q8: How satisfied are you with your franchisor's spending of the royalty fees you pay?

		% answering
A)	Extremely satisfied	46%
B)	**Mostly satisfied**	**31%**
C)	Somewhat satisfied	15%
D)	Not very satisfied	8%
E)	Not satisfied at all	0%

Q9: **In what ways could the parent company most improve? (Please check those that most apply, no more than three):**

- ❏ Communications
- ❏ Counsel/advice on administrative/management issues
- ❏ Effectiveness of marketing/promotions
- ❏ Evolution of products/services
- ❏ Frequency of marketing/promotional campaigns

- ❏ Quality of products/services
- ❏ Pricing of products/services to franchisees
- ❏ Technology (Point of sale systems, usage of computers/email/software, etc.)
- ❏ Training

Most frequent responses:

	% answering
Training	54%
Counsel/advice on administrative/management issues	38%
Technology	31%

Q10: **Is your income more, less or about what you expected prior to opening your business?**

	% answering	
More	**38%**	
Less	23%	**Summary: 76% are making about what they**
About what was expected	**38%**	**expected, or more.**

Q11: **Prior to opening your franchise, which (if any) of the following did you underestimate?**

- ❏ Amount of working capital required for your 1st year in business
- ❏ Difficulty in hiring/retaining quality staff
- ❏ Expertise required to run the business
- ❏ Impact of marketing/promotions

- ❏ Start-up costs
- ❏ Degree of stress
- ❏ Workload

Most frequent responses:

	% answering
Difficulty in hiring/retaining quality staff	54%
Degree of stress	31%
Workload	23%

Q12: **If you could turn back time to the day you signed your franchise agreement, would you make the same decision to buy your franchise?**

	% answering
Yes	**85%**
No	15%

*   Number of survey respondents: 13 from 13 different states
    Number of survey respondents as a % of total franchise units: < 1%

TACO JOHN'S

www.tacojohns.com
Email: contact@tacojohns.com

Fast-food Mexican restaurant.

OVERALL SCORE: 79

808 West 20th Street
Cheyenne, WY 82003
Fax: 307-638-0603
Total number of outlets: 377
Total number of franchise outlets: 370
International: No

OVERALL RANK: 36

Phone: 800-854-0819
Franchise fee: $25,000
Franchise term: Varies, generally 3 to 5 years
Initial investment: $495,000 to $709,500
Advertising/Marketing fee: 1/2% of net sales monthly
Royalty fee: 4% of net sales monthly

SURVEY AND RESULTS *

Q1: About how many hours per week do you dedicate to your franchise business?

		% answering
A)	**Less than 40**	**36%**
B)	41–50	27%
C)	51–60	18%
D)	More than 60	9%
E)	Passive investment	9%

Q2: How would you describe your relations/ communications with your franchisor?

		% answering
A)	Excellent	9%
B)	**Good**	**55%**
C)	Adequate	36%
D)	Fair	0%
E)	Poor	0%

Q3: In terms of how your franchisor views your communications with other franchisees, it is:

		% answering
A)	**Very supportive**	**73%**
B)	Not very supportive	9%
C)	No influence	18%

Q4: Is the franchisor fair with you in resolving any grievances?

		% answering
A)	Extremely fair	18%
B)	**Pretty fair**	**55%**
C)	Reasonably fair	18%
D)	Not very fair	9%
E)	Not fair at all	0%

Q5: Are territories equitably granted?

		% answering
A)	**Yes**	**64%**
B)	No	0%
C)	Not yet sure	36%

Q6: How would you describe the initial and ongoing training provided by your franchisor?

		% answering
A)	Excellent	36%
B)	**Good**	**55%**
C)	Adequate	9%
D)	Fair	0%
E)	Poor	0%

Q7: How well does the franchisor anticipate future trends in how it evolves and markets products and services?

		% answering
A)	Extremely well	27%
B)	**Pretty well**	**36%**
C)	Adequately	18%
D)	Not very well	9%
E)	Terribly	9%

Q8: How satisfied are you with your franchisor's spending of the royalty fees you pay?

		% answering
A)	Extremely satisfied	0%
B)	**Mostly satisfied**	**73%**
C)	Somewhat satisfied	27%
D)	Not very satisfied	0%
E)	Not satisfied at all	0%

Q9: In what ways could the parent company most improve? (Please check those that most apply, no more than three):

- ❏ Communications
- ❏ Counsel/advice on administrative/management issues
- ❏ Effectiveness of marketing/promotions
- ❏ Evolution of products/services
- ❏ Frequency of marketing/promotional campaigns
- ❏ Quality of products/services
- ❏ Pricing of products/services to franchisees
- ❏ Technology (Point of sale systems, usage of computers/email/software, etc.)
- ❏ Training

Most frequent responses:	% answering
Evolution of products/services	45%
Effectiveness of marketing/promotions (tie)	36%
Frequency of marketing/promotional campaigns (tie)	36%

Q10: Is your income more, less or about what you expected prior to opening your business?

	% answering	
More	27%	
Less	27%	**Summary: 72% are making about what they**
About what was expected	**45%**	**expected, or more.**

Q11: Prior to opening your franchise, which (if any) of the following did you underestimate?

- ❏ Amount of working capital required for your 1st year in business
- ❏ Difficulty in hiring/retaining quality staff
- ❏ Expertise required to run the business
- ❏ Impact of marketing/promotions
- ❏ Start-up costs
- ❏ Degree of stress
- ❏ Workload

Most frequent responses:	% answering
Degree of stress	64%
Workload	45%
Difficulty in hiring/retaining quality staff	36%

Q12: If you could turn back time to the day you signed your franchise agreement, would you make the same decision to buy your franchise?

	% answering
Yes	**82%**
No	18%

* Number of survey respondents: 11 from 9 different states

Number of survey respondents as a % of total franchise units: 2.92%

TCBY

www.tcby.com
Email: eliseh@mrsfields.com (Elise Hansen)

Frozen yogurt and other frozen desserts.

OVERALL SCORE: 40

9803 11th Place SE, A
Lake Stevens, WA 98258
Fax: 425-377-0963
Total number of outlets: 2,500+
Total number of franchise outlets: 2,500+
International: Yes (worldwide)

OVERALL RANK: 186

Phone: 800-336-6551, ext. 5611
Franchise fee: $25,000
Franchise term: 10 years
Initial investment: $158,800 to $398,000
Advertising/Marketing fee: 5% of gross sales
Royalty fee: 5% of gross sales

SURVEY AND RESULTS *

Q1: About how many hours per week do you dedicate to your franchise business?

		% answering
A)	**Less than 40**	**29%**
B)	41–50	14%
C)	**51–60**	**29%**
D)	**More than 60**	**29%**
E)	Passive investment	0%

Q2: How would you describe your relations/communications with your franchisor?

		% answering
A)	Excellent	0%
B)	Good	14%
C)	Adequate	21%
D)	Fair	29%
E)	**Poor**	**36%**

Q3: In terms of how your franchisor views your communications with other franchisees, it is:

		% answering
A)	Very supportive	21%
B)	Not very supportive	21%
C)	**No influence**	**57%**

Q4: Is the franchisor fair with you in resolving any grievances?

		% answering
A)	Extremely fair	7%
B)	Pretty fair	21%
C)	Reasonably fair	21%
D)	**Not very fair**	**43%**
E)	Not fair at all	7%

Q5: Are territories equitably granted?

		% answering
A)	**Yes**	**50%**
B)	No	0%
C)	**Not yet sure**	**50%**

Q6: How would you describe the initial and ongoing training provided by your franchisor?

		% answering
A)	Excellent	0%
B)	Good	29%
C)	**Adequate**	**36%**
D)	Fair	21%
E)	Poor	14%

Q7: How well does the franchisor anticipate future trends in how it evolves and markets products and services?

		% answering
A)	Extremely well	7%
B)	Pretty well	7%
C)	Adequately	29%
D)	**Not very well**	**50%**
E)	Terribly	7%

Q8: How satisfied are you with your franchisor's spending of the royalty fees you pay?

		% answering
A)	Extremely satisfied	0%
B)	Mostly satisfied	7%
C)	Somewhat satisfied	7%
D)	**Not very satisfied**	**57%**
E)	Not satisfied at all	29%

Q9: **In what ways could the parent company most improve? (Please check those that most apply, no more than three):**

- ❏ Communications
- ❏ Counsel/advice on administrative/management issues
- ❏ Effectiveness of marketing/promotions
- ❏ Evolution of products/services
- ❏ Frequency of marketing/promotional campaigns

- ❏ Quality of products/services
- ❏ Pricing of products/services to franchisees
- ❏ Technology (Point of sale systems, usage of computers/email/software, etc.)
- ❏ Training

Most frequent responses:	% answering
Communications	64%
Effectiveness of marketing/promotions (tie)	57%
Pricing of products/services to franchisees (tie)	57%

Q10: **Is your income more, less or about what you expected prior to opening your business?**

	% answering	
More	0%	
Less	**64%**	**Summary: 36% are making about what they**
About what was expected	36%	**expected, or more.**

Q11: **Prior to opening your franchise, which (if any) of the following did you underestimate?**

- ❏ Amount of working capital required for your 1st year in business
- ❏ Difficulty in hiring/retaining quality staff
- ❏ Expertise required to run the business
- ❏ Impact of marketing/promotions

- ❏ Start-up costs
- ❏ Degree of stress
- ❏ Workload

Most frequent responses:	% answering
Difficulty in hiring/retaining quality staff	50%
Degree of stress	36%
Impact of marketing/promotions (tie)	21%
Start-up costs (tie)	21%

Q12: **If you could turn back time to the day you signed your franchise agreement, would you make the same decision to buy your franchise?**

	% answering
Yes	29%
No	**71%**

* Number of survey respondents: 14 from 9 different states
Number of survey respondents as a % of total franchise units: < 1%

TUFFY AUTO SERVICE CENTERS

www.tuffy.com

Vehicle repair services.

OVERALL SCORE: 40

1414 Baronial Plaza Drive
Toledo, OH 43615
Fax: 419-865-7343
Total number of outlets: 199
Total number of franchise outlets: 199
International: No

OVERALL RANK: 187

Phone: 800-22-TUFFY
Franchise fee:
Franchise term:
Initial investment:
Advertising/Marketing fee
Royalty fee:

SURVEY AND RESULTS *

Q1: About how many hours per week do you dedicate to your franchise business?

		% answering
A)	Less than 40	0%
B)	41–50	18%
C)	51–60	18%
D)	**More than 60**	**64%**
E)	Passive investment	0%

Q2: How would you describe your relations/ communications with your franchisor?

		% answering
A)	Excellent	0%
B)	**Good**	**36%**
C)	Adequate	9%
D)	**Fair**	**36%**
E)	Poor	18%

Q3: In terms of how your franchisor views your communications with other franchisees, it is:

		% answering
A)	**Very supportive**	**40%**
B)	Not very supportive	30%
C)	No influence	30%

Q4: Is the franchisor fair with you in resolving any grievances?

		% answering
A)	Extremely fair	9%
B)	**Pretty fair**	**36%**
C)	Reasonably fair	27%
D)	Not very fair	9%
E)	Not fair at all	18%

Q5: Are territories equitably granted?

		% answering
A)	**Yes**	**73%**
B)	No	27%
C)	Not yet sure	0%

Q6: How would you describe the initial and ongoing training provided by your franchisor?

		% answering
A)	Excellent	9%
B)	**Good**	**27%**
C)	Adequate	9%
D)	**Fair**	**27%**
E)	**Poor**	**27%**

Q7: How well does the franchisor anticipate future trends in how it evolves and markets products and services?

		% answering
A)	Extremely well	0%
B)	**Pretty well**	**36%**
C)	Adequately	18%
D)	**Not very well**	**36%**
E)	Terribly	9%

Q8: How satisfied are you with your franchisor's spending of the royalty fees you pay?

		% answering
A)	Extremely satisfied	0%
B)	Mostly satisfied	27%
C)	**Somewhat satisfied**	**36%**
D)	Not very satisfied	18%
E)	Not satisfied at all	18%

Q9: **In what ways could the parent company most improve? (Please check those that most apply, no more than three):**

- ❏ Communications
- ❏ Counsel/advice on administrative/management issues
- ❏ Effectiveness of marketing/promotions
- ❏ Evolution of products/services
- ❏ Frequency of marketing/promotional campaigns

- ❏ Quality of products/services
- ❏ Pricing of products/services to franchisees
- ❏ Technology (Point of sale systems, usage of computers/email/software, etc.)
- ❏ Training

Most frequent responses:	% answering
Effectiveness of marketing/promotions (tie)	45%
Pricing of products/services to franchisees (tie)	45%
Communications	36%

Q10: **Is your income more, less or about what you expected prior to opening your business?**

	% answering	
More	0%	
Less	**82%**	**Summary: 18% are making about what they**
About what was expected	18%	**expected, or more.**

Q11: **Prior to opening your franchise, which (if any) of the following did you underestimate?**

- ❏ Amount of working capital required for your 1st year in business
- ❏ Difficulty in hiring/retaining quality staff
- ❏ Expertise required to run the business
- ❏ Impact of marketing/promotions

- ❏ Start-up costs
- ❏ Degree of stress
- ❏ Workload

Most frequent responses:	% answering
Amount of working capital required for your 1st year in business	73%
Degree of stress	64%
Start-up costs	55%

Q12: **If you could turn back time to the day you signed your franchise agreement, would you make the same decision to buy your franchise?**

	% answering
Yes	40%
No	**60%**

* Number of survey respondents: 12 from 6 different states
  Number of survey respondents as a % of total franchise units: 6.03%

TUTORING CLUB

www.tutoringclub.com

Tutoring services.

OVERALL SCORE: 61

14870 Highway 4, Suite B
Discovery Bay, CA 94514
Total number of outlets: 103
Total number of franchise outlets: 103
International: No
Advertising/Marketing fee: 1% of gross
revenues monthly

OVERALL RANK: 134

Phone: 888-674-6725
Franchise fee: $29,500
Franchise term: 5 years
Initial investment: $64,750 to $97,900
Royalty fee: 10% of gross revenues monthly

SURVEY AND RESULTS *

Q1: About how many hours per week do you dedicate to your franchise business?

		% answering
A)	**Less than 40**	**50%**
B)	41–50	36%
C)	51–60	7%
D)	More than 60	7%
E)	Passive investment	0%

Q2: How would you describe your relations/ communications with your franchisor?

		% answering
A)	Excellent	7%
B)	**Good**	**36%**
C)	Adequate	29%
D)	Fair	21%
E)	Poor	7%

Q3: In terms of how your franchisor views your communications with other franchisees, it is:

		% answering
A)	**Very supportive**	**57%**
B)	Not very supportive	14%
C)	No influence	29%

Q4: Is the franchisor fair with you in resolving any grievances?

		% answering
A)	Extremely fair	7%
B)	**Pretty fair**	**43%**
C)	Reasonably fair	36%
D)	Not very fair	7%
E)	Not fair at all	7%

Q5: Are territories equitably granted?

		% answering
A)	**Yes**	**71%**
B)	No	14%
C)	Not yet sure	14%

Q6: How would you describe the initial and ongoing training provided by your franchisor?

		% answering
A)	Excellent	7%
B)	**Good**	**36%**
C)	Adequate	7%
D)	Fair	14%
E)	**Poor**	**36%**

Q7: How well does the franchisor anticipate future trends in how it evolves and markets products and services?

		% answering
A)	Extremely well	0%
B)	Pretty well	29%
C)	Adequately	21%
D)	**Not very well**	**36%**
E)	Terribly	14%

Q8: How satisfied are you with your franchisor's spending of the royalty fees you pay?

		% answering
A)	Extremely satisfied	0%
B)	Mostly satisfied	21%
C)	**Somewhat satisfied**	**50%**
D)	Not very satisfied	14%
E)	Not satisfied at all	14%

Q9: **In what ways could the parent company most improve? (Please check those that most apply, no more than three):**

❑ Communications
❑ Counsel/advice on administrative/management issues
❑ Effectiveness of marketing/promotions
❑ Evolution of products/services
❑ Frequency of marketing/promotional campaigns

❑ Quality of products/services
❑ Pricing of products/services to franchisees
❑ Technology (Point of sale systems, usage of computers/email/software, etc.)
❑ Training

Most frequent responses:

	% answering
Effectiveness of marketing/promotions	64%
Communications	43%
Evolution of products/services	36%

Q10: **Is your income more, less or about what you expected prior to opening your business?**

	% answering	
More	7%	
Less	43%	**Summary: 57% are making about what they**
About what was expected	**50%**	**expected, or more.**

Q11: **Prior to opening your franchise, which (if any) of the following did you underestimate?**

❑ Amount of working capital required for your 1st year in business
❑ Difficulty in hiring/retaining quality staff
❑ Expertise required to run the business
❑ Impact of marketing/promotions

❑ Start-up costs
❑ Degree of stress
❑ Workload

Most frequent responses:

	% answering
Impact of marketing/promotions	64%
Amount of working capital required for your 1st year in business	50%
Start-up costs	29%

Q12: **If you could turn back time to the day you signed your franchise agreement, would you make the same decision to buy your franchise?**

	% answering
Yes	**77%**
No	23%

* Number of survey respondents: 14 from 9 different states
Number of survey respondents as a % of total franchise units: 13.59%

TWO MEN AND A TRUCK

www.twomenandatruck.com
Email: franchiseinfo@twomenandatruck.com

Moving and related products and services.

OVERALL SCORE: 68

3400 Belle Chase Way
Lansing, MI 48911
Fax: 517-394-7432
Total number of outlets: 123
Total number of franchise outlets: 119
International: No

OVERALL RANK: 93

Phone: 800-345-1070
Franchise fee: $32,000 or $72,000
Franchise term: 5 years
Initial investment: $94,300 to $351,000
Advertising/Marketing fee: 1% of gross receipts monthly
Royalty fee: 6% of gross receipts monthly

SURVEY AND RESULTS *

Q1: About how many hours per week do you dedicate to your franchise business?

		% answering
A)	Less than 40	21%
B)	**41–50**	**43%**
C)	51–60	7%
D)	More than 60	29%
E)	Passive investment	0%

Q2: How would you describe your relations/communications with your franchisor?

		% answering
A)	**Excellent**	**36%**
B)	Good	29%
C)	Adequate	21%
D)	Fair	7%
E)	Poor	7%

Q3: In terms of how your franchisor views your communications with other franchisees, it is:

		% answering
A)	**Very supportive**	**71%**
B)	Not very supportive	0%
C)	No influence	29%

Q4: Is the franchisor fair with you in resolving any grievances?

		% answering
A)	Extremely fair	23%
B)	**Pretty fair**	**38%**
C)	Reasonably fair	23%
D)	Not very fair	15%
E)	Not fair at all	0%

Q5: Are territories equitably granted?

		% answering
A)	**Yes**	**57%**
B)	No	29%
C)	Not yet sure	14%

Q6: How would you describe the initial and ongoing training provided by your franchisor?

		% answering
A)	**Excellent**	**36%**
B)	Good	29%
C)	Adequate	0%
D)	Fair	21%
E)	Poor	14%

Q7: How well does the franchisor anticipate future trends in how it evolves and markets products and services?

		% answering
A)	**Extremely well**	**38%**
B)	Pretty well	23%
C)	Adequately	15%
D)	Not very well	23%
E)	Terribly	0%

Q8: How satisfied are you with your franchisor's spending of the royalty fees you pay?

		% answering
A)	Extremely satisfied	14%
B)	**Mostly satisfied**	**43%**
C)	Somewhat satisfied	21%
D)	Not very satisfied	14%
E)	Not satisfied at all	7%

Q9: **In what ways could the parent company most improve? (Please check those that most apply, no more than three):**

❑ Communications

❑ Counsel/advice on administrative/management issues

❑ Effectiveness of marketing/promotions

❑ Evolution of products/services

❑ Frequency of marketing/promotional campaigns

❑ Quality of products/services

❑ Pricing of products/services to franchisees

❑ Technology (Point of sale systems, usage of computers/email/software, etc.)

❑ Training

Most frequent responses:	% answering
Counsel/advice on administrative/management issues	43%
Effectiveness of marketing/promotions	36%
Frequency of marketing/promotional campaigns (tie)	29%
Technology (tie)	29%

Q10: **Is your income more, less or about what you expected prior to opening your business?**

	% answering	
More	29%	
Less	**43%**	Summary: 58% are making about what they
About what was expected	29%	expected, or more.

Q11: **Prior to opening your franchise, which (if any) of the following did you underestimate?**

❑ Amount of working capital required for your 1st year in business

❑ Difficulty in hiring/retaining quality staff

❑ Expertise required to run the business

❑ Impact of marketing/promotions

❑ Start-up costs

❑ Degree of stress

❑ Workload

Most frequent responses:	% answering
Degree of stress	71%
Difficulty in hiring/retaining quality staff	57%
Workload	43%

Q12: **If you could turn back time to the day you signed your franchise agreement, would you make the same decision to buy your franchise?**

	% answering
Yes	**67%**
No	33%

*   Number of survey respondents: 14 from 11 different states

Number of survey respondents as a % of total franchise units: 11.76%

U.S. LAWNS

www.homeinstead.com
Email: info@uslawns.com

Landscaping services.

OVERALL SCORE: 76

4407 Vineland Road, Suite D-15
Orlando, FL 32811
Fax: 407-246-1623
Total number of outlets: 125
Total number of franchise outlets: 124
International: No

OVERALL RANK: 47

Phone: 407-246-1630
Franchise fee: $29,000
Franchise term: 10 years
Initial investment: $48,500 to $56,000
Advertising/Marketing fee: 1% of gross contract
buildings, up to a maximum of $225 per month
Royalty fee: varies

SURVEY AND RESULTS *

Q1: About how many hours per week do you dedicate to your franchise business?

		% answering
A)	Less than 40	13%
B)	41–50	13%
C)	**51–60**	**40%**
D)	More than 60	31%
E)	Passive investment	4%

Q2: How would you describe your relations/communications with your franchisor?

		% answering
A)	Excellent	25%
B)	**Good**	**46%**
C)	Adequate	13%
D)	Fair	4%
E)	Poor	13%

Q3: In terms of how your franchisor views your communications with other franchisees, it is:

		% answering
A)	**Very supportive**	**88%**
B)	Not very supportive	8%
C)	No influence	4%

Q4: Is the franchisor fair with you in resolving any grievances?

		% answering
A)	Extremely fair	30%
B)	**Pretty fair**	**39%**
C)	Reasonably fair	22%
D)	Not very fair	0%
E)	Not fair at all	9%

Q5: Are territories equitably granted?

		% answering
A)	**Yes**	**79%**
B)	No	13%
C)	Not yet sure	8%

Q6: How would you describe the initial and ongoing training provided by your franchisor?

		% answering
A)	Excellent	17%
B)	**Good**	**44%**
C)	Adequate	21%
D)	Fair	13%
E)	Poor	6%

Q7: How well does the franchisor anticipate future trends in how it evolves and markets products and services?

		% answering
A)	Extremely well	13%
B)	**Pretty well**	**63%**
C)	Adequately	13%
D)	Not very well	8%
E)	Terribly	4%

Q8: How satisfied are you with your franchisor's spending of the royalty fees you pay?

		% answering
A)	Extremely satisfied	9%
B)	**Mostly satisfied**	**48%**
C)	Somewhat satisfied	17%
D)	Not very satisfied	13%
E)	Not satisfied at all	13%

Q9: **In what ways could the parent company most improve? (Please check those that most apply, no more than three):**

❑ Communications
❑ Counsel/advice on administrative/management issues
❑ Effectiveness of marketing/promotions
❑ Evolution of products/services
❑ Frequency of marketing/promotional campaigns

❑ Quality of products/services
❑ Pricing of products/services to franchisees
❑ Technology (Point of sale systems, usage of computers/email/software, etc.)
❑ Training

Most frequent responses:	% answering
Effectiveness of marketing/promotions	54%
Communications	46%
Counsel/advice on administrative/management issues	42%

Q10: **Is your income more, less or about what you expected prior to opening your business?**

	% answering	
More	17%	
Less	22%	**Summary: 78% are making about what they**
About what was expected	**61%**	**expected, or more.**

Q11: **Prior to opening your franchise, which (if any) of the following did you underestimate?**

❑ Amount of working capital required for your 1st year in business
❑ Difficulty in hiring/retaining quality staff
❑ Expertise required to run the business
❑ Impact of marketing/promotions

❑ Start-up costs
❑ Degree of stress
❑ Workload

Most frequent responses:	% answering
Amount of working capital required for your 1st year in business	46%
Difficulty in hiring/retaining quality staff	42%
Degree of stress	33%

Q12: **If you could turn back time to the day you signed your franchise agreement, would you make the same decision to buy your franchise?**

	% answering
Yes	**79%**
No	21%

* Number of survey respondents: 24 from 15 different states
Number of survey respondents as a % of total franchise units: 19.35%

UNIGLOBE TRAVEL

www.uniglobefranchise.com
Email: salesinfo@uniglobetravel.com

Travel agency.

OVERALL SCORE: 67

OVERALL RANK: 98

5 Park Plaza, Suite 800
Irvine, CA 92614
Total number of outlets: 740 (301 in U.S.)
Total number of franchise outlets: 740 (301 in U.S.)
International: Yes (worldwide)
Advertising/Marketing fee: none
Royalty fee: varies

Phone: 800-863-1606 (U.S. headquarters)
Franchise fee: $1,500 for "conversion"agencies;
"conversion agencies", which are the only eligible
licensees of Uniglobe, are those converting an
existing travel agency to Uniglobe
Franchise term: 2 years
Initial investment: $3,925 to $17,075

SURVEY AND RESULTS *

Q1: About how many hours per week do you
dedicate to your franchise business?

		% answering
A)	Less than 40	17%
B)	**41–50**	**58%**
C)	51–60	17%
D)	More than 60	8%
E)	Passive investment	0%

Q2: How would you describe your relations/
communications with your franchisor?

		% answering
A)	**Excellent**	**42%**
B)	Good	25%
C)	Adequate	25%
D)	Fair	8%
E)	Poor	0%

Q3: In terms of how your franchisor views your
communications with other franchisees, it is:

		% answering
A)	**Very supportive**	**67%**
B)	Not very supportive	0%
C)	No influence	33%

Q4: Is the franchisor fair with you in
resolving any grievances?

		% answering
A)	**Extremely fair**	**42%**
B)	Pretty fair	33%
C)	Reasonably fair	25%
D)	Not very fair	0%
E)	Not fair at all	0%

Q5: Are territories equitably granted?

		% answering
A)	**Yes**	**50%**
B)	No	10%
C)	Not yet sure	40%

Q6: How would you describe the initial and
ongoing training provided by your franchisor?

		% answering
A)	Excellent	17%
B)	**Good**	**50%**
C)	Adequate	8%
D)	Fair	8%
E)	Poor	17%

Q7: How well does the franchisor anticipate
future trends in how it evolves and markets
products and services?

		% answering
A)	**Extremely well**	**33%**
B)	**Pretty well**	**33%**
C)	**Adequately**	**33%**
D)	Not very well	0%
E)	Terribly	0%

Q8: How satisfied are you with your franchisor's
spending of the royalty fees you pay?

		% answering
A)	Extremely satisfied	8%
B)	**Mostly satisfied**	**42%**
C)	Somewhat satisfied	25%
D)	Not very satisfied	25%
E)	Not satisfied at all	0%

Q9: **In what ways could the parent company most improve? (Please check those that most apply, no more than three):**

❏ Communications
❏ Counsel/advice on administrative/management issues
❏ Effectiveness of marketing/promotions
❏ Evolution of products/services
❏ Frequency of marketing/promotional campaigns

❏ Quality of products/services
❏ Pricing of products/services to franchisees
❏ Technology (Point of sale systems, usage of computers/email/software, etc.)
❏ Training

Most frequent responses:

	% answering
Counsel/advice on administrative/management issues (tie)	50%
Effectiveness of marketing/promotions (tie)	50%
Communications	42%

Q10: **Is your income more, less or about what you expected prior to opening your business?**

	% answering	
More	33%	
Less	**50%**	**Summary: 50% are making about what they**
About what was expected	17%	**expected, or more.**

Q11: **Prior to opening your franchise, which (if any) of the following did you underestimate?**

❏ Amount of working capital required for your 1st year in business
❏ Difficulty in hiring/retaining quality staff
❏ Expertise required to run the business
❏ Impact of marketing/promotions

❏ Start-up costs
❏ Degree of stress
❏ Workload

Most frequent responses:

	% answering
Degree of stress	58%
Difficulty in hiring/retaining quality staff (tie)	42%
Expertise required to run the business (tie)	42%

Q12: **If you could turn back time to the day you signed your franchise agreement, would you make the same decision to buy your franchise?**

	% answering
Yes	**58%**
No	42%

*   Number of survey respondents: 12 from 11 different states
   Number of survey respondents as a % of total franchise units: 1.62%

UNITED CHECK CASHING

www.unitedfsg.com
Email: wbarry@unitedfsg.com (Wayne Berry)

Check cashing services.

OVERALL SCORE: 58

400 Market Street, Suite 1030
Philadelphia, PA 19106
Total number of outlets: 140
Total number of franchise outlets: 140
International: No

OVERALL RANK: 146

Phone: 800-626-0787
Franchise fee: $27,500
Franchise term: 15 years
Initial investment: $194,700
Advertising/Marketing fee: none
Royalty fee: 2/10 of 1% on each debit transaction,
5% on "other" revenues, payable weekly

SURVEY AND RESULTS *

Q1: About how many hours per week do you dedicate to your franchise business?

		% answering
A)	Less than 40	10%
B)	41–50	15%
C)	51–60	35%
D)	**More than 60**	**40%**
E)	Passive investment	0%

Q2: How would you describe your relations/communications with your franchisor?

		% answering
A)	Excellent	5%
B)	**Good**	**36%**
C)	Adequate	31%
D)	Fair	14%
E)	Poor	14%

Q3: In terms of how your franchisor views your communications with other franchisees, it is:

		% answering
A)	Very supportive	19%
B)	Not very supportive	14%
C)	**No influence**	**67%**

Q4: Is the franchisor fair with you in resolving any grievances?

		% answering
A)	Extremely fair	5%
B)	Pretty fair	21%
C)	**Reasonably fair**	**32%**
D)	**Not very fair**	**32%**
E)	Not fair at all	11%

Q5: Are territories equitably granted?

		% answering
A)	Yes	43%
B)	**No**	**48%**
C)	Not yet sure	10%

Q6: How would you describe the initial and ongoing training provided by your franchisor?

		% answering
A)	Excellent	10%
B)	**Good**	**38%**
C)	Adequate	21%
D)	Fair	14%
E)	Poor	17%

Q7: How well does the franchisor anticipate future trends in how it evolves and markets products and services?

		% answering
A)	Extremely well	0%
B)	Pretty well	25%
C)	Adequately	23%
D)	**Not very well**	**38%**
E)	Terribly	15%

Q8: How satisfied are you with your franchisor's spending of the royalty fees you pay?

		% answering
A)	Extremely satisfied	0%
B)	Mostly satisfied	22%
C)	**Somewhat satisfied**	**28%**
D)	Not very satisfied	22%
E)	**Not satisfied at all**	**28%**

Q9: **In what ways could the parent company most improve? (Please check those that most apply, no more than three):**

- ❏ Communications
- ❏ Counsel/advice on administrative/management issues
- ❏ Effectiveness of marketing/promotions
- ❏ Evolution of products/services
- ❏ Frequency of marketing/promotional campaigns
- ❏ Quality of products/services
- ❏ Pricing of products/services to franchisees
- ❏ Technology (Point of sale systems, usage of computers/email/software, etc.)
- ❏ Training

Most frequent responses:	% answering
Evolution of products/services	57%
Effectiveness of marketing/promotions	52%
Communications (tie)	33%
Counsel/advice on administrative/management issues (tie)	33%
Quality of products/services (tie)	33%

Q10: **Is your income more, less or about what you expected prior to opening your business?**

	% answering	
More	19%	
Less	33%	**Summary: 67% are making about what they**
About what was expected	**48%**	**expected, or more.**

Q11: **Prior to opening your franchise, which (if any) of the following did you underestimate?**

- ❏ Amount of working capital required for your 1st year in business
- ❏ Difficulty in hiring/retaining quality staff
- ❏ Expertise required to run the business
- ❏ Impact of marketing/promotions
- ❏ Start-up costs
- ❏ Degree of stress
- ❏ Workload

Most frequent responses:	% answering
Amount of working capital required for 1st year in business	57%
Degree of stress	33%
Impact of marketing/promotions (tie)	24%
Start-up costs (tie)	24%

Q12: **If you could turn back time to the day you signed your franchise agreement, would you make the same decision to buy your franchise?**

	% answering
Yes	65%
No	35%

* Number of survey respondents: 21 from 9 different states

Number of survey respondents as a % of total franchise units: 15%

UNITED COUNTRY REAL ESTATE

www.unitedcountry.com

Real estate services, primarily focused on rural areas.

OVERALL SCORE: 83

Kansas City, MO
Total number of outlets: 462
Total number of franchise outlets: 462
International: No

OVERALL RANK: 23

Phone: 800-444-5044
Franchise fee:
Franchise term:
Initial investment
Advertising/Marketing fee:
Royalty fee:

SURVEY AND RESULTS *

Q1: About how many hours per week do you dedicate to your franchise business?

		% answering
A)	Less than 40	8%
B)	41–50	4%
C)	51–60	29%
D)	**More than 60**	**58%**
E)	Passive investment	0%

Q2: How would you describe your relations/communications with your franchisor?

		% answering
A)	**Excellent**	**58%**
B)	Good	21%
C)	Adequate	13%
D)	Fair	4%
E)	Poor	4%

Q3: In terms of how your franchisor views your communications with other franchisees, it is:

		% answering
A)	**Very supportive**	**70%**
B)	Not very supportive	0%
C)	No influence	30%

Q4: Is the franchisor fair with you in resolving any grievances?

		% answering
A)	**Extremely fair**	**48%**
B)	Pretty fair	38%
C)	Reasonably fair	10%
D)	Not very fair	0%
E)	Not fair at all	5%

Q5: Are territories equitably granted?

		% answering
A)	**Yes**	**64%**
B)	No	36%
C)	Not yet sure	0%

Q6: How would you describe the initial and ongoing training provided by your franchisor?

		% answering
A)	Excellent	40%
B)	**Good**	**44%**
C)	Adequate	4%
D)	Fair	0%
E)	Poor	13%

Q7: How well does the franchisor anticipate future trends in how it evolves and markets products and services?

		% answering
A)	**Extremely well**	**58%**
B)	Pretty well	29%
C)	Adequately	4%
D)	Not very well	4%
E)	Terribly	4%

Q8: How satisfied are you with your franchisor's spending of the royalty fees you pay?

		% answering
A)	Extremely satisfied	29%
B)	**Mostly satisfied**	**67%**
C)	Somewhat satisfied	4%
D)	Not very satisfied	0%
E)	Not satisfied at all	0%

Q9: **In what ways could the parent company most improve? (Please check those that most apply, no more than three):**

❑ Communications
❑ Counsel/advice on administrative/management issues
❑ Effectiveness of marketing/promotions
❑ Evolution of products/services
❑ Frequency of marketing/promotional campaigns

❑ Quality of products/services
❑ Pricing of products/services to franchisees
❑ Technology (Point of sale systems, usage of computers/email/software, etc.)
❑ Training

Most frequent responses:

	% answering
Effectiveness of marketing/promotions	38%
Technology	33%
Counsel/advice on administrative/management issues (tie)	25%
Training (tie)	25%

Q10: **Is your income more, less or about what you expected prior to opening your business?**

	% answering	
More	**46%**	
Less	25%	**Summary: 75% are making about what they**
About what was expected	29%	**expected, or more.**

Q11: **Prior to opening your franchise, which (if any) of the following did you underestimate?**

❑ Amount of working capital required for your 1st year in business
❑ Difficulty in hiring/retaining quality staff
❑ Expertise required to run the business
❑ Impact of marketing/promotions

❑ Start-up costs
❑ Degree of stress
❑ Workload

Most frequent responses:

	% answering
Difficulty in hiring/retaining quality staff (tie)	46%
Workload (tie)	46%
Degree of stress	38%

Q12: **If you could turn back time to the day you signed your franchise agreement, would you make the same decision to buy your franchise?**

	% answering
Yes	**88%**
No	13%

*   Number of survey respondents: 24 from 19 different states
Number of survey respondents as a % of total franchise units: 5.19%

THE UPS STORE

www.theupsstore.com
Email: usafranchise@mbe.com

Packing, shipping, and mailing services.

OVERALL SCORE: 61

6060 Cornerstone Court West
San Diego, CA 92121
Fax: 858-546-7493
Total number of outlets: 4,500+
Total number of franchise outlets: 4,500+
International: Yes (worldwide)

OVERALL RANK: 135

Phone: 877-623-7253
Franchise fee: $19,950 to $29,950
Franchise term:
Initial investment: $135,600 to $247,547
Advertising/Marketing fee:
Royalty fee:

SURVEY AND RESULTS *

Q1: About how many hours per week do you dedicate to your franchise business?

		% answering
A)	Less than 40	13%
B)	41–50	31%
C)	**51–60**	**38%**
D)	More than 60	19%
E)	Passive investment	0%

Q2: How would you describe your relations/ communications with your franchisor?

		% answering
A)	Excellent	13%
B)	Good	25%
C)	Adequate	19%
D)	**Fair**	**31%**
E)	Poor	13%

Q3: In terms of how your franchisor views your communications with other franchisees, it is:

		% answering
A)	**Very supportive**	**44%**
B)	Not very supportive	25%
C)	No influence	31%

Q4: Is the franchisor fair with you in resolving any grievances?

		% answering
A)	Extremely fair	0%
B)	**Pretty fair**	**44%**
C)	**Reasonably fair**	**44%**
D)	Not very fair	13%
E)	Not fair at all	0%

Q5: Are territories equitably granted?

		% answering
A)	**Yes**	**69%**
B)	No	19%
C)	Not yet sure	13%

Q6: How would you describe the initial and ongoing training provided by your franchisor?

		% answering
A)	Excellent	19%
B)	**Good**	**44%**
C)	Adequate	31%
D)	Fair	6%
E)	Poor	0%

Q7: How well does the franchisor anticipate future trends in how it evolves and markets products and services?

		% answering
A)	Extremely well	0%
B)	**Pretty well**	**56%**
C)	Adequately	19%
D)	Not very well	19%
E)	Terribly	6%

Q8: How satisfied are you with your franchisor's spending of the royalty fees you pay?

		% answering
A)	Extremely satisfied	0%
B)	Mostly satisfied	31%
C)	**Somewhat satisfied**	**50%**
D)	Not very satisfied	13%
E)	Not satisfied at all	6%

Q9: **In what ways could the parent company most improve? (Please check those that most apply, no more than three):**

❑ Communications   ❑ Quality of products/services

❑ Counsel/advice on administrative/management issues   ❑ Pricing of products/services to franchisees

❑ Effectiveness of marketing/promotions   ❑ Technology (Point of sale systems, usage

❑ Evolution of products/services   of computers/email/software, etc.)

❑ Frequency of marketing/promotional campaigns   ❑ Training

Most frequent responses:	% answering
Communications	63%
Effectiveness of marketing/promotions	44%
Pricing of products/services to franchisees	38%

Q10: **Is your income more, less or about what you expected prior to opening your business?**

	% answering	
More	0%	
Less	**63%**	**Summary: 38% are making about what they**
About what was expected	38%	**expected, or more.**

Q11: **Prior to opening your franchise, which (if any) of the following did you underestimate?**

❑ Amount of working capital required for your   ❑ Start-up costs

    1st year in business   ❑ Degree of stress

❑ Difficulty in hiring/retaining quality staff   ❑ Workload

❑ Expertise required to run the business

❑ Impact of marketing/promotions

Most frequent responses:	% answering
Difficulty in hiring/retaining quality staff	44%
Amount of working capital required for your 1st year in business	31%
Workload	25%

Q12: **If you could turn back time to the day you signed your franchise agreement, would you make the same decision to buy your franchise?**

	% answering
Yes	**75%**
No	25%

*   Number of survey respondents: 16 from 15 different states

    Number of survey respondents as a % of total franchise units: < 1%

V2K, THE WINDOW FASHION STORE

www.v2kwindowfashions.com

Seller and installer of software-designed window treatments for commercial and residential customers.

OVERALL SCORE: 53

1127 Auraria Parkway, Suite 204
Denver, CO 80204
Fax: 303-202-5201
Total number of outlets: 84
Total number of franchise outlets: 84
International: No

OVERALL RANK: 162

Phone: 800-200-0835
Franchise fee: $39,900
Franchise term: 10 years
Initial investment: $50,120 to $62,300
Advertising/Marketing fee: currently 2% of gross sales
Royalty fee: varies

SURVEY AND RESULTS *

Q1: About how many hours per week do you dedicate to your franchise business?

		% answering
A)	Less than 40	22%
B)	**41–50**	**50%**
C)	51–60	17%
D)	More than 60	11%
E)	Passive investment	0%

Q2: How would you describe your relations/ communications with your franchisor?

		% answering
A)	Excellent	22%
B)	Good	22%
C)	Adequate	22%
D)	**Fair**	**28%**
E)	Poor	6%

Q3: In terms of how your franchisor views your communications with other franchisees, it is:

		% answering
A)	**Very supportive**	**50%**
B)	Not very supportive	11%
C)	No influence	39%

Q4: Is the franchisor fair with you in resolving any grievances?

		% answering
A)	Extremely fair	17%
B)	**Pretty fair**	**56%**
C)	Reasonably fair	11%
D)	Not very fair	17%
E)	Not fair at all	0%

Q5: Are territories equitably granted?

		% answering
A)	**Yes**	**50%**
B)	No	11%
C)	Not yet sure	39%

Q6: How would you describe the initial and ongoing training provided by your franchisor?

		% answering
A)	Excellent	11%
B)	**Good**	**33%**
C)	Adequate	17%
D)	Fair	28%
E)	Poor	11%

Q7: How well does the franchisor anticipate future trends in how it evolves and markets products and services?

		% answering
A)	Extremely well	22%
B)	**Pretty well**	**39%**
C)	Adequately	6%
D)	Not very well	28%
E)	Terribly	6%

Q8: How satisfied are you with your franchisor's spending of the royalty fees you pay?

		% answering
A)	Extremely satisfied	6%
B)	**Mostly satisfied**	**29%**
C)	Somewhat satisfied	18%
D)	Not very satisfied	24%
E)	Not satisfied at all	24%

Q9: **In what ways could the parent company most improve? (Please check those that most apply, no more than three):**

- ❏ Communications
- ❏ Counsel/advice on administrative/management issues
- ❏ Effectiveness of marketing/promotions
- ❏ Evolution of products/services
- ❏ Frequency of marketing/promotional campaigns

- ❏ Quality of products/services
- ❏ Pricing of products/services to franchisees
- ❏ Technology (Point of sale systems, usage of computers/email/software, etc.)
- ❏ Training

Most frequent responses:	% answering
Effectiveness of marketing/promotions	67%
Frequency of marketing/promotional campaigns	44%
Training	33%

Q10: **Is your income more, less or about what you expected prior to opening your business?**

	% answering	
More	0%	
Less	**78%**	Summary: 22% are making about what they
About what was expected	22%	**expected, or more.**

Q11: **Prior to opening your franchise, which (if any) of the following did you underestimate?**

- ❏ Amount of working capital required for your 1st year in business
- ❏ Difficulty in hiring/retaining quality staff
- ❏ Expertise required to run the business
- ❏ Impact of marketing/promotions

- ❏ Start-up costs
- ❏ Degree of stress
- ❏ Workload

Most frequent responses:	% answering
Amount of working capital required for 1st year in business (tie)	50%
Expertise required to run the business (tie)	50%
Workload	28%

Q12: **If you could turn back time to the day you signed your franchise agreement, would you make the same decision to buy your franchise?**

	% answering
Yes	**61%**
No	39%

* Number of survey respondents: 18 from 10 different states
  Number of survey respondents as a % of total franchise units: 21.43%

VANGUARD CLEANING SYSTEMS

www.vanguardcleaning.com

Commercial cleaning services.

OVERALL SCORE: 30

655 Mariners Island Boulevard, Suite 303
San Mateo, CA 94404
Fax: 650-591-1545
Total number of outlets: 293 (all in California
at this time)
Total number of franchise outlets: 293 (all in
California at this time)
International: No

OVERALL RANK: 122

Phone: 650-594-1500
Franchise fee: $5,300 to $35,300
Franchise term: 10 years
Initial investment: $2,193.71 to $33,700
Advertising/Marketing fee: none
Royalty fee: 5% of gross monthly volume (there
is also an administrative fee of 15% of gross
monthly volume)

SURVEY AND RESULTS *

Q1: About how many hours per week do you dedicate to your franchise business?

		% answering
A)	**Less than 40**	**67%**
B)	41–50	22%
C)	51–60	0%
D)	More than 60	0%
E)	Passive investment	11%

Q2: How would you describe your relations/ communications with your franchisor?

		% answering
A)	Excellent	9%
B)	Good	18%
C)	Adequate	0%
D)	Fair	9%
E)	**Poor**	**64%**

Q3: In terms of how your franchisor views your communications with other franchisees, it is:

		% answering
A)	Very supportive	9%
B)	**Not very supportive**	**55%**
C)	No influence	36%

Q4: Is the franchisor fair with you in resolving any grievances?

		% answering
A)	Extremely fair	0%
B)	Pretty fair	18%
C)	Reasonably fair	9%
D)	Not very fair	27%
E)	**Not fair at all**	**45%**

Q5: Are territories equitably granted?

		% answering
A)	Yes	18%
B)	**No**	**45%**
C)	Not yet sure	36%

Q6: How would you describe the initial and ongoing training provided by your franchisor?

		% answering
A)	Excellent	0%
B)	Good	27%
C)	Adequate	9%
D)	Fair	0%
E)	**Poor**	**64%**

Q7: How well does the franchisor anticipate future trends in how it evolves and markets products and services?

		% answering
A)	Extremely well	0%
B)	Pretty well	11%
C)	Adequately	11%
D)	Not very well	33%
E)	**Terribly**	**44%**

Q8: How satisfied are you with your franchisor's spending of the royalty fees you pay?

		% answering
A)	Extremely satisfied	0%
B)	Mostly satisfied	22%
C)	Somewhat satisfied	11%
D)	Not very satisfied	0%
E)	**Not satisfied at all**	**67%**

Q9: **In what ways could the parent company most improve? (Please check those that most apply, no more than three):**

❑ Communications

❑ Counsel/advice on administrative/management issues

❑ Effectiveness of marketing/promotions

❑ Evolution of products/services

❑ Frequency of marketing/promotional campaigns

❑ Quality of products/services

❑ Pricing of products/services to franchisees

❑ Technology (Point of sale systems, usage of computers/email/software, etc.)

❑ Training

Most frequent responses:	% answering
Communications	73%
Training	45%
Counsel/advice on administrative/management issues	36%

Q10: **Is your income more, less or about what you expected prior to opening your business?**

	% answering	
More	25%	
Less	**63%**	**Summary: 38% are making about what they**
About what was expected	13%	**expected, or more.**

Q11: **Prior to opening your franchise, which (if any) of the following did you underestimate?**

❑ Amount of working capital required for your 1st year in business

❑ Difficulty in hiring/retaining quality staff

❑ Expertise required to run the business

❑ Impact of marketing/promotions

❑ Start-up costs

❑ Degree of stress

❑ Workload

Most frequent responses:	% answering
Degree of stress	45%
Workload	36%
Impact of marketing/promotions	27%

Q12: **If you could turn back time to the day you signed your franchise agreement, would you make the same decision to buy your franchise?**

	% answering
Yes	27%
No	**73%**

* Number of survey respondents: 11 from 1 different states (at time of survey, all Vanguard franchisees were located in the state of California)

Number of survey respondents as a % of total franchise units: 3.75%

VISITING ANGELS

www.visitingangels.com

Non-medical companionship and home care services for the elderly.

OVERALL SCORE: 80

28 West Eagle Road, Suite 201
Havertown, PA 19083
Total number of outlets: 225+
Total number of franchise outlets: 225+
International: Yes (Canada)

OVERALL RANK: 34

Phone: 800-365-4189
Franchise fee: $12,950 to $25,950
Franchise term: 10 years
Initial investment: $22,350 to $41,600
Advertising/Marketing fee: none
Royalty fee: varies

SURVEY AND RESULTS *

Q1: About how many hours per week do you dedicate to your franchise business?

		% answering
A)	Less than 40	22%
B)	41–50	22%
C)	**51–60**	**28%**
D)	**More than 60**	**28%**
E)	Passive investment	0%

Q2: How would you describe your relations/ communications with your franchisor?

		% answering
A)	**Excellent**	**56%**
B)	Good	28%
C)	Adequate	17%
D)	Fair	0%
E)	Poor	0%

Q3: In terms of how your franchisor views your communications with other franchisees, it is:

		% answering
A)	**Very supportive**	**78%**
B)	Not very supportive	0%
C)	No influence	22%

Q4: Is the franchisor fair with you in resolving any grievances?

		% answering
A)	Extremely fair	31%
B)	Pretty fair	25%
C)	**Reasonably fair**	**44%**
D)	Not very fair	0%
E)	Not fair at all	0%

Q5: Are territories equitably granted?

		% answering
A)	**Yes**	**61%**
B)	No	6%
C)	Not yet sure	33%

Q6: How would you describe the initial and ongoing training provided by your franchisor?

		% answering
A)	Excellent	33%
B)	**Good**	**44%**
C)	Adequate	22%
D)	Fair	0%
E)	Poor	0%

Q7: How well does the franchisor anticipate future trends in how it evolves and markets products and services?

		% answering
A)	Extremely well	39%
B)	**Pretty well**	**56%**
C)	Adequately	6%
D)	Not very well	0%
E)	Terribly	0%

Q8: How satisfied are you with your franchisor's spending of the royalty fees you pay?

		% answering
A)	**Extremely satisfied**	**44%**
B)	Mostly satisfied	28%
C)	Somewhat satisfied	28%
D)	Not very satisfied	0%
E)	Not satisfied at all	0%

Q9: **In what ways could the parent company most improve? (Please check those that most apply, no more than three):**

❑ Communications
❑ Counsel/advice on administrative/management issues
❑ Effectiveness of marketing/promotions
❑ Evolution of products/services
❑ Frequency of marketing/promotional campaigns

❑ Quality of products/services
❑ Pricing of products/services to franchisees
❑ Technology (Point of sale systems, usage of computers/email/software, etc.)
❑ Training

Most frequent responses:

	% answering
Effectiveness of marketing/promotions	44%
Counsel/advice on administrative/management issues	33%
Frequency of marketing/promotional campaigns (tie)	28%
Training (tie)	28%

Q10: **Is your income more, less or about what you expected prior to opening your business?**

	% answering
More	17%
Less	**44%**
About what was expected	39%

Summary: 56% are making about what they expected, or more.

Q11: **Prior to opening your franchise, which (if any) of the following did you underestimate?**

❑ Amount of working capital required for your 1st year in business
❑ Difficulty in hiring/retaining quality staff
❑ Expertise required to run the business
❑ Impact of marketing/promotions

❑ Start-up costs
❑ Degree of stress
❑ Workload

Most frequent responses:

	% answering
Degree of stress	61%
Amount of working capital required for your 1st year in business (tie)	44%
Difficulty in hiring/retaining quality staff (tie)	44%

Q12: **If you could turn back time to the day you signed your franchise agreement, would you make the same decision to buy your franchise?**

	% answering
Yes	**88%**
No	12%

* Number of survey respondents: 18 from 17 different states
Number of survey respondents as a % of total franchise units: 8%

WE THE PEOPLE FORMS AND SERVICE CENTERS USA

www.wethepeople.biz
Email: irad@wethepeopleusa.com

Legal document services.

OVERALL SCORE: 55

1501 State Street
Santa Barbara, CA 93101
Fax: 805-962-9602
Total number of outlets: 170
Total number of franchise outlets: 156
International: No
Advertising/Marketing fee: none currently

OVERALL RANK: 158

Phone: 805-962-4100
Franchise fee: $89,500
Franchise term: 10 years
Initial investment: $115,500 to $151,500
Processing fee is 25% of the purchase price
received by you for each legal document prepared
for your customers

SURVEY AND RESULTS*

Q1: About how many hours per week do you dedicate to your franchise business?

		% answering
A)	Less than 40	25%
B)	**41–50**	**33%**
C)	51–60	25%
D)	More than 60	17%
E)	Passive investment	0%

Q2: How would you describe your relations/ communications with your franchisor?

		% answering
A)	Excellent	25%
B)	**Good**	**33%**
C)	Adequate	25%
D)	Fair	8%
E)	Poor	8%

Q3: In terms of how your franchisor views your communications with other franchisees, it is:

		% answering
A)	**Very supportive**	**50%**
B)	Not very supportive	25%
C)	No influence	25%

Q4: Is the franchisor fair with you in resolving any grievances?

		% answering
A)	Extremely fair	17%
B)	Pretty fair	25%
C)	**Reasonably fair**	**50%**
D)	Not very fair	0%
E)	Not fair at all	8%

Q5: Are territories equitably granted?

		% answering
A)	**Yes**	**64%**
B)	No	9%
C)	Not yet sure	27%

Q6: How would you describe the initial and ongoing training provided by your franchisor?

		% answering
A)	Excellent	8%
B)	Good	17%
C)	**Adequate**	**42%**
D)	Fair	8%
E)	Poor	25%

Q7: How well does the franchisor anticipate future trends in how it evolves and markets products and services?

		% answering
A)	Extremely well	25%
B)	**Pretty well**	**33%**
C)	Adequately	25%
D)	Not very well	17%
E)	Terribly	0%

Q8: How satisfied are you with your franchisor's spending of the royalty fees you pay?

		% answering
A)	Extremely satisfied	17%
B)	**Mostly satisfied**	**42%**
C)	Somewhat satisfied	17%
D)	Not very satisfied	17%
E)	Not satisfied at all	8%

Q9: **In what ways could the parent company most improve? (Please check those that most apply, no more than three):**

❑ Communications

❑ Counsel/advice on administrative/management issues

❑ Effectiveness of marketing/promotions

❑ Evolution of products/services

❑ Frequency of marketing/promotional campaigns

❑ Quality of products/services

❑ Pricing of products/services to franchisees

❑ Technology (Point of sale systems, usage of computers/email/software, etc.)

❑ Training

Most frequent responses:

	% answering
Effectiveness of marketing/promotions (tie)	58%
Frequency of marketing/promotional campaigns (tie)	58%
Training	50%

Q10: **Is your income more, less or about what you expected prior to opening your business?**

	% answering	
More	8%	
Less	**75%**	**Summary: 25% are making about what they**
About what was expected	17%	**expected, or more.**

Q11: **Prior to opening your franchise, which (if any) of the following did you underestimate?**

❑ Amount of working capital required for your 1st year in business

❑ Difficulty in hiring/retaining quality staff

❑ Expertise required to run the business

❑ Impact of marketing/promotions

❑ Start-up costs

❑ Degree of stress

❑ Workload

Most frequent responses:

	% answering
Degree of stress	58%
Amount of working capital required for your 1st year in business	50%
Impact of marketing/promotions (tie)	42%
Workload (tie)	42%

Q12: **If you could turn back time to the day you signed your franchise agreement, would you make the same decision to buy your franchise?**

	% answering
Yes	**58%**
No	42%

*   Number of survey respondents: 12 from 8 different states

Number of survey respondents as a % of total franchise units: 7.69%

WILD BIRD CENTER

www.wildbird.com
Email: info@wildbird.com

Retail stores offering wild bird seed and related products.

OVERALL SCORE: 75

7370 MacArthur Boulevard
Glen Echo, MD 20812
Fax: 301-320-6154
Total number of outlets: approximately 100
Total number of franchise outlets:
approximately 100
International: Yes (Canada)
Advertising/Marketing fee: 1/2% of store sales

OVERALL RANK: 56

Phone: 800-WILDBIRD, ext. 203
Franchise fee: $15,000
Franchise term: 10 years
Initial investment: $90,900 to $135,300
Royalty fee: 4% of gross sales if territory
population is more than 60,000, 3% if territory
population is less than 60,000 (for first franchise)

SURVEY AND RESULTS *

Q1: About how many hours per week do you dedicate to your franchise business?

		% answering
A)	Less than 40	0%
B)	41–50	38%
C)	**51–60**	**62%**
D)	More than 60	0%
E)	Passive investment	0%

Q2: How would you describe your relations/ communications with your franchisor?

		% answering
A)	**Excellent**	**42%**
B)	**Good**	**42%**
C)	Adequate	8%
D)	Fair	0%
E)	Poor	8%

Q3: In terms of how your franchisor views your communications with other franchisees, it is:

		% answering
A)	**Very supportive**	**83%**
B)	Not very supportive	8%
C)	No influence	8%

Q4: Is the franchisor fair with you in resolving any grievances?

		% answering
A)	Extremely fair	27%
B)	**Pretty fair**	**45%**
C)	Reasonably fair	18%
D)	Not very fair	0%
E)	Not fair at all	9%

Q5: Are territories equitably granted?

		% answering
A)	**Yes**	**92%**
B)	No	8%
C)	Not yet sure	0%

Q6: How would you describe the initial and ongoing training provided by your franchisor?

		% answering
A)	Excellent	8%
B)	**Good**	**58%**
C)	Adequate	17%
D)	Fair	17%
E)	Poor	0%

Q7: How well does the franchisor anticipate future trends in how it evolves and markets products and services?

		% answering
A)	Extremely well	8%
B)	**Pretty well**	**42%**
C)	Adequately	33%
D)	Not very well	8%
E)	Terribly	8%

Q8: How satisfied are you with your franchisor's spending of the royalty fees you pay?

		% answering
A)	Extremely satisfied	8%
B)	**Mostly satisfied**	**58%**
C)	Somewhat satisfied	17%
D)	Not very satisfied	8%
E)	Not satisfied at all	8%

Q9: **In what ways could the parent company most improve? (Please check those that most apply, no more than three):**

❑ Communications
❑ Counsel/advice on administrative/management issues
❑ Effectiveness of marketing/promotions
❑ Evolution of products/services
❑ Frequency of marketing/promotional campaigns

❑ Quality of products/services
❑ Pricing of products/services to franchisees
❑ Technology (Point of sale systems, usage of computers/email/software, etc.)
❑ Training

Most frequent responses:	% answering
Technology	58%
Effectiveness of marketing/promotions	50%
Evolution of products/services	33%

Q10: **Is your income more, less or about what you expected prior to opening your business?**

	% answering	
More	9%	
Less	36%	**Summary: 64% are making about what they**
About what was expected	**55%**	**expected, or more.**

Q11: **Prior to opening your franchise, which (if any) of the following did you underestimate?**

❑ Amount of working capital required for your 1st year in business
❑ Difficulty in hiring/retaining quality staff
❑ Expertise required to run the business
❑ Impact of marketing/promotions

❑ Start-up costs
❑ Degree of stress
❑ Workload

Most frequent responses:	% answering
Impact of marketing/promotions	50%
Workload	42%
Degree of stress	33%

Q12: **If you could turn back time to the day you signed your franchise agreement, would you make the same decision to buy your franchise?**

	% answering
Yes	**83%**
No	17%

* Number of survey respondents: 12 from 8 different states
   Number of survey respondents as a % of total franchise units: 12%

WILD BIRDS UNLIMITED

www.wbu.com

Email: pickettp@wbu.com (Paul Pickett) or gilkersonl@wbu.com (Linda Gilkerson)

Retailer that offer bid feeders, bird seed, and other related items.

OVERALL SCORE: 68

11711 North College Avenue, Suite 146
Carmel, IN 46032
Fax: 317-208-4050
Total number of outlets: 303
Total number of franchise outlets: 303
International: Yes (Canada)

OVERALL RANK: N/A

Phone: 888-730-7108
Franchise fee: $18,000
Franchise term: 10 years
Initial investment: $90,570 to $152,619
Advertising/Marketing fee: none currently
Royalty fee: 4% of gross sales monthly

SURVEY AND RESULTS *

Q1: About how many hours per week do you dedicate to your franchise business?

		% answering
A)	Less than 40	0%
B)	41–50	25%
C)	**51–60**	**50%**
D)	More than 60	25%
E)	Passive investment	0%

Q2: How would you describe your relations/ communications with your franchisor?

		% answering
A)	**Excellent**	**63%**
B)	Good	13%
C)	Adequate	25%
D)	Fair	0%
E)	Poor	0%

Q3: In terms of how your franchisor views your communications with other franchisees, it is:

		% answering
A)	**Very supportive**	**75%**
B)	Not very supportive	13%
C)	No influence	13%

Q4: Is the franchisor fair with you in resolving any grievances?

		% answering
A)	**Extremely fair**	**50%**
B)	Pretty fair	25%
C)	Reasonably fair	13%
D)	Not very fair	13%
E)	Not fair at all	0%

Q5: Are territories equitably granted?

		% answering
A)	**Yes**	**75%**
B)	No	13%
C)	Not yet sure	13%

Q6: How would you describe the initial and ongoing training provided by your franchisor?

		% answering
A)	**Excellent**	**63%**
B)	Good	13%
C)	Adequate	13%
D)	Fair	13%
E)	Poor	0%

Q7: How well does the franchisor anticipate future trends in how it evolves and markets products and services?

		% answering
A)	Extremely well	13%
B)	**Pretty well**	**63%**
C)	Adequately	13%
D)	Not very well	13%
E)	Terribly	0%

Q8: How satisfied are you with your franchisor's spending of the royalty fees you pay?

		% answering
A)	Extremely satisfied	13%
B)	**Mostly satisfied**	**75%**
C)	Somewhat satisfied	0%
D)	Not very satisfied	0%
E)	Not satisfied at all	13%

Q9: **In what ways could the parent company most improve? (Please check those that most apply, no more than three):**

❑ Communications

❑ Counsel/advice on administrative/management issues

❑ Effectiveness of marketing/promotions

❑ Evolution of products/services

❑ Frequency of marketing/promotional campaigns

❑ Quality of products/services

❑ Pricing of products/services to franchisees

❑ Technology (Point of sale systems, usage of computers/email/software, etc.)

❑ Training

Most frequent responses: % answering

	% answering
Effectiveness of marketing/promotions	63%
Evolution of products/services	38%
Communications (tie)	25%
Pricing of products/services to franchisees (tie)	25%

Q10: **Is your income more, less or about what you expected prior to opening your business?**

	% answering	
More	13%	
Less	**63%**	**Summary: 38% are making about what they**
About what was expected	25%	**expected, or more.**

Q11: **Prior to opening your franchise, which (if any) of the following did you underestimate?**

❑ Amount of working capital required for your 1st year in business

❑ Difficulty in hiring/retaining quality staff

❑ Expertise required to run the business

❑ Impact of marketing/promotions

❑ Start-up costs

❑ Degree of stress

❑ Workload

Most frequent responses: % answering

	% answering
Impact of marketing/promotions	63%
Degree of stress	50%
Expertise required to run the business (tie)	38%
Workload (tie)	38%

Q12: **If you could turn back time to the day you signed your franchise agreement, would you make the same decision to buy your franchise?**

	% answering
Yes	**63%**
No	38%

* Number of survey respondents: 8 from 7 different states

    Number of survey respondents as a % of total franchise units: 2.64%

WIRELESS ZONE

www.wirelesszone.com
Email: info@wirelesszone.com

Retail store dedicated to wireless communications products and services.

OVERALL SCORE: 72

34 Industrial Park Place
Middletown, CT 06457
Total number of outlets: 220+
Total number of franchise outlets: 220+
International: No

OVERALL RANK: 71

Phone: 860-632-9494
Franchise fee:
Franchise term:
Initial investment:
Advertising/Marketing fee:
Royalty fee:

SURVEY AND RESULTS *

Q1: About how many hours per week do you dedicate to your franchise business?

		% answering
A)	Less than 40	27%
B)	41–50	13%
C)	51–60	20%
D)	**More than 60**	**40%**
E)	Passive investment	0%

Q2: How would you describe your relations/ communications with your franchisor?

		% answering
A)	**Excellent**	**47%**
B)	Good	20%
C)	Adequate	13%
D)	Fair	13%
E)	Poor	7%

Q3: In terms of how your franchisor views your communications with other franchisees, it is:

		% answering
A)	**Very supportive**	**73%**
B)	Not very supportive	7%
C)	No influence	20%

Q4: Is the franchisor fair with you in resolving any grievances?

		% answering
A)	**Extremely fair**	**40%**
B)	Pretty fair	27%
C)	Reasonably fair	33%
D)	Not very fair	0%
E)	Not fair at all	0%

Q5: Are territories equitably granted?

		% answering
A)	**Yes**	**80%**
B)	No	7%
C)	Not yet sure	13%

Q6: How would you describe the initial and ongoing training provided by your franchisor?

		% answering
A)	Excellent	7%
B)	**Good**	**40%**
C)	Adequate	13%
D)	Fair	20%
E)	Poor	20%

Q7: How well does the franchisor anticipate future trends in how it evolves and markets products and services?

		% answering
A)	Extremely well	7%
B)	Pretty well	33%
C)	**Adequately**	**40%**
D)	Not very well	20%
E)	Terribly	0%

Q8: How satisfied are you with your franchisor's spending of the royalty fees you pay?

		% answering
A)	Extremely satisfied	7%
B)	Mostly satisfied	27%
C)	**Somewhat satisfied**	**33%**
D)	**Not very satisfied**	**33%**
E)	Not satisfied at all	0%

Q9: **In what ways could the parent company most improve? (Please check those that most apply, no more than three):**

❑ Communications
❑ Counsel/advice on administrative/management issues
❑ Effectiveness of marketing/promotions
❑ Evolution of products/services
❑ Frequency of marketing/promotional campaigns

❑ Quality of products/services
❑ Pricing of products/services to franchisees
❑ Technology (Point of sale systems, usage of computers/email/software, etc.)
❑ Training

Most frequent responses:	% answering
Effectiveness of marketing/promotions	80%
Pricing of products/services to franchisees	53%
Communications (tie)	33%
Training (tie)	33%

Q10: **Is your income more, less or about what you expected prior to opening your business?**

	% answering	
More	27%	
Less	33%	**Summary: 67% are making about what they**
About what was expected	**40%**	**expected, or more.**

Q11: **Prior to opening your franchise, which (if any) of the following did you underestimate?**

❑ Amount of working capital required for your 1st year in business
❑ Difficulty in hiring/retaining quality staff
❑ Expertise required to run the business
❑ Impact of marketing/promotions

❑ Start-up costs
❑ Degree of stress
❑ Workload

Most frequent responses:	% answering
Difficulty in hiring/retaining quality staff	67%
Amount of working capital required for your 1st year in business (tie)	40%
Degree of stress (tie)	40%
Workload (tie)	40%

Q12: **If you could turn back time to the day you signed your franchise agreement, would you make the same decision to buy your franchise?**

	% answering
Yes	**80%**
No	20%

* Number of survey respondents: 17 from 15 different states
Number of survey respondents as a % of total franchise units: 7.73%

WORLD GYM

www.worldgym.com
Email: info@worldgym.com

Fitness and workout center.

OVERALL SCORE: 77

3223 Washington Boulevard
Marina del Rey, CA 90292
Fax: 310-827-6355
Total number of outlets: 275 (250 in U.S.)
Total number of franchise outlets: 275 (250 in U.S.)
International: Yes (worldwide)

OVERALL RANK: 46

Phone: 310-827-7705
Franchise fee: $13,000
Franchise term: 5 years
Initial investment: $156,000 to $1,200,500
(excluding real estate)
Advertising/Marketing fee: none
Royalty fee: $7,000 monthly

SURVEY AND RESULTS *

Q1: About how many hours per week do you dedicate to your franchise business?

		% answering
A)	Less than 40	0%
B)	41–50	18%
C)	51–60	27%
D)	**More than 60**	**55%**
E)	Passive investment	0%

Q2: How would you describe your relations/ communications with your franchisor?

		% answering
A)	**Excellent**	**55%**
B)	Good	27%
C)	Adequate	9%
D)	Fair	0%
E)	Poor	9%

Q3: In terms of how your franchisor views your communications with other franchisees, it is:

		% answering
A)	**Very supportive**	**55%**
B)	Not very supportive	9%
C)	No influence	36%

Q4: Is the franchisor fair with you in resolving any grievances?

		% answering
A)	**Extremely fair**	**45%**
B)	Pretty fair	18%
C)	Reasonably fair	36%
D)	Not very fair	0%
E)	Not fair at all	0%

Q5: Are territories equitably granted?

		% answering
A)	**Yes**	**82%**
B)	No	0%
C)	Not yet sure	18%

Q6: How would you describe the initial and ongoing training provided by your franchisor?

		% answering
A)	**Excellent**	**36%**
B)	Good	9%
C)	**Adequate**	**36%**
D)	Fair	0%
E)	Poor	18%

Q7: How well does the franchisor anticipate future trends in how it evolves and markets products and services?

		% answering
A)	**Extremely well**	**36%**
B)	**Pretty well**	**36%**
C)	Adequately	18%
D)	Not very well	0%
E)	Terribly	9%

Q8: How satisfied are you with your franchisor's spending of the royalty fees you pay?

		% answering
A)	Extremely satisfied	27%
B)	Mostly satisfied	27%
C)	**Somewhat satisfied**	**36%**
D)	Not very satisfied	0%
E)	Not satisfied at all	9%

Q9: **In what ways could the parent company most improve? (Please check those that most apply, no more than three):**

❑ Communications
❑ Counsel/advice on administrative/management issues
❑ Effectiveness of marketing/promotions
❑ Evolution of products/services
❑ Frequency of marketing/promotional campaigns

❑ Quality of products/services
❑ Pricing of products/services to franchisees
❑ Technology (Point of sale systems, usage of computers/email/software, etc.)
❑ Training

Most frequent responses:	% answering
Effectiveness of marketing/promotions	73%
Frequency of marketing/promotional campaigns	64%
Communications (tie)	27%
Technology (tie)	27%
Pricing of products/services to franchisees (tie)	27%

Q10: **Is your income more, less or about what you expected prior to opening your business?**

	% answering	
More	18%	
Less	27%	**Summary: 73% are making about what they**
About what was expected	**55%**	**expected, or more.**

Q11: **Prior to opening your franchise, which (if any) of the following did you underestimate?**

❑ Amount of working capital required for your 1st year in business
❑ Difficulty in hiring/retaining quality staff
❑ Expertise required to run the business
❑ Impact of marketing/promotions

❑ Start-up costs
❑ Degree of stress
❑ Workload

Most frequent responses:	% answering
Impact of marketing/promotions	55%
Amount of working capital required for your 1st year in business	45%
Difficulty in hiring/retaining quality staff (tie)	27%
Start-up costs (tie)	27%

Q12: **If you could turn back time to the day you signed your franchise agreement, would you make the same decision to buy your franchise?**

	% answering
Yes	**82%**
No	18%

* Number of survey respondents: 11 from 9 different states
Number of survey respondents as a % of total franchise units: 4%

WORLD INSPECTION NETWORK

www.wini.com
Email: joinwin@wini.com

Home inspection services.

OVERALL SCORE: 86

6500 6th Avenue NW
Seattle, WA 98117
Total number of outlets: 140
Total number of franchise outlets: 140
International: No
Advertising/Marketing fee: 3% of monthly
gross revenues, with a minimum of $125 per month

OVERALL RANK: 12

Phone: 800-967-8127
Franchise fee: $25,000 or $28,000 if financed
Franchise term: 5 years
Initial investment: $41,700 to $49,500
Royalty fee: 6% to 7% of monthly gross revenues,
with a minimum of $300 per month

SURVEY AND RESULTS *

Q1: About how many hours per week do you dedicate to your franchise business?

		% answering
A)	Less than 40	19%
B)	41–50	13%
C)	**51–60**	**50%**
D)	More than 60	19%
E)	Passive investment	0%

Q2: How would you describe your relations/ communications with your franchisor?

		% answering
A)	**Excellent**	**44%**
B)	**Good**	**44%**
C)	Adequate	13%
D)	Fair	0%
E)	Poor	0%

Q3: In terms of how your franchisor views your communications with other franchisees, it is:

		% answering
A)	**Very supportive**	**88%**
B)	Not very supportive	0%
C)	No influence	13%

Q4: Is the franchisor fair with you in resolving any grievances?

		% answering
A)	**Extremely fair**	**64%**
B)	Pretty fair	29%
C)	Reasonably fair	7%
D)	Not very fair	0%
E)	Not fair at all	0%

Q5: Are territories equitably granted?

		% answering
A)	**Yes**	**69%**
B)	No	19%
C)	Not yet sure	13%

Q6: How would you describe the initial and ongoing training provided by your franchisor?

		% answering
A)	Excellent	40%
B)	**Good**	**55%**
C)	Adequate	6%
D)	Fair	0%
E)	Poor	0%

Q7: How well does the franchisor anticipate future trends in how it evolves and markets products and services?

		% answering
A)	Extremely well	38%
B)	**Pretty well**	**56%**
C)	Adequately	6%
D)	Not very well	0%
E)	Terribly	0%

Q8: How satisfied are you with your franchisor's spending of the royalty fees you pay?

		% answering
A)	Extremely satisfied	13%
B)	**Mostly satisfied**	**44%**
C)	**Somewhat satisfied**	**44%**
D)	Not very satisfied	0%
E)	Not satisfied at all	0%

Q9: **In what ways could the parent company most improve? (Please check those that most apply, no more than three):**

❏ Communications
❏ Counsel/advice on administrative/management issues
❏ Effectiveness of marketing/promotions
❏ Evolution of products/services
❏ Frequency of marketing/promotional campaigns

❏ Quality of products/services
❏ Pricing of products/services to franchisees
❏ Technology (Point of sale systems, usage of computers/email/software, etc.)
❏ Training

Most frequent responses: % answering

Pricing of products/services to franchisees   29%
Frequency of marketing/promotional campaigns (tie)   21%
Training (tie)   21%

Q10: **Is your income more, less or about what you expected prior to opening your business?**

	% answering
More	19%
Less	25%
About what was expected	**56%**

Summary: 75% are making about what they expected, or more.

Q11: **Prior to opening your franchise, which (if any) of the following did you underestimate?**

❏ Amount of working capital required for your 1st year in business
❏ Difficulty in hiring/retaining quality staff
❏ Expertise required to run the business
❏ Impact of marketing/promotions

❏ Start-up costs
❏ Degree of stress
❏ Workload

Most frequent responses: % answering

Amount of working capital required for your 1st year in business   64%
Degree of stress   29%
Impact of marketing/promotions (tie)   21%
Start-up costs (tie)   21%

Q12: **If you could turn back time to the day you signed your franchise agreement, would you make the same decision to buy your franchise?**

	% answering
Yes	**88%**
No	13%

*   Number of survey respondents: 16 from 11 different states
    Number of survey respondents as a % of total franchise units: 11.43%

ZIEBART

www.ziebart.com
Email: info@ziebart.com

Retailer of automotive parts and services.

OVERALL SCORE: 59

1290 East Maple Road, P.O. Box 1290
Troy, MI 48007
Fax: 248-588-1444
Total number of outlets:
Total number of franchise outlets:
International: Yes (worldwide)

OVERALL RANK: 141

Phone: 800-877-1312
Franchise fee:
Franchise term:
Initial investment: Starting at $146,000
Advertising/Marketing fee:
Royalty fee:

SURVEY AND RESULTS *

Q1: **About how many hours per week do you dedicate to your franchise business?**

		% answering
A)	Less than 40	9%
B)	41–50	18%
C)	51–60	27%
D)	**More than 60**	**45%**
E)	Passive investment	0%

Q2: **How would you describe your relations/ communications with your franchisor?**

		% answering
A)	**Excellent**	**45%**
B)	Good	27%
C)	Adequate	9%
D)	Fair	9%
E)	Poor	9%

Q3: **In terms of how your franchisor views your communications with other franchisees, it is:**

		% answering
A)	**Very supportive**	**55%**
B)	Not very supportive	18%
C)	No influence	27%

Q4: **Is the franchisor fair with you in resolving any grievances?**

		% answering
A)	**Extremely fair**	**45%**
B)	Pretty fair	18%
C)	Reasonably fair	18%
D)	Not very fair	0%
E)	Not fair at all	18%

Q5: **Are territories equitably granted?**

		% answering
A)	**Yes**	**73%**
B)	No	18%
C)	Not yet sure	9%

Q6: **How would you describe the initial and ongoing training provided by your franchisor?**

		% answering
A)	Excellent	27%
B)	Good	18%
C)	**Adequate**	**27%**
D)	Fair	18%
E)	Poor	9%

Q7: **How well does the franchisor anticipate future trends in how it evolves and markets products and services?**

		% answering
A)	Extremely well	18%
B)	Pretty well	18%
C)	**Adequately**	**36%**
D)	Not very well	18%
E)	Terribly	9%

Q8: **How satisfied are you with your franchisor's spending of the royalty fees you pay?**

		% answering
A)	Extremely satisfied	10%
B)	**Mostly satisfied**	**30%**
C)	Somewhat satisfied	20%
D)	Not very satisfied	10%
E)	**Not satisfied at all**	**30%**

Q9: In what ways could the parent company most improve? (Please check those that most apply, no more than three):

❑ Communications
❑ Counsel/advice on administrative/management issues
❑ Effectiveness of marketing/promotions
❑ Evolution of products/services
❑ Frequency of marketing/promotional campaigns

❑ Quality of products/services
❑ Pricing of products/services to franchisees
❑ Technology (Point of sale systems, usage of computers/email/software, etc.)
❑ Training

Most frequent responses:	% answering
Evolution of products/services (tie)	45%
Pricing of products/services to franchisees (tie)	45%
Counsel/advice on administrative/management issues (tie)	36%
Effectiveness of marketing/promotions (tie)	36%

Q10: Is your income more, less or about what you expected prior to opening your business?

	% answering	
More	10%	
Less	**70%**	**Summary: 30% are making about what they**
About what was expected	20%	**expected, or more.**

Q11: Prior to opening your franchise, which (if any) of the following did you underestimate?

❑ Amount of working capital required for your 1st year in business
❑ Difficulty in hiring/retaining quality staff
❑ Expertise required to run the business
❑ Impact of marketing/promotions

❑ Start-up costs
❑ Degree of stress
❑ Workload

Most frequent responses:	% answering
Difficulty in hiring/retaining quality staff	55%
Degree of stress	45%
Amount of working capital required for 1st year in business (tie)	36%
Expertise required to run the business (tie)	36%

Q12: If you could turn back time to the day you signed your franchise agreement, would you make the same decision to buy your franchise?

	% answering
Yes	**64%**
No	36%

* Number of survey respondents: 11 from 6 different states
Number of survey respondents as a % of total franchise units:

INDEX

978-0-595-38094-7
0-595-38094-8